D0857948

# Maritime Transport

## The Evolution of International Marine Policy and Shipping Law

# Maritime Transport

## The Evolution of International Marine Policy and Shipping Law

**Edgar Gold**
Dalhousie University

**LexingtonBooks**
D.C. Heath and Company
Lexington, Massachusetts
Toronto

**Library of Congress Cataloging in Publication Data**

Gold, Edgar.
  Maritime transport.

  Bibliography: p.
  1. Maritime law—History. I. Title.
K1155.4.G64        341.7'566        80-8641
ISBN 0-669-04338-9

Published simultaneously in Canada

Printed in the United States of America

International Standard Book Number: 0-669-04338-9

Library of Congress Catalog Card Number: 80-8641

55, 310

*To Judy*

# Contents

# List of Tables

# Foreword

I am pleased to contribute the foreword to this monumental work on the history and development of maritime transport. This much-needed study provides a valuable background for the understanding of international marine policy and shipping law, which, in a variety of international settings, has been the subject of searching examination and reexamination in recent times. Only a meticulous analysis of the traditions of the great maritime states, which have come to the historical forefront from time to time and have thus shaped all aspects of maritime transport, can aid its understanding. This unique contribution to the subject meets all such requirements, and the learned author merits congratulations on his achievements.

This work will be of great interest to all for whom maritime transport is of importance. Not only will it provide valuable information for the maritime lawyer and policymaker, but it will also be an asset to legal and historical scholars who are interested in maritime matters. I recommend the book to the general reader as well because of its fascinating presentation.

At a time in history when the sea and the regulation of its uses is one of the international community's main preoccupations, a study such as this will surely aid not only attempts to unify divergent maritime law, but also the achievement of greater equity in ocean uses.

*Nagendra Singh*
Judge of the International Court of Justice
Vice-President of the Court
1976-1979

# Preface and Acknowledgments

This book unites the artificially created divergences among the various marine law and policy aspects affecting international maritime transport. This has been done by tracing the evolution of this most traditional ocean use and the rules within which it operates, from its hazy beginnings to the present, when it faces its greatest-ever challenge from competing ocean uses in an unequally divided world.

Much of this work is based on insights gained during my almost three decades of experience in the "ocean business" as mariner, lawyer, consultant, and academic. As a result, it is impossible to properly acknowledge my indebtedness to all those in every part of the globe who helped me, directly and indirectly, in compiling these insights. Their help, patience, and understanding is collectively but most gratefully acknowledged.

The work for this book was carried out with the encouragement of Professor Edward D. Brown of the Centre for Marine Law and Policy, University of Wales, Cardiff, and Professor Alastair D. Couper, head of the Department of Maritime Studies, also at the University of Wales. My gratitude goes to both—to the former, whose internationally acclaimed scholarship gave guidance to my efforts, and to the latter for providing a new and progressive interdisciplinary environment without which this type of study could not have been carried out.

The International Development Research Centre, Ottawa, awarded me a two-year research associate grant, which not only enabled me to work in Cardiff but also facilitated research in Europe, Africa, Asia, Latin America, and the Caribbean. Without such generous help, this work could not have been undertaken.

Completion of the book was greatly assisted by the resources of the Faculty of Law, Dalhousie University, where I have been a member of the faculty's Marine and Environmental Law Programme since 1975, as well as by the inspiring academic climate provided by my faculty colleagues under the leadership of Professor Ronald St. J. Macdonald, Q.C., dean of law until 1979, and Professor William H.R. Charles, the present dean.

Two scholars, colleagues, teachers, and true friends, Professor Douglas M. Johnston and Brian Flemming, Q.C., can take particular credit for whatever this book might achieve, as they shaped, nurtured, and encouraged my work in so many ways. To both I give my deep and sincere thanks.

I am most deeply grateful to Judge Nagendra Singh for honoring me by writing the foreword to this book.

Without logistic support, books such as this cannot be completed. My sincere gratitude for assistance far beyond the call of duty goes to my secretary, Suzanne McQuinn, now Administrator of the Dalhousie Ocean Studies Programme, who typed several versions of this study. Her editorial suggestions in particular were greatly appreciated. My thanks also go to Theodore McDorman for his assistance in preparing the index.

Last but not least, there is no doubt whatsoever that Judith Hammerling Gold, friend, wife, scholar, physician, and psychiatrist, was the major contributor to this work. Not only did she display endless love and forebearance for the middle-aged academic ambitions of the sea-captain she originally married, but, in addition, she constantly encouraged and helped him through the difficulties of writing this kind of book. Her practical criticism of the many stages of the book ensured its completion.

# Abbreviations

**A.M.C.**  American Maritime Cases Law Reports
**BIMCO**  Baltic and International Maritime Conference
**C.C.E.D. Penn.**  Circuit Court, Eastern District, Pennsylvania
**CIF**  Cost, insurance, and freight
**C.Rob.**  Charles Robbins Law Reports
**CAACE**  EEC Shipowners' Association
**CENSA**  Council of European and Japanese Shipowners
**CMI**  Comité Maritime International
**CRISTAL**  Contract Regarding an Interim Supplement to Tanker Liability for Oil Pollution
**EEC**  European Economic Community
**EEZ**  Exclusive Economic Zone
**Eliz.**  Queen Elizabeth I (Legislation)
**FAO**  Food and Agriculture Organization of the United Nations
**Fed.Cas.**  U.S. Federal Cases Law Reports
**GCBS**  General Council of British Shipping
**GESAMP**  Joint Group of Experts on the Scientific Aspects of Marine Pollution
**GNP**  Gross National Product
**grt**  Gross Registered Tonnage
**H.L.Cas.**  House of Lords Cases Reports
**IAEA**  International Atomic Energy Association
**IBRD**  International Bank for Reconstruction and Development (World Bank)
**ICC**  International Chamber of Commerce
**ICES**  International Council for the Exploration of the Sea
**ICJ**  International Court of Justice
**ICNT**  Informal Composite Negotiating Text (at UNCLOS III)
**ICS**  International Chamber of Shipping
**ICSU**  International Council of Scientific Unions
**IDA**  International Development Association
**IFC**  International Finance Corporation
**IHO**  International Hydrographic Organization
**ILA**  International Law Organization
**ILC**  International Law Commission
**IMCO**  Inter-Governmental Maritime Consultative Organization
**IMCOSAR**  IMCO Search and Rescue System
**INMARSAT**  International Maritime Satellite System
**INTERTANKO**  International Association of Independent Tanker Owners
**IOC**  International Oceanographic Commission

**IUMI**   International Union of Marine Insurance
**L.J.K.B.**   Law Journal of King's Beach Law Reports
**LNG**   Liquid Natural Gas
**LSI**   Law of the Sea Institute
**MEPC**   Marine Environmental Protection Committee (of IMCO)
**MSC**   Maritime Safety Committee (of IMCO)
**NSDAP**   Nationalsozialistische Deutsche Arbeiterpartei (Nazi party)
**OCIMF**   Oil Companies International Marine Forum
**OECD**   Organization for Economic Cooperation and Development
**P&I**   Protection and Indemnity
**P.C.I.J.**   Permanent Court of International Justice
**SCOR**   Scientific Commission on Oceanic Research
**Sess.**   Session
**SOLAS**   Safety of Life at Sea
**Stats.**   Statutes
**TOVALOP**   Tanker Owners' Voluntary Agreement Concerning Liability
   for Oil Pollution
**ULCC**   Ultra Large Crude Carrier
**UNCITRAL**   United Nations Commission on International Trade Law
**UNCLOS I**   United Nations Conference on the Law of the Sea, Geneva,
   1958
**UNCLOS II**   Second United Nations Conference on the Law of the Sea,
   Geneva, 1960
**UNCLOS III**   Third United Nations Conference on the Law of the Sea,
   1973-
**UNCTAD**   United Nations Conference on Trade and Development
**UNCTAD I**   United Nations Conference on Trade and Development,
   First Session, Geneva, 1964
**UNCTAD II**   United Nations Conference on Trade and Development,
   Second Session, New Delhi, 1968
**UNCTAD III**   United Nations Conference on Trade and Development,
   Third Session, Santiago de Chile, 1972
**UNCTAD IV**   United Nations Conference on Trade and Development,
   Fourth Session, Nairobi, 1976
**UNCTAD V**   United Nations Conference on Trade and Development,
   Fifth Session, Manila, 1979
**UNEP**   United Nations Environmental Program
**UNESCO**   United Nations Educational, Scientific, and Cultural Organization
**U.N.T.S.**   United Nations Treaty Series
**Vict.**   Queen Victoria (Legislation)
**VLCC**   Very Large Crude Carrier
**WHO**   World Health Organization
**WMO**   World Meteorological Organization

# Introduction

*Most comprehensively viewed, the international law of the sea comprises two very different sets of principles. One set of principles, establishing certain basic, overriding community goals, prescribes for all states the widest possible access to, and the fullest enjoyment of, the shared use of the great common resource of the oceans. The other set of principles, commonly described as jurisdictional, expresses certain implementing policies designed economically to serve the basic community goals of shared use by establishing a shared competence among states in a domain largely free from the exclusive public order of any particular state.*

—Myres S. McDougal (*American Journal of International Law* 54, 1960)

As this is written the Third United Nations Conference on the Law of the Sea (UNCLOS III), which has been in preparation as well as in session for more than a decade, slowly draws to a conclusion. Whether the final outcome of this enormous international search for consensus is a definitive convention or not has become almost an academic question. However, the ocean atlas of the Earth will be a very different one at the end of this most intensive of all law-reform movements. The end of the conference will thus mark the beginning of a new era for the oceans, great parts of which will now be subject to radically new controls, domination, regulation, and jurisdiction. Like everything else in the late twentieth century, the uses of the ocean will be complicated and fraught with conflict in a search for greater equity for the widely differing interests of people in a very unevenly divided world.

Strangely, however, in whatever form it will eventually take, the new law of the sea has in the past decade addressed itself to almost all areas of ocean use except the one that since before the dawn of history, has been preeminent—the use of the ocean as a means to transport people and their goods from place to place on this planet, so much more of which is water than is land. Marine transport has been discussed in an almost abstract manner, as if it did not really fit or belong within the public domain but needed to be confined to the more "private" region of international commerce, which was considered to be outside the scope of the law of the sea. This book intends to show that this is an anomaly and that there is a clearly discernible thread linking marine transport from the earliest times up to the present debate on the oceans.

There is little doubt that the law of the sea is divided into its "public" and "private" components. This is a relatively recent development historically; its origin lies in the national policies of the major maritime states, which saw the advantages of such a division. The traditional private or commercial aspect of ocean use was then conveniently sidelined in order to create a new area of dominance by new interest groups—within the same states—which dominated the public-law aspect. Although probably neither planned nor foreseen at the time, this division was to serve the traditional maritime states well in the battle to defend the concept of the "freedom of the seas" in later years. If the jurisdictional bridgehead were to fall, the commercial fortress would then be a second line of defense.

The complications caused by the existence of two law-of-the-sea components, which created not only two monolithic and strictly separated areas of international law and policy but also a gray area in between, is what faced the newly emerging nations of the Third World in the 1950s and 1960s. Their strength and unity in demanding a more equitable share in the manifold uses of the oceans was, therefore, required to be divided into completely different policy formulations in different forums. Only in recent years has this dilemma become clear to some of these countries, and it has had a direct result on the growing demands for a new international order. However, solutions are further complicated by the fact that the colonial past has imposed the twin structures of ocean law and policy on the governmental systems of most Third-World states. Only major policy changes, often precluded by other priorities, could change this difficult position, which itself contributes to the general development problem.

The traditional explanation of what we consider an anomalous division has always been that the more recent public-law-and-policy aspect of ocean use was to provide a service to the political aspirations of jurisdiction, whereas the traditional private-law component was to interpret the economic and commercial aspects of marine transport. This neat division appears nonexistent when one views the political and historical processes that have influenced ocean uses. There has hardly ever been a political or jurisdictional aspect in the law of the sea that has not had its effect on the commercial and economic use of the sea. The reverse is equally true. It is for these reasons that this examination and analysis will be historical in character as well as in methodology. It is felt that the history of the law of the sea has been frequently misinterpreted and largely misunderstood by those who seek to defend, as well as by those who wish to overturn, the status quo of traditional maritime power. We will attempt to show that marine transport has, throughout history, been a key concept, one that has waxed and waned vis-à-vis the many other oceanic considerations but that has always been the sign of the true maritime power.

It would be unoriginal to say in the late 1970s that the real difficulties of UNCLOS III have been largely politicoeconomic rather than legal. However, the conference was attempting to deal with difficulties that were being couched in terms of "have" versus "have-not" and North versus South, within a traditional legal framework that was inadequate even before such new demands were placed on it. Although the scientists have seen the sea as a biological whole for a long time, policy makers and lawyers still attempt to place their policies and legal drafts into neat compartments. We wish to focus attention on marine transport to show that no concept relating to the ocean can be isolated, that no maritime policy can be separated from others, and that the field of marine affairs—like the sea itself—is a *complete* unit that will only benefit mankind equitably if it is seen, understood, and left whole.

As has been stated, in the past decade ocean law has been undergoing its most searching examination ever. UNCLOS III, which started out as an ambitious law-making and codification exercise, slowly became a world ocean-law-reform movement, suffering from all the commensurate problems that plague not only law-reform movements but also all other world bodies in recent years. In this conference we witness a full display of the self-centered interest of over 150 nation-states, dozens of regional groupings, many similar-interest groups—in both politicoeconomic and geographic terms—and the difficult conference diplomacy of the North versus South, "have" versus "have-not" confrontation. However, the stakes are very high. The clarion call for new economic equity only thinly disguises the underlying demand for a greater share in everything the oceans have to offer. The oceans have much to offer. There are fish and other seafood for the 6 billion people of the world of the very near future; there is oil and gas for a world that is going to run out of such land-based resources even more rapidly; there are minerals to feed the wheels of an unequally industrialized world. These are the multiple uses of the sea—some ancient, some modern, and many still in the future. We speak here of the near future—there is hardly anything today that can be said to be in the distant future. These many uses include the sea as a dumping ground for human wastes as land-dumping sites become scarcer, and the use of the ocean's waters for tidal energy as we run out of other sources. We will have to turn the salty water of the ocean into fresh water to feed the arid land regions of the world, which soon will have to be utilized. The sea will soon be a new habitat for people escaping the problems of overpopulation, pollution, and land scarcity.

The most ancient of all uses of the sea—ocean shipping—will be under particular pressure in the new law of the sea; yet it has scarcely been considered in this, the largest of all international conferences. The purpose of this book is to examine this particular use. We wish to step back a little from the technocratic and legal urgencies of UNCLOS III and the many other forums where the ocean debate is taking place, and to look at the evolution of international maritime law and commerce, its problems, its inequities, and its greatness. We will attempt to return to basics—not to describe nor to reinterpret history, but to examine it with the hindsight of well over three millennia of constant ocean use.

# 1 The Origins of Shipping

*The Sea with its winds, storms, dangers, doesn't change; it calls for a necessary uniformity of juridical regimes.*

—Pasquale Stanislao Mancini, (Inaugural Lecture, University of Torino, 1861)

## The Setting and the Beginning: The Ancient Mariners

It is quite feasible that our planet has the wrong name. Ancient people named it Earth after the land they found themselves surrounded by. For centuries upon centuries, people believed that the planet's surface consisted almost entirely of earth and rocks with the exceptions of some small bodies of water, such as the Mediterranean. If they had known then that almost three-quarters of their planet were covered with water, they might more correctly have named it Ocean.

The very vastness of the oceans is astounding. It is possible to be on a ship over 1,500 miles from the nearest land and, at one point in midocean, to be over 3,500 miles from the nearest continent. The seas themselves contain 330 million cubic miles of water—80 times as much as all land above sea level.[1] Land's tallest peak, Mount Everest at 29,000 feet, could be sunk without trace in the sea's deepest depth, the Mariana Trench at 36,000 feet. Moreover, if all the irregularities on the surface of the earth, both above and below sea level, were to be smoothed out, no land would show at all and the seas would cover the entire globe to a depth of 12,000 feet.[2] Yet despite this overpowering magnitude of the watery mass on our planet, people have tried since well before the dawn of history to make use of the sea. It is certain that humans were making long voyages by sea many centuries before they were able to go more than a short distance on land.[3] At the same time the sea, as a cradle of life, has also sustained it. Recent archeological and historical discoveries tell us that at least 3,000 years ago fishing had already developed into a highly organized craft.[4] It has remained so ever since. Today over three-quarters of the world's population depends on fish for the greater part of its animal protein.[5]

But here we concern outselves with man, the sailor. We now know that there were sailors before there were farmers and shepherds; that there were

1

ships before people had settled in villages and made the first pottery.[6] Seafaring has been a vital part of human history and progress for a simple reason. The most efficient means for moving people and materials in any quantity is by flotation in some sort of craft in the water. We know that the simplest form of water craft, the 10-meter North American birchbark canoe, could carry 3,600 kilograms, including the weight of eight men. Such a cargo would require thirty-five porters on land, providing that each porter could carry 80 kilograms all day long.[7] If the cargo consisted of a large and heavy piece, which neither men nor beasts of burden could carry, then a ship was the answer. We know that a queen of ancient Egypt had a pair of stone obelisks with a total weight of 700 tonnes moved the entire length of Egypt on the Nile.[8] The Romans gave us the basic principle of marine transport when they determined it cost more to cart a large quantity of grain 75 miles than to ship it by sea from one end of the empire to the other.[9] The principle of marine transport has thus remained a central part of human life. Only the methods have changed.

The world has known so many types of ships that one has replaced another very quickly, and the older ones are forgotten. We have few records save an occasional rock drawing. The Egyptians are generally credited with inventing the sail some 8,000 years ago.[10] However, it is quite possible that ships were sailed in other areas of the then-unknown world, which has given us no records. Before the sail, it was necessary to paddle or punt. The sail—probably evolved from the wind catching soldiers' shields or palm-leaf shades on the craft—was, of course, the turning point. Ships became more sophisticated, larger, and faster in a relatively short time. We should note that the adoption of wind power for land use did not take place until almost 7,000 years after the first square sail was hoisted aboard an Egyptian ship.[11]

Western civilization undoubtedly began in the littoral areas of the Mediterranean, and shipping probably originated off its eastern shores. The records are scanty or nonexistent, but there is sufficient evidence that there was already much navigation in Minoan times and a little later, almost at the dawn of recorded history, in the Phoenician era.[12] The strong Mediterranean tradition has until recently discounted the existence of sea travel in other, then-undiscovered, areas of the globe. For example, it has been stated with some authority that navigation was nonexistent in early India.[13] However, recent archeological excavations contradict this notion. It was found that brisk seaborne trade existed between the Indus people and the Sumerians in the late Third and the Second Millennium B.C.[14] However, we really know very little about these very early times since almost no records have survived. We must rely on the dim tracts of potsherds, mysterious artifacts, and other such objects. A handful of words, "bringing of forty ships filled with cedar logs," written by an unknown scribe listing the accomplishments of Pharaoh Snefru of Egypt in about 2650 B.C., brings us across a threshold into the proper period of history.[15] These words tell us not only that the ancient pharaoh imported cedar logs from Phoenicia, but also that this early international trade was accomplished by ship.

However, the world's first articulate record of large-scale economic oceanic commerce only expressed in words what had been going on for centuries. There is ample archeological evidence that the whole "fertile crescent" of the then Middle East had been engaged in a vigorous seaborne trade for a long time.[16] Cedar from Lebanon, artifacts from Syria, minerals from Cyprus and Crete all found their way to Egypt by ship. The whole period between the Late Bronze Age and the founding of the Hellenic states saw extensive maritime activity in the Mediterranean area.[17] The new urban civilization, with all the trade and need for communication that it involved, then began to spread further westward. At the same time, as ships and marine technology became more advanced, the distances over which mariners could range increased. An unusually heavy reliance on seafaring developed with only a minimal use of land travel and trade.

The early Egyptian prominence in commercial shipping was eventually overshadowed by the Phoenicians, Judeans, Greeks, and Etruscans, who would become the principal seafaring peoples for the next era. In the last millennium B.C. in particular, the Phoenicians became the true masters of the Mediterranean Sea. They had colonized Cyprus by 900 B.C., although they had trade relations with the island long before.[18] By the beginning of the seventh century B.C., Phoenicians had settled in Spain and founded Carthage in North Africa. By 600 B.C. they had established trading colonies well down the Atlantic coast of Morocco. There is considerable argument whether Phoenician sailors in the service of Pharaoh Necho of Egypt actually circumnavigated Africa around 600 B.C.[19]—a story that is brought to us by the "father of history," the Greek traveler Herodotus:

> . . . Africa, except where it borders Asia, is clearly surrounded by water. Necho, Pharoah of Egypt, was the first we know of to demonstrate this. When he finished digging out the canal between the Nile and the Red Sea, he sent out a naval expedition manned by Phoenicians, instructing them to come home by way of the Straits of Gibraltar into the Mediterranean and in that fashion get back to Egypt. So, setting out from the Red Sea, the Phoenicians sailed into the Indian Ocean. Each autumn they put in at whatever part of Africa they happened to be sailing by, sowed the soil, stayed there until harvest time, reaped the grain and sailed on; so that two years went by and it wasn't until the third that they doubled the Pillars of Hercules and made it back to Egypt. And they reported, which others can believe if they want, but I cannot, to wit, that in sailing around Africa they had the sun on the right side.[20]

Some scholars doubt that this voyage took place. Seamen do not. The Phoenicians could easily have sailed down East Africa with the following

monsoon, around the Cape of Good Hope, then up the west coast with the
trade winds.

During this period Greek sailors founded Marseille and settled in Sicily,
Italy, North Africa, and along the Black Sea.[21] Their ships carried grain
from Egypt and the Crimea, wine from Asia Minor, fabrics from Tyre,
glassware from Sidon, pottery from the Greek cities. Etruscan seafarers,
under the stimulation of nearby Greek and Etruscan settlements in central
Italy, set about establishing a developed civilization.[22] Their ships had plied
along the Italian coast for a long time, but we have evidence of considerable
Etruscan seaborne trade and settlements during the sixth and seventh centuries B.C.[23] During this millennium, the sea traffic must have been enormous. Tyre, the main Phoenician city, apparently had a population of more
than 1 million; Carthage, another Phoenician stronghold, had 700,000; and
Alexandria, then a Greek city and the grain market for the ancient Mediterranean world, had 1 million.[24] As commerce flourished, two of the seven
wonders of the world arose over two of the world's busiest harbors—the
*Ptaros* (lighthouse) at Alexandria, and the Colossus of Rhodes. By the fifth
century B.C. the entire coast of the Mediterranen was thus dotted with colonies, settlements, and trading ports. And this is where the law of the sea
enters.

### Early Sea Law: The Custom of Phoenician, Greek, and Rhodian Sea Trade

It must be obvious that this large sea commerce caused a continuous body
of "international" custom to evolve over a long period of time. Even in antiquity trade could not flourish without regulations governing it, and
regulations there were. They evolved from the continuous body of custom
that dated back to the very earliest times. Empires rose and fell; states were
in one kind of political and legal chaos after another; but the sea law appeared to continue as a growing, maturing body of law throughout these
vicissitudes. It did so because it reigned on the sea where no king or chief-
tain exercised continuous control. The mariners of all waters had common
lives, fears, and experiences, guided by the sun by day and the stars at night
and regulated by the common custom of the sea merchants—the ancient sea
law. This formed a system by itself, which centuries later would be absorbed
in the various territorial laws of nation-states. However, for almost 5,000
years it lived its own separate existence—not a sovereign formulation, but
one that although only slowly and gradually codified, was obeyed by all—at
times even by the outlaw of the sea, the pirate.

Custom is, of course, the basis of all law whether on land or sea. Since
early times, strong rulers have often attempted to codify custom into laws,

with varying degrees of success. The Tigro-Euphrates Basin, which is surely the cradle of Western law, had one of the earliest codifications. This was the *Law of Babylon*, based on earlier Sumerian laws and codified by Hammurabi about 2200 B.C., which covered almost every aspect of life.[25] Interestingly, Hammurabi saw fit to include certain rules regarding marine collisions, bottomry, and reimbursement for leased watercraft.[26] Obviously, such customary law must have been important to be included in one of the most far-reaching legal codes of pre-Roman times. However, the first really "universal" sea law began with the Phoenicians and gradually shifted west and north with the expansion of commerce—a shift which itself illustrates the history of all maritime laws. No record of Phoenician sea law has remained, but it has been pointed out that "the demands of commerce as extensive as the Phoenician must have created a system of business law. Indeed, such commerce was possible only through the existence of such a law."[27]

The Phoenicians were a mysterious and secretive people. For over a thousand years they were the leading seafarers, settlers, and traders in the Mediterranean, but their story has only recently been written. Their accomplishments were impressive. Apart from roaming, trading, and colonizing the world for a thousand years and being the undisputed masters of the Mediterranean for at least three centuries, the Phoenicians invented the alphabet, built temples and cities, and developed the type of ship that was to be used well into the Middle Ages. As previously indicated, they probably circumnavigated Africa; also, 2,000 years before the Suez Canal, they had devised ship passage between the Mediterranean and the Indian Ocean. Their invincibility ended as enigmatically as it had begun when, in 332 B.C., they foolishly offended Alexander the Great, who then conquered their stronghold, Tyre, and put most of the inhabitants to the sword.[28] However, Phoenician sea law lived on and forms the basis of much maritime law to this day.

It is precisely for this reason that we are dwelling on the early antecedents of the law of the sea here. A full understanding of modern sea law is not possible without comprehending its basis. We have so far spoken of sea law, maritime law, and law of the sea interchangeably; this is deliberate, since no real difference existed then. We believe further that there are no real dividing lines today and that many of the modern problems have been created, or have persisted, because of the artificiality of such divisions. Such problems did not exist in antiquity, although the Mediterranean at the time of the Phoenicians, Greeks, Rhodians, and even the Romans was certainly a microcosm of the modern world in terms of uses of the sea. The conceived maritime law consisted of much of the basic modern admiralty law regulating carriage of goods by sea, general average, salvage, bottomry, seamen's compensation and discipline, early forms of marine insurances, and so on.

Was there, then, no "public" maritime law at all? Of course there was. Side by side with the evolution of the early merchant ship came the development of the warship. We have records of Egyptian war galleys, Phoenician warships, and Greek armed triremes.[29] Although these vessels were often instruments of conquest, they were designed also to protect the commercial interests of the various states. From earliest times, piracy—strictly defined as "an unauthorized act of violence committed by a private vessel on the open sea against another vessel with intent to plunder (*animo furandi*)"—was a well-practiced trade. It is always considered to be part of public international law. Yet Oppenheim points out that before international law existed in the modern sense of the term, a pirate was already considered an outlaw, a "*hostis humani generis.*"[30] Piracy is thus an "international crime"; a pirate is considered an enemy of every state and can be brought to justice anywhere.[31] The early warships of the Mediterranean had among their duties the protection of ships from piracy. Of course, they also had other duties that in modern terms were akin to piracy. For example, they would ensure that "their" merchant ships remained the dominant commercial force and thus exclude intruders and interlopers during certain periods.

But even here the pattern of interdependence between "private" and "public" maritime law was already discernible. Public law and public ships were needed to protect private ships and private trade in the common interests of international commerce. Even in antiquity the whole trade pattern was already apparent, with the differing interests of suppliers and manufacturers of goods, the sources of raw materials, the markets in the major urban areas, and last, but not least, the major maritime powers which carried out actual trade and transport.[32] All were welded together under customary commercial legal principles, protected by a variety of powerful navies created to keep public order on the seas. In other words, commercial interests and strategic domination were wholly interdependent. It seems that, despite what we may believe today, this pattern has not really changed too much. Only the law governing the two areas has been divided—at times even against itself!

After the Phoenicians, maritime supremacy in the Mediterranean world passed to the Greeks, who even today are a dominant maritime force. It has been observed that the international or intermunicipal law that appeared in Greece as early as 400 B.C. included:

> . . . Maritime provisions concerning the treatment of shipwrecked *nautodikai* (sailors) and jurisdiction of the admiralty court, embargo, blockade, piracy, etc. . . . disputes arising out of maritime contracts were subjected to specially appointed judges who constituted tribunals responding to some extent to the modern commercial courts of admiralty. . . . In most Greek states there was something of the nature of a prize court, to

which appeals would be made by those who felt they had been, *contrary to the law of nations*, deprived of their property.[33]

This again illustrates the interrelationship of the private- and public-law aspects of marine transport, which appeared to be well established in the Greek states. However, at this stage we also observe the first stirrings of territorial aspirations in the law of the sea. Lobingier correctly suggests that the Mediterranean as a theater of operation was the main contributing factor in the internationalization of maritime law.[34] The Mediterranean was bordered by many nations but used in common by all. However, during this period there was no longer one completely dominant power but rather many conflicting assertive states. Marine transport was thus often jeopardized by wars, raids, and dynastic changes. We find here the first assertions of exclusive ownership over parts of the oceans which seem to be a byproduct of political instability and upheaval.[35] Many nations denounced such claims, however. Athenian policy recognized unmolested navigation, and the great Pericles even assembled an international conference to recognize this.[36] However, at this stage the Greek triremes were no longer able to enforce unmolested navigation as well as Greek commercial domination, and Greece had to resort to expressing in legal terms what was once enforced by its war galleys.[37] This, too, is a pattern that was to be repeated many times in later history.

In the latter part of Greek history, Rhodes became the chief maritime power of the Aegean. It was a period of comparative stability. Rhodes, one of the large Greek islands lying eastward toward Egypt, reached the height of its prosperity about 300 B.C. The first comprehensive maritime code, which not only regulated Greek commerce for a very long time but also supplied the basis for almost all sea law for the next thousand years, was compiled by the Rhodians.[38] Only one of its provisions has survived, and this one only because it was preserved in the digest of Justinian.[39] There it was called the *lex Rodia de jactu* and contained one of the earliest known provisions relating to the principle of general average.[40] The Rhodian code probably dates from the third or second century B.C., and its principles were accepted both by the Greeks and, as already indicated, by the Romans. Assertions by some scholars that the code did not really form the basis of Roman maritime law have been resoundingly rejected.[41] There is little doubt that the Rhodian code was actually a codification of very ancient legal principles developed over a long period of time:

> These excellent [Rhodian] laws not only served as a rule of conduct to the ancient maritime states, but, as will appear from the attentive comparison of them, have been the basis of all modern regulations respecting navigation and commerce. The time at which these laws were compiled is not

precisely ascertained, but we may reasonably suppose it was about the period when the Rhodians first obtained the sovereignty of the sea, which was about 916 years before the era of Christianity.[42]

Various other Greek cities had their own codes, usually based on the Rhodian law. We know that the Athenians were familiar with bottomry bonds and enforced them, and that there were summary maritime courts charged with maritime infractions and with the punishment of crimes committed at sea.[43] Greek law, like the later medieval law, had a considerable customary content. It was said to be "based on constantly recurring business arrangements and on the fact that the courts accepted [maritime] documents as conclusive evidence. . . . Customs originating in agreements between shippers, merchants, bankers and crews gathered force, and were supported by tribunals."[44]

However, the real apex of all pre-Roman maritime legal development must be the *Maritime Code of Rhodes*, as fragmented as it is. We will see later how it formed the basis of a newer compilation of commercial maritime law entitled the *Rhodian Sea Law*, which appeared in the seventh or eighth century A.D.[45] As already suggested, this early Greek-Rhodian period also witnessed the first stirrings of the so-called public law of the sea. There is little direct evidence of either a Greek or a Rhodian concept of freedom of the seas, but some significant conclusions can be made on the basis of the active commercial activity of the Greek states—in particular, Rhodes.

The great wealth and prosperity of these states was almost wholly dependent on maritime commerce. As a result there was particularly strong activity by Rhodes to suppress piracy and other interference in trade and travel.[46] When Rhodes found that the Athenian Sea League, consisting of some seventy Greek states, was no longer beneficial to Rhodian trade, it seceded from the league, leaving Athens and its allies to the almost continuous wars of the era. As a result, Athens set out with a fleet of sixty ships to subdue the rebels, by then joined by other states, including Byzantium. Athens was soundly defeated.[47] Yet when Byzantium started to levy dues and tributes on Rhodian ships in Byzantine ports, Rhodes went to war against its former ally and was successful in eliminating any interference with the navigational rights and freedoms of Rhodian vessels.[48]

There is little doubt that Rhodes exercised definite and almost exclusive control over its adjacent seas. This is, of course, a remarkably modern phenomenon—a maritime power exercising control over its particular interest in the ocean and being able to enforce it. Thus the assumption that the "freedom of the seas" was already fairly well established in these early times is clearly a dubious one. In his great treatise, *The Maritime Law of Europe*, Azuni has already pointed out that these ancient states extended a very effective type of control and dominion over their coastal waters and fishing areas. This need undoubtedly stimulated much of the naval and maritime activities of the times. However, Azuni concludes:

> . . . every nation situated on the borders of the sea must have soon perceived that it had an equal right to navigation and fishing, and to common participation of the advantages which might result from these pursuits. . . . This truth acquires additional force, from the consideration of the impossibility of taking possession of the high seas. . . . Every nation has an equal right to launch its fleets on that element; there, every man has a right to navigate, to transport the productions of his soil or the fruits of his industry, and to plow the surface of the deep from pole to pole. . . .[49]

This eloquent early-nineteenth-century exposition of the freedom-of-the-seas principle was, however, not a correct statement of the maritime scene of antiquity. There is ample evidence that since early times considerable restrictions were placed on these freedoms by the most powerful maritime nations of the times. Carthage exercised rigid controls over its harbors and adjacent seas, thus severely restricting the movement of foreign traders.[50] Very few foreign vessels were ever permitted to enter Carthaginian ports. On the other hand, the very founders of Carthage, the Phoenicians, were probably the first great "free traders" and encouraged foreign trade as much as the later Greeks and Rhodians did. Nevertheless, the danger of pirates and brigands in the Mediterranean necessitated a considerable amount of control, and there is thus little doubt that almost all the states in antiquity claimed a certain amount of sovereignty over the sea. Again, the distinctions are of modern interest.

It also appears that the comparatively modern phenomenon of national economic development has its analogies in antiquity. The pattern is as follows. If we start off with Azuni's freedom of the seas, we find that, first, the aspiring maritime state with an embryonic fleet of merchant ships, few warships, but an economic need to trade, would seek to espouse this freedom and attempt to give it the force of international law because it would be advantageous to do so. However, in the second stage "freedom of trade" would become a liability. By then, the state would have developed its economy, which, for Mediterranean littoral states, was always a maritime one, having as its main aim the protection of its commerce and the regulation of competition. This could be done crudely, as by the early Egyptians, by simply destroying competing ships with a protective screen of warships. It could also be done with greater finesse, as by the later Carthaginians or Greeks, by placing severe restrictions on foreign vessels and trade, which virtually put such traders out of business since they needed to come to the markets in Carthage or in Greece.

During the next stage, the aspiring maritime state had developed into a maritime power and controlled both the sea and the trade by means of its ownership of large merchant and naval fleets and, of course, by being the locus of the major markets. At this time the freedom of the sea and maritime commerce would once again be espoused by a state which now had nothing to fear from it and which, on the contrary, could use its influence to advantage. The most serious competing forces had by this time been vanquished, and full international trade and seaborne commerce would prosper under the broad protective umbrella of the state, which had monopolized the sea for its own uses and could thus speak of such freedom with little cost to itself. Naturally, as such a major maritime state's powers faded vis-à-vis newly aspiring maritime powers, the cry to protect its failing freedoms became often more genuine as well as more anguished. The result was that this pattern would repeat itself with only a change of actors, as will be discussed in subsequent chapters.

In summary, at the decline of the Rhodian era we find that a well-established body of customary commercial maritime law, crudely but effectively codified, was accepted by almost all nations in the area. We also see the beginnings of what we might call "territorial maritime law" but find this so closely related to the commercial law that any distinctions are almost indiscernible.

### Codification of Early Sea Law:
### Roman Marine Policy

The contribution of the Romans to the world's legal systems need not be asserted here. In scope, as well as impact, it has had no equal and its influence is alive and well today in all the states of the world that subscribe to the civil-law system.[51] For our purposes, however, the most important fact is that the law of Rome can also be termed the earliest truly international law.[52] Surprisingly, however, the Romans did not find it necessary to promulgate purely Roman sea law as a codified system.[53] Only in the much later Byzantine era, with the reappearance of the Rhodian code as the *Rhodian Sea Law*, did any codification take place. For most of the important earlier age, Roman maritime law was not codified as a whole. Although the process of converting portions of customary maritime law into written law began quite early, the older customary law passed into medieval times basically unchanged. To understand this phenomenon, the political and economic history of imperial and republican Rome must again be consulted. As Sanborn explains:

In its earlier days the Latin language lacked words to express sea laws, and it is a matter of history that the Romans first built large ships in the time of the Punic Wars. We shall probably not be wrong if we infer that the Romans, knowing nothing of sea travel, lacked sea laws, and it will not be surprising to see that the sea laws of the later Roman Republic followed . . . those of Rhodes, so that the principles embodied in the two systems have become substantially universal.[54]

We spoke of Greek-Rhodian sea law and thus can now speak of Rhodian-Roman sea law, as the two bodies of law are difficult to separate. As previously indicated, it has been strongly disputed by some scholars who feel that such assertions detract from the importance of the jurisprudence of Rome.[55] In our view, however, in the first place it only adds to the brilliance of the Roman juriconsults that they did not see fit to interfere in the customary maritime legal system, which had operated perfectly adequately since very early times. In the second place, nonrecognition of the Rhodian-Roman link has been decisively refuted by several eminent scholars who have brought forth considerable evidence that further substantiates the link.[56]

The lack of a uniquely Roman sea law probably results from the early lack of interest in seafaring by the Romans, who were basically an agrarian society. It has been said that, unlike the Greeks, the Romans "never felt so favourably disposed toward maritime venture and regarded the sea with horror."[57] Yet in a comparatively short period of time the Romans became not merely seafaring people but masters of the Mediterranean, which they would eventually enclose within their borders and call, as a symbol of their mastery, *Mare Nostrum*.[58] The restless domineering energy of the Romans from their beginnings as simple immigrant colonists resulted in the expansion of Roman territory by sheer conquest until the boundaries included most of the known world during the next ten centuries.

This expansion would not have been possible without the use of the ocean. Roman interests in the sea, however, appear to have been motivated largely by defensive considerations, since the numerous wars with Carthage forced the Romans to take fuller advantage of ocean transportation.[59] Consequently, by the time of the Punic Wars Rome had become one of the mightiest naval powers, with the resultant development of a merchant navy. The importance of this connection between military and commercial shipping has been vital in the political and economic growth of every major power in history, with the possible exception of the United States of America.[60] Prime examples are the Rhodians, who had been the supreme shipping power in the Aegean; the Italian city-states such as Venice and

Genoa, which possessed a mighty naval power and finally vanquished the sea power of Islam; and, of course, in more modern times the very close relationship between the military and commercial shipping of Great Britain. In addition, we must not forget the present-day growth of sea power in the Soviet Union. Although a general discussion of sea power is beyond our scope here, this point has been well stated:

> In its narrowest sense, sea power means military power at sea, in other words, navies. But no one can study the history of nations in relation to the sea without realizing that the nations that have been maritime forces have usually not depended on naval power alone. . . . One condition recognized as fundamental to a nation being a sea power has been that a great and powerful navy is dependent for its financial support on a large and active merchant marine engaged in a flourishing commerce.[61]

There is little doubt that this principle of interdependence was at one of its peaks in Roman times. A significant feature of the *Pax Romana* was the almost unchallenged security of commerce throughout the known world. For the first time in history the Roman passion for law and order, coupled with complete control of the seas, had banished piracy and other oceanic brigandage. Under such conditions Roman commerce flourished. Voyages in the Atlantic Ocean, the Red Sea, and the Persian Gulf were frequent. There was regular communication with widely separated ports of the North Sea, the East Coast of Africa, the Indian Ocean, and even China and India.[62] Large grain fleets provisioned Rome, and the speed and distances covered by Roman ships could not be excelled until relatively modern times.[63] Obviously, such widespread oceanic activities needed a law of the sea. As earlier Roman law was bare of maritime provisions, the jurists had to resort to other sources. The source tapped was, of course, Rhodes. Almost six hundred years later, when Roman law still flourished in the East although it had long since vanished in the West, it was restated that "all nautical matters in litigation are decided by the Rhodian law unless some other is found contrary thereto. . . ."[64]

The eloquent Lobingier-Benedict dispute about the origins of Roman maritime law, already referred to, points out that like English maritime law it was never codified and that only a few fragments survive.[65] However, much of it was converted into written form and we have a very good idea of many Roman maritime provisions today.[66] Lobingier interprets the division of the scope and content of Roman maritime law as having been divided into five distinct yet completely interrelated divisions, which appear to be eminently more sensible than the more recent division of maritime law into two distinct areas. However, let us examine the ancient Roman divisions a little more thoroughly.

The first section deals with the sea (*mare*) and concerns what would today be called the public law of the sea. The Roman provisions relating to the sea itself, such as they were, are of considerable importance to our discussion here as they were to form the base from which the later freedom-of-the-sea proponents were to fight. It appears that expansionist Rome, which absorbed all the conquered territories surrounding the Mediterranean, did not actually claim exclusive jurisdiction over that sea. Some of the Roman juridical utterances were quite clear and unequivocal. According to Ulpian, one of the greatest of the Roman jurists:

> The sea, which by nature is open to all, cannot be subjected to private servitude. For the sea as well as the shore and the air which is common to all, and by no law may one be prevented from fishing in front of my buildings.[67]

Celsus, in early 200 A.D., considered that the "use of the sea is common to all men, like the air." He contrasted it with the land "over which the Roman people hold *imperium* (not just *dominium*)."[68] In the following century, Marcianus held that "by natural law air, running water, the sea and hence the seashore, are common to all."[69]

In retrospect, however, we must now question whether the Roman *Digests* were actual expressions of public international law of the sea and whether we really see the forerunner of what became known as the freedom-of-the-seas principle here. The political reality of the time was that Rome regarded all of its adjacent waters as well as the whole Mediterranean Sea as a "Roman Lake."[70] In examining the *Digests* it becomes clear very quickly that the concepts of freedom and common usage express the right of *the Roman people alone*. The true international-law aspect was absent because the waters were all under strict Roman control. It is extremely doubtful whether the enunciated freedoms would have been extended to non-Romans. In any case, there were few challenges to Roman controls throughout the heights of the Roman Empire. We have no evidence of any legal document of *mare clausum*, but the reality was exactly that—the sea under total Roman control, the expressions of freedom gratuitous and without challenge. Consequently, we find no basis of the freedom-of-the-seas principle in Roman times. Rome saw the sea in completely functional terms, and in that respect there is modern relevance. There were no real principles of sovereignty involved, but simply the uses of the sea for the benefit of Rome.[71]

The second division, ship (*navis*) brings us to the principal use of the ocean. Sanborn has pointed out as the main characteristic of maritime law that it "deals chiefly with the legal relations arising from the use of ships."[72] Without ships there would be no navigation and thus little need of a law of the sea. Roman law relating to ships classified water craft into freighters and passenger vessels, and further into seagoing and inland craft. These distinctions are still valid today, and modern admiralty law's chief distinctions from the "public" law of the sea is that it relates to the vessel rather than to the medium, that is, the sea through which it passes. This section of the law is concerned also with the personnel connected with the ships—the owner (both beneficial and otherwise), master and crew, pilot, shippers, and passengers. Again there is little difference from modern legal principles. Under the Roman term *privilegium*, the personification of the ship, so well known in modern *in rem* proceedings, was already established and is probably based on this ancient principle.

The next part concerned itself with cargo (*merx*)—after the sea and the ship the most important subject matter of maritime law. Once again, modern admiralty-law principles are remarkably similar. The Roman ship was not obliged to receive cargo but, once it did, the ship's personnel were responsible for the safekeeping of the goods. Even shipwreck was at first excluded as an excuse, but later the *Digests*, on Ulpian's authority, excluded shipwreck and piratical attack for reasons of *vis major*.[73] The common law notion of the "act of God" was probably born here. Jettison (*jactatio*) was a well-known method leading to the ancient Rhodian principle of general average or contribution (*contributio*) expressed by Paulus as: "When on account of lightening the ship, goods are jettisoned, what is sacrificed for all is supplied by the contribution of all."[74] On the other hand, Roman law apparently knew no principles of salvage, that is, compensation for assistance in saving. The appropriation of shipwrecked vessels or goods was forbidden.[75]

After sea, ship, and cargo, the next division obviously relates to the responsibilities (*obligationes*) of being in the business of shipping. Again, the analogy to modern transportation is astounding. The Roman master appears to have had implied authority to purchase necessary equipment, contract for urgent repairs, and even borrow money so that the voyage could proceed. There were no specific contracts of affreightment but the principles of hiring (*locatio*) of a vessel were much the same as they are today. The whole ship or part of a ship could be chartered, and compensation was for carriage to destination. Owing to the high risk involved in shipping, the ordinary Roman law relating to loans was not suitable; and a special maritime loan (*foenus nauticum*) was devised, which set special high interest rates for borrowing money on a maritime adventure.[76] We recognize, of course, the forerunner of marine insurance, which today forms a principal part of maritime law.

Finally, the Romans had the area of dispute settlement (*actiones*) for difficulties arising out of the four preceding sections. The Romans had developed a distinctive system of maritime jurisdiction and procedures.

Wrongs and injuries committed aboard ships were tried by the ordinary Roman law relating to all *delictu*. For example, collisions at sea were governed by the Roman statutes of damages, the *Lex Aquilia*, the negligent navigator being liable.[77] Today negligence is, of course, still the basis of all maritime-collision liability.

Thus it appears that the Romans had a very capable maritime legal system covering all aspects of ocean transportation starting with the sea as a medium; then the ship as a vehicle with the crew to operate it; the cargo as the purpose of the whole operation; the responsibilities relating to the operation; and, finally, the method to settle disputes arising out of it. We have looked at this division in some detail, as it appears to have a variety of modern consequences. Many of the principles established in the second through the fifth sections are still relevant today and form the basis of much of the "private" law as we know it. Only the first section—the sea—has assumed a paramount importance completely out of proportion to the place it occupied in Roman times. In retrospect, much difficulty would have been avoided had it remained in its more modest position! Once again, only history can assist us in understanding its changing role. However, the principle already alluded to in discussing the maritime power of the Phoenicians, Greeks, and Rhodians, that the "public" law of the sea decreases in importance as the power of the dominant maritime state increases, is further reinforced. The more domination, the less real need for public law. At the same time, private commercial law will flourish as commerce increases. This was certainly true during the whole Roman period, which lasted long after the extinction of the Western Empire when dominance had shifted to the East. Once again, the analogy to modern times is interesting.

## Ocean Chaos Leads to New Sea Law: Roman Decline and Mediterranean City-States

The twilight of the Roman Empire, which was eventually to result in a general breakup of Roman law and order on the oceans for a long period, saw also the first stirrings of coastal expansionism into the offshore areas—the antecedents of the territorial sea. By the time of Emperor Leo III (717-741) the notion that the seashore was common property had been discarded, with the emperor further decreeing:

> . . . that everyone shall be the actual owner of his land on the seashore and that no one shall be permitted to enjoy the advantages thereof without his permission nor interfere therewith in any way. . . . Would he be compelled to remain passive and permit strangers alone to enjoy the fishing privilege; or must he fish on other's lands not being able to use his own?[78]

Although not directly related to our area of discussion, this is a central and crucial point of friction that has plagued the international law of the sea ever since and that affects marine transport directly. How far can a coastal state expand its "power" into the open ocean and thereby impose its jurisdiction on those using these waters? This most basic problem in the law of the sea has never really been settled, and we will return to it later.

The disintegration of the Roman Empire was followed by a very productive period in the area of commercial maritime law—the era of the early maritime codes. At first Emperor Leo III promulgated a set of admiralty laws in addition to his great *Ecloga*.[79] This was a codification of all the sea laws.[80] However, during this period the old Rhodian code reappeared as the *Rhodian Sea Law*.[81] Incorporating parts of the old code, newer customs, and Roman usages, and catering to newer needs, this code was to remain prominent for at least six or seven centuries. For the times it was quite a comprehensive codification, particularly in the areas of loss at sea and commercial risks. However, by the ninth century there existed much uncertainty over the authorized sources of the law.[82] The empire was being assailed on all sides, and Roman law needed to be something more than a customary codification. Emperor Basil I (867-886) was concerned about this and had a large code drawn up, named the *Basilica*.[83] This was a curious instrument, consisting of customary provisions mixed with positive law depending on the will of the emperor rather than on the wishes of the merchants. Maritime law was treated by the editors of the *Basilica* in the fifty-third book of the code. It was basically a rearrangement and collection of maritime provisions of the Roman *Digests* together with a reinterpretation of the *Rhodian Sea Law*.

At this stage, however, Rome was crumbling from one end of its once-mighty empire to the other. Marine transport and any law connected therewith would sink to its lowest ebb during centuries of continuous wars, insurrections, invasions, and general lawlessness. Suddenly, after the death of Mohammed at Medina in 632, the Arab world virtually exploded outward and overran almost the whole Mediterranean area with a speed rivaled only by twentieth-century mechanized warfare. By 715 all of North Africa, Asia Minor, parts of Greece and Italy, and all of Spain had come under the power of Islam, bringing 650 years of Roman rule to a definite end.[84] At the same time, the Norman, Frankish, and Barbarian invasions removed Roman rule from the Italian peninsula. The Arabs were not a seafaring people, consisting rather of a nucleus of nomadic tribes, which had swept out of the Central and Northern Arabian peninsula.[85] This nucleus quickly grew into an alliance of converts and tribal groupings, which, under the uniting banner of Islam, conquered over half of the known world by sheer power and determination. However, the Arabs' thirst and respect for knowledge and learning resulted in their world quickly becoming the most civilized and materially advanced since the very height of Rome. But Islam and Christianity were on a collision course. When two great powers are in conflict, the sky over the whole world darkens. Over the Mediterranean, still the main ocean of the world at the time, it became very dark during this bloody period.

The Arabs, or, as they were known at the time, the Saracens, quickly became a naval power by using their allies and the seafarers of their conquered and converted countries. In an amazingly short time a Saracen fleet was able to defeat and destroy a massive Christian armada, which had set out to conquer Egypt in 652.[86] For the next 600 years a Saracen galley would be a force to be reckoned with in the Mediterranean. These were sorry years for commercial marine transport. There was still trade, but ships had to proceed in armed convoys (as would be the case during World War II) to escape the ever-present pirates and raiders which might legitimately fly Christian flags or Saracen standards.[87] There was little, if any, general sea law beyond survival of the strongest. It has even been suggested—facetiously, we hope—that there was something like the freedom of the seas by default.[88] All were free to do as they liked.

In the private-maritime-law area there was developments, however. The disintegration of the Roman Empire, the Islamic-Christian confrontation, and the general lawlessness of the time combined to make self-sufficiency and self-reliance of the Mediterranean coastal communities a necessity. This resulted in the ascendancy of the Mediterranean littoral city-states, which, as independent or semi-independent entities, salvaged what was left of the ocean trade after the decline of the Roman merchant fleets. This was, therefore, one of the most formative periods in the history of maritime law. The general political conditions of the times recognized a new organization of society, giving rise to new conditions and demands; the older customary rules were simply no longer good enough. Suddenly, after many centuries of domination by central powers, dozens of cities and trading communities had to think and act independently to survive. It was probably one of the world's first great "nationalistic" expansions, perhaps rivaled only by the postcolonial period of the present century. In the earlier period the motivations were of course very different, although some of the analogies are, once again, startling.

As already indicated, the political chaos of the era had as one result the self-sufficiency and independence of the Mediterranean coastal cities. A second factor added the necessary wealth and power to sustain this independence. Between 1096 and 1270, eight massive Crusades, ostensibly to recover the Holy Land for Christendom but in reality to release the expanding energy of Western Europe, gave the newly "independent" trading cities the commerical power they needed.[89] The ships of these cities provided not only the transportation for the first great passenger traffic in the history of marine transport, but also the lifeline of goods and supplies needed for the continuous wars of the Crusaders.[90] In the other direction, the new Western European demands for the luxury goods, spices, and raw materials of the Orient provided return cargoes. The result was a competitive world of trading centers with large fleets and wealthy cities.[91] Roman law and all the customary maritime rules were no longer adequate; consequently, maritime law was quickly codified and maritime courts sprang up in most of the cities. We witness here the real beginnings of modern international shipping law. The most important "codification" cities were:

1. *Venice*: The "Queen of the Adriatic" exploited its geographic position and relations with Byzantium to become one of the mightiest states of the times. At its height, Venice had 3,000 ships and 38,000 seamen out of a population of 200,000.[92] Venetian Doges promulgated sea laws of specific and detailed character as early as 1205, and the city remained a great trading port until modern times.

2. *Amalfi*: Now a sleepy resort near Naples, nine centuries ago this was a vigorous trading city of over 50,000 people, with colonies in Syria, Arabia, India, and Africa. The city's crest bore the inscription *Prima dedit nautis usus magnetis Amalphis*, and has led to the dubious conclusion that the Amalfitians invented the mariner's compass. For us, however, the *Tabula Amalfitana* is of importance. This maritime code, not rediscovered until 1843, discloses a comprehensive codification and record of maritime laws, commercial disputes, and sea controversies.[93]

3. *Trani*: Today unknown, Trani on the Adriatic coast was another important seafaring city of the time, one that provided sources of maritime law. The decisions of the "Consuls of the Cooperation of Navigators at Trani," purported to have been compiled around 1063, is an early case-law report of decisions of the "best instructed persons in maritime matters who could be found in the Adriatic Gulf."[94]

4. *Pisa*: Today removed from the sea and mainly known for one of its gravity-defying buildings, in the early twelfth century Pisa was another important trading center. Its *Constituum usus* is a juridical collection consisting mainly of maritime- and commercial-law rules. Some scholars consider it one of the most important and complete collections of early European maritime law.[95]

5. *Genoa*: This great rival of Venice, situated strategically at the head of the Gulf of Lions, is still an important Italian maritime city today. The medieval Genovese were a maritime superpower with far-reaching trade and a particular commercial inventiveness.[96] Only fragments of an 1154 maritime enactment remain, but later formulations appear to be so firmly based on earlier law that there is no doubt that such previous codifications existed. Archives in Genoa contain some of the earliest examples of bills of exchange and policies of marine insurance, and the famous Bank of St.

George, founded in the early thirteenth century and still in existence, is one of the oldest commercial maritime institutions in the world.[97]

6. *Marseille*: Still France's most important port today, it was already so in the eleventh century when it was a semi-independent trading post. We have records of maritime laws in the *Statutes of Marseille*, dated 1253 but again based on earlier rules.[98] Besides regulations concerning the carriage of goods and seamen's conditions, the statutes, because of Marseille's importance as the originating port of the Crusades, give us some of the earliest provisions relating to the carriage of passengers.[99]

7. *Jerusalem*: The Kingdom of Jerusalem, founded by Frankish crusaders in 1099, depended, as already indicated, on the supplies and trade provided by the Mediterranean merchants. The old Frankish procedure of trial by battle, adopted for many civil suits, appeared to be quite unsuitable for the settling of maritime cases. Therefore, in the mid-twentieth century, King Amalrich I (1161-1173) formed the *Assizes of Jerusalem (Assises de Bourgeois)* to administer the customary law of the merchants trading in the area.[100]

8. *Oleron*: This small island off New Rochelle near Bordeaux in the Bay of Biscay, a region that was then English territory, became a trade center in the twelfth century as a result of the Crusades originating in the North of Europe. This resulted in the first non-Mediterranean codification of maritime laws, which was, however, still based on the early Mediterranean customary laws. The code, known as the *Rolls of Oleron*, included, in addition to the codification, the actual judgments delivered by the maritime court of Oleron.[101] The origins of the code are not known, but it has been suggested, on the one hand, that it was first promulgated by Queen Eleanor of Aquitane, feudal lord of Western France in 1160,[102] and on the other, that the author may have been King Richard I (the Lionhearted) when he returned from his Crusades.[103] Whatever its origins, the code served northwestern Europe for several centuries and influenced European maritime law quite specifically, as will be seen later.

**Conclusions**

The Mediterranean world at the close of the thirteenth century was thus a very different one from that of a thousand years before, when Rome was at its height. However, despite almost continuous wars, piracy, invasions, and other forms of instability, the sea remained the key to the area's existence. The strengthening of Christian Europe and the Islamic Near East, which had brought the two powers into destructive confrontation at the end of a long period of Roman stability, plunged the known world into the Dark Ages. However, maritime commerce survived and was possibly even strengthened by new demands placed on it by the Crusades, the new developments in ship technology,[104] and the maritime knowhow of the self-sufficient and independent city-states, which, in turn, set up their own colonies and enclaves in alliance with ascendant princes and rulers.[105]

All this time the maritime law, without which trade would have been almost impossible, was being developed and nurtured into a growing and more widely accepted body of rules. The maritime law of this period was, therefore, well developed and based on mutual trust. It was probably the only civilized institution in an uncivilized period. In this chapter we have witnessed the evolution of maritime legal concepts in their gradual movements westward and northwestward as the pivot of commercial and political power was slowly shifting in the same direction. We shall now see how this movement was reflected in the next great period, which set the scene for the *real* antecedents of the more "public" law of the sea. It should be clear that, apart from the early gratuitous Roman statements, the period just discussed knew little of the public law of the sea and that the only freedom of the sea that existed was the one that encouraged anarchy.


**Notes**

1. Leonard Engel, *The Sea* (New York: Time Inc., 1961), p. 11.

2. Ibid. See also Cuchlaine A.M. King, *Introduction to Physical and Biological Oceanography* (London: Edward Arnold, 1975).

3. Peter Freuchen, *Peter Freuchen's Book of the Seven Seas* (London: Jonathan Cape, 1958), p. 127. Recent archeological evidence shows that seafaring in the Mediterranean began some 11,000 years ago, in the late Paleolithic era—some two millennia earlier than previous estimates. See *International Herald Tribune*, October 25, 1978, p. 14.

4. Elisabeth Mann-Borgese, *The Drama of the Oceans* (New York: Harry Abrams, 1975), p. 84.

5. Ibid., p. 87.

6. George F. Bass, ed. *A History of Seafaring—Based on Underwater Archeology* (New York: Walker, 1972), p. 12.

7. Ibid., p. 8.

8. Ibid.

9. Ibid.

10. G.E.R. Deacon, ed. *Oceans* (London: Paul Hamlyn, 1968), p. 132.

11. Mann-Borgese, *Drama of the Oceans*, p. 98.

12. Lionel Casson, *The Ancient Mariners* (New York: Macmillan, 1959), p. 21.

13. F.R. Sanborn, *Origins of the Early English Maritime and Commercial Law* (New York: Century, 1930), p. 3.

14. S.R. Rao, "Shipping and the Maritime Trade of the Indus People," *Expedition* 7 (1965):30.

15. Casson, *The Ancient Mariners*, p. 4.

16. William Culican, *The First Merchant Venturers* (London: Thames and Hudson, 1966). See also Lionel Casson, *Ships and Seamanship in the Ancient World* (Princeton, N.J.: Princeton University Press, 1971); and J.G. Landels, *Engineering in the Ancient World* (Berkeley: University of California Press, 1978).

17. Ibid.

18. Bass, *History of Seafaring*, p. 39.

19. Alan Villiers, *Men, Ships and the Sea* (Washington: National Geographic Society, 1973), p. 26.

20. Casson, *The Ancient Mariners*, p. 129.

21. Ibid., p. 141. See also Raphael Sealey, *A History of the Greek City States ca. 700-338 B.C.* (Berkeley: University of California Press, 1976).

22. Massimo Pallottino, *The Etruscans*, trans. J. Cremona (Bloomington: Indiana University Press, 1975), p. 91ff.

23. Ibid., p. 82ff.

24. John H. Wigmore, *A Panorama of the World's Legal Systems*, vol. 3 (St. Paul, Minn.: West Publishing Co., 1928), p. 876.

25. Wigmore, *World's Legal Systems*, vol. 1, p. 69; Bass, *History of Seafaring*, p. 18; C.S. Lobingier, "The Cradle of Western Law," *United States Law Review* 34 (1930):8-9.

26. C.S. Lobingier, "The Maritime Law of Rome," *Juridical Review* 47 (1935):1-2.

27. Ibid., p. 2.

28. Gerhard Herm, *The Phoenicians*, trans. C. Hiller (New York: Morrow, 1975), p. 226.

29. Casson, *Ships and Seamanship in the Ancient World*, p. 77ff.

30. L. Oppenheim, *International Law*, vol. 1: *Peace*, 8th ed., edited by H. Lauterpacht (London: Longman, 1974), p. 609.

31. Douglas Botting, *The Pirates* (Alexandria, Va.: Time-Life, 1978), p. 42ff. See also Edward Lucie-Smith, *Outcasts of the Sea* (New York: Paddington Press, 1978), p. 8ff.

32. Culican, *The First Merchant Venturers*; Wigmore, *World's Legal Systems*, vol. 3, p. 876ff.

33. Lobingier, "Maritime Law of Rome," p. 3.

34. Ibid., p. 32.

35. Ibid., p. 3.

36. Ibid. See also Sealey, *History of the Greek City States*.

37. Casson, *Ancient Mariners*, p. 35ff.

38. Lobingier, "Maritime Law of Rome," p. 3ff.; R.D. Benedict, "The Historical Position of the Rhodian Law," *Yale Law Journal* 18 (1909):223; K.-F. Krieger, "Die Entwicklung des Seerechts im Mittelmeerraum von der Antike bis zum Consolat de Mar," *Jahrbuch für Internationales Recht* 16 (1973):179.

39. Sanborn, *Early English Maritime Law*, p. 5.

40. Ibid.

41. Benedict, "Historical Position of the Rhodian Law"; Lobingier, "Maritime Law of Rome."

42. W.P. Gormley, "The Development of the Rhodian-Roman Maritime Law to 1681, with Special Emphasis on the Problem of Collision," *Inter-American Law Review* 3 (1961):317, 323.

43. Edward E. Cohen, *Ancient Athenian Maritime Courts* (Princeton, N.J.: Princeton University Press, 1973), p. 96ff.

44. Sanborn, *Early English Maritime Law*, p. 7.

45. Ibid. p. 35ff.

46. Sealey, *History of the Greek City States*, p. 439ff.

47. Ibid.

48. Gormley, "Rhodian-Roman Law," p. 321.

49. W.P. Gormley, "The Development and Subsequent Influence of the Roman Legal Norm of 'Freedom of the Seas'," *University of Detroit Law Journal* 40 (1963):561, 566.

50. Ibid., p. 567.

51. Wigmore, *World's Legal Systems*, vol. 1, p. 373ff.

52. Lobingier, "Maritime Law of Rome," p. 32.

53. Krieger, "Seerecht im Mittelmeerraum," p. 184.

54. Sanborn, *Early English Maritime Law*, p. 7.

55. Benedict, "Historical Position of the Rhodian Law." See also Grant Gilmore and Charles L. Black, Jr., *The Law of Admiralty*, 2nd ed. (Mineola, N.Y.: Foundation Press, 1975), p. 3; G.H. Robinson, "An Introduction to American Admiralty," *Cornell Law Quarterly* 21 (1935):46.

56. Gormley, "Rhodian-Roman Law," p. 2; Gormley, "Influence of Roman Legal Norms," p. 568.

57. Gormley, "Influence of Roman Legal Norms," p. 573.

58. P.T. Fenn, "Justinian and the Freedom of the Sea," *American Journal of International Law* 19 (1925):716, 722.

59. Gormley, "Influence of Roman Legal Norms," p. 574.

60. Ibid.

61. C.E. McDowell and H.M. Gibbs, *Ocean Transportation* (New York: McGraw-Hill, 1954), p. 30.

62. Sanborn, *Early English Maritime Law*, p. 9.

63. L. Goldschmidt, *Handbuch des Handelsrechts*, vol. 1, 3rd ed. (Stuttgart: Heine, 1891), p. 67.

64. Lobingier, "The Maritime Law of Rome," p. 6.

65. Ibid., p. 12.

66. Ibid., pp. 18-30.

67. Ibid., p. 18.

68. Ibid. See also Oppenheim, *International Law*, vol. 1, p. 582.

69. Ibid. See also Fenn, "Justinian and the Freedom of the Sea," p. 716.

70. H. Gary Knight, *Managing the Seas Living Resources* (Lexington, Mass.: Lexington Books, D.C. Heath and Co., 1977), p. 13.

71. Fenn, "Justinian and the Freedom of the Sea," p. 726; see also Edgar Gold, "The Rise of the Coastal State in the Law of the Sea," in *Marine Policy and the Coastal Community*, edited by D.M. Johnston (London: Croom Helm, 1976), p. 15.

72. Sanborn, *Early English Maritime Law*, p. xv.

73. Lobingier, "Maritime Law of Rome," p. 23.

74. Ibid., p. 24.

75. Ibid., p. 25.

76. Ibid., p. 27; see also Sanborn, *Early English Maritime Law*, p. 18ff.

77. Lobingier, "Maritime Law of Rome," p. 29.

78. Ibid., cited p. 19.

79. Ibid., p. 17.

80. Sanborn, *Early English Maritime Law*, p. 37ff.

81. Ibid.

82. Ibid.

83. Ibid., p. 39.

84. Peter Mansfield, *The Arab World—A Comprehensive History* (New York: Thomas Crowell, 1976), p. 35ff.

85. Ibid., p. 14ff.

86. W.O. Stevens and Allan Westcott, *A History of Sea Power* (Garden City, N.Y.: Doubleday, 1944), p. 40.

87. Ibid., p. 41ff.

88. Comment. "Territorial Seas—3000 Year Old Question," *Journal of Air Law and Commerce* 36 (1970):73, 76.

89. Mansfield, *The Arab World*, pp. 64-67.

90. Ibid.

91. Crane Brinton, John B. Cristopher, and Robert L. Wolf, *Civilization in the West* (Englewood Cliffs, N.J.: Prentice-Hall, 1964), p. 214.

92. Stevens and Westcott, *History of Sea Power*, p. 53; see also Wigmore, *World's Legal Systems*, vol. 3, pp. 881-883. For a most comprehensive analysis of Venice, see Frederic C. Lane, *Venice—A Maritime Republic* (Baltimore: Johns Hopkins Press, 1973).

93. Wigmore, *World's Legal Systems*, vol. 3, pp. 880-882; Krieger, "Seerecht im Mittelmeerraum," pp. 188-189.

94. Krieger, "Seerecht im Mittelmeerraum," p. 190.

95. Ibid. See also C. John Colombos, *International Law of the Sea*, 6th ed. (London: Longmans, 1967), p. 32.

96. Krieger, "Seerecht im Mittelmeerraum," p. 191; Wigmore, *World's Legal Systems*, vol. 3, pp. 884-885.

97. Wigmore, *World's Legal Systems*, vol. 3.

98. Krieger, "Seerecht im Mittelmeerraum," pp. 191-192.

99. Sanborn, *Early English Maritime Law*, pp. 59-60.

100. Krieger, "Seerecht im Mittelmeerraum," pp. 192-193.

101. Colombos, *International Law of the Sea*, pp. 32-33; Wigmore, *World's Legal Systems*, vol. 3, pp. 893-895.

102. Ibid.

103. Colombos, *International Law of the Sea*.

104. Douglas Phillips-Birt, *A History of Seamanship* (London: Allen and Unwin, 1971), p. 120ff.

105. Lane, *Venice—A Maritime Republic*, p. 44ff.

# 2

# The Evolution of Marine Transport

*Here commence the good customs of the sea. These are the good establishments and the good customs on matters of the sea, which the wise men who traveled over the world commenced to give to our predecessors, who put them into books of the wisdom of the good customs.*

—*Consulado del Mar* (ca. 1200)

## The Expansion of European Sea Trade

The gradual shift of maritime law from the eastern Mediterranean to the west, and then along the European west coast to the northwest, indicated the slow alteration not only of the external but also of the internal structures of sea commerce. There were many reasons for this apart from those basic ones already indicated. In commercial terms, there was a discernible intensification of international commercial intercourse, which not only sharpened competition between rival maritime city-states but also, for the first time, between individual traders and ship owners.[1] The result was greater specialization in ocean trade and the offer of commercial incentives to shippers and manufacturers. At the same time, the tight framework within which the maritime cities carried on their business was enlarged—at times even broken up completely. Also, for the first time marine transport and maritime trade began to evolve and to be conceived separately. The old-style "family" shipping/trading business now became a body corporate with interregional organization and international business relations.[2]

It is really a pity that so little research has been carried out on this first important era of "multinational corporations." Examples of particular prominence are the great Italian trading companies of the time, which established wide international links and invested in all aspects of commerce and ocean transport. The Florentine companies Bardi, Peruzzi, and Acciaiuoli had branches not only in the Mediterranean but also in northern and western France, Flanders, and England.[3] In the latter country, the Lombard merchant bankers were responsible for establishing what is still the world's main trading center in the City of London.

Interestingly enough, the growth of the great private trading companies occurred side by side with the rise of state control in some of the traditional maritime states such as Genoa and Venice. In the latter, for example, shipping and trade was an integral part of national policy strictly controlled by the Doge and his government.[4] Such policy, however, quickly resulted in an even greater search for a monopoly of sea trade; and the Italian city-states fought bitterly for centuries for trading rights and for domination over adjoining seas. Rather than building on their expertise in ocean trade, these cities turned their energies toward political power and sovereignty aspirations.[5] It is a phenomenon to which we shall return again and again.

The more immediate result was, however, a considerable movement of shipping business to the western Mediterranean, resulting in very rapid expansion of the Catalan-Castilian shipping industry with Barcelona as its center.[6] During the fourteenth and fifteenth centuries the Spanish ports were thus able to control the major share of world shipping. There is no doubt that this period witnessed the first really great internationalization of marine transport. Shippers and consignees cooperated with little consideration of nationality, borders, or sovereignty. Ship owners, masters, merchants, and sailors became a truly international group, which took the place of the old family concern. Former national, regional, and even municipal loyalties, which supported the local shipping industries, gave way to commercial competition. Attempts to regulate this were not successful. The analogy to the modern concept of flag preference is again clear.

This growing internationalization in shipping naturally brought with it new legal problems that could not be solved by traditional methods or the old codes. It was now commonplace to have a Spanish-owned ship with an Italian master and crew carrying a French cargo shipped by a Flemish merchant to an English consignee. The old formula for settling disputes in the home port at the end of the voyage according to generally accepted rules and codifications would no longer work. In some of these early commercial contracts, the various parties attempted to agree in advance to settle disputes according to an agreed-on law.[7] The idea of settling disputes "according to generally accepted commercial practices," to use the phrase probably established at this time, further emphasized the very subjective approach taken.[8] Another innovation that is still familiar today was the principle of third-party arbitration, under which the shipper and consignee agreed to place any disputes arising out of their voyage before respected merchants and mariners in a neutral location.[9]

It is interesting to note that these early forms of international dispute settlement preceded most other areas of international law by several centuries.[10] At a time when passports were unknown, when people traveled into strange territory at their peril, and when transnational disputes were still solved by the sword, ocean transportation thus had a clearly understood legal basis for the settlement of most conflicts. As a result, the maritime courts of most port cities dispensed commercial justice with a sophistication that would not be reached by other courts for a long time. Nevertheless, as indicated, the demand placed on the maritime tribunals exposed their inadequacies and dependency on the old codes and regional legislation. The tribunals had become more and more specialized in the area known as *ratione materiae* and were administered by an expert body of adjudicators, the *Consules Maris*.[11] However, a new all-embracing international maritime law was urgently needed.

### Barcelona and its Maritime Code

In the Spanish port of Barcelona, *Consules Maris* were first instituted in 1272 by an order of King Peter II of Aragon. Barcelona quickly became a leading dispute-settlement center in addition to being a major port.[12] By the late 1400s a papal official described its maritime laws as follows:

> In almost every maritime city the controversies of mariners and of merchants are settled by them or by laws derived from them with the greatest authority; and as formerly man spoke of laws of Rhodes, now everyone speaks of the laws of Barcelona.[13]

The law of Barcelona was in the form of a compilation entitled *Consolato Del Mare*, which consisted of a variety of coded laws and case decisions dating back to Rhodes by way of Rome. It was essentially an updating of all Mediterranean laws—a voluminous treatise consisting of almost 300 chapters and dealing with all aspects of shipping.[14] The *Consolato* was initially published in the Catalan language at about 1300, although the first printing is lost. It was an immensely popular codification because it appeared at the right time—the time of the expansion of truly international trade and commerce. It was also the first really comprehensive code that set out in considerable detail the answers to the manifold practical requirements of legal problems of the trade of the times.

Somewhat neglected by research, the *Consolato* has only very recently been reexamined and reveals itself as a masterpiece of casuistry drawing heavily on its Roman and pre-Roman sources.[15] The case decisions are all the more remarkable when one considers that they were made by the consuls, who were laymen—not judges—and were schooled only in the commercial and nautical practices of the times. The *Consolato*'s extensive vogue caused it to be translated into most of the "commercial" languages of the era. We have records of an Italian edition printed in Venice in 1566,[16] Dutch editions printed in 1705,[17] and a further Italian edition printed in 1755.[18] Its influence thus lasted almost five centuries and led Azuni to conclude that:

> It (the Consolato) contains the best laws that existed, and which were settled at the time by men of great experience, and consumate prudence,

who, with no other guide than reason and custom, made those excellent
regulations concerning navigation, and maritime contracts.[19]

Although the *Consolato* served as the most important maritime code for
this lengthy period, several other codifications existed elsewhere. We have
already referred to the *Rolls of Oleron* as an indication of the transfer of the
commercial pivot to the north and west in the thirteenth and fourteenth centuries. In the meantime, the Hansa League of the North Sea and Baltic had
risen to eminence and begun to dominate maritime commerce all the way
from Hamburg, Bremen, and Lübeck to Novgorod in Russia, with commercial enclaves in Italy, England, and Norway.[20] The league had become a
powerful trading entity and one of the first truly multinational enterprises.
At first the league adopted the *Sea Laws of Wisby*, named after a Baltic city
on the island of Gotland.[21] In the 1200s Wisby had some 12,000 merchants
and many ships, and it adopted its set of laws from the *Rolls of Oleron*.[22]
However, in 1361 the city was destroyed and plundered by the Danes; commerce then shifted then to the main Hansa League cities Hamburg, Lübeck,
and Bremen.

### The Hansa League

Although we have been talking about the Mediterranean almost exclusively,
seafaring in northern waters was not new. It is just that we know relatively
little about it. We have a reasonable idea that since Teutonic times the
seafarers of the north had dominated their stormswept waters but had used
them more for conquest than for trade. The Angles, Saxons, and Jutes were
followed by their northern cousins, the Vikings, who harried the coasts of
Europe between the eighth and tenth centuries.[23] The Vikings, great
seafarers and mariners, were even more remarkable settlers as they founded
colonies on most of the north-European coast.[24] It has been suggested that
if they had had a national organization under one head, they might well
have conquered all of Europe.[25] Nevertheless, the Vikings mixed with the
conquered peoples, founding a northern sea tradition that has never been
extinguished. These were again lawless times of plunder and piracy similar
to the anarchy existing in the Mediterranean at the same time. As in the
south, however, peaceful trading gradually gained the upper hand. This is
where the Hansa League finds its origin.

The demand for goods and wares from the Mediterranean shores and
the Orient resulted in the expansion of the northern trading cities and in the
rapid civilization of all the northern nations. The merchant guilds of the
cities banded together to repel piracy and plunder and formed what was
probably the strongest transnational alliance Europe has ever had—the

modern European Economic Community probably being no exception. At its height the Hansa League included sixty to eighty cities. It cleared northern waters of pirates and outlaws and completely controlled almost all exports and imports.[26] Flax, tallow, and wax from Russia; iron and copper from Scandinavia; hides and wool from England; fish, grain, and beer from Germany; and manufactured goods from the entire known world passed through Hansa warehouses, were carried on Hansa ships, and were sold on Hansa exchanges with the profits being paid into Hansa banks.

The league eventually adapted the old Wisby laws into an extensive code called the *Hansa Towns Shipping Ordinance*, which became the basis for most later continental law.[27] The Hansa code dealt with a wide variety of maritime law in considerable detail and a remarkable degree of sophistication. But why should this not have been so? The code, was, after all, based on at least two thousand years of practical experience in the field of marine transport. The center of maritime law making had during this extended period moved gradually around west to north, from Rhodes through Amalfi, Barcelona, and Oleron to Wisby and Lübeck. To illustrate what must easily be the greatest legal development in history, one can, as Wigmore did, take one aspect of maritime law and trace it through this journey. The following example is the ancient principle of *jettison*, which is not known in land-based law.[28]

In modern maritime law the act of casting goods overboard in a storm to save ship and cargo is still known as jettison. Those whose property is saved must pay the losses at a rateable share. This principle already existed in the Rhodian law in 700 A.D.; only the method differed. "If a captain is deliberating about jettison, let him ask the passengers who have goods on board, and let them take a vote on what is to be done."[29] This democratic feature of jettison has, of course, disappeared today; but the principle remains. However, article 48 of the *Tabula Amalfitana* states that

> If the merchants are greedy, as some people always are, and would rather die on the spot than sacrifice anything, so that by their extreme avarice they refuse to jettison, then the Captain after protest may proceed to jettison.[30]

Two centuries later, the *Consolato Del Mare* provides a set speech, which the captain must deliver in the presence of all on board before jettisoning can be lawful. Consent is required, and one of the merchants must first cast something into the sea before captain and crew can follow suit.[31] The same rule is found in the *Rolls of Oleron*, but the captain's speech has been shortened.[32] Finally, in the Wisby and Hansa laws, the principle appears again with little change but without the requirement of consent or speech. Wigmore points to the universality of the rule when he writes of the sea code of the Malay Islands, dating back to the 1200s, and the first Mohammedan sultan, which has similar explicit stipulations.[33]

Thus by the early 1500s the common law of the sea had evolved as an anonymous embodiment of community interest. Its force was not backed by sovereigns or states, and no single jurist was its author or even its craftsman. Its rules were enforced by special tribunals that were only rarely bound by land-based laws. Its strength lay in its uniformity, which would soon be lost, never to be recovered.

### Sovereignty Over the Open Seas: The Early Claims

During the lengthy period we have been describing, relatively little happened to the public maritime law in terms of its development. We have already attempted to show that it was not a very well-developed concept in pre-Roman times and that its importance has largely been exaggerated by many international lawyers. Some of this difficulty arises out of what Gormley correctly assesses as confusion between *jurisdiction* and *sovereignty*—two terms dear to the hearts of international legal scholars.[34] He agrees fully with the opinion of the eminent Myres McDougal, who holds that sovereignty has been confused with

> . . . the occasional and limited competence over certain particular events which is commonly called "jurisdiction" . . . The competence conferred upon the states by "freedom of the seas" is not an absolute competence, but a relative, shared competence which can survive only if it is exercised in accommodation with the similar competence of others.[35]

It is, therefore, probably quite true to say that the Romans exercised definite guardianship over the seas under their concept of *populi Romani esse* and that they regarded this guardianship as a sacred trust on behalf of the general welfare. However, this was not the same as the contemporary notions of sovereignty or jurisdiction. In any case, as already noted, it also was a rather one-sided guardianship—basically for the benefit of the Romans.

The power void created by the disintegration of the Roman Empire and the resulting oceanic appropriations and claims of the smaller states necessitated a certain revival of older public-law concepts as well as the creation of new ones. In retrospect, there was really very little of what we might remotely call the "national law of the sea." Mediterranean city-states simply claimed a certain jurisdiction over their adjacent waters. Such claims were then quickly transposed into principles of law by ever-willing legal scholars. Claims would include distance coordinates that depended on the area within which the particular state's navigational requirements were confined. Distances extending from 60 to 100 miles, including all the bordering seas, were common.[36] At times legal principles governing ownership of rivers would be transposed to the sea claims. If a state held both shores, then the waters in between could be claimed; if only one shore were held, then one-half to the midline could thus be claimed.[37]

Although always couched in imaginative legal terms, such claims were invariably enforced by the use of military power and led to many a sanguinary war. However, the motivation was always the same—to preserve a commercial status quo. This point has rarely been emphasized by later legal scholars, who might argue that the legal principle and not its motivation is of the essence. In that case, a very basic and probably irreconcilable conflict would exist between such a view and ours.

We are here at a crucial point in a book that examines the international law and policy of marine transport. The basic question is whether the principles of international law are hard and fast rules to the extent of abstraction and even absurdity, or whether, like all other law, they are a living and vibrant whole that is servant and not master to changing ocean policy? We go further and say that there were, in post-Roman times, hardly any hard and fast rules of international law of the sea at all. For example, when Venice, long before the thirteenth century the most eminent, wealthy, and powerful maritime city-state in the Mediterranean, claimed the whole Adriatic Sea—despite the fact that it was not in possession of both shores—enforced its claim, and levied tribute on foreign ships or banned them altogether from passing, what specific law of the sea was being broken?[38] Roman law? Rhodian law? Certainly Venice's act was discriminatory and unjustified—but was it really illegal? Had the law of nations advanced far enough at that stage to make it so?

We think not. For those who cling to the clear principles established by the Roman jurisconsults, the fact that Roman power was supreme and that it was easy to speak of freedom when only Romans would have its advantages must surely be bothersome. The Roman language was indeed clear and quite specific—we could even say that as far as Rome was concerned the stipulations were meant to have legal force. However, law cannot truly exist in a vacuum; a law that survives solely because it was drafted will become meaningless. Instead it must be clearly linked to the practices, actions, and policies of the times in which it was composed. We have already indicated in chapter 1 that this cohesion did not exist in Roman times, and we suggest that it did not exist in any tangible form until well into the sixteenth century. We have stated the proposition that the importance of the public aspect of maritime law decreases as the power of the dominant maritime state increases. The reverse is also true, and we are here examining the advent of the period during which the fragmentation of maritime power encouraged a greater emphasis and interest on the public international law of the sea. At the same time it should be emphasized strongly that there was little, if any, established public law of the sea at the beginning of this era.

It was for two basic reasons that the fifteenth century witnessed this increasing interest in the public-law aspect of ocean law. Not surprisingly, these were both political in expression although still very much commercial in motivation. The first, already alluded to, was the fragmentation of maritime power in most of the seas known to man at the time. The advent of the city-states in the Mediterranean and the north and west of Europe with their awesome commercial power, wealth, and influence, would result first in bitter commercial but soon in military confrontation, which would take place on the oceans.

The reasons for this are not difficult to fathom. History tells us that wealth, luxury, and power carry themselves the germs of decay and corruption.[39] The decline of the city-states was probably no different, but was greatly influenced by the sacrifice of permanent for immediate interests in their marine policies. It is a pattern with which political philosophers are particularly familiar. The rise of Venice, the "Queen of thé Adriatic," as a commercial and naval power, is an example.

Obviously Venetian foreign policy was guided solely by the city's commercial interests, but because of human nature this was soon not enough.[40] At first there was a modest expansionist policy to "protect" trade interests. Venice had already conquered Crete in 1204 and kept it for 400 years. Cyprus was seized in 1479; and political control was also extended to Treviso, Padua, Verona, and other north-Italian cities. But by 1350 Venetian trading vessels and warships were state owned, and its trading monopoly was being steadily extended throughout the whole Mediterranean.[41] Great trading fleets under strong naval escorts set forth each year from Venice to Alexandria, Syria, Constantinople, the Biscay Coast, England, and Belgium. Competition was fierce with other Italian trading cities and cities in Mediterranean France and Spain. At first this fierceness was expressed purely in competitive commercial terms, but new monopolistic policies eventually dictated stronger action. It was then only a short step to proclaiming such monopolies and backing these up by annexing adjoining seas, while expressing it all in legal terms.

In other words, this is an example of the classic form of unilateral action by a sovereign state. Venice, after declaring its monopoly of all the Levantine trade, also declared its exclusive jurisdiction over the whole Adriatic Sea.[42] Genoa followed suit by invoking a charter that granted it a similar monopoly and claiming the Ligurian Sea and the Gulf of Lions.[43] Many other cities made similar claims. The splendor and magnificence of the Venetian Doge's annual marriage with the sea is well known. He would cast a golden ring into the sea and speak the words *desponsamus te mare, in signum veri perpetuique domini"* as a symbol of Venice's perpetual mastery over the whole Adriatic Sea.[44]

Claims over the ocean mushroomed between 1300 and the mid-1500s. In addition to the Mediterranean where little "free" or nonannexed ocean remained, the cities and states on the Atlantic coast of western Europe and in the North and Baltic Seas engaged in similar practices. The rise and decline of Venice is a good analogy for most of them. In the Baltic Sea, the Sound and the Belts came under Danish jurisdiction, while the Gulf of Bothnia fell under Swedish rule.[45] In the North Sea the area between Norway and the Shetlands, Iceland, Greenland, and Spitzbergen were claimed by Norway and later by Denmark.[46] Obviously, multiple monopolistic claims over the same area would have to lead to conflicts, and so they did. For well over three centuries the claims, counterclaims and demands of these states led to endless discussions, many wars, and numerous treaties. Alliances were forged and shattered, and the commercial power and wealth accumulated over many centuries of relatively peaceful trading was expended in wars where everyone was a loser. The Hansa League, for example, after flourishing for over two hundred years, became tyrannical and arbitrary, engaged in countless wars, and lost respect and influence. As a result, the monopoly that the league had previously achieved by peaceful means, but had sought to extend by tyranny, was lost forever.

More important in this context is that, owing to the difficulty of the times, the public aspect of the law of the sea began its renaissance. The confusing series of claims, counterclaims, declarations, demands, and proclamations over the sea forced jurists to develop a new approach in public law. The well-developed private maritime law was neither designed nor adequate to deal with the new pressures. Old tenets of Roman law were resorted to and resurrected, rewritten, expanded, interpreted, and often misinterpreted. The pattern of legal development was in keeping with previous history. Public maritime law increased in importance with the decline of the dominant maritime powers.

## The Enlarged Oceans: The Age of Discovery

The second influence on the rise of the public law of the sea, although itself influenced by the first, was the rather sudden enlargement of the known world. From the days of the Phoenicians until the end of the fifteenth century all trade between Europe and Asia had to cross the land barrier of the eastern Mediterranean. Oriental goods were delivered by Moslem vessels at the head of the Arab/Persian Gulf to Red Sea ports and then followed traditional caravan routes across Arabia or Egypt to the Mediterranean, quadrupling in value during transit.[47]

Contact and trade between East and West, active in Roman times, was stimulated by the Crusades and by a greatly expanded European horizon accentuated by new trade interests and connections. Oriental goods were in demand in Europe, but the supply routes were unreliable and fraught with danger because of the continual Christian-Islamic hostilities. The capture of Constantinople by the Turks in 1453, together with the general instability of the trade routes in the eastern Mediterranean owing to piracy, Saracen attack, and city-state rivalries, revived the old desire among the nations of Western Europe to find the elusive water route to Asia either around Africa or else directly westward, off the edge of the known world. The results were the great voyages of discovery, particularly by the newly ascendant Iberian "superpowers," Portugal and Spain.

The great Mongol conquests of the thirteenth century under Ghengis Khan and Kublai Khan had succeeded in uniting most of Asia, the Near East, and eastern Europe, and had opened direct communication between Europe and the Orient, raising the prospect of an alliance against the Moslems. Africa, long familiar to the Arabs, was also slowly being opened up by European exploration. Between 1394 and 1460, Prince Henry the Navigator of Portugal had either personally explored or directed the exploration of much of West Africa.[48] Within the next half century the rest of Africa was opened up to Portuguese influence and trade. Once started, the discoveries occurred at a fast pace, leaving little of the globe unknown to man. By 1486 Bartolomeu Dias had rounded the Cape of Good Hope, followed a few years later by Vasco de Gama, whose voyages established complete Portuguese authority in East Africa.[49] In 1501 the voyage of Pedro Cabral established Portuguese trade connections in India.[50] Between 1513 and 1557 Portugal also established itself on the Chinese coast, in Canton and Macau.[51]

On the other hand, Spain took on the unknown seas to the west of the world. Christoforo Colombo, not surprisingly Genoese, in the service of Spain reached the "New World" on his first voyage in 1492; discovered most of the Caribbean islands on his second voyage (1493-1496); reached Trinidad and South America on his third voyage (1498-1500); and reached Central America on his last voyage (1502-1504).[52] Meanwhile, Amerigo Vespucci, in the service of Portugal, reached Brazil in 1501. Brazil had, however, already been claimed by Pedro Cabral in the name of Portugal in 1500, when Cabral was on his way to India.[53]

John Cabot, born in Genoa but resident in Venice and in the service of Bristol merchants, opened up the northern seas when, spurred on by Colombo's discovery, he reached the northern part of the North American continent in two voyages of 1497 and 1498.[54] In 1513 Vasco Nuñez de Balboa crossed the Isthmus of Panama and took possession of his discovery—the Pacific Ocean—for Spain.[55] Finally, Ferdinand Magellan, sent by the Spanish

Crown to find a route to the Moluccas, reached Brazil and Argentina, sailing into the South Seas and taking possession of the Philippines, then continuing westward and completely circumnavigating the globe for the first time.[56] In just over one generation the world was thus completely opened up for human endeavors, and a new age was ushered in. The great voyages were a navigational marvel—the culmination of development and innovation in ocean transportation over several thousand years.[57]

The age of discovery naturally brought with it new pressures on a traditional law of the sea that was ill suited to cope with such demands. The Iberian superpowers not only took possession of all newly discovered land territory but also of the newly opened-up oceans.[58] This was bound to lead to conflict and confrontation between the two great Catholic nations. As a result, several Popes issued edicts allocating the newly discovered regions to either Spain or Portugal with the object of maintaining peace between them.

Conveniently, from 1492 to 1503 a Spaniard, Alexander VI Borgia, occupied the Throne of St. Peter.[59] On May 3, 1493, just after Colombo's return from his first voyage, Alexander VI issued a Bull in which he conferred on Spain title to all lands discovered, or yet to be discovered, in the western seas.[60] More important to this discussion, on the very next day he issued another Bull in which he divided Spanish and Portuguese claims by a line running from north to south "one hundred leagues West of the Azores and the Cape Verde Islands." At the same time he granted a trade monopoly to Spain in its area so that no other nation could trade without a Spanish license.[61]

In other words, the waters of the world had been divided and allocated to two nations by papal decree, at that time the highest form of legal instrument. Stevens, writing about this extraordinary decree, said that it was ". . . small wonder that the French King, Francis I, remarked that he refused to recognize the title of the claimants until they could produce the Will of Father Adam, making them universal heirs."[62] Nevertheless, in 1494 the Treaty of Tordesillas between Spain and Portugal fixed the demarcation line more firmly at 370 miles west of the Cape Verde Islands, giving Portugal the Brazilian coast.[63] An additional clause made unauthorized trade in the area punishable by death. In theory, if not in effect, *mare clausum* had been established.

Obviously, such all-embracing claims would not go unchallenged. The challenge was to give birth to the first really viable principles of public law of the sea. Thus at the end of the sixteenth century we see a drastically enlarged world in which a vigorous and far-reaching international seaborne trade is carried out. We see the real beginnings of nation-states and national sovereignty, to which former commercial supremacy had to give way. The traditional private maritime law had been further developed as well as internationalized, but the intense rivalries of the major trading states, in addition to the greatly expanded world, brought political consideration into the forefront. This would require an entirely new effort in the making of a public law of the sea.

## Colonies and Conquests:
## Sea Trade and Maritime Conflict

In the course of the sixteenth century—the age of Charles V, Holy Roman Emperor of Germany; of his son Philip, King of Spain; of Francis I of France; and of Henry VIII and Elizabeth I of England—the map of the world was drastically altered, enlarged, and corrected. By the end of that tumultuous century, there was hardly any "unknown" world left.[64] All this was the product of the new era of marine transport, which had seen considerable progress in the art of navigation and nautical skill, as well as the development and perfection of better and larger ships and other new marine technology.[65] This was, of course, a response to the new maritime and commercial intercourse of the European states, which was being rapidly increased and extended. In many states various international establishments, such as shipping corporations, were formed by governments for the protection and encouragement of maritime commerce.[66] Treaties between states proliferated; and international rules, founded on reciprocal advantage, came to be recognized.[67] In addition, the external maritime and commercial relations of states and communities and of their subjects multiplied rapidly. This resulted in new demands being made on traditional principles of maritime law as well as on the common or consuetudinary law of nations.

From the commerical point of view, an age of unprecedented prosperity for the greatly enlarged world appeared imminent, but the political realities of the times were not conducive to such a development. The rise of the Iberian superpowers already mentioned, coupled with the strengthening of other European states—all governed by strong monarchs—resulted in a period of nationalism of the type that is common today. Although the actors and the methods have changed, the scenario is strikingly familiar. Like that of the city-states in the medieval Mediterranean, the commercial and military power of the various European states and their new-found nationalism was bound to lead to conflict. Much of this conflict was to take place on the ocean and would thus directly affect all aspects of marine transport for the whole period.

*The Iberian Decline*

After Portugal came under Spanish rule in 1580, Spain was able to claim dominion over all the seas.[68] However, as already indicated, it is easier to claim than to hold. There were immediate challenges to these Spanish claims. In addition, Spain, at that time unrivaled as the leading maritime nation in the world, was in difficulty. The confidence with which Spain had set out on its many discoveries in the New World quickly led to disappointment when further explorations revealed the vast continents to be populated with inhabitants who opposed the *conquistadores* bitterly.[69] There was no thoroughfare to the East and no lucrative commerce. Not until the conquest of Mexico by Cortez was some assurance of treasure given. The accumulated wealth of seven centuries then began to pour out of America in an endless procession of bullion ships across the Atlantic Ocean.[70]

But the 3,000-mile "lifeline" was a long one, and there were many enemies. First, the ocean—still a formidable opponent for the frail craft consisting mostly of impressed merchant ships designed for European trading—was of prime importance.[71] In addition, the challengers to Spanish supremacy—the French, Dutch, and English—began to prey on the Spanish fleets. Furthermore, Spain had to protect its coastline from raiders; guard its possessions in the Netherlands and Italy against independence-seeking inhabitants; and make war continually against Islam, the constant enemy.[72] The wealth of the Americas thus ended up in German or Genoese banking houses and was expended in the purchase of foreign luxuries and the waging of endless imperial wars. Agriculture, industry, and trade at home were neglected and in the overseas colonies were scarcely even attempted.[73] The most powerful nation in the world declined not so much because of the continued wars and challenges to Catholic supremacy but because it had:

> . . . depended for its support, not upon a widespread healthy commerce and industry that could survive many a staggering blow, but upon a narrow stream of silver trickling through a few treasure ships from America, easily and frequently intercepted by the enemy raiders.[74]

The detail given here is essential to the understanding of the background and the scenario for the next thrust in the law of marine transport. The slow decline of the Iberian states left a power vacuum in Europe that, when filled by a group of other states would lead to national rivalries. These would consequently lead to the foundation of much of the public law of the sea as it is known today. The historical analogy is again clear. The decline of the Roman Empire resulted in a fragmentation of maritime power that brought about the blossoming of the maritime codes of the private maritime law. The new, more nationalistic and political age would result in the formation of a new, public maritime law. This was basically brought about by the maritime development of two comparative newcomers on the maritime scene.

### The Commencement of English Maritime Power and Law

While the Iberians were expanding their bullion and spice routes, the English under the Tudor monarchy were slowly formulating a policy that would eventually lead to virtual British domination of seaborne trade. However, the beginnings were indeed modest. In the early sixteenth century English trade was inconsequential.[75] There were few seamen and fewer ships, and most of the island's commerce was carried out by the Hansa League and Italian trading houses. However, Henry VII (1485-1509), who displayed a "grasp for finance, commerce and the principles of economic power such as no European sovereign had evinced before,"[76] and probably few thereafter, saw the need for truly English maritime commerce. He passed navigation laws favoring English vessels (the first flag-discrimination rules in history invented by a nation that was to fight such laws bitterly in the twentieth century),[77] strengthened the embryonic Royal Navy, and negotiated more equitable commercial treaties with the Hansa League as well as with the Dutch and the Spanish.[78]

Although deeply religious and a friend of Spain, Henry VII nevertheless challenged and opposed the Iberian division of the New World, which did not consider the rights and claims of other nations.[79] Instead, he laid down the Doctrine of Effective Occupation, which has since become a part of the law of nations.[80] Under this principle he stated that he would only recognize the rights of other nations to lands actually in their possession. Accordingly, he stayed out of Spanish territories and sent John Cabot across the northern part of the Atlantic to find a new route for the spice trade. Instead, Cabot discovered "New Found Land."[81]

However, Henry VII's successors were no longer bound by religious ties and alliances to practice new commercial trade with ubiquitous diplomacy. Instead, English merchant adventurers attempted to open up legitimate trade with the West Indies.[82] When this met with Spanish opposition—often leading to capture and imprisonment—the English navigators turned to privateering, plundering, and even piracy. For example, Drake's voyage around the world (1577-1580) was undertaken at Elizabeth I's request, but his plundering on the way paid for the voyage.[83] Subsequently, relations between England and Spain deteriorated to open war in 1585, culminating in the defeat of the Armada, which, in no small way, further hastened the decline of Spain.[84] It ultimately destroyed Spanish maritime supremacy forever and "freed" the oceans for new masters. These were not long in arriving.

The reign of Elizabeth I (1558-1603), once the Spanish threat had been removed, was characterized by maritime commercial activity and exploration. The Willoughby expedition, searching for a northeast passage to India via the coast of northern Russia, had been unsuccessful in finding such a passage but had made a trade treaty with Tzar Ivan (the Terrible) in Moscow, leading to the foundation of the British Muscovy Company.[85] Another, better-known trading company also founded at this time was the British East India Company, which brought larger profits than any trade in which England had previously engaged.[86] The company's ships, the "East India Men," were really the first purposely built merchant ships designed for a specific trade.[87]

The Spanish vacuum in the Atlantic resulted in dozens of English ships trading to the West Indies and exploring the western shores of North America, still in search for the elusive Northwest Passage. Navigators had become convinced that they had to sail around the American continent to reach Asia. The shorter route to India and Cathay, which would avoid the still Spanish-Portuguese-monopolized Cape of Good Hope route, drew many famous English sailors. Among these were Sebastian Cabot, Martin Frobisher, John Davis, William Baffin, Humphrey Gilbert, and Henry Hudson.[88] The skill of English sailors and navigators increased as rapidly as the technology of the ships in which they sailed.[89] The sea had become an English occupation with the kind of government encouragement the Spanish and Portuguese seamen never received. Nevertheless, it would take many more years before England would become commercially independent. A start was made when, in 1578, Elizabeth I cancelled the special privileges of the Hanseatic traders in England and closed their great warehouses in the Steelyard of London.[90] However, as we will discuss further, the real pivot of the words "maritime commerce" was shifting to the Netherlands. Meanwhile, let us see what sort of maritime law was being followed by the English and their new merchant fleet.

The primary source of English sea law, even to the present time, was a collection of prior laws dating from Rhodes and the *Rolls of Oleron* called the *Black Book of Admiralty*.[91] The collection is thought to have been compiled in the early fourteenth century in the reign of Edward II and elaborated by Richard II and Henry IV.[92] It was basically a practical collection of rules of maritime law and practice for use in the Admiral's Court. Originally written in the Norman-French language, but later translated into English, the *Black Book* drew heavily on the Domesday Books of the English maritime boroughs, which, from earliest times, had administered the customary law of the sea to English and foreign mariners and traders.[93] The *Black Book* was constantly revised and expanded as circumstances required but served as an accepted maritime code throughout this expansive period in English maritime commerce. In Scotland a collection of "Sea

Lawes" was compiled by Sir James Balfour and consisted simply of local maritime legislation, the *Rolls of Oleron*, and the Wisby laws. It was compiled about 1579.[94]

The concept of protection against loss by maritime perils—in modern terms, marine insurance—had been in existence since Roman times. All the maritime codes made provisions for it, but it was perfected by the Hansa League in cooperation with the Lombard banking houses in London.[95] It has never since left that city. In 1578 the Hansa merchants lost their privileges by royal order. When the league attempted to retaliate against English merchants in the Hansa cities, an angry Elizabeth I had them deported from England in 1597.[96] However, the Hansa trade, including the marine-insurance business, was quickly taken over by English merchants. The first enactment relating to marine insurance to be placed on the statute book of England was put through the British Parliament in eight days in 1601 and forms the basis for all marine-insurance law in the Anglo-American world to this day. It was entitled *An Act touching Policies of Assurance used among Merchants* and was based largely on the assurance statutes of the Hansa League. In the preamble of the act, reference is made to the long-established practices of sea insurance, demonstrating how firmly the principles were already generally accepted. There is no more succinct definition of the whole object of marine insurance than this preamble:

> It hath been tyme out of mynde an usage amongste merchantes, both of this realme and of forraine nacyons when they make any great adventure speciallie into remote partes, to give some consideration of money to other persons (which commonlie are in noe small number) to have from them assurance made of their goodes, merchandizes, ship and things adventured, or some parte thereof, at suche rates and in suche sorte as the parties assurers and the parties assured can agree, which course of dealinge is commonlie called a policie of assurance, by whiche . . . it comethe to passe that upon the losse of perishinge of any shippe there followethe not the undoinge of any mann, but the losse lightethe rather easie upon many than heavilie upon few, and rather upon them that adventure not than on those that doe adventure, whereby all merchantes speciallie the younger sorte, are allured to adventure more willinglie and more freely.[97]

It is believed the Francis Bacon himself drafted the act and also sponsored the bill in the House of Commons.[98]

It appears, therefore, that in the Tudor period the maritime law of England was well established in conformity with most of the continental codes and was definitely the leader in the area of marine insurance. What about the more public maritime law? We have already suggested that the Iberian division of the world never was accepted and was openly challenged by many other European powers. In England this reached its peak during this particular period. Of course, famous English navigator-privateers, such as Drake and Hawkins, physically challenged Spanish assertions with impudence and success. This resulted in the Queen of England making one of the first recorded comprehensive statements on the freedom of the seas. When the Spanish Ambassador to England complained to Elizabeth I about the English raiders' flagrant violations of the Spanish *mare clausum*, he was told that the Spanish had brought these difficulties on their own heads since they, contrary to the "law of nations," had prohibited the English from carrying on commerce in these regions. The queen said that she was unable to understand why her subjects and others should be barred from the "Indies." She could not recognize the prerogative of the "Bishop of Rome" that "he should bind princes who owe him no obedience." Her subjects would continue to navigate "that vast ocean," since "the use of the sea and air is common to all; neither can any title to the ocean belong to any people or private man, for as much as neither nature nor regard of the public use permitteth any possession thereof."[99] This eloquent formulation of what is frequently still considered a hallowed principle of international law, was confirmed in 1602 when Elizabeth I gave similar instructions to her ambassadors to the Court of Christian IV of Denmark.[100]

However, we must question again whether at this stage we really see a proper formulation of international law or simply a repetition of our previously stated proposition that the importance of the public aspect of maritime law increases as the power of the dominant maritime state decreases (or vice versa). Again, we feel that the latter is the case. The maritime domination of Spain, although never really complete, was waning; and weaker states, such as England, were challenging this domination by all available means. Recourse to natural-law principles of basic freedom fit well into this type of challenge. However, we shall see how inconsistent England's earlier "freedom" principles became when that country itself achieved maritime dominance. The analogy, therefore, still fits perfectly. Now we must look at the rise of Holland as a sea power.

*The Rise of Dutch Sea Trade and*
*Commercial Power*

It has been said that if the English were drawn to the sea, the Dutch were driven to it, for the land could not produce enough to support their population. Recent advertisements for KLM, the Dutch National Airline, refer to "those surprising Dutch." This is probably true today and certainly so in the sixteenth and seventeenth centuries, when the Netherlands produced the world's best navigators, traders, scholars, and fighters.[101] They built better ships more cheaply and sailed them more skillfully than any other people since the Phoenician period.[102] Situated at the seaboard outlet of Europe's greatest rivers, the Dutch ports had for a long time been of importance as central distribution centers for the world's trade. By 1550 Dutch ships were already monopolizing European coastal trade routes (as they still do to a great extent today). Their great trading centers—Amsterdam, Leiden, Rotterdam, Bruges, and Lille—were the most civilized, liberal, cultured, and wealthy cities in the world.[103] In addition to their trading interests, they had also established a large fishing industry and had perfected a method of preserving fish for export to the Catholic Mediterranean.[104]

The rise of the "surprising" Dutch took place against a background of war and violence of almost unprecedented magnitude. The low countries were originally a loose collection of ducal powers, which came under the control of the dukes of Burgundy in 1384 through a variety of purchases, marriages, and cessions. Ultimately, the predominantly Calvinist area passed into the hands of the Holy Roman Emperor, Charles I, who annexed the seventeen provinces in 1548.[105] When Charles I abdicated in 1556, the Netherlands, like Spain, passed to his son Philip II (1556-1598). Rigid and cruel Spanish rule and the mass imposition of Catholicism quickly led to the outbreak of revolt in 1568. Conflict lasted almost continually for a period of eighty-eight years until 1648, when the Treaty of Westphalia recognized the independence of the Republic of the United Provinces of the Netherlands.[106] However, by 1580 the Dutch had already defeated the Spanish sufficiently to be semi-independent in the north, and had formed their own government, the States-General, which immediately recognized the importance of seaborne trade for Holland.[107] Dutch ships were continually harassed by the Spanish and Portuguese in European waters, and it was felt that the overseas trade to the East Indies would be a better commercial venture.

To eliminate the destructive competition that developed among the various Dutch trading groups, the States-General founded the Dutch East India Company in 1602.[108] This charter corporation was given the monopoly for all Far Eastern trade. It was a spectacularly successful venture. Between 1607 and 1620, investors earned a return of from 80 to 280 percent on their investment annually.[109] By 1610, the Dutch merchant and fishing fleet was estimated to consist of over 16,000 sailing vessels, with a total tonnage of almost 1 million, manned by some 160,000 crew members. In the meantime the States-General had also incorporated the Dutch West Indies Company to trade with some 800 ships in the Caribbean—once an exclusive Spanish enclave.[110] In a relatively short time, Dutch ships were to be found engaged in every kind of legal and illegal trade on all seas. At its peak, the value of merchandise shipped in Dutch ships was estimated to amount to over 1 billion gold francs per year.[111]

There is little doubt that marine transport proper, as we know and understand it today, really began at this time. The earlier traders, particularly the wealthy Italian merchant-ship owners, and later the Spanish and

Portuguese, dealt mainly with the more exotic high-value merchandise; the Dutch, however, offered vessels to carry everything and anything as long as the freight was economical. For the first time wheat, timber, hemp, fish, tar, ore, iron, and leather were starting to be transported in large quantities in ships built for that purpose.[112] This was a turning point in the history of marine transport. The Dutch middle-class burghers had an entrepreneurial skill that also appears surprisingly modern. They quickly saw that maritime trade must be a two-way affair that must not only benefit the wealthy and powerful, but must also involve the shipowner as a carrier performing a service. It is suggested that losing sight of this principle had resulted (and will always result) in the deterioration of ocean transportation—although transportation economists might voice this interjection with greater finesse.

In any case, by 1650 the Netherlands was the greatest shipping nation the world had seen up to that time.[113] Its position was entirely analogous to that of Great Britain just before World War I. In addition to owning and controlling the world's largest shipping fleet, the Dutch also had a virtual monopoly of much of the world's trade, which depended on marine transport. There was, however, one great difference between the Dutch position and that of their later rivals, the English. They had virtually no exports of their own, depending solely on "cross-trading." Thus, like all such traders since that time, they were at the mercy of third parties who could be wooed away by effective competition and price cutting.

The Dutch domination in maritime commerce obviously required regulation, and a fairly comprehensive system of maritime law had been long established. Much of this, however, was based on existing customs, usages, and other maritime codes. For example, the *Judgments of Damme*, in use in the Flemish area for a long time, was really such a collection.[114] It was an almost literal copy of the first twenty-four articles of the *Rolls of Oleron* and probably passed into the area in the thirteenth or fourteenth century. Other maritime usages were collected in the *Customs of Amsterdam* and of other maritime cities, which combined the Damme laws with certain parts of the Wisby laws.[115] There is evidence of the practice of marine insurance dating back to 1377 in Bruges, which was the most eminent center in that area of maritime law.[116] It was, however, in the public area of maritime law that Holland was to make its greatest contribution.

## The Birth of the Modern Law of the Sea: The Times of Grotius

As often happens, the circumstances surrounding this breakthrough of the public law were not really unusual. As previously mentioned, the Dutch had been sailing to the East Indies for some years in contravention of Portuguese claims to monopoly. They had avoided open confrontation and were instructed to fight the Portuguese only if attacked themselves. Unfortunately, this frequently occurred; and added to the general political situation in the Netherlands, persuaded the *Verenigde Oostindische Compagnie* (Dutch East India Company) to give secret orders to their captains to "cause the common enemy the maximum amount of damage both at sea and on land."[117] However, even before the formation of the company in 1602, two heavily laden Portuguese ships were captured, one off St. Helena and the other in the Strait of Malacca, the rich booty being conveyed to the Netherlands.[118]

The advantages of such action could not have been lost on the newly formed company. Before receiving the company's new instructions, the famous Dutch maritime hero, Jacob van Heemskerk, captured the Portuguese carrack *Catharina* in 1603.[119] The vessel was laden with treasures from the Indies, and the booty reached the Netherlands in 1603. The Dutch Admiralty Court had to adjudicate the booty claimed by the attorney-general of Holland, as well as by Admiral Heemskerk and the Dutch East India Company. Three citations for unknown claimants to the ship were made; when no one appeared, the vessel and its cargo were declared a good prize less than two months after their arrival in Holland. The ship and cargo were sold for almost 4 million guilders. After subtraction of expenses, payment of the crew and the admiral, and the state's percentage, the company retained a sum that was more than double the invested capital.[120]

This prize, which had been considered "the best, the real fruit of trade with the Indies," did not meet with general agreement, however.[121] There were serious objections that the government, instead of limiting its ships to honest trading and marine transport, had gone over to the quicker profit making of privateering. There was a considerable public outcry and an immediate danger to the East India Company when opponents to the new policy made plans to set up a rival company in France under the patronage of Henry IV.[122] Under these circumstances a powerful defense of the East India Company's action was urgently needed. What was required was a well-reasoned demonstration of the right to enrich oneself at the expense of the enemy. This question of "prize law" was to occupy the area of public maritime law into the twentieth century almost exclusively. However, in 1604 in Holland we first hear the name Hugo Grotius (de Groot).[123]

Grotius, who without exaggeration can be called the "Father of the Law of Nations," was born in Delft in 1583. He was a prodigy endowed with exceptional intellectual gifts and talents. He commenced the study of law at Leiden at the age of eleven and became a Doctor of Laws at Orleans, France at fifteen. He was a man of the late Renaissance with a reputation not only as a jurist, but also as a linguist, a Latin poet, and a philologist; he was learned in the physical sciences, mathematics, and navigation. It was Grotius who, at the age of twenty-one, was asked to write this defensive opinion for the East India Company. It is not certain whether Grotius actually appeared on behalf of his client company in the prize-court proceedings;[124] but what he did produce was the first systematic commentary on the law of prize and booty, *De Jure Praedae Commentaris*, in which Grotius argues that the seizure of Portuguese vessels as prizes is justified.[125] The manuscript was completed in 1606 but not published; events had overtaken the book, and the then-prevailing sentiment was that such a doctrinal justification was no longer necessary. The treatise, with the exception of one famous chapter, which will be discussed in this section, was thus "abruptly doomed to partial obscurity for a period of 265 years."[126]

In an examination of the international law and policy of marine transport, we cannot delve deeply into the very complex principles of the public international law to which the law of prize belongs. We shall thus examine only cursorily the scope and arguments advanced in *De Jure Praedae*. They were presented in three parts. In the first—the *Dogmatica*—Grotius, without reference to the actual case at hand, argued for the right to wage war at sea and to take prizes as the result thereof. He deduced this right from the very broad and systematic development of principles of natural law and the accepted law of nations. The second division—entitled the *Historica*—chronicles the Spanish tyranny, which resulted in the Dutch revolt. It points to the mistreatment of Dutch sailors by the Portuguese in the East Indies prior to 1603, as well as to other forms of Portuguese misconduct in the form of slander, agitation of the natives, violence, and murder. As a result, Grotius holds, the long-suffering and generous Dutch were simply compelled by reason of self-preservation to battle and rob the enemy.

In the third section—beginning with chapter XII, the famous *Mare Liberum*—Grotius attempts to prove that the Portuguese possessed no exclusive right to trade in the East Indies and that the waters in this area were free to be used by the Dutch traders. In the remaining chapters the author demonstrates that the capture of prizes under the circumstances was not only just but also in the interests of the Dutch Republic, which gained profits at the expense of the wealthy and monopolistic Portuguese.

Chapter XII, *Mare Liberum*, was brought out separately and anonymously in 1609 as an eloquent plea for the so-called principle of "freedom of the seas."[127] The chapter's prime purpose was to disprove Portuguese rights in the Indies, using arguments about proprietary rights such as title and possession, which Grotius reasoned the Portuguese never had. Furthermore, he restated the old argument that the Pope's spiritual powers did not extend to giving title to lands. The development of Grotius's argument is, however, of the greatest relevance to the public maritime law under consideration here. Grotius states that as the Portuguese had not "legally" occupied the Indies, they could not occupy the sea. They could obtain no title by prescription since this prescription is part of a civil law that cannot operate against the law of nations, by which *navigation is free to all* to fit the needs of humanity, and also since prescription could give no title to things incorporeal.[128] The air and the sea were so made by nature that they might be used by all, time after time, and thus ought to be free for all. It would be, in Grotius's opinion, absurd to assert that the sea belonged to the country whose navigators first sail it; for the law takes no more cognizance of the cutting of the sea by a vessel than does the sea, which immediately closes against it.

Here, in a nutshell, we have the one principle that was not only to dominate all international law of the sea until the present day, but would also present international marine transport—the very activity it was designed to facilitate—with some of its most acute problems in years to come. "Freedom" is a word with an appealing ring to it but with many different interpretations and meanings for different points of view.

This presents more of a problem to lawyers than to policymakers. Lawyers usually make use only of the language before them; for the sake of consistency and infallible reliability they are not supposed to look behind the words lest their own views color their opinions with subjectivity. In international law this is a particular problem, as illustrated here by the description of *Mare Liberum*'s antecedents. Do we really have a definitive statement of the "freedom of the seas principle," painstakingly researched and eloquently expressed by one of the greatest scholars of the times? Or do we simply have the very excellent opinion of a superb jurist on a particular set of circumstances? We are, obviously, inclined to believe the latter, and to say further that it might even have been better had *Mare Liberum* also been forgotten for another two and one-half centuries.

In any case, it seems obvious that Grotius never intended his argument to be so all-embracing and widely accepted.[129] In Grotius's later work, the famous *De Jure Belli ac Pacis (The Law of War and Peace)*, published in 1625 while he was in exile in France, the fiery nationalistic ardor of *De Jure Praedae* is missing and Grotius freely contradicts some of his earlier statements.[130] He was well aware of these differences and in 1637 dismissed the earlier work as a young man's book written out of fierce compassion for his fatherland.[131] And yet it was one chapter of an unpublished book by a twenty-one-year-old jurist that caught the emotional imagination of the world.

"Imagination" is here used pejoratively; in his *Apologeticus* in 1622, Grotius points out how he had tried to solve Dutch ocean-trade policy: free trade for themselves, for others as many limitations as possible.[132] Once again an ascendant maritime power attempted to assert itself vis-à-vis the fading dominant power, using the principle of the freedom of the seas as one instrument to do so. But as soon as the influence of the former dominant power was vanquished—by fair means or foul—freedom would be a redundant luxury that could quickly be dispensed with lest some newly ambitious state might seize on it to repeat the circle of history once more. Of course, the close link between the private and public aspects of maritime law must be apparent. The former contributes directly to the stability and the buildup of maritime trade, rendering the state the necessary "commercial acceptance" and viability in the international community; the latter is used either to guard the established dominance and the status quo or to assist in forging new monopolies.

### Mare Liberum *Ascendant: The Battle of the Books*

The fires of imagination, fed by the emotional appeal of the free-seas principle, were further fueled by the rapid changes occurring in the history of Europe during the time of Grotius. Not surprisingly, the challenge to the Dutch shipping and fishing supremacy would come from England. It has been indicated that in Elizabethan times the expansionist policy of the English was very similar to that propounded by the Dutch, as formulated by Grotius. The latter's English counterpart, predecessor, and considerable influence was Alberico Gentili (1552-1608), who in 1598 in his *De Jure Belli* exclaimed that "the sea is open to all because of its nature and its use is common to all, just as that of the air."[133] Like Grotius, Gentili based his arguments largely on principles laid down by the Roman jurists as well as the publications of great thinkers of earlier generations, such as Baldus de Ubaldis and the great Spaniards Francisco de Vitora, Domingo de Soto, Francisco Suarez, Fernando Vazquez de Manchaca, and Diego de Covarruvias.[134] However, it is often forgotten that the Roman jurists looked at a world very different from the Europe of the seventeenth century, with its collection of strong autonomous states and entirely different economic considerations.

For England, the new economic consideration was its fisheries, which turned that country away from the previously propounded free-seas principle and, at the same time, against its former allies, the Dutch. After the Reformation, English fish consumption had steadily declined, which directly affected the English fisheries.[135] As already observed, the Dutch fishing industry had rapidly expanded both in size and in productivity and efficiency. Despite specific legislation to protect the English fishery, such as the prohibition on buying fish from foreigners and on eating meat on certain days, the English industry declined further.

Under Elizabeth I protectionist measures were considered but dropped in favor of the free-seas principle, which assisted the expansion of overseas trade.[136] However, this policy was drastically changed under James I (1603-

1625), who came from Scotland, where foreigners had traditionally been forbidden to fish in adjacent waters.[137] James I completely altered the whole power equilibrium of the times. He concluded a peace treaty with Spain, and the United Provinces of the Netherlands became the enemy of England. This was the real beginning of England's struggle for economic and maritime world supremacy, which would be reached within the next century and maintained for at least another. In 1609, scarcely a year after the appearance of *Mare Liberum*, James I issued the following proclamation, which except for its language has a certain modern ring to it:

> . . . that from the beginning of the month of August next coming, no person of what nation or qualitie soever, being not an naturall born subject, be permitted to fish upon any of our coasts and seas of Great Britaine, Ireland, and the rest of isles adiacent, where most usually heretofore any fishing has bene, until they have orderly demanded and obtained licenses from us.[138]

The Dutch reacted with shrill protest, disputing England's right to subject Dutch vessels to the payment of tolls putting forward the argument that the sea was free and open to all. A special Dutch delegation, of which Grotius was a prominent member, opened negotiations in 1610; but no conclusions or agreements were reached.[139]

At first the dispute resulted in the "Battle of Books," in which English scholars attempted to reply to Grotius's *Mare Liberum*. The first such effort came in 1612, when William Welwood published his *Abridgement of all the Sea Laws*, in which he maintained the English view of the dispute in a rather simplistic manner.[140] Grotius prepared a reply but it—like the *Jure Praedae*—was never published.[141] On the other hand, the distinguished English lawyer and scholar John Selden prepared his superbly erudite *Mare Clausum* as a direct reply to Grotius in 1617 or 1618 and offered it to James I. However, its publication was delayed until 1635, when it was published by direct order of Charles I.[142]

An examination of Selden's position reveals once again a remarkably modern analogy. He sought to point out that in accordance with natural law, as well as with the law of nations, the sea, like the land, could be occupied. He suggested that the right of foreign ships to navigate waters belonging to other nations, was analogous to similar privileges at times imposed on landed proprietors. He categorically rejected Grotius's proposition that it was impossible to establish limits or frontiers in the sea, by maintaining that parallels of latitude and meridians of longitude could serve as borders as well as could walls, rivers, or trenches. However, although Selden supported coastal-state expropriation, he also took the position that a state could not forbid navigation of its seas by foreign vessels.

Today there is little doubt that Selden's arguments were logically superior to Grotius's, displaying not only immense legal learning but also a broad understanding of history, geography, and nautical science.[143] Nevertheless, his efforts were powerless to stem the tide in favor of the Grotian doctrine, which was soon to overtake England once again. The Battle of Books continued for some years; in addition to Welwood and Selden, their countrymen Robert Callis, Gerard Malynes, and Sir John Borough also defended *Mare Clausum*.[144] So did the Spaniard Pedro Calixto Ramirez;[145] the great Portuguese jurist Serafin de Freitas;[146] and several Venetian and Genoese jurists.[147] Grotius's *Mare Liberum*, on the other hand, was defended by his countrymen Theodor Graswinckel and Jan Pontanus, as well as by Jacques Godefroy and Claude Marisot of France.[148] Nevertheless, as already intimated, victory belonged to Grotius's position. However, more serious battles were to come.

*Conflict on the Seas: England Versus Holland*

Under Charles I (1625-1649) English claims with respect to sovereignty over the sea reached their all-time zenith. Charles considered himself to be "lord of the surrounding seas," which extended to the Continent and in which non-English vessels were barely tolerated.[149] He saw to it that a much more effective naval fleet was built up in order to support and enforce claims. The Dutch disputed these claims and further strengthened their already strong fleet.[150] As a result, English claims were not very effective. However, continuous friction and clashes on the seas were putting the two states on a collision course.

Holland was at its greatest height. The huge Dutch trading companies controlled much of the world's trade and had driven out the Spanish and Portuguese almost everywhere.[151] In the East, Batavia was founded in 1619; Ceylon was taken from the Portuguese between 1638 and 1659, as was Malacca in 1641. By 1652 the Dutch had established themselves on the Cape of Good Hope. In the West Indies, the Dutch West India Company had created a virtual monopoly and had taken the islands of St. Eustace, Curacao, and St. Maarten between 1634 and 1648.

On the other hand, the English were badly neglecting their own colonies in the New World, which ended up depending on Dutch trade and Dutch vessels for most of their imports and exports.[152] The Dutch completely controlled the trade in sugar, tobacco, and slaves; English merchants complained that they had established colonies so that the Dutch could grow rich on their trade.[153]

It was obvious that there would be commercial pressure in England to change this state of affairs and to urge a more restrictive trade and shipping policy. This resulted in three bloody wars between the former allies in the period 1652-1674. First, during the Commonwealth under Cromwell, came the Navigation Act of 1651, which required that goods produced in English colonies be shipped in English ships.[154] The hated concept of "flag preference," so well known today, had appeared again. Its appearance is also part of a pattern. Flag preference is a last-resort measure used by a state to protect an inefficient or inadequate merchant fleet against superior competition. The result in this instance was the first Anglo-Dutch War, which lasted for two years;[155] was fought entirely at sea by such famous Admirals as Blake, Monk, Tromp, and de Ruyter; and was generally indecisive.[156] In the end, the Treaty of Westminster resulted in an uneasy peace and an indemnity payment to England by the Dutch.

The second Anglo-Dutch War (1665-1667) was more serious. It showed the weakness of the Dutch and started their decline as a great ocean power. They had neglected their navy and had difficulties in breaking the blockade off the Dutch coast by powerful English naval squadrons. The English had learned the old Mediterranean lesson that, in order to have an effective merchant fleet, the first priority is a powerful navy.[157] The Dutch, with their trading mentality, had never accepted this.

At the end of the war, the English acquired New Amsterdam, soon to be New York; but the Dutch received Surinam in South America instead. In the Far East the Dutch agreed to confine their trade to the islands, leaving India to England. In the third war (1672-1678), the Dutch were forced to fight on land and were opposed by France as well as by England. The odds were too much and the Dutch were saved only when they opened their dykes to keep out the invading armies.[158]

This was really the beginning of the end for Holland as a world maritime power, and henceforth the Dutch were to occupy a secondary position in the area of marine transport. It is significant that Holland's fate was determined not on the oceans but on the battlefields of Europe, where many "commercial" decisions would be made.

### Conclusions: Maritime Law and Policy at the End of the Seventeenth Century

We have ranged far and wide in describing maritime commerce and law in this tumultuous century. Our purpose in examining the political, commercial, and legal components in marine transport during this period in considerable detail was twofold. First, the actual historical perspective is essential in understanding the rise of the modern maritime powers, in particular England. The second purpose is to show how political—and, even more so, commercial—marine policy played the main role in determining what a state could or could not do.

The rules of public maritime law could and would change as required by the state, which was the real rule maker. Despite the greatness of Grotius and the scholarship of his proponents and opponents, there were few new, widely accepted, *effective* rules of public maritime law. There were, however, antecedents of what would become very important legal principles in later years. There was also a strong thrust for "free seas," but this was used by states as a *forum conveniens* for the propagation of maritime commercial monopolies and the preservation of the status quo. The overemphasis on *mare liberum* has persisted ever since, but there has never been a real examination of the mind of Grotius when he wrote *De Jure Belli ac Pacis*, which set out almost all there was to be known about the law of nations for all times.

The private rules of maritime law continued to be further developed—still fairly international, but less so than before, nationalism being the enemy of uniformity. Although private-law rules, more than ever, were of great importance for the efficient functioning of maritime commerce, public rules were being put forward with increasing strength to maintain such maritime commerce or obtain new sources. The end of the seventeenth century thus brings us into an entirely new area of ocean transportation in which the interrelationship between the private and public maritime law would assume new dimensions and perspectives.

## New Oceanic Rivalries: France as a Maritime Power

In the preceding discussion of marine transport we have characterized the sixteenth century as a period of expansionism and the seventeenth century as an era of development of ocean trade. However, the eighteenth century could undoubtedly be called the age of consolidation of both the expansionistic and the trade periods. It was an era of immense historical interest, and it is important not to range too widely, but to concentrate instead on the legal and policy aspects of ocean transportation, which are the primary focus here. This may result at times in possible distorted abbreviation, which is inevitable under the circumstances. It is impossible to describe here in historical detail each and every aspect that may have ever affected the area under examination. We must confine ourselves to highlights and refer the reader to the general history of the age for greater detail.

"Sea power," which we construe not as the narrow term referring basically to naval strength, but rather in the broader and more acceptable definition of *overall* shipping and trading strength, was vested in three states at the beginning of the eighteenth century.[159] We have already referred to England and Holland, and will return to these "powers" again. The third nation, a late arrival on the scene of commercial shipping, was France.

Prior to the reign of Louis XIV (1643-1715), France had already become a prosperous commercial state, but apart from the European coasting trade it had little shipping interest. The unification of French power under Louis XIV laid the foundation for a vigorous maritime commerce, which would reach its zenith in a relatively short period. Early in the seventeenth century, France started certain overseas explorations of the gentleman-adventurer type favored by the Portuguese and Spanish. As a result, Quebec was settled in 1608, which in turn led to a thin trickle of French ships to the Americas.[160]

The turning point came, however, when Cardinal Richelieu, the shadow ruler of France from 1624 to 1642, adopted a new and decisive commercial policy for the country. He encouraged French shipping and founded the famed Company of One Hundred Associates to compete with England and Holland in the Americas.[161] In addition, he also arranged for charters for the funding of French trading companies to settle West Indies islands. However, the cardinal's ground work for expansion was barely laid when his objective was overshadowed by France's greater political ambitions of becoming the supreme power on the Continent.

Many conflicts and wars later, but before Richelieu's death, this ambition had been achieved. It was now up to the succeeding Bourbon monarchs to develop France as a maritime power. After Louis XIV commenced his reign in 1660, Jean-Baptiste Colbert, his Controller-General of Finance and one of the most brilliant administrators of all times, laid out a farsighted policy to strengthen France as a maritime and commercial power. If all previous maritime commercial expansionism (except, possibly, that of Rome) had been somewhat haphazard and dictated by extraneous influences, then here for the first time was a clearly envisaged policy—a plan—which in the period 1662-1683 put France on the path to becoming one of the leading mercantile nations in the world, only to be thwarted in the end by political ambitions that instead would lead the country to almost continuous war.[162]

Colbert's policy was three-pronged—first, increased agricultural and industrial production; second, expansion of merchant shipping and the navy; and last, directly linked to shipping, the consolidation of world markets and expansion of French colonies. A French East India Company, as well as a West India Company, was organized.[163] The merchant fleet was expanded considerably and was soon trading worldwide, and the navy was built up to exceed that of England in size.[164]

Colbert's efforts were just starting to benefit France when Louis XIV's ambitions and aspirations interfered. The monarch wanted to expand France at the expense of his neighbors and invaded the Spanish Netherlands in 1667. From that year until Louis XIV's death in 1715, France was at war. Almost continuous hostilities required the expenditure of all the resources generated by Colbert's policies, and also left little for any further development of France's commerce and colonies. Much of the merchant fleet was impressed into military service, and few trading vessels left France after 1670.[165]

Despite this setback, from which France was not to recover for at least a century, the underlying strength of French maritime commerce had been established. But the crucial momentum of the period during which this strength should have been consolidated was lost.

### The French Codification of Maritime Law: Model for the Future

Obviously, an administrative system as well ordered as Colbert's would also examine the maritime law of France. The result was a codification considered by many to be the "Maritime Code of Europe" and one of the most highly respected marine-law formulations of all times.[166] Before Colbert, there had been disarray in France, not only in maritime law but also in commerce generally. Although the ancient codes, such as the *Rolls of Oleron* and the *Guidon de la Mer*, had been perfectly adequate for a long period of time, the extension of navigation and commerce, as well as the introduction of new arrangements and types of business, required additional regulation founded on an enlarged experience.[167] In France the result had been a severe fragmentation of jurisdictions, all with certain powers in matters relating to maritime commerce. Provinces and principalities, port cities and admiralty districts, all dispensed a variety of judgments based on a confusing array of law and local regulations.

This imperfect state of the maritime, as well as the commercial, laws of France was quickly remedied by the ambitions of Louis XIV and the actions of Colbert. As James Reddie suggests:

> After having almost created a navy, and raised it to a state of splendour corresponding to the extent of his power, after having founded various establishments for the protection and encouragement of the national commerce and manufactures, and of the navigation and maritime commerce of his subjects, it only remained for Louis to confirm and regulate that internal and maritime commerce by a system of laws adapted to the circumstances of the times.[168]

This task was brilliantly accomplished by Colbert. The *Ordonnance du Commerce* of 1673 and, a few years later the *Ordonnance de la Marine* of 1681 more than corresponded to the fondest wishes of the French monarch.[169] The *Ordonnance du Commerce*, drawn up to regulate the operation of commerce generally, was without question the first such undertaking in any of the major states of the times. For the first time transactions of merchants, bankers, agents, and brokers; of the bookkeeping methods; bills of exchange; incorporations; personal and real execution; business failures and bankruptcies were all examined and regulated in an orderly and consistent manner that laid the groundwork for a powerful commercial system.

It is, however, generally agreed that the *Ordonnance de la Marine* surpassed the commercial ordinance in excellence. Only the genius of a Colbert could perceive the real advantages of collecting and arranging all the materials of maritime law previously enumerated, turning them into a code that would complete the law already in existence and would reconcile and digest the great variety of ancient customary usages into one consistent and uniform body of positive legislation. The *Ordonnance* was strongly influenced by previous legal developments, in particular Rhodian-Roman law, as well as by the Wisby, Oleron, and Hansa codes plus, of course, the numerous regional and subregional codes that had been adapted in many parts of Europe. Many scholars consider the *Ordonnance* to herald the beginning of the modern period, as it was undoubtedly the first great national legislative effort after the Hansa code to achieve truly international status. Furthermore, both ordinances formed the basis of the renowned *Code of Napoleon* of 1806.[170] Azuni describes the *Ordonnance de la Marine* as follows:

> . . . the formation of a Code of particular laws, in which should be united everything necessary to instruct mariners in their duties, to establish the police of ports, bays, and rivers, to determine, at the same time, the rights, privileges, and prerogatives of the admiralty, the order to be observed in its judicial proceedings, the functions and duties of judges, and officers, employed to maintain and preserve a just system in maritime, and mercantile, affairs. All this has been admirably performed in the Marine Ordinance of August, 1681, which is, without contradiction, the most masterly act of legislation, promulgated by that incomparable monarch, and had become, in some sort, the common law of all the neighbouring nations.[171]

As has already been indicated, this piece of maritime legislation, the most complete and methodical that any nation had until then produced, quickly gained international acceptance. During the long period in which he presided as Chief Justice of England's Court of King's Bench, the great Lord Mansfield frequently used the French code, deriving from it many of his famous enlightened views of equity and expediency in matters connected with commerce.[172] In 1829 a notable American judge, evaluating the development of international maritime law, concluded:

> . . . that the Ordinances of Louis XIV afford evidence of the general maritime law of nations, they have been respected by the maritime courts of all nations, and adopted by most, if not all of them, on the continent of Europe. . . . Why should not such parts of it as are purely of the general maritime character, which are adopted to the commerical state of this country, and are not inconsistent with the municipal regulations by which our courts are governed, be followed by the courts of the United States in questions of a maritime nature. . . . Neither justice nor policy requires it. . . . I fear myself not only at liberty, but bound to adopt and apply it to the present case. . . .[173]

The code itself consisted of five lengthy books divided as follows:

1. The rights, duties, and powers of the admiral; the institutions charged with the policy and protection of maritime commerce; the jurisdiction vested in the admiral.
2. The law regulating the rights and duties of persons employed in maritime commerce; the law relating to the vessel as a property.
3. The law relating to every type of maritime contract.
4. The law regulating the protection of harbors and coastal areas.
5. The law relating to wreck.[174]

It is important to note that *all* aspects of marine transport are treated as a complete unit. There is no splitting of private from public maritime law; no shipping/commercial law separate from "law of the sea." It would have been totally inconceivable to Colbert, the master administrator, to break his policies into fragments. The interrelationship among *all* components of the code and the subject matters they dealt with was entirely clear.

### War at Sea: The Development of New Legal Rules

Unlike the earlier law, however, the public-law component is now more prominent, although it is still part and parcel of the overall policy. The foremost principle of this public law was the law relating to the status of vessels during the many wars that had become an almost integral part of the era. Grotius's earlier principles relating to the taking of prizes and booty at sea had become much more refined. Rules relating to visitation and search; neutral commerce; confiscation of hostile vessels; contraband of war; duties of the captor; and the adjudication and division of prizes would now occupy maritime courts with increasing regularity.[175]

Such rules were basically unknown in earlier times, when capture usually meant the loss of ship and goods for the owners and death or slavery for those who had the misfortune to be captured. History does, of course, repeat itself. The international law relating to war has in recent years fallen into disregard; and we appear to have reverted to the earlier, cruder methods of war at sea, as evidenced by the mass destruction of shipping in World War II. Nevertheless, the French code was an important forerunner of a whole aspect of international law that occupied marine transport for a very long period. Its relevance was still more commercial than strategic, however. The importance of attack on and seizure of enemy vessels could be phrased no more eloquently than in the words of Oppenheim:

Whereas in land warfare all sorts of violence against enemy individuals are the chief means, in sea warfare attack and seizure of enemy vessels are the most important means. For together with enemy vessels a belligerent takes possession of the enemy individuals and enemy goods thereon, so that he can appropriate vessels and goods, as well as detain those enemy individuals who are liable to be interned as prisoners of war. For this reason, and compared with attack and seizure of enemy vessels, violence against enemy persons, the other means of sea warfare, play only a secondary part, although they are certainly not unimportant. For a weak naval Power can even restrict the operations of its fleet to mere coast defence, and thus totally refrain from directly attacking and seizing enemy vessels.[176]

It was a sign of the world's greater sophistication in trade, as well as war, that this part of the law of the sea would become more developed, reaching its climax by World War I. It would then slowly decline, in particular during the "all-out war" aspect of World War II, during which very often not even the barest principles laid down earlier were observed. However, this period did witness the early development of the rules relating to the conduct of and against ocean transportation in times of war. As indicated already, the reasons behind these new public-law rules were commercial, illustrating the close link between the private- and public-law aspects once again. In the public sector there were now five major maritime powers (England, Holland, France, Spain, and Portugal) engaged in endless wars and conflicts, very often fought on the sea. At the same time, all five were engaged in a considerable international seaborne trade, which was well governed by sets of private maritime-law rules accepted by all. Although ascendant nationalism had begun to whittle away at the uniformity of such rules, they nevertheless still complied with the basic international character. Opposed to this widespread aspect of marine transport was the ever-growing destruction of merchant vessels on the high seas by an increasing number of warships under many flags that engaged in every conceivable act of belligerency ranging from sheer piracy to privateering to the legitimate act of ocean warfare. The concept of sea power, well known since antiquity, was assuming a new meaning.

In earlier times the warship fulfilled two very simple roles—as an instrument of limited conquest and as the protector of trading ships. In this new era these roles were greatly expanded. The buildup of a powerful navy, particularly in France and England, was based on the policy of "mastery of the sea," which often removed belligerency from land borders to the oceans. The term *sea power* now had a newer, wider interpretation that included not only the navies of nations but also their *total* strength and interest in the sea—their extent of coastline, extent of adjacent and inland waters, overseas bases and colonial possessions, and merchant shipping and seaborne trade.[177] With this breadth of meaning, sea power now not only referred to naval warfare but also included the rise and decline of the great maritime powers as well as the rivalry for ocean trade and sea control. Among the traditional western maritime nations, such rivalry had always been a dominant motive; the histories of such states reveal an almost continuous relationship between the development of their commerce and their changes of foreign-policy.

Added to this newer perspective were the very real problems of the almost-continuous wars and conflicts at sea. Several dominant powers were now vying for supremacy, all of them with considerable commercial interests to protect. There is little doubt that even at this stage such interests prevailed at the highest levels of policy making or, at least, amounted to a powerful "lobby" influencing national decisions. It thus quickly became apparent that certain spatial, as well as physical, limitations placed on belligerent acts at sea would benefit all states mutually. Such a community interest has, of course, always been reflected in the making of specific rules of international law or the law of nations, which Oppenheim defines as:

. . . the body of customary and treaty rules which are considered legally binding by States in their intercourse with each other.[178]

As previously indicated, during this time the law of nations witnessed a considerable development of rules relating to the laws of naval warfare; restrictions on the right of capture of enemy property; neutrality of vessels; and so on. It is beyond the scope of this book to delve into this area of international law except to say that it was sufficiently important to occupy a major part of the international law of the sea. Traditional international lawyers would henceforth speak of the divisions of international law applicable in times of peace and in times of war.[179]

Nevertheless, although it is almost always maintained that the international law of the sea in time of war belongs fully to the public aspect of maritime law, we would even question that. The very intricate and technical body of law that sprang up in relation to the multitude of cases heard by prize courts and similar tribunals consisted of a mixture of public and private legal aspects. At stake were, of course, always one or more ships and the related crew and cargo. In other words, private commercial interests were centrally involved. If ship, crew, and cargo were captured, destroyed, damaged, seized, or even prevented from proceeding on their "legitimate" business, then commercial interests were affected—albeit by the public action of another power.

This, in turn, led directly to (1) new pressures on marine-insurance interests, which had to assume these additional risks to ship and cargo; (2) dangerous navigational practices that had to be used in order to escape capture and seizure; and (3) new pressures on the hiring practices, training, and welfare of seamen, who were now exposed to additional dangers. There is little doubt that these considerations related directly to the private-maritime-law areas of marine insurance, navigational safety, and seamen's affairs—all of which had to be adjusted to the difficulties of the times. In other words, even in this very public area of maritime law, the private-public division is far from complete, illustrating once again the close interrelationship between the two aspects.

### Coastal-State Protection and Marginal-Seas Jurisdiction

During this period another well-known concept of the public law was further developed. This was the concept of the "territorial sea," which had existed since early Mediterranean times but had found expression only in a variety of irregular and invariably unilateral expressions of sovereignty over adjacent seas. Frequently, however, sight has been lost of the fact that the extended territorial sea—which started out, as in the case of Venice, for example, as a sort of "protection zone" for the claimant state,[180] and then became a type of "fisheries protection zone" (quite analogous to its modern counterparts)[181]—had by this time become a "coastal protection zone" in order to protect against the belligerencies of the times.[182] Although we disagree with parts of the statement, the great Elihu Root's definition of the territorial sea, as he saw it, illustrated the "protection" aspect of the zone perfectly:

> These vague and unfounded claims (of the eighteenth, seventeenth and earlier centuries) disappeared entirely and there was nothing of them left. . . . The sea became, in general, as free internationally as it was under the Roman law. But the new principle of freedom, when it approached the shore, met with another principle, the principle of protection, not a residuum of the old claim, but a new independent basis and reason for modification, near the shore, of the principle of freedom. The sovereign of the land washed by the sea asserted a new right to protect his subjects and citizens against attack, against invasion, against interference and injury, to protect them against attack threatening their peace, to protect their revenues, to protect their health, to protect their industries. This is a basis and the sole basis on which is established the territorial zone that is recognized in the international law of today. Warships may not pass without consent to the zone, because they threaten. Merchant ships may pass and repass because they do not threaten.[183]

It thus appears that even a concept such as "territorial sea," which superficially appears to be firmly rooted in public-maritime-law principles, is on close examination found to be related to the rules laid down for the conduct of the international law of the sea in time of war. We have suggested that the latter, in turn, has a direct bearing on maritime commerce and thus on private maritime law. If the attempt to establish this link appears ponderous or labored, it will be more forcefully made by examining the concept of the territorial sea as it appeared during this period.

The Battle of the Books, followed by the more-serious battles described above, really ended in a sort of "academic stalemate" (again, very much like the real battles). As previously stated, Grotius—by then an ambassador in the service of the Swedish court—was unable to reply to Selden and his followers, lest he prejudice Sweden's maritime claims.[184] However, Pontamus, a fellow countryman of Grotius, while in the service of Denmark, did write a reply.[185] He abandoned Grotius's distinction between sovereignty and ownership, reasoning that the former included the power of exclusion. Instead, he advanced a more practical compromise based on the distinction between the high seas and the "adjacent" sea and argued that the latter could be reduced to ownership and fully exclusive jurisdiction, while the former must remain free. Pontamus was, therefore, quite likely the originator of the concept of the territorial (adjacent) sea as we understand it today.[186]

This differentiation between the high sea and the territorial sea became the common ground for European juridical thought in the next century. In other words, the jurists had found concepts that were suitable to accommodate the claims of coastal states, particularly those relating to fisheries and coastal protection from belligerency—the concept of the territorial or adjacent sea—while simultaneously restating or preserving the so-called freedom of the high seas. This was a neat package but one that, once again, was dictated by the exigencies of the times, by political and commercial realities, rather than by continuing a really discernible trend from Roman or even pre-Roman sources, as has often, and erroneously been claimed.[187]

In 1702, almost a century after Grotius's *Mare Liberum*, another eminent Dutch jurist, Cornelius Van Bynkershoek, published a treatise entitled *De Dominio Maris*, which firmly closed the old controversy and at the same time set out the doctrine of freedom of the high seas and sovereignty over waters adjacent to coastal states.[188] Bynkershoek opposed Selden's wide and open-ended claims, putting forward instead a more practical limit of the breadth of the territorial sea. By following certain of Grotius's theories, as well as a number of already well-formulated rules of diplomatic practice, he suggested that sovereignty must be extended outward from the coastline. Under this doctrine he specifically disregarded Grotius's distinction between *dominium* and *imperium*, which had misled many jurists since Roman times, and instead stated quite simply that the adjacent sea is assimilated to the land territory—thus bypassing the difficult questions relating to ownership and sovereignty.[189] The width of the territorial sea, unsettled to this day, was in Bynkershoek's words simply expressed as "the territorial sovereignty ends where the power of arms ends." (*"Terrae potestas finitur ubi finitur armorum vis."*[190]) He is therefore credited with having formulated the famous "cannon-shot rule."[191] As the maximum breadth of the territorial sea was later limited to three nautical miles, Bynkershoek was, for a long period, also credited with inventing the "three-mile cannon-shot rule."[192] The distance of three miles was roughly equivalent to one nautical league, which was considered to be the marine breadth that could be claimed by any nation. Research undertaken in recent years has revealed that the cannon-shot three-mile limit was completely erroneous.[193] It was shown that the cannon-shot rule was practiced long before Bynkershoek, but in a much narrower and different sense than as a measure of territorial rights.[194] In short, the cannon-shot rule was a matter of *actual* control as opposed to the more-theoretical legal control. One of the researchers, Bernard G. Heinzen, explains:

> . . . that the cannon shot rule as it existed in the seventeenth and eighteenth century practice . . . merely provided that, for the purpose of *preserving the neutrality* of the coastal state, the range *of guns actually stationed on the shore* were under the protection of the coastal state.[195]

In other words, a nation effectively claimed only adjacent sea areas that could actually be "covered" by the range of shore batteries. The relationship between one marine league and the cannon-shot rule is also not supported by the ballistics of the period in question.[196] Until the latter part of the nineteenth century, the maximum range of the most powerful gun was barely half a league, and the effective range barely half a mile, even under the best possible conditions.[197] There is thus little doubt that the rule was much more limited in scope than an attempt to exercise full jurisdiction over the adjacent sea. As a rule of public maritime law, it was clearly subservient to the commerical considerations that had brought it into existence in the first place. These were simply to protect neutrality in times of war by providing "protection" for the vessels of all belligerents in an area within cannon range of shore. One of the effects of the rule was to establish an intricate set of rules and ceremonials relating to the striking and showing of flags in certain adjacent sea areas.[198]

Nevertheless, there is little doubt that the cannon-shot rule helped establish the public-maritime-law proposition that states could exercise a certain amount of control over adjacent waters in order to preserve preexisting national rights and interests. The cannon-shot/three-mile relationship was accepted by many eminent jurists in a number of states for many years.[199] Its acceptance thus encouraged the development of much more comprehensive rules as time passed. A more acceptable view is that the practice of the Scandinavian states at this time, in establishing a uniform belt of defined measure along their entire coasts, was a more clearly discernible forerunner of the later territorial seas.[200] These claims varied in distance from four to six miles and were enforced not only to preserve neutrality but more specifically to "protect" coastal fisheries. They were expressed well into the nineteenth century by Sweden, Denmark, and Norway.[201] The Napoleonic wars, however, appear to have provided the real spark for the adoption of the law of the modern territorial sea. Before turning to that important era in the development and expansion of the law and policy of marine transport, we pause to summarize briefly the maritime law at the end of the 1700s.

## Conclusions: Maritime Law and Policy at the End of the Eighteenth Century

This period was significant for most states because of their growing sense of nationality. This led to the centralization, unification, and codification, in the name of royal governments, of all their diverse jurisdictions formerly held by princes, bishops, cities, guilds, and so on, which had since earliest days shared not only the power of legislation but also that of justice. Wigmore points out that this movement was, at the same time, disintegrating and absolving the Common Papal as well as the Common Roman law into individual national laws.[202] Maritime law also underwent this nationalizing process, although it had already begun in the mid-sixteenth century, reaching one of its heights with Colbert's *Ordonnance de la Marine* in 1681. The French code consisted of French law enforced in the Royal Court of Justice, which had a monopoly of jurisdiction and dispensed with the ancient courts of the sea. For France, a new national spirit ended the common law of the sea once and for all. Other maritime states followed suit. Holland issued the *Marine Ordinance of Rotterdam* in 1721;[203] Prussia passed a similar instrument in 1727;[204] Spain in 1737—with the *Ordinances of Bilbao*;[205] and Venice in 1786—the *Code of Mercantile Marine*.[206] Even England had, between 1650 and 1681, gradually abolished the local sea courts despite tenacious opposition; their jurisdiction was transferred to the Admiralty in other national courts.[207] It seemed, therefore, that within the comparatively short period of two centuries, the uniform common law of the sea, which had its roots almost in prehistoric times, had almost disappeared. Perhaps it would be more accurate to say that it was "absorbed" into national laws. The basic "common" principles, although often adapted to particular needs, were preserved in this metamorphosis. The uniform link or thread remained basically untouched.

In the more public area of maritime law, certain new developments had taken place; these were, however, really a complement to traditional commercial needs and inadequacies in the private-law area. Because of the warlike atmosphere of the whole period, which had as its byproduct the buildup of several powerful navies, an intricate new system of "sea law in time of war" was developed and constantly refined, particularly in areas such as prize law, neutrality, search, capture, and seizure. Although claims over ocean areas still prevailed to a certain extent, the *mare liberum* idea, so expertly expounded by Grotius in the previous decade, found more or less common favor and adoption. At the same time, however, the idea of the territorial sea also found expression. Although originally another byproduct of the belligerency of the era as a coastal-protection zone, it also served another purpose. It was able to satisfy the expansionist maritime and coastal states who wanted sovereignty in their adjacent seas for the more traditional expansionist reasons.

It should be noted that the territorial sea never satisfied all demands, nor was it ever a perfect compromise, as is proved by its unsettled state to this day. But the territorial sea, as developed during this time, did appear to fulfill various commercial, political, and strategic needs, and thus passed into the law of the sea. Therein lies also the increasing public content of maritime law. Although commercial interests still underlay almost all political and strategic considerations in this period, the lessening of the impact of such interests is apparent. National policy, as will be seen in the case of England, may still be exactly the same as commercial policy; but this equation need no longer be a foregone conclusion. It is quite likely that most policy related to the territorial sea was made in this period by decision makers who also decreed commercial policy.

Nevertheless, a change is apparent. Purely strategic and political expansionist policies would soon take their own paths after being born in entirely different and/or new policy-making institutions. The monarch and his close-knit council, a relatively simple decision-making body, was giving way in most of the maritime states to powerful ministries, which created a much more complex bureaucratic system and widely differing constituencies of interest. Interests represented by a Minister of Defense might now vary widely from those of his counterpart responsible for the smooth operation of national commerce. If we add to this an absolutist monarch, who might for dynastic or other political reasons (as was so often true in the cases of France and Spain) superimpose his own policy, then the system becomes indeed intricate. The old-style "commerce for the common good," which dictated a simpler policy made by a relatively small group of directly interested decision makers and protected by a uniform system of private law, had given way to the newer demands of more far-flung commerce, larger populations, colonial ambitions, strategic requirements, and a much larger circle of interested policy makers who required a more public expression of law in international terms. The beginnings of the divergence between private and public law can thus be found in the history of eighteenth-century marine transport, although in a very preliminary way. As the divergence and eventual complete separation of the two areas of law is a central theme in this book, we must now examine this phenomenon against the background of the nineteenth century, which will bring us to England's oceanic ambitions and successes, the Napoleonic Wars, and the rise of the United States in the area of marine transport.

## Notes

1. K.-F. Krieger, "Die Entwicklung des Seerechts im Mittelmeerraum von der Antike bis zum Consulat de Mar," *Jahrbuch für Internationales Recht* 16 (1973):179.

2. Ibid., p. 199.

3. Ibid., p. 200.

4. W.O. Stevens and Allan Westcott, *A History of Sea Power* (Garden City, N.J.: Doubleday, 1944), pp. 51-52.

5. For a comprehensive analysis of this phenomenon, see Fernand Brandel, *The Mediterranean*, trans. S. Reynolds, 2 vols. (New York: Harper and Row, 1972).

6. Krieger, "Seerecht im Mittelmeerraum," p. 199ff.

7. Frederic R. Sanborn, *Origins of the Early English Maritime and Commercial Law* (New York: Century, 1930), p. 42ff.

8. Ibid.

9. Ibid.

10. Krieger, "Seerecht im Mittelmeerraum," p. 196ff.

11. Sanborn, *Early English Maritime Law*, pp. 77-89.

12. Ibid.

13. John H. Wigmore, *A Panorama of the World's Legal Systems*, vol. 3 (St. Paul, Minn.: West Publishing, 1928), p. 885.

14. Stanley S. Jados, *Consulate of the Sea and Related Documents* (University, Ala.: University of Alabama Press, 1975).

15. Ibid.

16. Wigmore, *World's Legal Systems*, vol. 3, p. 890.

17. Ibid.

18. Ibid.

19. Cited in W. Paul Gormley, "The Development of the Rhodian-Roman Maritime Law to 1681, with Special Emphasis on the Problem of Collision," *Inter-American Law Review* 3 (1961):317, 333.

20. Wigmore, *World's Legal Systems*, vol. 3, pp. 897-900.

21. Sanborn, *Early English Maritime Law*, p. 76.

22. The Laws of Wisby are reprinted in *Federal Cases* 30 (1897):1189; and the Laws of Oleron in *Federal Cases* 30 (1897):1171.

23. Robert Wernick, *The Vikings* (Alexandria, Va.: Time-Life, 1979), p. 66ff.

24. Ibid.

25. Gwyn Jones, *A History of the Vikings*, pt. 4 (New York: Oxford University Press, 1968).

26. Stevens and Westcott, *History of Sea Power*, pp. 90-92.

27. "The Laws of the Hansa Towns" have been reprinted in *Federal Cases* 30 (1897):1197.

28. Sanborn, *Early English Maritime Law*, pp. 108-111.

29. Wigmore, *World's Legal Systems*, p. 902.

30. Ibid., p. 903.

31. Ibid.

32. Ibid. See also James Reddie, *Researches, Historical and Critical in Maritime International Law*, 2 vols. (Edinburgh: Thomas Clark, 1844).

33. Wigmore, *World's Legal Systems*, p. 904.

34. W. Paul Gormley, "The Development and Subsequent Influence of the Roman Legal Norm of 'Freedom of the Seas'," *University of Detroit Law Journal* 40 (1963):561, 585.

35. Myres S. McDougal and William T. Burke, *The Public Order of the Oceans* (New Haven: Yale University Press, 1962), p. 82.

36. T.W. Fulton, *The Sovereignty of the Sea* (Edinburgh: Blackwood, 1911), p. 3.

37. Ibid., p. 4.

38. Ibid.

39. Stevens and Westcott, *History of Sea Power*, p. 53.

40. Ibid., p. 67. See also Frederic C. Lane, *Venice—A Maritime Republic* (Baltimore: Johns Hopkins Press, 1973).

41. Ibid.

42. Fulton, *Sovereignty of the Sea*, p. 4; Edgar Gold, "The Rise of the Coastal State in the Law of the Sea," in *Marine Policy and the Coastal Community*, edited by D.M. Johnston (London: Croom Helm, 1976), p. 16.

43. Ibid.

44. Frans De Pauw, *Grotius and the Law of the Sea*, trans. P.J. Arthern (Bruxelles: Editions de l'Institut de Sociologie, 1965), p. 8.

45. R. Lapidoth, "Freedom of Navigation—Its Legal History and Its Normative Basis," *Journal of Maritime Law and Commerce* 6 (1975):259.

46. Ibid.

47. Stevens and Westcott, *History of Sea Power*, p. 69.

48. Ibid., p. 73. See also Samuel E. Morison, *The European Discovery of America—The Southern Voyages A.D. 1492-1616* (New York: Oxford University Press, 1974); and Richard Humble, *The Explorers* (Alexandria, Va.: Time-Life, 1978).

49. Ibid.

50. Stanley Wolpert, *A New History of India* (New York: Oxford University Press, 1977), p. 136.

51. Stevens and Westcott, *History of Sea Power*, p. 75.

52. Morison, *Southern Voyages*, pp. 3-122; see also Samuel E. Morison, *Admiral of the Ocean Sea*, 2 vols. (New York: Time, 1962).

53. Humble, *The Explorers*, p. 104.

54. Samuel E. Morison, *The European Discovery of America—The Northern Voyages A.D. 500-1600* (New York: Oxford University Press, 1971), pp. 157-210.

55. Humble, *The Explorers*, pp. 132-133.

56. Morison, *Southern Voyages*, pp. 313-473.

57. Humble, *The Explorers*, p. 6.

58. Stevens and Westcott, *History of Sea Power*, p. 84.

59. *An Encyclopedia of World History*, 4th ed. edited by W.L. Langer (Boston: Houghton Mifflin, 1968), p. 422.

60. Stevens and Westcott, *History of Sea Power*, p. 84.

61. Ibid.

62. Ibid.

63. Ibid.

64. Humble, *The Explorers*, pp. 6-8.

65. Patrick Brophy, *Sailing Ships* (London: Hamlyn, 1974), p. 30ff.; *The History of the Sailing Ship* (New York: Arco Publishing Inc., 1975), p. 103ff.; George F. Bass, *A History of Seafaring* (New York: Walker, 1972), p. 225ff.

66. Arthur Nussbaum, *A Concise History of the Law of Nations* (New York: Macmillan, 1962), pp. 27-35.

67. Ibid. See also Clive Day, *A History of Commerce* (New York: Longmans, 1919), p. 139ff.

68. Stevens and Westcott, *History of Sea Power*, p. 85.

69. Ibid., p. 86.

70. Ibid.

71. *The History of the Sailing Ship*, ch. 5.

72. Stevens and Westcott, *History of Sea Power*, p. 86.

73. Ibid.

74. C.E. McDowell and H.M. Gibbs, *Ocean Transportation* (New York: McGraw-Hill, 1954), p. 11.

75. Ibid.

76. Ibid.

77. Ibid.

78. Stevens and Westcott, *History of Sea Power*, ch. 7.

79. Ibid.

80. McDowell and Gibbs, *Ocean Transportation*, p. 12.

81. Morison, *Northern Voyages*, pp. 157-210.

82. Stevens and Westcott, *History of Sea Power*, pp. 111-113.

83. For a comprehensive examination of Drake's voyage, see Derek Wilson, *The World Encompassed* (New York: Harper and Row, 1977).

84. Stevens and Westcott, *History of Sea Power*, ch. 7.

85. McDowell and Gibbs, *Ocean Transportation*, p. 12.

86. R.J. Cornewall-Jones, *The British Merchant Service* (London: Samson Low, 1898), ch. 6.

87. Ibid.

88. Morison, *Northern Voyages*.

89. *History of the Sailing Ship*, ch. 3, 4.

90. Victor Dover, *A Handbook to Marine Insurance*, 7th ed., revised by R.H. Brown (London: Witherby, 1970), p. 12.

91. C. John Colombos, *International Law of the Sea*, 6th ed. (London: Longmans, 1960), pp. 34-35.

92. Ibid.

93. Ibid.

94. Ibid., p. 35.

95. Dover, *Handbook to Marine Insurance*, p. 12.

96. Ibid.

97. 43 Eliz., ch. 12.

98. Dover, *Handbook to Marine Insurance*, p. 14.

99. Fulton, *Sovereignty of the Sea*, p. 107.

100. Ibid., p. 108.

101. McDowell and Gibbs, *Ocean Transportation*, p. 13.

102. Ibid. See also Brophy, *Sailing Ships*, ch. 4.

103. Stevens and Westcott, *History of Sea Power*, p. 92.

104. McDowell and Gibbs, *Ocean Transportation*, p. 13.

105. Langer, *World History*, pp. 406-408.

106. Ibid.

107. Ibid., pp. 474-476.

108. McDowell and Gibbs, *Ocean Transportation*, p. 13.

109. Ibid.

110. Ibid.

111. Ibid., p. 14.

112. Ibid.

113. Stevens and Westcott, *History of Sea Power*, p. 102.

114. James Reddie, *An Historical View of the Law of Maritime Commerce* (Edinburgh: Blackwood, 1841), p. 222ff.

115. Ibid., p. 228.

116. Dover, *Handbook to Marine Insurance*, p. 22.

117. De Pauw, *Grotius and the Law of the Sea*, p. 15.

118. Ibid.

119. Ibid., p. 16.

120. Ibid.

121. Ibid.

122. Ibid.

123. Hamilton Vreeland, *Hugo Grotius* (New York: Oxford University Press, 1917).

124. De Pauw, *Grotius and the Law of the Sea*, p. 18.

125. Ibid.

126. Alison Reppy, "The Grotian Doctrine of the Freedom of the Seas Reappraised," *Fordham Law Review* 19 (1950):243, 259.

127. De Pauw, *Grotius and the Law of the Sea*, p. 21.

128. Vreeland, *Grotius*, p. 55.

129. De Pauw, *Grotius and the Law of the Sea*, p. 42; Reppy, "Grotian Doctrine Reappraised," p. 269.

130. Ibid.

131. De Pauw, *Grotius and the Law of the Sea*, p. 42.

132. E. Laspeyres, *Geschichte der volkswirtschaftlichen Anschauungen der Niederländer und ihrer Literatur zur Zeit der Republik* (Leipzig: Hirzel, 1863), p. 160. See also G.H. Crichton, "Grotius on the Freedom of the Seas," *Juridical Review* 53 (1941):226; Fujio Ito, "The Thought of Hugo Grotius in the 'Mare Liberum'," *Japanese Annual of International Law* 18 (1974):1.

133. Oppenheim, *International Law*, vol. 1, pp. 90-91.

134. Ibid.

135. S.A. Riesenfeld, *Protection of Coastal Fisheries under International Law* (Washington, D.C.: Carnegie Endowment, 1942), p. 9.

136. Fulton, *Sovereignty of the Sea*, pp. 108-115.

137. Riesenfeld, *Protection of Fisheries*, p. 9.

138. De Pauw, *Grotius and the Law of the Sea*, p. 11.

139. Ibid.

140. Fulton, *Sovereignty of the Sea*, p. 352; Reppy, "Grotian Doctrine Reappraised," p. 264.

141. De Pauw, *Grotius and the Law of the Sea*, pp. 44-45.

142. Oppenheim, *International Law*, vol. 1, p. 585.

143. Reppy, "Grotian Doctrine Reappraised," p. 271.

144. Reddie, *Maritime International Law*, vol. 1, p. 84ff.

145. Ibid.

146. C.H. Alexandrowicz, "Freitas versus Grotius," *British Year Book of International Law* 35 (1959):162.

147. Reddie, *Maritime International Law*, vol. 1, p. 84ff.

148. Ibid.

149. De Pauw, *Grotius and the Law of the Sea*, p. 11.

150. Ibid., p. 46.

151. McDowell and Gibbs, *Ocean Transportation*, p. 13.

152. Ibid., p. 15.

153. Ibid.

154. Navigation Act, 1651. *Stats. Interregnum*, 9 Oct. 1651.

155. 1652-1654. Langer, *World History*, p. 474.

156. Stevens and Westcott, *History of Sea Power*, pp. 130-139.

157. Ibid., pp. 144-147; see also David Howarth, *The Men-of-War* (Alexandria, Va.: Time-Life, 1978).

158. Stevens and Westcott, *History of Sea Power*, pp. 148-149; Langer, *World History*, p. 474.

159. Stevens and Westcott, *History of Sea Power*, p. 1.

160. McDowell and Gibbs, *Ocean Transportation*, p. 16.

161. Ibid.

162. Crane Brinton, J.B. Christopher, and R.L. Wolff, *Civilization in the West* (Englewood Cliffs, N.J.: Prentice-Hall, 1964), pp. 334-335.

163. McDowell and Gibbs, *Ocean Transportation*, p. 16.

164. Stevens and Westcott, *History of Sea Power*, ch. 9.

165. Ibid.

166. Gormley, "Maritime Law to 1681," p. 340.

167. Reddie, *Law of Maritime Commerce*, p. 341ff.

168. Ibid., p. 345.

169. The "Marine Ordonnances of Louis XIV" have been reprinted in *Federal Cases* 30 (1897):1203.

170. Reddie, *Law of Maritime Commerce*, p. 362.

171. Gormley, "Maritime Law to 1681," p. 340.

172. Reddie, *Law of Maritime Commerce*, p. 313.

173. *The SENECA, Federal Cases* 21, no. 12,670 (C.C.E.D. Penn. 1829):1081 at 1084.

174. Wigmore, *World's Legal Systems*, vol. 3, pp. 915-918.

175. L. Oppenheim, *International Law*, vol. 2, 7th ed., edited by L. Lauterpacht (London: Longman, 1952), ch. 4.

176. Ibid., p. 465.

177. McDowell and Gibbs, *Ocean Transportation*, pp. 30-32.

178. Oppenheim, *International Law*, vol. 1, pp. 4-5.

179. Ibid.

180. Venice, when claiming part of the Adriatic Sea, gave as a reason the need to "protect" commerce from piracy.

181. During the time of Charles I of England.

182. Oppenheim, *International Law*, vol. 2, ch. 4.

183. Philip C. Jessup, *The Law of Territorial Waters and Maritime Jurisdiction* (New York: Jennings, 1927), cited p. 5.

184. Riesenfeld, *Protection of Fisheries*, p. 19.

185. Ibid.

186. Ibid., p. 20.

187. Jessup, *Law of Territorial Waters*; R.D. Benedict, "The Historical Position of the Rhodian Law," *Yale Law Journal* 18 (1909):223.

188. Reddie, *Maritime International Law*, vol. 1, p. 215.

189. Bernard G. Heinzen, "The Three Mile Limit: Preserving the Freedom of the Seas," *Stanford Law Review* 11 (1959):597, 602; J.K. Oudendijk, *Status and Extent of Adjacent Waters* (Leiden: Sijthoff, 1970), ch. 5.

190. Comment, "Territorial Seas—3000 Year Old Question," *Journal of Air Law and Commerce* 36 (1970):73, 79.

191. William L. Walker, "Territorial Waters: The Cannon Shot Rule," *British Year Book of International Law* 22 (1945):210.

192. Ibid.

193. Ibid., pp. 230-231.

194. Ibid.; see also Heinzen, "Three Mile Limit," pp 602-603.

195. Heinzen, "Three Mile Limit," p. 603.

196. Walker, "Territorial Waters," p. 231.

197. Carlo M. Cipolla, *Guns, Sails and Empires* (New York: Pantheon, 1965), ch. 11.

198. Colombos, *International Law of the Sea*, pp. 52-55, 166.

199. Ibid., p. 92.

200. Comment, "Territorial Seas," pp. 80-81.

201. Ibid.

202. Wigmore, *World's Legal Systems*, vol. 3, pp. 914-918.

203. Ibid., p. 914.

204. Ibid.

205. Ibid.

206. Ibid.

207. Ibid. See also Sanborn, *Early English Maritime Law*, p. 262ff.

# 3

# The Making of a Maritime State

*Whosoever commands the sea commands trade; whosoever commands the trade of the world commands the riches of the world, and consequently the world itself.*

—Sir Walter Raleigh (ca. 1610)

## England's Path to Maritime Leadership amid Political Instability

We have already glanced rapidly at certain early aspects of the rise of England as a commercial maritime power. During the eighteenth century this ascent was further consolidated and would reach its greatest height in the 1800s. England's commercial growth, however, was steady and somewhat plodding, beset by a variety of commercial as well as political difficulties and lacking both the spectacular achievement of the Dutch in the seventeenth century and the daring and glamor of the earlier Elizabethan days.

English-Dutch conflict ended with the expulsion of James II in 1688 and with the accession of the Dutch William III (of Orange) to the English throne.[1] However, this accession resulted in England being drawn into the war of the League of Augsburg (1688-1697) against France.[2] Louis XIV of France not only attempted to return to James II his lost throne but also, when the exiled monarch died, recognized his son, the Pretender, as the legitimate king of England. For over 125 years after this, England was at war with France.[3] This long series of conflicts began and ended with the English fear of an expansionist France—in the beginning under Louis XIV, and in the end under Napoleon. The significance of this period for this book is crucial, because sea power—in its broadest meaning—was a factor of paramount importance. Even when battles were fought on land rather than at sea, England's ability to cut France off from its overseas possessions resulted in the transfer of many new territories to an England on the threshold of becoming the British Empire. Through the eighteenth century England's colonial possessions increased enormously, the only important setback being the loss of the American colonies. Despite the fact that the French navy under Colbert had at first so greatly strengthened itself that it outnumbered the combined fleets of England and Holland, the French were unable to contain English expansionism and sea power.[4] When the War of the Spanish Succession (1701-1714) began, England was *one* of the sea powers; but at the end of the era England was recognized as *the* power of the sea.[5]

The leading, all-pervading role England was to take in all matters connected with the seas had a pronounced influence on the law of the sea of "modern" times, which we are now entering. In an examination of the international law and policy of ocean law and transportation, which finds its origins in prehistory, the point can obviously be made that the eighteenth and nineteenth centuries belong to the modern era. There are various reasons for examining England's rise on the ladder of the world's sea powers. The fact that it was to occupy this place is, of course, one of the reasons. However, even more important is the illustration of England's *completeness* as a maritime power in terms of shipping, maritime commercial infrastructure, trade monopolies, and strategic considerations. It was this "maritime tradition" that would dominate England's (and most other traditional maritime states') ocean policy right up to the present time. Behind the obvious maritime power lies the *invisible* power that is acquired, nurtured, refined, maintained, and protected over a long period of time in a benevolent policy climate. This is also the area that provides the most problematic difficulties to all who wish to challenge such maritime dominance. We will have to return to this theme when we attempt to look at the maritime aspirations in the 1960s and 1970s of the developing world, which had the greatest difficulty in dealing with this invisible opponent.

In 1650 England's overseas possessions consisted of an insecure strip of land on the Atlantic coast of the North American continent, mainly owing to the more-or-less active occupation of the colonies of Massachusetts, Maryland, and Virginia; several West Indian Islands, of which the most important were Barbados, Antigua, and St. Kitts; and some scattered trading posts in the Far East and in India. As has been indicated, these were dwarfed by the overseas possessions of Spain, Holland, and France. But by the end of the Napoleonic Wars in 1815, although England had lost the thirteen American colonies, its overseas holdings had increased to include Canada and Jamaica in the Americas; Gibraltar, Minorca, and Malta in the Mediterranean; the Cape Colony in Africa; and all of India, Australia, and New Zealand. This considerable expansion was purely the result of sea power in its widest sense.[6] Between 1686 and 1788, English-owned shipping increased from 340,000 tons to 1,055,000 tons, a direct reflection of new, far-flung trade routes and colonial interests.[7]

It must be remembered that the much-discussed Navigation Acts, which had been a direct cause of war with the Dutch, continued to dominate English commercial thinking for most of the eighteenth century. In 1707 the Act of Union had brought Scotland into the empire, and Scots shipping was then able to participate in the "reserved" trades with considerable success.[8] However, these discriminatory practices were not confined to Britain. Sweden imposed even more drastic measures to protect its shipping.[9] Spain continued to prohibit all direct trade with its colonies, but because it was unable to trade adequately itself, the result was a vast illicit trade that further bolstered non-Spanish shipping but often led to friction and war.[10] Holland still excluded all foreigners from its East Indies, and France pursued the same policy in the Canadian and West Indian colonies.[11] France's superb administrators devoted a large share of their considerable energies to building up a flourishing merchant navy and profitable foreign commerce by establishing an intricate system of protective tariffs, subsidies, navigation rules, and privileged companies.[12] As a result, the French and British East Indian Companies fought each other bitterly even when their governments were at peace.[13] Commercial rivalry lay behind every war, and colonies changed hands as prizes with each peace treaty. It was a grand game of winners and losers in which most of the major powers were players. But those who played best would prosper most, and in these stakes Britain was the unquestioned winner. Each war would leave Holland, whether British ally or enemy, a little weaker, until its eventual relegation to second-string power. Every war would also check the development of French commerce, which was the only real rival to that of Britain. After all, France's population was three times that of England; and France held Martinique, Guadeloupe, and Santo Domingo, the three best sugar-producing islands in the West Indies. Reflecting Louis XIV's policies in 1715, French commerce was estimated to be worth $72 million.[14] By 1785 it had climbed to approximately $330 million, compared with English commerce worth about $265 million.[15] However, every peace treaty added new markets that were open only to British commerce. British ships trebled during the last four decades of the seventeenth century, and trebled again during the first three-quarters of the eighteenth century. Successful war was directly related to the growth of shipping because naval and financial strength, which had turned England into Britain and then into Great Britain, was derived from expanding maritime commerce. Naval strength combined with an insular position to protect British commerce and to give it virtual monopolies during the lengthy wars that ravaged continental Europe for decades. Industrial and commercial success led to financial innovation. The Bank of England had been founded in 1694,[16] the national debt had been funded, and the insurance business was rapidly turning London into the center of the world for marine and other assurances.[17] The increasing use of commercial bills of exchange cheapened interest rates and provided facilities for the accumulation and uses of capital. Money and specie were streaming into Britain, which had learned how to multiply money; in turn, a very large percentage of the accumulation of wealth was prudently reinvested in foreign trade and the shipping that conveyed it. As Ernest Fayle so succinctly points out:

Thus, while war opened new markets to British goods and new ports to British ships, the consequent growth of British shipping was an actual growth, based firmly on the possession of an ever-increasing volume of goods for export and on the activities of the rapidly increasing body of wealthy traders restlessly seeking an outlet for their accumulated capital. It was not merely because the British fleets were usually victorious that Britain outstripped France in the race for ships, colonies, and commerce, but because British trade and shipping followed the lines of natural economic development, while French industry and commerce were still, to a great extent, half official; stimulated into activity by royal rescripts, subsidies, and grants of privilege and at the same time shackled with a host of medieval regulations and impostes.[18]

## The Gain of English Colonies from France

By the middle of the eighteenth century British shipowners became convinced that the Navigation Acts were no longer of help to British shipping. They had served their purpose. In any case, the acts had to be continually relaxed during the many wars to allow the employment of neutral vessels.[19] Such vessels became necessary in the more dangerous trades, to take the place of British vessels employed as military transports and privateers, and to permit the use of foreign seamen to replace British sailors who had joined the Royal Navy either by bounty inducement or by a press gang. Perhaps an even more important consideration was the theory that the Navigation Acts' protection raised freight rates and restricted trade.[20] However, before Britain could raise itself to its greatest height, more wars of "commercial and colonial consolidation" had to be fought. As already indicated, at the end of the war of the Spanish Succession in 1713, England had become *the* sea power. At the Peace of Utrecht, England retained Minorca and Gibraltar, seized during the war, and received Nova Scotia, Newfoundland, and the Hudson Bay Territory from France.[21]

After approximately twenty-five years of uneasy "peace" between the two countries, the Anglo-French struggle for India commenced in the 1740s. Colbert's *Compagnie des Indes Orientales* was flourishing, with its Indian base at Pondicherry and its trading connections into Siam and China.[22] At the same time, the English East India Company had in 1717 secured and strengthened its hold on the subcontinent.[23] The inevitable clash occurred in 1746. After the outbreak of the War of the Austrian Succession, the French, strengthened in their participation in Indian intrigue under the guidance of Joseph Duplix, captured Madras.[24] Although the city was restored to the British by the Treaty of Aix-la-Chapelle in 1748, bitter rivalry continued. In 1751 Robert Clive seized Arcot for Britain and recaptured Calcutta in 1757 during the Seven Years War.[25] This was the end of the French in India. By 1763 Pondicherry had been captured by British forces; it was eventually restored to France as a limited trading post only according to the Treaty of Paris in 1763. In 1769 the French East India Company was dissolved.[26]

The Seven Years War (1756-1763) between Britain and France, which began with an obscure boundary dispute in North America, was really the first worldwide struggle for sea power and commercial supremacy between two great states.[27] At stake were the colonial empire in America, the West Indies, West Africa, and India. Most of the hostilities took place at sea, and the French were losers almost everywhere. Britain took Florida, Havana in Cuba, and Manila in the Philippines, as well as Canada. The British returned some islands to Spain. France, under the peace treaty, received back its best sugar islands except Tobago. In addition to Florida, Britain also took control of all territory "East of the Mississippi" for what was to be a short-lived period. However, even the Seven Years War did not stop British trade, which actually increased during that period.[28]

### The Loss of English Colonies in America

The ascendency of Britain as a world power was not without its setbacks, the greatest of which was loss of the thirteen British colonies in America. The overt cause was commercial. British commerce had become increasingly protectionist, with enforcement by a variety of mercantilist devices. There was a complete lack of understanding of the requirements of the American settlements, which by the end of the seventeenth century were already much more than the collection of colonized plantations the British considered them. Yet as late as 1726 an official British communique stated that:

> All advantageous projects or commercial gain in any colony which are truly prejudicial to and inconsistent with the interest of the Mother Country, must be understood to be illegal and the practice of them unwarrantable; because they contradict the end for which the colonies had a being.[29]

Yet in the thirteen colonies English settlers, traders, and shipowners were indeed engaged in advantageous projects and commercial gain—why should they have been different from their compatriots at home? However, George III decided to tax them out of business and to restrict American trade generally. This type of mercantilist policy was, of course, difficult to enforce. There were many violations of the mountain of restrictive legislation, and American opposition mounted.[30] As a result, the thirteen colonies were becoming a nation dissatisfied with its government, which lay across the Atlantic Ocean and which appeared not to understand the importance of its American satellite.

When we speak of nationality here, we do so in the modern sense, which was certainly not understood at the time—neither by the British nor by the "revolutionaries" who were "hot for their rights as Englishmen."[31] They were being treated differently from other Englishmen, and they revolted against what they considered injustice. If British indifference prior to the American War for Independence (1775-1783) had been folly, the war itself was simply stupid. At the outbreak of the war the colonies had a population of 2 million, while the British Isles had less than 8 million. The great distance, the size of the colonial territory, and the outside help the Americans received made any attempt to hold the colonies by force quite hopeless. Nevertheless, war it was to be—and despite its obvious continental implications, much of it was again fought at sea or was dependent on sea power and successful blockade. Spain, still bitter about the loss of Jamaica and Gibraltar to Britain, and France, which had lost Canada in the Seven Years War, came to the aid of the colonies. It must also be remembered that between 25 and 30 percent of British ships were owned in North America, thus directly reducing British shipping by that amount.[32] the French and Spanish fleets had recovered from their previous losses and were able successfully to blockade the British Isles in the latter part of the war.[33] The United States of America thus came into existence through commercial shortsightedness and astute use of sea power as well as at the battlefields of Bunker Hill, Valley Forge, and Yorktown.

*The Defeat of Napoleon by English Sea Power*

The loss of the thirteen colonies was Britain's only real setback. During the Napoleonic period Britain established itself as a supreme sea power once and for all. A futile reaction against overtaxation, a politically excluded middle class, an unwieldly and inefficient machinery of government—which was a far cry from Colbert's visions—and an ever-growing national deficit, resulted in the French Revolution of 1789. For more than a decade, France was once again the center of a world in turmoil. Under Napoleon Bonaparte, France became an empire ranging from Schleswig-Holstein to Naples, from Estremadura to Greece; but that empire would eventually end in the snows of Russia and the bloodsoaked soil of Waterloo.

Although it would be wrong to say that "Napoleon's power ends at the shore,"[34] the British—in conflict with France almost continually during this period of turmoil—controlled the sea. After Trafalgar, where Admiral Nelson destroyed two-thirds of Napoleon's great fleet before the other third could come into action, there were no further challenges to British mastery of the sea. At the end of the period Britain retained the islands and territories that it had occupied during the wars—the Cape Colony in South

Africa, Ceylon, Malta, and Helgoland—all important strategic outposts for a fledgling empire with worldwide trade routes and commercial connections.

Nevertheless, the Napoleonic wars were costly to all sides. Although French expansionism is always cited as a root cause, the wars actually consisted again of the rivalry between two commercial superpowers, which the world since prehistory had never been able to support. Although British sea power reigned supreme, French influence did not end at the shore. Although they abandoned any policy of opposing the British at sea with great fleets, the French sought to destroy seaborne commerce by supporting a large number of privateers.[35] France was in a perfect position to carry out this policy. The port of London carried more than half of all British trade;[36] of the 13,000 to 14,000 annual vessel entries to and departures from British ports, more than two-thirds had to pass through the English Channel.[37] French privateers sailing from continental French ports could reach their prey very quickly, and some of the British losses were very serious. For example, just one large French privateer, captured in 1799, had taken some 160 prizes in four years, claiming for its owners some $5 million.[38] British ships were forced to sail in convoys under warship protection. Fleets of 200 to 1,000 vessels were not uncommon and were obviously costly in time and money. However, French efforts were more of a nuisance than anything else. French commercial vessels were literally swept from the seas, and by 1800 France's imports and exports to Asia, Africa, and America amounted to less than $400,000.[39]

After a brief interval of peace, in 1803 Napoleon, now the absolute ruler of France, reopened his new "commercial war" against Britain. He had realized the futility of a direct contest with the British on the seas, but he knew that the commercial supremacy of his enemy depended on the trade lifeline. He knew that there were only three ways in which he could conquer England. First, by direct invasion—impractical because of the strength of the British fleets. Second, by a strike at Britain's eastern empire—to which the unsuccessful Egyptian campaign was preparatory. Finally, by the "commercial strangulation" of the "nation of shopkeepers" by the exclusion of British goods from continental Europe.

Napoleon concentrated his efforts on the last scheme, with considerable impact. In the first instance, the wares and ships of British commerce were excluded from France. However, the Napoleonic conquests extended the prohibition to most of Europe. By 1809 English trade had ceased from all but Turkey, Sicily, and Portugal.[40] Napoleonic decree after decree attempted, with complete thoroughness, to close all gaps through which British trade might flow to and from Europe.[41] Napoleon's plan was to have European trade carried out only by neutrals—such as the newly independent Americans—or by his allies. The end result would be the total exclusion of an England starved into submission.

The emphasis once again had shifted to the seas. However, these measures did not work. English goods were in demand despite the hostilities. Prices doubled and trebled, and smuggling proliferated.[42] Napoleon had to clothe his armies in English cloth and had to sell licenses to evade his own decrees. At the same time, the British did not stand by idly and allow their trade to slip into the hands of the American rebels or Napoleon's allies. Interference in trade, which had brought on the American Revolution, would lead to not only the ire but also the unity of all of Britain. Various English Orders in Council matched Napoleon's decrees.[43] British policy was to drive Napoleon's allies from the sea and to make neutral commerce comply with this policy. An order in 1807 required any neutral vessel trading with the continent to stop at a British station, to land and reship its cargoes, and to pay certain duties both coming and going.[44]

Neutrals were thus placed in an intolerable position. Obedience to the orders of one belligerent meant exposure to the other. The Americans, who had profited greatly from these hostilities at first, were soon forced to declare open war on Britain in 1812, because their efficient ships were in difficulties.[45] Prizes, confiscations, and contraband declarations were frequent; and commercial losses were high for all who supported Napoleon, both allies and neutrals.[46] At the same time British trade grew, and British industry expanded behind the ever-growing wooden wall of British ships.

## The Congress of Vienna and the New European Public Order

There is relatively little new to add about maritime law during this difficult period. It was all-out war at sea; and the international law of the sea already referred to, relating to prizes and similar matters, was further developed. The rules of conduct on the sea were also strengthened but frequently broken, as the fight was becoming more one-sided all the time. The loser in desperation and the winner in arrogance often dispensed with legal principles. Private maritime law was changing only slightly, keeping pace with new demands of expanded English fleets and withering in a France cut off from the sea. The *Ordonnance de la Marine*, Colbert's masterpiece, had been revised after the Revolution,[47] and then again,[48] in a revised version, was incorporated into Napoleon's codes.[49] But as indicated, there was little need for it.

Later in this chapter we will examine briefly how the two areas of law fared during this whole period. For now, it should be noted that the trend dividing the two areas continued, particularly during the almost-continuous periods of belligerency. As previously suggested, the root causes of such conflicts were as commercially motivated as they had ever been—by maritime and colonial commercial expansionism for Britain, by continental and political supremacy and commercial control for France, and by commercial independence for the new United States of America.

However, although such policies could still be formulated fairly simply, they could no longer be put into practice as easily in a world that had become much more complex. The comprehensiveness of governing an enlarged populace in an expanded world required new administrative measures and much delegation of policy making and implementation—no matter how autocratic a monarch might be. Bureaucracy—perhaps invented by Colbert, whose visions of administrative perfection would, however, soon be lost—was in its infancy, having been born only a scant century earlier. In the previous era priorities of commerce were not necessarily priorities of military expediency, and the whole decision-making process was changing accordingly. During the period now under discussion, the "art of governing" was being perfected in a grand manner, which would reach one of its all-time heights during the glittering Congress of Vienna (1814-1816).[50] This meeting resulted in the *Concordat*, which divided up Europe. Although commercial considerations were hovering in the background, public political policies in the grand manner dictated *public* internationalism, to be practiced by the unprecedented array of autocracies that now governed Europe.

The congress itself was one of the most brilliant international assemblies of modern times and probably stage-managed all that was to happen to the world, at least during the next century. As guests of the Emperor Francis of Austria, most of the rulers of Europe attended, surrounded by a host of lesser potentates, ministers, and claimants. For example, the chief negotiators were: for Austria, Prince Metternich; for Prussia, Hardenburg and Wilhelm von Humboldt; for Great Britain, Castlereagh and Wellington; for Russia, Tzar Alexander I; for the Papacy, Cardinal Consalvi; and for France, Talleyrand.[51] Napoleon managed to interrupt the congress with his Hundred Day Campaign in 1815—but he was finally defeated and banished.[52] Peace was made; Europe was divided; colonial possessions were restored, retained, or traded; and a new age of conservative autocracy was ushered in. A devastated Europe was given a certain stability that would also result in the sort of discontent that facilitated further war and revolution.

That is not the point here, however. What we are trying to indicate is that governing in the grand manner had taken on different aspects and considerations. National policy, although even more centrally directed, was now composed of many different and often competing aspects. Commercial well-being was now a matter for rulers, ministers, and politicians; the merchant had faded in prominence as an influence on policy making, to be replaced, in many countries, by the industrialist and manufacturer, whose interests were often quite different.[53]

These policy changes were usually directly reflected in the laws, decrees, and orders that implemented them. In the area of ocean transportation, such laws were almost exclusively in the public domain.[54] The law regulating ocean *trade*, as it affected merchant, carrier, banker, insurer, and seaman, was definitely not a priority at the Congress of Vienna nor in any of the council chambers of European governments. It was slowly being relegated to a secondary role and would henceforth occupy such a position.

Priorities were changing quickly; and political and strategic factors, both at home and in overseas possessions, were dictating new approaches. For most European countries, commerce was no longer "fashionable" nor something on which great amounts of energy needed to be expended. Commerce was considered to be sufficiently self-motivated and self-perpetuating that whatever loose regulation it needed could be supplied by lesser government bodies.[55] As long as commerce could provide a convenient tax base for government ambitions, necessary employment for the expanding population, and new markets for imports and exports, it was left to its own devices. Ocean transportation, as a part of the commercial structure, fitted well into this laissez-faire philosophy. It had never been comfortable with mercantilism and restrictions and was happiest when there was little governmental direction.

Private maritime law would soon become simply a body of accepted laws in the private intercourse of maritime commerce. Public maritime law, on the other hand, was becoming an integral part of the "greater law of nations," which was itself becoming more and more accepted by the burgeoning number of nation-states of the world. The crack that had appeared in the cohesion of the two areas in the previous century was now becoming a split, and would soon be a schism that would never again be bridged. The barely perceptible, peripheral public rules of pre- and post-Roman times were becoming an all-embracing part of even larger sets of rules in the era of the new nation-states.

### The Worldwide Expansion of British Commerce and Sea Trade

The foregoing does not mean, however, that commerce was not a primary consideration for any of the European powers. For a Britain on the threshold of becoming a new empire, it was the very crux of its existence. The British government had been rather slow in learning the lessons of the American Revolution and the Napoleonic Wars. British shipowners did find a certain consolation when, in 1782, the Americans—who had been vigorous competitors—were excluded from the reserved trades,[56] but the general pessimistic view was that British commercial prosperity had come to an end.[57]

The pessimists could not have been more wrong, however. The loss of the thirteen colonies, the Napoleonic Wars, and the antecedents of a new "industrial age" would continue to lift British shipping into a position of unchallenged supremacy. First, a greatly improved agriculture was able to support a considerably enlarged British population.[58] Second, the construction of a network of canals multiplied the volume of internal British transport and brought goods to ports and markets at a greatly increased speed.[59] Third, the use of coal as an industrial fuel, and the introduction of machinery into the textile trade, increased the volume of British surplus export products by an unprecedented amount.[60] The resultant growth in shipping is reflected in the increase of tonnage clearing British ports from about 900,000 tons just before the American War of Independence, to over 1.7 million tons—of which 90 percent was British—just before the outbreak of the Napoleonic Wars.[61]

Finally, of course, came the boost that British commerce and shipping received from the lack of progress in a continental Europe laid waste after more than two decades of conflict. French and Dutch ships and those of their allies, as well as many neutral vessels, were swept into British ports as prizes or kept out of service by successful British blockade. At the same time, British industry advanced by leaps and bounds, and its products were carried all over an expanded world by an ever-growing British fleet.

Thus despite constant involvement in war, shipping clearances at British ports grew from 1.7 million tons in 1792 to an average of 2.7 million tons in the period 1816-1820.[62] At the end of 160 years of conflict, which had begun with the first Anglo-Dutch War and the promulgation of the Navigation Acts, Great Britain was in a position of absolute supremacy in terms of shipping, colonies, and commerce—a supremacy such as the world would not witness again for at least another century. The next step was, as always, for the new dominant power to consolidate its position to ensure its survival.

British trade at the end of the Napoleonic era was still confined to a limited number of shipping lanes over which commodities moved between the British Isles and British colonies. Between 1815 and 1850, the British took steps not only to expand these routes but also to supply the commercial leadership that was to make the empire supreme. First, there was an ever-increasing demand for the abolition of the Navigation Acts, which British shipowners—now supported by industrialists and manufacturers—considered restrictive to trade.[63] They argued that free trade was absolutely necessary for an island state that depended on import from and exports to all parts of the world.

Although the slogan of "free trade" was appealing, in reality the dominant maritime power once again simply wished to dispense with restrictions that might not only stifle its own expansionism but also inhibit the foreign overseas trade, which was dominated if not controlled by Britain. As before, "freedom" was a gratuitous gift of supreme benefit to the giver. Consequently, in 1849 British ports were opened to ships of all nations granting similar rights to British ships.[64] The British knew, of course, that they could now compete with superiority on all the world's trade routes.

The next step in the free-trade fight (which was not without its opponents) was to have the multitude of tariffs and taxes revised downward.[65] In 1823, for example, there were some 1,500 customs laws in effect in Britain.[66] When the British tried to lower rates on certain goods, other countries countered by claiming that they had no means to pay for increased British imports as long as certain British tariffs, particularly those on grain, remained in force. The "corn laws" were subsequently revised downward in 1846.[67] Other commodities received similar treatment, and consequently from the 1850s until World War I trade was more or less free. This period also coincides with the greatest heights of the British Empire.

Another reason for Britain's interest in free trade and the growth of world commerce was that it had now become a nation of creditors. The protection of investment, so familiar today, would at times almost supersede the interest in protection of shipping. Even better, they moved hand in hand. By 1815 London had become the world's financial capital. A European statesman is reported to have said at the close of the Congress of Vienna: "There were six powers in Europe—Great Britain, France, Russia, Austria, Prussia and the Baring Brothers."[68] Baring was a synonym for the London investment market.

Since the days of Cromwell's Commonwealth, Britain had steadily accumulated capital from trade. Increased production and exports, government loans, and marine-insurance premiums had all added to British capital. As always, investors of capital like to operate out of a comparatively safe and stable place; and international financiers and bankers flocked to London during the European wars. Immigrants such as Alexander Baring and Nathan Rothschild were instrumental in mobilizing these increasing capital resources.[69] The Barings floated huge loans to pay French reparation and occupation costs, and the Rothschilds financed the acquisition of the Suez Canal for Britain.[70]

The expanding colonial empire required an increasing amount of equipment and materials and large British loans for land settlement; mining development; railroad construction; and ports, factories, utilities, roads, canals, and docks. Many of these credit transactions were either directly or indirectly linked to the movements of goods between countries. As the principal supplier of manufactured goods and the world's largest ocean carrier, Britain benefited greatly. Trade quickly became more complex and sophisticated.

The old colonial trade staples—sugar and other such products from the colonies, and unlimited manufactured goods and slaves in the other direction—changed with the total abolition of the slave trade in 1807.[71] The colonies became much more than an area to be exploited, despoiled, and operated by slave labor. They were now a much more integral part of the British trading system and the London capital market.

Of course, marine transport was the physical methodology on which this whole new prosperity rested. As money flooded to and from the London market, the goods and industries financed by the money floated from one end of the world to the other on British ships. British industrial development was assured by an abundant supply of cheap coal, coke, and iron ore, as well as by a large workforce of laborers and skilled workers. High-grade ores were imported from Sweden to be mixed with the low-grade British ore. The great woolen-textile industry depended on imported raw materials—wool from Australia and New Zealand, cotton from the United States. The completed textiles were then exported worldwide.

In addition to ores, cottons, and wools, four-fifths of all wheat; two-fifths of all meat; and all the rice, tea, coffee, bananas, and citrus fruit came into Britain by ship.[72] Of course, the basic foodstuffs for the expanded European population, as well as most industrial raw materials, came primarily from the United States, Canada, Argentina, Australia, and New Zealand, all of which were closely tied to Britain in economic, cultural, and political terms. In terms of marine transport, only the United States and Argentina did not fly the British flag on their vessels. Of the two, only the fledgling United States was able to offer any shipping competition to Britain.

Although the American Revolution had virtually eliminated the shipping of the thirteen colonies, the new state had as one of its greatest assets a great shipbuilding industry consisting of scores of small yards from Maine to Georgia. This industry had an abundance of good lumber available as well as some of the most skilled craftsmen in the world. Nor was it a new industry—as early as the 1770s, out of a total of 600,000 tons of British-owned shipping, over one-third had been constructed in North America.[73]

After independence the U.S. merchant fleet blossomed, and the years from 1810 to 1840 have been called the "most glorious period in American maritime history."[74] During this period American ships carried some 90 percent of U.S. imports and exports, and by 1860 only two countries in the world owned merchant fleets of note, with Great Britain's fleet of 5.7 million tons only slightly larger than the 5.3-million-ton U.S. fleet.[75] On the other hand, the greater speed and carrying capacity of the American ships more than compensated for the difference.

This was the era of the great American packet shipping companies. The history of such operators as the American Black Ball, Swallow Tail, and

Red Star Lines gives eloquent strength to these developments. Americans were building cheaper, better, faster, and larger ships than their former colonial masters. American shipbuilders contributed as much to the development of the sailing ship in three decades as those of other countries had in four centuries.[76] Some of the most noteworthy changes in design, rig, handling, and carrying capacity occurred between 1820 and 1850.[77] At a time when Massachusetts builders had evolved a ship of 450 tons handled by a crew of 18, the British "East Indiaman" of 1,500 tons with a crew of 125 could carry only twice as much freight at half the speed. Thus another reason for a repeal of the British Navigation Acts was that British shipowners wished to employ superior American ships.[78] However, British shipyards soon began to catch up, and the great era of the clipper ships ensued.

However, even before the repeal of the Navigation Acts, U.S. ships were given special privileges by the British; and a healthy and mutually beneficial trade and competition evolved.[79] By the 1820s American ships were clearly within the British commercial sphere of influence and trading pattern in all parts of the world. American shipping was financed and insured in the London market, with acceptable profits being returned to the great ports of the United States. The lessons of the revolution had finally been learned. Only the advent of the steamship, to be discussed later in this chapter, would result in the gradual decline of American shipping.

*The Consolidation of European
Maritime Law*

There is thus little doubt that by the second part of the nineteenth century Great Britain was not only the master of the seas but also the leading trading nation of the world. The end of the Napoleonic upheaval also saw a conservative group of nation-states facing a period of comparative stability. Europe had been neatly divided up by the Congress of Vienna, and the map of the world at the end of the Napoleonic era has been aptly summarized as follows:

> Africa was a Dark Continent, as yet little noticed by the countries of Europe except as a source for slaves. The Near or Middle East, still a part of the Turkish Empire, had lost all importance as a link between East and West, waiting for the Suez Canal and petroleum to plunge it back into the vortex of world affairs. India was still governed by the British East India Companies; China, a slumbering giant, was yet to be torn by the Opium Wars; and Japan, the hermit nation, permitted extremely limited trade through the port of Nagasaki to the Dutch. In America, the United States was free, developing a flourishing trade that complemented more than it rivaled Britain's commerce, while Canada remained secure as a British colony.

To the South, the vast regions of Central and South America were on the verge of revolt.[80]

By the mid-1850s little had changed except that trade had greatly increased, slavery had finally been discontinued, and most colonies had become more settled and were considered to be a central part of the world's trading pattern. However, before moving into the next great era of expansionism in marine transport, we might quickly examine how the maritime law stood at the end of the first half of the nineteenth century.

In the private-maritime-law area there were really no notable changes. In France, the *Ordonnance de la Marine,* which had quickly become the most celebrated maritime code of Europe, continued to gain in repute. Commentaries on the *Ordonnance* by practicing admiralty counsel and judges such as Valin, Pothier, and Emerigon further enriched the collection.[81] The turmoil in France, both during and after the revolution, left little room for legal innovation in French maritime law. As already indicated, French maritime influence would fade and wither during this long period of hostilities.

Nevertheless, in 1800 a commission was established with a task of compiling a new code of commerce and marine matters. By 1807 a new *Code de Commerce* was approved by the emperor and enacted.[82] The new promulgation was more political than practical for a country that had reduced its shipping to privateers, smugglers, and blockade runners. The new code consisted of four books: first, laws regulating commerce in general; second, laws peculiar to maritime commerce; third, failures and bankruptcies; fourth, the competency of tribunals in commercial affairs and of the mode of judicial procedure.

In most respects, the new imperial code was similar to its better-known predecessors—Colbert's codes. In the period after Napoleon, the newer code was enlarged and further refined and became the accepted maritime law of France. French laws during the Napoleonic period were, however, exported to the many states that were occupied by, annexed by, or allied with France. In the Netherlands, for example, French occupation brought French maritime law, which, after 1815, was incorporated into the maritime codes of the new Kingdom of the Netherlands.[83]

Germany—still a disunited collection of free cities, principalities, and dukedoms, together with the kingdom of Prussia—had a proliferation of maritime laws, all of which were generally based on ancient codes, local customs, and the old Hansa laws. The Prussian Code of Maritime Law, issued in 1727, was modified in 1756 and then completely revised by order of King Frederic-William II in 1794. It was translated into Latin in 1800 and finally published in 1803, and is one of the most detailed codes of Europe by a state that had, as yet, little maritime presence. The great maritime jurist and commentator, Pardessus, observed about this code:

In doing justice to the science of the juri consults who concurred in the composition of this great work it is impossible to avoid remarking, that it contains too many details, definitions, interpretations, and doctrines; and that, if other codes err, or are defective, from the brevity which, in fact, leaves blanks in them, the Prussian code has gone into the opposite excess. But it is nevertheless one of the most remarkable works, and one of the most useful to juri consults, which has been published in our modern times; and it contains numerous and wise enactments relative to maritime law.[84]

The maritime law of the greatest maritime power of the day—Britain—was as modest as its shipping was great. As already indicated, the origin of English shipping law was obscurely derived from continental sources and set out in the *Black Book of the Admiralty*. However, the growing importance of English shipping and commerce obviously necessitated a certain growth in maritime jurisprudence. Consequently, this development was reflected on the one hand in the statutory laws relative to trade and navigation encompassing all the acts of Parliament relating to such subjects, and on the other to the common or consuetudinary law, also known as marine law and the law of merchants.

As in other branches of English law, there was no legislative codification such as existed on the continent. On the statutory side, the acts do not lay down any legal principles of the law, which are generally taken for granted or presumed to be preexistent in the common law of the land. Such acts were not passed to lay a foundation or to establish a part of a systematic whole but rather in a haphazard manner to correct occasional abuses or defects in the common law.[85] Examples are acts relating to the transference of property in British vessels, seamen's rights, marine-insurance provisions, shipping documentation, and so on.[86] In addition, the notorious Navigation Acts—to protect British shipping—also belong to this group, although an argument could be made that they rightly belong to the area of public maritime law. In other words, over the years, as requirement dictated, statutory maritime law was slowly built up into an ill-defined body of rules, which was rather haphazard but appeared to work.

The common law—the law merchant or *lex mercatoria*—is harder to describe, as the common law always is. Blackstone's words may assist:

In mercantile questions, such as bills of exchange and the like, and all marine causes relating to freight, average, demurrage, insurance, bottomry and others of a similar nature, the Law Merchant which is a branch of the Law of Nations is regularly and constantly adhered to. So, too, in all disputes relating to prizes, to hostages, and ransom bills, there is no other rule of decision but this great universal law, collected from history and usage and such writers of all nations and languages as are generally approved of and allowed.[87]

Again we see a slow buildup of maritime case law and rules of procedure in admiralty courts as used by skilled practitioners and able commercial judges in an atmosphere of learned deliberation. Nevertheless, the link between the two areas of law is still apparent. But it was an age of innovation, and much modern admiralty law is still founded on the precedents of that early period. To the uninitiated it was almost incomprehensible, to most foreigners—used to the neat European codes—unbelievable; but it worked and helped to lay the foundations that made English admiralty law and English courts internationally accepted.

As previously observed, the age of greater nationalism in the late 1700s and early 1800s left its imprint on the maritime law. There was certainly less uniformity. As well as in the states already noted, new maritime laws had also already been promulgated in Russia,[88] the Scandinavian nations,[89] Scotland,[90] the Italian city-states,[91] and of course the United States of America.[92] It appeared that an assertion of individual nationalism invariably had to be accompanied by the issuance of new laws regulating maritime trade. It was a sign of the times.

The public maritime law received only very limited development during this period. The three-mile limit of the territorial sea appeared to have become widely accepted by most states that found it advantageous during the long periods of war. It was introduced into English jurisprudence by Sir William Scott in the *Twe Gebroeders*, which held that Britain accepted both the cannon-shot and the three-mile limits.[93]

Almost all public law during this period was, of course, concerned with prizes and neutrality; and new rules relating to the rights of belligerents as well as neutrals in maritime war were worked out. The rules were intricate and still commercially oriented, but less so since Britain, now very much the dominant power, had less to fear from receiving quid pro quo for any breaches of the rules. The public maritime law was becoming less a mutual commercial affair and more a politically motivated body of rules of behavior. In addition, as already noted, the sheer bitterness of the wars made secondary commercial considerations quite unthinkable. Only neutrals needed the protection of these new rules, which basically depended on maritime policies and regulations laid down in London rather than on any "law of nations." The dominant power tolerated only those rules that would not interfere directly or indirectly with its own maritime ambitions. We have already examined the success of such ambitions, which would be even further consolidated in the next time period.


*Shipping Competition and Innovation*


The end of the Napoleonic period left Great Britain in a position of unquestioned supremacy in terms of shipping, as well as of international finance and commerce.[94] However, although the dominant maritime power always seeks to consolidate and preserve its position, the general freedom of British trade resulted in a certain inefficiency. As is often the case, those who gain from a certain enterprise appear to believe that a profitable business will continue to move forward of its own momentum. British shipping fell into this trap, with research and development stifled by the automatic increases in British shipping tonnage in the 1830s and 1840s, which appeared to preclude further or special exertions.[95]

However, as already shown, the supremacy of British shipping was being effectively challenged, particularly by the efficient and innovative Americans. Sailing vessels were still the main carriers of world commerce and, both in the building and operating of these, the British were being rapidly outclassed.[96] Design progress was being stifled by obsolete tonnage-measurement systems that penalized vessel breadth and resulted in very deep and full-bottomed ships that were capable of carrying cargo much in excess of the registered tonnage but were also very slow and unwieldly.

A report of a Board of Trade Commission, appointed in 1847, showed that British shipping was being overtaken by its competitors, particularly in the design of ships, the training and discipline of crews, and the nautical training of officers.[97] The report spoke of poor workmanship, defective stores and equipment, professional incompetence, and drunkenness. It appeared that British shipping was, once again, looking to the Navigation Acts for protection and depending on the lead gained during the Napoleonic turmoil.

As previously indicated, the navigation laws had already been substantially modified. They could not be enforced consistently against American ships, which were given special privileges under the acts by 1830.[98] By this time, in any case, the economic realities of the times were making the acts more and more redundant. At the same time, the government and the bulk of British shipowners were still firmly wedded to the old provisions. In addition, at the end of the Napoleonic period, Portuguese and Spanish colonies in South and Central America exploded in revolt, the result being a number of new and fiercely independent republics. These insisted on much of their commerce being carried in their own ships, and the Navigation Acts had to be amended accordingly.[99] New direct trade to South America caused severe competition for the traditional West Indian market, which had to adjust to its losses by removing shipping restrictions and allowing imports of European, American, and African goods in ships of the producing country, and exports in vessels of the purchasing state.[100]

The Navigation Acts were revised and further consolidated in 1845,[101] at a time when at least half the total trade was governed by exceptions to the acts rather than by the acts themselves.[102] However, they embodied the old conservative, mercantilist-protectionist spirit in its final death throes.

As already shown, newer interests and pressures prevailed—free-trade movements swept away most protectionist measures—and by 1847 the entire body of the Navigation Acts, with the exception of the coasting-trade provisions, was repealed.[103] Six years later the coasting trade was also opened up to the vessels of all states.[104]

Despite the wail of the pessimists, the acts were not long mourned. British shipowners were suffering too much from competition, particularly from the Americans. The discovery of gold in California in 1847 had given a further stimulus to American shipowners, as there was still no continental railroad. In 1849 alone, some 90,000 people sailed for San Francisco from the Atlantic U.S. coast via Cape Horn.[105] Larger and faster ships had become paying propositions. This resulted in the famous "California Clippers" built by the Nova Scotia-born Donald MacKay and other great U.S. shipbuilders. At a time when hardly any British merchant ships exceeded 1,000 tons, vessels like MacKay's *Flying Cloud* measured 1,800 tons and held the San Francisco record of ninety-eight days.[106] His *Sovereign of the Seas* measured 2,400 tons.[107] However, with only gold dust as the return cargo, these great clippers would cross to China to pick up a cargo for New York or Boston—and, after the repeal of the Navigation Acts, for British ports. The China tea trade was one in which speed was of the essence. The first of the new season's teas on the London market realized the highest prices. The American speedsters took full advantage of this trade and quickly became the foremost tea carriers for the London market.

With the discovery of gold in Victoria, Australia in 1851, another rush of immigrants commenced, carried almost exclusively on American ships. However, British shipowners were learning. Many were purchasing U.S.-built ships. James Baines of Liverpool, for example, owned the MacKay-built *Lightning,* whose Melbourne to Liverpool passage of sixty-three days would never be equaled under sail.[108] Not only were the U.S.-built ships bigger and better, they were also very much cheaper, being built out of an inexhaustible supply of softwood at a time when hardwoods such as oak and teak were becoming not only costly but also scarcer.[109] There were, on the other hand, serious defects in the softwood ships, which after about two voyages would become waterlogged and slow. With proper management, the expensive hardwood ship was more economical in the long run. By the late 1850s, British shipyards, catering to more progressive customers, were producing ships that were more than a match for their American rivals.

The first British Merchant Shipping Act of 1854, which greatly extended the powers of the Board of Trade, in particular with respect to ship construction and equipment, also heralded the beginning of state responsibility for the general welfare of the shipping industry and for enforcing the performance of its duties towards the public.[110] One of the first revisions was the promulgation of more rational rules for tonnage measurement, which gave British builders the freedom they needed.[111] By the 1860s British tea clippers were running the Americans out of the China trade.

In the Indian and Australian trade, a whole new generation of British ships, the famous "Blackwall frigates," came into being. Builders such as Hall of Aberdeen, Steele of Greenock, and Pile of Sunderland; and owners such as Richard Greene, Money Wigram, Joseph Saunders, and Duncan Dunbar combined to raise the British fleet to new heights. By 1860 British tonnage had increased to almost 6 million tons, but American tonnage still stood at 2.5 million tons.[112] At the same time, the total American-flag tonnage, including inland-river craft, stood only about 0.5 million tons less than the British Empire total.[113] However, less than twenty years later American tonnage had halved while British shipping had increased by almost the same ratio.[114]

One of the main causes of this extraordinary decline of American shipping was, of course, the American Civil War. Between 1861 and 1865, over 0.5 million tons of U.S. shipping was transferred to the British flag.[115] The war itself caused not only a reduction in shipping expansion but also direct losses to both Federal and Confederate shipping. However, another cause of decline was perhaps even more fundamental. This is well stated by Ernest Fayle as being caused by:

> . . . the immense development of the West and the Middle West which followed the War of Secession. Apart from a few of the New England states, the faces of the American people had always been set westwards, and when the political quarrels arising from the question of slavery had been disposed of, capital and enterprise found a far better return from the exploitation of the vast undeveloped resources of the western states than they could obtain from investment in shipping.[116]

However, even these two very significant causes would probably have been less marked had not American shipping also been overtaken by the greatest-ever development in marine transport—the change from sail and wood to steam and iron.

### Shipping-Technology Revolution: From Sail to Steam

As early as 1807, the *Clermont,* by steaming up the Hudson River on a summer afternoon, had become the first steamship engaged in a commercially successful operation.[117] But although the wooden, paddle-wheel steamship, ideal for river and inland navigation, was an American invention, the use of steam for oceangoing ships was perfected by the British.[118]

It should be clear by now that shipping is a notoriously conservative, tradition-bound, and cautious industry. At first steam power was derided and considered and invention of the devil. Iron steamships were derisively dismissed as tin kettles; seamen, no less conservative than their masters, would not go near them. Yet steam-powered and iron ship construction would not be halted; they moved along, albeit slowly and at times quite separately. However, the launching of the *Great Britain* in 1845 is considered a landmark in the whole history of shipping, for the vessel was the first iron-hulled, double-bottomed, screwpropelled, steam-powered Atlantic liner.[119] Although the sailing ship would be around for another six or seven decades, its death knell had been loudly and clearly sounded.

Between the *Clermont* voyage and the launching of the *Great Britain*, progress in steam propulsion for ships had been rapid. After many experimental voyages, numerous technical and financial failures, and a notable lack of support and interest from government, effective steamship service between Europe and North America began in 1836 with the launching of the *Great Western* (1,340 gross tons) and the *British Queen* (1,862 gross tons).[120] The reliability of the new steamships brought with it the coveted mail contracts, which fully established such shipping lines as Cunard, the Peninsula and Oriental Steam Navigation Company (P&O), and the Royal Mail Steam Packet Company.

Although good shipbuilding lumber was becoming ever scarcer and more expensive in Britain, the iron hull gained acceptance slowly also. The Royal Navy had acquired three steamships in the 1820s but rejected iron-hulled ships with considerable skepticism. Such hulls were considered to be more susceptible to solid cannon balls than was the traditional wooden vessel.[121] Such a governmental stand severely limited research and experimentation, which thus had to be confined to the private sector.

When the *Great Britain* was stranded off the coast of Ireland in 1846 and remained on the beach all winter with relatively little damage, the skeptics slowly realized the potential of the iron hull. At the same time, quite a while before the regular construction of iron-hulled ships, sailing vessels were being constructed with iron frames and wooden planking. Builders, as well as owners, were becoming convinced of the advantages of iron as a shipbuilding material. Although iron was heavier than wood, its greater strength allowed such a reduction in hull thickness that an iron ship weighed about 25 percent less than a wooden vessel of the same dimensions.[122] This resulted in additional cargo capacity, a fact that endeared iron to vessel owners. In the case of the steamship, the owners had to make provisions for a large bunker capacity; but iron construction permitted the building of considerably larger vessels. The structural limit of a wooden vessel was about 300 feet, but iron held no such limitations.

By 1858 the famous *Great Eastern,* constructed by the great engineer

Brunel, had arrived on the scene with an incredible length of 680 feet and unbelievable tonnage of 18,914 gross registered tons (grt).[123] The vessel was not a commercial success but was a great experiment in ship construction. Such large tonnages would not reach commercial viability until the very end of the nineteenth century, but by 1875 steamers in the 3,000-5,000-ton range were regular paying propositions.[124]

The next step was the screw propellor, which was a much more viable propulsion system than the delicate and cumbersome paddle wheel. However, propellors vibrated and were therefore not successful in wooden hulls—a further incentive for iron construction. The propellor was soon followed by the remarkable compound engine, with its great saving in fuel.[125] This innovation was followed in turn by the surface condenser, which made it unnecessary to carry large quantities of fresh water for the boilers.[126] All these changes increased the cruising range, as well as the carrying capacity, of the new steamships, which could compete with the sailing ships only if they reduced their running expenses. Most of the early steamers still carried considerable sail as auxiliary power, but iron was now the standard construction material for sailing ships as well and would remain so until the end of sail.[127]

By the 1860s the iron steamship had come into its own; British shipyards, which had completely cornered the construction market, could not keep up with the demand. During this period, over 30 percent of all British ships in existence and over 50 percent of ships under construction were made of iron.[128] As British wooden sailing ships were replaced by iron sailing ships, and iron sailing ships by iron steamships, the redundant vessels were sold to other states that were building up their own fleets. This meant that Britain was always about one innovation ahead.

The most remarkable fact of this expansionistic period was that there was an almost total lack of British-government policy behind this great leap forward in shipping progress. The private sector—builders and owners—alone and without government assistance, finance, or even support, engineered the greatest revolution in the whole history of ocean transportation. National policy was forced lamely to follow the entrepreneurial innovation of British shipowners and shipbuilders who would thrust Britain into the forefront of the world's shipping nations once again.

It would be pure conjecture to speculate whether this lack of government interference, or even interest, was a positive or negative contribution to the progress achieved. It was, of course, a manifestation of the change in direction of national policy that had taken place in most of the world's powers after the Congress of Vienna. Britain had its national policy objectives firmly fixed on a worldwide empire with an unprecedented system of colonial satellites linked to the causal nationalism of the British Crown. The fact that this objective rested on a firm commercial base was recognized and encouraged, but was no longer part and parcel of national political policy. It was seen that commerce and shipping could well take care of themselves and that interference was neither necessary nor desirable.

Even this might be considered a policy if it had been expressed in such terms, but it seldom was. Commercial interests had become quite separated from political considerations, which had moved into the forefront of national thinking. Commercial strength was merely the vehicle that supported national ambitions. Commercial power was in the private sector, whereas national strength was definitely of public interest. The Board of Trade, already mentioned, was to look after the former, while the imperial government steered the latter. At times the two interests were even at variance. One of the best examples of this was the British policy vis-à-vis the construction of the Suez Canal, which would revolutionize ocean transportation even further.

### The New Route to the East: The Suez Canal

Probably no single event more completely revolutionized the great trade routes to the East than did the Suez Canal.[129] Until the Middle East wars of the 1950s and 1960s, the canal was the most frequented route for vessels bound for all ports in India, China, Australia, Southeast Asia—about half the ports of the world.[130]

As already mentioned, the idea of the canal was not new. It is fairly certain that Pharoah Necho (612-596 B.C.) commenced a canal from the Nile to the Red Sea, which started in the vicinity of present-day Suez, passed through the Bitter Lakes to Lake Tumsah, and thence turned westward to Bubastis on the Nile.[131] Herodotus describes the canal's watergates and tells us of the four-day passage through this ancient waterway.[132] It apparently silted up over the next centuries, but was again dug out in the reign of the Caliph Omar in the seventh century, when Egypt fell under Arab rule.[133]

Sand again choked up the waterway over the years, but the idea always remained. In 1798 Napoleon had the area surveyed, but he received erroneous engineering information claiming that the Red Sea water levels were considerably higher than those of the Mediterranean. Consequently, further examination was dropped.[134] Nevertheless, it was ultimately France, despite Britain's strongest-possible objections, which successfully carried out the construction of the modern Suez Canal.[135]

Between 1831 and 1838, Ferdinand de Lesseps, then a French consular agent in Egypt, started thinking about the project and carried out endless negotiations with the Ottoman government—all to no avail.[136] Between 1838 and 1854, he continued his efforts and in 1854 was finally successful in obtaining a construction concession from the viceroy of Egypt, Mohammed Said Pasha.[137]

Returning to France, de Lesseps tried to raise the required capital for the gigantic project. He held public meetings in most of the great commercial centers of England in order to raise money and gain acceptance for the canal. The British government, under Lord Palmerston, opposed him bitterly and considered the whole idea to be a danger to British expansionism and sea power.[138] The reasons were never made entirely clear, but the de Lesseps canal just did not seem to fit within the general planning of British ocean policy of the times.

However, the canal did receive a generally favorable response from the British shipping industry, which was still engaged in the sail-versus-steam battle.[139] The progressives and steam proponents immediately saw the great advantage of a fast route to the East. The sailing-ship diehards were naturally opposed, as were those merchants who saw not only a reemergence of the importance of the great Mediterranean trading cities, but also vigorous competition, as byproducts of the canal.[140] The Royal Navy was not convinced about the canal and supported the government's stand fully in a decision that was clearly against the commercial interests of the country.[141] In retrospect it is clear that it could have been a disastrous decision had Egypt not experienced its later financial difficulties.

In any case, de Lesseps was able to raise one half of the 200-million-franc capital in France, where public response and interest was considerable.[142] On December 15, 1858 a general company was constituted to pierce the Isthmus of Suez; and work commenced on April 25, 1859.[143]

The work took ten years, owing to many delays caused by the continued interference and opposition of Britain and the perennial ineptitudes and weaknesses of the Egyptian government.[144] Nevertheless, on November 17, 1869, the Suez Canal, available under the same terms for everybody, was opened for navigation. The water link between the Mediterranean and the Red Sea had once again been established.

The total cost of construction had been just over £20 million, and there were immediate financial difficulties as lenders and shareholders demanded a quick investment return.[145] Transit charges rose rapidly but were soon reduced because of the rapid increase in canal users. By 1874 shareholders were already receiving a 25-franc dividend on a 500-franc share, and interest rose steadily after that.[146] Also, by 1874 a new British Government, under Lord Beaconsfield, had recognized the real potential of the canal as England's "high road to India."[147]

In the relatively short period since the opening of the new waterway, the majority of users clearly were British ships; and the canal's strategic importance increased quickly. The British, taking advantage of the improvidences and inefficiencies of the Egyptian government in 1875, secured all of that government's shares, valued at £4 million.[148] Within twenty years these shares were worth £23 million.[149] This was not only a good investment but also secured for Britain a large, almost commanding voice in the management of the canal. This was valuable indeed, since by 1895, out of the approximately 3,000 vessels (totaling almost 8.5 million tons) that used the canal, some 80 percent were British.[150]

Thus the shortsighted and bumbling British policy, which had for the first time totally disregarded commercial considerations, was in effect saved by Egyptian mismanagement. The Suez Canal became as firm a part of British imperialism as were that country's far-flung colonies. Sailing vessels would henceforth be confined to routes that were unprofitable for steam or to situations where time and distance were not of prime relevance.

Enormous benefits were conferred on ocean transportation by the construction of the Suez Canal. First, from the investors' point of view, dividends would rise to over 20 percent per year.[151] Second, the canal shortened the route to India by one-third, with a commensurate shortening of distance to points further east. Third, the canal furthered the growth of the world's steam tonnage at a rate that would have been impossible without it. Fourth, the canal made possible the movement of bulk cargoes, such as rice, wheat, petroleum, and coal, that were formerly excluded from trade with the East. Further indirect benefits were the drop of European prices of Eastern products by 25-35 percent within fifteen years of the opening of the canal.[152] This increased the demand for such goods; stimulated their production; and added to the prosperity of all engaged in the trade from manufacturer to seller, with a large part of the benefits again being conferred on the ocean carrier.

### Maritime Commerce, Law, and Policy and the Industrial Revolution

However, the Suez Canal was only one of many improvements in transport and communications that would, in the latter half of the nineteenth century, cause a commercial revolution that has been equated in importance with the Industrial Revolution itself.[153] It was probably the very fulfillment of the Industrial Revolution as well as its outgrowth. The real effects of the steam locomotive and the steamship began in the earlier part of the century but would not be felt until the latter part. The scope and area of world markets would thus be widened rapidly as the result of speedier and more regular transportation systems and a new network of telephone, telegraph, and ocean-cable services. The first Atlantic submarine cable was laid in 1893,[154] but in 1874 a cable had already been laid to Pernambuco to link Brazilian coffee production with world markets.[155] The year 1869, in which the Suez Canal was opened, also witnessed the completion of the U.S. transcontinental railroad system.[156] In 1874 the Universal Postal Union (UPU) was founded, making international correspondence certain as well as inexpensive.[157] There is thus little doubt that, in the five decades prior to World War I, the face of the world was changed more completely, and, certainly more rapidly, than in its entire history.

A large percentage of these changes was directly attributable to marine transport, which had taken the greatest "leap forward" in its history. The shipping statistics of the times are astounding; nowhere is this better reflected than in figures for the fleet of Great Britain at its height of sea power and Victorian imperialism. In 1837, when Queen Victoria came to the throne of England, the country's shipping register showed a total of 19,269 sailing vessels (many under 100 tons) plus 554 steamships, with a total tonnage of 2,312,000 grt.[158] When the Queen celebrated her Diamond Jubilee in 1897, there were 2,452 sailing vessels of over 100 tons, totaling 2,189,840 tons, and 6,655 steamships over 100 tons, totaling 10,213,569 tons, on the British Register.[159] In addition, some 2,130 sailing vessels and steamships with a tonnage of 1,079,467 tons were owned in the British colonies, making a grand-total British tonnage of 13,482,876 tons, which was just over half of the world's total tonnage of 26.5 million grt of shipping in 1897.[160] Thus by the end of the nineteenth century there was little doubt that Britain was not only the dominant sea power but also a commercial and colonial empire on which the sun truly never set.

In 1862 the Companies (Limited Liability) Act passed in Britain making possible the development of the modern shipping company.[161] Henceforth, anyone with money to invest could buy shares in a shipping enterprise, knowing that at worst he was risking only what he put in and that the company's creditors could not lay claim to any of his other assets. The circle from which most of the great shipping companies could draw capital was thus greatly widened to include any and all with money to invest in one of the best investments the country could offer.

In any case, shipping was no longer confined to the great liner companies but had become diversified into all aspects of marine-transport services. Although the regular "cargo liners" and passenger liners would continue to dominate the major trade routes for some years, world trade on more irregular routes was also growing rapidly. Seasonal products such as wheat and cotton; rough and bulk cargoes such as timber, iron, and coal, which were usually bought and sold in ship-size consignments; and the many new ports that were off the beaten trade routes, or that did not offer sufficient commercial inducement for the liner services, gave birth to the irregular trader or "tramp" vessel. These were "odd job" ships, which quickly gained for themselves a large proportion of world commerce.

Although the sailing vessel had at first been relegated to this service by the steamer, sailing ships were soon hard pressed by the tramp steamers, which could make more voyages and were independent of wind and weather. Once worldwide coal-bunkering depots became well established, tramp steamers' schedules could easily be calculated, adding greater certainty to the fixing of time charter parties.[162] Improvements in world communications added to the effectiveness of these "cross-trading" ships.

An unknown seventeenth-century English writer noted that "the coal trade is indeed the refuge and mother of our entire shipping industry."[163] A well-known American expert on transport and trade spoke of "coal—the key to the carrying trade."[164] Coal was, indeed, another cornerstone of British oceanic dominance. As European and British shipping increased with the rising European demand for foodstuffs and raw materials, shipowners needed an outward-bound cargo that "would move in volume, one to supplement exports of high-value but low-tonnage manufactured goods and thereby to help to balance the volume moving in both directions."[165] This development led the British, sitting on top of some of the world's largest coal reserves, to exploit this great resource. From 3.2 million tons in 1850 British coal exports rose steadily to 29 million tons in 1890 and to 64 million tons in 1907.[166] Exports were so great that British trade statistics divided the world into ten coal markets:

1. Germany and all European countries to the north, including Russia;
2. France and all countries to the south, including those bordering the Mediterranean;
3. the West Coast of Africa;
4. British South Africa;
5. the East Coast of Africa, including Mauritius, Arabia, Persia, Aden, and so on;
6. the Indian continent;
7. the rest of Asia;
8. the countries of North and South America;
9. Brazil, Uruguay, and Argentina;
10. the western part of South America and the western part of the United States of America.[167]

Britain, therefore, controlled the supply of this vital resource at a time when there was no substitute and when all industrial power and most ocean-going ships depended on coal. As steamships increased, so did the demand for coal and worldwide bunkering stations. Britain met the supply and established a wide network of coaling stations.[168] With the world's largest fleet, Britain itself was, of course, the greatest consumer of bunkering coal. In 1870, still the age of sail, British coal-bunker exports stood at 3.2 million tons, rising to 8.1 million tons for 1890, and reaching a peak of 21 million tons in 1913, when they made up almost one-quarter of total British coal exports.[169]

## Conclusions: A Maritime State Created

At the end of the nineteenth century, Britain therefore was:

1. the world's largest seapower, in terms of naval and merchant ships;
2. the financial center of the world, in terms of investment, capital, and assurance;
3. the largest commercial country in the world, in terms of exports and imports;
4. the major colonial power with possessions on all continents;
5. in control of most of the world's communications—by ownership or major shareholding in the main telephone, telegraph, and cable networks;
6. a major shareholder in the Suez Canal;
7. the main supplier of coal—the main industrial power source.

This unprecedented prominence as a major power was achieved without question by Britain's mastery of the sea. Although the aims of British policy during this historical period were not always clear, a combination of extrinsic and intrinsic influences shaped this oceanic thrust, which was not to be halted by conservative government of "mercantilist" commerce. The laissez-faire attitude towards trade, governed by the handsome return on investments combined with the Protestant ethic of the Victorian Age, would make Britain into one of the most formidable powers in world history. It was a commercial juggernaut which moved on ten thousand ships—buying, selling, trading, annexing, and conquering with pounds sterling rather than with shot.

Resistance was feeble or nonexistent. The other European powers were licking their post-Congress of Vienna wounds at a time when British commerce was already in its ascendency. When they had recovered sufficiently to compete, they quickly fell into the already well-established trading pattern and, instead of beating it, joined it. This was a stable time for most of the European powers, although a variety of smaller wars, such as the Franco-Prussian war of 1870-1871, only increased the peaceful stability of the British Empire, which could only benefit from the instability of its rivals.

However, the unprecedented spread of imperialism and colonialism (which was certainly not confined to Britain) sowed the wind that the world would reap in the whirlwind of two world wars. The final result would be the horizontal explosion of the world of nation-states in the present era, and the division of the world into developed and developing countries. Eurocentricity, Christian ethics, civilization, and trade (not necessarily in that order) had as byproducts many of the problems we are facing today. The imposition of European rules and values, whether by cannon, missionary, or trading company on the Asian, African, and South American continents, would have results that would not only change the whole economic and political aspect of the world, but would also topple old empires and establish new ones. The pattern established in Roman and pre-Roman times had not really changed.

This examination of the international law and policy of marine transport has ranged far and wide. The excursions have been necessary—if anything, they have been briefer than history really permits. The purpose in showing the wider context here has been to illustrate the *real* infrastructure of marine transport as well as its strengths, depths, and resilient traditions. At the end of the nineteenth century, the "freedom of the seas" had a much, much wider meaning than Hugo Grotius could possibly have envisaged. It now encouraged and encompassed the freedoms to trade, to conquer, to colonize, to monopolize, to Christianize, and to subjugate. It accepted as a Christian ethic that commerce was of community benefit and that the community was the world under one's control. If the world's greatest commercial empire were the end, then shipping was the means, and freedom the great causal umbrella that heaped benefit on all who stood beneath it. There was now little need for coastal extension of state sovereignty—commerce and trade, of mutual benefit to all who could and would invest in it, took precedence.

The public maritime law during this period confined itself to setting up new rules for the regulation of coastal and international fisheries and for consolidating and refining the rules relating to naval warfare and war at sea.[170] European international lawyers were engaged in the technical exercise of demarcation and limitation of boundaries, while smugly consolidating what they considered to be "their" European law of nations.[171] There were, of course, no other nations or other people with similar rights under this law of nations. As Professor Verzijl quite confidently asserts:

> . . . there is one truth that is not open to denial or even doubt, namely, that the actual body of international law, as it stands today, not only is a product of the conscious activity of the European mind, but also has drawn its vital essence from a common source of beliefs and in both these aspects it is mainly of western European origin.[172]

In other words, the civilizations of Africa and Asia, under colonial rule and domination, had nothing to contribute to the international law of the late nineteenth century. The conscious activities of African and Asian minds henceforth would be directed mainly toward liberation. At the same time, the European law of nations would be imposed on the non-European world lock, stock, and barrel. Yet in later years the newer nations of Africa, Asia, and Latin America were supposed to follow this "law of nations," which had never been "their" law but which

> ... is a law of Christian Europe. It has roots in the *Republica Christiana* of medieval Europe. It is based on the value of the Occidental culture, on Christian and often Catholic values.[173]

Most of the "public" law-of-the-sea rules, established by the end of the nineteenth century, were a product of this Eurocentricity which had taken the principles of expediency established by Grotius and his contemporaries and had turned them into "principles of permanent world law" in a world which at that time consisted of Great Britain, Europe, and the United States, with the rest of the world being under colonial rule and/or imperialist subjugation. The traditional law of nations can thus be attacked on the ground of universal validity. The public law of the sea, as part of such international law, is thereby weakened. However, seen in the context of our preceding examination, its role as a tool of expediency by the dominant maritime power once again becomes clear. It was in the private-maritime-law area that further developments would occur, developments that would occupy a role of considerable importance in the next half century.

## Notes

1. William L. Langer, ed., *An Encyclopedia of World History,* 4th ed. (Boston: Houghton Mifflin, 1968), p. 465.

2. W.O. Stevens and Allan Westcott, *A History of Sea Power* (Garden City, N.Y.: Doubleday, 1944), p. 152.

3. Ibid.

4. Ibid.

5. C.E. McDowell and H.M. Gibbs, *Ocean Transportation* (New York: McGraw-Hill, 1954), p. 16.

6. Ibid., pp. 30-32.

7. Ralph Davis, *The Rise of the English Shipping Industry* (London: Macmillan, 1962), p. 27.

8. Ibid., p. 28.

9. Ibid., pp. 30-31.

10. C. Ernest Fayle, *A Short History of the World's Shipping Industry* (London: George Allen and Unwin, 1933), p. 167.

11. McDowell and Gibbs, *Ocean Transportation,* pp. 16-17.

12. Ibid., p. 16.

13. Fayle, *History of the World's Shipping Industry,* ch. 7.

14. McDowell and Gibbs, *Ocean Transportation,* p. 17.

15. Ibid.

16. Langer, *Encyclopedia of World History,* p. 466.

17. Dover, *A Handbook to Marine Insurance,* 7th ed., edited by R.H. Brown (London: Witherby, 1970), p. 16.

18. Fayle, *History of the World's Shipping Industry,* pp. 193-194.

19. Ibid., p. 194.

20. Ibid.

21. McDowell and Gibbs, *Ocean Transportation,* p. 19.

22. Langer, *Encyclopedia of World History,* pp. 572-573.

23. Stanley Wolpert, *A New History of India* (New York: Oxford University Press, 1977), p. 142 ff.

24. Ibid., pp. 175-177.

25. Ibid.

26. Ibid., p. 180.

27. McDowell and Gibbs, *Ocean Transportation,* p. 19.

28. Ibid.; see also Fayle, *History of the World's Shipping Industry,* p. 194.

29. J.B. Condliffe, *The Commerce of Nations* (New York: Norton, 1950), p. 103.

30. Bernard Bailyn et al., *The Great Republic: A History of the American People* (Boston: Little, Brown, 1977), ch. 7.

31. McDowell and Gibbs, *Ocean Transportation,* p. 20.

32. Ibid.

33. Ibid.

34. Ibid., p. 19; see also the classic interpretation of this question in A.T. Mahan, *The Influence of Sea Power upon History,* 22nd ed. (Boston: Little, Brown, 1911).

35. Clive Day, *A History of Commerce,* 2nd ed. (New York: Longmans, Green, 1919), p. 343.

36. Ibid.

37. Ibid.

38. Ibid.

39. Ibid.

40. Ibid., p. 344.

41. Ibid.

42. Ibid.

43. Ibid.

44. Ibid.

45. Ibid.; see also Bailyn, *The Great Republic,* pp. 377-382.

46. Day, *History of Commerce,* p. 344.

47. James Reddie, *An Historical View of the Law of Maritime Commerce* (Edinburgh: Blackwood, 1841), p. 361.

48. Ibid.

49. John H. Wigmore, *A Panorama of the World's Legal Systems*, vol. 3 (St. Paul, Minn.: West Publishing Co., 1928, p. 1031ff.

50. Langer, *Encyclopedia of World History,* pp. 650-651.

51. Ibid.

52. Ibid., p. 651.

53. Condliffe, *Commerce of Nations,* pp. 124-126.

54. See, for example, Fayle, *History of the World's Shipping Industry,* ch. 8.

55. Ibid.

56. Ibid., p. 195.

57. Ibid.

58. Ibid.

59. Ibid.

60. Ibid.

61. Ibid.

62. Ibid.

63. Day, *History of Commerce,* pp. 370-371.

64. Condliffe, *Commerce of Nations,* p. 215.

65. Ibid.

66. Ibid.

67. Ibid.; see also, Day, *History of Commerce,* pp. 369-370.

68. L.H. Jenks, *The Migration of British Capital to 1875* (New York: Knopf, 1927), p. 36.

69. Condliffe, *Commerce of Nations,* pp. 203-205.

70. McDowell and Gibbs, *Ocean Transportation,* p. 25.

71. Fayle, *History of the World's Shipping Industry,* p. 217.

72. McDowell and Gibbs, *Ocean Transportation,* p. 26.

73. Ibid., p. 21.

74. Ibid.

75. Ibid.

76. Ibid.; see also *The History of the Sailing Ship* (New York: Arco, 1975), ch. 6; Patrick Brophy, *Sailing Ships* (London: Hamlyn, 1974), p. 66ff.

77. Ibid.

78. Ibid., McDowell and Gibbs, p. 22.

79. Ibid., p. 23.

80. Ibid., p. 27.

81. Reddie, *Historical View of the Law of Maritime Commerce,* p. 354ff.

82. Wigmore, *World's Legal Systems,* vol. 3, p. 1031ff.

83. Reddie, *Historical View of the Law of Maritime Commerce,* p. 332.

84. Ibid., pp. 402-403.

85. Ibid., ch. 11.

86. Michael Thomas and David Steel, *The Merchant Shipping Acts,* vol. 2: *British Shipping Laws,* 7th ed. (London: Stevens, 1976).

87. Reddie, *Historical View of the Law of Maritime Commerce*, p. 426.
88. Wigmore, *World's Legal Systems,* vol. 3, p. 918.
89. Ibid.
90. Ibid.
91. Ibid.
92. Reddie, *Historical View of the Law of Maritime Commerce,* p. 478ff.
93. [1800] 3 C. Rob. 162.
94. McDowell and Gibbs, *Ocean Transportation,* p. 24.
95. Ibid.
96. Fayle, *History of the World's Shipping Industry,* p. 231.
97. Ibid., pp. 231-232.
98. McDowell and Gibbs, *Ocean Transportation,* p. 23.
99. Ibid.
100. Ibid.
101. Fayle, *History of the World's Shipping Industry,* p. 233.
102. Ibid.
103. Ibid., p. 234.
104. Ibid.
105. Ibid.
106. Ibid.
107. Ibid.
108. McDowell and Gibbs, *Ocean Transportation,* p. 21.
109. Fayle, *History of the World's Shipping Industry,* p. 236.
110. The Merchant Shipping Act, 1854. 17 and 18 Vict., ch. 103.
111. Fayle, *History of the World's Shipping Industry,* p. 236.
112. McDowell and Gibbs, *Ocean Transportation,* p. 21.
113. Ibid.
114. Gerard J. Mangone, *Marine Policy for America* (Lexington, Mass.: Lexington Books, D.C. Heath and Co., 1977), p. 75ff.
115. Fayle, *History of the World's Shipping Industry,* pp. 238-239.
116. Ibid. For a magnificent panorama of this movement, see Frederick Merk, *History of the Westward Movement* (New York: Knopf, 1978).
117. McDowell and Gibbs, *Ocean Transportation,* pp. 27-28.
118. Ibid., p. 28; David Howarth, *Sovereign of the Seas* (New York: Atheneum, 1974), p. 310ff.
119. McDowell and Gibbs, *Ocean Transportation,* p. 27.
120. Ibid., p. 28.
121. Ibid.; see also Howarth, *Sovereign of the Seas,* p. 310ff.
122. Fayle, *History of the World's Shipping Industry,* p. 239.
123. Ibid., p. 240.
124. Ibid.
125. McDowell and Gibbs, *Ocean Transportation*, p. 28.

126. Ibid.

127. Fayle, *History of the World's Shipping Industry*, p. 240.

128. McDowell and Gibbs, *Ocean Transportation*, p. 29.

129. Day, *History of Commerce*, pp. 308-309.

130. McDowell and Gibbs, *Ocean Transportation*, pp. 78-79.

131. R.J. Cornewall-Jones, *The British Merchant Service* (London: Sampson Low, 1898), p. 306.

132. Ibid., p. 307.

133. Ibid.

134. Ibid.

135. Ibid.

136. Ibid.; see also David McCulloch, *The Path Between the Seas—The Creation of the Panama Canal, 1870-1914* (New York: Simon and Schuster, 1977), ch. 2.

137. Cornewall-Jones, *The British Merchant Service*, pp. 308-309.

138. Ibid., p. 307; see also R.R. James, *The British Revolution, 1880-1939* (New York: Knopf, 1977), pp. 27-28.

139. Ibid.

140. E.W. Zimmerman, *Ocean Shipping* (New York: Prentice-Hall, 1922), p. 45.

141. Ibid.

142. Condliffe, *The Commerce of Nations*, p. 324; Cornewall-Jones, *The British Merchant Service,*, p. 308.

143. Cornewall-Jones, *The British Merchant Service.*

144. Ibid.

145. Zimmerman, *Ocean Shipping*, p. 46ff.

146. Ibid.

147. Ibid.

148. Cornewall-Jones, *The British Merchant Service*, p. 314.

149. Ibid.

150. Ibid.

151. Day, *History of Commerce*, pp. 308-309.

152. Ibid.

153. Condliffe, *The Commerce of Nations*, p. 293.

154. Ibid.

155. Ibid.

156. Ibid.

157. Ibid.

158. Zimmerman, *Ocean Shipping*, p. 220ff.

159. Ibid.

160. Ibid.

161. The Companies Act, 1862. 25 and 26 Vict., ch. 89.

162. Fayle, *History of the World's Shipping Industry*, ch. 10.

163. Zimmerman, *Ocean Shipping,* p. 223.

164. Ibid., ch. 13.

165. McDowell and Gibbs, *Ocean Transportation,* p. 51.

166. Ibid.

167. Ibid., pp. 51-52.

168. Ibid.

169. Ibid.

170. See, for example, Oppenheim, *International Law,* vol. 2. (New York: Macmillan, 1962), ch. 6.

171. Cited in Gormley, "Maritime Law to 1681", p. 340.

172. J.H.W. Verzijl, "Western European Influence on the Foundations of International Law," *International Law in Historical Perspective,* 8 vols. (Leiden: Sijthoff, 1968), pp. 435-436.

173. Josef L. Kunz, "Pluralism of Legal Value Systems and International Law," in *The Changing Law of Nations* (Toledo, Ohio: University of Ohio Press, 1963), pp. 48-56.

# 4 The Creation of Maritime Power

*The colony of a civilized nation which takes possession either of a waste country, or of one so thinly inhabited, that the natives easily give place to the new settlers, advances more rapidly to wealth and greatness than any other human society.*

—Adam Smith (*The Wealth of Nations, 1776*)

## The Commencement of the Division Between Commercial Rules and Public Policy

We have seen that the "common law of the sea" had disappeared, apparently forever, through its absorption into the various national laws of the early 1800s. The rampant nationalism of the post-Congress of Vienna world allowed for little "internationalism" in either political or legal terms. The strengthening of the various nation-states, the comparative stability of the era, and the separate evolution of the various maritime powers—in particular Great Britain—all dissipated the ancient maritime-law common links rapidly.[1] All this occurred at the worst possible time for marine transport, which in the later 1800s—particularly after 1830—was operating under the most changed economic conditions in two thousand years.

We have already spoken of the great shipping advances and progress in international communications, but all stages of the shipping progress were affected—the building, loading, routing, and discharging; the bills of lading; the marine risks; the crew; the navigation rules, port customs, wharfage, banking, and brokerage; and the laws of purchase and sale of ships. The paradox of expanded ocean commerce operating under rigid national codes has been described as

> A curious phenomenon: on one side, immense spaces are opened to navigation and foster exchanges on almost a world wide scale; their utilization normally requires uniform juridical rules, thus safeguarding the freedom of communication and stability in business; but, at the same time, antagonistic powers meet face to face and create a parcelling out of the law with conflicts of all kinds which result in a harmful corollary.[2]

This resulted directly in the resurrection of the "common maritime law" in a new form and from a different direction. All the distinct but related shipping interests described here were, within a relatively short period of time, standardized by powerful associations and similar-interest groups whose viewpoint and interests were conceived as international rather than national. In the various maritime countries, these groups—consisting mainly of shipowners, merchants, bankers, and insurers—found that, regardless of national persuasion, they were united by vital common interests, overriding the diversities of national laws.

This new thrust at maritime-law uniformity thus came once again from those who operated the marine-transport system and those who operated within it. There was one important exception, however. The international efforts at standardization confined themselves almost exclusively to the private-maritime-law field in every sense of the word. Only legal and policy matters relating to "maritime commerce" would henceforth come under the scrutiny of the newly termed "ocean industry." Legal and policy matters relating to those areas that could be deemed to be in the public domain would be left to the governments of the sovereign states. Although private and public maritime law had been diverging for some time, as described already, it was at this time that the real wedge was driven between the two areas.

In retrospect, this was an unfortunate but probably unavoidable development in the whole history of the law and policy of international marine transport. Private-law matters would now truly belong in the private sector, whereas public law and policy relating to the oceans would from now on be completely under the jurisdiction of the foreign ministries of the major maritime states. Obviously, foreign policy and private commercial interests would now have to develop quite separately without influencing each other to any great extent. The result would be the separate development of public maritime law, with which we are still struggling today. The most ancient of all ocean uses would now be split away from total ocean considerations and, furthermore, would never again exert the global influence it had achieved since earliest history. It would be reduced to a "lobby," albeit at times a very powerful one, and would develop its own sphere of influence. It would build a new body of law and knowledge—but one based, of course, on many of the ancient rules that had been preserved in national custom and national law.

For private maritime law, this was to be an era of spectacular development; but public law, or the law of the sea, as it now came to be known, blossomed at the same time.[3] However, both sets of rules now traveled on parallel roads that never met. It can easily be maintained that the development of the private law, for example, was only possible within the almost "inbred" atmosphere of the commercial similar-interest groups in which it grew. These groups were basically left alone to get on with the great ocean business of the late nineteenth and early twentieth centuries. They knew their own requirements and problems and were thus considered to be best qualified to act independently, without interference from the public sector.

At first glance, then, it seems that this development was not really unsatisfactory. The ocean family's favorite son, marine transport, had left the fold, struck out on his own, and done very well indeed. However—and here once again we benefit from hindsight—the favorite son quickly became so busy, so self-sufficient, and so independent, that he no longer even needed to keep in touch with the family. Even that would have been a reconcilable breach, but the family itself was not dormant. Its other offspring were nurturing and developing their own strengths, all in the benevolent shadow of the growing influence of the ever-larger family of nations.[4]

It is this aspect which was not foreseen by the good and sound shipping men who struck out on their own in the latter half of the nineteenth century. It is unlikely that it could have been foreseen, despite all the deliberation involved in a move that hardly occurred overnight. In any case, the private-maritime-law area would first experience new heights before plunging slowly to its present-day nadir.[5] Nevertheless, the separate development of public and private maritime law would result in disadvantages to both that could and should have been perceived much more clearly within the past century. In the post-World War I era, certainly the growing world awareness of the ocean as a total resource must have been apparent to the shipping industry.[6] Yet the "successful son" made no attempt to rejoin the "family," which by then had many offspring, all clamoring for attention and receiving it within the confines of the ever-growing family of nations, which, within a comparatively short period of time, would regard the oceans as the last manifestation of the "common heritage of mankind."[7] Sadly, marine transport continued to be left out of most of these momentous considerations. We will have to examine its separate path, and some of the reasons, in some detail.

Despite what we have just said, it would be fundamentally erroneous to assume that marine transport was functioning in an unfriendly atmosphere during this time—far from it. During this period the world provided the best environment marine transport has ever experienced since its distant beginnings. The family of nations had established a supporting international law of the sea which, with the so-called freedom-of-the-sea principle, allowed the merchant ships of the world to roam freely and without interference in a maximum amount of ocean space.[8] At the national level, there was the added encouragement of minimal commercial interference, almost to the extreme of benign neglect.

The great error made by the shipping industry, however, was that it expected this beneficial setting to continue forever. For many years, of course, there were few indications that the status quo might be in danger. On the other hand, marine transport did (and to a great extent still does) neglect its research capacity.[9] Little attempt was made to keep ahead, or even abreast, of international political, social, and economic developments. As we will see shortly, the attempts at uniformity and consolidation of the shipping industry were limited to a search for direct industrial advantages, ranging from the straightforward—at times almost crude—"lobby" such as the various national chambers of shipping, to the broader interests of the various national maritime-law associations under the broad umbrella of the Comité Maritime International (CMI), which at least ostensibly serves the community interest in marine transport, rather than self-interest.

Nevertheless, on closer examination almost all of these organizations are oriented towards furthering a particular or specific interest and are limited to working toward such ends according to their own terms of reference.[110] In the past they have often leaned over backward to avoid any involvement with the political or economic policies that would eventually affect their very existence. As already indicated, there was little research capacity, and attendance at international maritime conferences dealing with other areas was limited to the occasional observer. The organizations themselves were invariably formed by busy practitioners in the shipping industry and almost prided themselves on having as little administrative machinery as possible.[11]

This was the free-entrepreneurial spirit of the world shipping industry, which would reach its greatest heights during this period—the successful son who ignored his family and invested all his efforts in furthering his own ends, rarely looking around and never looking back. This attitude was not really a studied or premeditated policy, but it was aided and abetted by the beneficial political climate of the period.[12] Although the era would witness two world wars, many minor wars, and remarkable political changes, the commercial expansionism of the time depended—in peace as well as war—on marine transport. The shipping industry expanded at a rate not even experienced in the late seventeenth and early eighteenth centuries, when a newly expanded world was fully opened up to human endeavors.[13] Military might, colonial expansion, and commercial enterprise were the slogans of this newer period. These slogans depended on the successful effort of moving goods and people from one part of the globe to the other.

Thus we cannot blame the shipping industry for being less farsighted than it might have been. There was simply no time, certainly not in the late nineteenth and very early twentieth centuries, to stop and reflect. Such an attitude would have been labeled as misguided pessimism in an optimistic age.[14]

Nevertheless, the winds of change were apparent even then. The wind that sowed colonial expansion would reap the whirlwind of independence in the post-World War II period; and the commercial expansionism of the time would result in the deep differences existing between the North and South today, just as marine transport is now facing its greatest-ever challenge to its favored-son position in the family of nations.[15] In a later chapter this book will examine how the industry will fare in this changing atmosphere. Here, however, we must look at what happened to marine transport during the period under discussion and, in particular, at its institutional responses to the rampant nationalism of the day.

### The Emergence of New Maritime States

Although chapter 3 examined the evolution of the modern shipping industry very much in British terms, there was also considerable progress in shipping in other maritime states. However, for a long time Britain was able to maintain its lead and even to consolidate it further.[16] Nevertheless, as political conditions in Europe stabilized, most of the European states began to catch up with Britain both in general economic terms and in shipping.[17]

By the end of the nineteenth century, international competition at sea had become exceedingly keen.[18] In the previous century, international oceanic rivalry was reflected largely in the many legislative restrictions on ocean trade and in the multitude of armed conflicts for the possession and control of certain trades and markets which would then be brought under such regulation. But in the late nineteenth century, maritime rivalries were carried out by relatively peaceful methods in a "free-enterprise" world. As Ernest Fayle suggests, the rivalries "took the form of competition in efficiency, which was all to the good, and the rate-cutting competition, the effects of which were sometimes very bad."[19]

In particular, there were now more players in the game. The Scandinavians, particularly the Norwegians, had perfected tramp shipping.[20] The old maritime tradition of the descendants of the Vikings had reappeared, and their shipping industry was highly developed. They maintained (and still maintain) a fleet much larger than required for their own purposes, and thus they were able to start the profitable tramping and cross-trading system in the world's general cargo-carrying trade.[21] Greece, the other maritime state with traditions dating to the "pre-Argonaut" times of the ancient Mediterranean, proved equally adept at this type of trade. The Greeks were often able to undercut British trade in the Mediterranean by using cheaper, second-hand tonnage.[22]

Germany, France, Italy, the Netherlands, and the United States had all focused or refocused on their shipping industries.[23] These countries concentrated almost exclusively on the liner trades in the hope of making inroads on the British monopolies in this area of the shipping industry. After all, the great international liner routes were the world's lifelines at a time when the Wright brothers had not yet flown. The liners, calling at numerous ports to collect cargo and passengers, presented one of the best returns on commercial investment available at the time.[24]

Competition became truly aggressive. The great German lines, for example, were highly efficient and well run. They formed a common competitive policy as soon as they saw that the British could only be beaten by a "united" competition.[25] By the time of World War I the ten largest German lines, which controlled 60 percent of all German tonnage, had formed themselves into one association for the purpose of rate wars and other competition.[26] Although national governments were not usually directly involved in shipping policy, in several countries they were called on to extend lavish aid to the industry. The old Navigation Act principles of the previous century had, of course, long since broken down or been discarded. However, new "coasting-trade" restrictions had appeared in France, Russia, and the United States.[27] Governments offered encouragements, such as shipbuilding bounties on tonnage constructed, navigation bounties on mileage traveled, reimbursement for Suez Canal dues, and special rates on goods carried on state railways that had been or would be carried on national vessels.[28]

At this time, however, an almost direct ratio existed between the amount of subsidy received and the inefficiency of operation.[29] In other words, it was a reflection of the great free-enterprise spirit of the time that the least government aid resulted in the most efficient and competitive shipping service—a lesson for us today, perhaps. Throughout this period, for example, Britain, the Netherlands, Norway, and Denmark received almost no government assistance, yet prospered greatly.[30] As Fayle suggests:

> Insofar, therefore, as it held its own, British shipping did so strictly on its merits, backed by the natural advantages of its position. The central situation of Great Britain, rendering its ports natural entrepots for the world's trade; an indented coastline bringing the great centres of production within easy reach of the ports; abundant coal supplies to furnish the motive powers of industry and provide shipping itself with cheap bunkers, and with outward cargos for the tramps; the demands of the dense and rapidly growing population for foodstuffs and raw materials; the accumulation of capital in the small country and the employment of the surplus in shipping, in commerce, and in foreign investment—all these things, and the aptitudes derived from them, counted for much more maintaining the status of the British mercantile marine than any subsidy system could have done.[31]

As already indicated, the United States continued to decline in importance as a maritime power. American concentration on developing the great wealth of the country's interior hastened this demise.[32] Despite various government subventions, which in the post-Civil War period amounted to over $25 million, the number of ships continued to decline.[33] In any case, the subventions had many opponents in the U.S. Congress, who claimed that such subsidies would thwart competitiveness and innovation with the resultant nonproductivity and high cost being passed on to the U.S. taxpayers.[34] In retrospect, the farsightedness of these critics was remarkable. By 1890 less than 1 million tons of U.S. shipping was engaged in foreign trading, although close to 6 million tons of shipping were providing service in the U.S. coastal trade, which had been reserved for U.S.-flag vessels.[35] Of all the maritime powers, only the newly united Germany was really in competition with Great Britain. However, Germany had a fleet only about one-quarter the size of the British fleet.[36]

The breakdown of the world's maritime powers would remain roughly the same until 1914, as shown in table 4-1. Of the countries listed, only Japan would not really come into contention until the early part of the twentieth century. Since then, the meteoric rise of that fleet, despite its almost total destruction in World War II, is well known.[37]

**Table 4-1**
**World's Gross Steam Tonnage, 1914**
*(percentages)*

| Groups of Nations | Percentage | |
|---|---|---|
| Group A: | | |
| British Empire | 47.7 | (United Kingdom: 44.4) |
| Group B: | | |
| Germany | 12.0 | |
| Group C: | | |
| Norway | 4.5 | |
| France | 4.5 | |
| United States | 4.3 | (not including coastal and Lakes fleet) |
| Japan | 3.9 | |
| Netherlands | 3.5 | |
| Italy | 3.4 | |
| Group D: | | |
| Austria-Hungary | 2.5 | |
| Sweden | 2.3 | |
| Spain | 2.1 | |
| Greece | 1.9 | |
| Denmark | 1.8 | |
| Group E: | | |
| All other powers | 5.6 | |

Source: *Lloyd's Register of Shipping, 1915. See also Brassey's Naval and Shipping Annual*, 1924, pp. 207-209, cited in C. Ernest Fayle, *History of the World's Shipping Industry* (London: George Allen and Irwin, 1933), p. 276.

### New Aspects of International Marine-
### Transport Law and Policy

Here, however, we are looking at the period between the second half of the 1800s and the years just before World War II. In addition to the growth of the various national fleets, there were a number of significant developments that had considerable effect on international marine transport. These were: the growth of shipping cartels, liner conferences, and shipowners' associations; a long overdue interest in maritime safety; the new thrust at advancing international uniformity in maritime law; and, finally, the explosion of knowledge about the oceans and the ocean environment that resulted from the very rapid expansion of oceanography and hydrography.

Despite the continuing prominence of British shipping, the increasing competition from the "other half" in world shipping had turned international ocean trade into a very different system from that of the previous century. The shipping industry was now truly operating within the modern competitive corporate structure familiar to us today. Conditions a century ago were quite different, however. Business ventures were still experimental, and free enterprise was often not equal to successful venture. The wide fluctuations of supply and demand for cargo space, which often depended on a resource boom here and a small colonial war there, would produce disproportions in the industry, which in turn would send freight rates soaring or plunging. The world's tonnage rapidly increased to a figure beyond its normal requirements, with a short-lived boom usually followed by a prolonged slump.[38] This cyclical trend has been with the shipping industry ever since, and the present-day slump seems to indicate that the industry has learned little. However, a century ago the results were often more radical. As Fayle points out:

> A great deal of money was made during the good years by tramp ship owners; but during the bad years a great deal was lost, especially by companies who were sufficiently imprudent to forget that shipping is a wasting asset and continued to distribute dividends out of earnings that should have been devoted to writing off the depreciation of their fleets.[39]

Although the greatest fluctuations in freight and profit would be experienced in the tramp trades, the liner companies were the most vulnerable to the new rate-cutting competition. They had to provide regular service whether loaded or empty; a liner could not be diverted from an unprofitable market. In addition, they had a heavy overhead owing to the infrastructure necessary to keep the whole intricate operation going. A new company could compete with the established lines simply by undercutting the established rates. Once the new arrival was established, rates would again rise until a new competitor arrived. It was a deadly game of winners and losers, and in the 1800s there were many losers.[40]


## Shipowners, Cartels, and Conferences


The efforts of the liner companies to guarantee for themselves an absolute minimum revenue led to two important institutional innovations for world shipping. First, in order to eliminate competition, shipping cartels arose. These might be the result either of the complete absorption of a number of small lines by a large one, or of the "conglomerate" approach, which allowed a number of lines to operate independently but under one financial direction. These mergers, pioneered by the Germans but perfected by the British, lessened international competition and led to greater efficiency in shipping service, the reduction of administrative costs, and a more widely spread investment risk.[41] There were obviously many disadvantages to this type of cartelization, but these will not be discussed here.[42] The important point here is the growing independence of the shipping industry *as a group,* or as groups, in the international arena at this time.

The second innovation was the formation of the "liner conferences." The liner conference is simply "an association of lines engaged in a particular trade for the purpose of regulating freights in their trade."[43] As already discussed, fierce competition resulted after the opening of the Suez Canal in 1869, in particular on the profitable Indian trade. This led to the first successful liner conference, the Calcutta Shipping Conference of 1875, in which all lines in the trade agreed to apply the same rates between Calcutta and British ports.[44] This was quickly followed by separate British conferences for Madras-United Kingdom and Bombay/Karachi-United Kingdom.[45]

The basic problem facing shipowners at the time was excess capacity resulting from the change from smaller, usually slower, sailing ships to larger and more reliable steamships. The 1875 Calcutta conference, for example, typified the early conference system. In that agreement seven British shipowners agreed among themselves, first, to regulate the number of sailings each would make and, second, to fix minimum rates from all British ports to Calcutta and return, regardless of the size of the consignment or of the shipper.[46] The members of this group undertook to sail their vessels on a given date regardless of whether they were fully loaded. The fixing of uniform rates was to be the compensation for any loss. At that time, no rebates of any kind were offered to shippers. There was continued expansion and when continental-European shipowners began to participate in the lucrative Indian trade, separate conferences were formed for trade between

India and European ports.[47] It should be noted, however, that particularly in this trade the British conferences were soon working in combination with cargo cartels such as the Indian Tea Association, formed in 1892, and were able to keep out non-British lines almost completely until the early part of the twentieth century.[48]

Although the conferences varied considerably in their details, they generally supported: (1) independence of lines; (2) no financial mergers; (3) grouping by trade rather than by ownership.[49] Thus lines that were part of a larger cartel might each be members of a separate conference; and a single conference might comprise lines belonging to many cartels, often owned in several countries. The many good and bad points of the conference system will not be examined here, because such discussion would require knowledge of the very complex area of shipping economics. The conference system has been eloquently discussed for many years and will continue to be a central theme of international marine-transport debates for many years to come.[50] It is undoubtedly the single most important development in the business-operating aspects of shipping in the last century.

The proponents of the conference system will always refer to the regularity and quality of shipping services provided as well as to the security of investment achieved. They will maintain that with assured fixed sailings and freight rates, the international transportation of general cargo has been carried out to the best advantage of all concerned.[51] On the other hand, the opponents will present facts that show the conference system to be a well-organized monopoly with discriminatory practices that result in higher costs, lack of competition, rate disparities, inefficiencies, and a general weakening of the shipper's bargaining position in the carriage transaction.[52]

The aspect of conference methods that is probably most frequently cited as questionable is the system of ''deferred rebates,'' which firmly ties shippers to the conference. Under this system, a shipper who made exclusive use of the conference for his goods for a fixed period would be credited with 5-10 percent deferred rebates on the freights that he had already paid. The catch is that the refund would not be payable until the conclusion of the forthcoming half-year period and would be forfeited completely if, in the interim, he shipped any cargo on nonconference vessels.[53]

Nevertheless, the conference system quickly became well established, and by the end of the nineteenth century and the early twentieth century in the outward-bound trades, conference agreements covered a major part of shipments to South America, Africa, India, Australasia, and the Far East. On the homeward trade, however, the fierce competition from tramping and cross-trading ensured the relative freedom of cargoes from the system.[54] On many routes the monopoly of the conferences would never be complete.[55] There were always competitors who would try to break into the system, and this could be used to the advantage of shippers.

The conference system serves here to illustrate the tendency toward greater organization of the shipping industry at the private, nongovernmental level. This tendency was also reflected in the establishment of the various shipowners' associations. The forerunner of these was the Liverpool Steam Shipowners' Association, founded in 1858 and comprising members operating out of all the major British ports.[56] By 1878 the Chamber of Shipping of the United Kingdom had come into existence and would become the model for similar organizations in other maritime states.[57] The purpose of these associations was to formulate policy on shipping matters and to express the shipping industry's views on a variety of national and international areas of concern to its members' interests. The original object of the Chamber was to "consider and discuss questions affecting shipping . . . and to endeavor to procure when required united action on the part of shipowners."[58] It quickly became an advisory body to the British government on shipping matters and, together with the older Liverpool Association, which did not join the Chamber until 1963, was deemed to be the representative and voice of British shipping.[59] In other words, it was a powerful lobby with which almost all shipowners and local shipowners' associations, as well as the newly created Protection and Indemnity (P&I) Clubs became associated.

The P&I Clubs are another example of the "independent but united" approach of the shipping industry of the late 1800s. They were formed to provide insurance on a mutual basis against third-party risks and other legal liabilities, which had become a byproduct of the new complexities of the burgeoning international marine-transport industry.[60] Traditionally, the marine-insurance policy of a ship covered only three-quarters of the liability for damage done to another ship.[61] One of the purposes of the P&I Clubs was to cover the other one-quarter, which could not be placed in the normal hull-insurance market. However, it is today generally accepted that the real development of the P&I Club was spurred on by the many new legal liabilities shipowners were facing vis-à-vis new legislation relating to loss of life and personal injury claims, as well as to the excess, over and above the sum insured, of liability for damage done and received in collision.[62] In the future, P&I insurance would become of vital importance as it would include coverage against every new liability that came along.[63]

In 1874 the Steamship Owners' Mutual Protection and Indemnity Association was formed in Newcastle,[64] although the Britannia Steamship Insurance Association Ltd., which was founded in 1855 and provided some P&I coverage almost from the beginning, is the oldest shipowners' mutual club still in existence.[65] Several other clubs were formed in quick succession in the 1870s and 1880s.[66] Although at first established for the "mutual" benefit of British owners, the clubs quickly opened their doors to "selected" foreign owners who could comply with the requirements set out in the "Articles of Association" of the various clubs.[67] This would result in Great Britain becoming a leader in another area of shipping. In addition to having the largest fleet and shipping infrastructure, Britain had already taken a very substantial lead in the general marine-insurance market, which it has maintained to this day. The P&I Clubs, with growth implications quite unforeseen at the time, would also establish P&I insurance firmly in London where, even today, some 70 percent of the world's P&I coverage is still arranged.[68]

P&I would soon establish an entirely new area of maritime law built around the many new risks that were now subject to claims.[69] These were, among others, loss of life and personal injuries; collisions; cargo risks; harbor and port installation damages; wreck and wreck-removal risks; salvage and general average; risks relating to distressed and sick seamen; fines and legal fees; war risks; freight war risks.[70] In other words, shipowning was becoming a more complex business than ever before. There were more ships trading to more ports, carrying more cargo and passengers, and employing more persons in the whole infrastructure. Obviously, this much more complicated world had successfully challenged old legal principles and other safeguards—not only in the area of sea transportation—to the extent that such safeguards were simply no longer adequate in the face of a drastically changed environment. We will return later to the maritime law area built around P&I coverage. For now, the foregoing should be sufficient to illustrate another aspect of the growing "internal institutionalization" of the shipping industry, particularly in Great Britain, which continued to maintain its leadership position in the shipping world.


*Safety at Sea*

One aspect of shipping that had received little attention during its long history was the safety of the ships themselves. From the very beginning, the ship was the vehicle on which the owner's profit depended. It was therefore in the owner's interest to ensure that his ship was capable of proceeding from point A to point B. In the very early days, when the owner/merchant usually travelled on the vessel, his own interest in self-preservation usually dictated the highest common safety denominator. However, there were few rules and regulations and, until a surprisingly recent time, no construction standards at all.[71]

The increased sophistication of shipping actually resulted in less safety, since the owner now stayed at home and sailors' lives were cheap. Vessel and cargo were now always well insured—often overinsured—so that a profit could frequently be made on a total loss. As shipping competition intensified, cost cutting was the result. Safety standards, already inadequate, were often the easiest to cut. The marine-insurance industry, although already well established by the latter half of the nineteenth century, was powerless or unwilling to impose its own regulations. After all, insurance was another profit-making business; as long as losses paid out did not exceed premiums paid in, the underwriters maintained that they had little further to say. This was the age of *Pax Victoriana*, when the Protestant ethic of free enterprise was at its height, tolerating little regulation, fewer rules, and even less interference. In any case, the maritime states' governments were more concerned with promotion of the commercial interests of shipowners than with enforcing their obligation to the general community or to the men who sailed in their ships.

There were, of course, many shipping companies that did not take advantage of the unacceptable side of this liberty; but unfortunately there were many others that did. The sailor's lot had probably never been worse when compared to life ashore.[72] For some reason, the shipping industry has always taken an almost perverse pride in maintaining that cruel discipline, inhuman conditions, and inadequate compensation provided the only environment in which sailors could adequately perform their work. This "human element" in shipping was never studied and rarely considered.[73] By the mid-1880s many ships were sent to sea badly built, ill-found, grossly overloaded and often overinsured.[74] These were the "coffin ships," which frequently took their unfortunate crews to the bottoms of the oceans of the world.

As often happens, reform came through the agitation of one man who, if seamen were religious, would long ago have become their patron saint. This was Samuel Plimsoll, a little-known coal merchant who became a member of the British Parliament in 1868. Instead of keeping his own counsel and counting his profits, he wrote a book about the "coffin ships."[75] This caused considerable controversy as it was considered an attack on the Holy Grail of profit making in Victorian England. A Royal Commission on Unseaworthy Ships, appointed in 1874, went on to prove every one of Plimsoll's allegations.[76] A bill was introduced in Parliament to bring the shipowners under control; before it was passed, however, Prime Minister Disraeli announced that the government could not proceed with it. Plimsoll lost his temper in the House of Commons and in a most un-Victorian outburst, did more for safety at sea than he could have accomplished in a lifetime of patient reform work. Although he had to apologize to the House, his outburst brought public opinion to his side. The bill was revived and became law in 1876.[77] The Board of Trade was now empowered, as a responsible government agency, to survey ships; pass them as fit for sea; and have them marked with a load line indicating the legal limit to which they could be submerged.[78] Fittingly, this line has been known every since as the Plimsoll line.

In the next thirty years, Plimsoll's act was extended until most aspects of ship safety had come under government jurisdiction.[79] This was, nevertheless, a very slow process. The British Board of Trade was given the legal authority to enforce the safety of ships, including the determination and fining of any vessels loaded below Plimsoll's marks.[80] At the same time, the responsibilities of measuring the load line still fell on the shipowner; no general formula for measurement was devised until the last decade of the nineteenth century.[81] Only in 1890 was Lloyd's Registry entrusted by the Board of Trade with the task of assigning load lines to ships.[82]

We cannot give a detailed account of the development of Lloyd's of London from its origins of a small obscure coffee house on Tower Street to the premier marine-insurance market of the world.[83] By the late 1800s, Lloyd's had already been in existence for very close to two centuries and was undoubtedly the very center of the world's marine-insurance market.[84] In 1871 the first Lloyd's Act was passed, which incorporated the society and replaced the old trust deed of 1811.[85] The 1871 statute restricted the insurance activities of the members to "marine" business, but this was substantially broadened in the later 1911 act.[86] Ostensibly, Lloyd's as an institution has no functions other than providing underwriting facilities and regulating the underwriting business in order to assure maximum security to the insured. However, in addition to offering extracurricular services such as shipping intelligence, provided by over 1,500 agents and subagents throughout the world, the society has also contributed toward the general safety of shipping.[87] Although safety considerations for insured vessels by the insurer cannot be considered altogether altruistic, Lloyd's has proved time and time again that it has contributions to make to more general shipping safety. As Fayle concludes:

> Many causes have combined in modern times to reduce progressively the risks of maritime adventure—the progress of shipbuilding and engineering science; the regulations as to construction, equipment, manning and stowage, laid down under the British Merchant Shipping Acts and corresponding legislation abroad; the survey and charting of all seas by the British and foreign admiralities; better lighting and buoying of the coasts, and more stringent regulations. In most of these movements Lloyds have cooperated by assistance or advice, and in matters more strictly within their own sphere they have had much to do with amendments of marine insurance laws, which have gradually stamped out the fraudulent casting away of ships and cargoes which was rampant at the beginning of the nineteenth century and not unknown in later times . . . .[88]

However, Lloyd's most lasting contribution to the safety of ships and of those who sailed in them was undoubtedly the founding of the Society of Lloyd's Register in 1834.[89] Despite its name, the society is wholly independent of Lloyd's Corporation, which is, however, strongly represented on the society's committee together with other organizations representing ship-building, marine engineering, shipping, and commerce.[90] Based on older register books, the "Lloyd's Register of British and Foreign Shipping" was a detailed description of all sea-going vessels to assist the underwriters in assessing risks.[91] Although the service is, once again, of primary interest to the underwriter, it is in fact of greater significance to ships' safety. The Register Book, in addition to describing ships, also assigns a "class" sym-bol, which indicates the construction rules according to which each vessel has been built. Accordingly, it became essential for vessels, in order to ob-tain reasonable insurance, to be classed by Lloyd's. Within a few years other classification societies were founded in Scotland, the United States, France, Norway, and so on.[92] To be classified, therefore, vessels were now required to be built, as well as equipped, under the strictly enforced supervi-sion of classification-society surveyors. Only materials approved and tested by the society could be used; in order to retain its class, a vessel had to be surveyed periodically to ensure that hull and machinery remained in an ac-ceptable condition.[93]

It was, therefore, not surprising that the Board of Trade in 1890 handed over the responsibilities for assigning load lines to British ships to Lloyd's Register and the other British classification societies. In subsequent years, classification societies in other countries began to perform similar functions for their flag vessels.[94] This system of classification, as well as the load-line assignment by the society, has remained unchanged every since. In the 1890s it was, however, a great step forward for those whose interests lay in the promotion of safety at sea. It is particularly noteworthy in the context of this book that this important aspect of shipping had once again devolved on a private-sector organization, which was able to accommodate the varying in-terests of maritime commerce, ship construction, and marine insurance under a basic and commonly accepted umbrella of safety. There were, of course, no international safety regulations and few national rules. There was simply this peculiar system of tacit acceptance of rules laid down by private organizations basically for the benefit of underwriters seeking to reduce their risks.

The public-sector interests, represented in Britain by the fledgling Board of Trade, continued to have an uphill battle.[95] In most of the other maritime states there were, at this stage, hardly any comparable governmental organizations in existence.[96] However, in their efforts to raise the standards of safety and shipboard working conditions, organizations such as the Board of Trade were almost continually strongly opposed by the industry itself. The most common accusations were that hard and fast safety laws would cramp the development of the shipping industry and aid foreign com-petition from states where rules were less strict and that, in any case, it was unfair to punish a whole industry for the sins of a small minority.[97] In the late nineteenth and early twentieth centuries, such arguments were often persuasive enough to thwart contemplated legislation.[98] Only legislation such as the international rules for preventing collisions at sea, first put into legal form by the British Parliament in 1863, was considered to be "of general benefit" to the industry as a whole, and thus could quietly pass into international maritime law without causing great controversy.[99]

### The First International Maritime Conference

In 1889 the world's maritime states met for the first time to discuss common problems at an international conference. This was the International Marine Conference held in Washington, D.C. in late 1889 on the invitation of the United States.[100] Of the thirty-seven states invited, twenty-seven attended the Washington conference. The following subjects were to be discussed:

1. rules for the prevention of collisions and rules of the road;
2. regulations to determine the seaworthiness of vessels;
3. draft to which vessels should be restricted when loaded;
4. uniform regulations regarding the designation and marking of vessels;
5. saving life and property from shipwreck;
6. necessary qualifications for officers and seamen;
7. lanes for steamers and frequented routes;
8. night signals for communicating information at sea;
9. warnings of approaching storms;
10. reporting, marking, and removing dangerous wrecks or obstructions to navigation;
11. notice of dangers to navigation;
12. the uniform system of buoys and beacons;
13. the establishment of a permanent international maritime commission.[101]

This ambitious agenda, which to this day has not been completely fulfilled, could, of course, not be carried out within the confines of a two-and-a-half-month conference. Although most of the agenda items were for the "common good," the conference soon became immersed in a very technical discussion of the proposed marine-collision regulations. These were to be the basic achievement of the conference, an achievement that should not be underestimated, as the new regulations would form the basis of all such future rules.[102] Furthermore, the conference did show that the maritime powers could get together to solve common problems, given sufficient time, preparation, and willingness to negotiate. As already indicated, many of the agenda items would have to wait much longer for solutions, but the 1889 conference was nevertheless an important forerunner of international safety conferences, as well as an attempt to fill a void that would not in fact be filled until after World War II.[103]

The conference's agenda item 13—the establishment of an international maritime commission—is of particular interest to us in this historical analysis. This was a noble, if impossible, attempt; some six decades would pass before a similar attempt finally succeeded, and then only with limitations that will be described later on. The report of the committee charged with dealing with this matter in 1889 speaks eloquently for itself and sets out the difficulties, which reflect both the lack of uniformity prevailing in international shipping matters and the extremely nationalistic approach taken by the maritime powers of the day. It appeared almost inconceivable that any state, particularly the maritime superpower Great Britain, would relinquish any of its "maritime sovereignty" at that time (or for some time to come):

> We have considered whether such a commission [the establishment of a permanent international marine commission] could be instituted with the practical result and in such a manner as to lead to its adoption by the maritime powers. However desirable such a result would be, a majority of the committee do not believe it to be possible to carry it into effect and are of the opinion that it cannot be regarded as one of practical feasibility at the present time. In coming to this conclusion, we have been guided, amongst others, by the following considerations: an international commission could not be invested with any legislative power. It would be a consulting body only, constituted with a view of preparing universal legislation on maritime matters of international importance. Apart altogether from the difficulty connected with the formation of such a body, the questions as to its domicile, as to who are to be its members, and how and by whom the members are to be compensated for their labours—difficulties which by themselves seem to be entirely insurmountable for the present—it seems to the committee that such a consulting body of experts would not serve the purpose for which it is intended to be created, viz. that of facilitating the introduction of reforms in maritime legislation, because the advice given by such a commission would not in any way enable the governments of the maritime nations to dispense with the necessity of considering the subjects laid before them and laying the proposals made to them, if adopted, before the legislative bodies of different states.[104]

Despite the new approaches to ships' safety, the main consideration was—as should be obvious from its origin—more commercial than humanitarian. The shipping industry of the Victorian era was still far from philanthropic. Although the "coffin ships" were gone, conditions for seamen were improving only very slowly. Although worse conditions existed under other flags, the British certainly did not lead the world in this respect. Apart from their low wages and appalling living conditions, the death rate of British seamen was exceedingly high until well into the twentieth century.[105] Such medical and sanitary rules as existed were only infrequently enforced, despite the fact that trained seamen were starting to be in short supply owing to the ever-increasing demand of the expanding industry.[106] In 1890 the Shipping Federation of Great Britain was formed by the British Shipowners' Association specifically to deal with their manning problems and relationship with their crews.[107] It was really formed as a response to the more frequently raised demand by seamen for better wages and conditions, which finally culminated in unionization and the great Seamen's Strike of 1911.

Much of what has been said about Britain would be applicable to other seafaring countries as well. British legislation became the blueprint for legislation in most of the maritime countries of the world. Britain, with its Victorian Protestant ethic, had proved its success in shipping (and in many other spheres); and the rules, regulations, laws, and customs facilitating that success would become a desired British export item.

## The Expansion of Knowledge of the Oceanic Environment

For the Great Britain of the Victorian Age, the establishment of the world's largest military and merchant fleet was thus part and parcel of her overall marine policy, ill defined as it was. It was a time of relative stability, and the Royal Navy was needed to fight few wars. Some of its efforts were turned to expanding human knowledge of the oceans. During the nineteenth century, British naval vessels surveyed every ocean of, and all the coasts of, the world with an unparalleled meticulous patience.[108] They completed what had been started by earlier voyages and issued navigation charts and sailing directions that were either unique or better than any others in existence. This was not an entirely new development. Since the earlier voyages of discovery, the Royal Navy had been deeply involved in hydrography. The best-known examples are, of course, the voyages of Captain James Cook, R.N., between 1771 and 1775, which resulted not only in the opening up of the "lost continent"—Australia—but also in the charting of vast tracts of hitherto-unknown oceanic and coastal areas, particularly in the South and North Pacific.[109] Cook's traditions were to be carried on by a generation of Royal Navy hydrographers.[110] The nineteenth century was, however, the real birth of the science of hydrography. As David Howarth so eloquently explains:

> It was a huge and romantic undertaking, so expensive in time and money and ships that nobody else could possibly have done it, and the fund of information collected might well have been treated as a naval secret. In war it would have been priceless. But war seemed inconceivable, and the charts and pilots were published for any seafarer to use. They still are. Some other nations since then have made their own, at least of their home waters,

but the original British surveys are hard to beat. . . . Many of them are still based on the charts that were drawn by Victorian officers who crossed and recrossed every ocean, under sail or in the early steamships, observing the sun and stars and sounding with leaded line—who landed with infinite patience on every rock and reef and rowed into every creek and harbour.[111]

Again it could be argued that this was hardly philanthropy, since a greater knowledge of the ocean would largely benefit the greatest user—Great Britain. Such an argument is too narrow, however. The expansion of human knowledge of the oceans was a part of *Pax Britannica*—a part of the unwritten and unspoken British policy for the oceans. If the commercial aspects of marine transport were to be left entirely to the private sector, then the new ocean sciences would become the prerogative of the Royal Navy as the representative of the public sector. But hydrography was not the only result of this policy. The Royal Society, that prestigious body which encouraged much of the expansion in the world's scientific knowledge since its foundation, had already seen the Royal Navy's surveying expeditions as a vehicle for acquiring other scientific data.[112] For example, the voyage of the *Beagle,* which sailed on a five-year routine survey of South America in 1831, took along a young scientist named Charles Darwin—with results well known to us all.[113]

However, the real ocean science—oceanography—was born with the scientific naval voyages, in particular the *Challenger* expedition.[114] The *Challenger,* a wooden corvette, was put at the Royal Society's disposal in 1872 and sailed on a remarkable four-and-a-half-year voyage manned by a naval crew and a group of distinguished scientists and naturalists.[115] The vessel crisscrossed the Atlantic and Pacific Oceans; became the first steamer to cross the Arctic Circle; and along the entire route collected botanical, zoological, and geological information; sounded the ocean depths; took samples of the ocean bottom; made meteorological and magnetic observations; and measured the temperature and chemical content of the sea. The reports of the voyage filled fifty published volumes—the first systematic storehouse of human knowledge of the oceans.[116] The rather terse and stern instructions issued to the *Challenger* expedition by the British Admiralty and the Royal Society were as follows:

(1) To investigate the physical conditions of the deep sea and the great ocean basins (as far as the great southern ice-barrier) in regard to depth, temperature, circulation, specific gravity and penetration of light.

(2) To determine the chemical composition of the seawater at various depths from the surface to the bottom, the organic matter in solution and the particles in suspension.

(3) To ascertain the physical and chemical character of deep-sea deposits and the sources of these deposits.

(4) To investigate the distribution of organic life at different depths and on the ocean floor.[117]

We know that such directions are still keeping oceanographers occupied today in their search to broaden knowledge of the oceans. Nevertheless, British ocean policy, no matter how conceived, opened the door to oceanic knowledge at a time when it was needed. The real importance and consequences of ocean science would, however, not become apparent until much later in the twentieth century.

## The Search for Uniformity of Maritime Law

The Comité Maritime International (CMI) has already been mentioned. In order to discuss this important organization, we have to go back a little in history. We have discussed the consolidation and institutionalization that took place in the shipping industry, particularly in Great Britain, during this period. But we have not discussed specifically any of the efforts to achieve greater *international* uniformity in the maritime law, which in its national expression was exerting a stifling influence on the development of the industry. Despite Great Britain's continued prominence as a maritime power, the other maritime states were sharpening their competitive edges; marine transport was moving into one of its most truly international stages. Although British law was widely accepted, legal disputes related to shipping were increasing. Many problems were directly caused by the lack of uniformity in shipping laws. This was a particular problem in Britain, mainly because of a great flowering of maritime and commercial law under the tutelage of such eminent lawyers as Lord Mansfield, Lord Stowell, and Judge Shaw Willes in the late eighteenth and nineteenth centuries.[118] This had led to a preoccupation with the "British" common law and the virtual exclusion of other legal approaches that diverged from the British system.[119] The outcome was that new approaches toward greater uniformity would move to continental Europe.[120]

The year 1863, already denoted as the year in which international agreement on uniformity of collision at sea regulations was first achieved, was also notable for two other achievements. First, in France, de Courcy published his formidable treatise, *Réforme International du Droit Maritime,* in which he completely updated international maritime law, thereby newly revealing the fundamental identity of maritime law in most countries.[121] At almost the same time, the great Italian Jurist Pasquale Stànislao Mancini proposed to the Italian Parliament that it should make a greater effort to reduce the diversity in national legislation by international agreement.[122] Mancini's proposal was wholeheartedly endorsed.[123] Some years later, a similar proposal was also endorsed by the government of the Netherlands.[124] Continental lawyers soon saw the advantages in what their jurists and governments were advocating—and not only in the maritime field. It was seen that the sacrifice of specific advantages gained from national legislation might result in a more uniform, stable, and secure legal regime on a broader international level. The result was the formation, as well as the diversification, of several associations directly concerned with furthering such aims, particularly in matters relating to the sea.

The National Association for Social Science, founded in London in 1857, was given the task of studying the ancient maritime principle of general average and, in 1864, produced the first codification of general average.[125] In 1873 the Association for the Reform and Codification of the Law of Nations was founded; it would eventually change its name to the International Law Association (ILA), and under the latter name still flourishes today.[126] The ILA took over the work on general average and sponsored the famous York/Antwerp Rules of 1890.[127]

In 1873, the Institut de Droit International was founded in Ghent, Belgium.[128] The Institut was, of course, to be the promoter of the Hague International Conventions. The Belgian government, through the initiative of one of its ministers, Auguste Beernaert, organized an international congress in Antwerp in 1855, and one in Brussels in 1888, with the very ambitious purpose of drawing up an all-encompassing international maritime code for the whole world.[129] It has been suggested that this was probably overambitious, as it "overran the goal through an excess of generosity and, consequently, an absence of realism, without any concrete result."[130] As with the 1889 Washington conference, despite useful discussions, the time was not yet right for ambitious and far-reaching uniformity in international maritime law. National considerations, particularly in Great Britain and in the now truly "United" States of America, were still blocking international agreement.[131]

Discussions continued in most maritime states, but no real means of coordinating similar views and uniform approaches was found. It had been appreciated that initial cooperation could not really proceed at a very broadly based level that might question in any way the almost sacrosanct sovereignty of the world's nation-states of the late nineteenth century. It was further understood that international agreement could be achieved in areas of mutual benefit requiring international cooperation. However, these areas were usually specifically definable, perhaps technical, but always painstakingly researched with much of the groundwork being completed before the congress ever convened. This had resulted in the only success of the 1889 conference—the new international collision regulations. It was seen, therefore, that the lesson to be learned from all these efforts, and the way to succeed in achieving greater national uniformity in maritime law, was to

. . . work within precincts and prepare the work in a thorough manner, limit the process of unification to certain matters of maritime law which lend themselves better than others to amalgamation, assemble the greatest number of elements in comparative law, sift out the common denominator, sound the tendencies of the various national communities, progress by stages. . . .[132]

We have been inured by history to the fact that fundamental changes are often created by one person with the necessary combination of vision and ideas as well as energy and persistence. The creation of the Comité Maritime International was no exception. A young Belgian maritime lawyer, Maître Louis Franck of Antwerp, had been deeply interested in the idea of unifying maritime law but felt that such uniformity could only be achieved by the establishment of a successful and internationally accepted body that would not only establish but also maintain such uniformity. Franck realized that he needed to achieve consensus in three areas of support. First, he had to obtain the active cooperation of the practitioners in maritime commerce, since they alone faced the problems created by the lack of international uniformity in their everyday enterprise. Second, national associations of such practitioners had to be established in the major maritime countries. Such associations would then come under the umbrella of the central international organization. Finally, a method had to be found to convey to governments, via the central international organization, the proposals which could then be enacted as unifying legislation. This was a tall order at a time of extreme nationalism in a world dominated by one major maritime power, which had no part and relatively little interest in Franck's visionary ambitions.[133]

Undeterred, Franck first enlisted the support of two of the most eminent men in his own country: Auguste Beernaert, by then prime minister of Belgium, and Charles Le Jeune, an average adjuster and marine insurer of considerable influence. This triumvirate of politician, commercial man, and jurist, with the support of the ILA, formed the Belgian Association of Maritime Law in 1896.[134] It is perhaps best to cite Louis Franck's own words describing the aims of the association:

Our object was to give to the sea, which is a natural tie between the nations, the benefit of a uniform law, which will be rational, deliberate, equitable in its inception and practical in its text. We have considered that in our work, the shipowner, the merchant, the underwriter, the average adjuster, the banker, the parties directly interested, should have the leading part: that the task of the lawyer was to discern what in this maritime community was the general feeling, which, among these divergent interests, is common to all; to discern also which of the various solutions are the best; to contribute to the common work his science and his experience, but that ultimately the lawyer should hold the pen and that the man of practice should dictate the solution.[135]

Such aims must have struck a responsive chord in the multitude involved in the day-to-day operation of international marine transport throughout the world. As a result, barely a year after the formation of the Belgian association, several other national associations, modeled after it, were founded.[136] This grouping then formed the International Maritime Committee—better known as the Comité Maritime International—at its first conference, which opened in Brussels on June 6, 1897.[137] In the first CMI constitution, its aims are expressed by Louis Franck as follows:

> . . . to promote by the establishment of national associations, by conferences, by publications, by any other activities or means, the unification of international maritime and commercial law and practice, whether by treaty or convention or by establishing uniformity of domestic laws, usages, customs or practices.[138]

The function and purpose of the constituent-member national associations were defined as:

> . . . the national associations shall use their utmost endeavor to enlist the recognized specialists in commerce and law in their respective countries, and should be in a position to maintain relations with their governmental authorities, so that they shall truly represent all commercial and maritime interests in their countries. . . .[139]

It is important to note the basic nonjuridical personality of the CMI and the group of national associations out of which it was formed. This was to be the CMI's great strength in the years to come. In retrospect, it appears also to have been one of its weaknesses. During its early formative years, and then throughout its history, the CMI found it expedient to operate on the basis of "consensus" within its relatively small "interested circle," which "without juridical mold made a very important impact on the unification of maritime law.[140] It should be emphasized that despite certain limited support from politicians in various countries, the CMI was (and still is) a completely independent body—that is, independent of political interference in either the perjorative or beneficial sense. It was created as a body for the mutual benefit of like-minded professionals and practitioners, all of whom made their livings out of international marine transport and who created the CMI to make this operation work more smoothly. Unlike the ILA, the CMI did not look at uniformity of law in the altruistic sense of contributing to lasting world stability and peace. They were concerned mainly with strengthening and furthering the benefits they derived from ocean commerce. There was absolutely nothing wrong with such an approach. Many of the benefits were, after all, passed along the line to all who toiled in the industry. The CMI members were obviously the best-qualified group to speak for the industry; they were a similar-interest pressure group par excellence.

The CMI would henceforth meet at regular intervals at conferences held in different parts of the world.[141] At these meetings delegates from the various national associations would assemble at their own expense in order to discuss preparatory work carried out by some national associations or by international ad hoc subcommittees. If a specific area of maritime law was under discussion, a draft agreement in the area might be approved or rejected by a majority vote. Until such a vote took place, all work was conducted on an entirely private level, often requiring several years of preparatory work. In the words of the late Albert Lilar, an eminent former CMI president:

> Work bearing the stamp of prudence and measure; work in depth, too, as prior to having reached the stage of an international draft convention, national associations and the international sub-committees, and the international conferences themselves, had assembled, confronted, sorted out, cleared away the massive elements of comparative law of the raw material of their labours to finally extract the common denominator and bring about a large accession. Work essentially realistic and practical and devoid, if not often ideal, at least of false hopes and Utopian speculations, forged, as it was, of material duly tested by the very people who manipulated through the vicissitudes of economic life.[142]

Obviously, all these efforts would be of litle use unless some force of international law were given to the agreements which were reached. The founders of the CMI realized that what was needed was an organ, beyond the private interest in which they had worked, that not only would be permanent but also would always be ready to receive the new drafts coming from the CMI and to call on the international community to approve international conventions on the subjects proposed. At the same time, it was felt very strongly that such a body, while being political, should not have powers or interests that might influence the private-level decisions that had already been reached. In other words, a political conduit was required that would facilitate eventual international enabling legislation. At this stage the CMI's political friends came into their own. The Belgian government was persuaded to become this organ—to accept CMI drafts, to call national governments to diplomatic conferences, and finally to act as a depository of the instruments of ratification. To cite Lilar again:

> Thus was born, in 1905, from happy circumstances and without a civil status (!) the "Conference Diplomatique du Droit Maritime", promotor of international conventions, all signed in Brussels from the drafts deliberated and presented by the CMI.[143]

This important link between the CMI and the diplomatic conferences would continue into the 1970s and would contribute most of the international maritime law we have today.[144] It was indeed a fruitful marriage, which will be further discussed later. In later years the CMI would have to work with other partners, but the "Antwerp/Brussels axis" would remain the most basic foundation of international maritime law for almost a century.

## Conclusions: Maritime Law and Policy at the End of the Nineteenth Century

The end of the nineteenth and beginning of the twentieth centuries thus witnessed another great era in the history of marine transport. During a period of relative stability, the world had reached an unprecedented stage of scientific, technical, and commercial expertise in all matters related to the oceans. Britain, still the dominant oceanic superpower, was now being actively challenged by other powers in the full confidence of their post-Congress of Vienna nationhood. The ambitious thrust of Protestant-ethic commercialism was on a collision course with other states' ambitions in a world that was much more complicated than ever before. Private maritime law was taking a great leap forward, again reflecting the growing complexity of the world in general and of marine transport in particular. In this section we will return to our side-by-side method examining the private and public maritime law, which would soon be in almost direct conflict during a period of instability, confrontation, and world war.

The next chronological period was one of the most formative eras in the social, commercial, political, and legal history of the world. The social upheavals, commercial expansionism and rivalry, and political conflicts of this time are all well chronicled and can be referred to only in passing. Even a summary of the great changes and expansion in national and international law cannot be given. We will simply continue our analysis of the legal and policy aspects of marine transport against the background of this rich social, political, commercial, and legal mosaic, which pervaded every aspect of human endeavor during this period, when new heights of material achievement were reached before the world was plunged into the maelstrom of the bloodiest war in history. As always, the ocean would play a preeminent role.

The nineteenth century was primarily renowned for the extraordinary growth of ocean commerce. For example, the total value of the world's import and export trade climbed from about $1.5 billion in 1800 to $4 billion by the mid-1800s.[145] By the beginning of the twentieth century, however, this figure had reached almost $24 billion.[146] This meant that during a hundred-year period that witnessed only a three-fold increase in the world's population, international commerce increased sixteen-fold. This incredible growth was, of course, facilitated by the rapid progress in manufacturing, the vast increase in output of coal and iron, and the increased capacity of marine transport. At the end of the Napoleonic period Great Britain was not only the main commercial, industrial, and colonial power, but was also in virtual control of the world's oceans. At the close of the nineteenth century, Britain and its colonies still controlled about one-quarter of the world's foreign trade but faced increasing rivalry and challenge from other states. The United States, with its Civil War wounds healed, already showed all the signs of the commercial and political giant that country was to become.[147] Germany, after unification and victory in the Franco-Prussian War, had achieved considerable industrial development and had opened up great resources in coal and iron that made it Britain's fiercest competitor.[148] As a late arrival in the colonial field, Germany felt that its future lay on the oceans, as a means of securing access on favorable terms to world markets and raw materials.[149]

In the latter part of the nineteenth century, the Congress of Vienna powers—Austria, Britain, Russia, and Prussia (which had become Germany in 1871)—were thus joined by a new phalanx of powers—the United States, Italy (united in 1867), a rejuvenated France, Belgium, the Scandinavian kingdoms, the Netherlands, and (quite late) Japan. Each power realized that its continued growth and prosperity would depend on commercial expansion. This might be accomplished to some extent by developing cheaper and more competitive means of production, along with superior business knowhow and organization, but it would have to be aided and abetted by political means such as colonial activity and expansion; securing control or obtaining special privileges in unexploited areas and backward states; and, most importantly, building up a sizable merchant fleet.[150] Naturally, since the oceans joined the continents and formed the great highways of trade, this political-commercial expansion would give rise to the increased importance of sea power in the broadest sense of the term. Admiral Mahan, best remembered as the greatest of all naval strategists and historians, but also an acute political observer, summed up the international situation in 1897 as

An equilibrium on the [European] continent, and, in connection with the calm thus resulting, an immense colonizing movement in which all great powers were concerned.[151]

This was certainly true until a few years before the outbreak of World War I, when colonial rivalries had once again been superseded by rivalries within Europe. However, sight has often been lost of the fact that European tensions were also largely the product of activities and ambitions in more distant spheres. In fact, international developments in the last five or six decades—whether they have taken the form of colonial enterprise or national liberation, of armament competition or disarmament negotiations, or of actual armed conflict—have all found their common denominator or at least their common origin in economic and commercial interest.[152] As already indicated, commerce and rapid communication methods had drawn the nations of the world closer together; paradoxically, these developments also increased the possibilities of conflict. This paradox provides the operating scenario of marine transport during a period that can accurately be described as the era of "a rivalry for world power."

## Empires and Colonies, Ships and Trade Routes: The Rivalry for World Power

This book will eventually concern itself with Third-World problems related to marine transport, law and policy. As the Third World grew out of the dominated colonial world which reached the climax of its development in the period we will now examine, we must rapidly survey this phenomenon, particularly in the period 1870-1914. The rivalry for world power that would lead to the terrible bloodshed of World War I and, inevitably, to the holocaust of World War II, was primarily based on the race for empire—a race in which every government seemed to think that the possession of colonies was a sign of greatness. This imperialism—a strange combination of free-enterprise commercialism, nationalistic prestige, and racist theory about superior and inferior races, often contained an element of sincere religious—even humanitarian—policy. This was reflected in the impulse to assume the "white man's burden" and to spread the gospel of Victorian enlightenment and progress to the "less fortunate part of the globe."[153] But commerce was still the basis; and as free trade gave way to refurbished mercantilism, business required more and more colonies in order to enlarge the market for manufactured goods as well as to provide new fields for investment. In order to illustrate better the global scenario in which marine transport had to operate during this period, we should examine the setting a little further.

### Great Britain: The Leader Challenged

Britain was still the veritable center of the globe at this time, controlling not only the destinies of its island people but also those of its millions of imperial subjects. In Africa, Britain controlled more than one-third of the continental area and more than three-fifths of its population.[154] We have already referred to British policy concerning the Suez Canal; by 1882, with the British Residents guiding the Khedive's government, Egypt had become a British protectorate.[155]

The discovery of gold in South Africa and its subsequent new wave of immigrants created tensions between the early Boer settlers and the newcomers that led to the 1899 Boer War between Britain and the Republics of Transvaal and Orange Free State. This difficult three-year war resulted in loss of British prestige and a confrontation between Britain and Germany, but also in eventual British rule for South Africa, which was enlarged in 1910 by the addition of the British Cape Colony and Natal.[156] This meant that Britain controlled every strategically important part of Africa and exercised full control over all oceanic trade routes to and from that continent.

In Asia, the situation was not very different. Queen Victoria, the empire's stern mother figure, was proclaimed Empress of India in 1897—a move that symbolized the importance of that colony in commercial and strategic terms.[157] The British also controlled all of Malaya and the door to China, Hong Kong. In addition to its control of the many West Indian islands, Britain had a small foothold on the mainland of Central and South America, in British Honduras and British Guiana.

Of course, the great self-governing dominions—Australia, Canada, and New Zealand—continued to have very close links with the mother country; and all followed the British parliamentary and governmental system. They were no longer colonies in the strict sense of the world, but were in many respects (at that time, certainly) extensions of British imperial thinking, while at the same time forming a central part of the empire. In terms of trade, they were the suppliers of raw materials and importers of manufactured goods and were thus absolutely and completely dependent on well-protected ocean trade routes and a vigorous, reliable marine-transport system. Thus with respect to colonialism and imperialism—and without examining the important moral and philosophical questions—the British Empire continued to hold its own in this period—certainly until 1914. Commercial consideratons, the profit-oriented "Protestant ethic," and a discernible genuine (no matter how conceived) wish to spread a vaguely defined "Englishness" to the far-flung corners of the empire, were still the main considerations of British endeavors internationally.[158] International policy was still ill defined, although quite well understood in Whitehall to be to preserve the status quo at all costs and not to tolerate "real" competition that might harm it. This would inevitably lead to confrontation and even conflict with "competitors," and the oceans would once again figure prominently in such disputes. On the eve of World War I, however, British shipping superiority was still evident. In 1914 British shipping tonnage (vessels over 100 gross tons) stood at just over 21 million gross tons out of a world tonnage of 49 million tons.[159] The shipping policy of Great Britain up to World War I was fairly comprehensively summed up by a Board of Trade departmental committee in 1918:

The commercial treaties which govern our maritime relations cover a period of over 250 years, during which our policy has gradually changed from the mercantilism of the Navigation Laws to the freedom of more recent times. Most of these treaties are relatively modern, but some, especially those with the older maritime Powers such as Sweden, Denmark, Spain and even France, Holland and the United States, go far back and bear the impress of the policy underlying them. Since the middle of the last century, the navigation policy of this country has been based on the great ascendancy of the British mercantile marine and the widespread carriage of our trades, which make protection both unnecessary and undesirable. Our object was to obtain free access to the ports and the trade of foreign countries. It was therefore inexpedient to give British shipping privileged treatment at home since such action could only have afforded foreign countries an excuse for similarly differentiating in favour of their own vessels. In view of its relative size, the British mercantile marine stood to gain more from free access to foreign countries than foreign flags stood to gain from free access to British ports; and conversely a policy of mutual restriction would for the same reasons have caused more harm to British than to foreign shipping. The navigation policy of our modern commercial treaties may be summarized as follows:

(1) General freedom of navigation, i.e. liberty to come with ships and cargoes to places in the territory of the contracting parties (national treatment);

(2) National treatment as regards the stationing, loading and unloading of vessels in ports, docks, roadsteads and harbours;

(3) National treatment as regards duties of tonnage, pilotage, lighthouse, quarantine or other analogous duties levied for the profit of Governments, public functionaries, private individuals, corporations or establishments of any kind;

(4) Prohibition of differential flag treatment; and

(5) General most-favoured-nation treatment in all matters relating to navigation.[160]


*France: A Subsidized Shipping Industry*

However, as already implied, there were other "empires." In 1914, perhaps a little surprisingly, the second-largest colonial empire belonged to France. In Asia the French controlled the rich rice-growing Indochina peninsula. In Africa they ruled extensive areas in the West-Africa tropical coastal bulge and in Equatorial Africa to the south of the bulge, as well as Madagascar, the large Indian Ocean island off the east coast of Africa. France had held Algeria since 1830 and acquired Tunisia in 1881 and Morocco in 1911 as French protectorates.[161] These areas in particular attracted a large number of French immigrants, setting the scene for eventual conflicts.[162] In addition, France held some important West Indian islands, several South Pacific islands, and the small Cayenne enclave in northern South America.[163] France's colonial system, such as it was, was quite simplistic. French colonial administrators hoped to assimilate native populations—to turn them into colonial Frenchmen—often at considerable cost to the metropolitan power. Although in some ways the idea might have been a generous one, it was also quite unrealistic.[164]

French shipping, for such a far-flung empire, was important, but not to the exclusion of almost everything else as was the case with Britain. The clear commercial prerogatives, so essential for British shipowners, were never as clear cut for their French counterparts who could and would rely on governmental aid, which the British were precluded from doing. It has been suggested that France has granted more aid to her shipping and for a longer period than any other country, and that this clearly conceived policy has given rise to more conflicting opinions than could be found in the maritime industry of other nations.[165] Critics of this French policy have maintained that construction and navigation bounties did not actually increase the total amount of tonnage, that ships sailed without cargoes in order to obtain liberal navigation bounties, and that the French merchant fleet decreased rather than increased during the 1881-1918 period when its navigation bounties were in force.[166]

To counter these arguments, there are actually no reliable figures for this period. In 1914 France was in fifth place in the world shipping scale with its fleet of 2.3 million gross registered tons, but there is no way to determine how French shipping would have compared without subsidies.[167] This argument remains unsettled to this day. The basic free-enterprise position contends that the less governmental involvement, the better for shipping, with the resultant point often made that subsidized shipping is bound to be unprofitable.[168] Usually overlooked is the fact that government interest in shipping is also one sure sign of a premeditated government shipping policy and that the main thrust of such a policy is rarely dictated by a profit-making motive. This will become remarkably clear in the examination of the post-World War II period later in this book. During the period under discussion, however, the French government considered the military and political importance of French merchant ships to be such that it had to be maintained at all costs and that it was to the advantage of France to do so.[169]

*Germany: Nationalistic Pride and*
*Commercial Expansionism*

Among the real newcomers to colonial competition and imperialistic ambitions, the Germans were by far the most important. Germany was the up-and-coming power—led by businessmen seeking new contracts on new horizons and by nationalistic militarists seeking new glory. The unification of Germany brought a vast new power potential to bear in continental Europe. The 1866 defeat of the great army of Austria on the field of Königgrätz by the Prussians under William I, assisted by Bismarck and Moltke, ended the Congress of Vienna era once and for all.[170] As has been suggested, "the world that had been so painstakingly restored in 1815 and that assumed a Hapsburg hegemony over central Europe—a hegemony dependent on the containment of revolutionary forces—was destroyed."[171] The rise of Prussia, and then of Germany, was rapid; Prussia would soon be the only real competitor of Great Britain, which served as the example. In Bismarck's own words:

> Our colonial efforts suffer from the fact that with us it is rarer for capital and energy to be united in one hand than it is in England. As a rule the German capitalist is unsure of himself, a 'homonovus', who does not yet dare to move toward far-seeing ventures, but energetic entrepreneurial spirit is widely disseminated among our unpropertied. . . . The holders of great German fortunes (unlike their English counterparts) still feel oppressed by the fear that they might lose what they have not yet possessed for a long time. This state of affairs is to a large extent responsible for the fact that we are the disadvantaged vis-à-vis England in the colonial competition.[172]

The twin spearheads of German nationalistic and commercial expansionism would obviously find their main outlets in the buildup of the merchant fleet and the establishment of overseas territories. German shipping expansion in the pre-1914 period was, without question, the result of a variety of economic forces in the shape of industrial and territorial expansion and the outward movement of German nationals and interests.[173] To keep this in perspective, it should be noted that German overseas colonial investment never reached the proportions of Great Britain's. As late as 1913-1914, 53 percent of German foreign investments were still concentrated in European countries, whereas the comparative British figure was 5 percent.[174] However, a clearly discernible German shipping policy developed very quickly with the government exerting a strong influence on the entire shipping infrastructure.[175]

This influence was, however, quite different from that exerted by the French government. Generally speaking, the German government did not expend state funds on the development of shipping but used more-indirect stimulation. This placed the shipping industry in a special category in the national economy together with official, as well as popular, sympathy with the development of German sea power within the full meaning of that term. Germany was still an autocratic country, and commerce did not question government policy but operated within it. This was invariably done with relatively sophisticated central planning of the German overseas and international traffic system, which combined the rail, canal, and ocean movement of cargo and passengers. The merchant fleet was assigned its proper place in the distribution system and the whole industry—shipbuilders, shipowners, and shipping banks—were allied through a variety of methods in a common "German" cause. The idea was to compete with other states, particularly Britain, and not with each other. Shipping was thus a part of German national industrial policy, which consisted of parallel development of production, distribution, and financing of foreign trade. Shipping statistics demonstrate a certain success of this policy. By 1914 Germany had crept up to second place, with a fleet of just over 5.5 million gross registered tons, or about one-quarter the size of the British fleet.[176]

In the colonial race the Germans did not fare so well. In Africa they acquired Togoland and the Cameroons on the west coast, South West Africa, and Tanganyika on the east coast. In the Pacific they had only a few small islands and part of New Guinea, but they exercised a very strong control over South Pacific trade in general. Most of the colonies were too poor and primitive to contribute much to the German economy; they mainly satisfied the German national appetite for prestige.[177] This would prove to be a dangerous and costly appetite, which, when combined with the overall German military-expansionist trade policy, would set Germany on an almost unavoidable collision course with Britain, the greatest imperialist and colonial power.

### United States: The Giant Awakens

Once the ravages of the Civil War had healed, the United States rapidly began to take on the vestments of international power. There was little doubt that this fledgling giant would be infected by the ambitions of imperialism, although to a lesser extent than the European powers. The mysterious sinking of the U.S. battleship *Maine* in Havana Harbor in 1898 touched off the Spanish-American War; as a result, the United States won control of the former Spanish islands, Cuba and Puerto Rico, in the Caribbean, and of the Phillipines in southeast Asia.[178] In 1898 the United States also annexed Hawaii.

In the mid-1850s, however, there was already active consideration of a shorter sea route between the two coasts of the United States, to replace the treacherous route around Cape Horn.[179] The answer appeared to be a canal through the narrow neck of Central America. The question was where to put it. During the California gold-rush days, the feasibility of a canal in Nicaragua was considered. This almost led to a war between Britain and the United States when a British warship seized San Juan del Norte in 1848 and renamed it Graytown.[180] The Clayton-Bulwer Treaty of 1850 diverted this crisis by specifically binding the United States and Great Britain to *joint* control of any canal in Nicaragua or, by implication, anywhere in Central America.[181] This was an important treaty, because it blocked the foothold for the British Empire in Central America and precluded any chance of a British-controlled canal in the Western Hemisphere as a counterpart to the Suez Canal in the East. Within a comparatively short period of time, four other proposals for cutting through the Central American isthmus appeared. One of these was a proposal for a route through the Isthmus of Tehuantepec in southern Mexico, but the other three all involved the area that was then part of Colombia and is now Panama.[182]

The pressure to build a canal had grown steadily, particularly with the advent of the steamship. Global trade was increasing at a rapid rate, and Asia was being opened up for western commerce. By 1854 Commodore Perry of the U.S. Navy and his famous squadron of Black Ships had forced Japan to open its doors to international trade.[183] It seemed that there had to be a better route to Asia from North America. In the 1870s a Wall Street financier named Frederic Kelley calculated that a canal through Central America could mean an annual saving to American trade as a whole of no less than $36 million—in reduced insurance, interest on cargoes, wear and tear on ships, wages, provisions, crews, and so on, with a total saving for all maritime nations of about $48 million.[184] It was asserted that this saving would be enough, irrespective of canal tolls, to pay for the entire canal construction in a few years, even if such a canal were to cost the staggering sum of $100 million, a possibility almost no one foresaw at the time.[185] In order to avoid the Cape Horn voyage, overland passage across the Panamanian and Nicaraguan isthmus flourished; but this was unsatisfactory and did not solve the problem.

It has been suggested that the first really serious consideration of the present-day Panama Canal began with the U.S. Navy Survey-Expedition of 1870.[186] But it was a French company, under the leadership of the indefatigable Ferdinand de Lesseps of Suez Canal fame, that managed to obtain a ninety-nine-year concession from the government of Colombia to construct a canal across Panama.[187] Work was begun in 1881, but disease and bankruptcy stopped it ten years later. The venture appeared to face complete failure, and a new company sought to sell the remaining assets. However, by this time the U.S. political system had seized on the canal issue as a *cause célèbre* and the U.S. Congress appointed a Canal Commission to report on possible canal routes through Panama.[188] The United States-British joint venture in the Clayton-Bulwer Treaty was renounced by the Hay-Pauncefote Treaties of 1900-1901, which gave the United States sole rights of construction, maintenance, and control.[189]

However, the United States was having difficulties with an intransigent Colombia, of which Panama was still a part. In early 1903 Colombia and the United States signed the Hay-Herran Treaty, which gave the United States a "canal zone." This treaty, however, was not ratified by the Colombian Senate.[190] At this stage the United States reacted in the best tradition of the European imperialist powers. By November of 1903 Panamanian elements in Colombia, fearing a choice by the United States of the alternate Nicaraguan route and assured of full American support, staged a revolution against the Colombian government and proclaimed an independent Republic of Panama.[191] As part of a well-planned scheme for imperial expansion, which delighted U.S. President Theodore Roosevelt, American warships were in attendance and prevented Colombian forces from landing to quell the uprising. The United States hastened to recognize the independence of the new Republic of Panama. Only a few days later, the Hay-Bunau-Varilla Treaty between the new republic and the United States granted the latter in perpetuity a zone five miles wide on either side of the future canal with full jurisdiction.[192] The United States guaranteed the neutrality of the canal and received the right to fortify the area. Total payment was $10 million, with $250,000 to be paid annually.[193] A few months later the United States acquired the property of the French canal company for $40 million.[194]

At this time, American engineering opinion still favored a sea-level canal; but in 1906 the Isthmian Canal Commission reported in favor of a lock canal, construction of which commenced in 1907.

On August 15, 1914 the canal was opened for traffic. The cost had been enormous both in financial terms and in terms of human lives. The United States' expenditures totaled $350 million, perhaps not a great deal by present standards but nevertheless four times the cost of the Suez Canal.[195] Adding to this figure the French expenditures before the Americans entered the picture brings the total cost to $639 million—the greatest national expenditure in history up to that time.

This lengthy discussion of the Panama Canal has been presented as an illustration of what a marine policy that is truly well conceived can mean. Nevertheless, as previously suggested, the Panama Canal had other costs as well. Between 1904 and 1914, 5,609 lives were lost from disease and accidents; if the deaths during the French period are added, the total is probably about 25,000—or 500 lives for every mile of the canal.[196]

On the other hand, the canal was a technical masterpiece and, with the Suez Canal, one of the most important additions to international marine transport. The problem of frequent landslides and the advent of World War I restricted canal traffic somewhat in the early years, but by 1924 the canal was handling 5,000 ships a year with traffic approximately equal to that of Suez.[197] In 1915 annual tolls were about $4 million, a figure that would rise to $100 million by 1970.[198] The story of this fantastic venture has only recently been fully told, and in his conclusion the author David McCulloch, comments:

The creation of a water passage across Panama was one of the supreme human achievements of all time, the combination of a heroic dream of 400 years and of more than 20 years of phenomenal effort and sacrifice. The fifty miles between the oceans were among the hardest ever won by human effort and ingenuity, and no statistics on tonnage or toll can begin to convey the grandeur of what was accomplished. Primarily the Canal is an expression of that old and noble desire to bridge the divide, to bring people together. It is a work of civilization.[199]

Even more recently, the United States has renounced its treaty rights and will allow the canal to revert to Panama at the end of the century.[200] The United States' first successful attempt at European-style imperialism will end with this reversion.

We have already spoken of the decline of the American merchant fleet, which had once almost rivaled that of Britain in foreign-trade capacity.[201] With the great continental thrust westward and the Civil War as root causes, this change, once started, could apparently not be checked. The total-world-tonnage figures show the United States in third place in 1914 with a gross tonnage of 5.4 million tons; but because this figure includes U.S. coastal and inland-waters vessels, it is quite misleading.[202] In fact, in 1914 just over 1 million gross tons of U.S. shipping was available for foreign trading.[203] The change in foreign-trade shipping capacity really shows the decline that had already begun in the 1830s, as can be seen in table 4-2.

This considerable change resulted in the United States relying more and more on foreign vessels to carry U.S. exports and imports at a time

**Table 4-2**
**Changes in U.S. Foreign-Trade Shipping Capacity, 1830-1914**

| Year | Tonnages of U.S. Vessels Available for Foreign Trade | Percentage (by Value) of U.S. Foreign Trade Carried in U.S. Vessels |
|------|------|------|
| 1830 | 537,563 | 90 |
| 1840 | 762,838 | 83 |
| 1850 | 1,439,694 | 72 |
| 1860 | 2,379,396 | 66 |
| 1870 | 1,448,846 | 35 |
| 1880 | 1,314,402 | 17 |
| 1890 | 928,062 | 13 |
| 1900 | 816,795 | 9.3 |
| 1910 | 782,517 | 9 |
| 1914 | 1,066,288 | 9.7 |

Source: Sir Osborne Mance, *International Sea Transport* (London: Oxford University Press for Royal Institute of International Affairs, 1945), p. 82. Information based on various U.S. government reports. Reprinted with permission.

when these were increasing at a considerable rate annually.[204] The United States had become a world power. Although the acquisiton of an empire inspired some Americans, particularly President Theodore Roosevelt, many others saw in such ambitions a betrayal of the democratic principles on which the country had been built.[205] Americans have always taken such principles very seriously. An empire to spread trade and enlightenment might have been necessary for the island British; an empire to master foreign parts and gain prestige may have been a necessity for France and Germany; but such reasons simply did not sit well with the boisterous giant the United States had become by 1914. By then it already was a great industrial nation, with a highly mechanized agriculture and the financial resources that were making New York a serious rival to London.[206] The tremendous influx of European manpower had contributed to American individualism—the "American way of life"—and had made the United States the great bastion of free-enterprise commerce. Despite the problems of crass materialism, political naivete and crudeness, and the presence of so-called robber barons in American business life, Americans cooperated to build and to develop a new world power that would eventually overshadow all others.

Only in shipping did the United States lag far behind—and it has really never caught up.[207] The relative political stability in the world in the period between 1815 and 1914 added to the hiatus in U.S. shipping created by western expansion in the continental United States and by the Civil War.[208] U.S. commercial interests were happy to rely on foreign shipping and saw no reason to expend their special energies on a shipping industry that was adequately supplied by other maritime states. The voices that were raised in warning of the danger of this reliance were very much in a minority.[209] Attempts made to stimulate the construction and operation of American ships by the grant of federal-government subsidies were not well received. The American people were generally unwilling to levy taxes for this particular industry at a time when government expenditures were required in so many other areas of the infrastructure of this massive country.[210]

The vulnerability of a large commercial state without a reliable merchant fleet was forcibly brought home to the people of the United States by the rapid withdrawal of foreign shipping that occurred as a result of World War I. American trade was almost immediately completely disorganized; domestic prices for goods with an exportable surplus lapsed dramatically; freight rates on the available ships increased ten-fold and higher.[211] Not even the barest minimum of vessels from the merchant marine was available to be used as naval auxiliaries and transports in the event of the United States entering the war. The first action to remedy this situation was the establishment of the United States Shipping Board under the Shipping Act of 1916.[212] This board was given the tall order of creating and developing a naval auxiliary and reserve and a merchant marine, as well as of regulating sea transport. This in turn resulted in the incorporation of the U.S. Shipping Board Emergency Fleet Corporation with a capital of $50 million, charged to "purchase, construct, equip, lease, charter, maintain and operate merchant vessels in the commerce of the United States."[213]

In other words, a virtual national emergency had induced the most "free-enterprise" of all nations to introduce massive government ownership and operation of international shipping. The Emergency Fleet Corporation, originally intended as a regulatory and advisory body that would control, for example, the entry of U.S. shippers into the various conference systems, was soon expanding its terms of reference. The entry of the United States into World War I prompted the Shipping Board to commence actual shipping operations; at one time it controlled some 4,500 vessels totaling 24.5 million tons.[214] At the end of World War I, regular sailings of ships under the U.S. flag had been established on some forty trade routes.[215]

Although the United States would never really be a merchant-marine superpower like Great Britain, the lesson of the consequences of over-reliance on foreign shipping had been well learned and would henceforth influence U.S. shipping policy. American marine-transport policy was embodied in the famous Jones Act of June 5, 1920, which clearly states as its object the maintenance of a merchant marine "of the best equipped and most suitable types of vessels sufficient to carry the greater portion of American commerce and to serve as naval or auxiliary military ships in time of war or national emergency and, ultimately, to be owned and operated by citizens of the United States."[216]

## Italy, The Netherlands, and Belgium: The Smaller Empires

There were, at this time, also several smaller empires. Italy, unified and freed from Austro-Hungarian domination, was left out of the real African partition but managed to get Libya in North Africa and two colonies on the Horn of Africa—Eritrea and Somaliland.[217] These bordered Ethiopia, a fact that would have implications for future conflicts. With colonial policies that were haphazard at best, Italy really belonged to the prestige-only group. There is ample evidence that Italy never received any commercial advantages from its colonies but saw them rather as areas for colonization by metropolitan Italian settlers.[218] Nor was Italian marine policy very well expressed—certainly not before Mussolini's Fascists came to power. The country's dependence on imports of raw materials, a long coastline, and its geographical situation as a transit country, dictated the establishment of a flourishing merchant marine. The maritime traditions of the great medieval

Italian city-states had not been forgotten; and by 1914 Italy had a respectable merchant fleet, which, with a tonnage of 1.7 million gross tons, was the world's seventh largest.[219]

Two smaller maritime "empires," the Netherlands and Belgium, also deserve some consideration. The once-great Dutch fleet was in eighth place in 1914 with a tonnage of 1.5 million gross tons.[220] The Netherlands still controlled its old East India colonies as well as several small islands in the Caribbean and the Surinam colony on the mainland of South America. Belgium had a relatively small fleet of less than 0.5 million tons in 1914, but had done very well in the division of Africa under the energetic rule of King Leopold II (1865-1909).[221] King Leopold has been aptly described as a

> . . . repository of all the mixed motives that impelled Europe to launch the great thrust across the seas: a passionate traveller, an adventurous "manque", a man filled with nationalist ambition (in 1861, four years before his accession to the throne, he lamented that Belgium's neutrality limited her European destiny, but added, "the sea washes our coast, the Universe is before us"), in whom the poetry of discovery was supplemented by a growing practicality and rapacity. . . .[222]

Through a series of rather brilliant political maneuvers, with German and French assistance, he managed to outfox Britain completely and gain control of Africa's "jewelled navel"—the Congo Basin. First, during the 1885 Berlin Conference on Congo affairs, arranged by Germany and France, agreement was reached to provide freedom of navigation on the Congo and Niger Rivers and free trade in the Congo Basin, as well as the abolition of slavery and the slave trade.[223] At first the area had been placed under the jurisdiction of an International Association for the Exploration and Civilization of Central Africa, which had also been envisaged and established by King Leopold as a multinational enterprise.[224] Shortly after the Berlin Conference, however, Belgium assumed sovereignty over the Congo area, which then became the king's own personal possession for full commercial exploitation. In 1908 the Belgian Parliament simply annexed the area, which then became the Belgian Congo.[225] The Congo annexation process typifies the colonial imperialism of the times as well as the colonial methodology often adopted.

The purpose of the present discussion of the imperialism of the period has been to illustrate the link between the international ambitions of the major powers and international marine transport, which continued to be the vehicle of control as it had been throughout its history. We have attempted to show that there were now more actors involved, as well as more competition in every sphere of commercial ambition. Before concluding this setting of the scene in which the next act of the public-versus-private maritime-law drama will unfold, we must briefly refer to another "empire," which does not fit precisely into the present discussion but, because of its future importance, cannot be omitted either. We are, of course, referring to Japan.

## Japan: Rising Sun in the Far East

Before 1854, Japan had repelled all attempts for "friendly" relations with the western powers. The United States in particular had made over fifty attempts and was often violently repelled by the antiforeign element of the Japanese shogunate.[226] Commodore Perry's arrival with his U.S. naval squadron in 1853 was the catalyst for change in Japanese policy. The United States feared French and Russian overtures to Japan; in 1854, during Perry's second trip to Edo Bay, he secured the opening of two Japanese ports for foreign trade and also opened limited regulated trade.[227] Treaties between Japan and Britain, Russia, and the Netherlands quickly followed; and by 1859 foreign merchants had become established at Yokohama, although the antiforeign element continued to cause difficulties until 1868.[228] This was the beginning of the Meiji Period (1868-1912), during which Japan entered the modern era. Within an incredibly short period of time the remnants of military rule and feudalism were abolished; and a strong, centralized bureaucratic government, imitating the Occidental system, was established.[229] Rapid industrialization based on Western models took place; as a consequence, the wealth and population of Japan multiplied.

Almost from the beginning of this modernization period, the government of Japan has had a clear shipping policy dictated by the economic and geographical situation of Japan, which compelled it to be a shipowning nation. The teeming population confined to a relatively small and unproductive area; the necessity for importing a great part of the food requirement; the need for exports to balance imports; the lack of native raw materials—all these factors contributed to the remarkable expansion of the Japanese shipping industry. Soon after the Sino-Japanese War of 1894, the Japanese government embarked on a subsidy program supplemented by credit facilities for shipbuilding and ship operation. Two decades later, in 1914, the Japanese merchant fleet, with a tonnage of 1.7 million gross tons, had reached the sixth place in the world fleet.[230] The war with China, mainly for control of Korea, also showed Japan's imperialist ambitions, which at this time were still gestating.

## Conclusions: Maritime Policies and World Power on Collision Course

Thus the world on the eve of the first disastrous world war was very different from that which had existed in the relative stability of the post-Congress of Vienna decades. The rivalry for world power that had brought the major powers to the brink of war was still best illustrated by international-trade figures. Commerce was the real reflection of power because power could be sustained only by trade. Figures showing the international trade of the nine major powers in the period 1881-1910 (table 4-3) reveal that only two of the nine, Russia and Austria-Hungary, were not maritime states in the true sense of the word. These figures show the share of the leading countries in world trade but are based, for simplicity and clarity, on the figures for "special" trade including, therefore, only those exports produced in the country and those imports retained for home consumption.

Table 4-3 shows clearly that Great Britain still retained its position as the world's leading commercial power. The slackening of development that had caused concern in England at the end of the nineteenth century was followed by a period of recovery and a sharp rise in import and export values.[231] The import trade in particular continued to give Britain its primacy in the world's foreign commerce. Nevertheless, there is no doubt that British trade declined *relatively* during this period. This is particularly true when it is compared to the sharply contrasting commercial records of the United States and Germany. The latter country's methodical growth in all spheres of international trade and its maintenance of economic progress continued despite the heavy military burden resulting from the buildup of a great army as well as a navy that could (and would) rival the Royal Navy itself.[232]

All in all, the rivalry for world power was carried along with the almost apocalyptic race for colonies and overseas markets. The imperialist thrust of the great powers revealed that colonies were often lucrative propositions, particularly when they supplied the metropolitan industries with cheap

**Table 4-3**
**World Trade, 1880-1910**
*(annual average trade value in millions of dollars)*

|                 | 1881-1890 | | 1891-1900 | | 1901-1910 | |
|                 | Imports | Exports | Imports | Exports | Imports | Exports |
|-----------------|---------|---------|---------|---------|---------|---------|
| Great Britain   | 1,650   | 1,170   | 1,725   | 1,190   | 2,525   | 1,700   |
| Germany         | 825     | 780     | 1,140   | 880     | 1,800   | 1,470   |
| United States   | 705     | 780     | 780     | 1,050   | 1,185   | 1,655   |
| France          | 880     | 680     | 835     | 710     | 1,065   | 995     |
| Netherlands     | 465     | 375     | 660     | 550     | 1,020   | 835     |
| Belgium         | 302     | 261     | 362     | 309     | 578     | 453     |
| Austria-Hungary | 247     | 302     | 302     | 337     | 464     | 459     |
| Russia          | 234     | 311     | 276     | 339     | 386     | 503     |
| Italy           | 269     | 206     | 255     | 219     | 480     | 343     |

Source: Report, British Board of Trade, 1911. See also Clive Day, *A History of Commerce* (New York: Longman's, Green, 1919, 2nd. ed.) p. 583.

and abundant raw materials. On the other hand, the existence of exotic and distant colonies offered prestige, nationalistic fervor, and often a diversion that turned people's thoughts away from more pressing problems at home. At the same time, the unacceptable face of imperialist domination, which from the start contained a certain self-destruct mechanism, would give the liberal element a chance to criticize the hypocrisies of the system. More importantly, though, the power struggle in Africa and Asia would contribute to the outbreak of World War I.

### The Growth of the Law of Nations: Last Hope for Humanity?

We now return to a more specific examination of maritime law as it developed during this period. In the public-law area there were some spectacular changes, whereas private law grew more steadily and methodically. The two fields were now undoubtedly separate, although both still influenced such national ocean policy as existed. Rather than complementing each other, however, the public and private maritime law would now emanate from very different interest groups and would at times be almost on opposite sides.

There is little doubt that the modern law of nations, or the public international law, flowered during the period under discussion.[233] The "European Concert" of the great powers, which ensured almost a century of comparative stability, also encouraged a vigorous international intercourse. Because the old customary law of nations was inadequate, new principles evolved quickly. The new law of nations most often spread in the form of international canons and through the development of the law of treaties. At a time when the prevailing international political and commercial cooperation dispensed with grandiose peace treaties and similar alliances, the number of nonpolitical treaties multipled rapidly. Thus in the latter part of the nineteenth century there were commercial, consular, and extradition treaties; and agreements on financial and tax matters; on postal, telegraphic and railway communication; on ocean fisheries; on copyrights and patents.[234] One source states that between 1815 and 1914 some 16,000 treaties were concluded; another estimate gives the number of treaties in existence in 1917 at 10,000.[235]

As a result of this amazing growth, international legal treaties became more and more businesslike and technical in nature. Even more important was the spread of multilateral conventions in the state practice of the period. These were new in that they tended to lay down general rules for the *conduct* of states, which previously had seldom been the case. They were thus actually "law-making" treaties; and in order to enlarge the area affected by their lawmaking, they often extended their range of action by allowing for the accession of states that had not been original signatories.[236] Despite their often specific and even technical nature, which affected the private sector of states, they were nonetheless "making law" at the public level. In other words, the diplomatic arm of a sovereign state made a decision on behalf of the state to *agree* to the content of a particular treaty or convention, and indicated its agreement by its signature. There was the added implied obligation that ratification of the treaty should then follow, which would then bring this new international law into the municipal law of the particular state.[237] This meant that to a great extent a public-law political-diplomatic decision would be made on a private subject. Of course, those interested in the private subject would often be consulted, or might even lobby for their desired political-diplomatic action; but the final decision was no longer theirs. Unlike the ancient "law merchant," which by nature contained its own simple policy, the international law now had a variety of new considerations to weigh in arriving at its particular policy. This meant that political decisions might, under certain circumstances, be in conflict with commercial considerations.

One of the first important multilateral treaties was the famous Paris Declaration of Maritime Law of 1865 and the Paris Treaty of the same year.[238] The declaration abolished privateering once and for all, and prohibited the capture of enemy goods, except contraband, on neutral ships, and of neutral goods, except contraband, on enemy ships. It also required blockades to be effective, that is, to be maintained by a force sufficient actually to prevent access to the coast held by the enemy. This was a very important declaration to which all the states of the world were invited to accede. Most of the major maritime powers did so, one exception being the United States, which considered privateering to be a necessary method of naval warfare for states that did not possess large navies.[239]

In other areas, juridically even more refined multilateral treaties were inaugurated by a large number of conventions, which established the idea of transferring the treaty partners into a working community. Of these, the Geneva Convention for the Protection of the Wounded in War of 1864, and the Universal Telegraphic Union of 1865, were early examples.[240] The General Postal Union of 1875, which in 1878 would become the Universal Postal Union; the International Convention on Railway Traffic of 1890; the International Sanitary Convention of 1903; and the International Radio-Telegraphic Convention of 1906 were other noteworthy achievements indirectly related to marine transport.[241] Only the United States was consistently unable to become a part of this new trend in international law. Despite the early republic's idealized conception of international law, the newer isolationist element power in the U.S. Senate prevented U.S. accessions to international treaties.[242]

We will not go into the complex field of international law any further here. What we are attempting to illustrate is that written regulations penetrated into international relations to such an extent that little was left to custom, on which the whole law of nations had originally been built. At the same time, the new written international laws were almost all created in the public area, either superseding customary rules or catering to new requirements in a more complex politicized world. Only in the law of the sea did some vestiges of custom remain.

## The Public Law of the Sea Further Developed

During this period the public maritime law was concerned mainly with three of its aspects: fisheries, neutrality in ocean warfare, and the territorial sea. Although the last of these directly affected the first two, it can be treated separately, because fisheries and neutrality in ocean warfare were also quickly being absorbed into the written-treaty area.[243] That is probably a simplified or even superficial statement, but it is impossible here to discuss in detail the complex field of fisheries, which on the one hand has been eloquently discussed elsewhere,[244] and on the other still faces numerous unsolved problems.[245]

During the first half of the nineteenth century, the three-mile limit had achieved considerable support in state practice.[246] At first Great Britain and most of its colonies adopted the three-mile limit mainly by a process of assimilating and expanding on the one cannon-shot rule. This rule had been cited in the famous case of *The Anna,* which held that the boundary of territorial waters was considered to be three miles.[247] The rule was further affirmed in later cases and legislation.[248] During the latter half of the century some states attempted to assert general jurisdiction beyond three miles, but they were strongly opposed in their claims.[249]

Nevertheless, by 1900 the three-mile limit had been positively adopted as law by twenty of the twenty-one states that were acknowledging or claiming a territorial sea at that time. These states were Argentina, Austria-Hungary, Belgium, Brazil, Chile, Denmark, Ecuador, El Salvador, France, Germany, Great Britain, Greece, Honduras, Italy, the Netherlands, Norway, Russia, Sweden, Turkey, and the United States.[250] Spain, the twenty-first state, claimed six miles.[251] Prior to 1910, Mexico, Japan, and Portugal joined the "three-mile club."[252] Thus by the beginning of the twentieth century, the legal concept of the three-mile territorial sea was well established in international law. It was also evident that a number of states made much broader claims for particular "functional" purposes, such as customs and excise control, fishery control, and the movement of naval vessels.[253] But it has been pointed out that two theories about the degree of sovereignty that could be exercised by the coastal states also arose at this time.[254]

These would have serious future implications. The first of these held that the coastal state had actual and complete *ownership* of the coastal waters, with all the rights and obligations that went with such ownership. The other theory held that the territorial sea remained primarily a part of the high seas, subject only to limited rights of the coastal states.

Although at first this controversy appeared to be more academic than practical, it would eventually (and to this day) prevent "any measure of agreement sufficient to establish an indisputable rule" in the area.[255] The whole difficult story of the territorial waters in the law of the sea is well known today, but during the time under discussion it really only affected fisheries and a variety of functional uses of the coastal sea belt. The "great ocean business" of the Victorian era was not at all impaired or even inconvenienced by such considerations. Free navigation in international waters was considered to be of community benefit throughout this period.

This obviously begs the question about the so-called freedom-of-the-seas principle, which probably reached its fullest extent of use during this period. Grotius and his followers had asserted that the sea had to remain free because, first, it could not be effectively occupied by a navy, and, second, because nature does not give the right to anyone to appropriate things that may inoffensively be used by everyone, are inexhaustible, and thus are sufficient for all. The advent of modern naval power had abolished the first argument, and the second was now increasingly questioned in a more skeptical and critical world.[256] Oppenheim gives perhaps the most eloquent summary of what we consider to be the *functional* rule of the freedom of the open sea, which *served* ocean transportation during this time:

> The real reason for the freedom of the open sea is represented in the motive which led to the attack against maritime sovereignty, and in the purpose for which such attack was made—namely, the freedom of communication and especially commerce, between the states which are separated by the sea. The sea being an international highway which connects distant lands, it is the common conviction that it should not be under the sway of any state whatsoever. It is in the interest of free intercourse between states that the principle of the freedom of the open sea has become universally recognized and will always be upheld.[257]

The last few words of this citation are arguable and obviously inaccurate today. Even Oppenheim could not have foreseen, when he wrote his great treatise, that marine transport as an ocean use would eventually have to compete with other ocean uses.

## The Continuation of the Search for Uniformity in Private Maritime Law

We have already shown the steady growth in size and importance of world shipping during the period under consideration. Obviously, there must also have been certain developments in the private maritime law. The modest attempt at unifying or reunifying the very diverse maritime laws, begun with the creation of the Comité Maritime International, continued vigorously. There was, indeed, an overall thrust toward greater unification of laws in general.[258]

The complexities of the modern era had produced a great deal of legislation in all the major countries of the world, and international intercourse was plagued by quickly growing conflicts between various national laws. All this came at a time of extreme nationalism, when ideas of sovereignty and national prestige barely permitted the admission that another state's laws or a different legal system might be superior. Attempts at unification, particularly in commercial law, had to face these difficulties. At the Antwerp Congress, called by King Leopold I of Belgium to discuss the assimilation of mercantile law in 1885, these problems were already very apparent.[259] Although the conference was attended by all the major commercial maritime states, the leading state, Great Britain, sent only an unofficial delegation, which attended on behalf of the English Bar. Unification of law was an idea quite alien to the English system, as it appeared to apply the supposition

.... that a nation should at a given moment send delegates to a conference to negotiate a uniform law by means of reciprocal concessions entailing perhaps sacrifice of time-honoured legal notions in favour of provisions of systems of law reared in a different legal and political atmosphere, all of which is apt to strike the English mind as profoundly unpractical.[260]

England simply assumed that the unification of law meant the acceptance of English law by other states. Compromises in the interests of international harmony could not be made by the world's leading state. A good illustration is an excerpt from a report on the Antwerp Congress:

"You English seem to think it negotiating to grant your gracious permission to adopt your laws *telles quelles,*" exclaimed an exasperated Frenchman in reply to an Englishman who thought he had given a sufficient reason for his dissent in saying that the proposals differed from English law.[261]

One of the British delegates really gives the game away when, in commenting in his report on the French outburst, he reveals the true notions of superiority of Victorian England, which with a little more restraint might have prevented much friction and even conflict:

... in pleading guilty we must ask the enlightened foreigner to remember that we old fashioned English have no code of laws yet, and that the principles of our law still lie hidden in the bosoms of our great lawyers, who do not seem to think very highly of systems which would lower the standard

of intelligence necessary for discovering the sense and sequence of our
beautiful case-law. Hence as regards England it is doubtful whether this
Congress and its successors are destined to bear much fruit in the way contemplated by the Belgian government, that is to say in the way of unification. All that can be expected on the part of England is an acceleration of
that natural assimilation towards which similar circumstances and similar
desiderata are causing contemporary legislation to tend.[262]

For most of the continental European countries, unification of laws had
become necessary as well as practical. Unification was achieved, for example, by the influence and bodily adoption in several states of the French
codes.[263] The Scandinavian states, Germany, the Netherlands, Belgium, and
France had, by further example, virtually identical Bills of Exchange
laws.[264] Progress at Antwerp and several other similar meetings was
therefore blocked by the lack of interest of Great Britain and, to some extent, of the United States.[265] Nevertheless, the general process of unification
of law continued—and has continued to this day.[266] Only in the area of
maritime law was any real progress made. At the Antwerp Congress
maritime-law questions had been well prepared; and preliminary work on
conflict-of-laws problems relating to liability of shipowners, collisions,
general average, insurance, and bottomry bonds was vigorously discussed—although without any real decisions being taken.[267]

The CMI would continue to be the only international organization
dedicated exclusively to the furtherance and unification of private maritime
law on a global scale. Having already examined the antecedents of the CMI
and its methodology, we must now look at its early achievements prior to
World War I, which also reflect the development of private maritime law
during this whole period. Between its foundation year, 1897, and the commencement of World War I, the CMI staged ten international conferences,
which discussed a great variety of maritime-law subjects and achieved consensus and codification in two important areas.[268] It will be best to illustrate
this important work by quickly outlining each of the meetings:

Ist      Conference:  Brussels 1897
         Agenda:    CMI organization
                    Marine collisions
                    Shipowners' liability

IInd     Conference:  Antwerp 1898
         Agenda:    Shipowners' liability

IIIrd    Conference:  London 1899
         Agenda:    Collisions in which both ships are to blame
                    Shipowners' liability

IVth     Conference:  Paris 1900
         Agenda:    Assistance, salvage and duty to tender assistance
                    Jurisdiction in collision matters

Vth        Conference:   Hamburg 1902
           Agenda:       International code on collision and salvage at
                         sea
                         Jurisdiction in collision matters
                         Conflict of laws as to ownership of vessels
                         Mortgages and liens on ships

VIth       Conference:   Amsterdam 1904
           Agenda:       Conflicts of laws in the matter of mortgages and
                         liens on ships
                         Jurisdiction in collision matters
                         Limitation of shipowners' liability

VIIth      Conference:   Liverpool 1905
           Agenda:       Limitation of shipowners' liability
                         Conflict of laws as to maritime mortgages and
                         liens
                         Agenda for the Brussels diplomatic conference,
                         1905

VIIIth     Conference:   Venice 1907
           Agenda:       Limitation of shipowners' liability
                         Maritime mortgages and liens
                         Conflict of laws as to freight

IXth       Conference:   Bremen 1909
           Agenda:       Conflict of laws as to freight
                         Compensation in respect of personal injuries
                         Publication of maritime mortgages and liens

Xth        Conference:   Paris 1911
           Agenda:       Limitation of shipowners' liability in the event
                         of loss of life or personal injury
                         Freight

XIth       Conference:   Copenhagen 1913
           Agenda:       Safety of navigation
                         International code of affreightment
                         Insurance of enemy property[269]

This short summary serves to show the variety of maritime-legal problems faced by the CMI as well as the persistent difficulties in particular
areas, which would reappear at regular intervals at the CMI conferences.
Even more interesting is the arrival of new areas of maritime law, which had
appeared as byproducts of the greater sophistication of marine transport

unheard of in traditional maritime law but now frequently legislated in municipal laws, and for other types of claims related to liability toward individuals.[270] This reflects the great increase in the international carriage of passengers, not only in terms of travel mobility but also owing to the great exodus from some of the Mediterranean countries, Ireland, Scandinavia, and so on to the New World.

Shipowners were now facing greater liabilities from directions that could not have been foreseen by the ancient maritime law. This resulted in an unsatisfactory "patchwork quilt" of national municipal laws and regulations, which often hindered rather than facilitated the international aspect of the trade.[271] The difficulty was further exacerbated by the actual law-making process. A new piece of national legislation, covering some aspect of shipping, would often be superimposed by the responsible ministry on the industry in order to cover some kind of shortcoming in the marine-transport process. There might be some sort of consultation with the industry—perhaps a suggestion for the needed legislation might even have come from the shipowner—but there was little if any international consultation. The final legislative decision would come from the political arm of government and might be in conflict with prevailing shipping practice. Municipal private maritime law thus often originated from public sources serving political interests rather than international uniformity.

This difficulty has faced the CMI since its foundation. The law of merchant shipping was, quite naturally, one of the first branches of private law to attract attention for possible unification. It was seen that such unification was not simply desirable but virtually necessary because of the great importance of marine transport to the economy of most countries, which suffered from the repercussions of existing conflicts among maritime laws.[272] It was, however, much harder to achieve the required consensus. Yet for many years the CMI, with its amazingly modest resources and infrastructure, but with very rich resources in the abilities of its international professional membership, was able to whittle away resistance to uniformity in subject after subject.

This progress was possible because "in all countries the bulk of shipowners, underwriters, merchants, bankers, and maritime lawyers [were] practically unanimous in the opinion that an international law for the sea [was] required by modern commerce."[273] This statement by Maître Franck, the first CMI president, referred strictly to the private law of the sea, however. With the vision for which he won fame, Franck had seen that the public and private areas were now definitely separated and that this schism could not be breached In future the private law, which represented the practical aspect of ocean commerce and transportation, would have to fight for itself to receive attention and consideration in the public sector, which was more concerned with political expediency than with practicalities. Franck, well aware of the difficulties faced by the 1885 Antwerp Congress, saw the fight for uniformity of ocean law as an uneven struggle between these two sectors, with failure to agree as the inevitable result. He went on to say:

> What were the causes of this failure? It appeared to me that they were to be found in indifference of business circles, and in the practical difficulties with which reforms of this kind were meeting in the various Parliaments. The businessmen refused, less by reason than by instinct, to adopt the system of reforms which came from purely legal and official circles, whereas the government did not feel inclined to bring before Parliament Bills involving substantial changes in the commercial laws of their countries without having the least security that other Parliaments would follow and make the same changes in their laws.

> How could these obstacles be removed? The objection of the businessman was a perfectly sound one. Good law cannot be made without contact with practical life. The man who has to live under the proposed new law must be consulted on it. But how can this rule of common sense be applied in a matter essentially international when there is neither international electorate, nor international Parliament, nor a common international ground, on which these questions may be discussed and thrashed out?[274]

This "rule of common sense" became the aim of the CMI. From the beginning, the CMI operated strictly separately from the public sector, in a private-club environment. The public sector became involved only when a subject had been thoroughly discussed, dissected, revised, and redrafted over a period of years, and only after careful lobbying to gain support of the political factor in each country concerned. Only then was a diplomatic conference called—only then did private and public sectors meet.

Even this is not, strictly speaking, correct. Private law could be made by public delegations, although delegation members might simply have switched hats at the diplomatic conference. The *real* public law of the sea, referred to earlier, was of no concern to private law, which was basically confined within the three-mile limit, leaving all that lay outside to the public and political system of sovereign states and the international legal intercourse between them. The difficulty of private maritime law making must be apparent from this ponderous system of relying on a two-step method of obtaining private-law consensus, and of operating only within the narrowest confines of commercial-interest uniformity.

Nevertheless, there was progress. For example, the truly international problem of collisions at sea, already discussed at the Washington conference in 1889 and at the CMI conferences of 1897, 1899, 1900, 1902, and 1904, was finally brought to a diplomatic conference in Brussels in early 1905.[275] An adjourned meeting of this conference met later in this same year, also in Brussels; delegations signed a protocol providing for the submissions to the governments represented of two draft conventions related to collisions at sea and marine salvage.[276] A third session of the conference met at Brussels four years later, in 1909, and was attended by most of the maritime states. After an adjournment the conference met again in 1910 and was finally able to conclude the two conventions, which were then opened for signature and ratification.[277]

The conference had also considered two draft conventions relating to the limitation of shipowners' liability and maritime liens respectively, but no final consensus could be reached on these proposals. Nevertheless, the collision and salvage conventions were a remarkable achievement and were quickly signed by all the major maritime nations, receiving sufficient ratification to enter into force.[278] They are still in force and still represent the best international expression of law in these areas, despite the fact that one of the most important maritime countries, the United States, has been unable to ratify the collision convention. It is impossible to discuss in detail here the complex commercial-political reasons that make the United States the only major maritime nation not adhering to this important convention.[279] But the U.S. failure to agree once again illustrates the difficulties faced by attempts to create uniformity in maritime law. It was also, more seriously, a sign of future difficulties for the CMI.

**Conclusions: The Eve of World War I**

This chapter has consisted of another far-reaching discussion of marine transport—this time in the period running from the latter part of the nineteenth century until immediately before World War I. In retrospect, we see a world full of promise and potential at the end of the century of relative peace, progress, and stability that had begun with the final act of the Congress of Vienna. We see a vigorous and prosperous marine-transport system reaching all parts of the globe, many parts of which had been divided up among the major powers in their colonial race.

Superimposed on the prosperity of the era is the rivalry for world power, which with its destructive prestige-oriented ideology was setting the major powers on an almost unavoidable collision course toward a conflict in which there would be no winners. At the same time, there appears to have been a great surge in the law of nations and new developments in the law of the sea—a public law of the sea. On the private side, maritime law was becoming more and more isolated and confined to commercial interests, with little dialogue or communication with the public sector. National marine policies were now more important but were also dictated by very different interests in many of the major maritime states. The next chapter examines the further development of the international law and policy of marine transport in the period when the world arose from the ashes of destruction of World War I, and then plunged to the new depths of World War II.

**Notes**

1. John H. Wigmore, *A Panorama of the World's Legal Systems,* vol. 3 (St. Paul, Minn.: West Publishing Co., 1928), pp. 914-918.

2. Albert Lilar and Carlo van den Bosch, *Le Comité Maritime International* (Anvers: CMI, 1972), pp. 2-3.

3. See, for example, C. John Colombos, *International Law of the Sea,* 6th rev. ed. (London: Longmans, 1967), ch. 1.

4. See, for example, Arthur Nussbaum, *A Concise History of the Law of Nations* (New York: Macmillan, 1962), ch. 6.

5. Lilar and van den Bosch, *Comité Maritime International,* pp. 2-8.

6. Stefan A. Riesenfeld, *Protection of Coastal Fisheries under International Law* (Washington: Carnegie Endowment, 1942), ch. 3; Douglas M. Johnston, *The International Law of Fisheries—A Framework for Policy-Oriented Inquiries* (New Haven: Yale Univesity Press, 1965), pt. 1; Myres S. McDougal and William T. Burke, *The Public Order of the Oceans—A Contemporary International Law of the Sea* (New Haven: Yale University Press, 1962), ch. 1, 7.

7. Shigeru Oda, *The Law of the Sea in Our Time. I: New Developments 1966-1975* (Leiden: Sijthoff, 1977), pp. 13-20.

8. Oppenheim, *International Law,* vol. 1, 8th ed., edited by H. Lauterpacht (London: Longmans, 1955), pp. 589-590.

9. For example, neither the CMI nor the ICS has developed any significant research capacity, particularly in areas of *wider* ecopolitical concern to the industry.

10. Nagendra Singh and Raoul Colinvaux, *Shipowners,* British Shipping Laws, vol. 13 (London: Stevens, 1967), ch. 5.

11. For example, the CMI is administered only as a sideline by a firm of average adjusters in Antwerp.

12. C.E. McDowell and H.B. Gibbs, *Ocean Transportation* (New York: McGraw-Hill, 1954), ch. 6.

13. Ibid.

14. J.B. Condliffe, *The Commerce of Nations* (New York: Norton), pt. 2.

15. Edgar Gold, "The 'Freedom' of Ocean Shipping and Commercial Viability," *Law of the Sea: Neglected Issues,* edited by John K. Gamble, Jr. Proceedings, Law of the Sea Institute, 12th Annual Conference, 1978 (Honolulu: Law of the Sea Institute, University of Hawaii, 1979), pp. 248-258.

16. David Howarth, *Sovereign of the Seas* (New York: Atheneum, 1974), pt. 5.

17. McDowell and Gibbs, *Ocean Transportation,* ch. 2.

18. Ibid.

19. C. Ernest Fayle, *A Short History of the World's Shipping Industry* (London: George Allen and Unwin, 1933), p. 271.

20. Ibid., pp. 271-272.

21. Ibid.

22. Ibid.

23. Ibid.

24. McDowell and Gibbs, *Ocean Transportation,* pp. 47-50.

25. Sir Osborne Mance, *International Sea Transport* (London: Oxford University Press, 1945), p. 71ff.

26. Fayle, *History of the World's Shipping Industry,* p. 273.

27. Ibid.

28. Ibid.

29. Ibid., pp. 273-274.

30. Ibid., p. 274.

31. Ibid., p. 275.

32. Gerard J. Mangone, *Marine Policy for America* (Lexington, Mass.: Lexington Books, D.C. Heath and Co., 1977), p. 81.

33. Ibid.

34. Ibid.

35. Ibid., p. 82.

36. Fayle, *History of the World's Shipping Industry,* p. 276.

37. Mance, *International Sea Transport,* pp. 125-126; see also OECD, *Maritime Transport 1977* (Paris: OECD, 1978), p. 135.

38. Fayle, *History of the World's Shipping Industry,* p. 277.

39. Ibid.

40. Ibid., pp. 277-278.

41. Ibid., p. 278.

42. See, for example, S.G. Sturmey, *Shipping Economics: Collected Papers* (London: Macmillan, 1975), p. 9ff.

43. Fayle, *History of the World's Shipping Industry,* pp. 278-280; S.G. Sturmey, *British Shipping and World Competition* (London: Athlone Press, 1962), ch.13; Sturmey, *Shipping Economics,* p. 33ff; B.M. Deakin, *Shipping Conferences: A Study of their Origins, Development and Economic Problems* (Cambridge: Cambridge University Press, 1973).

44. Ibid., Deakin, pp. 23-25.

45. Ibid.

46. Ibid.

47. Ibid., p. 27.

48. Ibid., p. 25.

49. Ibid., p. 23ff.

50. See the recently completed but not yet in force Convention on a Code of Conduct for Liner Conferences, *International Legal Materials* 13 (1974):912.

51. Fayle, *History of the World's Shipping Industry,* p. 279.

52. Sturmey, *Shipping Economics,* ch. 4.

53. Fayle, *History of the World's Shipping Industry,* p. 279.

54. Ibid.

55. Ibid., p. 280.

56. Ibid.

57. Singh and Colinvaux, *Shipowners,* p. 138.

58. Ibid., p. 139.

59. Ibid., pp. 140-141.

60. Ibid., p. 207ff.

61. Victor Dover, *A Handbook to Marine Insurance,* 7th ed., edited by R.H. Brown (London: Witherby, 1970), ch. 7. See also the landmark case of *de Vaux* v. *Salvador,* 5 L.J.K.B. (1836):134.

62. Dover, *A Handbook to Marine Insurance,* pp. 505-506.

63. Ibid., pp. 513-518.

64. Singh and Colinvaux, *Shipowners,* pp. 215-216.

65. Dover, *A Handbook to Marine Insurance,* p. 507.

66. Ibid., pp. 507-508.

67. Ibid.

68. The remainder are handled by three Scandinavian associations and associations in Japan, United States, and Italy.

69. E.R. Hardy Ivamy, *Marine Insurance,* 2nd ed. (London: Butterworths, 1974), pp. 240-250.

70. Singh and Colinvaux, *Shipowners,* pp. 217-228.

71. Ibid., pp. 165-169.

72. Fayle, *History of the World's Shipping Industry,* pp. 286-288.

73. Serious research into this wide area has only begun in the late 1970s. See David H. Moreby, *The Human Element in Shipping* (Colchester: Seatrade Publications, 1975).

74. Fayle, *History of the World's Shipping Industry,* p. 284.

75. Howarth, *Sovereign of the Seas,* p. 326.

76. Ibid.

77. Merchant Shipping Act, 1876. 39 and 40 Vict., ch. 80.

78. Fayle, *History of the World's Shipping Industry,* p. 285.

79. Ibid.

80. Ibid.

81. Singh and Colinvaux, *Shipowners,* pp. 170-172.

82. Ibid.

83. Raymond Flower and Michael W. Jones, *Lloyd's of London: An Illustrated History* (Newton Abbot: David and Charles, 1976).

84. Ibid.

85. Lloyd's Act, 1871. 34 and 35 Vict., ch. 21.

86. Lloyd's Act, 1911. 1 and 2 Geo. V, ch. 62.

87. Fayle, *History of the World's Shipping Industry,* p. 282.

88. Ibid.

89. Singh and Colinvaux, *Shipowners,* p. 166.

90. Fayle, *History of the World's Shipping Industry,* p. 283.

91. Singh and Colinvaux, *Shipowners,* p. 165.

92. Ibid., pp. 173-174.

93. Ibid., p. 167ff.

94. Ibid., p. 173.

95. Fayle, *History of the World's Shipping Industry,* pp. 285-286.

96. Ibid., p. 287.

97. Ibid., p. 285.

98. Ibid.

99. Sea Regulations of 1863 authorized under the Merchant Shipping Act of 1862. 25 and 26 Vict., ch. 63, table C.

100. *Protocol of Proceedings of the International Marine Conference 1889,* 3 vols. (Washington, D.C.: U.S. Government Printing Office, 1890).

101. Ibid., vol. 1, p. ix-xiii.

102. David R. Owen, "The Origins and Development of Marine Collision Law," *Tulane Law Review* 51 (1977):759, 786.

103. With the establishment of IMCO.

104. *Proceedings, International Maritime Conference,* vol. 3, p. 347.

105. Fayle, *History of the World's Shipping Industry,* p. 287.

106. Ibid., p. 288.

107. Singh and Colinvaux, *Shipowners,* p. 137.

108. Howarth, *Sovereign of the Seas,* p. 325.

109. J. C. Beaglehole, *The Life of Captain James Cook* (Stanford: Stanford University Press, 1974); Allan Villiers, *Captain James Cook* (New York: Scribner, 1967).

110. Susan Schlee, *The Edge of an Unfamiliar World: A History of Oceanography* (New York: Dutton, 1973).

111. Howarth, *Sovereign of the Sea,* p. 325.

112. Founded under the patronage of Charles II in 1675. See ibid., ch. 17.

113. Alan Moorehead, *Darwin and the Beagle* (New York: Harper and Row, 1969).

114. Schlee, *Edge of an Unfamiliar World.*

115. Ibid.

116. Brenda Horsfield and Peter B. Stone, *The Great Ocean Business* (London: Hodder and Stoughton, 1972).

117. Ibid., p. 47.

118. Singh and Colinvaux, *Shipowners,* p. 154.

119. Ibid., p. 155.

120. Ibid.

121. Lilar and van den Bosch, *Comité Maritime International,* p. 6.

122. Ibid.

123. Ibid.

124. Ibid.

125. Ibid.

126. Singh and Colinvaux, *Shipowners,* p. 155.

127. Ibid.

128. Lilar and van den Bosch, *Comité Maritime International,* pp. 6-7.

129. Ibid.

130. Ibid.

131. Sir Leslie Scott and Cyril Miller, "The Unification of Maritime and Commercial Law through the Comité Maritime International," *International Law Quarterly* 1 (1947): 482, 483; Louis Franck, "Collisions at Sea in Relation to International Maritime Law," *Law Quarterly Review* 12 (1896):260, 273.

132. Lilar and van den Bosch, *Comité Maritime International,* p. 8.

133. Thomas Barclay, "The Antwerp Congress and the Assimilation of Mercantile Law," *Law Quarterly Review* 2 (1886):66, 77.

134. Lilar and van den Bosch, *Comité Maritime International,* p. 10.

135. Singh and Colinvaux, *Shipowners,* cited p. 156.

136. Lilar and van den Bosch, *Comité Maritime International,* p. 12.

137. Ibid.

138. Singh and Colinvaux, *Shipowners,* cited p. 156.

139. Ibid.

140. Lilar and van den Bosch, *Comité Maritime International,* pp. 12-13.

141. Ibid., p. 14.

142. Ibid.

143. Ibid., p. 16.

144. Ibid., p. 14; Singh and Colinvaux, *Shipowners,* p. 154.

145. W.O. Stevens and Allan Westcott, *A History of Sea Power* (Garden City, N.Y.: Doubleday, 1944), p. 271.

146. Ibid.

147. Ibid.

148. Ibid.

149. Ibid.

150. Ibid., pp. 271-272.

151. Ibid., cited p. 272.

152. For an enlightening analysis of this area see Hugh Seton-Watson, *Nations and States: An Enquiry into the Origins of Nations and the Politics of Nationalism* (Boulder, Colo.: Westview, 1977).

153. As per Rudyard Kipling, cited by Crane Brinton, John B. Christopher, and Robert L. Wolff, *Civilization in the West* (Englewood Cliffs, N.J.: Prentice-Hall, 1964), p. 570.

154. Ibid.

155. Ibid.

156. Ibid., pp. 570-572.

157. Stanley Wolpert, *A New History of India* (New York: Oxford University Press, 1977), pp. 248-249.

158. Brinton, Christopher, and Wolff, *Civilization in the West,* p. 570ff.

159. Mance, *International Sea Transport,* p. 68.

160. Ibid., pp. 73-74.

161. Alistair Horne, *A Savage War of Peace—Algeria, 1954-1962* (New York: Viking Press, 1977), pt. 1.

162. Ibid.

163. Brinton, Christopher, and Wolff, *Civilization in the West,* p. 572.

164. Ibid.

165. Mance, *International Sea Transport* p. 70.

166. Ibid.

167. Ibid., p. 68.

168. Fayle, *History of the World's Shipping Industry,* p. 304.

169. Mance, *International Sea Transport,* pp. 70-71.

170. Fritz Stern, *Gold and Iron—Bismarck, Bleichröder and the Building of the German Empire* (New York: Knopf, 1977), p. 88.

171. Ibid.

172. Ibid.

173. Mance, *International Sea Transport,* p. 71.

174. Stern, *Gold and Iron,* p. 434.

175. Mance, *International Sea Transport,* p. 71.

176. Ibid., p. 68.

177. Brinton, Christopher, and Wolff, *Civilization in the West,* pp. 572-573.

178. Stevens and Westcott, *History of Sea Power,* p. 272ff.

179. David McCulloch, *The Path Between the Seas: The Creation of the Panama Canal—1870-1914* (New York: Simon and Schuster, 1977); Walter la Feber, *The Panama Canal* (New York: Oxford University Press, 1978).

180. McCulloch, *Path Between the Seas,* p. 38.

181. Ibid.

182. La Feber, *The Panama Canal,* ch. 2.

183. Brinton, Christopher, and Wolff, *Civilization in the West,* p. 574.

184. McCulloch, *Path Between the Seas,* p. 39.

185. Ibid.

186. Ibid., p. 26ff.

187. Ibid., ch. 4.

188. Ibid., ch. 9.

189. Ibid., p. 265.

190. Ibid., p. 332.

191. William L. Langer, ed. *An Encyclopedia of World History,* 4th ed. (Boston: Houghton Mifflin, 1968), pp. 856, 853.

192. McCulloch, *Path Between the Seas,* pp. 392-394.

193. Langer, *World History,* p. 856.

194. Ibid.

195. McCulloch, *Path Between the Seas,* p. 610.

196. Ibid.

197. Ibid., p. 611.

198. Ibid., p. 612.

199. Ibid., pp. 613-614.

200. La Feber, *The Panama Canal,* ch. 6.

201. McDowell and Gibbs, *Ocean Transportation,* p. 21.

202. Mance, *International Sea Transport,* p. 68.

203. Ibid., p. 82.

204. Ibid.

205. Brinton, Christopher, and Wolff, *Civilization in the West,* p. 573.

206. Ibid.

207. Mangone, *Marine Policy for America,* p. 105ff.

208. Ibid., pp. 82-83.

209. Ibid., p. 81.

210. Ibid.

211. Ibid., p. 83; Mance, *International Sea Transport,* p. 82.

212. Mance, *International Sea Transport,* p. 82.

213. Ibid.

214. Ibid., pp. 82-83.

215. Ibid.

216. Ibid.; Merchant Marine Act, 1920. 41 U.S. Stats. 988 (1919-1921).

217. Brinton, Christopher, and Wolff, *Civilization in the West,* p. 573.

218. Mance, *International Sea Transport,* pp. 77-78, 123-124.

219. Ibid., p. 68.

220. Ibid.

221. Ibid., p. 68.

222. Stern, *Gold and Iron,* p. 402.

223. Ibid., pp. 407-408.

224. Ibid.

225. Brinton, Christopher, and Wolff, *Civilization in the West,* p. 573.

226. Langer, *World History,* p. 919.

227. Ibid.; see also Edwin O. Reischauer, *The Japanese* (Cambridge, Mass.: Harvard University Press, 1977).

228. Ibid.

229. Ibid.

230. Mance, *International Sea Transport,* p. 68.

231. Ibid., p. 582

232. R.R. James, *The British Revolution, 1880-1939* (New York: Knopf, 1977), p. 287.

233. Hersch Lauterpacht, *International Law: Collected Papers*, vol. 2, edited by E. Lauterpacht (Cambridge: Cambridge University Press, 1975), pp. 95-144.

234. Arthur Nussbaum, *A Concise History of the Law of Nations* (New York: Macmillan, 1962), p. 196.

235. Ibid., pp. 196-197.

236. Ibid, p. 198.

237. Ibid.

238. Ibid., p. 192.

239. Ibid.

240. Ibid., p. 198.

241. Ibid.

242. Ibid.

243. Ibid., p. 192.

244. See, for example, Johnston, *The International Law of Fisheries.*

245. See, for example, Brian J. Rothschild, ed., *World Fisheries Policy*, (Seattle: University of Washington Press, 1972); Edward Wenk, Jr., *The Politics of the Ocean* (Seattle: University of Washington Press, 1972).

246. H.S.K. Kent, "The Historical Origin of the Three-Mile Limit,"*American Journal of International Law* 48 (1954):537; Bernard G. Heinzen, "The Three-Mile Limit: Preserving the Freedom of the Seas," *Stanford Law Review* 11 (1959):597.

247. [1805] 5 C. Rob. 373, 385.

248. Comment, "Territorial Seas—3000 Year Old Question," *Journal of Air Law and Commerce* 36 (1970):73, 82. See also *Gann* v. *The Three Fisheries of Whitstable* [1865] 11 H.L. Cas. 192, and The Territorial Waters Jurisdiction Act 1878, 41 and 42 Vict. c. 73.

249. Heinzen, "The Three-Mile Limit," p. 630.

250. Ibid., pp. 632-634.

251. Ibid., p. 634.

252. Ibid., pp. 634-635.

253. Comment, "Territorial Seas," p. 82.

254. Ibid., pp. 82-83.

255. H.A. Smith, *The Law and Custom of the Sea* (London: Stevens, 1959), p. 25.

256. William E. Masterson, "Territorial Waters and International Legislation," *Oregon Law Review* 8 (1929):307.

257. Oppenheim, *International Law*, vol. 1, p. 593.

258. A.N. Yiannopoulos, "The Unification of Private Maritime Law by International Conventions," *Law and Contemporary Problems* 30 (1965):370.

259. Barclay, "The Antwerp Congress," p. 66.

260. Ibid., p. 67.

261. Ibid., p. 68.

262. Ibid.

263. Ibid.

264. Ibid.

265. Yiannopoulos, "Unification of Maritime Law," p. 375ff.

266. See *Yearbook of the United Nations 1976* (New York: U.N., 1978), p. 822ff.

267. Barclay, "The Antwerp Congress," pp. 74ff.

268. Lilar and van den Bosch, *Comité Maritime International*, p. 22ff.

269. Ibid., pp. 108-110.

270. Singh and Colinvaux, *Shipowners*, pp. 212-213.

271. Lilar and van den Bosch, *Comité Maritime International*, p. 26.

272. Yiannopoulos, "Unification of Maritime Law," p. 371.

273. Louis Franck, "A New Law for the Seas," *Law Quarterly Review* 42 (1926):25, 28.

274. Ibid., p. 26.

275. Louis Franck, "Collisions at Sea in Relation to International Maritime Law," *Law Quarterly Review* 12 (1896):260; Lilar and van den Bosch, *Comité Maritime International*, p. 24.

276. Ibid.

277. Ibid.; Franck, "New Law for the Seas," p. 29.

278. Lilar and van den Bosch, *Comité Maritime International*, p. 118.

279. Comment, "The Difficult Quest for a Uniform Maritime Law: Failure of the Brussels Conventions to Achieve International Agreement on Collision Liability, Liens, and Mortgages," *Yale Law Journal* 64 (1955):878, 879, 880.

# 5 World Shipping in War and Peace

*Interdiction of enemy trade has always been the great weapon of sea power.*

—W.O. Stevens (*A History of Sea Power*, 1944)

*War is a continuation of policy only in the sense in which death is a continuation of life, or a breakdown in a machine is a continuation of its smooth running. War is a breakdown of policy.*

—R.G. Collingwood (*The New Leviathan*, 1942)

## Prelude to World War I: Preparations in Europe and Adventures in Asia

The prelude to World War I was not, as historians usually claim, the pistol shot that killed an Austrian Archduke in Sarajevo in 1914, but rather a sea battle fought far from the Europe that was to be the war's main theater.

The Treaty of Shimonoseki of April 17, 1895, which ended Japan's victorious war with China, gave Port Arthur, the Liao-tung peninsula, the Pescadores Islands, and Formosa to Japan.[1] In addition, China had to withdraw from Korea, which would henceforth be under Japanese influence. However, Japanese ambitions in the area were thwarted by the European powers, which began to exploit the defenseless China for themselves. Japan had acquitted itself well in its war with China but was as yet no match for the European powers and had to bide its time during a period of intensified commercial and colonial rivalry in the Far East.[2]

Russia, together with Germany and France, were able to prevent Japan from fully exploiting its victory over China. At first Russia, in return for protecting China against Japan, was able to obtain a number of territorial concessions from China. In 1898 Germany seized Kiao-chau and extorted a ninety-nine-year lease of the port with exclusive development privileges throughout the Shantung peninsula. Russia pushed through a twenty-five-year lease of Port Arthur; England seized Wei-hai-wai as a "precautionary measure"; and France secured a new naval base in Kwang-chau Bay in southern China.[3] When the Chinese masses, in the summer of 1900, reacted against the "foreign menace" in what became known as the Boxer Rebellion, a combined multipower expedition to relieve the legations at Peking was successfully launched.[4] In this expedition, Japanese troops displayed superior deftness, discipline, and endurance and gained confidence in their ability to cope with the armies of the European powers.

In 1904 Japan demanded that Russia remove its troops from Manchuria and recognize Japanese predominance in Korea. Japan then almost immediately declared war on Russia. Control of the sea was vital for Japan, and the ensuing Russo-Japanese War was fought mostly at sea, culminating with the Battle of Tsushima when the Japanese navy swept the Russian Imperial Fleet out of existence.[5] U.S. President Theodore Roosevelt offered to mediate; and, in accordance with the Treaty of Portsmouth, New Hampshire, of September 1905, Russia withdrew from Manchuria in favor of China; recognized Japan's paramount position in Korea (which Japan would fully annex in 1910); and handed over its privileges in Port Arthur and the Liao-tung peninsula to Japan.[6]

It is quite clear that the war thwarted Russia's policy of imperialistic expansion in the Far East and established Japan firmly on the mainland of China. What is less-often recognized is that the war, resulting in a military debacle for Russia, seriously and permanently disturbed the balance of power in Europe and caused a loss of equilibrium that would result in World War I.[7] This prelude to the War is recounted here in order to emphasize the closely intertwined relationship between clearly defined marine policies and the expansionist-colonialist commercial ambitions of the major maritime powers. An understanding of the modern "maritime state" is incomplete without a full comprehension of the colonialist-political infrastructure on which it was founded. Many developing states with maritime aspirations fail to grasp this lesson of history, which accordingly becomes part and parcel of the whole development gap. This problem will be discussed again later.

The Russo-Japanese War greatly weakened Russia's prestige and position in Europe and left the "Dual Alliance" of France and Russia greatly outweighed by the military strength of Germany and Austria. Great Britain, which as a leading power had steered its own course in isolation from the European powers, was now forced to become involved owing to the power imbalance created by the Russian defeat. The result was the intensification of German-British rivalry, which had already begun in the latter part of the nineteenth century. This rivalry was particularly evident in international commerce and sea power.[8] Along with the buildup of the German merchant fleet, a powerful navy—the guardian of such a fleet—had also been developed very quickly.

As long as Bismarck was chancellor, German expansion had remained fairly reasonable, but the young Kaiser Wilhelm II had a vision of his country as a world power.[9] For him, England was both rival and lesson. Mastery of the sea appeared to be the answer. The kaiser was undoubtedly influenced by Admiral Mahan's theories and distributed the epoch-making book to his admirals.[10] German naval development found stimulus as well as justification in the rapid economic growth of the country. In addition to the German merchant fleet, which took second place only to that of Britain by 1914, industrial production by that time had attained a value of $3 billion. By way of comparison, British industrial production in 1914 stood at $4 billion, that of the United States at $7 billion.[11] However, Germany had passed both the United States and France in the volume of foreign commerce.

The expansion of German sea power was a natural result of this growth. The German Naval Bill of 1900 had already declared that

> . . . to protect her sea trade and colonies . . . Germany must have a fleet so strong that a war, even with the greatest naval power, would involve such risks as to jeopardize the position of that power.[12]

This bill, passed in an emotionally charged atmosphere of anti-English feeling aroused by the Boer War, contained specific provisions that allowed considerable and steady increases of German naval strength under the able guidance of Admiral von Tirpitz.[13] In a comparatively short period of time, Germany had built a battle fleet that could (and would) seriously challenge that of Britain.

On the other hand, Britain's fleet had been allowed to age; had it not been for the energies of Admiral Sir John Fisher, First Sea Lord from 1904 to 1910, the tradition-ridden Royal Navy might have been in serious trouble. Against considerable opposition, Fisher was able, in his five years as First Lord, to blow "away a century's dust and cobwebs."[14].

> "Scrap the lot" was the phrase of the period: he wrote it across a list of 154 ships, including 17 battleships, which he said were only devices for wasting men. He insisted that only four types of ships were needed for the kind of war that might be fought in the future: battleships of 21 knots, driven by turbines (a new British invention) and armed entirely with 12-inch guns; armoured cruisers of 25½ knots; destroyers of 36 knots; and submarines.[15]

Fisher also opposed the tradition of the Royal Navy as a worldwide force. He said that no navy, however large, could police the whole world and also be ready in European waters for a major war.[16] As a consequence, oceans that had known a Royal Navy presence for over a century were now left empty as the fleets returned to home waters. As David Howarth notes:

> Plenty of people saw in this the downfall of the Empire; and perhaps they were right, insofar as it was only the beginning of it then. But Lord Fisher insisted downfall was coming certainly and soon unless the navy were concentrated for the defence of Britain.[17]

History has painted Fisher as a cruel and intolerant autocrat who mercilessly wrecked the careers of men who got in his way.[18] Nevertheless, his single-minded rule reformed the Royal Navy in half a decade from a nineteenth-century force into the most modern sea power in history. By 1914, Britain had twenty-seven new battleships and a further twenty on the stocks.[19] The lengthy coal-bunkering process of warships had been by-passed, and Fisher had oil-fired boilers fitted to most of the smaller ships despite admonitions by the First Lord of the Admiralty that "the substitution of oil for coal is impossible, because oil does not exist in this world in sufficient quantities."[20] Fisher had also foreseen the importance of submarine warfare, but Britain was far behind Germany in this respect at the outbreak of the war. This was because of the conservatism of the cautious element in the Royal Navy, which considered submarine warfare to be "underhand, unfair and damned un-English."[21] The Germans did not suffer from such misgivings, and the war at sea would be a vicious and unforgiving one.

## The War at Sea: The Disappearance of International Law

On June 28, 1914 a Serbian nationalist assassinated the Austrian Archduke Franz Ferdinand, an event that immediately led to a series of sharp diplomatic exchanges between Austria-Hungary, Serbia, and Russia. The commitments of the Triple Alliance and the Triple Entente came into play; Germany and Italy were called on to support Austria-Hungary, and France and Britain were aligned with Russia. Italy did not accept its commitment; and on August 4, 1914, before any further diplomacy could find a solution, the German army marched into Belgium. Belgian neutrality had been guaranteed by Britain since 1839, and consequently Britain declared war on Germany the same day. The so-called "war to end all wars" had begun.

Although it was not to be the last war, World War I certainly changed the world. It is, of course, one of the best-chronicled wars in history, and will not be discussed at length here, except for a few words about the war at sea, which was fought with a devastating bitterness reminiscent of the Dark Ages in the Mediterranean. Marine transport had to cope with entirely new problems during these war years. Principles of international law disappeared very quickly in the first all-out war of the modern era.

At the very beginning of the war, Great Britain took an action that clearly contravened accepted standards of international law, by declaring the North Sea a "military area" and laying mine fields there.[22] As a result, neutral vessels, unless guided by the British, would enter the North Sea at their own peril. Germany retaliated by declaring the waters around the British Isles and Ireland to be a *Kriegsgebiet* (war zone) with similar dangers to neutral vessels.[23] Britain retaliated by completely blockading Germany. All passage of neutral vessels to and from Germany was barred, with the ultimate objective of preventing any commodities from entering or leaving Germany. Neutral ships were subject to visit and search in British-controlled ports.

On the other hand, Germany, invoking the right of reprisal under international law, extended its submarine warfare in order to enforce its "war zones," so that any vessel, whether enemy or neutral, found in such a zone would be torpedoed without warning.[24] The explanation was that any warning might expose the submarine to detection and destruction. The most notable example of this "new" type of warfare was the sinking in 1915 of the British passenger liner *Lusitania* with a loss of more than 1,100 people.[25] Even the ancient law of angary, under which a state could seize and use the property of neutrals for purposes of warfare, was revived. Neutral ships were simply requisitioned by the belligerents, particularly Great Britain and the United States; but even neutral powers such as Italy, Portugal, and Brazil frequently requisitioned German ships.[26]

These contraventions against accepted legal principles created a whole new field of jurisprudence, which continued until well after the war. The prize courts heard case after case relating to confiscation, requisition, contraband, damage, loss, and injury; and lawyers and legal scholars debated fine points of prize law for decades.[27] Although all this makes fascinating reading, it is of little relevance today and is only of passing historical interest. The conception of war as a contest between governments only, which was first described by Rousseau and which had prevailed in all previous wars,[28] was entirely abandoned under a new concept of "total warfare." Not only would the life and health of citizens of the warring countries be affected by food shortages caused by maritime blockade, but war against civilians generally became an unfortunate but accepted byproduct of this total war.[29] Seizure and confiscation of private enemy property was widespread and was aided by the rapid passage of municipal enabling legislation.[30] Although the rights of neutrals had already been badly impaired in the Napoleonic Wars, little remained of such rights in World War I despite vigorous protests, particularly by the United States prior to its entry into the war.[31] Military areas, long-distance blockade, and indiscriminate submarine warfare forced the neutrals either to take sides or to stay out of the area altogether—often leading to their own loss and the suffering of their populations from resultant shortages.

*The End of Battleship Warfare*

Apart from a series of isolated encounters in various parts of the world, the British and German navies did not clash head on until 1916 at the famous

Battle of Jutland. This was really the first and last appearance of the German battle fleet, the building of which had done so much to embitter Anglo-German relations before the war. When the confrontation finally came, the Royal Navy could have "won the war" at Jutland but missed its chance because of the overcautious attitude of its commander, Admiral Sir John Jellicoe, one of the most overrated of all British naval heroes.[32] Despite a seven-to-four advantage, the British battle fleet of 150 vessels, ranging from dreadnought battleships to destroyers, could not defeat the 100-vessel fleet of the German force. On the contrary, 14 British vessels totaling 112,000 tons were sunk with the loss of some 7,000 men, against German losses amounting to 11 warships totaling 60,000 tons with some 3,000 men.[33] In the end, it was probably an indecisive battle because the British did not pursue their initiative and the Germans retreated to their bases from which their great fleet would never emerge again en masse during the war. The Royal Navy, however, was now truly put on a war footing; and Admiral Fisher's predictions had come true. Jutland would not soon be forgotten. In the words of one of the war's naval-strategic experts:

> It would seem a fair deduction that one reason for technical errors committed on the day of Jutland is to be found in the fact that, due to a long period of comparative naval inactivity, the functions of high naval command had become sluggish in disuse, and practice in the art of "fleet control" on the field of battle had been neglected.[34]

In actual fact, the modern battle fleet was a monster that had totally outgrown its use except in the eyes of the admirals who sought to perpetuate it. A battle fleet was such an immense industrial investment and source of national prestige that no state could afford to lose it. Strategically, however, it was of less importance. Indeed, it has been pointed out that the "British battle fleet never fought as a tactical unit except at Jutland when it was engaged in the work it was built to do for a total of forty minutes!"[35] However, the real lesson of Jutland was not only the uselessness of the battleship (a lesson that many states did not finally learn until World War II) but that bigger and stronger battle fleets were not the answer. Certainly in Germany, with its fleet cooped up in its estuaries, the answer appeared to lie in constructing a weapon system of greater certainty and lower cost. The answer was the submarine with its deadly stealth, as perfected by the Germans in both world wars. Again Admiral Fisher had been prophetic, and again the Royal Navy had not listened. When German submarines started to create their havoc, the Royal Navy was caught off balance.[36]

## The Beginning of Submarine Warfare

The German submarine campaign started in earnest in February 1915 as a result of the German retaliatory establishment of the war zone. The intention was to impose a total commercial blockade of Great Britain and to enforce it with the submarine fleet.[37] This was an entirely new phase in the long history of marine transport. Merchant ships were now viewed as commercial extensions of the belligerents, which therefore had to be destroyed. It was warfare against commerce—not, as in the past, to take prizes and rob the enemy's goods on the high seas, but purely and simply to destroy the enemy's goods, supplies, and citizens by sinking the *carrier* on the seas.

The famous "peace conferences" of 1899 and 1907 had already discussed a variety of warlike actions, the treatment of prisoners and wounded, and other aspects of the "law of war," which at that time many still believed could be followed.[38] In retrospect these conferences inspire cynicism because many of the Geneva and Hague conventions and declarations were indeed followed by nation-states to a certain extent on a quid pro quo basis if and when it suited them to do so.

During the 1907 conference, several agreements dealt with maritime aspects of war, particularly with respect to neutrals. But these aspects, the substance of which was never ratified, were probably unrealistic and obsolete even when they were written. For example, neutrals were not supposed to prevent the manufacture, transit, or export of arms and other war materials for belligerents or to restrict them in the use of communication systems that were situated on neutral territories.[39] Another agreement, which illustrated an almost naive belief in the international law of neutrality, dealt with the right of capture in maritime war and granted the inviolability of neutral and belligerent mailbags, including those of an official character.[40] A further agreement attempted to set up an international prize court. Although there were a few accessions, there were almost no ratifications.[41]

The Draft Convention on the International Prize Court had, as a sequel, a naval conference held in London in 1908-1909, which was to formulate an international prize law that in turn would provide the terms of reference for the proposed court.[42] The result was the Declaration of London of 1909, which—still unrealistically favorable to neutrals—attempted to regulate such matters as blockade, contraband, flag transfer, convoy, and search visitation of ships. Strangely, perhaps ominously, both the conference and the declaration failed to give adequate consideration to the employment of submarines, the deployment of mines, and other methods of modern naval warfare that by 1909 were well known and comparatively well developed.

Thus, some five years before the outbreak of World War I, which was to wreak havoc of unprecedented dimensions on the world's maritime fleets, the methods that would create this destruction were scarcely discussed.[43] We would suggest that this, too, is part of the state's maritime policy, although largely in the negative sense. It appeared that the newer naval-warfare methods were almost mutually blocked out by most of the maritime states in their international policies. The "gentlemanly" art of war still prevailed at most of these conferences immediately prior to World War I. Contingency plans for "commerce warfare" did not exist; or, if they did, they were not brought forward at gatherings that simply confined themselves to "black letter" discussions of legality and illegality of certain warlike actions in the public international law of the sea.

This is another area where the gulf that by then separated the public from the private maritime law is apparent. At a time when the international shipping industry was attempting to unify its rules through the actions of organizations such as the ILA and the CMI, military naval technology was being perfected not to unify but to destroy world shipping. In an atmosphere of almost-unhurried inevitability, the parties now no longer communicated about the drama that was about to unfold. While members of the shipping industry talked among themselves about unification of commercial rules and private law, the naval armament and submarine designers were perfecting unheard-of methods of destruction in relative secrecy. At the same time, the foreign ministries were still attempting to write elaborate international treaties containing intricate and unrealistic terms from another, more-gentlemanly age to "regulate" the war at sea. At the apex were the politicians of the various belligerents-to-be, all vying for nationalistic prestige in a power game that would soon be beyond their control.

Again—in retrospect—we can ask whether anything could have been done differently. It is hard to say. Perhaps if the CMI had been a little less painstaking in avoiding any involvement in "public" or political questions relating to the sea, it might have been able to exert some of its considerable influence on the forces that were hurtling the world into one of the most destructive oceanic conflagrations of all time. Even if that would not have been possible, the belligerents might at least have been better informed about the deadly methods of destruction that were being developed in the shipyards and arsenals of the world at that very time. Further information *might* have resulted in fewer losses if such information could have been absorbed by shipbuilders in time. Faster vessels, better construction (such as better compartmentalization), and better life-saving methods and equipment could have been the result.

Although this may be considered mere speculation, U.S. maritime policy, which established the U.S. Shipping Board Emergency Fleet Corporation in 1916, appears to lend credence to this view.[44] The U.S. government, as a public body, created a fleet to deal with the menaces of the modern war at sea. Although commercial transportation and not altruism were the motives for this U.S. policy, the fact remains that from 1916 on the United States made serious attempts to improve its ships vis-à-vis the submarine menace.[45] What the United States learned in 1915 and 1916 must have been—or at least could have been—known to the maritime states, and through them to the CMI, long before. The subject could in fact have been legitimately discussed at the Salvage Conference of 1910, which chose instead to confine itself to strictly private legal aspects of salvage and excluded any discussion about the reasons that vessels might have to be salved in the first place.[46] We might add that we appear to have learned relatively little since then—even today the "constructive" and "destructive" aspects of merchant shipping are rarely brought together. Naval secrecy and shipping-industry egocentricity still cooperate on their almost parallel courses.

It appears evident from the limited supply of some thirty submarines at the outbreak of World War I that Germany did not really contemplate their use as commerce destroyers.[47] To the German navy as well as to the allied navies, the deployment of submarines in this fashion was an innovation as well as a surprise. The Battle of Jutland gave the German navy the incentive to look at this alternative method of naval warfare, which proved to be a highly "successful" alternative. Between 1914 and 1918, Germany built almost 1,000 submarines and lost just over 400.[48] After 1916, German shipyards were devoted entirely to submarine construction and perfected their product to a high degree of capability. There are no accurate statistics for World War I on exactly how much shipping was destroyed by German submarines. We do know that the total allied and neutral war losses amounted to 12 million gross tons, as shown in table 5-1. The total figure represents just over one-quarter of the world fleet at the beginning of World War I and does not include German and Austrian losses.

There is little doubt that the majority of these war losses resulted from German submarine warfare. In the first year of the war alone, almost one million tons of merchant ships were sunk.[49] After January 1917, when submarine warfare became quite unrestricted, the figures rose quickly. By the early summer of that year, 1.25 million tons had ben destroyed; by autumn, 2.75 million.[50] Ships were being lost more rapidly than they could be replaced. Germany's General von Hindenburg declared on July 2, 1917 that "the war is won for us if we can withstand the enemy attack until the submarine has done its work." It was indeed doing its work.[51] By mid-1917 British food supplies were good for only four to six weeks, and ships were being sunk indiscriminately in an enormous barred zone with limits extending from the Dutch coast to Cape Finisterre and including also the entire Mediterranean.[52]

Against this offensive, allied countermeasures were chiefly defensive and less than effective. Many merchant ships were armed, and this led the Germans to react with more indiscriminate actions against merchant ships. How could submarine commanders distinguish armed enemy from unarmed neutral vessels? One of the answers appeared to be the well-secured and -defended convoy; but Admiral Jellicoe, who had returned as First Sea

**Table 5-1**
**Allied and Neutral Losses in the 1914-1918 War**

| State | Losses in Gross Tons |
|---|---|
| Great Britain | 7,753,311 |
| British Colonies | 169,712 |
| United States | 343,090 |
| Belgium | 85,842 |
| Brazil | 20,328 |
| Denmark | 210,880 |
| France | 722,939 |
| Greece | 349,661 |
| Italy | 745,766 |
| Japan | 119,764 |
| Netherlands | 201,797 |
| Norway | 976,516 |
| Spain | 157,527 |
| Sweden | 180,415 |
| Total | 12,037,548 |

Source: *Lloyd's Register of Shipping*, 1919. See also E.W. Zimmerman, *Ocean Shipping* (New York: Prentice-Hall, 1922), p. 580.

Lord to the Admiralty, opposed this method.[53] Thus a convoy system, which had been successfully used throughout history, was neglected for three long years. Jellicoe said that even if convoys could be organized, there were not enough destroyers to defend them.[54] As David Howarth concludes:

> It was the most damning confession of lack of foresight the Navy has ever made. The Navy was still using shipyards and manpower to make its enormous battle fleet even stronger: by the end of that same year it had no less than forty-three Dreadnoughts watching the German fleet, which had only twenty-four. It was short of small ships solely because it spent so much time and money building big ones, though most of the big ones never fired a shot at any enemy. And for that reason Britain was reduced before the year was out, to six weeks' reserve of food, and the Grand Fleet itself, ironically, had to cut short its exercises for lack of oil.[55]

In actual fact, the German submarine menace was not defeated by direct Allied action but by more-indirect methods. When Germany embarked on its policy of indiscriminate attack on all merchant ships in 1917, it was taking well-calculated risks. The Germans knew that the torpedoing of neutral ships carrying nonmilitary cargoes to the allies and neutrals might well bring the United States into the war. But the hope was that German submarines would destroy so much vital food and raw materials that Britain would be starved into surrender. In 1917, Admiral von Capelle, head of the German Admiralty, declared that in his personal view "the U-boat would bring peace within six months" and that America's aid would be "absolutely negligible."[56] As we know, however, in staking everything on this policy Germany burnt its bridges. On April 6, 1917 the United States entered the war against Germany. Suddenly the energies of the North American giant were thrown at an already staggering Germany, and the blockade tables were turned completely.[57]

### Allied Victory at Sea

Britain alone had not been able effectively to "blockade" all goods entering Germany despite a complete embargo on German trade that allowed the British, in the words of Prime Minister Asquith, "to detain and take into port ships carrying goods of presumed enemy destination, ownership or origin."[58] Despite these British efforts, there had been a considerable increase in direct and indirect trade with Germany through neutrals. For example, although U.S. exports to Germany in 1915 were $154 million less than in 1913—that is, they had just about ceased—U.S. exports to the Netherlands and the Scandinavian countries had increased during the same period by $158 million.[59] European neutral states simply substituted imports for home use and exported their own products to Germany.

All this ceased immediately when the United States entered the war. An effective long-range blockade was commenced, and by the end of 1917 the German people were suffering from malnutrition.[60] Virtually no ships could get through to Germany or to neutrals who might supply the Germans.[61] By early 1918 the blockade had created an almost complete absence of imported raw materials, had virtually crippled vital war industries, and had brought about a marked lowering of national morale and efficiency owing to continued food shortages and consequent rationing.[62] This, combined with more effective antisubmarine warfare, defeated Germany. When the United States entered the war, the problem of escort ships was also solved. The U.S. Navy had many destroyers, frigates, corvettes, and auxiliary vessels that could be used in convoy work. Admiral Jellicoe, who still resisted, was finally—very belatedly—dismissed.[63]

The convoys that were organized worked as effectively as they always had. Sinkings of merchants ships declined, and German submarine losses increased.[64] Despite a belief to the contrary, Britain—and, for that matter, the Royal Navy—had been saved by a rather ill-conceived U.S.-government shipping enterprise and by the U.S. Navy.[65] In a historical analysis of the international law and policy of marine transport, the historian should avoid any attempt to be wise after the event. But David Howarth correctly sums up this problem of naval policy—still applicable today—when he suggests that

. . . it is strange that the high command of navies—not only the British navy—was given so many chances for that spurious kind of wisdom. The creation of the race-built ship and the reliance on gunnery in John Hawkins's time under Queen Elizabeth—that was one supreme stroke of imagination and forethought in naval war. Perhaps the creation of the Polaris submarine and its successors was another. But in between, elder seamen have mainly been distinguished for dogged conservatism, whether they are fishermen or admirals.[66]

## Conclusions: The End of World War I

Despite the appalling destruction of over 12 million tons of shipping during the war, the world's fleet was actually greater in 1919 than it had been in 1914.[67] But statistics cannot tell the real story of the uncounted losses of human life on the oceans, which, along with the deaths on the fields of Flanders and the Somme, destroyed a whole generation. Shipping, however, with its extraordinary resilience, recovered even while it was being destroyed in the greatest onslaught to which it had ever been exposed.

There were several factors that contributed to this recovery. British shipyards had finally received some long-overdue government assistance during the last two years of the war and were thus able to produce new ships for a fleet that lost almost 8 million tons during the war.[68] The expansion of the Japanese shipbuilding industry was another important factor. Japan was on the Allied side during World War I and increased its fleet by some 36 percent between 1914 and 1919, as can be seen from table 5-2.

Table 5-2, however, shows the most important factor in the rapid recovery of world shipping from the losses of the "commerce" war: the enormous building program embarked on by the United States after its entry into the war, which increased the U.S. oceangoing fleet by a staggering 400 percent. This was a response to Allied appeals for assistance as well as the U.S. hope of regaining its old position as a shipping power. In addition to the nearly 8-million-ton increase in the U.S. fleet during the war years, a further 2 million tons were "controlled" by the U.S. Shipping Board.[69] This tonnage consisted of (1) seized German and Austrian ships; (2) commandeered neutral vessels; (3) foreign vessels on long-term charters; and (4) vessels built for the board in foreign yards.[70] In June 1920 the board still controlled a total of 1,400 vessels with a tonnage of just over 9 million tons.[71] It was the culmination of one of the most successful and far-reaching national marine policies ever undertaken by any state, and was a display of the capability of what would soon be the world's most powerful country in every sense of that word.

Table 5-2 also shows that the losers, Germany and Austria-Hungary, lost about 36 percent and 32 percent, respectively, of their fleets in the war.

**Table 5-2**

**Changes in Shipping Tonnage in the Principal Maritime States of the World, 1914-1919**

*(vessels over 100 gross tons, exclusive of sail)*

| | 1914 | 1919 | Change | |
|---|---|---|---|---|
| | *(Thousands of* | *(Thousands of* | *(Thousands of* | |
| *State* | *Gross Tons)* | *Gross Tons)* | *Gross Tons)* | *Percentage* |
| Great Britain | 18,892 | 16,345 | − 2,547 | − 13.5 |
| British Colonies | 1,632 | 1,836 | + 231 | + 14.1 |
| U.S.A. (ocean-going) | 2,027 | 9,773 | + 7,746 | + 382.1 |
| Austria-Hungary | 1,052 | 713 | − 339 | − 32.2 |
| Denmark | 770 | 631 | − 139 | − 18.1 |
| France | 1,922 | 1,962 | + 40 | + 2.1 |
| Germany | 5,135 | 3,247 | − 1,888 | − 36.8 |
| Greece | 821 | 291 | − 530 | − 64.6 |
| Italy | 1,430 | 1,238 | − 192 | − 13.4 |
| Japan | 1,708 | 2,325 | + 617 | + 36.1 |
| Netherlands | 1,472 | 1,574 | + 102 | + 6.9 |
| Norway | 1,957 | 1,597 | − 360 | − 18.1 |
| Spain | 884 | 709 | − 175 | − 19.8 |
| Sweden | 1,015 | 917 | − 98 | − 9.7 |
| Other states | 2,427 | 2,552 | + 125 | + 5.2 |
| Total | 43,404 | 45,737 | + 2,393 | + 5.5 |

Source: *Lloyd's Register of Shipping*, 1919. See also E.W. Zimmerman, *Ocean Shipping* (New York: Prentice-Hall, 1922), p. 581.

Nevertheless, there was an overall increase in the world of 5.5 percent. The table, however, does not indicate that under normal circumstances there would probably have been a natural growth in the fleet amounting to between 5 and 7 million tons per year.[72] Even if we take the modest lower figure and allow for normal attrition and marine losses, the fleet should have increased by some 20 million tons. In fact, it increased only by just over 2 million tons. The war had taken its toll.

The armistice of November 11, 1918 concluded the war but also laid the groundwork for the next world war by humiliating a shattered and defeated Germany and dismantling the sick giant, Austria-Hungary. The whole map of Europe was altered, and countries changed hands as if they were chattels. The Ottoman Empire ceased to exist and became the trimmed-down modern Turkey. Russia, in the throes of a revolution, would become the Union of Soviet Socialist Republics; the old czarist ambition of oceanic dominance would disappear for some years as the new government became established.[73] World War I had not only swept away millions of lives but had also finally laid to rest the "European Concert" of the post-Congress of Vienna era. Another world war was only just over two decades away, but in the intervening period the world had to repair the damages of World War I and embark on a rather uncertain voyage into the future. As always, marine transport would be a vital part of such a venture.

## Petroleum: New Energy Source with Revolutionary Shipping Implications

One of the most important developments in the history of marine transport belongs to the period we are now entering. This concerns a natural-resource product that from a modest beginning would rise to be of all-embracing importance. We are, of course, referring to petroleum or oil, and its many byproducts.

Oil seeping from the ground had been noted since prehistoric times. In the ninth century, Arabic records already speak of *naft* (from the classical *naptha*) and contain observations about oil springs and combustible mineral oil used for lighting.[74] Associated with petroleum deposits is natural gas—the mysterious "eternal flames" of Persian, Greek, Egyptian, and Roman temples. Humans have thus used oil and gas for a long time. As Mangone describes:

> In Europe oil seepages, in tar sands and from springs, were surely known and used from the Middle Ages onward, primarily for their adhesive pitch and their alleged medicinal or healing qualities. The intrepid sixteenth century Spanish captains who crossed the Atlantic and reached the Pacific ocean caulked ships with residues of crude oil seeping from the water-edge or sands in Cuba, Texas, California and Peru. The North American Indians used petroleum for paint and medicinal purposes for many tribes were well aware of its combustible qualities when they observed flaming creeks and springs. The drillers of salt wells in the early nineteenth century in New York and Pennsylvania often were annoyed by the black smelly oils, as well as the gas, that often gushed up with the brine.[75]

Nevertheless, man was quite slow to realize the true potential of what would become almost the "ultimate resource." In 1830 a natural oil well spouting some fifty feet was discovered on the banks of the Cumberland River but was stated to be useful "only medicinally, and bottled and exported for that purpose."[76] But by 1847 the Scots chemist James Young obtained lubricating oil from a small petroleum spring in Derbyshire, and in 1854 the Canadian physician and geologist Abraham Gesner had patented a distilling process for coal oil which he called "kerosene."[77] The sudden interest in this "new" product, which appeared to offer possibilities beyond its use as a proprietary medicine, led to the formation in 1854 of a "Rock Oil

Company," which drilled the first oil well near Titusville, Pennsylvania a few years later.[78] By 1860 it had been fully realized that oil—the "fossil fuel"—could be effectively burned for illumination after distillation. The stage was set for the petroleum revolution. Apart from its many other implications, in the shipping world this was a development that ranked with the invention of the sail and the development of the iron steamship.

Of course, oil had a few other uses as well! Soon after 1860, the United States started to export oil with little idea that this new trade would become one of the great features of international commerce. Besides Pennsylvania, oil was found in West Virginia, Ohio, Kentucky, and California. In the latter state, production rose from 12,000 to one million barrels between 1876 and 1895.[79] Texas oil started to be produced in 1890, and by 1901 one Texas well equaled half the entire U.S. production.[80] By 1882 the United States was producing over 80 percent of all the crude oil in the world and exporting two-thirds of its production.[81]

Drilling for oil in other parts of the world was also successful. By the end of the nineteenth century Russia had surpassed U.S. oil production and accounted for almost half the world's production.[82] The first tank ship had sailed in the Caspian Sea oil trade in 1877. The demand for petroleum continued to soar rapidly. First it was for illumination; then for heating; then, of course, for fueling the internal-combustion engine that would completely revolutionize transportation throughout the world on land, on sea, and—ultimately—in the air. The world's appetite for the new "black gold" would soon be insatiable, and more and more uses would be found for the product and its many byproducts.

However, the chief obstacle to the development of the oil trade in this early period was the difficulty of transportation. Neither land nor sea transportation had developed any methods of handling large amounts of liquids in bulk. When oil was first transported by sea, it was shipped in forty-gallon barrels—a dangerous, wasteful, and uneconomical practice.[83] Another development was the five-gallon tin container packed in twos and fours—but this was also an expensive way to move a low-value bulk product. It was the shipping industry that came up with a solution, as it had for every transportation problem in its long history. The answer was the tank ship or tanker—a vessel specifically built to carry bulk liquid cargoes. The first tanker built to carry bulk petroleum was launched in 1886,[84] and by 1911 Lloyd's Register showed some 280 vessels designed to carry bulk oil.[85] A whole new ocean-transportation system had arrived, with all the commensurate problems—technical, legal, commercial—such a system would be expected to have.

In addition to its importance as a new cargo at sea, oil was equally important as a fuel for ships' engines. When the oil-burning steam engine was first developed at the turn of the century, its potential was not really seen. The first oil-burning steamship was in operation in 1902, and before World War I only about one percent of the world's oceangoing fleet used oil as a fuel.[86] By the end of the war, however, this had risen to 15 percent and was increasing rapidly.[87] In addition to new construction, coal burners were quickly being converted for the use of oil. Suddenly the great advantages of oil in marine propulsion seemed clear, and there was an almost frantic change from coal to oil.

There were, of course, many advantages in using the new fuel. For example, using oil permits more cargo to be carried both in weight and space; the steaming radius of the vessel is increased; the vessel can be operated at greater speed and efficiency with lower fuel costs; and time and handling costs for bunkering are greatly reduced. The following may serve as an illustration:

> A 5,000 ton deadweight coal burning ship, 2,000 rated horsepower, steaming at 12 knots per hour [sic] will require approximately 37 days time and 1,060 tons of coal to make a round trip between New York and French Channel ports. This shows that 21% of the ship's deadweight capacity would be required for her fuel. The same ship burning oil could make the trip in 34 days, and requiring only 587 tons of oil, or less than 12% ship's deadweight capacity for fuel. Thus an oil burning ship's cargo capacities increased by 9% or 468 tons per voyage. By storing the oil in double bottoms, which is standard practice, a 5,000 ton deadweight capacity ship can carry 689 tons, or 27% more cargo per trip than a coal burning ship of equal deadweight.[88]

A further important consideration was labor cost, even in these earlier days. Indeed, this factor is said to have been instrumental in persuading many shipping companies to change from coal to oil. From two-thirds to three-quarters of the firemen and coal trimmers were made unnecessary by such a change. For a large passenger vessel such as the *Mauretania,* this reduced the engine-room crew from 300 men to 30.[89] The vessel's 192 coal fires were eliminated, together with a whole generation of firemen and trimmers whose services had become redundant.

*The Establishment of the Major*
*U.S. Oil Companies*

Almost as fast as shipping was switching to oil for its propulsion systems, other industries were put on an oil basis. Although coal would remain an important energy source until well after World War II, oil was a new fuel, which provided the energy source for almost all industrial advancement after World War I. The phenomenal demand for oil was quickly recognized by the great entrepreneurs of the late-nineteenth-century United States, and the great oil companies—the so-called seven sisters—were born.[90] First came John D. Rockefeller, who established a joint-stock company called the Standard Oil Company with a capital of $1 million in 1870.[91] At that time Rockefeller had been in the oil business only seven years and already controlled 10 percent of it. By 1893, with the establishment of the Standard Oil Trust, Rockefeller virtually controlled the U.S. oil industry and was almost untouchable by state and federal governments. By 1885, Standard Oil was well established overseas, absorbing rival after rival.

This was too much for even the liberal free-enterprise spirit of the United States. Standard's autocratic and monopolistic actions had aroused public and political ire—even the Protestant profit-making ethic of the times could not absorb the fact that Standard had made nearly $1 billion in profits in a quarter century.[92] President Theodore Roosevelt made new antitrust laws—aimed specifically at the Standard Oil Trust—more effective, and in 1906 a massive suit was launched against the company. The battle went through the whole U.S. court system, with the U.S. Supreme Court handing down a historic decision in 1911.[93] In his opinion, U.S. Chief Justice White described how the "very genius for commercial development and organization" that had created Standard Oil Trust had also created a monopoly the purpose of which was to drive "others from the field and exclude them from their right to trade."[94] The Court held that Standard Oil had to divest itself of all its subsidiaries within six months. Rockefeller's thirty-year wonder had ended, in future the international oil industry would be oligopolistic rather than monopolistic.

The fascinating history of the international oil industry has only partly been told.[95] It is a very secretive business. Obviously, not even a brief summary is possible here. On the other hand, the industry was to become one of the most central factors in the international law and policy of marine transport, and we must at least look quickly at some of the antecedents of the "seven sisters" which would play such a central role in the energy supply and oil transportation of the future.

The dissolution of Standard Oil was drastic. American antitrust laws had always been quite effective—at least on the surface. Although some of the old component subsidiaries were returned to the original operating state, some thirty-eight companies were still owned and operated by the Rockefeller group.[96] The price of oil actually increased, and shares went up quickly. Anthony Sampson suggests that:

> There were some critics—including the young Walter Lippman—who believed that it would have been more in the public interest to have left the monopoly and controlled it firmly from Washington. The breakup looked like a radical reaffirmation of free enterprise, but it funked the problem of the government's control.[97]

However, of the thirty-eight "survivors," some would soon surpass the original parent company in terms of profits. The oil industry was, after all, rapidly expanding to provide the fuel for world industry and the gasoline for automobiles, airplanes, and war machines. Three of the survivors would become members of the seven sisters. The biggest of these was Standard Oil of New Jersey (Esso/Exxon) which, after the parent's dissolution in 1911 would become (and remain) the biggest oil company in the world.[98] Primarily an oil-trading company, Esso had little oil of its own and was forced to look outside the United States for sources. Its success in this search is, of course, legendary; and it would soon, like an "invisible government," become a major force on the world's political scene.

The second offspring was Standard Oil Company of New York (Socony-Vacuum-Mobil) which was another marketing company with very wide international links. The third member of this triumvirate was the Standard Oil Company of California (Socal). Rockefeller acquired the original company in 1895 for less than $1 million, shortly after the discovery of the Los Angeles oil field had depressed oil prices owing to overproduction. By 1919 this company accounted for over one-quarter of all U.S. oil production. It has always been a producing company, as opposed to Mobil, which is a marketing company.

The most complete breakthrough of the Rockefeller monopoly occurred in Texas before Standard Oil's dissolution. Texas had vigorous antitrust legislation. Quite early it had thrown Standard Oil out of the state when a secret subsidiary was discovered.[99] In 1901 the first of the great Texas oil discoveries took place, financed by the Mellon banking interests, which would become Rockefeller's formidable rivals. The company that was eventually formed was called Gulf after the surrounding Gulf of Mexico. Its success is well known, and it became one of Standard's most serious competitors. The other "independent" U.S. oil company, and the fifth member of the "seven sisters," was the Texas Company (Texaco), founded in 1901 in Texas. By 1904 Texaco was producing nearly 5 percent of all U.S. oil.[100] It was also one of the first truly international oil companies and set up its transportation department at a very early date. In 1908 a Texaco tanker, the *Texas*, was already operating in the trans-Atlantic oil trade.[101] These, then, were the five U.S. oil giants—still household words today. As Anthony Sampson concludes:

> It was a very American industry. Though the companies sold much of their oil abroad, and built up networks of distributors and agents, it was the United States that was the source of nearly all their production. It was not till the First World War that the companies were beginning seriously to look outside America for supplies. But in the meantime there were growing up in Europe two oil companies who had cornered supplies from the other side of the world, who were coming into growing conflict with the Americans.[102].

*The Establishment of the Major*
*International Oil Companies*

The two European oil companies mentioned by Sampson—the last two members of the seven sisters—are, of course, Shell and British Petroleum. We must remember that prior to World War I the British were very much the masters of the whole world, particularly in political and commercial terms. Yet they had somehow missed out on the oil boom, which had been taken over by their brash, rebellious children, the Americans. When the full potential of oil became apparent, the British realized that they were vulnerable because they were far from the oil-producing areas. They knew that they would have to bring the precious liquid to Britain from remote parts of the world. From the very beginning, therefore, the marine transport of oil was an important primary factor for the British rather than the tertiary factor—after production and land transportation—it had been for the United States. Sampson suggests that:

> For the British, oil was a long distance industry which acquired from the beginning an association with national survival and diplomacy, and oil soon seemed part of the Empire itself.[103]

In fact, the beginnings of the Shell Oil Company can be found in an oil-transportation system and not in an oil field. In 1892 a tank ship designed especially for passage through the Suez Canal carried a cargo of oil from Russia to Singapore and points east. The vessel was named *Murex* after a seashell, and the owner was Marcus Samuel, an Englishman. By 1893 the *Conch,* the *Clam,* and other vessels followed despite almost violent opposition from Standard Oil, which saw the new company as a serious rival.[104] Standard Oil's British friends, who had even resorted to opposing Samuel's concepts because he was Jewish, were defeated.[105] Rejecting Standard's offer to buy him out, Samuel formed the Shell Transport and Trading Company in 1897. It was still a family business and would have to withstand severe difficulties before Shell merged in 1906 with another newcomer. This was a Dutch commercial company operating in the East Indies. It was given a royal charter in 1890 and henceforth called itself Royal Dutch. For some sixteen years an intricate battle for the control of markets was fought by Standard, Shell, and Royal Dutch. The loser in the battle was finally Shell, which in 1906 merged with Royal Dutch on a 60-40 basis.[106] By that time Samuel had been knighted, had become Lord Mayor of London, and had also lost interest in his earlier ventures. The "sixth sister" would henceforth be known as Royal Dutch Shell—a giant company with large European markets, Asian oil fields, and the largest tanker fleet in the world.

However, Britain was not satisfied. Despite the British public's belief to the contrary, Shell was now no longer a British company. Despite Dutch neutrality, the Anglo-German rivalry made Shell suspect. As already pointed out, all this came at a time when the British merchant fleet—and also the Royal Navy, to the extent that Admiral Fisher could get his way—were switching to oil fuel. British suspicions and policy were given a clear airing by Winston Churchill, then a young politician and First Lord of the Admiralty, when he made a historic speech in the House of Commons. It was really an attack on Shell, full of innuendoes and more than a little tinged with the anti-Semitism of the time:

> It is their policy—what is the good of blinking at it—to acquire control of the sources and means of supply, and then to regulate the production and the market price . . . we have no quarrel with Shell. We have always found them courteous, considerate, ready to oblige, anxious to serve the Admiralty and promote interests of the British Navy and the British Empire—at a price.[107]

In any case, only three months before the outbreak of World War I, the British government announced that it would purchase a controlling 51-percent interest in the new Anglo-Persia Oil Company, which owned very promising oil fields in the Middle East. This, of course, was also the work of Churchill in his ambition to make Britain less dependent on "foreign" oil interests. With this benevolent and financial government interest, the Anglo-Persia Company grew rapidly. It was a new kind of industrial enterprise, enjoying special British-government protection, which in turn dissuaded it from selling out to foreigners. After changing its name to Anglo-Iranian, it eventually became the British Petroleum Company (BP) and had considerable success in the production, refining, and marketing of its product, which was in abundant supply in the Persian part of the gulf area and which was available to BP on very cheap concessionary terms.[108] BP also became the main supplier of the Royal Navy, establishing a worldwide bunkering service as well as a large tanker fleet.[109]

*Ocean Transportation of Oil: The*
*Commencement of the Age of*
*the Tank Ship*

There were, of course, a few other oil companies; but the seven sisters had all become major powers in the international oil industry by the time of World War I. They would dominate the world's oil industry over the next decades.

They were the forerunners of the modern transnational corporations—integrated completely—controlling not only their oil production but also the refining process, byproducts, transportation, and marketing. As Sampson notes:

> With their own fleet of tankers, they could soon operate across the world in every sector of the industry, from the "upstream" business of drilling and producing at the oil fields, to the "downstream" activity of distributing and selling at pumps or the factories.[110]

World War I added awareness to the world's states of the great importance of oil for survival and led to what has been called "oleaginous diplomacy."[111] The battles on land, at sea, and in the air were fought with tanks, ships, and planes—all hungry for fuel. It was no wonder that the French Premier Clemenceau said: "Oil is as necessary as blood,"[112] or that Marshall Foch said: "We must have oil or we shall lose the war,"[113] or that Britain's Lord Curzon stated that: "The allies floated to victory on a sea of oil."[114] It is true. The Allies had oil supplies and tankers to transport the oil, and they won the war. The Germans had neither, and lost. In retrospect, this shows very clearly the interlinking relationship between industrial enterprise, commercial viability, political consideration, and ocean-transportation policy.

Lord Curzon's expression can be expanded to say that the developed world floated to modern prosperity on a sea of oil. At the same time, the oil was beginning to float on many ships; the era of the tank ship, begun by Samuel before the turn of the century, was now truly ushered in and would have profound influences on all aspects of marine transport. In 1900 there were 109 tankers of over 2,000 tons, totaling just over 0.5 million tons deadweight; by 1911 there were 300 tankers; by 1914 the tanker tonnage stood at over 1.5 million tons. By the end of World War I in 1919, there were 467 tankers totaling over 3.5 million tons; this would increase to 1,571 vessels totaling over 16.5 million tons by 1939.[115] Thus in less than four decades a completely new marine-transport system had not only been established but had, in actual tonnage, added over one-third of the total 1914 world tonnage to the world fleet.

The changeover from coal to oil would continue on land and on sea, and as a result world demand for oil would increase rapidly. For example, between 1920 and 1969 world use of oil increased from 200 million tons to 2 billion tons.[116] This demand would increase at the steep rate of 5 percent per year, and over half of all the oil had to be moved by sea.[117] The tanker had become very much part of the world's marine-transport systems, and we will return to its development later. We must now, however, continue our examination of world shipping at the close of World War I.

## World Shipping in the Interwar Years

It has been calculated that the shipbuilding capacity of the world's shipyards multiplied by about 2.5 times because of World War I.[118] This extra capacity continued for some time after the war. After all, the war had impressed on governments the importance of sufficient shipping. In many countries, particularly the United States, Australia, Canada, and Japan, which had established heavy government involvement in the industry during the war, the war-measures shipping boom was perpetuated. At the very least, shipowners received every possible encouragement, ranging from public opinion to actual government assistance, not only to replace their losses but also to increase their fleets.[119] A very short-lived postwar boom in freight rates in 1919-1920 further stimulated construction. In addition, under the harsh terms of the Versailles Peace Treaty, most of the remaining German tonnage was transferred to Allied flags; thus the German companies were forced to rebuild their depleted fleets quickly.

Yet no one foresaw the predictable economic results—a pattern from which the shipping industry has often suffered. By mid-1920, oceangoing tonnage had increased by 15 percent while the volume of trade had greatly diminished owing to the severe economic dislocations caused by the war.[120] The obvious result was the worst slump in the history of shipping, which was to last for well over a decade before the world was sufficiently recovered from one world war to prepare for another.[121] Strange as it may seem, the great shipping depression occurred at a time when the shipping policies of the various nation-states were more apparent than ever. How could this happen? To provide at least a partial answer, we must look at what had happened to the shipping policies of the major maritime states since we last considered this aspect.

Hindsight shows, of course, that this period not only shaped much of the shipping policy of the maritime states but also provided the important infrastructural climate in which marine transport would operate to this day. In other words, despite the forthcoming destruction of shipping in World War II, decisions made at this time shaped the "maritime aspect" and interests of these states, in which there would be relatively few changes in the next half decade. We would go on to suggest that an understanding of what Third-World states today consider the undesirable effects of international marine transport cannot be complete without a thorough analysis of this particular period in world shipping. Economic analysis and commercial statistics—so often put forward as proof of these undesirable inequities by organizations such as the UNCTAD Shipping Division—are not enough. They are, obviously, the end results of certain policies that simply cannot be seen in their true perspective without a look at their antecedents. Surprisingly, this is seldom if ever done.

It is even more of an anomaly if one considers the fact that most Third-World states are fully aware of all or most of the political-commercial aspects of their colonial history, which often has been the very raison d'être for freedom and independence. However, ocean transportation has never received this searching examination and remains largely an international infrastructure composed of invisibles and tip-of-the-iceberg end results.[122] Although we are not certain whether the full story can, at this stage, even be written, if and when it is told it will be a major contribution to the scanty literature on the subject.[123] As already stated, we cannot even attempt a cursory analysis here and will confine ourselves simply to a brief examination of what was happening to ocean transportation in the major maritime states between the two wars.

*Great Britain: Still the Leader*

Great Britain was still the uncontested leader despite the appalling destruction of its merchant fleet in World War I. A summary of British shipping policy in 1918 was given earlier; despite the stress of the great shipping slump, British shipping interests did not advocate any changes in this policy until the late 1930s.[124] It is probably fair to say that British shipping bore relatively little responsibility for the shipping-slump difficulties. Between 1914 and 1931, British tonnage increased by only 3 million tons, accounted for mainly by the growth of the British tanker fleet.[125] On the other hand, British shipping during the same period decreased from just over 45 percent of the world total to just under 34 percent.

One might say, somewhat cynically, that if the other maritime states had kept their shipping as it was in 1914 and had allowed Britain to remain the world's leading maritime state, then there would have been no shipping slump. However, other states rapidly expanded their shipping for a variety of reasons, and the British fleet was not spared the ill effects of "overtonnaging." The British Chamber of Shipping appointed a Committee on Shipping Policies in 1932 to look into the matter.[126] Not surprisingly, the resultant report set out the standard free-enterprise principles of British shipping and called for the "restoration and development of a prosperous world trade, cooperation and the removal of trade barriers, and fair access to an open freight market"—displaying a remarkable naiveté as well as trust in a system that, although it had served the British well, had done so only when it was basically under their control.[127]

However, the report also recognized some of the root causes of the slump by attributing the "appalling conditions of the industry mainly to the direct and indirect action of governments both in bringing ships into existence for political and not for commercial reasons, and in keeping them running at a heavy loss at the expense of the taxpayers."[128] "State aided ships were like dumped goods," the report thundered, "and had no place in trade''; they were "a standing menace to the freight market and hampered the working of all ships operating on an economic basis.''[129] These last words really sum up the British point of view, which was then as now shared by a number of other traditional maritime states. Marine transport had, in other words, become not only a vital part of the general commercial system but also one that, like all other sectors of that system, had to pay its own way. It was almost inconceivable to the British that this was not necessarily a view to which all must be converted, or that economic and political considerations were, after one of the most disastrous wars in history, not necessarily compatible. At the rather unsuccessful 1933 World Monetary and Economic Conference, Britain presented its type of policy by demanding an agreement as follows:

> 1. That State subsidies to aid the construction of shipping for, or its maintenance on, competitive routes are uneconomic; that such subsidies can only lead to the granting of similar subsidies by other countries and to protective measures in respect of shipping, which would deprive world trade of the economic and efficient sea transport it has so far enjoyed; and that they will disorganize a broad freight market, increase the burdens on national budgets, and lessen the power of maritime countries to pay in services for imports and loans.
>
> 2. In these circumstances the countries concerned should move as rapidly as possible towards diminuation and ultimate abolition of state assistance to shipbuilding and ship operation on competitive routes.[130]

At the same time, the British steadfastly rejected any outright retaliatory methods of keeping the state-subsidized shipping menace of other states at bay, despite the fact that British shipowners demanded the use of such methods.[131] It was rightly felt that such actions not only were crude but also would expose British shipping—which was vulnerable in many international trades—to retaliatory disadvantages. Furthermore, Britain still had such international commercial control of the shipping infrastructure that it could exercise "invisible retaliation" quite effectively.

Specifically, British shipping policy was opposed to subsidies because:

> 1. the cost to the Treasury would be very great (perhaps £20 to 30 millions a year for subsidies on the scale of those of competitors);
>
> 2. they would tend to foster inefficiency;
>
> 3. they might lead to a competitive race in subsidies;
>
> 4. by creating more unwanted tonnage they would leave the last state of the shipping industry worse than the first;
>
> 5. they would encourage Government interference in the conduct of shipping; and

6. they would tend to give an unfair advantage to British shipping in receipt of assistance over other British shipping forced to rely on its own resources.[132]

There is, however, ample evidence that British shipping subsidies did exist but took the form of mail contracts, marine-insurance writeoffs, merger securities, and building assistance, particularly under the Trade Facilities Act.[133] More open subsidies and assistance were facilitated by the passage of the British Shipping (Assistance) Act of 1935, which allowed direct help to tanker shipping, which had been most adversely affected by the slump.[134] This act was extended effectively until the beginning of World War II and provided, in addition to direct subsidy, advances to assist in scrapping, construction, and modernization as well as generous loans, grants, guarantees, indemnities, and so on.

Almost on the eve of World War II, the British Shipping (Assistance) Bill, drafted in 1939, sought to provide—apart from further subsidy provisions—the power for the Board of Trade to purchase, maintain, and repair ships for the purpose of creating a reserve of shipping.[135] The outbreak of the war interrupted any further efforts in this area. Such efforts would have resulted in an almost complete reversal of British shipping policy, which had consistently opposed any and all direct government involvement in shipping. It can be said, therefore, that the basic British shipping policy—consisting of efforts to maintain a satisfactory international political milieu in which British shipping could continue its dominant position with complete commercial independence—was, with a few exceptions (or lapses), continued until World War II. Before the outbreak of the war, therefore, Great Britain was still the uncontested leader in the world shipping fleet, with a tonnage of just under 18 million gross tons, making up just over 27 percent of the world fleet.[136]

## United States: Free Enterprise and Protectionism

The situation in the United States was very different. There maritime commerce was built up in a strangely paradoxical fashion, which pitted the most free of free-enterprise systems against fairly frequent direct government involvement.[137] We have already discussed the part of U.S. history that had turned the country away from maritime interests in favor of continental development. American unpreparedness in shipping, owing to World War I, had almost a shock effect on U.S. shipping policy, from which the country has probably never quite recovered. We have also spoken of the resultant remedial action of the U.S. Shipping Act of 1916, the subsequent creation of the U.S. Shipping Board, and the tremendous buildup of the U.S.

merchant fleet—much of it government owned and controlled—by the end of World War I.

It is probably true that U.S. shipping has never "paid its way" independently since that time. This statement implies no position on government involvement in shipping. We are simply stating the fact that since World War I the U.S. shipping industry has been unable to compete in international marine transport without U.S.-government help.[138] Although it is often suggested that this reflects poorly on U.S. shipping operations, we would point out that it is a reflection of higher U.S. shipping costs which are themselves largely a reflection of the superior U.S. standard of living.[139] What we are saying here must be seen in that context and that context alone.

We have already referred to the well-known Jones Act of 1920, which established U.S. shipping policy firmly at a time when the demand for shipping throughout the world was falling off drastically.[140] The act continued the existence of the U.S. Shipping Board and transferred to it all government-owned vessels, which were to be sold to private American interests.[141] Furthermore, the board was given wide regulatory powers, such as the power to determine the number of steamship lines to be established, the types of vessels to be used, and the frequency of sailings from U.S. ports. Vessels could be sold only to U.S. citizens who agreed to abide by the board's regulations. If no buyer was found, the board would operate the vessel itself. A maximum annual amount of $25 million was set aside to aid construction of commercial vessels in the United States. Any vessels chartered or transferred to foreigners would have to be maintained under the board's full control. Further controls were exercised by the board over unfair conference practices, many of which were prohibited outright.[142] The board also had the power to impose restrictive practices, such as preferential rules for the use of U.S. vessels and discriminatory tonnage dues for foreign vessels; but these measures were seldom put into practice, mainly because of their political, as well as commercial, implications.[143]

Nevertheless, by 1926 the U.S. Shipping Board had to report to the U.S. Senate that unless substantial further direct and indirect federal aid were forthcoming, a privately owned and operated American merchant fleet could not be realized.[144] The crux of the difficulty lay in operating and construction costs. For example, it was stated that for ships of equal size, each with a crew of thirty-six, the comparative monthly crew costs were $3,270 for the United States, $1,308 for Great Britain, and $777 for Japan.[145]

The result was a new U.S. Merchant Marine Act in 1928, which authorized substantial loans to empower the U.S. Shipping Board to assist in the construction of new ships as well as in the modernization of existing vessels.[146] There were further restrictions relating to the carrying of U.S. mails and to manning of U.S. vessels, but the act unquestionably was a shot in the arm for the U.S. shipbuilding industry.[147]

All this, of course, came at the height of the world shipping slump when ships of all nations were lying idle. However, U.S. shipping policy appeared to enjoy full public support despite its heavy costs. The board had sold many vessels at very low prices, often at only a fraction of construction cost; it had also lost heavily in operating its own fleet, all the time advancing large sums to the shipbuilding industry.[148] The board rarely lost less than $6 million a year in its ship operations and, in 1924, lost $41 million.[149] However, by 1931 loans amounting to $145 million had been approved; and new constructions and improvement totaling $312 million had been authorized.[150] These costs of maintaining a U.S. merchant fleet were, therefore, extraordinarily high; few countries other than the United States could have absorbed such losses.

That, at least, is the orthodox and often-quoted view. Even economists frequently overlook the "invisible" benefits from this heavy U.S. investment. For example, between 1914 and 1927 the increase of U.S. vessels in the Far Eastern trade from 5 to 140 led to an increase in trade from $380 million to $1.8 billion.[151] When world wheat prices appeared on the brink of collapse in 1924, the U.S. Shipping Board was quickly able to dispose of the U.S. wheat surplus, saving U.S. agriculture some $1 billion.[152] During another emergency, the British coal strike, U.S. commercial losses amounting to over $200 million were averted by the availability of U.S. shipping.[153] In more straightforward commercial terms, however, the U.S. Shipping Board had reduced freight rates to U.S. shippers by some $2 billion by 1933 and had earned $3 billion "which would otherwise have been paid to foreign carriers."[154]

Economists would certainly view our "marriage" of direct U.S. Shipping Board losses and indirect benefits with some alarm, but the intention here is not to do violence to shipping economics. We are simply stating the policy as it was presented to the U.S. Congress during the 1930s when these important provisions were made. There is absolutely no doubt that U.S. shipping policy of this period reflected the general attitude of the country as a whole. As General Mance suggests:

> The man in the street in America accepted the argument which had been advanced by so many countries besides his own on the credit side of the mercantile marine and, in accordance with the prevailing spirit of economic nationalism, added that as foreign Powers were building "uneconomical" ships why should the first Power in the world, moreover possessed with the largest resources, stand tamely aside?[155]

On the other hand, when the actual costs, losses and inefficiencies of the U.S. Shipping Board were examined in purely commercial terms, rather than against the background of the overall benefits, it became clear that there were problems. In 1935 President Franklin D. Roosevelt, in a message to

Congress, recognized this and stated that in future all subsidies should be
called by their right name—that is, the basic difference between American
and foreign shipping costs, consisting of building and operating expenses.[156]
He saw that the shipbuilding-loans program had been unsuccessful and that
mail contracts were inflating mail-freight costs by up to 900 percent, but he
went on to say that:

> The American people want to use American ships; their Government owes
> it to them to make certain that such ships are in keeping with our national
> pride and national needs.[157]

However, national pride was suffering from the Great Depression, and
national needs were at that time severely reduced. Few benefits but much inefficiency, loss, and unjustifiable profit making could be shown. The new
president and his "New Deal" Democratic Congress were intent on re-
examining U.S. maritime policy as a whole. By 1933, the Shipping Board,
which had been an independent entity since its formulation in 1916, was
reduced in size and had become a section in the U.S. Commerce Department.[158] An investigation by a select committee of Congress also revealed
considerable waste and inefficiency in the privately owned merchant fleet
under government subsidies.[159] The final result was the famous U.S. Merchant Marine Act of 1936, which after many drafts, some fifteen models,
numerous compromises, and stormy debates in both houses, was finally
passed into law by presidential approval on June 29, 1936.[160] The
significance of this new act is adequately summarized by Professor
Mangone:

> The Act started from the old premise that the United States had to main-
> tain an "adequate" merchant marine for carrying a substantial part of
> American trade over essential routes and be convertible to national defense
> needs in time of emergency. To achieve that objective, the Act provided for
> "parity" between U.S. and foreign trade lines through direct public con-
> struction and operating subsidies to compensate the American shipping in-
> dustry for its higher costs of materials and manpower. Moreover, the old
> construction loan and revolving fund was continued at a 3.5 percent in-
> terest rate on all new loans. In a period of massive unemployment Congress
> also made every effort to protect the jobs of American seamen by severely
> limiting the number of aliens that could be employed on U.S. flag vessels
> and by regulating the hours, the conditions of work, and the minimum
> wages of the crews. It also legislated the practice that all American exports
> financed in whole or part by any instrumentality of the government should
> be carried by U.S. flag vessels. Finally, as a national defense measure,
> special compensation went to shipbuilders incorporating Navy-recommended
> design features on any subsidized vessel while—in the case of emergency—
> all vessels constructed with subsidy aid were subject to repurchase by the
> United States at cost less depreciation.[161]

There is no doubt that the 1936 act was the first comprehensive formulation of U.S. shipping policy and perhaps the first maritime-policy formulation anywhere. In the United States the act reworked and improved subsidy programs and became a model for all later shipping legislation. The act also dissolved the U.S. Shipping Board after two decades of controversial existence and created instead the five-member U.S. Maritime Commission, which under the chairmanship of Joseph P. Kennedy commenced work in 1937, its aims being to

> . . . study, perfect and adopt a long range program of replacement and additions to the American merchant marine so as to create an adequate and well-balanced merchant fleet, including vessels of all types, to provide shipping services on all routes essential for maintaining the flow of foreign commerce to the United States, the vessels in such fleet to be so designed as to be readily and quickly convertible into transport and supply vessels in a time of national emergency.[162]

Kennedy, who chaired the new commission for only one year before moving on to become U.S. Ambassador to the Court of St. James, made his mark on U.S. shipping when his commission produced the *Economic Survey of the American Merchant Marine* in 1937.[163] This is certainly one of the most important documents in American ocean-transportation history and might well be required reading today for all who have difficulty in reconciling the visible and invisible economic aspects of ocean shipping. On the one hand, the report clearly enunciates the relationship between ocean transportation and the state, recognizing that shipping in the United States is not a commercial enterprise in the orthodox sense of the word, but *an instrument of national policy maintained at a large cost to serve the total needs of commerce and defense.*[164] In order to survive, U.S. shipping thus requires substantial government support, which in turn requires a certain amount of government control with some measure of inflexibility, curtailment of investments, and continuing subsidy needs as a result.[165] On the other hand, the commission also recognized the considerable increase in American foreign trade since World War I as being a direct effect of the expansion of the U.S. shipping industry. This resulted in large part from the establishment of regular U.S. shipping lines on routes that before the war had depended on foreign shipping and indirect transshipment services.

Thus the commission promulgated, at this early stage, the lesson which almost half a century later most states still have not learned: that there can be a reconciliation between the visible costs and the invisible effects of shipping, provided that the beneficiary is willing to pay the costs. In other words—not shipping at any price for shipping's sake, but shipping at any price if the benefits are worth it. To us, this appears to be the real crux of the debate about whether to support the shipping industry or not, rather than the many well-worn polemical chestnuts that are constantly resurrected in the continuing argument in this important area. For the post-World War I United States, the commercial prosperity of the nation found a direct contributor in its shipping industry, but the U.S. people had to pay for this contribution out of the large benefits they were receiving. The trouble had been that much of the U.S. policy had been half-hearted and thus less than fully realized.

The commission found, for example, that the U.S. merchant fleet was basically obsolescent—that the defense needs of the country alone dictated almost complete replacement at the rate of 260 vessels of 1.5 million tons per year by 1942, at a total cost of $2.5 billion.[166] It was further found that subsidized U.S. shipping (excepting tankers) carried only just under 17 percent of U.S. foreign trade. About 13 percent was carried in unsubsidized U.S. vessels, but the remaining 70 percent was still being carried in foreign vessels. If tankers were included in the statistics, just over 35 percent of all U.S. foreign trade was carried on U.S. vessels.[167] The report does not address itself, except by implication, to the silent question of what would have happened to U.S. commercial prosperity if the subsidized U.S. fleet had been more efficiently operated or had been larger. The commission recommended the expansion of operating subsidies at an annual cost of $15-$20 million and building subsidies at an annual cost of $10 million.[168] The resulting bill to amend the 1936 act was approved by the president in 1938.[169] The new act also made provisions for a mortgage fund of $200 million for a massive shipbuilding program, which had barely gotten under way when World War II broke out. At that time, the United States stood firmly in second place with a fleet of just under 9 million gross tons, making up about 14 percent of the world's fleet.[170]

*France, Greece, and Norway: Subsidies*
*and Free Enterprise*

Before moving on, we must look at some other maritime states and their marine policies and developments during this period. France, as we have seen, had never been reticent in providing assistance to its shipping industry, which had rarely been "profitable" in any real sense. The destruction of World War I had resulted in a large new-building program, and the French fleet (vessels over 2,000 tons) had increased by 109 percent by 1931.[171] The fleet was hard hit by the slump and world-trade depression; and the French government became more and more involved in the operation of French shipping, particularly in the buildup of a large subsidized tanker fleet for reasons of national defense. In 1935 a further marine-reconstruction program was approved by the government when it was found that the French commercial fleet was not only old and slow but also completely uneconomic and uncompetitive.[172]

French shipping companies, in particular the "big three"—the Compagnie Générale Transatlantique, the Chargeurs Réunis, and the Messageries Maritimes—were linked by a highly specialized agency that basically operated all French shipping.[173] Subsidies were quite high, ranging from 45 million francs in 1923-1924 to 1 billion francs in 1929; they covered construction, operating, and mortgage-fund costs.[174] However, French shipping continued to have many problems, particularly on the highly competitive trade routes; and the difficulties of the slump years were not really overcome. From fifth place in the world fleet in 1914, France fell to sixth place by 1933 and to eighth place by 1939.[175] The highly centralized French policy system simply could not operate properly, owing to the continuous political and financial difficulties during this period.[176]

Greece, a country that from the dawn of history had never been out of shipping, was steadily building up its modern shipping capacity during this period. Although Greece has no colonies or protectorates and thus little need for communication by sea with areas remote from Greece, the physical geography of the country has not only favored ocean transportation but has always forced a large number of Greeks to seek their livelihood from the sea. Some 46 percent of the Greek fleet was lost in World War I, and consequently the fleet expanded between 1914 and 1931 by almost 100 percent.[177] By 1939 Greece occupied a respectable ninth place on the world shipping ladder, with a fleet of about 1.8 million tons.[178] There was no government support for Greek shipowners who operated generally older tonnage as cheaply as possible under individual or family ownership. The Greek system was thus in almost complete contrast to the U.S. or French systems; it was characterized by complete entrepreneurial free enterprise dating back to the very early traders of the Mediterranean.

Another free-enterprise shipping state was Norway, which was in fourth place in the world fleet after 1914 but had doubled its fleet between the two wars.[179] Since Viking days shipping has been a vital element in the progress of the Norwegian nation, and no other country has anywhere near Norway's ratio of shipping tonnage to population.[180] The growth of Norwegian shipping has been "fairly earned as a result of enterprise."[181] Apart from some very modest construction subsidies, the government gave little direction to the industry.[182] As a true cross-trading state, Norway recognized quite early that it could not afford to enter any subsidy war and that it was to the advantage of Norwegian owners to have their ships built in foreign shipyards, which gave them beneficial loans and subsidies to do so.[183] As a result, the Norwegian fleet was built up rapidly and efficiently—but only as long as it could make money. In a shipping slump, the fjords of Norway would be filled with idle ships awaiting better days.

*Germany, Italy, and Japan: Shipping*
*in the Service of Nationalism*

Three other maritime powers require a brief consideration, not least because they would compose the Axis side in World War II. Germany, having "lost" World War I had lost not only the war but also the greater portion of its fleet, either in the war at sea or by confiscation during and after the war.[184] One part of the shortsighted Versailles settlement had handed over most of what was left of German shipping to the Allies. However, German shipping bounced back from that setback with incredible vigor. The German government quickly committed itself to replacing one-third of the surrendered German tonnage with a provision of 12 billion marks, later increased to 18 billion.[185] By 1925 the government had set up a loan fund of 50 million marks for new construction. This was exhausted in 1925 but was regularly reconstituted until 1934.[186] By then Germany had once again crept up to fifth place on the world shipping ladder, with just under 4 million gross tons.[187]

The NSDAP (Nazi party) under the leadership of Adolf Hitler had also come into power in 1933. The new Nazi government had as one of its platforms proposed measures to rescue the German shipping industry from its extreme difficulties resulting from the trade depression, which had exacerbated the problems faced in the postwar period. Immediate direct- and indirect-subsidy systems were put in place, and finally the entire industry was incorporated into the state-controlled and highly complex economic system. This system divided all German trade and industry into thirteen separate sections.[188] Shipping would become section XII—"Transport and Communications." Various subgroupings within section XII covered the interests and control of shipowners, brokers, pilots, port services, legal questions, and so on. The main administrative part of section XII was known as the "*Spitzenvertretung der deutschen Schiffahrt*," the main duty of which was to maintain a liaison between German shipping and other transport systems.[189] Although the various shipping companies were allowed considerable decentralized freedom in their business practices, they were very much part of an overall German shipping policy, which in turn was very closely linked with the general political policy of the expansionist Nazi government, which controlled all aspects of German enterprise. It thus became the most highly centralized state-controlled shipping system outside the Soviet Union. As General Mance sums up:

> . . . Ships and shippers alike came within the scope of exchange control regulations; subsidies were granted for shipbuilding and ship operation, partly to relieve unemployment, partly to form a tanker fleet; and a general expansion of the commercial fleet was undertaken for the benefit of German foreign trade. Currency manipulation made it possible to build ships for foreign account at a time when German shipyards were complaining of the powerful competitive effect of devalued currencies abroad.[190]

Thus by 1939 Germany had a fleet of just under 4.5 million tons but had maintained its fifth place in the world fleet.[191] It is worth noting that at the outbreak of World War I, Germany was in second place, but with a fleet of only 1 million tons more than in 1939.

Italy, which had been on the Allied side in World War I moved in the opposite political direction between the wars. Its shipping industry, like that of Germany, had become an arm of the expansionist policies of the fascist government under Benito Mussolini. For Italians, shipping subsidies were not novel, as the country depended to a great extent on a flourishing marine-transport system. The government quickly laid down two basic principles for Italian shipping and the commensurate state interests. First, the state was obligated to produce a marine-transport system for its citizens; and second, the state must have the power to require its citizens to discharge its obligations.[192]

Between 1931 and 1932 the Italian government put these principles into practice, not only by providing subsidies and loans to shipping but also by implementing a scheme of rationalization for the whole Italian fleet. This involved an interesting linkage between fascist autocracy and corporate capitalism that was probably unique in the history of world shipping. Mance describes it as follows:

> Four main groups were formed as joint-stock companies to handle shipping in different parts of the world: the Atlantic and South America; the Levant, the Black Sea, Egypt, India, the Far East; the Mediterranean and East Africa; the Adriatic and the Dodecanese. Sixty per cent of the capital of these companies was to be held by Italian subjects or recognized Italian bodies. An Institute for Industrial Reconstruction was formed at the same time to promote the formation of the four joint stock companies referred to above, in each of which the Institute was to hold the majority of the shares and nominate the majority of the directors. The Institute itself was authorized to subscribe to the share capital of a new joint stock company called Società Finanziaria Marittima (Finmare), whose object would be to take up shares in the four operating companies; to attend to their technical co-operation and to give them the necessary financial assistance. The Institute could transfer to this company its shareholding in the operating company. The Institute was empowered to issue, within certain limits, bonds guaranteed by the State as to both capital and interest.[193]

Although Italy had maintained its seventh place in the world fleet between 1914 and 1931, the actual tonnage increase had been an astounding 136 percent. By 1939 Italy had moved up to sixth place with a fleet of just under 3.5 million tons.[194]

Another maritime state that would be changing sides in the forthcoming conflagration was Japan—newly but quickly emerging from self-imposed isolation. As already noted, the importance of shipping for Japan was seen as early as 1868; but serious attempts to rationalize Japanese shipping as an industry were not made until 1936.[195] There had been a certain amount of government assistance and subsidy to shipbuilding and ship operation between 1894 and the slump, but World War I had caused severe depression and much disturbance in the Japanese shipping industry.

The new, expansionist political policies of Japan in the early 1930s resulted in commensurate shipping expansionism and eventual centralization. Although in 1932 Japan had a very high proportion of old ships in its fleet, new government policy directed at modernization and the rapid expansion of shipbuilding facilities resulted in a remarkable growth of the fleet. By 1933 it occupied third place in the world with over 4 million tons, an increase of 153 percent since 1914.[196] By 1939 the fleet was still in third place with a tonnage of over 4.5 million tons.[197]

Such an achievement, which was in reality only a sign of things to come in the post-World War II period, had a variety of causes. First was the achievement orientation of the Japanese. During this period, this mentality was also closely linked to the nationalistic-expansionist superiority complex fostered by the military leadership of the Empire of Japan.[198] But there were also more tangible factors such as skilled and efficient, but low-cost, labor; highly rationalized production and able management; benevolent, paternalistic state direction; and, last but not least, the very close cooperation between the Japanese shipping industry and the great industrialist, merchant, and financial interests of the country. Credit facilities were easily available, yet strictly controlled, and operated by special banks of a semi-official nature.[199] All this took place against the background of a new political awareness that Japan was not only destined, but had a right, to be a major power in the world and the dominant power in the Pacific arena. Japan would indeed realize its destiny, but the lessons of a further global war would first have to be learned.

## Conclusions: The Eve of World War II

Thus, on the eve of a new holocaust, international shipping had recovered somewhat from the Great Depression as well as from the shipping slump, which had many causes but was not helped by the overexpansion of nationalist-inspired shipping in the post-World War I years. In retrospect, it seems obvious that Great Britain had too many ships and had dominated world shipping for too long, and that the other states wanted a larger slice of what had been mistakenly seen as a very fruitful business but was in fact a fragile economic system. Expansionism of non-British shipping without a reduction of British shipping led to the great slump. Contributing to the difficulty was, the new nationalist spirit, which inspired shipping involvement, ownership, and operation by the governments of many states, particularly the United States and British Empire members such as Australia and Canada.[200] As a result, by 1933 between 12 and 13 million tons of shipping lay idle and a large amount of the remaining tonnage was being operated at a loss.[201] The proportion of laid-up tonnage in relation to known tonnage is best illustrated in table 5-3.

On the other hand, between 1914 and 1933 national fleets had increased enormously, ranging from a 13 percent increase for Great Britain to a 415 percent increase for the United States.[202] As usual, shipping survived. From a 1914 total tonnage of just under 50 million tons, the world fleet had increased to almost 68 million tons by 1933 at the height of the slump.[203] By 1939 it had leveled off to just over 65.5 million tons.[204]

For the world shipping industry, however, this had been a tumultuous period. Not only had it faced one of the most destructive wars in history, followed by an extensive period of commercial depression, but it was also now exposed to a whole variety of new socioeconomic-political processes in a very nationalistic world of nation-states. Heavy government involvement in marine transport, resulting from national marine policies that saw a national fleet as a natural extension of political policy and ambitions, had become the rule rather than the exception. Whether in the form of actual state ownership and/or operation, or of direct and indirect subsidy payments, such government involvement ended the great commercial era which had lasted well over a century. The lone voices raised in opposition to the trend, such as those of Great Britain and, to a lesser extent, Greece and Norway, appeared to be almost out of step with reality.

Marine transport as a commercially viable enterprise was now only one side of the coin. The *indirect* benefits of shipping, as reflected in the various marine policies, were now of much greater relevance. It was seen that if

**Table 5-3**
**Proportion of Laid-Up Tonnage in Relation to Known Tonnage in 1933**

| Country | Percentage |
|---|---|
| United States | 30 |
| France | 29 |
| Netherlands | 26 |
| Germany | 22 |
| Italy | 19 |
| Norway | 17 |
| United Kingdom | 16 |
| Japan | 5 |

Source: Sir Osborne Mance, *International Sea Transport* (London: Oxford University Press for Royal Institute of International Affairs, 1945), p. 66. Official source not cited. Reprinted with permission.

these indirect benefits were sufficient, then marine transport—as a system—could even operate at a loss. The profit motive was not an important consideration.

This was not a new development—newly realized, but not new. The Roman Empire at the height of its power would have found it strange to be questioned about the profitability of its merchant ships. They were simply a *part* of the greatness that was Rome—a part that made the contribution it could. However, the diversified interests of the United States of the 1920s and 1930s were unable, perhaps even unwilling, to see U.S. shipping policy in quite that way. Had they done so, the industry might have faced fewer difficulties; but this was probably impossible at the time. Only the Germans, the Italians, and to some extent the Japanese clarified their ocean-transportation policies along these lines. Unfortunately, the ultimate political aims of these states would lead to disaster, destroying not only their policies and their fleets, but also, inevitably, the countries themselves.

## International Maritime Law
## in an Unstable Era

We have paid little attention to the developments in maritime law during this period, and this is entirely intentional. As often happens during periods of international turmoil, war, and other difficulty, international law is relegated almost to a secondary level. This may be an unfortunate commentary on the human condition, but it is nevertheless accurate.[205] For example, during the comparatively short period of the "war to end all wars"—1914-1918—most international law virtually ceased to exist.[206] This was true despite the considerable buildup of international law, both public and private, since the turn of the century. Rampant nationalism, no matter what form it took, had little need for legal rules and humanitarian niceties. Yet there was further development and some progress in both aspects of maritime law, especially during the difficult 1930s. On the other hand, particularly in the area of public maritime law, this period spawned some of the difficulties still faced by the law of the sea even today.

We have already analyzed the separation of the traditional functional commercial transportation system from the political-purpose policy of marine transport during this period. However, in the law of the sea—the public maritime law—an even more important separation also became discernible at this time. This was the separation of the traditional function of shipping from the *use of marine space* in legal terms. This division probably goes back to the Napoleonic wars and the nationalistic era of the late nineteenth century, but it became most dominant during the period under discussion here.

In other words, despite their operation in a total marine system—of which they are an integral part—ships would now be governed by a variety of legal provisions frequently at variance with each other. For example, a ship on a commercial ocean voyage might be governed by certain laws relating to that commercial activity, either in the form of public municipal laws promulgated by nation-states, or of private laws in the form of international shipping conventions formulated by the CMI and legislated by the state of the vessel's flag. Paradoxically, however, the actual passage of a vessel through areas such as the territorial sea would now be determined by a superimposed set of public maritime laws that might well completely disregard the traditional functional purpose of the ship in favor of the virtually theoretical principle of state sovereignty in the form of extended coastal-state jurisdiction.[207]

There is little doubt that the future of the law of the sea, from this period on, would depend on the interplay between these opposing aspects, which would henceforth reduce shipping to one of the many *uses* of the sea. The "favored-son" position that shipping had occupied for centuries would be lost forever. Of course, none of this was seen by those whose interests lay in the area—and how could it have been? As already suggested several times, the two "interest groups"—a loose term, but acceptable here—were now separated from each other on two parallel courses that would never meet. Spokesmen for the "favored son," such as the CMI, would tend to look inward at the shipping system in their new search for uniformity, which was basically intended to make the business of shipping easier internationally. They could not see that their protégé's status was being whittled away steadily in an ever-increasing array of competitive interests. Or could they have? Perhaps, when we finally have a definitive history of the CMI we may be closer to an answer.

In any case, on the public side, maritime law was now truly a constituent part of the legal science known as public international law, which would occupy future generations of a new breed of international lawyer with fascinating new theories, doctrines, and analyses as well as new international legal tribunals and cases.[208] It was a science founded, or course, by Hugo Grotius; nurtured and developed in the intervening centuries; and distinguished, above all, by an abiding faith in the principle that international law would lead to international peace.[209] Despite its scars and cracks, it was a principle of such nobility that it has survived as a sign of human strength in adversity. Adversity was certainly the starting point for the public law of the sea during this period.

After the end of World War I, the leaders of a shattered world met in Paris in 1919 for a peace conference that was to lay the groundwork for continuing peace.[210] The horrors of the war were still vividly in the minds of the seventy delegates representing some twenty-seven victorious powers.

The terms of reference were the 10 million dead and 20 million wounded of the Great War, and the total direct cost of the conflagration, which had been figured at over $180 billion with added indirect costs of over $150 billion.[211]

Yet the peace conference itself appeared to lay the groundwork for the next conflagration, a mere two decades away. Instead of the modest and moderate peace that experienced statesmen such as President Woodrow Wilson and Prime Minister Lloyd George privately wanted to make, election promises and secret alliances resulted instead in revenge on, and humiliation for, the vanquished, with inherent dire results for the rest of the world. Germany and Russia were fomenting in revolution—one being drawn to the far right on the political scale, the other exchanging czarist feudalism for Bolshevist egalitarianism.

Nevertheless, the peace conference formulated plans for a League of Nations, which came into being in 1920.[212] The league was to devote itself to disarmament, labor legislation, health, international cooperation, and administration. Its activities began early in 1920 after the ratification of the disastrous Treaty of Versailles.[213] From the beginning, the league's work was hampered by the absence of the United States, which refused to join for reasons that will not be examined here.[214] The absence of the United States deprived the league not only of fresh "non-European" ideas but also of a moderating factor. The symptoms of weakness that soon set in were further accentuated by the economic crisis of the 1930s and by the open defiance of league covenants, such as the Japanese invasion of Manchuria in 1931 and the Italian invasion of Abyssinia (Ethiopia).[215] The efforts of the league finally received their death knell with the outbreak of World War II. Nevertheless, this brief summary probably does violence to a great idea in an unwilling world. Nussbaum summarizes the league's functions as follows:

> The political functions of the League were dual. On the one hand it was entrusted with specific duties relative to the execution of the peace treaties; on the other hand the League was dedicated—in the words of the covenant—to the achievement of "international peace and security". This meant in the first place the maintenance of status quo as set up by the peace treaty; but broader policies looking toward the establishment of a peaceful atmosphere under the rule of international law were at the same time envisaged and emphasized in the Covenant.[216]

*The Law of the Sea and the*
*League of Nations*

If the league was unsuccessful in bringing about its broad objectives of world peace and international political stability, it did have some greater success in its "functional" roles. One of these related to the law of the sea.

The league had established a number of committees in order to facilitate discussion and debate of controversial areas in the international sphere.[217] One of the most important of these was the Committee of Experts for the Progressive Codification of International Law.[218] A subcommittee of this group was given the task of studying specific problems related to the international law of the sea. We should note how far removed from the actual marine-transport process this new public maritime law had become. A highly political body such as the League of Nations, with specific political aims, set out to codify even more specific aspects of the international law of the sea. Consultation with the users of ocean space would have been almost unthinkable. In any case, the subcommittee chose the old and thorny problem—the breadth of the territorial sea—as its main concentrated area of study and actually drafted a convention establishing a coastal sea of six miles by 1925.[219] In 1927 the question was submitted to the League of Nations Assembly, which finally adopted the following agenda on the "coastal sea," to be discussed at a codification conference to be held in the Hague in 1929-1930:

1. Limitation of the breadth of the territorial sea to three miles.

2. Recognition of the claim of certain States specifically mentioned to a territorial sea of greater breadth.

3. Acceptance of the principle of a zone on the high seas contiguous to the territorial sea in which the coastal State would be able to exercise the control necessary to prevent, within its territory or territorial sea, the infringement of its customs or sanitary regulations or interference with its security by foreign vessels, such control not to be exercized more than twelve miles from the coast.[220]

The Hague Conference, which met twice in 1929-1930, attracted thirty-eight coastal/maritime state delegations.[221] It was really the first formal international public-law-of-the-sea conference in history, and it failed.[222] Although only a few states claimed more than the three-mile territorial sea limit, the conference could find no common ground on the breadth of the territorial sea.[223] Hindsight shows us how this failure heralded the difficulties that this and many other parts of the law of the sea would face over the next half century. If we must name a villain, it would probably have to be Great Britain. Still the major maritime power, Britain appeared arrogantly unwilling to consider any changes or compromises in accepted customary law-of-the-sea principles, which, as we have seen, were neither as customary nor as widely accepted as was generally believed. Together with a few other conservative maritime allies, Britain steadfastly refused to recognize either the right of coastal states to exercise jurisdiction in a contiguous zone,[224] or even the truly historical and customary claims of the Scandinavian countries of a four-mile territorial sea.[225]

This uncompromising attitude antagonized many states that would have been willing to codify the three-mile limit and thereby save the world a great deal of future trouble.[226] As a result, the conference became so deadlocked that a formal vote could not even be taken, although informal expressions of preferences indicated clearly that some twenty out of the thirty-eight states represented would have agreed to a three-mile zone.[227]

It must be pointed out that Great Britain and its allies, supporting the three-mile limit without a contiguous zone, owned over 70 percent of the world's shipping tonnage.[228] In other words, the narrowest possible territorial sea was somehow seen as a protection for shipping—the "favored son." Were the resultant bitterness and long memories of the "defeated" coastal states worth it? Would a contiguous zone or even a wider territorial sea have altered shipping patterns radically? It seems unlikely. In any case, the point here is that there was little if any communication between the public-law sector and the shipping interests. Yet the damage was done, and the question of the territorial sea remains unanswered to this day although until well after World War II the three-mile territorial sea became generally accepted in state practice.[229]

In other, more functional, areas, however, the public law of the sea during this period had a little more success. For example, basic legal principles relating to passage through international canals and waterways were worked out at a number of international conferences.[230] Ship passage through various important international straits was also formalized and facilitated by legal principles.[231] An International Maritime Ports Convention was able to lay down rules and guidelines relating to the legal status of ships in foreign ports, to port dues and formalities, and to so-called free ports.[232] Furthermore, the right of landlocked states to a maritime flag was also established.

Finally, we must return to the so-called freedom of the seas, which had existed in relatively uneasy peace since the end of the sixteenth century but was far from an established principle of international law. During this period it was generally considered that because no state exercised jurisdiction over the high seas, the ship on such seas would be subject only to the jurisdiction of its flag state.[233] This interpretation was, however, seriously challenged by the rather curious decision of the Permanent Court of International Justice in the famous *Lotus* case.[234] In a seven-to-six decision, the court held that the criminal courts of Turkey *had* jurisdiction to try and punish the French navigating officer of a French vessel (in a Turkish port) for alleged criminal negligence in relation to a collision between the French vessel and a Turkish vessel on the high seas of the Mediterranean, resulting in death and injury of Turkish nationals in the Turkish vessel. This decision caused considerable controversy for a number of years and led to very involved study and discussion under CMI auspices, which finally resulted in a 1952 convention that basically reversed the court's decision.[235]

*Private Maritime Law*
*Further Isolated*

For private maritime law, the period between the world wars was a very fruitful one. The Comité Maritime International continued its leadership in the field and held eight conferences between 1921 and 1937. The CMI's important and progressive work is best illustrated by a brief outline of each of the meetings:

XIIth    Conference:  Antwerp 1921
         Agenda:     International conventions relating to collisions
                        and salvage at sea
                     Limitation on shipowners' liability
                     Maritime mortgages and liens
                     Code of affreightment

XIIIth   Conference:  London 1922
         Agenda:     Immunity of state-owned ships
                     Maritime mortgages and liens
                     Exonerating clauses in bills of lading

XIVth    Conference:  Gothenburg 1923
         Agenda:     Compulsory insurance of passengers
                     Immunity of state-owned ships
                     International code of affreightment
                     International convention on bills of lading

XVth     Conference:  Genoa 1925
         Agenda:     Compulsory insurance of passengers
                     Immunity of state-owned ships
                     International code of affreightment
                     Maritime mortgages and liens

XVIth    Conference:  Amsterdam 1927
         Agenda:     Compulsory insurance of passengers
                     Letters of indemnity
                     Ratification of Brussels conventions

XVIIth   Conference:  Antwerp 1930
         Agenda:     Ratification of the Brussels conventions
                     Compulsory insurance of passengers

Jurisdiction and penal sanctions in matters
of collision at sea

XVIIIth    Conference:  Oslo 1933
           Agenda:    Ratification of the Brussels conventions
                      Civil and penal jurisdiction in matters of colli-
                      sion on the high seas
                      Provisional arrest of ships
                      Limitation of shipowners' liability

XIXth      Conference:  Paris 1937
           Agenda:    Ratification of the Brussels conventions
                      Civil and penal jurisdiction in the event of
                      collision at sea
                      Provisional arrest of ships
                      Commentary on the Brussels conventions
                      Assistance and salvage of and by aircraft at
                      sea.[236]

In addition to discussing, studying, and negotiating this ever-changing
list of subjects, which is almost a barometer of marine transport, the
CMI was also able to send four conventions to the Brussels Diplomatic
Conference for international approval. First, in 1924, the Convention on
Limitation of Liability of Owners of Seagoing Vessels was adopted after
having first appeared on the CMI's agenda as far back as 1897.[237] The
new convention reconciled the conflict of views that had existed between
the British and the continental systems. The former made the shipowner
liable for the acts and omissions of his master; however, his responsibility
was limited by a fixed amount, regardless of whether the ship was lost or
not.[238] On the other hand, the latter based the shipowner's liability on the
value of the "maritime adventure" (ship, freight, and accessories), so
that his responsibility disappeared with the abandonment of such adventure.[239]

Of great importance was the adoption in 1924 of the Bills of Lading
Convention—the famous "Hague Rules"—relating to the carriage of goods
by sea.[240] This convention solved a number of great problems in international contracts of affreightment caused by the diversity of national con-
tractors and the excessive use of "negligence" and "exemption" clauses,
which gave little or no protection to the shipper of goods.[241] The United
States had pioneered reforms in this area by the adoption in 1893 of the
Harter Act, which was a compromise between the conflicting interests of
shipper and carrier.[242] The need for uniform international legislation was
quickly recognized, but it was to take several decades of difficult negotiations before agreement could be reached. The International Law Association first studied the subject and adopted the Hague Rules at its 1921

Hague meeting.[243] These rules were eventually molded into a convention by the CMI and finally emerged in 1924 as the International Convention for the Unification of Certain Rules of Law Relating to Bills of Lading.[244] It was a remarkable achievement.

The third convention adopted in Brussels in 1926 concerned the unification of the highly technical legal rules relating to maritime liens and mortgages. It basically recognized the principle that a mortgage or lien, if contracted in one state according to its laws, was entitled to be recognized in all the other signatory states.[245]

Finally, in 1926 a further convention relating to the immunity of state-owned ships was also achieved. A serious problem had been created by the exemption from jurisdiction, recognized by international law, of publicly owned vessels.[246] As we have seen, such ownership had become increasingly common as the result of government involvement in shipping during and after World War I. The new convention corrected this anomaly, which had resulted in much litigation,[247] by declaring categorically that, as a general rule, ships and cargoes owned or operated by governments for commercial purposes should, with respect to legal action and remedies, be subject to common maritime law.[248]

Despite these achievements, an examination of the CMI's agenda during this period reveals that private shipping interests represented by the Comité and related bodies were becoming more and more isolated from broader international, as well as national, shipping and other marine policies. By now they were clearly restricted to general technical, legal, and commercial terms of reference and had little access to wider marine-policy decisions. In any case, it is fairly certain that by this time the CMI and its satellites no longer sought to influence international marine policy in the public sector of international law.[249] And yet, year after year, the ocean—the main linking factor—was being steadily viewed in much wider terms than mere marine-transport use. It was beginning to be seen as a functional system providing multiple uses, at a time when the traditional users appeared to be withdrawing into their narrow shell of self-interest. Of course, as previously discussed, these were very difficult times for international cooperation or legal unification, let alone political cross-semination. Nevertheless, despite war and depression, revolution and recession, marine transport survived and prospered, expanded and consolidated, innovated and developed in the face of all adversity. As the lights went out all over the world, it was business as usual on the oceans.

## Prelude to World War II: Aggression in Asia and Africa, Unrest in Europe

Politically, World War II probably began with the Versailles Treaty which concluded World War I, although the actual shooting war would not commence for a further two decades. In any case, for World War II there was little of the clear peace/war demarcation that had been discernible in earlier armed conflicts. At the same time, the "economic" causes of World War II are often ignored. Yet the war occurred after the failure of an elaborate attempt in the 1920s and 1930s to reconstruct the mechanisms of international economic collaboration. Henceforth, the discipline of economics would be given the undeserved title of the "dismal science."[250] This failure could be linked directly to the abortive attempts in the 1930s by Japanese, Italian, and German nationalist aggression to create radically new systems of political and economic power.

If we look for another starting date for World War II—in economic terms—we would probably choose September 18, 1931, when Japan invaded Manchuria.[251] This invasion came at the worst possible moment in the period of global instability. The world trading system, which was slowly being restored after World War I, and the many subsequent years of economic crisis, had left Great Britain, still the world's financial center, in severe financial crisis. Britain had to abandon gold parity for sterling a few days after the Manchurian invasion.[252] The economic and political reconstruction, of which the League of Nations had been the keystone, collapsed; and political and economic events became almost completely interdependent. The League of Nations appeared powerless, and most of its efforts to prevent further conflicts were in vain. The disarmament conference called by the league in 1932 only resulted in Japan's withdrawal from the league in early 1933.[253] Later in the same year Germany followed suit.[254] The failure of the 1933 International Monetary and Economic Conference in London precipitated a series of higher tariffs and extended the quota system and foreign-exchange controls. Only a few months later, in early 1934, the Hitler government moved to put Germany on a footing of preparedness for war.[255] Drastic trade restrictions were pursued, and the German trade drive in the Balkan countries was begun with the idea of creating an economic-bloc tributary to the German rearmament program in central and eastern Europe.

At this stage world events were quickly drawn into the maelstrom of inevitable world conflict. Italy attacked Ethiopia in 1935. The league condemned this action and even put into effect certain economic sanctions which, however, stopped short of affecting oil.[256] Italy then withdrew from the league, and German supplies were poured into Italy. Next, in the summer of 1936, the civil war that broke out in Spain became a dress rehearsal for the world war yet to come.[257] Italy and Germany supported the Fascist rebels with massive infusions of war material and men. On the other hand, the Soviet Union supported the Loyalist government. A weakened policy, curiously described as "nonintervention," was followed by Britain, France, and to some extent the United States. As a result, Spain, one of the most populous and promising states in Europe, would be isolated under a tight Fascist dictatorship for almost four decades.[258]

By mid-1937 Japan had marched into Northern China, the next step in the Japanese "grand plan" to dominate the Asian part of the Pacific.[259] Then it was Germany's turn in 1938, when Austria was absorbed into the German Reich. The betrayal of Czechoslovakia by France and Britain resulted in that unfortunate country's subjugation under German rule by early 1939, just a few days before Italy invaded Albania. As we know, the tension over the free city of Danzig, orchestrated by Germany, finally led to the German invasion of Poland on September 3, 1939, which forced the totally unprepared Britain and France to declare war on Germany.[260] World War II had commenced in earnest.

This brief catalog of events, which omits the many intricate, complex, and important stages that preceded the actual outbreak of the war, is intended simply to indicate the severe economic damage that had been done well before 1939. This damage was the result of nationalist trade policies that had severely altered the whole trade pattern of the world.

Obviously such changes would have to affect marine transport severely. Condliffe astutely refers to "three major aspects of the economic consequences" of what he calls the period of "war preparedness."[261] First came the stage of "psychoeconomic reorganization," during which the potential aggressors—Japan, Germany, and Italy—were completely reorganizing their economies many years before the actual outbreak of war. In retrospect it appears that the major powers either ignored, misinterpreted, or missed altogether the significance of this stage. For Japan, Germany, and Italy, trade was henceforth the instrument of national policy with totalitarian aims. The buildup of national fleets in these countries, referred to previously, can now clearly be seen as a constituent part of this process. Stocks of civilian goods were allowed to run down as all manpower, research, capital resources, and technology were diverted to war preparation.

The second aspect was the stage of "garrison economic self-sufficiency" in the totalitarian countries, which was, of course, at complete odds with the carefully nurtured, fragile economy built up over several centuries. Bilateral barter agreements, in which economic objectives would be subject to prior political and military considerations, were substituted for multilateral world trade exchanges. The traditional circuits of trade were gravely impaired by such policies.

Finally, the war itself brought out an aspect that can be called a system of "econogeographical detachment." Aggressive German, Italian, and Japanese actions resulted in large conquered parts of the world being absorbed into the conquerors' areas of interest and thus effectively detached from traditional trading systems. All this, of course, followed one of the greatest economic depressions in world history, which had left most of the world mentally, physically, and economically unprepared for a further conflagration.

The general picture is equally accurate for a specific example such as marine transport. We have already seen how the merchant fleets of Japan, Germany, and Italy had been steadily expanded as a part of their new systematic expansive policy. At the same time, the other maritime states were vigorously attempting to disengage all the government interest and support they had reluctantly given to the shipping industry during World War I.[262]

In Great Britain, as we have seen, the industry continued to be left to its own devices with the commensurate disastrous results of the economic depression on shipping. The United States, having built up its mighty World War I fleet, was plunging into almost mercantilist (and soon to be political) isolation, moving rapidly away from any governmental policy concerning shipping, despite the intent of the 1936 Merchant Marine Act.[263] For the United States, there were simply too many other pressing priorities. Shipping had to wait in line for support like any other industry. In the 1930s the line was very long.

France, as we have seen, had some government support for shipping but also had some priorities which, at that time, lay far inland across the Saar and the Rhine. There is little doubt that the Allied countries had made some grave errors in reacting to the Axis pretensions, particularly in maritime matters.[264] Unquestionably, Italy, Japan, and Germany had seen their opportunities and based their hopes, at least partly, on the decreased effectiveness of Allied sea power in the broadest sense of that term.[265]

The lengthy *Pax Britannica* of the nineteenth century had been based almost completely on Britain's undisputed mastery of the sea and control of sea communications, which allowed the maintenance of a far-flung colonial empire, the defense of the British Isles, and the isolation of enemies from trade. Although neither discerned nor accepted by Britain, these powers had seriously weakened in the periods before and after World War I. In any case, the rival maritime powers—Japan, the United States, Germany—disputed the superiority of the hitherto unquestioned "mistress of the seas."

Second, the rapid spread of industrialization and policies of economic self-sufficiency had made other states less vulnerable to the paralyzing effect of any blockade. Third, the development of new instruments of war, particularly the submarine, had proved in World War I that an island nation, dependent on shipping for its very existence, could be seriously endangered. Of course, air power had added a new dimension to this vulnerability.[266]

There was one final invisible weakening effect. Like all great powers, Britain, having built up its greatness by conservative, almost plodding devotion to empire and trade, had lulled itself into a false sense of security, which had stifled progress and innovation and had attempted instead to preserve a status quo that was quickly disappearing because it had become redundant. The belief that "what was good policy in 1838 must be good in 1938" simply could not nurture the hard policies that were required before World War II.[267] The warnings of the previous war had been ignored or forgotten despite the fact that Britain's youth had bled to death on the fields of Flanders or had disappeared into the unforgiving waters of the North Atlantic. The laissez-faire free-enterprise system, with a liberal dose of government assistance—as adopted by the United States—could easily have worked in Britain but was unthinkable in the pre-World War II years.

On the other hand, had a forecast of exactly what World War II would bring been possible, it would not have been believed anywhere, let alone in pre-World War II Great Britain, which uncomprehendingly was seeing its empire and world control crumbling.[268] Yet as in most of the previous great wars, this war would once again be a trial of strength on the seas with marine transport, as always, playing its preordained central role.

**Total War at Sea: The Struggle for Control of the Oceans**

Strictly speaking, World War II has little to do with a historical analysis of the international law and policy of marine transport. The war will thus not be examined in any detail here. But it is probably correct to say that, as in the Dark Ages, law virtually ceased to exist on the seas during World War II; what policy there was existed strictly for the benefit of the belligerent states' general war policy. We have already seen that private maritime law had diverged from the general law of the sea to the extent that it had become isolated in its own self-interest. At the same time, it had continued to build up its own body of rules of law and attempted to unify such rules through greater international cooperation. Its public interests stopped there, and its efforts had to be basically discontinued during the war years.[269]

As the private maritime law had diverged from the public law of the sea, there had been a discernible convergence of ocean uses other than transportation under the public-law aegis. Ancient and traditional uses such as fisheries had now been joined by new uses related to nonliving resources of the sea bed, in particular petroleum. In the years immediately before the war, these resources were becoming accessible as well as exploitable.[270] Thus the three-thousand-year-old problem of coastal-state jurisdiction came into the forefront once again. The 1930 Hague conference had examined these problems in detail, with particular reference to the law of territorial waters, but had been unable to reach any agreement. It can be said, therefore, that the public law of the sea at the outbreak of the war was in such a state of disarray that it was unable to exert any influence whatsoever on the war at sea. It seems unlikely, however, that even the most stable and accepted law of the sea could have exerted such influence. There is no doubt that the traditional international law relating to disputes, war, and neutrality disappeared completely during this savage all-out war. The law of war had, in any case, begun to fade quickly in World War I. By 1939 it had disappeared altogether. For example, Admiral Dönitz's orders to his *U*-boat commanders in 1940 were quite explicit:

> . . . do not rescue people or take them with you. Do not trouble about the steamers' boats. Weather conditions and distance from land are immaterial. Think only of your own boat and endeavour to achieve the best success as soon as possible! We must be hard in this war . . . .[271]

Such orders effectively marked the end of German observance of the well-established, but always fragile, prize laws and the beginning of unrestricted, ruthless submarine warfare. Soon survivors would be machine-gunned in the water.[272] The observance of neutrality on the seas during the war would be left to the whim of the belligerents. It was, in any case, difficult to be neutral in a world war. Indiscriminate sinkings of neutral vessels led neutral countries to seek sides eventually. Principles relating to the humanization of warfare at sea, worked out only a short time before the war, also disappeared quickly.[273] The arsenal of the belligerents now included weapons with destructive force never before contemplated—ranging from unsweepable mines to fragmentation bombs.[274] The civilized niceties of nineteenth-century warfare had disappeared forever. As a result, the war took a terrible toll on the oceans of the world.

World War I had demonstrated the increasing importance of sea control. Wartime mastery of the seas enables the controlling belligerent to use the oceanic communicating highways freely for supplying its armed forces and for trade, and prohibits such use to its foes. Control of the sea was thus seen as vital, whether secured by weapons operating on, beneath, or above the surface of the ocean. The securing of this control was the marine policy of the warring nations during this time. When Germany and Japan lost the war at sea, they lost the whole war.[275] The various war theaters illustrate this fact. In the African conflict, troops, supplies, and weapons for the warring factions had to cross the Mediterranean, in which, certainly in the early years of the war, neither party could establish control.[276] In the Pacific arena, the southern thrust of Japan into Malaya, the Philippines, and the Pacific islands, almost to the back door of Australia, was possible only through mastery of the sea.[277] The Battle of the Atlantic, as its name implies, became for Britain a conflict to maintain sea communications, and for the United States a struggle to keep up an uninterrupted flow of munitions, foodstuffs, and manpower overseas.[278] The costs were terrible.

## The Perfection of Commerce Warfare

At the beginning of the war the pattern was immediately discernible. Germany would continue the policy of "commerce warfare" it had practiced so successfully in World War I. The German navy at that time consisted of a very small battle fleet, which despite some spectacular exploits would soon be eliminated or neutralized. On the other hand, in 1939 Germany started the war with some sixty operational submarines, which commenced their operations with spectacular success.[279] In a manner reminiscent of World War I, on September 3, 1939, a German U-boat sank the English passenger liner *Athenia* off the Irish coast.[280] On September 17, 1939 the British aircraft-carrier *Courageous* was torpedoed and sunk in the eastern approaches to the English Channel. In one of the most daring raids of the war, submarine *U-18* penetrated the British naval anchorage at Scapa Flow and sank the battleship *Royal Oak*—a veteran of the Battle of Jutland.[281]

This illustrated the problems faced by the Royal Navy, which had not foreseen the future of submarine warfare and had wasted its efforts on outdated and vulnerable capital ships.[282] It would have to pay a terrible price for its lack of clear policy. By the end of 1939—after only four months of war—over 750,000 tons of allied and neutral shipping had been sent to the bottom of the Atlantic by U-boats, mines, aircraft, and surface raiders.[283] And this was only a foreshadowing of things to come. In addition to submarines, shipping now had to contend with a whole new generation of sophisticated mines. In November 1939 Germany started to sow the new secret "magnetic" mines, which were laid by aircraft, sank to the bottom, and were brought up only by the magnetic attraction of a large steel hull passing within thirty to fifty feet. Until effective countermeasures were finally found, these mines caused heavy losses.[284]

In 1940, the first full year of the war, merchant-ship losses mounted quickly, with a monthly average of over 300,000 tons being lost, totaling almost 4 million tons by the end of the year.[285] Of this loss, over half was the result of submarine action, which was responsible for the loss of some 400 ships.[286] During that year, the German conquest of Norway and France and the entry of Italy into the war had also extended the Axis submarine campaign. German U-boats and aircraft could now attack shipping from a coastline extending from the North Cape to North Africa. At the end of 1940, Allied merchant-shipping losses outweighed new shipping construction by over 3 million tons, but the U-boat fleet had increased to seventy-five, losing only three vessels during the year.[287]

While Germany was broadening its domination over Europe, Japan extended its authority southward into Indochina, ostensibly to tighten the blockade of China but in actual fact moving toward the precious oil and rubber resources of Southeast Asia.[288] By September 1940 Japan had joined the German-Italian Axis in a tripartite pact. Tokyo's link with Berlin and Rome gave a very clear impression of a unified Fascist juggernaut rolling toward global domination.[289]

### United States: Isolation and Assistance

All this time the United States, one of the world's newest major powers, continued to exist in almost neutral isolation imposed by a series of neutrality acts and a vociferous isolationist "America First" movement, which intended to keep the United States out of the "European War" at all costs.[290] At sea, between the outbreak of the war and Germany's *Blitzkrieg* in 1940, the United States hugged its shore and induced its Latin American neighbors to join in declaring a very large neutrality/buffer zone between Europe and the Western Hemisphere.[291]

Although Britain, France, and to a lesser extent Germany purchased goods and strategic materials in the United States, the terms were strictly "cash and carry." Under the neutrality laws, U.S. citizens could not provide credit or ships for the belligerents.[292] Hopes that there would not be a "real" world war involving the United States slowly dissipated between 1940 and 1941, when the majority of Americans began to realize that their country must stand behind Britain. The isolationists, who continued in prominence for some time, ensured that the rough rule of "all aid short of war" would be followed.[293] However, this "head in the sand" attitude could not last.

Despite the fact that the British Empire and much of what it stood for was anathema to American thinking, the German threat was more imminent. In particular, President Franklin D. Roosevelt saw that the German threat of political and economic penetration could not be held by piling up home defenses.[294] In July 1940, at the Havana Conference of the American Republics, steps were taken to ensure that the transfer of any American territory to a non-American power would not be possible.[295] At the same time, the U.S. Congress brought forth legislation for a two-ocean navy and a $10-billion defense program.[296] In September 1940 the famous "destroyers for bases" deal was passed by the U.S. government.[297] In retrospect, this appears to have been the exact instant when oceanic dominance passed from the British Empire to the United States. This deal exchanged some fifty overaged but operative U.S. destroyers, badly needed by the deficient Royal Navy, for 100-year leases of eight bases, extending from Newfoundland to

British Guiana and including facilities in Bermuda, the Bahamas, Jamaica, Antigua, St. Lucia, and Trinidad. These new bases strengthened control over the Caribbean and pushed American sea defenses right out into the Atlantic and, eventually, into the battle for that ocean.

By the winter of 1940-1941, Britain's situation appeared desperate and German invasion imminent. British assets in the United States were dwindling rapidly and could not pay for the materials urgently required. Roosevelt, sensing U.S. public support, chose involvement when he proposed an almost unlimited British access to American production and offered credit to what he called the "arsenal of democracy."[298] The main legal instrument by which the United States would become the mobilizing center of the whole Allied war effort was the Lend-Lease Act of March 11, 1941, which signaled the effective abandonment of the attempt to isolate the United States from the European conflict.[299] The act was passed to enable the United States to supply war material, food, and other goods to any country that the president might designate as aiding the defense of the United States. The purpose of the act was to enable designated countries to concentrate their manpower and other resources on immediate military aims by drawing from the United States the necessary supplies to sustain their struggle. It also enabled the United States to supply this aid without involving the recipient countries in financial difficulties hitherto experienced.

*Battle of the Atlantic: Submarines Versus*
*Shipyards*

Lend-Lease was a vast operation for which no parallel can be found in history. It had a profound impact in showing the virtually limitless power of ocean transportation. For the four and one-half years of the war, an immense volume of war materiels and civilian supplies was transferred by an unprecedented "bridge of ships" to the Allied countries.[300] Lend-Lease deliveries by the United States were valued at over $50 billion, of which almost two-thirds consisted of actual munitions, weapons, and military goods.[301]

There is no question that this fragile bridge spanning the Atlantic Ocean won World War II. Without this lifeline there would have been no Stalingrad, El Alamein, or D-Day. It was also, without a shadow of doubt, international marine transport's finest hour, when the skill, knowledge, innovation, and courage of five millennia of seamanship came together. The odds were terrible and the losses appalling. The Germans knew that to win the war they had to win the Battle of the Atlantic, and they threw everything into this effort.[302] Between 1939 and the end of the war, the German submarine fleet had been built up from its modest beginnings to over 1,200.[303]

Never before had merchant shipping been required to run such a gauntlet. The statistics speak for themselves, as shown in tables 5-4 and 5-5. Taking into account all losses to merchant shipping, some 4,600 ships, totaling over 20 million tons and manned by over 40,000 men, were lost during the war. Over one-third of the 1939 world fleet was thus wiped out.

Nevertheless, with its traditional resilience, shipping not only survived but actually increased in the face of these incredible odds.[304] However, the traditional method of simply increasing shipyard capacity was not enough. Although the output of British shipyards had been drastically increased from prewar-slump levels, they could not produce more than 1.25 million tons per year. As can be seen from the statistics, this was not nearly enough to counteract losses.

In February 1942, when allied shipping was taking its worst pounding, President Roosevelt called a high-level White House shipping conference and set in motion "the greatest shipbuilding program in world history."[305] Admiral Land was placed in charge of the newly formed U.S. Warship Administration, which was to produce 24 million tons of new shipping by the end of the year.[306] Not only was this twenty times the output of 1940, but Admiral Land noted that "to meet the stiff quota of 750 ships before the end of the year, and about 1,500 vessels in 1943, American yards would have to increase their delivery of ships from one to three per day."[307] By the end of the war the United States had built ninety-nine new shipyards with a total work force of 1.5 million.[308]

However, yards alone were not enough. New construction methods for ships had to be developed. Shipbuilding had traditionally been a highly

**Table 5-4**
**British Shipping Losses, 1939-1945**

|  | Number of Ships Lost | | Number of Crew Lost | |
|---|---|---|---|---|
| Year | By Submarine | By All Action | By Submarine | By All Action |
| 1939 | 50 | 95 | 260 | 495 |
| 1940 | 225 | 511 | 3,375 | 5,622 |
| 1941 | 288 | 568 | 5,632 | 7,838 |
| 1942 | 452 | 590 | 8,413 | 9,736 |
| 1943 | 203 | 266 | 3,826 | 4,606 |
| 1944 | 67 | 102 | 1,163 | 1,512 |
| 1945 | 30 | 45 | 229 | · 323 |
| Total | 1,315 | 2,177 | 22,898 | 30,132 |

Source: Trade Division Records, British Admiralty, Public Records Office Doc. ADM 199-2073-194. See also Terry Hughes and John Costello, *The Battle of the Atlantic* (New York: Dial Press, 1977), ch. 15.

**Table 5-5**
**Allied and Neutral Shipping Losses, 1939-1945**
*(in tons)*

| Year | By Submarine | By All Action |
|------|-------------|---------------|
| 1939 | 421,156 | 755,392 |
| 1940 | 2,186,158 | 3,991,641 |
| 1941 | 2,171,070 | 4,328,558 |
| 1942 | 6,266,215 | 7,790,697 |
| 1943 | 804,277 | 1,218,219 |
| 1944 | 358,609 | 530,510 |
| 1945 | 281,716 | 437,015 |
| Total | 12,489,201 | 19,052,032 |

Source: *Official History of the War at Sea* (London: HMSO, 1946). See also Terry Hughes and John Costello, *The Battle of the Atlantic* (New York: Dial Press, 1977), ch. 15.

skilled, painstaking, and lengthy process. Industrialist Henry J. Kaiser and his colleagues decided to apply car assembly-line mass-production techniques by working to a standard design and using all welded construction and prefabrication methods. In less than a year ship-construction methods advanced by a century, laying the groundwork for the modern construction techniques the industry was to use in the postwar years. Using an old British tramp-streamer blueprint dating back to 1879, U.S. shipyards produced, as their principal standardized vessel, the famous 10,000-ton "Liberty" ship. The first of these remarkable vessels was launched in September 1941, and by the end of the war some 2,700 had been built.[309] Construction time ranged from six months in the early period to just over a week in the latter part of the war.

The Germans had, of course, foreseen the importance of their "commerce warfare" but had seriously miscalculated the tremendous industrial capacity of the United States. As Hughes and Costello point out:

In May, 1942 Dönitz had set out the targets he had established for his U-Boat arm to win the war: "The total tonnage the enemy can build will be about 8.2 million tons in 1942, and about 10.4 million tons in 1943. This would mean that we would have to sink approximately 700,000 tons per month in order to offset new construction; only what is in excess of this amount would constitute a decrease in enemy tonnage. However, we are already sinking these 700,000 tons per month now." Dönitz revealed the flaw in his calculations with the statement that: "The construction figures quoted are the maximum amounts ever mentioned by enemy propaganda as a goal of the shipbuilding programme. Our experts doubt that this goal can be reached and consider that the enemy can only build about five million tons in 1942." He was wrong. The United States alone was building ships faster than the Germans were sinking them by the late summer of

1942. In the autumn of that year there was a net gain for the first time of over 700,000 tons in Anglo-American tonnage, and this was repeated in the next quarter. In the first quarter of 1943 it was doubled to one and one-half million tons and the balance of new construction over losses never fell below two million tons throughout 1944.[310]

To illustrate this point further, table 5-6 dramatically shows the gains by new construction and losses of merchant ships between 1939 and 1945. It shows, in effect, how the war was really won.

Thus by 1943 the tide was turning for the Allies, particularly in the war at sea. Convoy-protection methods had finally, if belatedly, been improved and perfected; and shipping losses were decreasing while submarine losses increased. Whereas only 22 U-boats had been sunk in 1940, 35 in 1941, and 87 in 1942, losses rose sharply to 217 in 1943 and 239 in 1944.[311] The Germans had lost the Battle of the Atlantic, which had probably caused greater loss than all the sea battles in history combined.

## Conclusions: Victory at Sea

One of the most important turning points in World War II occurred, of course, when the United States entered the war in 1941, after the Japanese attack on Pearl Harbor. During the crucial months of 1940 and 1941, Asian affairs appeared to be far removed, less volatile, and less important than what was happening in the Atlantic arena. The United States knew only that Japan posed some kind of indefinable threat.

**Table 5-6**
**New Construction and Losses of British and U.S. Shipping, 1934-1945**
*(number of ships of 1,600 gross tons and over)*

| | | New Construction | | | |
| Year | Losses | British Empire | United States | Total | Net Change |
|---|---|---|---|---|---|
| 1939 | 810 | 231 | 101 | 332 | −478 |
| 1940 | 4,407 | 780 | 439 | 1,219 | −3,188 |
| 1941 | 4,398 | 1,169 | 815 | 1,984 | −2,414 |
| 1942 | 8,245 | 1,843 | 5,339 | 7,182 | −1,063 |
| 1943 | 3,611 | 2,201 | 12,384 | 14,585 | +10,974 |
| 1944 | 1,422 | 1,710 | 11,639 | 13,349 | +11,927 |
| 1945 | 458 | 283 | 3,551 | 3,834 | +3,376 |
| Total | 23,351 | 8,217 | 34,268 | 42,485 | +19,134 |

Source: Trade Division Records, British Admiralty, Public Records Office Doc. ADM 199-2073-194. See also Terry Hughes and John Costello, *The Battle of the Atlantic* (New York: Dial Press, 1977), p. 304.

U.S. Secretary of State Cordell Hull believed that Japan would honor the Nine-Power "Open Door" Treaty of 1922, which required Japanese withdrawal from Asia's mainland.[312] As leverage, the United States imposed a very tight trade embargo on Japan, which did have a considerable effect on the Japanese economy. However, by the summer of 1941 the two nations were drifting toward war.

When Japan completed its occupation of Indochina, the U.S. government froze Japanese assets in the United States. Japan's leaders, fully aware of their limited resources, realized that they had to fight the United States in order to achieve their planned expansion and domination. Last-minute negotiations failed, and on December 7, 1941 the Japanese attack on Pearl Harbor not only caught the United States off guard but also seriously crippled U.S. Pacific naval forces.[313]

This was the event that dissolved the nation's doubts and propelled it into total war. The awesome industrial machine and the economic power of the United States could now be fully utilized and would finally overwhelm the Axis on all fronts. It was close at times, however, not only on the Atlantic Ocean but also in other theaters of the world war. One of the most formidable American leaders in the war would write in 1945:

> The nation is just emerging from one of its gravest crises. This generation of Americans can still remember the black days of 1942 when the Japanese conquered all of Malaysia, occupied Burma, and threatened India while the German armies approached the Volga and the Suez. In those hours Germany and Japan came so close to economic domination of the world that we do not yet realize how thin the thread of Allied survival had been stretched. In good conscience this nation can take little credit for its part in staving off disaster in those critical days. It is certain that the refusal of the British and Russian peoples to accept what appeared to be inevitable defeat was the great factor in the salvage of our civilization. Of almost equal importance was the failure of the enemy to make the most of the situation.[314]

We have deliberately shown only selected aspects of the war as it relates to the central theme of our examination. Obviously, the wholesale destruction of a great part of the world fleet and the development of a whole array of new ship-construction methods, together with the perfecting of a shipping supply route, all in the face of almost insurmountable odds, are low and high points in international marine transport, which would have widely felt effects in the postwar years. In any case, these are the directly visible effects of shipping policy with wartime urgencies. Less visible, but equally important for the future of shipping, was the emergence of the United States as a leading world power, which had proved its great industrial capacity at a time of world crisis. The United States perfected the conversion of production and trade from peacetime to wartime channels using raw materials from every available source. Command of the seas enabled these supplies to be drawn from the whole free world. Thus even the economies of neutral countries were affected by the demands of Allied war production. The trading circuits of the prewar world, with Great Britain as the centre were, however, completely broken; and the United States became the focusing, operating, financial, and decision-making center of world trade. The former European center of gravity of world trade had been effectively shifted to the Western Hemisphere. The era during which Western Europe had dominated world politics and global economics was at an end, and it would be a number of years before the Western European states would recover even some of their former strength. The extraordinary productivity and industry, as well as the political prestige of the United States and the quickly rising world power of the Soviet Union, would soon divide the world into two camps with an impoverished Western Europe reduced to a buffer zone between two new superpowers.

**Notes**

1. W.O. Stevens and Allan Westcott, *A History of Sea Power* (Garden City, N.Y.: Doubleday, 1944), p. 269.

2. Ibid.

3. Ibid., pp. 288-289.

4. Ibid.

5. Ibid., pp. 298-302.

6. Ibid.

7. Ibid., p. 304.

8. Ibid.

9. Fritz Stern, *Gold and Iron: Bismarck, Bleichröder and the Building of the German Empire* (New York: Knopf, 1977), p. 451ff.

10. Stevens and Westcott, *History of Sea Power*, p. 304.

11. Ibid.

12. Ibid., p. 305.

13. Ibid.

14. David Howarth, *Sovereign of the Seas* (New York: Atheneum, 1974), p. 335.

15. Ibid.

16. Ibid.

17. Ibid.

18. Ibid., p. 336; see also R.R. James, *The British Revolution—1880-1939* (New York: Knopf, 1977), pp. 318-319.

19. Howarth, *Sovereign of the Seas*, p. 337.

20. Ibid., p. 336.

21. Ibid., p. 346.

22. Stevens and Westcott, *History of Sea Power*, ch. 17; Arthur Nussbaum, *A Concise History of the Law of Nations* (New York: Macmillan, 1962), p. 230.

23. Ibid., Stevens, p. 397; Nussbaum, p. 230.

24. Ibid., Nussbaum, p. 231.

25. Stevens and Westcott, *History of Sea Power*, p. 398.

26. Nussbaum, *History of the Law of Nations*, p. 231.

27. C. John Colombos, *International Law of the Sea*, 6th rev. ed. (London: Longmans, 1967), ch. 21.

28. Jean Jacques Rousseau, *The Social Contract* (New York: Carlton House, n.d.), p. 63.

29. Nussbaum, *History of the Law of Nations*, p. 231.

30. Ibid.

31. Ibid.

32. Stevens and Westcott, *History of Sea Power*, p. 348ff.

33. Ibid., p. 383.

34. Ibid., p. 386.

35. Howarth, *Sovereign of the Seas*, p. 345.

36. Ibid., p. 346.

37. Stevens and Westcott, *History of Sea Power*, p. 397ff.

38. Nussbaum, *History of the Law of Nations*, pp. 229-230.

39. Ibid.

40. Ibid.

41. Ibid.

42. Ibid.

43. See also L. Oppenheim, *International Law*, vol. 2, 7th ed., edited by H. Lauterpacht (London: Longman, 1952), particularly ch. 4.

44. Gerard J. Mangone, *Marine Policy for America* (Lexington, Mass.: Lexington Books, D.C. Heath and Co., 1977), p. 85.

45. Stevens and Westcott, *History of Sea Power*, p. 404.

46. Albert Lilar and Carlo van den Bosch, *Le Comité Maritime International* (Anvers: CMI, 1972), p. 24.

47. Stevens and Westcott, *History of Sea Power*, p. 401.

48. Ibid.

49. Howarth, *Sovereign of the Seas*, pp. 346-347.

50. Ibid.

51. Stevens and Westcott, *History of Sea Power*, p. 394.

52. Howarth, *Sovereign of the Seas*, p. 347.

53. Ibid.

54. Ibid.

55. Ibid.

56. Stevens and Westcott, *History of Sea Power*, p. 400.

57. Ibid.

58. Ibid., p. 396.

59. Ibid.

60. Ibid.

61. Ibid., p. 397.

62. Ibid., p. 396.

63. Howarth, *Sovereign of the Seas*, p. 347.

64. Ibid.

65. Stevens and Westcott, *History of Sea Power*, pp. 406-407.

66. Howarth, *Sovereign of the Seas*, pp. 347-348.

67. C. Ernest Fayle, *A Short History of the World's Shipping Industry* (London: Allen and Unwin, 1933), p. 293.

68. Ibid.

69. Zimmerman, *Ocean Shipping*, p. 584.

70. Ibid.

71. Ibid.

72. Ibid.

73. For an extensive analytical examination of this important area, see Donald W. Mitchell, *A History of Russian and Soviet Sea Power* (New York: Macmillan, 1974).

74. Mangone, *Marine Policy for America*, p. 168.

75. Ibid., p. 169.

76. Clive Day, *A History of Commerce* (New York: Longmans, Green, 1919), p. 561.

77. Mangone, *Marine Policy for America*, p. 168.

78. Day, *History of Commerce*, p. 561.

79. Mangone, *Marine Policy for America*, p. 171.

80. Ibid.

81. Ibid.

82. Ibid.

83. C.E. McDowell and H.M. Gibbs, *Ocean Transportation* (New York: McGraw-Hill, 1954), p. 58.

84. Ibid., p. 57.

85. Ibid., p. 58.

86. Zimmerman, *Ocean Shipping*, p. 180.

87. Ibid.

88. Ibid., pp. 184-185.

89. Ibid.

90. For a fascinating exposé of the oil industry see Anthony Sampson, *The Seven Sisters. The Great Oil Companies and the World they Shaped* (New York: Bantam, 1976).

91. Ibid., p. 28.

92. Ibid., p. 33.

93. *Standard Oil Company of New Jersey et al.* v. *United States.* 221 U.S.S.C.R. 619 (1911).

94. Ibid., p. 645.
95. Sampson, *Seven Sisters*, Introduction.
96. Ibid., p. 38.
97. Ibid., p. 39.
98. Ibid.
99. Ibid., pp. 44-45.
100. Ibid., pp. 48-49.
101. Ibid.
102. Ibid., p. 50.
103. Ibid., p. 52.
104. Ibid., p. 55.
105. Ibid.
106. Ibid., p. 58.
107. Ibid., cited p. 62.
108. Ibid., p. 67.
109. Ibid., p. 69.
110. Ibid., p. 70.
111. Ibid., p. 72.
112. Ibid., cited p. 72.
113. Cited, ibid.
114. Cited, ibid.
115. Fayle, *World's Shipping Industry*, p. 297; A.D. Couper, *The Geography of Sea Transport* (London: Hutchinson, 1972), p. 112.
116. Couper, *The Geography of Sea Transport*, p. 110.
117. Ibid.
118. Fayle, *World's Shipping Industry*, p. 294.
119. Ibid., pp. 294-295.
120. Ibid., p. 294.
121. Ibid.
122. As studied by the UNCTAD Division of Shipping and Invisibles, which includes insurance, freight rates, agency fees, brokerage rates, and so on.
123. There has been no major examination of the industry overall since 1945.
124. Sir Osborne Mance, *International Sea Transport* (London: Oxford University Press, 1945), p. 74.
125. Fayle, *World's Shipping Industry*, p. 297.
126. Mance, *International Sea Transport*, p. 74.
127. Ibid.
128. Ibid.
129. Ibid., pp. 74-75.
130. Ibid., pp. 75-76.
131. Ibid.
132. Ibid., pp. 120-121.

133. Ibid.; see also Trade Facilities Act, 1921. 11 and 12 Geo. V., ch. 65 as amended.

134. British Shipping (Assistance) Act, 1935. 25 Geo. V., ch. 7.

135. Mance, *International Sea Transport*, p. 122.

136. Report, *Committee of Inquiry into Shipping* ("Rochdale Report") (London: HMSO, 1970), p. 9.

137. Mangone, *Marine Policy for America*, pp. 87-88.

138. Ibid.; Mance, *International Sea Transport*, p. 85.

139. Ibid.

140. Merchant Marine Act, 1920 ("Jones Act"). 41 U.S. Stats. 988 (1919-1921).

141. Mance, *International Sea Transport*, p. 83.

142. Ibid.

143. Ibid., p. 84.

144. Ibid.

145. Ibid.

146. Merchant Marine Act, 1928. 45 U.S. Stats. 689 (1927-1929).

147. Mangone, *Marine Policy for America*, p. 87.

148. Mance, *International Sea Transport*, p. 85.

149. Ibid.

150. Ibid.

151. Ibid.

152. Ibid., pp. 85-86.

153. Ibid., p. 86.

154. Ibid.

155. Ibid.

156. Ibid.

157. Cited, ibid.

158. Mangone, *Marine Policy for America*, p. 88.

159. Ibid.

160. Merchant Marine Act, 1936. 49 U.S. Stats. 1985 (1935-1936).

161. Mangone, *Marine Policy for America*, p. 88.

162. Mance, *International Sea Transport*, p. 87.

163. Report presented on November 16, 1937.

164. Mance, *International Sea Transport*, cited p. 88.

165. Ibid.

166. Ibid., p. 83.

167. Ibid.

168. Ibid.

169. Ibid., p. 90.

170. "Rochdale Report," p. 9.

171. Fayle, *World's Shipping Industry*, p. 297.

172. Mance, *International Sea Transport*, p. 71.

173. Ibid., p. 117.

174. Ibid.

175. "Rochdale Report," p. 9.

176. Mance, *International Sea Transport*, p. 71.

177. Fayle, *World's Shipping Industry*, p. 197.

178. "Rochdale Report," p. 9.

179. Ibid.

180. Mance, *International Sea Transport*, p. 81.

181. Ibid.

182. Ibid.

183. Ibid.

184. Ibid., p. 119.

185. Ibid.

186. Ibid.

187. Fayle, *World's Shipping Industry*, p. 297.

188. Mance, *International Sea Transport*, p. 72.

189. Ibid., pp. 72-73.

190. Ibid., p. 73.

191. "Rochdale Report," p. 9.

192. Mance, *International Sea Transport*, p. 77.

193. Ibid., p. 78.

194. "Rochdale Report," p. 9.

195. Mance, *International Sea Transport*, p. 79.

196. Fayle, *World's Shipping Industry*, p. 297.

197. "Rochdale Report," p. 9.

198. Mance, *International Sea Transport*, p. 80; see also Edwin O. Reischauer, *The Japanese* (Cambridge, Mass.: Harvard University Press, 1977), ch. 19.

199. Ibid., Mance, p. 80.

200. Fayle, *World's Shipping Industry*, pp. 294-295.

201. Mance, *International Sea Transport*, p. 66.

202. Ibid., p. 67.

203. Ibid., p. 68.

204. "Rochdale Report," p. 9.

205. See, for example, W. Friedmann, *Law in a Changing Society*, 2nd ed. (New York: Columbia University Press, 1972), p. 465ff.

206. Ibid.; E.G. Trimble, "Violations of Maritime Law by the Allied Powers during the World War," *American Journal of International Law* 24 (1930):79.

207. Oppenheim, *International Law*, vol. 1, p. 460ff.

208. Hersch Lauterpacht, *International Law: Collected papers*, vol. 2, ed. E. Lauterpacht (Cambridge: Cambridge University Press, 1975), pp. 145-158.

209. See, for example, ibid., vol. 1, pt. 2, entitled "General Rules of the Law of Peace," p. 179.

210. Nussbaum, *History of the Law of Nations*, p. 251.

211. *Encyclopedia of World History*, 4th ed., edited by William L. Langer (Boston: Houghton Mifflin, 1968), pp. 976-977.

212. Ibid., p. 1121.

213. Nussbaum, *History of the Law of Nations*, p. 252.

214. Ibid.

215. Ibid., p. 253.

216. Ibid.

217. Ibid.

218. Ibid., p. 258.

219. Mance, *International Sea Transport*, p. 14.

220. Ibid.; see also William E. Masterson, "Territorial Waters and International Legislation," *Oregon Law Review* 8 (1929):306, 307-310.

221. Hunter Miller, "The Hague Codification Conference," *American Journal of International Law* 24 (1930):674.

222. C. John Colombos, "The Unification of Maritime International Law in Time of Peace," *British Year Book of International Law* 21 (1944): 96.

223. Bernard G. Heinzen, "The Three-Mile Limit: Preserving the Freedom of the Seas," *Stanford Law Review* 11 (1959):197, 637; Jesse S. Reeves, "The Codification of the Law of Territorial Waters," *American Journal of International Law* 24 (1924):486; Special Supplement, *American Journal of International Law* 24 (1924):25, 234.

224. Heinzen, "Three-Mile Limit," p. 637.

225. Ibid.

226. Ibid.

227. Ibid.

228. Ibid., p. 638.

229. Ibid., p. 639ff.

230. Mance, *International Sea Transport*, pp. 15-19.

231. Ibid., pp. 19-22.

232. Ibid., pp. 22-26.

233. Myres S. McDougal, William T. Burke, and Ivan A. Vlasic, "The Maintenance of Public Order at Sea and the Nationality of Ships," *American Journal of International Law* 54 (1960):25, 27.

234. P.C.I.J. Series A, No. 10 (1927); see also J.L. Brierly, "The LOTUS case," *Law Quarterly Review* 44 (1928):154.

235. Convention on Penal Jurisdiction in Matters of Collision or other Incidents of Navigation, May 10, 1952.

236. Lilar and van den Bosch, *Comité Maritime International*, pp. 110-112.

237. Ibid., pp. 24-26.

238. Colombos, "Unification of Maritime Law," p. 100.

239. Ibid.

240. Ibid., pp. 100-101.

241. Ibid.

242. "Harter Act," 27 U.S. Stats. 445 (1893).

243. A.N. Yiannopoulos, "The Unification of Private Maritime Law by International Conventions," *Law and Contemporary Problems* 30 (1965):370,386-390.

244. Lilar and van den Bosch, *Comité Maritime International*, pp. 26-28.

245. Colombos, "Unification of Maritime Law," p. 101.

246. Comment, "The Difficult Quest for a Uniform Maritime Law: Failure of the Brussels Conventions to Achieve International Agreement on Collision Liability, Liens and Mortgages," *Yale Law Journal* 64 (1955):878, 893-903.

247. Ibid.

248. Ibid.; Lilar and van den Bosch, *Comité Maritime International*, pp. 28-30.

249. Sir Leslie Scott and Cyril Miller, "The Unification of Maritime and Commercial Law through the Comité Maritime International," *International Law Quarterly* 1(1947):482.

250. J.B. Condliffe, *The Commerce of Nations* (New York: Norton, 1950), ch. 16; J.K. Galbraith, *The Age of Uncertainty* (London: André Deutsch, 1977), ch. 8.

251. Condliffe, *Commerce of Nations*, p. 527.

252. Ibid.

253. Ibid.

254. Ibid.

255. Ibid.

256. Ibid., p. 528.

257. Hugh Thomas, *The Spanish Civil War*, rev. ed. (New York: Harper and Row, 1977).

258. Ibid.

259. Condliffe, *Commerce of Nations*, p. 528.

260. Langer, *World History*, p. 983.

261. Condliffe, *Commerce of Nations*, p. 528.

262. Mance, *International Ocean Transport*, p. 146.

263. Mangone, *Marine Policy for America*, p. 88.

264. Stevens and Westcott, *History of Sea Power*, p. 427.

265. Ibid.

266. Ibid., p. 428.

267. Howarth, *Sovereign of the Seas*, p. 351.

268. Ibid., p. 350.

269. The CMI had suspended its operations during the war.

270. Mangone, *Marine Policy for America*, p. 176.

271. Terry Hughes and John Costello, *The Battle of the Atlantic* (New York: Dial Press, 1977), cited in appendix.

272. Ibid., p. 219.

273. Nussbaum, *History of the Law of Nations*, pp. 266-267.

274. Hughes and Costello, *Battle of the Atlantic*, p. 219.

275. Stevens and Westcott, *History of Sea Power*, p. 428.

276. Ibid.

277. Ibid.

278. Barrie Pitt, *The Battle of the Atlantic* (Alexandria, Va.: Time-Life, 1977).

279. Hughes and Costello, *Battle of the Atlantic*, p. 304.

280. Ibid., pp. 5-6.

281. Pitt, *Battle of the Atlantic*, p. 8.

282. Howarth, *Sovereign of the Seas*, p. 351.

283. Hughes and Costello, *Battle of the Atlantic*, p. 304.

284. Ibid., pp. 48-50.

285. Ibid., p. 304.

286. Pitt, *Battle of the Atlantic*, pp. 178-179.

287. Hughes and Costello, *Battle of the Atlantic*, p. 304.

288. Stevens and Westcott, *History of Sea Power*, p. 452.

289. Bernard Bailyn et al., *The Great Republic* (Boston: Little, Brown, 1977), p. 1169.

290. Ibid., p. 1170.

291. Ibid., p. 1169.

292. Ibid., pp. 1169-1170.

293. Ibid.

294. Ibid.

295. Langer, *World History*, p. 1143.

296. Bailyn, *The Great Republic*, p. 1170.

297. Ibid.

298. Ibid.; see also Robert E. Sherwood, *Roosevelt and Hopkins: An Intimate History* (New York: Harper and Brothers, 1948), pp. 278-290.

299. "Lend-Lease Act," 55 U.S. Stats. 31 (1941-1942).

300. Condliffe, *Commerce of Nations*, p. 533.

301. Ibid., p. 532.

302. Hughes and Costello, *Battle of the Atlantic*, ch. 15.

303. Ibid., p. 304.

304. Ibid.

305. Ibid., p. 214ff.

306. Ibid., p. 215.

307. Ibid., p. 216.

308. Ibid.

309. Ibid.

310. Ibid., p. 218.

311. Ibid.

312. Bailyn, *The Great Republic*, p. 1171.

313. Ibid.

314. George C. Marshall, cited by Condliffe, *The Commerce of Nations*, p. 530.

# 6 The Internationalization of Marine Transport

*Come then, comrades, the European game has finally ended; we must find something different. We today can do everything so long as we do not imitate Europe, so long as we are not obsessed by the desire to catch up with Europe.*

—Frantz Fanon (*The Wretched of the Earth*, 1965)

*. . . each state, whether coastal or not, has an interest in the fullest possible access, either for itself or for others on its behalf, to all the inclusive uses of the ocean, such as navigation, fishing, cable-laying and so on, for the richest possible production of values.*

—Myres S. McDougal (*Yale Law Journal* 67, 1958)

## Introduction: A New Economic System Emerges from the War

We now come to the era of recent or modern history, and obviously we cannot examine the entire world panorama as it unfolded in the post-World War II period. We are examining legal and policy aspects of international shipping, knowing full well that, like all other systems, marine transport was inextricably linked to the broader political, economic, and international legal questions of this important period. Thus we must be selective, at the risk of subjectivity. We will simply continue our examination of marine transport during this period against the background of our central theme of public- and private-law divergence. In addition, we will analyze the alienation of shipping policy from the other public ocean policies, which were converging to form the modern law of the sea at this time. To do this, we intend to look at the following selected aspects of post-World War II history: the changes in the world's general trading system and the emergence of newly independent states; the establishment of the United Nations and some of its special agencies; the continuing work of the *Comité Maritime International* (CMI) and the recovered world shipping industry; and the important new spatial approaches in the law of the sea.

Economists generally agree that economic power is based on population, resources and raw materials, technical skills, and industrial organization.[1] At the end of World War II, the United States and the Soviet Union were more favorably placed than were the Western European states, which had always depended on *outside* sources of economic power. On the continent of Europe their systems were destroyed and could be rebuilt only with massive infusions of aid from the United States. Otherwise, they would be absorbed into the centralized socialist system of which the Soviet Union was to be the apex.

For Great Britain the problems were more complex. World War II not only had caused widespread physical destruction and almost irreplaceable losses in youthful manpower, but also had come at a time when the British Empire was inevitably declining.[2] As we have seen, the concentration of economic, financial, strategic, and political British power reached its peak in the last quarter of the nineteenth century. It then leveled off and started to decline with the advent of Germany and other states in Western Europe that had wrested much of this power away by the time World War I commenced. The Great Depression and two destructive wars took much of what was left and threw it to the United States and the Soviet Union.

This oversimplification of a very involved and complex process should, at least, suffice to help explain the subtle and not-so-subtle shifts in economic power that were occurring.[3] After all, one of the most essential elements of European political-economic strengths had been the complete dominance of vast areas in Asia and Africa by trade and investment backed up by military force. From there, all ocean trade routes had led to the ports of Western Europe. The economic development of the colonies, even those that had remained politically independent, was generally determined by the demands of European markets. As Professor Condliffe suggests:

> This nineteenth century organization of world order was a remarkable achievement. Vast empires had been lightly held. The combination of naval force and skeleton garrisons at posts commanding strategic waterways had been sufficient to keep open the sea lanes. The threat of punitive expeditions had sufficed to maintain authority that was directly exercised by European states and to ensure economic access where authority remained in the hands of local rulers. It is a significant fact that Britain, the greatest colonial power and the greatest trading country, did not find it necessary to resort to conscription before 1914. The real instrument of domination was economic power buttressed by skillful administration.[4]

*The Problems of Freedom and Independence*
*for the Colonial Peoples*

There is little doubt that the breakdown of these "imperial" systems, with their well-established trading patterns, was one of the major elements in the great political changes that took place after World War II. The trading system that had been based, if not built, on the economic and political subordination of dependent colonies was shattered.[5] Salvage was not possible, although attempts were made.[6] Certainly the British, French, and Dutch attempted, either by granting concessions or by suppression, to hold off the independence of their colonial possessions. However, on the whole, World War II accelerated the independence movement in Africa and Asia with remarkable speed.

Being on the losing side, Japan was stripped of all its conquests, which were divided among the United States, the Soviet Union, Korea, and China.[7] Britain's colonial "crown jewel," India, achieved its own independence, though at the cost of partition.[8] Burma, Ceylon, and Malaya also gained independence. After bitter struggle, over three centuries of Dutch rule in the East Indies ended with the independence of the new Republic of Indonesia. The French possessions in Indochina would finally be subdivided into Vietnam, Laos, and Cambodia—again after many struggles and wars of independence. The Philippine Republic became independent in 1946. Italy lost both conquests and colonies to independence movements and, in the Middle East, Transjordan followed Iraq, Syria, and Lebanon in attaining independence. Egypt had become completely independent from British influence; and the British mandate in Palestine had been handed over to the United Nations, which created an independent Israel in 1948.

Thus five years after the end of World War II, with the exception of a few enclaves in Asia and the Caribbean area, only Africa south of the Sahara remained under foreign domination. By the late 1950s and early 1960s, most of Africa had also become independent.

This emergence of literally scores of new nation-states on the global political scene would, obviously, have profound effects on all aspects of international affairs. The resultant radical changes in world shipping and trading patterns would, as always, be of central importance, although this was not always recognized. This was because the lack of clear policy by the former colonial powers and the comparative suddenness and wholesale nature of emancipation had produced an extraordinarily varied conglomeration of new nations. The new states had to make the most out of their new-found freedoms within the confines—whether political, economic, or geographical—created by their former masters for the former masters' benefit.

So much has been eloquently said about colonial emancipation, root causes of developmental problems, and other difficulties of emerging nations, that we can once again be selective as well as illustrative.[9] Economic development, a phrase hardly coined in the late 1940s and early 1950s was, of course, the key, and remains so today. In terms of development—or industrialization—almost all the emerging, newly independent states of Africa and Asia were deficient in terms of education, agriculture, transportation, and communication.[10] Even among the twenty Latin American and

Caribbean republics, independent already for many years, there were considerable developmental gaps between, say, Uruguay, one of the most advanced, and Haiti, one of the least developed. Not only had the colonial masters failed to prepare their dependent colonies for independence on even the most basic level, but they had also frequently altered the indigenous systems to such an extent that when independence came many problems were simply further compounded.[11]

Self-sufficient village economies had been destroyed so that labor could be furnished for foreign-owned and foreign-directed enterprises. Social structures had been wiped out by the introduction of alien money economics; tribal and racial structures had been eliminated by political boundaries agreed on in European conference halls with little or no consideration for the immediate, let alone ultimate, effects. Western-style increased productivity was soon swallowed up by massive population increases.[12]

By that time it was too late to turn back the clock. Governments of newly independent states had only two choices—either to face hardship, disease, and famine on a massive scale, or to continue their search for modern economic methods of production. The latter would involve the eternal treadmill of developmental problems, which have continued into the most recent period.

Although the colonial master had left, the imperialist vanished, and the alien settler departed, their spirits had been transposed into the indigenous desire for a higher (Northern) standard of living, for Northern machines and comforts, and for general Northern prosperity.[13] Very quickly this large grouping of new states, with its ever-swelling ranks in terms of both population and statehood, would become a completely different world—a developing world, a Third World[14]—in time even splitting up into Fourth and Fifth worlds,[15] all clamoring for greater equity in an unequal world, all dependent on the generosity of the remaining two worlds—particularly the "First" world, consisting of the advanced industrial nations many of which had so directly created their problems in the first place.[16]

Although we cannot stray too far into the awesome complexities of international development here, we intend nevertheless to make particular reference to the Third World in our examination of international marine policy and shipping law, despite the fact that the developing nations, particularly in these early post-World War II stages of independence, had not the slightest influence on either such law or such policy.[17] It can be stated as flatly as that. We know, of course, from pre-World War II shipping statistics, that nations that could then have been considered "developing" did not figure very prominently. Some of the more advanced Latin American republics, such as Argentina, Brazil, Chile, and Uruguay were exceptions, but only in a very modest sense.[18] Although the pattern of world shipping would be drastically changed in the aftermath of World War II, these changes occurred *within* a comparatively small and select group of major maritime states, which had mostly been the imperialist colonial powers before colonial independence.

### Development and Marine Transport

In other words, these changes in marine policy and shipping trends did not have any beneficial effect on the newly independent nations of the Third World. If anything, the effect was deleterious and often downright damaging to the fragile economic systems of the new states. During the colonial period these states had been entirely dependent on the supply of shipping transportation by the metropolitan power. This dependence had often been part and parcel of the colonial master's overall marine policy. The colony was considered to be a part of the mother country's trading pattern and trade routes and was thus assured a reliable and reasonably priced shipping service over which the colony, nevertheless, could not exercise any control whatsoever.

As we have seen, for some of the colonial powers such shipping services were heavily subsidized and were thus "true services" to and from the colony. For others, which followed full commercial requirements, the service was at least assured of protective treatment for government cargoes and passengers. Independence changed all of this overnight. Almost at once the frail young nations were subject to the whims of the international shipping industry with all its commensurate commercial complexities. No longer was there an assurance of reliable shipping services subsidized at a reasonable cost. Third-World cargoes would henceforth be subject to the full sweep of the international freight market, the shipping conference system, and the costly charter market.

Freedom is, of course, an emotionally charged word, conveying many different meanings to those of differing points of view. Less frequently is the cost of freedom calculated in commercial terms. Perhaps this is not even possible; but if it were, then the developing countries paid (and are still paying) a very bitter price for their freedom and independence. And yet we are not denying that freedom is probably worth *any* price. But in practical terms, it was a high price—the immediate and stark division of the world into developed and developing states, with all the latter's burgeoning problems.

We must address this problem here, even if only in passing, because marine transport was one of the real difficulties facing the new nations right from the beginning of independence. It was not (and still is not) seen as a primary problem when compared to hunger, disease, and basic education difficulties. A slightly more realistic examination might have revealed that both transport and communications were centrally interlinked with the more visible and pressing problems.[19] After all, development problems caused dependence on outside assistance; and nowhere were the Third-World states more vulnerable and dependent than in international transportation.

Most of the developing states, particularly in Asia and Africa but also to a lesser extent in Latin America and the Caribbean, had poorly developed internal transportation systems and even worse regional international systems.[20] Thus air and sea transport was required for almost all international trade and passenger carriage. Obviously, air transportation, particularly in the early years of independence, would only cater to a very limited group. Marine transport was, therefore, the key to economic survival for most of the young nations.[21] However, marine transport had been developed, as we have discovered, into a system in which only a small and select group of richer nations participated. This system had created complex infrastructures, which had developed completely outside any of the new nations' spheres of influence.

That is not to say that the Third World had no maritime traditions. On the contrary, the very ancient mariners of Egypt, the Fertile Crescent, the African Coast, India, China, and Southeast Asia had passed their trade down through the ages to their descendants.[22] However, the descendants had either been forced to continue their primitive seaborne trade without any modernization or incentive, or they had become the sailors—the labor—in the fleets of the latecomer colonial masters. The masters had kept the shipping business very much to themselves, sending their own people out to the far-flung corners of their empires to run European-style shipping businesses strictly controlled by investment-conscious boards of directors in the European capitals.[23] If the shipping industry trained indigenous workers to be managers, then they were trained to operate a European-style industry and to look to some European capital for orders, guidance, and priority. If such trainees remained after independence, they could not be expected to solve transportation problems because they were not trained to do so and thus often exacerbated the difficulties faced by their new nations.

Almost all the new states had one or two raw material exports on which their whole economy depended.[24] To get these products to the world markets required shipping, which was controlled by well-established conferences and other cartels, which in accordance with well-tried economic models charged "what the market could bear." A country with only one market simply has to bear a lot, and year after year the developing states would pay out precious foreign exchange for their export freight rates, which were, to add insult to injury, often carried on a cost, insurance, and freight (CIF) basis.[25]

Of course, lack of industrial and manufacturing capacity ensured that the new states would also have to depend on international shipping for all or most of their imports, which were continually increasing owing to Northern-style marketing tactics, which assured ever-increasing consumer demands for imported goods. If this appears to paint the shipping states (that is, the former colonial powers) in a subjectively negative light, it is our intention to do so. The practices of the international shipping industry and the marine policies of the maritime states are hardly a matter for pride. The fact that a United Nations organization would eventually have to lay down a "code of conduct" in a so-far unsuccessful attempt to regulate these practices lends credence to our subjectivity.[26]

We will return later to this important theme in our examination. We must add, however, that many of these difficulties could have been reduced considerably by a change of attitude of the Third-World governments, which suffered most from these difficulties. Despite the fact that there were many pressing priorities and immediate problems, marine transport should have been much higher on the list of developmental concerns. There was an absence of marine policy, clearly defined or otherwise, and at times a complete lack of understanding of the invisible costs to the country incurred through the lack of shipping infrastructure.[27] Shipping had in the past been something alien—part of the former colonial masters' structural super-imposition—and its internationalism did not fit in well with the surging, emotional nationalism of new-found independence and sovereignty. The leaders of the new countries, trained as they often were at the great universities of Europe and North America, had little interest in the technicalities of international marine transport and even less time to train someone in the field who would not only understand the country's transportation problems but also comprehend the international structure.

By this time the divergence between the public aspects of marine law and policy and the private, commercial side of shipping law and policy were already well defined in the developed world, and this would create additional specific problems for the developing states. The divergence had been passed to them via the former colonial powers, which had created a governmental administrative structure accordingly. Public marine law and policy was a matter for foreign affairs, which would, after independence, be the leading ministry during the difficult early years. However, shipping law and policy would belong to a subgroup in a ministry dealing with commerce, trade, transport, or communications and would thus rank much lower in the priorities of emergent power.

As already suggested, this divergence was harmful and costly to the developed maritime states. Obviously, then, such cost and harm would be much greater in the Third World, where all losses, human and otherwise, were much more harmful. It was thus not unusual to find that by the time a new state had been independent for some years, its marine affairs were spread over a number of ministries and government departments. Law of the sea, shipping law, fisheries resources, shipping policy, marine research, port administration and development, coastal protection, and so on might all be looked after by quite separate entities without the benefit of any centrally planned marine policy whatsoever.[28]

We are not advocating here the central planning of the socialist economic systems. But we maintain that the ocean is a single inalienable unit and that *all* ocean uses and *all* marine affairs can be realized only by a fairly close interlinking of the decision-making process relating to it. For the Third World, this process has not yet begun. However, we must leave this area for the moment to look at what was happening to the larger world in the aftermath of World War II.

### The Creation of the United Nations: Search for World Peace and Stability

The fact that only two decades would pass from the conclusion of the "war to end all wars" until the majority of the world states were embroiled in a new world war, which reached new depths of inhumanity and destruction, led to a demand for some sort of supreme international organization that could accomplish what the ill-fated League of Nations had been unable to do. Added to this motive was a new urgency created by the technological advances in warfare achieved during World War II. The development of the atomic bomb and, soon after, of its "doomsday brother" the hydrogen bomb, which would rapidly become a part of the arsenal of the major powers, required that some sort of international peace-keeping mechanism be recreated to prevent the world from reaching the brink of all-out war and possible global destruction.

The idea of creating a new intergovernmental body to replace the League of Nations arose early in World War II and was probably first publicly expressed in June 1941 in London in an inter-Allied Declaration by five Commonwealth States and eight European governments-in-exile.[29] In January 1942, in Washington, the formal Declaration of United Nations was signed by twenty-six states, all of whom had subscribed to the principles of the Atlantic Charter (1941), pledging their full support for the defeat of the Axis powers.[30] At a meeting in Moscow in 1943, the representatives of the United States, Great Britain, China, and the Soviet Union proclaimed that they

. . . recognized the necessity of establishing at the earliest applicable date a general international organization, based on the principle of the sovereign equality of all peace-loving states, and open to membership by all such states, large and small, for the maintenance of international peace and security.[31]

In 1944 a further four-power conference, at Dunbarton Oaks in Washington, laid the groundwork for further concrete suggestions for discussions at a subsequent conference of all the "united nations."[32] Meeting at San Francisco from April 25 to June 25, 1945, representatives of fifty states participated in the drafting of the United Nations Charter, which was formally signed at the end of the conference.[33] Within four months the charter had been ratified by enough signatories and by the five permanent members of the Security Council, and could enter into force.[34] On January 10, 1946 the U.N. General Assembly convened its first regular session and accepted an invitation by the United States to establish a permanent home for the United Nations in New York.

The development of the U.N. organization is a part of well-known modern history that needs little elaboration here. But it is of considerable interest to note that of the fifty-one founding states of the United Nations, some thirty-one could be classified as belonging to the "developing" category.[35] One must add, however, that this group comprised eighteen Central and Latin American states; six Middle Eastern states; two Caribbean states; three Asian states; and only two African states.[36] The great bulk of what would become the Third World had not yet gained independence. However, the world at that time was still undergoing the euphoria of victory; and thoughts of underdevelopment, North-versus-South confrontation, and new economic orders were still some two decades away. Nevertheless, the benefit of hindsight shows that the three-to-five ratio of what could be classified as "old-line" powers to underdeveloped states, even at that time, was an almost accurate prediction of what was to come.

To simplify matters, the U.N. system was conceived as comprising:

1. the principal organs;
2. subsidiary organs established by the United Nations to deal with particular aspects of U.N. responsibilities;
3. a series of specialized and related agencies;
4. a number of ad hoc global conferences dealing with issues singled out by the organization as having particularly pressing importance.

This institutional structure was and still is the product of very complex negotiations in which an attempt was made to find an equitable balance both of the conflicting claims of national sovereignty and international responsibility and of the rights of the large and small states.

Naturally, a world organization such as the United Nations, with its various organs and specialized agencies, would have some significance for marine transport. Suprisingly, in the early days after the establishment of the United Nations, this significance was hard to find and was more peripheral than central. This is not to say that the importance of marine transport was not recognized by the United Nations—far from it. Already in 1946, at Washington, a group of maritime states prepared a draft convention for the possible establishment of an international maritime organization.[37] This meeting took place at the specific request of the U.N. Economic and Social Council (ECOSOC).[38] In other words, the work left incomplete at the 1889 Washington Maritime Conference was finally to be continued. However, considerable difficulties remained. In 1948 a full maritime conference was convened under the auspices of ECOSOC at Geneva. During the two-month conference, the Convention of the Inter-Governmental Maritime Consultative Organization (IMCO) was worked out; it was finally adopted and opened for signature on March 6, 1948.[39] IMCO is unique in being the only intergovernmental organization solely concerned with shipping. Its purposes are best set out as laid down in the convention:

Article 1: The purposes of the Organization are:

a.) To provide machinery for co-operation among Governments in the field of governmental regulation and practices relating to technical matters of all kinds affecting shipping engaged in international trade, and to encourage the general adoption of the highest practicable standards in matters concerning maritime safety and efficiency of navigation;

b.) to encourage the removal of discriminatory action and unnecessary restriction by Governments affecting shipping engaged in international trade so as to promote the availability of shipping services to the commerce of the world without discrimination; assistance and encouragement given by a Government for the development of its national shipping and for purposes of security does not in itself constitute discrimination, provided that such assistance and encouragement is not based on measures designed to restrict the freedom of shipping of all flags to take part in international trade;

c.) to provide for the consideration by the Organization of any matters concerning unfair restrictive practices by shipping concerns in accordance with Part II;

d.) to provide for the consideration by the Organization of any matters concerning shipping that may be referred to it by any organ or specialized agency of the United Nations;

e.) to provide for the exchange of information among Governments on matters under consideration by the Organization.[40]

Even these comparatively modest purposes were too much for most of the maritime states; it would be ten long years until Japan's ratification completed the twenty-one ratifications required for the convention to enter into force.[41] There was, of course, a fully discernible fear by the traditional maritime states that the war had completely changed shipping patterns and trade and that competition would soon arise from the establishment of new fleets in new countries. The fear that IMCO might become an international regulatory agency, which might take a very serious look at traditional shipping methods, was directly related although at that time quite unfounded.[42]

As we have seen, the strategic importance of marine transport had once again been brought to the fore in World War II, which had taken such a heavy toll of merchant shipping. At the end of the war, as a part of the task of reconstruction, special attention was devoted to the establishment of relatively modest shipping in a number of Latin American, Asian, and to a lesser extent African states.[43] Before the war, all shipping to and from these states had been the prerogative of the major maritime states. However, the practices of the traditional shipping industry ensured the need for many of the newer states also to develop, in addition to their shore-based industry, their own national shipping. Active encouragement for the expansion of shipping resulted in a modest proportion of these states' seaborne trade being carried in their own ships. As Singh and Colinvaux conclude:

> The entry of newcomers into the field of international shipping, however, had repercussions among the shipping circles of the established maritime countries who had for long years carried the overseas trade not merely of their own country but also of their dependent territories in distant areas. Some thought this intrusion to be quite unnecessary, on the ground that all shipping services which the commerce of the world needed, were being provided already by the existing maritime Powers. Others saw in these efforts a threat to their own dominating position. Serious objection was taken by the leaders of the industry to some of the measures of government assistance which the nascent merchant navies were being accorded.[44]

Obviously, it was not altogether in the interests of the maritime states to see a U.N. organization established that was solely concerned with international shipping and had any capacity other than a purely advisory or technical one. Some states opposed the establishment of the organization altogether and would eventually append lengthy reservations to their instruments of ratification when IMCO was finally established.[45] Others attempted to water down the effectiveness of the organization so that they could control its vital organs as much as possible.[46] In retrospect it appears that international shipping displayed amazingly little foresight and even less sensitivity in following a broad and ill-defined policy of delaying tactics, which would become the standard methods of the developed states in the future whenever the status quo even appeared to be endangered. Besides harming IMCO, this policy also added to the self-centered reputation with which the shipping industry would be burdened for some years—eventually at great loss to the industry as a whole. We will return to this important theme, as well as to IMCO, later in this chapter.

Several of the other "early" U.N. specialized agencies had interests of some significance to ocean transportation.[47] Among these were the following.

1. Food and Agricultural Organization (FAO):[48] Established in 1946 and given considerable responsibility relating to ocean fishing, including fishery technology. Also involved in marine transport during famine and in disaster relief.

2. International Bank of Reconstruction and Development (IBRD):[49] Established in 1946 to promote the international flow of capital for productive purposes such as ports, shipping, and transportation infrastructures.

3. International Civil Aviation Organization (ICAO):[50] Established in 1946 to promote international cooperation and development of principles of air navigation and air transport; thus, in theory, ICAO is IMCO's sister organization. However, it never received the resistance from the aviation industry that IMCO received from the shipping industry, and it has thus been a much more effective and viable organization.

4. International Telecommunication Union (ITU):[51] Established in 1946 but based on a convention already in effect in 1934. The ITU's prime purpose was to foster international cooperation for the improvement and rational use of telecommunications; it has, of course, a certain effect on marine communications.

Thus, within a decade of the conclusion of World War II, the establishment of the United Nations and of some of its specialized agencies ushered in a hopeful new era of international cooperation and a great variety of human endeavors. Unfortunately, marine transport was effectively left out, having received its long-awaited recognition only to be thwarted in becoming established by the overprotective concerns of the major shipping states. Of course, the delaying and other anti-IMCO tactics, which could not have been a part of any overall public marine policy by these states, originated from the private sector of the shipping industry, which had by this time diverged so far from overall interests that it really had become nothing more than an effective pressure group with fairly high-placed connections. Rather than viewing its interests against the background of the *whole* changing maritime panorama, international marine transport in the traditional maritime states could now only propagate its own narrower policies. These consisted simply of rebuilding their devasted fleets up to and beyond prewar standards and of getting back to "their" shipping business in the traditional way without allowing any newcomers on the scene or much interference, national or international, in regulating their traditional trade.

## The Law and Policy of World Shipping in the Aftermath of World War II

International shipping did return to normal very quickly after the war. By 1947 international seaborne trade was almost back to the prewar figure of 480 million metric tons, and by 1950 it had reached 550 million metric tons.[52] By that year the world fleet had also surpassed the 1939 total of 67 million gross tons by 3 million.[53] Of course, the biggest fleet changes had occurred in the United States, which had increased its total fleet from 8.9 million tons to 11.6 million tons in the decade 1939-1950, *despite* all its war losses.[54] The total British Empire fleet had, despite its almost 60 percent destruction, grown by just over 1 million tons to 22 million, thus still making up 31.6 percent of the world fleet.[55]

The losers in the war, Germany, Italy, and Japan, had declined by 30 percent on the world-fleet ladder. In other words, the appalling losses of World War II notwithstanding, the world fleet had not only recovered but had actually increased quickly within five years of the end of the war. Not only had the world fleet changed drastically in its distribution, but its trading pattern and composition had also altered considerably. Despite the war, the world's tanker tonnage increased by 50 percent, to 25.3 million tons deadweight, between 1939 and 1950; in the latter year, tank ships constituted almost one-quarter of all ships in operation.[56] This was only a sign of things to come. By 1955 this figure had risen to 30 percent, although well over 60 percent of all ships being built or constructed in the world were tankers.[57]

The actual trading pattern was also changing. The Asian share of imports and exports was rising rapidly and the African share slightly. Western European trade had declined while North American trade had doubled between 1938 and 1946.[58] There was thus no question that marine transport had recovered fully from the ravages of World War II and was progressing with renewed vigor in a comparatively short time. As we have noted, however, the world's fleet was still very much distributed, albeit unevenly, among the dozen or so traditional maritime states. By 1950 the only newcomer to the group was Panama, with some 3.4 million tons, for reasons that will be discussed later.[59]

As already noted, international law virtually ceased to operate during World Wars I and II. For the CMI and private maritime law, the World War II interruption lasted from 1939 to 1946, when activities once more got underway. As a result, problems that had been left in abeyance and new subjects were tackled together at the following CMI conferences during the early post-war period.[60]

XXth        Conference:   Antwerp 1946
            Agenda:       Ratification of the Brussels conventions,
                              including the convention on the immunity
                              of stateowned ships
                          Revision of the conventions on liability of
                              owners of seagoing vessels and on bills
                              of lading
                          Examination of the three draft conventions
                              adopted at the XIXth conference in Paris
                          Assistance and salvage of and by aircraft at
                              sea
                          York and Antwerp rules

XXIst       Conference:   Amsterdam 1949
            Agenda:       Ratification of the Brussels conventions
                          Revisions of the York/Antwerp rules, 1924
                          Limitation of shipowners' liability (gold
                              clauses)
                          Combined through bills of lading
                          Revision of the draft convention of provi-
                              sional arrest of ships
                          Draft of creation of an international court
                              for navigation by sea and air

XXIInd      Conference:   Naples 1951
            Agenda:       Brussels conventions
                          Draft convention relating to provisional arrest
                              of ships
                          Limitation of liability of the owners of sea-
                              going vessels and bills of lading (revision of
                              the gold clauses)
                          Revision of the convention of maritime
                              hypothecation and mortgages
                          Liability of carriers by sea toward passengers
                          Penal jurisdiction in matters of collision at
                              sea

XXIIIrd     Conference:   Madrid 1955
            Agenda:       Limitation of shipowners' liability convention
                          Liability of sea carriers toward passengers
                          Stowaways
                          Marginal clauses and letters of indemnity

It thus appears from even a cursory glance at the agendas of the CMI
conferences during this period that the Comité had renewed its work with its

customary vigor but was now completely devoted to the study and unification of generally the most technical aspects of private maritime law. At a time when international shipping was undergoing great changes, when IMCO was being founded, when many new states with differing maritime interests were appearing on the scene, the most viable maritime organization was, in effect, isolated from this new mainstream. That is not to say that the CMI was not doing worthwhile work—on the contrary. By 1952 the committee was able to produce, as the fruits of many years of labor, three new drafts for the *Conference Diplomatique*, which in turn resulted in the adoption of three new international conventions in May 1952.

The first of these was the Convention on Penal Jurisdiction in Matters of Collision or Incidents of Navigation.[61] It finally laid to rest the controversial and unfortunate decision in the *Lotus* case.[62] The convention attributes exclusive competence to the judiciary or administrative authorities of the state of which the ship flies the flag. Such authorities are given the competence to deal with any action resulting from a collision or any other event likely to engage the penal or disciplinary responsibility of those serving on the ship, with the exception of the right of each state to institute proceedings against their nationals serving on board a foreign ship. The convention prohibits any arrest or detention of the ship by any authority other than the flag state. The new convention thus laid down its rules as an affirmation of the high-seas freedom under which all nations have equal rights on the high seas and no one may assert a right of jurisdiction over the subjects of other nations.[63]

The second of the ''1952 Brussels Conventions'' was the Convention on Civil Jurisdiction in Matters of Collision, which deals with the concurrence of civil jurisdiction in maritime matters, the frequency of which produced effects that were quite harmful to the general operation of maritime transportation.[64] This was remedied by the convention by limiting the number of competent courts and laying down rules for the expeditious award of damages to the claimant. The convention thus aptly complements the 1910 collision convention.[65]

The third convention of 1952 is probably one of the most important achievements in the quest for the unification of maritime law. This is the Convention on the Arrest of Sea-Going Ships,[66] which not only sets out the rules in the vital *in rem* procedure area,[67] but also, at the same time, succeeded in unifying legislative systems of considerable dissimilarity.[68] The CMI had been working in this field since the 1930s and had reached a basic agreement in Paris in 1937 that could not be followed up because of the onset of the war.

Obviously, the arrest of ships, apart from being a unique legal proceeding, is of great concern to shipowners and to all involved in the voyage of the ship. Unified regulations relating to the procedure were thwarted by an array of divergent national laws, which made consensus almost impossible.[69] However, the postwar intensification of marine traffic, which gave rise to a virtual multiplicity of arrest and subsequent litigation, led to new attempts to find common ground.[70] Eventually a compromise was achieved at the Naples conference of the CMI in 1951, which then led to the 1952 convention. In this broad historical examination of the international law and policy of marine transport, we cannot go into details of substantive law, which in most instances is well chronicled.[71]

The arrest of ships is, for example, a very technical legal procedure that cannot be detailed here. It illustrates, however, the *international* aspect of shipping and the necessity for creditors/claimants in one state to be able to press their interests directly against the property of a debtor who is outside the claimants' jurisdiction. The former, of course, was interested in making arrest of vessels easier, whereas the latter (usually the shipowner) wished to restrict arrest or at least to avoid untimely or unnecessary arrests. At the same time, both parties have an overall interest in facilitating international commercial exchanges, of which their dispute is only a byproduct. The arrest convention was not able to resolve many of the existing problems, and even its rather modest compromise was unacceptable for many states.[72] Its progress lay simply in defining which courts should have jurisdiction to determine a case when an arrest occurs. Cases for arrests are limited and strictly defined, reducing to a great extent the conflicts of law existing in the area.[73]

## The Law of the Sea: The Divergence of Ocean-Use Interests

As we have seen, the 1930 Hague Codification Conference was unable to settle any of the new jurisdictional problems created by both clear and subtle changes occurring in ocean use between the wars. Retrospectively, it can perhaps be said that 1930 was probably too early for these problems to be discussed at a global conference. On the one hand, the traditional oceanic states were still too powerful to permit any inroads on what they considered their historic ocean rights. On the other hand, the coastal states, which felt that they had certain other rights, were either unable to press their claims strongly enough or could not muster enough potential strength to have their views accepted. There is no doubt that this impasse led to much instability in the public law of the sea in the few remaining years before World War II broke out. However, the general difficulties of the period relegated this oceanic problem to fairly low priority, and there were few further high-level discussions on the subject before the war. World War II precluded all further negotiations.

Nevertheless, the 1930 conference, so often dismissed today as an unimportant failure, was an important milestone in the context of our overall analysis.[74] The conference set out, for the first time, to discuss functional approaches to the traditional public law of the sea. Despite its outcome, the conference thus served clear notice to the world's ocean users that the public law of the sea did not simply consist of the spatial or jurisdictional content, as had hitherto been understood.

We doubt that the law of the sea had ever been meant to be interpreted within such a narrow legalistic category; that had certainly never been the intention of great jurists such as Grotius.[75] But even if it had been so—even if we had moved historically from a period we might call "oceanic juridical convergence," existing up to the Napoleonic period, to a period of "oceanic juridical divergence" in the next era—then the 1930 conference marked an almost imperceptible return to "oceanic convergence." Yet it would not be the uniting juridical convergence that was now, more than ever before, needed. At a time when *all* the uses of the ocean would be slowly coming under the scrutiny of a rapidly changing political world (a situation that already was well underway by 1930), the most traditional use—marine transport—had effectively become isolated from the mainstream of the public law of the sea, which had evolved slowly from its modest beginnings into the sophisticated legal system needed to meet the needs of the world's oceanic endeavors.

Thus the cannon-shot coastal-protection rule had become the law of territorial seas; the ill-assorted combination of colonial conquest, prize laws, and protection of neutrality had evolved into the law of the high seas built on the vague principle of "freedom of the seas." By 1930 Professor Gidel would divide what he called "international maritime law" into public, administrative and criminal, and commercial law. But even these more acceptable subdivisions largely concern ships—what they can and cannot do, what can and cannot be done to them, what can and cannot be done by and to those on board, their cargoes, their liabilities, questions of ownership, and so on. The rights of the coastal states had, for reasons we have already discussed, become subservient to the overall importance of the ship in international commercial intercourse. That had led directly to the juridical divergence we have discussed.

If we accept (which we do not) that this divergence was beneficial to the operation of international marine transport during this time, then we must immediately add that it could only operate while shipping was the main ocean use and was accepted by the general world to be so. As soon as shipping had to compete with other uses, this divergence would lead to difficulties, misunderstandings, and eventual conflict. The other most traditional use—fisheries—can illustrate this point best.[76] Fisheries, evolving from the dawn of history, have almost continually been seen as an ocean use requiring "converging juridical approaches."[77] Both at the international and national levels, the "law of fisheries" has become highly integrated, ranging from legislation of coastal fisheries between sovereign states, to the protection of the resource itself, to the regulation of the actual operation. We hasten to add that this integrative process has had frequent difficult problems and has been far from uniform or even universally accepted. Nevertheless, it has never become nearly as *disintegrated* as the law of the sea relating to ocean-shipping uses.

By the 1930s, however, ocean interests were changing. They were shifting from the particular interest of the ship to the more wide-ranging interests of coastal states—albeit still disguised as an endeavor for extending state sovereignty horizontally outward into ocean space. This obviously could be interpreted as "expansionism for expansionism's sake" and, perhaps partly for that reason, was unsuccessful at the Hague in 1930.

Nevertheless, the attempt was made to establish a nine-mile contiguous zone within which coastal states could exercise limited jurisdiction for quite functional reasons.[78] However, even this compromise failed, as most of the traditional maritime states felt that the acceptance of such new rights would eventually lead to the creation of a belt of territorial sea that would include the contiguous zone. Why was this view taken? Was the motive to preserve the widest possible "freedom of the seas"? If so, was such a principle still of prime community interest for the world? Might consultation with shipping interests—with the isolated private-maritime-law system—have revealed that functional coastal zones hardly interferred with the freedom of shipping?

It is quite likely that no such communications ever took place and that the maritime states went to the conference table simply to preserve the vaguely defined status quo, which they were prepared to defend (and are still defending) at great costs eventually to themselves and to the very international community they appointed themselves to protect. Thus, as the uses of the ocean once again converged in a community of interest, the law relating to the ocean was now in two separate houses. Nevertheless, in the years before World War II, there were clear signs that new ocean uses would soon be clamoring for greater attention in the marine policies of the world's nations and that international law would have to find answers and solutions that it was now almost incapable of finding.

In addition to changing uses of the seas, there were also early indications of environmental pressures on the oceans, which, almost forgotten today, date back to 1924 when the Chamber of Shipping of the United Kingdom recommended the establishment of a prohibited zone, 150 miles wide, within which ships could not discharge oil and oily water.[79] However, this and other proposals were not followed up; and further efforts were negated by the difficulties of the pre-World War II period. We will return to the important subject of marine oil pollution in more detail later. In any case, as already stated, most international law—whether public or private—basically ceased during the world war. However, the end of the war ushered in a whole new era for the public law, which would on the one hand have wide-ranging effects on marine transport, and on the other be virtually ignored, or even misunderstood, by those representing shipping interests.

In the summer of 1937, the Pure and Superior Oil Company built a large platform in fifteen feet of water about one mile from the U.S. coast off Louisiana in the Gulf of Mexico. The company built an oil rig on the platform, began drilling, and found oil at just under 6,000 feet.[80] This success heralded the beginning of the oil industry's offshore-oil technology; and it changed the whole marine policy of the United States—turning it from a conservative maritime state into a progressive coastal state. Internationally, this was the beginning of a whole new era in the law of the sea. For marine transport, its most serious competitor ever—oceanic resources—had arrived on the scene. By the 1940s the amazingly innovative U.S. oil industry had perfected the technology necessary to exploit petroleum resources at much greater depths than fifteen feet and far beyond its three-mile territorial sea limit—out on its continental shelf.[81] Once again we must be selective, as the voluminous literature on the continental shelf and its antecedents obviates the need for any detailed examination of this area of the law of the sea here.[82] We will, therefore, discuss the continental shelf only insofar as it relates to our examination of the international law and policy of marine transport during this period.

The fact that the offshore submarine areas might contain valuable resources had been known to coastal states for a number of years. Mines had tunneled out under the sea for a long time, and in 1858 the British Cornwall Submarine Mines Act declared minerals won from mines and workings under the open sea adjacent to but not part of the County of Cornwall as "part of the soil and territorial possessions of the Crown."[83] Accordingly, well before the three-mile territorial sea became the generally accepted limit, coastal states had ostensibly exercised some dominion over the seabed and its subsoil off their adjoining coasts. However, the continental shelf is made up of both the seabed and its subsoil. Access through the seabed to the subsoil had new legal implications; by 1932 Professor Gidel had stated unequivocally that the surface of the seabed had the same legal position as the water column above it, and that therefore only very lengthy prescriptive use or acquiescence of other states would give a coastal state any right to claims of self-jurisdiction over it.[84]

However, the urgencies of World War II dictated a different approach. The war was depleting U.S. oil reserves at an alarming rate, and the U.S. Department of the Interior consequently suggested to President Roosevelt in 1943 that an interdepartmental study should examine how the United States might best obtain access to the petroleum reservoirs known or expected to exist beneath the continental shelf off the U.S. coast.[85] At the same time, there was growing concern for the conservation of another important resource, fisheries in the U.S. contiguous seas; and an interagency study was quickly mounted.[86]

The result was, of course, the two famous proclamations—one on fisheries and one on the continental shelf—made by President Harry S. Truman on September 28, 1945, which "opened an entirely new chapter in the history of international law."[87] The first of these asserted the right of the United States to establish "fisheries conservation zones" in the areas of the high seas contiguous to its coasts "wherein fishery activity had been or in the future may be developed and maintained on a substantial scale."[88] The proclamation stated that unilateral methods would only be used where U.S. fisheries were involved and that bilateral and multilateral agreements would be sought with foreign fishing interests.

More significant, of course, was the second U.S. proclamation—usually called the Truman Proclamation—which stated in one of its relevant sections that "having concern for the urgency of conserving and prudently utilizing its natural resources, the Government of the United States regards the natural resources of the subsoil and seabed of the Continental Shelf beneath the high seas but contiguous to the coast of the United States as appertaining to its jurisdiction and control."[89] As Dr. Garcia-Amador points out:

> Aside from the internal aspect and repercussions of this claim, its international aim is clear and unambiguous, namely to proclaim an exclusive right of jurisdiction and control for purposes of conserving and utilizing the natural resources of the bed and subsoil of the submarine area in question.[90]

In this respect, the U.S. step followed those taken by Great Britain and Venezuela, which in 1942 were able to agree on the Treaty of the Gulf of Paria, in which the two countries fixed their respective rights over the seabed and subsoil of the submarine areas between the island of Trinidad and the Venezuelean coast.[91] The treaty did not award exclusive sovereignty over the areas but rather assigned rights "which had been or may hereafter be lawfully acquired" by the two countries. The Gulf of Paria Treaty, as well as the Truman Declaration, clearly excluded any claim over the superjacent waters of the area. Article 6 of the Paria Treaty states that "nothing in this Treaty shall be held to affect in any way the status of the waters of the Gulf of Paria or any rights of passage or navigation on the surface of the seas outside the territorial waters of the contracting parties."[92] In the U.S. proclamation the statement reads:

The character of the high seas above the waters of the Continental Shelf and the right to their free and unimpeded navigation are in no way thus affected.[93]

Without question, these statements pay much more than lip service to the traditional tenets of the so-called freedom of the seas. They were, after all, made by Great Britain and the United States, the two most powerful maritime states in the world. Marine transport, although a prime concern for these states, was, certainly in the case of the United States, once again fading in importance in terms of overall marine policy.[94] As we have seen, U.S. marine policy has always been the *sum* of the various competing marine interests, with its various components waxing and waning as dictated by the particular national requirements of the day. At the end of World War II, the United States was gradually phasing out its heavy involvement in international shipping and, at the same time, grasping the important future implications of living and nonliving marine resources in the U.S. coastal areas. On the other hand, U.S. defense requirements still dictated comparatively free high seas, but U.S. resource policy was definitely expansionist and would henceforth set much of the world on a similar path—a development neither realized nor contemplated during the period of actual U.S. policy formulation.

British policy—such as it was—was much more inflexible, predictable, and to a great extent consistent with past positions. As it had done at the 1930 conference, Britain would almost consistently oppose all assertions of jurisdiction over marine areas outside the three-mile limit as being an encroachment on the freedom of the high seas. The Paria Treaty dealing with a (then) British colony can thus be seen as an exception to the rule, but one that was basically forced on Great Britain by the inevitability of Venezuelan expansionism. In retrospect, it is probably unfair to compare the policies of the United States and Great Britain at that time. Britain was trying to preserve its quickly fading importance and traditional status quo, whereas the more astute United States, having emerged from World War II as the most powerful state in the world, was able to discern a more viable future trend in oceanic-resource implications at a time when future resource needs were not even fully realized. This was, however, a dangerous game that could not be restricted to the great powers who were attempting to attain the best of both worlds. Within a decade or so, a great majority of the world's nations had followed the U.S. example and begun to assert their rights to the resources of "their" continental shelves.[95] Almost by default, a new rule of international law had appeared with implications unforeseen by the United States and undesired by both the United States and Britain.

The problems that arose were that many states, most particularly in Latin America, used the U.S. initiative, not only to make similar continental-shelf claims but also to enunciate claims to more specific—but nevertheless extensive—marine jurisdictions.[96] In the case of El Salvador, for example, the claim took the form of a full-blown, constitutionally enshrined, 200-mile territorial sea.[97] Other states, such as Argentina and Mexico, made claims to an "epicontinental sea" encompassing not only the continental shelf but also the superjacent waters.[98] More famous than these unilateral declarations was the trilateral decision made in 1952 by Chile, Ecuador, and Peru to establish a "maritime zone," which they declared to extend not less than 200 miles from their coast.[99] These and other Latin American claims to extend maritime jurisdictions varied significantly in both form and content; but most, unlike the Salvadorian legislation, purported to claim something less than complete territorial jurisdiction. On the other hand, they clearly attempted to exert more control over their coastal marine areas than ever envisaged in the U.S. proclamations or the Paria Treaty. A recent monograph has characterized these early Latin American claims in quite contemporary language as

> . . . early proposals for a multi-purpose functional zone within which the coastal state would exercise exclusive jurisdiction for designated purposes, but allegedly without prejudices to existing rights of navigation and associated rights under the regime of the High Seas.[100]

The literature of these claims is voluminous and, at best, confusing. Only recently has an attempt been made to view these in their true perspective as contributions to the modern law of the sea.[101] Much of the reasoning employed was a heady mixture of preexisting historical rights, geographical disadvantage, cultural references, and natural law. More important in this context is the economic content and purpose of some of the reasoning. After all, this was long before the term "developing country" was even invented. Yet these were indeed developing countries—many very poor, with few resources and enormous economic problems. None had a place of any prominence in international marine transport, although some had modest fleets.[102] It is interesting that many of these states were quite clear in asserting that their claims were made in order to accomplish the economic goals of further development and economic independence.[103] Just as the use of the ocean for international transportation had built and *developed* many of the world's great industrial states, these newer, poorer states were looking to other uses of the sea to attain some of their own modest developmental goals. In the 1952 Santiago Declaration on the Maritime Zone,[104] ratified by Chile, Ecuador, and Peru and later acceded to by Costa Rica, the parties agreed that:

> 1. Governments are bound to ensure for their peoples access to necessary food supplies and to furnish them with the means of developing their economy.

2. It is, therefore, the duty of each government to ensure the conservation and protection of its natural resources and to regulate the use thereof to the greatest possible advantage of its country.

3. Hence it is, likewise, the duty of each government to prevent exploitation of the said resources outside the area of its jurisdiction from jeopardizing the existence, integrity and conservation to the prejudice of nations so situated geographically, that their sea is an irreplaceable source of essential food and economic materials.[105]

In retrospect, this is strikingly contemporary language. It is also remarkable evidence of the disillusionment that began to be experienced by developing countries in the aftermath of World War II, and during the postwar period of optimism, about the prospects for international cooperation for greater human welfare and international equity. In the next few years, Latin American states, which still formed the nucleus of what would become the developing world, pursued this theme continuously and consistently in asserting their claims for greater oceanic jurisdiction in their offshore areas.[106] By 1956 the Latin American states were able to adopt a resolution, with only the United States dissenting, which stated that "each state is competent to establish its territorial waters within reasonable limits, taking into account geographical, geological, and biological factors as well as the economic needs of its population, and its security and defence."[107] Within two decades, a drastically enlarged world would be very close to recognizing such rights in a forum that, significantly, would virtually exclude the most traditional use of the sea—marine transport—from its deliberations. The intervening period would, however, be fraught with problems and difficulties relating to the law of the sea, which would soon receive its most comprehensive scrutiny ever by the nations of the world.

In discussing the last two decades in this examination we are presented with greater problems of selectivity. We are now dealing with the era of massive amounts of information. If we are to look at the international law and policy of marine transport for the 1958-1968 decade, a period that has occupied complete studies, we must confine ourselves to subjective selections of highlights of what we consider significant developments, perhaps even culminations in the areas under examination. We will have to look at several different, yet frequently interlinked, areas against the overall background of technological achievement and political development, which dictated that this decade would be of significant importance for the further evolution of the law and policy of international marine transport.

### IMCO: The First Difficult Decade

The initial area to be examined is the first decade of actual operation of the Inter-Governmental Maritime Consultative Organization (IMCO). Under article 60 of the IMCO convention, it could not enter into force until twenty-one states, of which seven had a total tonnage of not less than 1 million gross tons of shipping, had become parties. It took ten years to reach this requirement. The delay was due to the fear of the major maritime states that the new organization might not confine itself to technical questions alone and might eventually branch out into regulatory or even commercial matters. In retrospect it is clear that although this apprehension was well founded, it nevertheless displayed the lack of clear *overall* marine policy which existed in most of the maritime states at the time. Nations that were usually politically astute, such as Denmark, Norway, and Sweden, had proposed in a variety of forums that IMCO should only exist if it were confined to purely technical matters.[108]

This attitude in the mid- and late 1950s displayed an almost naive lack of understanding of what was happening in the political world at the time. Even during the working sessions on the IMCO convention, there was ample evidence that the great majority of states present were in favor of allowing the organization to consider maritime questions of general principle.[109] It was felt that the time was right for the establishment of an all-embracing general maritime organization under the aegis of the United Nations. Yet most of the major maritime states consistently opposed the establishment of such a body. These states appeared simply to have accepted the views of their shipping-industry lobbies that the scope of the proposed organization would have harmful results.

Of course, in an industry that, because of the history already chronicled here, had become characterized by the dominance of private interests, there was now a genuine fear of the sudden imposition of an organization that was expected to function on the intergovernmental level—reducing private interests to observer status. The feeling that executive policies regarding the operation of privately owned shipping were matters best left to the shipping industry, and to nongovernmental organizations such as the CMI exacerbated these doubts. Nevertheless, even considering that its more recent history had placed the shipping industry into its self-reliant shell of egocentricity, there appeared to be an almost astounding lack of perspective for both the industry and its supportive governments.[110] Even a limited amount of perspective in the late 1950s would have revealed quite clearly that there were considerations involved that transcended the interests of any single group. In the narrowest view, the vagaries of world trade; the lack of progress of underdeveloped economies; the interests of merchants, shippers, consumers, insurers, passengers, and seamen demanded a new degree of international coordination. IMCO was to provide such a service with relatively modest terms of reference: to safely and efficiently facilitate the flow of maritime commerce in the interests of world trade by ensuring a continuous consultative flow among governments. Nevertheless, the final vote creating the convention, and ultimately the organization, was twenty-one in favor and one against, with seven abstentions.[111]

### The Maritime-Safety-Committee Problems of 1959

Even the establishment of IMCO did not end its problems. When the organization held its first assembly in 1959 in London, two difficult policy problems—ostensibily legal but in reality delaying tactics—immediately arose. Under article 12 of the IMCO convention the organization was to be composed of an assembly, a council, a maritime-safety committee, and required subsidiary organs. It was at once clear that the council and the maritime-safety committee (MSC) would be playing leading and important roles in the work of the organization. Article 28(a) provided that the MSC should consist of

> . . . fourteen members elected by the Assembly from the Member Governments of those nations having an important interest in maritime safety, of which not less than eight shall be the largest ship-owning nations. . . .[112]

Accordingly, the United States, the United Kingdom, Norway, Japan, Italy, the Netherlands, France, and the Federal Republic of Germany were elected to the MSC. Almost immediately, objections were made to the election of France and West Germany on the grounds that, in terms of shipping tonnage, these two states were not as large as Liberia, which ranked third on the world tonnage scale, or Panama, which ranked eighth.[113] The election had certainly not been incorrect but was a calculated procedural maneuver intended to deprive Liberia and Panama of membership in one of IMCO's most important committees.[114]

Several of the traditional maritime states, in particular Great Britain, had become concerned about the very rapid rise of the Liberian and Panamanian fleets, which had occurred because these states offered relatively easy ship-registration facilities without necessarily requiring beneficial Liberian or Panamanian ownership of the registered tonnage.[115] The flags of these states had become known as "flags of convenience," a phenomenon to which we will return in greater detail later.[116] In any case, much of the Panamanian and Liberian fleets were, in fact, beneficially owned by citizens of the United States for a variety of reasons which will also be discussed later. The IMCO dispute, however—mainly between the United Kingdom, France, Norway, and the Netherlands on one side, and Liberia, Panama, India, and the United States on the other—was finally submitted to the International Court of Justice for an advisory opinion on the following question:[117]

Has the Assembly, in not electing Liberia and Panama to the Maritime Safety Committee, exercised its electoral power in a manner in accordance with the provisions of Article 28(a) of the Convention of March 6, 1948 for the establishment of the Inter-Governmental Maritime Consultative Organization?[118]

At stake was, of course, the principle of a state's freedom to fix the conditions for the grant of its nationality to ships, for the registration of ships, and for the right of ships to fly its flag.[119] The opponents of the election argued that only reference to actual ship registry would meet the requirement of the IMCO convention, and that to look behind the law of the flag was to invite "international legal anarchy" and the "disruption of the legal order which has already been established."[120] The proponents of the election predictably argued that a "genuine link" had to be established between registration and ownership and that registration alone proved nothing.[121] This argument had been accepted elsewhere in the debate on flags of convenience, below, but it was not accepted by the International Court in this case.[122] By a nine-to-five vote the court held that the nonelection of Liberia and Panama to the MSC meant that the IMCO assembly had failed to comply with this requirement under the convention.[123] Under the circumstances, the decision was probably entirely correct, as it preserved the sovereign rights of states to affix their nationality to ships as they wished. On the other hand, it would also give the beneficial-owner state certain advantages that were entirely unpredictable at that time.

The second difficulty faced by IMCO at its first meeting was caused by a statement by India that raised two thorny legal issues: flag discrimination and reservation to multinational conventions.[124] These issues, neither of which has ever been entirely solved, have been well documented and discussed elsewhere.[125]

*IMCO's Early Contributions to Maritime Safety*

Despite this and other early difficulties, despite its modest and narrow mandate, despite one of the smallest U.N. budgets,[126] and despite a very slowly increasing membership,[127] IMCO took its place in the international organizational structure and in a relatively short time became a valuable part of international shipping as a whole. Its limitations were entirely those of its membership; and its organizational structure, as a technical advisory body, precluded even the slightest regulatory step that might have been of general benefit to the industry. The major shipping states reluctantly appeared at IMCO to debate questions of general international maritime safety, arriving finally at the lowest common denominator agreeable to all.

At a time when the organization's aviation counterpart, the International Civil Aviation Organization (ICAO) was taking giant steps in the regulation of international civil aviation,[128] IMCO was basically a convenient clearinghouse for the debate of safety questions. Legal matters, or anything concerning commercial policy—so closely interlinked with the general welfare of international shipping—were never discussed. Nevertheless, the organization's membership slowly increased; and some notable achievements in the maritime safety field were reached in IMCO's first decade.[129]

By 1959 the MSC had begun preparing for the International Conference on the Safety of Life at Sea (SOLAS), which would take place with considerable success under IMCO auspices in 1960.[130] It was only the fourth conference in history that looked at the general safety of ships, life-saving appliances, and fire-fighting equipment.[131] Thus merchant shipping had finally found an internationally acceptable and relatively independent body, which had as one of its main concerns the safety of ships and those who sailed in them. It had been a long wait since Samuel Plimsoll's early efforts. Prior to the establishment of IMCO, the United Kingdom had been entrusted with looking after international maritime-safety questions and had convened conferences dealing with such issues in 1913, 1929, and 1948.[132] It seemed appropriate, therefore, that IMCO would now take over responsibility for all international administration dealing with maritime safety and related aspects that had previously been entrusted to an individual government. For example, the International Convention for the Prevention of Pollution of the Sea by Oil, in 1954,[133] which had been concluded as the result of a conference held by the United Kingdom government, had come into force in July 1958 and was now made the responsibility of IMCO.[134]

The problem of marine pollution, to which we will return later, would present IMCO, as well as international marine transport in general, with questions of increasing complexity. During IMCO's first decade, conferences on the subject were held in 1961 and 1966, in order to update and revise the original 1954 convention, which was quickly proving inadequate to deal with the increasing problem of ship-generated pollution during the 1960s.[135] On other safety questions IMCO was able to produce a new set of Regulations Preventing Collisions at Sea in 1960;[136] a new Convention for the Facilitation of Maritime Traffic in 1965;[137] and a new Convention on Load Lines in 1966.[138] On a smaller scale, the organization carried out essential and valuable work related to safety matters such as construction standards, radio-safety regulations, lighthouse maintenance, carriage of dangerous cargoes, code of safe practice for bulk cargoes, safety of nuclear-powered ships, and new life-saving appliances.

In general terms, this was a very successful slate for the first decade of operation of a U.N. specialized agency born with distrust and suspicion after a ten-year gestation period. In the next chapter we will discuss IMCO's progress in the present period.

These first formative years of the new international shipping organization showed the difficulties it would face and the limitations within which it would have to operate. On the one hand, the major maritime states regarded IMCO as a danger if it moved outside narrow technical, advisory, and consultative terms of reference into a more regulatory area where it might become an unbiased spokesman for *all* aspects of the industry—particularly the users of shipping services. On the other hand, those shipping-service users, along with, eventually, many states in the developing world, saw the organization as a sort of "shipowners' club" controlled by and operated for the benefit of the world's major shipping states with little power, competence, or even concern for other interests in international marine transport.[139] The final draft of the IMCO convention reveals such differences in approach among the participating governments that it was not surprising that the commercial and economic-policy objectives of the organization were effectively diluted or discarded altogether.[140]

Thus although the convention includes in its aims the "removal of discriminatory action and unnecessary restrictions by governments," very little has been attempted by IMCO in this field. In other words, the truly impartial U.N. shipping organization once envisaged, which would on the one hand promote adherence to standards of fair competiton along the lines specified in the Havana Charter for a projected (but unsuccessful) International Trade Organization;[141] and on the other would be a successor to the World War II United States Maritime Authority, providing cooperation in technical and operation matters, did not really get off the ground.

Obviously, technical and operational coordination was valuable and even essential, but it was only part of the total problem faced by international marine transport during this period.[142] "Shipper" states, coastal states, and the newly independent developing states, would thus be forced to look at other forums in their search for a more equitable division of the international-shipping cake. This search would have consequences for the traditional shipping states which were, if not foreseeable, certainly projectable at this time.[143] As we have already seen, however, international shipping—both as an industry and within the states that spoke for it—had by this time almost completely lost its flexibility and had instead placed itself in the vulnerable position of having to defend an almost indefensible status quo.

### The United Nations and the Law of the Sea

If IMCO represented one of the most important developments in the progress of international marine transport as far as centralization and international regulation were concerned, the First and Second United Nations Law of the Sea Conferences (UNCLOS I and II) of 1958 and 1960 are important milestones in the public international law of the sea. UNCLOS I and II have already been analyzed, criticized, commented on, dissected, and reported on by a whole generation of scholars and diplomats of every description and persuasion.[144] This work will be surpassed only by the massive documentation of UNCLOS III in the future. Therefore, we do not see the need to repeat what has been done expertly and eloquently elsewhere. We will simply, as briefly as possible, confine ourselves to the two conferences' effects on the international law and policy of marine transport.

Our task is made easier by the fact that despite the title of these gatherings—United Nations Conference on the Law of the Sea—they really affected marine transport only obliquely. Shipping was no longer a central consideration for this type of international discussion. We have attempted to show the slow divergence of the two maritime laws. We have seen that the first laws were customary rules of a commercial nature. These eventually gave birth to public policy related to the ocean, which was rather haphazardly transposed into what we have here called the "public" maritime law. The divergence began at that time and has continued ever since.

The post-Congress of Vienna period saw a rapid acceleration of this movement, and World War I and its subsequent political dislocations turned the divergence into an actual separation. Any links that might have existed between the two systems were given the final blow by the Great Depression and World War II. The two Geneva Law of the Sea Conferences merely confirmed this fact. They were simply no longer of central importance to marine transport as a part of the marine system as a whole. The traditional transportation function—that is, the very heart of shipping—had now become separated from the use of marine space in terms of law.

Although both transportation function and use of marine space are part of the single, and in our opinion inseparable, *marine system*, they were now administered by completely divergent legal systems. On the one hand, shipping was governed by private laws relating to its commercial purpose and activity, but ships' actual ocean passages were now governed or regulated by a set of public laws, which at times totally disregarded the commercial function for which shipping was created in the first place. The fundamental contradiction that had thus crept into the *total marine system* would cause difficulties for *all* future attempts to unify all aspects of the law of the sea.

There is little doubt that UNCLOS I and II failed, because this almost fatal flaw was transposed into the policy perceptions of the major maritime states. Policies are, after all, simply extensions of perceptions; and the major states, if they had clear perceptions of their own positions (which was doubtful), had certainly little understanding of the perceptions of the many new actors in the drama that was about to unfold at Geneva.[145]

On the one hand there were, of course, the maritime states—the states with shipping traditions and historic maritime interests. These were the reluctant founders of IMCO and creators of the CMI, who felt that the maritime status quo was theirs alone to preserve and defend at any price. They had already lost the United States—once their ally but now the creator of the continental-shelf doctrine and flag-of-convenience concept and, at this time, staring coldly across an "iron curtain." Behind that curtain was the other super power, still enigmatic and isolated, not yet clearly enunciating maritime interests or ambitions for itself or its satellites, but nevertheless having a considerable history of maritime interest.[146] In the so-called South were the new states of Africa, Asia, Latin America—on the verge of taking their rightful place in the drastically enlarged family of nations. Superimposed on these divisions were whole substrata of other perceptions. There were coastal states, island states, landlocked states, fishing states, transit states, wide-shelf and narrow-shelf states—all with different interests in the use of the single marine system, which had once simply belonged to the ships.

Yet after UNCLOS I began in Geneva on February 24, 1958, some 700 delegates from 86 nations produced four conventions, nine resolutions, and an optional protocol in an eight-week period, all in the hope of producing a generally accepted and acceptable public code for the oceans.[147] Surprisingly, they almost succeeded. It was probably a blessing in disguise that they did not succeed, as the agreements produced did not adequately reflect the equitable principles in ocean law and policy that would be required, as well as demanded, within the next decade.

As we have seen, the 1930 Hague Conference for the Codification of International Law, sponsored by the League of Nations, had made a serious but unsuccessful attempt to set out generally acceptable rules for the marginal seas. Not only could that conference not agree on a uniformly accepted breadth, but it was also totally unable even to state what the present law was commonly understood to be.[148] The difficulties of the late 1930s, followed by World War II, prevented any further activity. But the problem remained, and the international community continued to discuss it informally, particularly in the postwar years, when new pressures on an already inadequate law continued to mount.[149] The U.S. Continental Shelf Declaration, followed rapidly by a large number of Latin American territorial-sea claims and declarations, undoubtedly hurried the efforts to convene a new conference on the subject.[150]

The task of clarifying some of these law-of-the-sea questions was finally assigned to the International Law Commission (ILC), the organ set up by the United Nations to assist in the codification and "progressive development" of international law.[151] At its first session in 1949, the ILC considered a memorandum from the Secretary-General of the United Nations which stated among other things that:

> It must be a matter for consideration whether, of all the branches of international law, that of the law of the sea does not lend itself to comprehensive treatment by way of codifying the entire branch of the law. A codification—in its widest sense—of the entire field of the law of the sea in a unified and integrated "restatement" or similar, more ambitious, instrument, would go far toward enhancing the authority both of the work of codification and of international law as a whole.[152]

It is interesting to note that the Secretary-General's terms of reference for the ILC spoke of law of the sea in its totality; the ILC certainly had the power, perhaps the very last chance, to attempt the reintegration of the two maritime laws which had by that time drifted so far apart.

This was not to be, however, for three probable reasons. First, an overriding problem was the fact that the law concerning ships was now no longer even considered a part of the law of the sea. Second, the ILC, consisting of the world's most eminent international scholars of public international law, could not really be expected to concern itself with private-law matters—or could it? Third, the failure of the 1930 codification conference had forced the ILC to concentrate on the age-old problem of the demarcation of the marginal seas. In retrospect, this probably sealed the fate of the whole conference. Rather than working up from the actual uses of the ocean, the conference was expected to work down from the thorniest problem—the problem of the regime of the territorial sea. In addition, at a later stage the ILC also selected for specific treatment the questions concerning the continental shelf as well as those relating to fishing and conservation of living resources.[153]

In 1956, after many drafts and interim reports, the ILC submitted its final report, which was to serve as the blueprint for UNCLOS I.[154] There is no doubt that the ILC report was as comprehensive a piece of work as could be expected from a scholarly organization after seven and one-half years of intensive work. The report's recommended rules and commentaries thereto did not purport to be codifying international law alone. The ILC rightly maintained that the distinction between codification and creating new and progressive international law could not be maintained, because any elaboration of accepted international law would necessarily involve the formulation of new law as well. For this reason, the ILC recommended that an international United Nations conference be held to examine the law of the sea:

> . . . taking account not only of the legal but also of the technical, biological, economic and political aspects of the problem, and to embody

the results of the work in one or more international conventions or such other instrument as it may deem appropriate.[155]

This proposal was approved without hesitation by the Eleventh General Assembly of the United Nations in 1957.[156] The General Assembly, in a resolution, then decided to convene UNCLOS I in 1958.[157] The conference was to work with the ILC's seventy-three-article report as its main point of departure. The United Nations in its resolution used the same language as that in the previously cited ILC proposal.

### The First and Second U.N. Law of the Sea Conferences

Thus after many years of careful and meticulous legal planning and preparation, which had nonetheless ignored—whether by design or otherwise—one of the most important economic, as well as legal, aspects of ocean use, an international conference was now expected to examine *all* aspects of the law of the sea and come up with a new rule book in a matter of weeks. This impossible mission merely displayed the ineptitude of states in the late 1950s in coming to grips with the complexities that were to face them in the coming years. Given the clear recognition that the law of the sea was no longer simply a legal problem but also one with important technical, economic, biological, and political aspects, it seems anomalous that the task of preparing the groundwork for the new law of the sea was given to the ILC, which was then only able (or willing?) to deal with the legal aspects. But this was entirely consistent with the international mentality of that time.

For marine transport this was, of course, the end of the line. Only its use of ocean space, the "freedom of the sea," became the catch phrase of UNCLOS I—to be fought over and defended with, at times, an acrimonious persistence.[158] On the other hand, the true purpose of marine transport was not really considered at all. At UNCLOS I, shipping was considered to serve political rather than economic functions.

As a result, only the most optimistic observers would call UNCLOS I a "successful" conference.[159] Its most crucial purpose, that of defining the territorial sea, remained unfulfilled. A very general view acknowledged the territorial sea to extend no further than twelve miles.[160] As a result, UNCLOS I served simply as a reaffirmation of essentially traditional, but far from generally accepted, international law. Many states, realizing that their rights were untouched by the various conventions, refrained from adherence—or, for that matter, from rejection. In 1960 UNCLOS II, called solely for the purpose of defining the territorial sea, once again failed to accomplish this purpose.[161]

At UNCLOS I and II, the territorial-sea convention failed because no compromise could be worked out between states that—for economic, biological, technical, and political reasons—wished to extend their exclusive rights into their coastal marginal seas, and those states who opposed this—usually for political reasons.[162] Fishery resources, in particular, were of great concern to many coastal states. Coastal-state interest in the protection and preservation of this resource clashed with the political concerns of the superpowers and the major maritime states. Neither side had really made its case well, because neither had a full understanding of the future implications of its position. On the one hand, the type of resource-protection, environmental-orientation, and economic-development-concern language used by those who wanted greater equity in ocean use, was simply out of place at an international conference prepared by the ILC at that time. Although today such terms are part of the everyday language of international diplomacy, understood by most and acted on by many, in the late 1950s and early 1960s such expressions were considered to be merely poorly disguised evidence of somewhat sinister territorial expansionism, regional eccentricity, and precocious attacks on inviolate Grotian principles.[163]

On the other hand, like Horatio at the bridge, the traditional maritime states were there to defend such principles, whatever they may have meant, in the late 1950s.[164] The whole issue was further confused by the great political difficulties of the times such as the Cold War confrontation; the Middle East crisis; and the wars of liberation taking place in Africa, both north and south of the Sahara, and in south, southeast, and east Asia.[165] Lack of agreement on the boundary of the territorial sea within which the coastal state was acknowledged as having sovereignty, subject to the right of innocent passage, made the landward boundary of the high seas beyond such waters also uncertain. However, UNCLOS I recognized that the waters beyond this line, wherever it may be, were *res communis* and thus not subject to acquisition by any state.[166] The high seas were henceforth to be subject to an international regime as set out in article 2 of the 1958 Geneva Convention on the High Seas, which provides:

> The high seas being open to all nations, no State may validly purport to subject any part of them to its sovereignty. Freedom of the high seas is exercised under the conditions laid down by these articles and by the other rules of international law. It comprises, *inter alia*, both for coastal and noncoastal States:
>
> 1. Freedom of navigation;
> 2. Freedom of fishing;
> 3. Freedom to lay submarine cables and pipelines;
> 4. Freedom to fly over the high seas.
>
> These freedoms, and others which are recognized by the general principles of international law, shall be exercised by all States with reasonable regard to the interests of other States in their exercise of the freedom of the high seas.[167]

Thus the "freedom of the seas" had been codified; and the politics of freedom, so prevalent at UNCLOS I, had been given a place in the annals of international law. For those who felt that this was a total victory for the principles of freedom of the seas, it was indeed a hollow triumph.[168] If anything, the attempted codification of principles, which were either meaningless or not generally accepted, only hurried the subsequent extension of coastal-state sovereignty over the seas with which we are faced today.

*The Geneva Law of the Sea Conventions:*
*Effects on Marine Transport*

From the shipping standpoint, what had been achieved? What had been preserved? What exactly was the meaning of "freedom of navigation" in 1958? This analysis of the historical development of the international law and policy of marine transport is supposed to answer questions, not ask them. But these questions contain answers within them. The freedom of navigation—of the seas generally—in the late 1950s, 1960s, and to some extent even today, had become, at best, an abstract principle behind which the major maritime states could rally in order to prevent a more equitable division of ocean use and resources. What Hugo Grotius had purposefully designed as a juridical principle, to protect the weak from the assertions and claims of the strong, had become an aberration. Even if we concede that the principle of the freedom of the seas was established to assist the communal development and benefit of international commerce in the seventeenth, eighteenth, and nineteenth centuries, then we must surely remember that it was created for the general and communal benefit of *all* nations. As soon as it lost this characteristic and became instead beneficial only to selected nations, it lost the very life that Grotius had breathed into it. It became a meaningless framework for endless emotional polemics and has remained so ever since.

In any case, for international marine transport, both before and after UNCLOS I and II, little had changed. Neither commercial viability nor ships' use of ocean space was affected. However, the real aims and the real problems of the coastal states, which would play such an important role in UNCLOS III, were not yet apparent. Except for the Latin American coastal states, which had clearly seen their stake in international ocean development at an early stage, but were almost ridiculed at UNCLOS I and II,[169] most of the coastal states either supported traditionalism, either real or perceived, or took little part in the debate.

Even a principle as related to marine transport as "innocent passage" had little *direct* relevance to actual ocean use by ships. Article 14 of the 1958 Territorial Seas Convention provided explicitly that the rights of innocent passage extend to "ships of all states," as long as passage is innocent and does not prejudice the "peace, good order and security of the coastal state." Nothing could more specifically define the very purpose of merchant shipping, which operates at its commercial best when peace, good order, and security exist. Therefore, if the purpose of marine transport is to provide viable commercial transit of goods from point A to point B, it will always be innocent in peacetime. Accordingly, the "new" law of the sea had neither widened nor restricted anything that had not existed since the Mediterranean was a Roman lake. Only rarely has a coastal state ever interfered with actual international coastal shipping. And such interference, although clearly in contravention of international law, has usually occurred to make a certain political point,[170] not to interfere with shipping per se.

The Geneva Law of the Sea Conferences were, therefore, neither the type of legal conference envisaged by the ILC, nor the complete international political congresses we are familiar with today. They fell somewhere in between, and this was probably their undoing. A drastically expanded world demanded new oceanic solutions but received, instead, four "public" law-of-the-sea conventions that would be redundant in less than a decade. However, for international shipping it was business as usual.

## The New Law of the Sea and the Nationality of Ships

We would be remiss if we did not address ourselves to the one aspect of UNCLOS I that did directly concern international shipping and that was, if not a *cause célèbre*, certainly a tempest in a teapot. We have referred to the difficulties faced by IMCO in 1959 when it elected its MSC and to the problems related to flag of registry, which eventually ended up in the International Court of Justice. These difficulties were created by earlier decisions, both at UNCLOS I and by the International Court.

We refer here to what may be called the "flag debate," at the heart of which was the problem of nationality of ships. The nationality of ships had never caused great problems; accordingly, the law governing it was loose and vague at best.[171] This had facilitated the establishment of "convenient nationality," or "flags of convenience," as they became known.[172] In the post-World War II period there had been a remarkable increase of flag-of-convenience registrations of ships.[173] Such a flag is basically one flown by a ship engaged in international navigation, which is not the flag of the state with which the ship is most closely associated.[174] In other words, in most instances the vessel flies one flag but is owned by nationals under another.

The reasons for the acquisition of a flag of convenience vary and are often misunderstood. Although we can only give brief details, some elaboration is required. First and foremost, there is an economic motivation, which might take several forms. In the postwar period, many states looked at the shipping industry as a considerable source for taxation—at times forgetting that it was still a high-risk industry, which had been rebuilt from the ravages of the world wars. However, the shipping boom of the 1950s, which has already been mentioned, produced high profits and, as a result, consistently higher taxation.[175] This prompted many shipowners simply to register their ships in another country where there was only minimal taxation or none at all. That has always been the primary motivation for flag-of-convenience registration.[176]

Second, in the "convenience state" there may also be greater freedom of operation resulting from less demanding labor-legislation requirements.[177] Other reasons may be the lack of currency exchange and investment controls in the flag-of-convenience state.[178]

The most widespread belief, however, is that flag-of-convenience states allow owners to bypass the more stringent safety requirements of their own states.[179] It is this image of substandard flag-of-convenience vessels that has received the widest publicity and is the least founded on fact. There have been (and still are) substandard vessels on all registries, and the safety record of flag-of-convenience states has only been marginally worse than that of the rest.[180] As already noted, safety at sea is as much an international matter for bodies such as IMCO and the marine-insurance industry as it is for flag states.

In any case, there was a phenomenal rise in flag-of-convenience registration after World War II.[181] At the outbreak of the war, Liberia, the main flag-of-convenience state today, had no shipping tonnage at all. Yet by 1958 it ranked third on the world shipping scale.[182] During the same period, Panama increased its fleet from 715,525 grt to 4,357,800 grt, to rank eighth on the scale.[183] As can be seen from table 6-1, by 1958 the combined tonnages of Liberia and Panama were only about 5 million tons behind that of Great Britain.

Naturally, during these high-profit, but nonetheless competitive, years for international shipping, there was considerable resentment against flags of convenience, which gave competitors a certain advantage. Although there were few restrictions on shipowners who wanted to "leave the flag" of the most traditional shipping states, the exodus mainly occurred from the United States,[184] and, to a lesser extent, from Greece. There was also concerted opposition to flags of convenience by various seamen's labor movements which, quite rightly, saw the threat of vessels that were free from labor contracts and collective agreements.[185] Nevertheless, the trend could not be halted; and an attempt was accordingly made at UNCLOS I to lay down more specific rules relating to the ownership of vessels.

One might ask what such a very technical aspect of private maritime law was suddenly doing on the agenda of a conference that had virtually ignored

**Table 6-1**
**The 1958 World Shipping Ladder**

| State | Gross Registered Tons |
|---|---|
| 1. United States | 25,589,596[a] |
| 2. Great Britain | 20,285,776 |
| 3. Liberia | 10,078,778 |
| 4. Norway | 9,384,830 |
| 5. Japan | 5,465,442 |
| 6. Italy | 4,899,640 |
| 7. Netherlands | 4,599,788 |
| 8. Panama | 4,357,800 |
| 9. France | 4,337,935 |
| 10. Federal Republic of Germany | 4,077,475 |

Source: *Lloyd's Register of Shipping*, 1958. See also K.R. Simmonds, "The Constitution of the Maritime Safety Committee of IMCO." *International and Comparative Law Quarterly* 12(1963), p. 61.
[a]Includes U.S. reserve and inland fleet.

all other aspects of private maritime law? The impetus for its appearance was undoubtedly the *Nottebohm* case,[186] between Liechtenstein and Guatemala before the International Court of Justice, which raised certain highly controversial aspects of nationality.[187] The facts of the case had nothing whatsoever to do with shipping but concerned a claim by Liechtenstein against Guatemala for compensation owing to that country's arrest, detention, and expulsion of Mr. Nottebohm, a German-born Liechtenstein citizen, and also for the seizure of his property. In its judgment, the court found that although Nottebohm was a naturalized Liechtenstein subject and although

> . . . it is for Liechtenstein, as it is for every sovereign State, to settle by its own legislation the rules relating to the acquisition of nationality. . . nevertheless, a State cannot claim that such rules . . . are entitled to recognition by another State unless it has acted in conformity with this general aim of making the legal bond of nationality accord with the individual's genuine connection with the State which assumed the defence of its citizens by means of protection as against other States . . . Nationality is a legal bond having as its basis a social fact of attachment, a genuine connection of existence, interest and sentiments, together with reciprocal rights and duties. It may be said to constitute the juridical expression of the fact that the individual upon whom it is conferred either directly by the law or as a result of an act of the authorities, is in fact more closely connected with the population of the State conferring nationality than with that of any other State. Conferred by a State, it only entitles that State to exercise protection vis-à-vis another State, if it constitutes a translation into juridical terms of the individual's connection with the State which has made him its national.[188]

It was, therefore, in the interests of the opponents of the flag of convenience concept to have these principles transposed and made applicable to international shipping. The International Law Commission, which, of course, reflected not only the scholarship but to a great extent also many of the views of the major maritime states, made this transition easy when it declared that "the attribution of an identity and a nationality to sea-going ships is a corollary of the principle of the free use of the high seas."[189] Although ships have had an identity since prehistory, the concept of nationality for ships was of more recent origin and was far from being as clear cut as the ILC maintained.[190] However, that august body was not to be stopped and went on to state categorically and with little basis

> . . . that ships should have nationality is necessary if the principle of the freedom of the seas, the most important consequence of which is the absence of state sovereignty over the high seas, is to be made compatible with the maintenance of a minimum degree of legal order on those same seas.[191]

There was certainly no general agreement with this proposition, although many prominent international legal scholars who ought to have known better leapt on the ILC bandwagon in support.[192] Some genuinely believed that the *Nottebohm* decision was transferable from individual to ship and made eloquent arrangements to back up their points.[193] They did not seem to realize that they were being manipulated by an unusual solidarity of shipowners and seafarers from the traditional maritime states who cared little what flag fluttered from the stern of the ship as long as they maintained effective control. In other words, what was undoubtedly a purely commercial dispute had been translated into an international legal problem, with a surprising phalanx of legal scholars as unwitting tools. The whole problem was therefore brought to a head by considerations far removed from the legal technicalities of the ship's nationality. It has been observed that

> . . . neither side (i.e. shipowners and seamen) appears much concerned over what flag flutters from the stern. But the conflict is being waged with no less vigour because it evolves around dollars and cents.[194]

Once again the real commercial motivations behind this dispute were basically ignored, and the legal argument alone was brought forth at UNCLOS I. The ILC had proposed that, although each state had the right to fix the conditions for the grant of its nationality to ships, there must nevertheless exist a "genuine link" between the state and the ship.[195] But the ILC was unable to supply any precise definition of this "genuine link." However, the ILC's motivation and inspiration was entirely clear—to drive the "flags of convenience" from the seas. The debate ended in a stalemate. The genuine-link proponents received their wish in the High Seas Convention, which in article 5 reads:

> 1. Each State shall fix the conditions for the grant of its nationality to ships, for the registration of ships in its territory, and for the right to fly its flag. Ships have the nationality of the State whose flag they are entitled to fly. There must exist a genuine link between the State and the ship; in particular, the State must effectively exercise its jurisdiction and control in administrative, technical and social matters over ships flying its flag.
>
> 2. Each State shall issue to ships to which it has granted the right to fly its flag documents to that effect.

On the other hand, the opponents were not that unhappy, because the vagueness of the language, the lack of definition of the genuine link, and the increasing popularity of flags of convenience all made the whole argument rather pointless. At stake was, of course, the question of a state's sovereignty and its fullest rights to grant its nationality to ships under rules it alone controls. It was a point not lost on the few new states at UNCLOS I. The clearest and most outspoken opponent of the genuine-link theory observed:

> To derive from application of criteria of this type to the competence of states to confer nationality upon individuals, principles assumed to be relevant to limiting the competence of states to attribute nationality to ships is, if not an exercise in irrelevancy, certainly a disguised mode of stating that because certain limits have been imposed on states with respect to individuals for some problems, other limits ought to be imposed with respect to ships for other problems.[196]

It is interesting to note that this whole debate, which was quite out of place at UNCLOS I, was really a sort of "reverse flag discrimination" indulged in by the traditional maritime states in their fear of a new competitive spirit. It is also not surprising that this strange mixture of commercial motivation and legal rhetoric did not work. It simply served to show the world, particularly the newly independent world, another side of the unacceptable face of international marine transport at its monopolistic worst. The whole maneuver certainly did not sweep the flags of convenience away. On the contrary, between 1958 and 1968 the Liberian and Panamanian share of the world's fleet rose from just over 15 million grt to just over 32 million grt, and was approaching 20 percent of the world fleet.[197] We will have to return to the flag-of-convenience phenomenon again, but table 6-2 should put it in proper perspective when compared with the shipping statistics during the period under discussion in this chapter.

**Table 6-2**
**Growth of Certain National Fleets, 1958-1968**

| Flag | Millions of Gross Registered Tons | | Percentage Increase in Tonnage, 1958-1968 | Percentage of World Fleet | |
|---|---|---|---|---|---|
| | *1958* | *1968* | | | |
| United Kingdom | 19.2 | 20.6 | 8 | 19.2 | 11.5 |
| France | 4.3 | 5.4 | 27 | 4.2 | 3.0 |
| Italy | 4.9 | 6.5 | 32 | 4.9 | 3.6 |
| Spain | 1.3 | 2.3 | 71 | 1.3 | 1.3 |
| Other Western Europe | 27.6 | 49.3 | 79 | 27.6 | 27.5 |
| Japan | 5.5 | 18.9 | 245 | 5.5 | 10.5 |
| United States[a] | 9.5 | 12.0 | 27 | 9.5 | 6.7 |
| Argentina | 1.0 | 1.1 | 17 | 1.0 | 0.6 |
| Brazil | 0.8 | 1.3 | 53 | 0.8 | 0.7 |
| Other Latin America | 1.8 | 1.8 | 5 | 1.8 | 1.0 |
| Liberia[b] | 11.1 | 27.1 | 144 | 11.1 | 15.1 |
| Panama[b] | 4.4 | 5.4 | 23 | 4.4 | 3.0 |
| Lebanon[b] | 0.0 | 0.4 | 735 | 0.0 | 0.2 |
| USSR | 3.2 | 9.8 | 210 | 3.2 | 5.5 |
| Poland | 0.5 | 1.4 | 190 | 0.5 | 0.8 |
| Yugoslavia | 0.4 | 1.3 | 233 | 0.4 | 0.7 |
| Other Socialist states[c] | 0.4 | 2.9 | 553 | 0.4 | 1.6 |
| India | 0.7 | 2.0 | 207 | 0.7 | 1.1 |
| Pakistan | 0.2 | 0.5 | 215 | 0.2 | 0.3 |
| Other Commonwealth[d] | 1.9 | 3.9 | 105 | 1.9 | 2.2 |
| All other states | 1.5 | 5.5 | 256 | 1.5 | 3.0 |
| World | 100.1 | 179.5 | 79 | 1.5 | 3.0 |

Source: Report, Board of Trade, United Kingdom, 1970. See also Report, *Committee of Inquiry into Shipping*. ("Rochdale Report") (London: HMSO, 1970), pp. 46, 57.
[a]Excluding U.S. inland and reserve fleet.
[b]Flag of convenience.
[c]Including North Korea and North Vietnam.
[d]Excluding South Africa.

## The Changing Political World: Emergence of the Third World

The years between the end of World War II and the conclusion of UNCLOS II in 1960 had, of course, seen many remarkable changes. Perhaps the most important of these was the emergence of the many newly independent states of Asia and Africa during that period. In 1945, of the fifty founding members of the United Nations, only two such states—Ethiopia and

Liberia—were members; by the end of the 1960s there were forty such members. Joined by their developing counterpart states in Latin America, they had formed the "Group of 77" which would in the 1970s dominate most international forums. However, during UNCLOS I and II many of the new states were not represented at all; and the four conventions that were issued by the conference received participation from only fourteen Afro-Asian states.[198]

Obviously, however, the law of the sea was not of prime concern for many of these new states, which had to face much more pressing problems of newly won independence for which their former colonial masters had ill-prepared them. Again, this is a well-documented subject.[199] The "decade of independence," as the mid-1950s to mid-1960s can accurately be called, saw the virtual doubling of the world's nation-states.[200] The aftermath of World War II, the unusual conditions of the Cold War, and the strong current of self-determination had resulted in large-scale liberation of colonial territories in Africa and Asia.[201] There is little doubt that the relatively sudden arrival of these many new states in the international community made the traditional 1815-style law of nations almost redundant. Already inadequate to deal with the pressures within the developed group of states, this traditional law was even less adequate to accommodate the perceptions, attitudes, and values of the new states. The previously accepted norm related to state succession, providing that a new state will be bound by all the existing rules of international law already established as custom by the practice of other states,[202] was simply not acceptable to most of these new states. And why should it have been? As one African scholar recently pointed out:

> International law as developed by the Concert of Europe was meant to serve the specific interest of the Concert. Is it not conceivable that the interests of Europe could very well be different from or even contrary to that of the new nations who are today expected to adhere to the old 1815 international law rule which was made for only a select group of European states? Since the States of Western Europe are no longer the majority in the new international society, is it not reasonable that their common denomination of interests should not continue to be the only standard of behaviour to be imposed on other equally sovereign states? Indeed, acceptance of a contrary position would mean for them the recognition of superiority of Western interests over their own. If this be so, their independence loses its purpose and their sovereign quality its meaning.[203]

However, it can be asserted that even the anachronistic international law of "Christian" Europe could have been accepted, at least for some time, had it not contained, in addition to the visible legal dogma, also strong underlying economic principles that were clearly biased toward the developed world. This, as we have seen, was not the result of specific intent but of the historical development of world trade and prosperity, which in turn had created the complete development of the industrialized nations, and thus distinguished these from the "developing" nations in Africa, Asia, and Latin America. There is no question that the major part of international relations during this period was neither legally nor politically, but essentially economically, motivated.[204] The coinage of the phrase "developing nations" reflected this overall economic concern.

We have seen that the industrialized revolution, colonialism, and commercial enterprise had set Great Britain and its European neighbors on the course for industrialization. Soon the former colony that became the United States was able to match and then surpass its former mother country. Within a single century—from the mid-1800s to the mid-1900s—the real income of these developed states had been raised over ten times.[205] Despite the fact that this commercial and industrial prosperity was often derived from the colonies, these were left far behind in the quickening pace of discovery, invention, industrialization, development, and scientific knowledge.[206] The industrialized states of Western Europe and America would become the "First World," distinguished from the planned but highly developed economies of the "Second World" of Eastern Europe. That left the many states of Asia, Africa, and Latin America, which had been the former colonies and which would now become the "Third World."

The Third World would henceforth contain the greatest mass of humanity with the lowest standard of living. However, as was only recently pointed out, the "superiority" of the developed countries is of relatively recent origin.[207] Only a few centuries ago, the flow of technology was quite the reverse. Countries that are today classified as "underdeveloped" have, in the not too distant past, contributed to the world: the use of fire; the taming and domestication of animals; the evolution of agriculture and irrigation; the invention of pottery; the art of weaving; the smelting of ores and use of metals; the manufacture of paper and the technique of printing; the decimal system of numerals and methods of calculation; the use of gunpowder; the invention of the marine compass; the use of the crankshaft and the windmill.[208] One wonders what might have occurred had the inventors of this early technology protected themselves with the kind of transnational "patent wall" that faces the Third World today.

The gulf that separates developed and developing countries is basically a technological one. It is also of relatively recent origin. Only 125 years ago the United States, Britain, Canada, the Netherlands, and Switzerland were the only countries with average per-capita income of about $200, which was only slightly higher than the current average for Third-World states.[209] In other words, it is technology alone that has transformed the world into what it is today.

*The Third World and Marine Transport*

The developmental problem is one of great magnitude, and the discussion here will of necessity be superficial. Although this book deals with marine transport, and although we have intended to make particular reference to the Third World in our examination, we find ourselves near the end of the book, yet only now are we actually taking up the subject of the Third World. The earlier chapters, which have illustrated the great history of the international law and policy of marine transport, have been silent about development, about the Third World, and about the inequality of developing national states. That silence should illustrate the gap between developed and developing states that existed when the scores of new states arrived on the international scene in the late 1950s and the 1960s.

Centuries of established commercial practice, trading traditions and political integration, had welded the First and Second Worlds into an industrial colossus that had little in common with the new states. In the international shipping infrastructure, this gap was as wide as anywhere.[210] Yet history shows us that many of the states of the Third World had great maritime traditions. We remember the Egyptians and the Arabs who started it all in the "cradle of life"—the Mediterranean; the Indians and Southeast Asians mastering the Indian Ocean and Southeast Asian seas in their frail craft; the Chinese, whose maritime history is still being unearthed today;[211] the Africans, sailing along and exploring the coast of their immense continent; the South Americans exploring the great Pacific Ocean and the Caribbean Seas.[212] We have seen how their maritime traditions just vanished, or how they were reduced to servitude by new colonial masters. By the 1960s these states were all "developing" in the true sense of the word, dependent on massive foreign aid and the vagaries of the international market structure, of which marine transport was, of course, an integral part. The problem was then really perceived for the first time by their more fortunate brethren of the North, who saw how quickly the gulf between rich and poor appeared to widen. It was up to the developed world to cope with this increasing problem.

A massive shift of resources from one system to another was, of course, not unknown to the post-World War II period. The Marshall Plan had helped a devastated Europe onto the road to a prosperity that would, within three decades, rival that of the donor. Vis-à-vis the Third World, however, political necessity and economic expediency were not as closely united as in the reconstruction of Europe. The Third World was quickly perceived as a welfare case—politically unstable, economically unreliable, and emotionally unpredictable.[213] Even one such trait would discourage international investment; a combination of all exacerbated the problem. Despite the fact that considerable aid and assistance flowed to the developing countries, the gap widened. Very early in the post-World War II period, the question was taken to the United Nations, which in turn added problems as it sought solutions. Within the very broad framework of the United Nations, international development emerged as a policy objective as broad as international peace and security. In any case, both were interlinked. Thus since 1946 numerous U.N. resolutions have called on the world, as well as on international agencies and organizations, to assist the Third World in its endeavor to develop. To give some examples up to 1968:

1. U.N. Resolution 304(IV) of December 16, 1949, establishing the expanded Program of Technical Assistance;[214]
2. U.N. Resolution 1240(XIII) of October 14, 1958, establishing the U.N. Special Fund;[215]
3. U.N. Resolution 1710(XVI) of December 19, 1961, proclaiming the first U.N. Development Decade;[216]
4. U.N. Resolution 1714(XVI) of December 19, 1961, establishing the World Food Program;[217]
5. U.N. Resolution 1995(XIX) of December 30, 1964, the United Nations Conference on Trade and Development (UNCTAD);[218]
6. U.N. Resolution 2186(XXI) of December 13, 1966, establishing the U.N. Capital Development Fund.[219]

Of these resolutions, the one that established UNCTAD would prove to be the most far-reaching, and is also most directly related to our overall discussion. When UNCTAD I met in Geneva in 1964, the economic difficulties, trade inequalities, and living disparities of many of the developing states were for the first time set against the economic superiority, trade monopoly, and living affluence of the developed countries.[220] It was found, for example, that the joint income of the Third World, with over two-thirds of the world's population, was not much more than one-tenth of that of the developed, industrialized world.[221]

Our historical analysis has shown how much marine transport has contributed to that prosperity. From time immemorial, it has been the backbone of commercial viability as well as the provider of the technical means for achieving it. But we have also seen how world shipping has been concentrated within a relatively small group of countries. Although domination of world shipping by one state, such as that achieved by Great Britain in the eighteenth and nineteenth centuries, was no longer the case, shipping in the late 1950s and 1960s was still firmly concentrated in the First and Second Worlds. Table 6-3 illustrates this point clearly, showing that in 1968, four years after UNCTAD I, the Third World's share of the world's merchant fleet was a mere 7.4 percent.

To lend further credence to this disparity, one should note that, at the

**Table 6-3**

**Distribution of the World Merchant Fleet in 1968**

|  | *Percentage* |
|---|---|
| *Developed countries* | |
| Developed market economies | 59.7 |
| Socialist bloc (Europe and Asia) | 8.7 |
| "Flags of Convenience" | 16.8 |
| *Developing countries* | |
| Africa | 0.4 |
| Asia | 4.3 |
| Latin America | 2.7 |

Source: Report, Board of Trade, United Kingdom, 1970. See also Report, *Committee of Inquiry into Shipping* ("Rochdale Reports") (London: HMSO, 1970), pp. 19, 46, 57.

same time, the Third World's part in international seaborne trade was far from unimportant, as table 6-4 illustrates. Table 6-4 shows only too clearly that most of the Third-World states are net importers of shipping services and thus experience a considerable deficit under the balance-of-payments item of marine transport. Having no shipping of their own, they are completely dependent on foreign shipping; in order to export their products, they rely almost exclusively on marine transport. The problem is further exacerbated because the major export of developing countries consists of primary commodities and raw materials, which are not only heavy and voluminous but also are of low unit value and must be shipped over long distances.[222] Developing countries are thus caught in a difficult bind, from which they have neither the means nor the ways to extricate themselves.

*UNCTAD: New Directions for Shipping Law
and Policy*

Obviously, shipping problems would be translated into very specific demands by Third-World states at UNCTAD I.[223] They recognized the

**Table 6-4**

**Third-World Share in International Seaborne Trade**

|  | Total Goods Loaded (Percentage) | Total Goods Unloaded (Percentage) |
|---|---|---|
| 1959 | 61.4 | 22.9 |
| 1967 | 63.1 | 18.7 |

Source: UNCTAD, DOC. TD/B/C. 4/50, February 24, 1969.

primary importance for their own development of reasonable access to shipping. What they did not, and probably could not, recognize was that the very history of marine transport not only had excluded them from consideration but also would work against them in many other less discernible ways.

The divergence of the maritime laws chronicled herein was at the heart of this difficulty. As we have seen, along with maritime law, marine policy had also diverged into what had now become spatial-political ocean policy and commercial maritime policy. The latter was now very much in the private sector and, certainly in the developed market economy countries, almost out of reach of government action, even if such action could create changes (which was doubtful). The demands by Third-World states, at forums such as UNCTAD I, for a more equitable distribution of the world's resources—and marine transport is certainly as important a resource as any—would thus cause great difficulties to even the most open-minded nations in the developed world. What was demanded could no longer be given, at least not without causing considerable internal difficulties for the developed countries.

These states had allowed their private-sector industries to develop with an independence nurtured at times by benign neglect. When the Third-World states demanded access to some of the technology that had created the industrial base in the North, they found that much of this technology was protected by a "patent wall" that even the most powerful governments in the developed world would not have been able to break.[224] When the Third World demanded more equitable access to international marine transport, they came face to face with a system that, with a tradition dating back to prehistory, had basically evolved within the private sector and guarded its trading advantage and its methods jealously. This problem, at the time of UNCTAD I, was aptly described by Gosovic:

> The economic and commercial aspects of shipping were almost virgin territory at the time of the Geneva conference, a forbidden land into which neither international organizations nor the developing countries had easy access. On the international scene it was one of the several untouched strongholds of anachronistic private enterprise and its credo of laissez-faire, with liner conferences enjoying all oligopolistic privileges. Generally, data was scarce and there was a dearth of published materials on the economics of ocean transport. This was primarily due to the secrecy which shrouded the practices of liner conferences, price fixing and costs. The absence of reliable figures prevented developing countries from fully substantiating their grievances and suspicions about certain shipping practices.[225]

The developing countries' main grievances relating to shipping, as voiced at UNCTAD, fell into four broad areas: (1) the unilateral fixing of ocean freight rates; (2) discriminatory shipping-conference practices; (3) inadequacy of shipping services (including the possible development of Third-World merchant marines); (4) inadequacy of existing international shipping legislation.

First, serious questions were raised by developing countries about the practice of unilateral freight-rate fixing.[226] They complained that freight rates were not only excessive but also discriminatory, although they recognized that they had little ability to judge the justifications of rate increases, since these were always decided unilaterally and secretly without any consultation with shippers. The developing countries, therefore, proposed that a scrutiny of the practices related to freight rates should be undertaken as the core of UNCTAD's activities in shipping.

Second, and related to the first grievance, was the question of the practices of shipping conferences, which had become widespread and dominated every trade route by the 1960s.[227] In this respect, the developing countries were highly critical of the problems caused by monopoly practices, in particular by liner conferences, which had led to the almost complete absence of free competition.

Third, the question of adequacy of shipping services was also raised. Third-World states complained that the market-economy system of providing shipping services was not a service at all, as it depended purely on the profitability of a particular route.[228] They argued that shipping was a vital service to them and that, regardless of profitability, they needed reliable marine transport. As the major shipping states appeared to be unable or unwilling to provide it, they would need assistance in building up their own merchant marines.[229] Finally, serious questions were also raised about the inadequacy of international shipping legislation. As Gosovic explains:

> The developing countries argued that the rules of international private maritime law were written by traditional sea powers (particularly the United Kingdom), and were unduly favourable to shipowners. Therefore, they asked for a review of these rules and of the economic and commercial aspects of shipping legislation and practices, a review which would take account of the interests of shippers and shipowners alike. They referred primarily to those aspects of shipping legislation which had a negative effect on their trade and development, in particular bills of lading, charter parties, limitation of shipowners' liability, and international marine insurance.[230]

As would be expected, there was vigorous opposition and almost shrill alarm in response to these demands and proposals at UNCTAD I. In particular, the major shipping states—all members of the UNCTAD B Group—opposed the placing of any of these matters on the conference's agenda of work.[231] They argued that efficient marine transport at low cost could be secured only through free competition between shipowners and that any regulatory interference with their present activities would lead to higher costs and poorer services. They added that shipping could be operated only on a basis of "sound economic investment" and that they alone were best qualified to provide efficient international shipping services as they had done for a long time.[232]

Of course, the delegations representing developed countries cannot really be blamed for these rather weak responses to the very valid points made by the Third-World states. Their governments had obviously not formed any clear policy, and consultation with the shipping industry had usually been minimal. On the other hand, if the shipping industry was actually represented on these delegations, which was often the case, they were usually only capable of arguing as a self-interest group that had to protect the status quo at all costs. In the case of the Scandinavian countries, for example, this hard-line attitude, which resulted from bowing to shipping interests was a marked contrast to their otherwise liberal and enlightened attitude vis-à-vis the Third World.[233] However, the two sides labored under one basic misunderstanding. The developing states not only were united as a group but also almost all spoke with a voice of sovereign governments, which saw access to international marine transport as a vital part of their national economic criteria. In other words, although these states did not really understand the complex historic infrastructure of international shipping, they had at least a national and, therefore, an international policy with which to approach the subject.

Of course, on the other side no such policy existed and for most of the shipping states would have been unthinkable. As we have seen, shipping had remained largely a private industry. Even in the Socialist-bloc states, national fleets were operated on almost exactly the same lines as in the West, with the exception of the corporate investment-profit structure.

As a result, when the developing countries demanded that a basically private industry should henceforth come under international regulation, these states were astonished. When it was asked that their governments act forcefully to convince shipowners of the need for reform and innovation, they were dumbfounded. When it was requested that unilateral or secret collusion procedures between shipowners should be internationalized, publicized, and used to assist consultation between user and provider of shipping, they were scandalized. After all, was this not a direct attack on the "law merchant," Adam Smith, the Protestant ethic, and free enterprise? They were suddenly faced with demands and requests couched in language using expressions such as justice, equity, equality, nondiscrimination, consultation, and social benefits, at a conference that had been touted as one in which international trade would be discussed. It suddenly seemed that the two sides were talking in quite different languages. The developing countries had sent their national delegations to UNCTAD—free to speak for sovereign states. On the other hand, the developed states had sent their traders and shipowners, or at least those who could speak only for them.

However, a number of developed countries not only were in sympathy with the developing states, but also combined this sympathy with their own more practical interests as users of shipping services. For example, Australia, Canada, and the United States consistently saw themselves in this role. Australia, without a foreign-going fleet of its own, was almost totally dependent on all the vagaries of the international shipping industry. Canada, a former shipping power, had because of specific government policy divested itself of its fleet but had remained a major trading nation dependent on international shipping. The United States, despite its high position on the world shipping ladder, always regarded itself more as a major direct trading nation than as a maritime state.[234]

This and other support paved the way for the establishment of a special organization within UNCTAD, which was to be given the task of examining international shipping questions. During UNCTAD I's deliberations, the subject of "invisibles"—an ingenious name covering such items as shipping, insurance, balance of payments, tourism, and transfer of technology—was given to the conference's Third Committee for study.[235] This body, quickly realizing that shipping required special attention, set up a separate Working Group on Shipping to deal with the many complex technical and policy issues involved. This eventually resulted in the establishment of the UNCTAD Permanent Committee on Shipping.[236] In the words of the distinguished representative of India to the Conference, Dr. Nagendra Singh:

> The deliberations of the *ad hoc* Working Party were so revealing and the conclusions reached so fundamental to both the developed and developing countries that after some discussion and exchange of views it was recognized that there was a need for a permanent organ where such deliberations could continue to take place periodically for the benefit of all regions of the world. The *ad hoc* "Working Party" had thus prepared the ground for the Permanent Shipping Committee of UNCTAD when the IIIrd Committee received the report of the Working Party and adopted it and the Conference accepted it.[237]

Obviously, the establishment of the forty-five-member UNCTAD Committee on Shipping and its permanent Secretariat in UNCTAD's Division of Invisibles was as vigorously opposed by the major maritime states as placing the shipping item on the conference's agenda had been in the first place.[238] In retrospect, this opposition appears to have been both futile and shortsighted; it only added to the unity of the newly established "Group of 77".[239] This opposition also served to typecast the maritime states as intransigents opposed to all change.[240] In other forums the developed states, in general, lost much persuasive bargaining power because of the unfortunate and futile role they adopted at UNCTAD. Unhappily, this pattern would repeat itself many times within the next decade.

After its establishment, the new Shipping Committee of UNCTAD was given the task of establishing reasonable consultation machinery in order better to document and understand the problems that existed in international shipping.[241] It was to meet regularly and provide a comprehensive report at the next UNCTAD meeting in 1968. Thus UNCTAD I ended in an aura of relative optimism with the developed world vowing that it would do much to eradicate the inequalities caused by the developmental gap. Detailed machinery to put this plan into action was set in motion by the conference, which became an integral and permanent part of the U.N. General Assembly. The results were to be examined four years later.

In the intervening years, the principles arrived at by UNCTAD I, which were, among other things, "to employ international machinery for the promotion of the economic and social advancement of all peoples,"[242] were repeated and further considered at other regional conferences, for example one at Algiers, which resulted in the Charter of Algiers, calling for rapid help and assistance in all economic matters for the poorer countries of the world.[243]

UNCTAD II took place in New Delhi in 1968.[244] It was in many ways a forum of disappointment and bitter recrimination, as it had quickly become apparent that the high hopes for the Third World, raised by UNCTAD I four years earlier, had not been realized. For the first time the poor confronted the rich in frustration and anger, when it was shown that economic progress for the developing world had been minimal and that their developmental progress had, in some cases, actually been reversed.[245] At the same time, it was seen that the developed world had prospered further. In addition, the ranks of the Group of 77, by then a misnomer,[246] had been further swelled by newly independent states as the last vestiges of colonialism were being cast off. In any case, the momentum and good will of UNCTAD I was gone, apparently forever.

On the shipping side at UNCTAD II, the struggle between the two unequal sides with their irreconcilable approaches continued. More than any other part of this conference, however, the Committee on Shipping could point to certain limited success. But even this achievement was blurred by the delaying tactics that had become so much a part of the United Nations procedure by this time and could be resorted to by any delegation that did not wish to appear intransigent but nonetheless wanted to stop proceedings.[247] It appeared at times as if the maritime states had realized that UNCTAD would be a convenient forum at which the Third-World states could air their frustrations related to shipping (and other economic and commercial matters), but that the *real* shipping decisions would continue to be taken at the CMI meetings or at IMCO, which, as we have seen, was at that stage basically under the control of the major shipping states.

Many of these procedural problems were further illustrated in the establishment of a new organization charged especially with international trade law. This was the United Nations Commission on International Trade Law (UNCITRAL). UNCITRAL was created in 1966 by a United Nations Resolution and was meant to be a highly competent small group charged with the technical examination of legislation related to international trade.[248] Policy questions were not to be part of UNCITRAL's mandate.

However, at UNCTAD II the maritime states proposed that the examination of international shipping legislation being undertaken by UNCTAD, which they opposed, should now become a task for UNCITRAL.[249] This, of course, caused lengthy debates and an acrimonious vote in UNCTAD's Shipping Committee.[250] The difficulties continued; and at times it appeared that the two sides were drawn further apart with Third-World states, secure in the unity of the Group of 77, becoming every more fiery and emotional in their rhetoric and, consequently, at times quite unrealistic in their demands. The developed states, on the other hand, were ill prepared to deal with this type of debate and eventually had in time, little choice but to withdraw from an unending polemical debate by the use of various time-consuming procedural maneuvers.[251]

It was all rather futile, and much could have been achieved if the terms of reference for each side had been a little more forthcoming toward the other. On the developed-state side, even a greater understanding and a less patronizing air of "rich toward poor" would have helped; this could only have been achieved by some clear-cut national policies in fields such as shipping. On the Third-World side, there should have been much more understanding of the operation of the very systems they were attacking and criticizing. Developing states should have realized quite clearly that most of the First-, and probably all of the Second-World states simply could not change a traditionally conceived and principally "private" system by government decree. However, this understanding seemed to be lacking at UNCTAD II, which ended quite inconclusively. We will return to this important organization once again in the next chapter as it continued to be a forum of hope for the Third World. In Nagendra Singh's words:

> Such organizations are indeed twice blessed first by the developing States for what they get out of them and second by the developed States for the sympathy and good will they evoke when reaching agreement. This feeling is undoubtedly there valued more in terms of what would have happened without the existence of such an organisation and this aspect has unfortunately to be discovered hidden beneath the humdrum routine of life. Be what it may, there can be little doubt that this is the golden age of international organisations and with them alone is in sight the golden age of mankind.[252]

## The Ocean Environment:
## Marine-Pollution Law and Policy

In addition to the worldwide problems related to international development, a new area of emphasis had arisen during the 1960s, particularly in
the developed regions. This was the era of resource orientation and environmental concern. The resource-hungry industrialized world had become
concerned about the quality of life at a time when the developing world was
still concerned with life and survival alone. Development and environment
are not necessarily compatible, as we shall see in the next chapter. In this
chapter, however, we must examine this environmental concern, which
received its impetus from the oceans of the world. We are referring, of
course, to the comparatively new phenomenon of marine pollution, which
within the last two decades has become a central part of the world's concern
for the protection of the environment.[253]

Sea pollution is caused by increasing human use of the ocean as a dumping ground for waste, which in turn causes harmful effects on the life-giving
capacity of the sea, on which we increasingly depend. At the end of the
1960s, for example, it was estimated that well over half of the world's
population depended solely on food from the sea for their supply of essential nutrition.[254] The ocean's importance as a potential food source was
clearly expected to increase in the future. In their concern, however, the
world's nation-states naturally chose to concentrate specifically on the
elimination of one particular source of pollution—that caused by oil—and
in particular on oil pollution that was ship-generated. This pollution source
was, in reality, only a small part of the overall problem,[255] but it appeared to
be the one that was easiest to deal with at the international level. Land-
generated pollution, by far the greatest problem, involved the sort of international cooperation between sovereign states that was simply not available
in the 1960s and would have to be attempted again in the 1970s.

Ship-generated pollution originating from the deliberate dumping of oil
into the ocean by seagoing vessels, from accidental spillages, and from shipping accidents and casualities was highly visible, easily documented, and
lent itself well to the general environmental concern of the time. It led to
debate, still inconclusive, which would have effects ranging far from the
prevention of such pollution, would invade many facets of international
discussion over the next decade, and would probably contribute directly to
the rise of the coastal state in the law of the sea.[256] The oil-pollution issue
also further contributed to the retrenchment of shipping interests on the international scene, as that industry had not learned the lessons of history well
enough to cope with this new phenomenon.

General concern about oil pollution appears to have originated in the
first decade after World War I, when first the United States and then the

League of Nations undertook to obtain explicit international agreement on measures to combat ship-generated oil pollution.[257] In 1926 an international conference held in Washington at the invitation of the U.S. government was attended by thirteen maritime states.[258] Despite vigorous debate, the very modest draft convention failed to achieve any ratification. In later years, oil pollution, particularly on the shores of the Atlantic Ocean, was very considerable during and after World War II as a direct result of the many torpedoed, sunken, and otherwise damaged vessels.[259]

By the 1950s, however, as we have seen, a rising world economy, resulting in an ever-increasing demand for petroleum fuels, led to renewed concerns about the pollution problem.[260] However, nothing concrete was achieved until 1954, when at the invitation of Great Britain a Conference on Oil Pollution from Ships was held in London.[261] The result was the International Convention for the Prevention of Oil Pollution in 1954, which took a further four years to enter into force in 1958.[262]

Although viewed as an abrogation of the freedom of the seas by many maritime states, it was indeed a modest convention. Exempting certain categories of vessels, it prohibited discharges of oil and oily mixtures within certain geographically defined zones extending generally fifty miles from land. These zones encompassed both high seas and territorial waters; but offenses under the convention were made punishable only under the "law of the territory in which the ship is registered," although coastal states could take limited action against offending vessels in their territorial seas. Beyond this area, a coastal state could only report violations to the flag state concerned. Under the convention, the flag state was obliged to conduct an investigation and impose sanctions. At the conference, however, no agreement could be reached on exactly how high-seas surveillance was to be carried out. Other convention articles provided that ships of contracting states be fitted with certain "pollution-avoiding" equipment and that the main ports of contracting states be equipped with facilities for the disposal of oily substances. The 1954 convention thus had few real "teeth" and depended almost completely on the full cooperation of participating states for enforcement. In other words, it was really a self-policing type of convention, which only paid lip service to an ever-increasing problem.[263]

We have already seen that the formation of IMCO in 1958 resulted in that organization accepting the responsibility not only for the 1954 convention but also for oil pollution in general. In 1959 another international conference on the subject of oil pollution, held in Copenhagen, resulted in a number of relatively minor recommendations aimed at extending the effectiveness of the 1954 convention.[264] However, one recommendation was that IMCO should prepare for a further intergovernmental oil-pollution conference, which should aim to extend considerably the prohibited ocean zones. This preparatory work resulted in the Second Conference on Oil

Pollution, held in London in 1962, which adopted many of the 1959 recommendations. These amendments, although marginal at best, did not achieve sufficient acceptance to bring them into effect until 1967.[265]

The question of pollution was also considered, if only in passing, by UNCLOS I in 1959, which in its Convention on the High Seas, requires states

> . . . to draw up regulations to prevent pollution of the sea by discharges of oil from ships or pipelines or resulting from exploitation of the sea bed and its subsoil, taking account of existing treaty provisions on the subject.[266]

Of course, this provision was drafted with the 1954 Oil Pollution Convention especially in mind; but it did not require the adherence of states. Another article in the Geneva High Seas Convention also deals with radioactive pollution, pointing to the fact that all legislative attempts so far had dealt only with oil pollution. It would take a further decade and a half before other pollutants would finally be included in international antipollution legislation.[267] All attempts to control pollution problems by international regulatory measures continued to be consistently opposed by the shipping industry. As a matter of fact, it can be said that in this field was found the most united posture in the recent history of that industry. The policy was to oppose antipollution moves on all fronts. However, this stand was to become even more assailable because of one of the most publicized shipwrecks in modern history.

### The Torrey Canyon *Incident: New Implications for Maritime Law*

In March 1967 the tanker *Torrey Canyon* grounded off the southwest coast of Cornwall, England, thus bringing the physical lessons of oil pollution home to one of the staunchest opponents of international regulatory measures against pollution. In 1967 the *Torrey Canyon* was still considered a very large vessel, carrying some 120,000 tons of crude oil on board.[268] To illustrate the international aspect of the incident: the ship was owned by a Bermudan-registered corporation, but was itself registered in Liberia under charter to a U.S. corporation, and was subchartered to a British company. Master and crew were Italian nationals. The salvage company involved was Dutch. The vessel grounded on a well-charted reef within the contiguous zone, but outside the territorial waters, of Great Britain.[269]

The subsequent investigation found that the grounding was caused solely by the human error of the master, not by the "flag of convenience" fluttering from the vessel's stern, as hinted by the British prime minister.[270]

The grounding caused the largest single oil spill in maritime history up to 1967. Some 80,000 tons of crude oil spread along British and French coasts, causing pollution in a 200-mile-plus arc.[271] The oil was released subsequent to the initial grounding and after the vessel had been bombed on orders of the British government after a decision that no other way was left to deal with the unsalvageable wreck.[272]

In every respect, whether scientific, technological, or legal, the *Torrey Canyon* disaster caught the maritime world completely unprepared. For example, scientific research into oil dispersal was then at best still experimental. Yet over 2.5 million gallons of various chemical dispersants were used, often with more disastrous effects on the marine environment than the crude oil itself. Damage claims in Great Britain amounted to £6 million, and to 40 million francs in France.[273] Most of these claims found no settlement.

However, there is no question that for those concerned with pollution the incident was a blessing in disguise. Public concern, aroused by the wide variety of problems caused by the wreck, resulted in relatively rapid action by various governments as well as by several international organizations. Suddenly the antipollution campaign was no longer only the concern of environmentally conscious individuals and organizations, which had persuaded a few governments to voice their own concerns. The campaign was quickly taken over by a large number of states who saw the dangers of a major oil spill to their own vulnerable coastlines. Such states consisted not only of coastal states without shipping interests, but also of shipping states with coastal interests.[274]

The *Torrey Canyon* added a whole new perspective to the pollution debate. At the specific request of Great Britain, IMCO convened a special council session in 1967 to examine all the problems raised by this disaster.[275] Up to that time IMCO had been forced to confine itself strictly to technical and advisory matters, leaving legal questions related to international shipping to the CMI, which, as we have seen, represented the interests of the international shipping industry. Obviously, many of the questions raised by the *Torrey Canyon* disaster were of a juridical nature, and IMCO consequently set up a legal committee. This was a significant move; for the first time an international organization, without special private or self-interest, had become involved in the public-law and -policy aspects of the pollution problem. In other words, the public and private aspect of maritime international law, which had by now been almost irretrievably separated, were forced together by this specific maritime problem.

Perhaps only marine pollution, with its very special characteristics, could have brought this about. Artificial though the separation had become, public maritime law was now concerned with political policy in regard to ocean space and its uses, whereas private maritime law confined itself to the commercial questions related to one particular use—that of marine transport. However, oil pollution generated by ships bridged both—it was directly related to the use of ocean space and the commercial activities of using it. Yet it had deleterious effects on both. It was an undesirable byproduct of marine transport and had no commercial benefit whatsoever. It also affected other uses of ocean space and caused damage to the coastline property of coastal states. Therefore, the complete legal system, ranging from the rights of the private littoral property owner in coastal states to the right of a maritime state to use ocean space, was affected by the pollution phenomenon. The difficulty, however, was and still is that the international law and policy of marine transport could no longer cope with this type of problem, which required a unified solution.

Public law and policy and private law and interests had diverged too far. Yet both were needed to provide answers and compromises rather than lead to further confrontation on two levels. It had to be recognized that pollution was an undesirable but unavoidable byproduct of industrialization. What was needed, therefore, was to reduce this byproduct to its lowest common denominator. In order to do this, both the public and private sectors had to seek mutually acceptable answers. This required recognition that ships not only carry large quantities of pollutants but also are propelled by fuel-burning machinery. They do not operate for the sake of operating but to provide a commercially viable cargo service from point A to point B. It is commercially viable because there is demand for the cargo, which can be carried by ship as the most efficient and economic mode of transportation.

So far so good. The ship operator gains from the profits he makes from carrying the goods, the cargo owner gains from the marketability of his goods, and the consumer benefits from having the goods available at competitive market prices. The whole process is facilitated by the free and unhindered use of ocean space allowing the carrier to proceed by the most direct routes available.

Now add the pollution factor. First, consider the *Torrey Canyon* type of disaster. The ship is lost; the shipowner collects his insurance. The cargo is lost; the cargo owner collects his insurance. However, there is now widespread oil pollution, which also affects other users of ocean space. After all, the "freedom of navigation" consists simply of the right for the vessel to proceed expeditiously and unhindered through ocean space. It does not consist of a license to pollute.[276] Usually, the released pollutants will also affect the coastlines of innocent third parties. Should they suffer?

Second, consider the deliberate pumping of pollutants into the oceans. Even if such an act were necessary as part of the efficient operation of international shipping—which we believe has never been the case—then such an act is nothing but a blatant insistence that there is indeed a freedom to pollute the oceans.[277]

It appears, therefore, that given the fact that marine transport will have this pollution byproduct, both public policy and private interest must work to achieve the lowest common denominator of pollution possible. First of all, deliberate dumping could easily have been banned altogether, as the technology has been available for decades to prevent such action.[278] However, the shipping industry was not able to divorce itself from its singularly commercial approach even to this question.

For the major-disaster type of pollution incident there were no easy answers. Considering the fact that most of these accidents are due to human error, technology alone could not prevent them, although technological progress in the shipping industry has been hampered too much by the self-same commercial approach taken by the shipping interests. In general shipping-safety matters, this approach has resulted in the lowest common denominator of safety becoming the international standard, in contrast to aviation, where the highest common denominator of safety has become the standard.

However, in the post-*Torrey Canyon* period, public law and policy and private law and interests were confronted with this problem and could handle it only with approaches that were basically unacceptable to each other. The question of whether marine pollution regulations, whether promulgated by international organization or by coastal states, abrogated the freedom of navigation was really not important. Yet many of the maritime states pursued this point as if the actual pollution problem were a secondary consideration. The result was, or course, that they appeared to support the proposition that the freedom of navigation did, indeed, include a license to pollute. On the other hand, the coastal and other nonmaritime states proposed regulatory restrictions that were not only unrealistic but often unnecessary. Thus the free-seas concept was used crudely and unbecomingly by both sides in the dispute.[279]

*Marine-Pollution Liability: IMCO and the CMI*

On the private-law side, important questions relating to liability and compensation for oil-pollution damage had to be worked out. Insurance and reinsurance risks had to be evaluated, and questions related to limitation of liability had to be negotiated. However, as there was now no common forum where both public and private matters could be approached, IMCO's brand new legal committee naturally asked the CMI for assistance. After May 1967 the two organizations therefore worked in cooperation but, of course, as separate entities.[280] The CMI and one of two IMCO working groups concerned themselves with questions related to private international law, while IMCO's other working group addressed questions of public international law.[281]

The distinction should be noted carefully. Nevertheless, there is no question that the cooperation between IMCO and the CMI was highly desirable and long overdue, since it at least attempted to bring private shipping and associated interests together with the public interests of a U.N. specialized agency. In retrospect, it seems clear that the CMI did not, or probably could not, realize at that time that it had the opportunity either to become a viable part of an expanded international maritime-law-making machinery, or to be reduced to a shipping-interest lobby par excellence. In order to achieve the former position, it would have had to accept that international maritime law making, which the CMI had been carrying out expertly for some seventy years, would also have to involve a certain amount of international maritime-law reform, considering the expansion of the world states with maritime interests.

It is probably a reflection of the CMI's orientation that it chose the second route. As we have said, the CMI, with its modest budget and small secretariat, was basically a clearing house for the views of the various constituent national maritime-law associations. There was little administrative capability to make quick policy decisions on the future of the organization. That decision would have to wait until 1972.

It was, therefore, not surprising that IMCO-CMI cooperation quickly ran into difficulties.[282] It is also not surprising that these difficulties related basically to questions of private maritime law, which were not considered to be in the interests of public policy. The most fundamental difference consisted of whether an international convention concerning oil pollution should be based on fault or on strict liability, and, if the latter, whether such liability should be imposed on the owner (operator) of the vessel, on the cargo interests, or on both.[283]

This question of liability has been the crux of the difficulties that have prevented international agreement to date. The Preliminary Report of the International *Torrey Canyon* Subcommittee under the chairmanship of Lord Devlin, the president of the British Maritime Law Association, called for absolute liabilty, compulsory insurance, and a limitation fund based on deadweight tonnage.[284] This highly progressive report, from the antipollution point of view, was unfortunately not accepted by the CMI member associations when they were asked to give their views on the matter.[285] Out of eighteen states that gave their comments, five favored strict liability, six wished to keep the existing fault liability, one state suggested strict liability on cargo only, and six wanted to preserve fault liability with a shift in the burden of proof to the shipowner to establish absence of fault.[286]

We will return to the difficult question relating to marine pollution in chapter 7. This question would continue to plague many different aspects related to the international law and policy of marine transport. In almost no other area were the two sides—public law and policy and private law and interests—brought into a sharper confrontation, and nowhere were they more closely related. Added to the futility of this dispute was the fact that much of it took the form of either defending or abrogating the Grotian principles of the freedom of the seas. Nowhere were these traditional principles more maligned nor misunderstood, misinterpreted, and misused than in the oil-pollution debate. The "father of international law" who wrote about the limitless inexhaustibility of the ocean would not have written so had he known of the vulnerability of the seas. Had he known, he would probably have been on the side of the coastal states that wished to protect rather than pollute the ocean.

**Maritime Law and Policy in a New Era**

For international marine transport, the decade from the late 1950s to the late 1960s was a diverse and complex one. We have seen how most aspects relating to the seas had come under the scrutiny of a drastically enlarged world, much of which demanded, perhaps even dictated, changes, progress, and a more equitable distribution of the world's oceanic resources—both visible and invisible. By the late 1960s there was certainly little doubt that marine transport was seen as one of these resources and that access to it was the prerequisite of development and prosperity. Yet, as we have also seen, never was this resource more ill prepared to face these new demands. Never had it been more isolated in its incomprehending self-interest—separated from most considerations of public law and policy and increasingly painted in terms of intransigence and anachronistic status quo preservation.

We know that the industry had become the victim of its own history and that it had been forced into a role from which there was little chance of extrication. Marine transport, which had actually given birth to all other oceanic considerations, was now isolated and forced to fight for its own survival, together with other ocean uses that were receiving a much more sympathetic hearing and understanding in the gathering places of the world's nations.

Somehow or other, the spark that in the past had prompted this great industry to rise to the occasion and cause fundamental changes to be made, could no longer be ignited. Perhaps the possibility existed when the marine-pollution debate first arose, but the opportunity appeared to have been lost. Private maritime law and interests had indeed become "private," without even a feeling of participation in, or obligation toward, the making of international ocean policy.

However, despite this complete separation and the considerable pressures asserted against the shipping industry during this decade, private maritime law flourished. The CMI was able to continue its productive effort in achieving, or at least in attempting to achieve, the uniformity of international maritime law as it became necessary. Accordingly, the CMI held four international conferences between 1958 and 1968, and obtained agreement on several new conventions in addition to cooperating with IMCO on the marine-pollution questions to which we have already referred. First, the following conferences were held during the period:

| | | |
|---|---|---|
| XXIVth | Conference: | Rijeka 1959 |
| | Agenda: | Liability of operators of nuclear ships |
| | | Revision of international convention for the unification of certain rules of law relating to bills of lading |
| | | Letters of indemnity and marginal clauses |
| | | Revision of the international convention for the unification of certain rules of law relating to assistance and salvage at sea |
| | | International statute of ships in foreign ports |
| | | Registry of operators of ships |
| XXVth | Conference: | Athens 1962 |
| | Agenda: | Damages in matters of collision |
| | | Letters of indemnity |
| | | International statute of ships in foreign ports |
| | | Registry of ships |
| | | Coordination of the convention of limitation and on mortgages |
| | | Demurrage and despatch money |
| | | Liability of carriers for luggage |
| XXVIth | Conference: | Stockholm 1963 |
| | Agenda: | Bills of lading |
| | | Passengers' luggage |
| | | Ships under construction |
| XXVIIth | Conference: | New York 1965 |
| | Agenda: | Revision of the conference on maritime liens and mortgages[287] |

In 1957 the CMI also successfully concluded the new Convention on Limitation of Liability of Owners of Seagoing Vessels.[288] We have already examined the controversy of this historical area of maritime law. Obviously, it is far from being simply a technical matter, as it is often taken to be, and was one of the aspects of maritime law questioned by many of the "ship-user states" at UNCTAD's Shipping Committe.[289] Yet the CMI was concerned only with reconciling divergent legal approaches to the principle rather than with the principle itself. The new convention was to supersede the 1924 convention and would basically codify the British approach to the principle.[290]

If the principle of limitation itself was accepted, then the new convention was obviously a better one, as it considerably raised the money value of the limitation fund for both personal injuries and property claims.[291] On the other hand, it also extended the right to limit liability to a whole group of persons in positions ancilliary to actual ownership of the vessel. It would now apply even to fault of shore personnel as long as they were concerned in the management of the ship. The CMI's claim that the new convention "outstrips its predecessor with gigantic strides by a humanitarian spirit, as well as by a more marked concern for equity and realism which is likely to serve international commerce,"[292] must thus be accepted cautiously. In particular, it must be remembered that "international commerce" was not fully represented at the convention's conclusion.[293] The CMI also saw to the conclusion of the little known Convention on Stowaways,[294] which, obviously, is concerned with problems that are not only administrative but, at times, highly political as well as humanitarian. In 1961 a Convention on Carriage of Passengers by Sea was concluded under CMI auspices, which finally brought human life in line with goods carried at sea.[295] Although the latter had received considerable juridical attention in the past, the former had not. But it was a controversial decision. As the CMI admits:

> . . . and yet, what difficulties there are to be surmounted, some the result of older habits strongly anchored in customs, others, of the fear of openly consecrating certain exonerations and limitations of liability which, nevertheless, are, in practice, customary in the wording of steamship tickets.[296]

It is interesting to note that at a time when the passenger liner was giving way to aircraft as the main mode for passenger transportation, the shipping industry would finally promulgate rules for protecting passengers at sea.

On the other hand, in 1962 the conclusion of the Convention on Liability of Operators of Nuclear Ships brought the CMI into the atomic age.[297] The utilization of nuclear energy for economic purposes, such as marine transport, had raised the possibility of considerable risks of accidents involving nuclear vessels; and the whole subject had been laid before the CMI in 1957. The organization worked in fairly close cooperation with the International Atomic Energy Agency (IAEA), which is the specialized agency of the United Nations charged with dealing with matters relating to nuclear energy.

The result of this convention is significant, as it successfully constituted a compromise between the needs of countries producing nuclear-powered vessels and those of states that receive such vessels in their ports and territorial seas. It is a universally applicable convention covering all nuclear accidents and damage caused by all vessels of contracting states. It establishes the strict liability of the vessel's operator, using the principle of liability of *ubi emolumentum ibi onus.*[298] It was exactly this principle that was found so unacceptable by the shipping industry in major incidents of marine pollution. In the Nuclear Ships Convention, limitation of liability was established but with an upper limit of about $100 million per nuclear incident. It was in many ways a remarkable convention and a brilliant display of the depth of international commercial expertise available within the CMI when directed to a new maritime matter requiring innovative solutions bridging the broad political and commercial spectrum. Within a mere five-year period, the CMI, in cooperation with a U.N. agency, was able to produce a highly satisfactory legal instrument, which displayed an almost complete uniformity of public maritime law and policy and private maritime law and interest. How unfortunate it seems that this unifying effort could not have been available more frequently during this difficult period.

In addition to achieving the nuclear convention, the CMI also did the following: concluded, in 1967, a new International Convention for the Unification of Certain Rules Relating to the Carriage of Passengers' Luggage at Sea;[299] amended, in 1967, the International Convention for the Unification of Certain Rules relating to Assistance and Salvage at Sea of 1910;[300] and concluded, in 1967, a new International Convention Relating to the Registration of Rights in Respect of Vessels Under Construction.[301] Furthermore, the conclusion of a new International Convention for the Unification of Certain Rules Relating to Maritime Liens and Mortgages, in 1967,[302] was the result of further international efforts, at the 1965 CMI New York Conference, to achieve acceptable international uniformity in this difficult, as well as technical, area of maritime law.

Even this very rapid overview of what had happened to private maritime law during this decade should show its continued resilience and viability but also its isolation and separation from the public law of the sea. The opportunities for unification between the two fields that were opened up by the establishment of the UNCTAD Shipping Committee, the debate on the marine-pollution question and even that on the Nuclear Ships Convention, could no longer be used to advantage by the international shipping industry, which had lost the momentum to create change and progress in all but its own self-imposed and self-defined areas. Even as the 1967 conventions were concluded, a whole new oceanic decade was being ushered in in the General Assembly of the United Nations from which the private side of the international law and policy of marine transport would be further isolated and separated.

## Notes

1. J.B. Condliffe, *The Commerce of Nations* (New York: Norton, 1950), pp. 556-557.

2. Ibid.

3. Ibid.

4. Ibid., p. 557.

5. Ibid.

6. Ibid., p. 559.

7. Ibid., p. 563; see also William L. Langer, ed., *Encyclopedia of World History,* 4th ed. (Boston: Houghton Mifflin, 1968), p. 1135ff.

8. Stanley Wolpert, *A New History of India* (New York: Oxford University Press, 1977), ch. 22, 23.

9. One of the best recent examinations of this difficult area can be found in Hugh Seton-Watson, *Nations and States: An Enquiry into the Origins of Nations and the Politics of Nationalism* (Boulder, Colo.: Westview, 1977). For some multidisciplinary views see Ronald St. J. Macdonald, Douglas M. Johnston, and Gerald L. Morris, eds., *The International Law and Policy of Human Welfare* (Alphen aan den Rijn: Sijthoff and Noordhoff, 1978).

10. See, for example, J.K. Nyerere, "The Economic Challenge: Dialogue or Confrontation?" *International Development Review* 18 (1986):2; Patrick J. McGowan, "Economic Dependence and Economic Performance in Black Africa," *Journal of Modern African Studies* 14 (1976):25; D. Goulet, "Development . . . or Liberation?" *International Develoment Review* 13 (1976):10.

11. Ibid.

12. Mary Ellen Caldwell, "The Legal Factor in the Food-Population Equation," in *International Law of Human Welfare,* edited by Macdonald, Johnston, and Morris, p. 601.

13. Although this is not strictly correct, the debate on the "new international economic order" is now frequently seen in geographical terms as a "North-versus-South" confrontation.

14. This is the popular conglomerate term for the vast group of states that profess not to belong (in geographical or econopolitical terms) to the First World—the developed countries of Western Europe and North America (OECD)—or the Second World—the Socialist states of Eastern Europe.

15. Now frequently used to designate the less and least-developed among the developing states.

16. Walter Rodney, *How Europe Undeveloped Africa* (London: Scribner, 1972).

17. At that time, the CMI had no membership associations in states which belonged to this group. Even developing-country membership in IMCO rose only very slowly.

18. Even by 1950 "other countries" to which that group of states would statistically belong only controlled some 18 percent of world shipping. See C.E. McDowell and H.B. Gibbs, *Ocean Transportation* (New York: McGraw Hill, 1954), p. 105.

19. Timothy M. Shaw, "The Elusiveness of Development and Welfare: Inequalities in the Third World," in *International Law of Human Welfare,* edited by Macdonald, Johnston, and Morris, p. 81.

20. Ralph W. Ochan, "Marine Policy and Developing Landlocked States: The Search for a New Equity in the Law of the Sea" (Master's thesis, Faculty of Law, Dalhousie University, Halifax, Nova Scotia, Canada).

21. Ibid.; see also Ronald Hope, "The Political Economy of Marine Transportation," in *Marine Policy and the Coastal Community,* edited by D.M. Johnston (London: Croom Helm, 1976), p. 103.

22. Alan Villiers, *Men, Ships and the Sea* (Washington: National Geographic, 1973).

23. McDowell and Gibbs, *Ocean Transportation,* p. 2.

24. Generally bulk commodities such as sugar, ores, coffee, and copper.

25. Requiring the exporters to deliver the cargo at the consignee's port of delivery and carrying all costs and responsibilities until such delivery.

26. Convention on a Code of Conduct for Liner Conferences," *International Legal Materials* 13 (1974):912.

27. Hope, "Political Economy of Marine Transportation," p. 105.

28. To the best of our knowledge there are no developing countries at present that have instituted coastal "marine-affairs" planning.

29. Arthur S. Banks, ed., *Political Handbook of the World: 1977* (New York: McGraw-Hill, 1978), p. 535.

30. Ibid.

31. Ibid., p. 536.

32. Ibid.

33. Ibid.

34. Justus Buchler et al., *Introduction to Contemporary Civilization in the West,* vol. 2, 2nd ed. (New York: Columbia University Press, 1954), pp. 1232-1233.

35. Banks, *Political Handbook: 1977*, pp. 581-583.

36. Ibid.

37. Clive Parry, "The Inter-Governmental Maritime Consultative Organization," *British Year Book of International Law* 25 (1949):437.

38. Ibid., p. 438.

39. Ibid., p. 446.

40. The full IMCO convention is appended in ibid., pp. 447-457.

41. IMCO convention, art. 60.

42. Nagendra Singh and Raoul Colinvaux, *Shipowners,* vol. 13, British Shipping Laws (London: Stevens, 1967), pp. 362-363.

43. Ibid., p. 361.

44. Ibid.

45. Ibid., p. 129.

46. By ensuring that the council and the maritime-safety committee of IMCO were heavily weighted with members from the traditional shipping states (IMCO Convention, arts. 17-32).

47. See Banks, *Political Handbook of the World* for fuller details.

48. Ibid., pp. 556-557.

49. Ibid., pp. 558-559.

50. Ibid., p. 560.

51. Ibid., pp. 566-567.

52. Report, *Committee of Inquiry into Shipping* ("Rochdale Report") (London: HMSO, 1970), p. 12.

53. McDowell and Gibbs, *Ocean Transportation,* p. 105.

54. Ibid.

55. Ibid.

56. Ibid., pp. 105-106.

57. Ibid., p. 106.

58. Condliffe, *Commerce of Nations,* pp. 558, 707.

59. McDowell and Gibbs, *Ocean Transportation,* p. 105.

60. Albert Lilar and Carlo van den Bosch, *Le Comité Maritime International* (Anvers: CMI, 1972), pp. 112-115.

61. Ibid., p. 34.

62. P.C.I.J., series A, no. 10 (1927).

63. Lilar and van den Bosch, *Comité Maritime International,* p. 36.

64. Ibid., pp. 36-37.

65. Ibid., pp. 22-24.

66. Ibid., pp. 38-46.

67. Grant Gilmore and Charles L. Black, Jr., *The Law of Admiralty,* 2nd ed. (Mineola, N.Y.: Foundation Press, 1975), pp. 35-36.

68. Lilar and van den Bosch, *Comité Maritime International,* p. 40.

69. Ibid.

70. Ibid.; see also A.N. Yiannopoulos, "The Unification of Private Maritime Law by International Conventions," *Law and Contemporary Problems* 30 (1965):370, 395.

71. Gilmore and Black, *Law of Admiralty,* p. 35ff.

72. Lilar and van den Bosch, *Comité Maritime International,* p. 44.

73. Ibid.

74. Comment, "Territorial Seas—3000 Year Old Question," *Journal of Air Law and Commerce* 36 (1970):73, 94; Bernard G. Heinzen, "The Three-Mile Limit: Preserving the Freedom of the Seas," *Stanford Law Review* 11 (1959):597, 639.

75. See, for example, Frans De Pauw, *Grotius and the Law of the Sea* (Bruxelles: Université de Bruxelles, 1965), pp. 14, 67ff.

76. Stefan A. Riesenfeld, *Protection of Coastal Fisheries under International Law* (Washington: Carnegie Endowment, 1942), p. 265ff.

77. Douglas M. Johnston, *The International Law of Fisheries* (New Haven: Yale University Press, 1965), ch. 3.

78. *Official Documents of the 1930 Hague Codification Conference, Report of the Second Committee, American Journal of International Law* 24 (1930):234, 235.

79. Joseph C. Sweeney, "Oil Pollution on the Oceans," *Fordham Law Review* 37 (1968):115, 118. See also Colombos, *International Law of the Sea,* pp. 430-431.

80. Gerard J. Mangone, *Marine Policy for America* (Lexington, Mass.: Lexington Books, D.C. Heath and Co., 1977), pp. 175-176.

81. Ibid., p. 176.

82. See, for example, Myres S. McDougal and William T. Burke, *The Public Order of the Oceans* (New Haven: Yale University Press, 1962), ch. 6; M.W. Mouton, *The Continental Shelf* (The Hague: Nijhoff, 1952).

83. Cornwall Submarine Mines Act, 1858. 21 and 22 Vict., ch. 109.

84. Mangone, *Marine Policy for America,* cited p. 178.

85. Ibid.

86. Ibid.

87. Ibid.; see also Donald C. Watt, "First Steps in the Enclosure of the Oceans—The Origins of Truman's Proclamation on the Resources of the Continental Shelf, 28 September, 1945," *Marine Policy* 3 (1979):211.

88. Ibid., p. 31.

89. Ibid., p. 178.

90. F.V. Garcia Amador, *The Exploitation and Conservation of the Resources of the Sea,* 2nd ed. (Leiden: Sijthoff, 1963), p. 97.

91. League of Nations Treaty Series, vol. 205, no. 4829.

92. Ibid., article 6.

93. U.S. Dept. of State Bulletin, September 30, 1945, p. 484.

94. Mangone, *Marine Policy for America*, ch. 3.

95. Ibid., p. 179.

96. Douglas M. Johnston and Edgar Gold, *The Economic Zone in the Law of the Sea: Survey, Analysis and Appraisal of Current Trends* (Kingston, R.I.: Law of the Sea Institute, University of Rhode Island, 1973), Occasional Paper no. 17, p. 1.

97. Constitution, art. 7 of September 1, 1950. See *International Boundary Study—Series A—Limits in the Seas* (Washington: U.S. Government Bureau of Intelligence and Research), no. 36, 3 January 1972.

98. Garcia Amador, *Resources of the Sea,* p. 98.

99. Agreements between Chile, Ecuador, and Peru. Signed at the First Conference on the Exploitation and Conservation of the Marine Resources of the South Pacific, Santiago, 18 August 1952. Reproduced in *New Directions in the Law of the Sea,* vol. 1, edited by S.H. Lay, R. Churchill and M. Nordquist (Dobbs Ferry, N.Y.: Oceana, 1973), p. 23.

100. Johnston and Gold, *The Economic Zone,* p. 1.

101. Alberto Szekely, *Latin America and the Development of the Law of the Sea,* 2 vols. (Dobbs Ferry, N.Y.: Oceana, 1976 and 1978).

102. "Rochdale Report," p. 18.

103. Johnston and Gold, *The Economic Zone,* p. 2.

104. Garcia Amador, *Resources of the Sea,* p. 73.

105. Ibid.

106. Ibid., pp. 73-78.

107. McDougal and Burke, *Public Order of the Oceans,* cited p. 443.

108. David J. Padwa, "The Curriculum of IMCO," *International Organizations* 14 (1960):524, 533.

109. Ibid., p. 531.

110. Ibid., p. 530.

111. Ibid., p. 532.

112. IMCO Convention, article 28(a).

113. K.R. Simmonds, "The Constitution of the Maritime Safety Committee of IMCO," *International and Comparative Law Quarterly* 12 (1963):56, 61, 62.

114. Ibid.

115. B.A. Boczek, *Flags of Convenience—An International Legal Study* (Cambridge, Mass.: Harvard University Press, 1962).

116. Ibid.

117. D.H.N. Johnson, "IMCO: The First Four Years (1959-1962)," *International and Comparative Law Quarterly* 12 (1963):31, 40.

118. Simmonds, "Constitution of Maritime Safety Committee of IMCO," p. 63ff.

119. Ibid.

120. Ibid.

121. Ibid.

122. L.F.E. Goldie, "Recognition and Dual Nationality—A Problem of Flags of Convenience," *British Year Book of International Law* 39 (1963):220.

123. *Constitution of the Maritime Safety Committee—Order of 5 August 1959,* I.C.J. Reports (1959):267.

124. Johnson, "IMCO: First Four Years," pp. 40-42.

125. Ibid.

126. In the area of $1 million for many years. See IMCO, *Annual Reports,* 1959-1976.

127. Ibid.

128. Banks, *Political Handbook: 1977,* p. 560.

129. It would take twenty years (to 1978) before the one-hundredth state joined the organization.

130. Johnson, "IMCO: First Four Years," pp. 43-48.

131. Ibid., p. 43.

132. Ibid.

133. 372 U.N.T.S. 3.

134. Edgar Gold, "Pollution of the Sea and International Law: A Canadian Perspective," *Journal of Maritime Law and Commerce* 3(1971):13, 19.

135. Ibid.

136. International Regulations for Preventing Collisions at Sea, 1960, applied from September 1, 1965 until superseded in 1977.

137. Convention on Facilitation of International Maritime Traffic, 1965, in force since March 5, 1967.

138. International Convention on Load Lines, 1966, in force since July 21, 1968.

139. Probably an unjust criticism, as the organization was simply a victim of its own inflexible convention.

140. Padwa, "Curriculum of IMCO," p. 540ff.

141. Condliffe, *Commerce of Nations,* p. 612.

142. For example, ICAO was able to look at the "totality" of aerospace use.

143. Leading eventually to the radicalization of the North-South encounter.

144. See for example, Max Sørensen, "Law of the Sea," *International Conciliation no. 520,* November 1958; D.W. Bowett, "The Second United Nations Conference on the Law of the Sea," *International and Comparative Law Quarterly* 9 (1960):415.; D.H.N. Johnson, "The Geneva Conference on the Law of the Sea," *Yearbook of World Affairs* 13 (1959):68; Philip C. Jessup, "The United Nations Conference on the Law of the Sea," *Columbia Law Review* 59 (1959):234; Arthur H. Dean, "The Geneva Conference on the Law of the Sea: What was Accomplished," *American Journal of International Law* 52 (1958):607.

145. Ibid.

146. Donald W. Mitchell, *A History of Russian and Soviet Sea Power* (New York: Macmillan, 1974). See also A. Kolodkin, "Territorial Waters and International Law," *International Affairs* 8 (1969):78 (Moscow).

147. United Nations Conference on the Law of the Sea, *Official Records,* vols. 1-7, U.N. no. 58.V.4, 1958.

148. Heinzen, "The Three-Mile Limit," p. 637.

149. Ibid., pp. 637-639.

150. Garcia Amador, *Resources of the Sea,* p. 97ff.

151. Sørensen, "Law of the Sea," p. 195.

152. Ibid., pp. 195-196.

153. Ibid., p. 226ff.

154. Ibid., p. 196.

155. Ibid., p. 197.

156. U.N. General Assembly Resolution 1105(XI), February 21, 1957.

157. Ibid.

158. See, for example, Arthur H. Dean, "The Second Geneva Conference on the Law of the Sea: The Fight for Freedom of the Seas," *American Journal of International Law* 54 (1960):751.

159. Sørensen, "Law of the Sea," p. 193.

160. L.A. Teklaff, "Shrinking the High Seas by Technical Methods—From the 1930 Hague Conference to the 1958 Geneva Conference," *University of Detroit Law Journal* 39 (1962):660, 667ff.

161. Bowett, "The Second United Nations Conference on the Law of the Sea," p. 428ff.

162. Myres S. McDougal and William T. Burke, "The Community Interest in a Narrow Territorial Sea: Inclusive versus Exclusive Competence over the Oceans," *Cornell Law Quarterly* 45 (1960):171, 251.

163. Johnston and Gold, *The Economic Zone,* pp. 3-4.

164. Dean, "Fight for Freedom of the Seas."

165. Johnston and Gold, *The Economic Zone,* p. 4.

166. Convention on the High Seas, art. 2.

167. Ibid.

168. Dean, "Fight for Freedom of the Seas."

169. McDougal and Burke, Public Order of the Oceans, p. 496.

170. Such as the arrest of whaling and fishing vessels by Ecuador in the post-World War II years. See also W. Paul Gormley, "The Unilateral Extension of Territorial Waters," *University of Detroit Law Journal* 43 (1966):695.

171. Myres S. McDougal, William T. Burke, and Ivan A. Vlasic, "The Maintenance of Public Order at Sea and the Nationality of Ships," *American Journal of International Law* 54 (1960):25; H. Meijers, *The Nationality of Ships,* (The Hague: Nijhoff, 1967).

172. Boczek, *Flags of Convenience;* ibid., Meijers.

173. Goldie, "Recognition and Dual Nationality"; "Rochdale Report," p. 51ff.

174. Edgar Gold, "Flags of Convenience: The 'Offshore' Registration of Ships," in *New Directions in Maritime Law 1978*, edited by Edgar Gold (Halifax, N.S.: Faculty of Law, Dalhousie University, 1978), pp. 86-88.

175. Ibid.

176. Ibid.

178. Ibid., pp. 88-90.

179. B.M. Metaxas, "Some Thoughts on Flags of Convenience," *Maritime Studies and Management* 1 (1974):162.

180. Ibid.

181. Note, "PanLibHon Registration of American-owned Merchant Ships: Government Policy and the Problem of the Courts," *Columbia Law Review* 60 (1960):711.

182. Simmonds, "Maritime Safety Committee of IMCO," p. 61.

183. Ibid.

184. Note, "PanLibHon Registration."

185. McDougal, Burke and Vlasic, "Public Order at Sea," p. 30.

186. *Nottebohm Case (Liechtenstein* v. *Guatemala)*, [1955] I.C.J. Reports 4.

187. D.H.N. Johnson, "The Nationality of Ships," *Indian Year Book of International Affairs* 8 (1959):3, 5.

188. [1955] I.C.J. Reports, 20, 23.

189. Johnson, "Nationality of Ships," p. 6.

190. Meijers, *Nationality of Ships;* Nagendra Singh, *Maritime Flag and International Law* (Leiden: Sijthoff, 1978).

191. Johnson, "Nationality of Ships," cited p. 6.

192. Jessup, "United Nations Conference on the Law of the Sea," pp. 255-258; Sørensen, "The Law of the Sea," pp. 201-206.

193. Ibid.; cf. McDougal, Burke, and Vlasic, "Public Order at Sea," p. 29ff.

194. McDougal, Burke, and Vlasic, "Public Order at Sea," p. 30.

195. A.D. Watts, "The Protection of Merchants Ships," *British Year Book of International Law* 33 (1977):52, 84.

196. McDougal, Burke, and Vlasic, "Public Order at Sea," p. 39.

197. "Rochdale Report," p. 57.

198. Afghanistan, Burma, Cambodia, Ceylon, Ghana, India, Indonesia, Laos, Liberia, Malaya, Nepal, Pakistan, Philippines, Thailand.

199. Augustin Cueva, "A Summary of Problems and Pespectives of Dependency Theory," *Latin American Perspectives* 3 (1976):12; Cadman Atta-Mills, "Africa and the New International Order," *Africa Development* 1 (1976):2; Pierre Uri, *Development Without Dependence* (New York: Praeger, 1976).

200. T.D. Elias, *Africa and the Development of International Law* (Leiden: Sijthoff, 1972), p. v.

201. Ibid.

202. Okon Udokang, *Succession of New States to International Treaties* (Dobbs Ferry, N.Y.: Oceana, 1972).

203. Ochan, "Marine Policy and Developing Landlocked States," p. 15.

204. Sudhir Sen, *United Nations in Economic Development—Need for a New Strategy* (Dobbs Ferry, N.Y.: Oceana, 1969.)

205. Edgar Gold, "The International Transfer and Promotion of Technology," *International Law and Policy of Human Welfare,* edited by Macdonald, Johnston, and Morris, p. 549.

206. Ibid.

207. S.J. Patel, "The Technological Dependence of Developing Countries, *Journal of Modern African Studies* 12 (1974):1, 3.

208. G. Blackett, "Technology and World Advancement," *Advancement of Science* 14 (1957-1958):3.

209. In 1952-1954 prices.

210. Singh, *Maritime Flag and International Law,* pp. xv, 105.

211. Charles O. Hucker, *China's Imperial Past* (Stanford: Stanford University Press, 1975), p. 187ff.

212. Victor W. von Hagen, *The Ancient Sun Kingdoms of the Americas* (Cleveland: World Publishing Co., 1961), p. 373ff.

213. Timothy M. Shaw, "The Elusiveness of Development and Welfare: Inequalities in the Third World," in *International Law and Policy of Human Welfare,* edited by Macdonald, Johnston, and Morris, p. 81.

214. N.S. Rembe, *Africa and the International Law of the Sea,* (Alphen aan den Rijn: Sitjhoff & Noordhoff, 1980). See also "Expanded Programme of Technical Assistance for Economic Development of Under-Developed Countries," U.N. General Assembly Resolution 304(iv), November 16, 1949.

215. "Establishment of the Special Fund," U.N. General Assembly Resolution 1240(xiii), October 14, 1958.

216. "United Nations Development Decade: A Programme for International Economic Co-operation" (I), U.N. General Assembly Resolution 1710(xvi), December 19, 1961.

217. "World Food Programme," U.N. General Assembly Resolution 1714(xvi), December 19, 1961.

218. B. Gosovic, *UNCTAD: Conflict and Compromise* (Leiden: Sijthoff, 1971), p. 19.

219. "Establishment of the United Nations Capital Development Fund," U.N. General Assembly Resolution 2186(xxi), December 13, 1966.

220. Gosovic, *UNCTAD,* p. 28ff.

221. *Proceedings of the United Nations Conference on Trade and Development,* vol. 1, Final Act and Report, U.N. no. E/Conf. 46/141, p. 6.

222. Gosovic, *UNCTAD*, ch. 6.

223. Ibid.

224. T. Vaitsos, "Patents Revisited: Their Function in Developing Countries," *Journal of Development Studies* 9 (1972):71; Ulf Anderfeldt, *International Patent Legislation and Developing Countries* (The Hague:Nijhoff, 1971).

225. Gosovic, *UNCTAD*, p. 138.

226. Ibid., pp. 142-146.

227. Ibid., pp. 146-150.

228. Ibid.

229. Ibid. For a most incisive analysis of these areas see Nagendra Singh, *Achievements of UNCTAD I (1964) and UNCTAD II (1968) in the Field of Shipping and Invisibles* (Delhi: Chand, 1969).

230. Gosovic, *UNCTAD*, 150.

231. This refers to countries that are OECD members—the "Western" and "Northern" developed states.

232. Gosovic, *UNCTAD*, pp. 146-150.

233. Ibid., p. 139, n. 4.

234. Ibid.

235. Singh, *Achievements of UNCTAD*, p. 44ff.

236. Ibid.

237. Ibid.

238. Gosovic, *UNCTAD*, p. 140.

239. Originally composed of 77 states, this group contained all the developing states of Africa, Asia, and Latin America. Although today there are some 120 members in the group, the original name persists.

240. Gosovic, *UNCTAD*, p. 139.

241. Ibid.

242. Paraphrasing the U.N. Charter's Preamble. *UNCTAD I Proceedings,* p. 3.

243. Ministerial Meeting of the Group of 77, Algiers, 1967. U.N. Doc. T.D. 138.

244. *United Nations Conference on Trade and Development, Second Session, New Delhi, 1 February-20 March 1968.* Summary Records of the 37th to 81st Plenary Meetings, U.N. Doc. T.D./SA37-81.

245. Ibid.

246. There were then already almost a hundred member states.

247. Gold, "Transfer of Technology," p. 560.

248. General Assembly Resolution 2205(xxi), December 17, 1966.

249. Gosovic, *UNCTAD*, p. 248.

250. Ibid., p. 249.

251. Ibid.

252. Singh, Achievements of UNCTAD, pp. 7-8.

253. James Barros and Douglas M. Johnston, *The International Law of Pollution* (New York: Free Press, 1974).

254. Roy I. Jackson, "Fisheries and the Future World Food Supply," in *World Fisheries Policy*, edited by Brian J. Rothschild (Seattle: University of Washington Press, 1972), p. 3ff.

255. Douglas M. Johnston, "Marine Pollution Control: Law, Science and Politics," *International Journal* 28 (1972-1973):69.

256. Edgar Gold, "The Rise of the Coastal State in the Law of the Sea," in *Marine Policy and the Coastal Community,* edited by Douglas M. Johnston (London: Croom Helm, 1960), p. 13ff.

257. McDougal and Burke, *Public Order of the Oceans,* p. 849.

258. C. John Colombos, *The International Law of the Sea,* 6th rev. ed. (London: Longmans, 1967), pp. 430-431.

259. V. Nanda, "The *Torrey Canyon* Disaster: Some Legal Aspects," *Denver Law Journal* 44 (1967):400, 403.

260. McDougal and Burke, *Public Order of the Oceans,* pp. 849-850.

261. E.D. Brown, *The Legal Regime of Hydrospace* (London: Stevens, 1971), p. 130ff.

262. See 372 U.N.T.S. 3.

263. Edgar Gold, "Pollution of the Sea and International Law: A Canadian Perspective," *Journal of Maritime Law and Commerce* 3 (1971):13, 19.

264. Ibid.

265. Ibid., p. 20.

266. Convention on the High Seas, 1958. 450 U.N.T.S. 82, art. 24.

267. Ibid., art. 25.

268. 1967 A.M.C. 569.

269. L. Oudet, "The 'Torrey Canyon' Commision of Inquiry," *Journal of the Institute of Navigation* 23 (1970):239.

270. Richard Petrow, *The Black Tide* (London: Hodder and Stoughton, 1968), p. 42.

271. Nanda, "Torrey Canyon Disaster," p. 400.

272. Petrow, *Black Tide,* p. 56.

273. Plinio Manca, *International Maritime Law,* vol. 1 (Antwerp: European Transport Law, 1970), p. 190.

274. D.P. O'Connell, "Reflections on Brussels: IMCO and the 1969 Pollution Conventions," *Cornell International Law Journal* 3 (1970):161, 184.

275. U.N. Doc. TD/32/Rev. 1, 23-24.

276. L.J.H. Legault, "Freedom of the Seas: A Licence to Pollute?" *University of Toronto Law Journal* 21 (1971):211.

277. See, for example, R.C. Page and A.W. Gardner, *Petroleum Tankship Safety* (London: Maritime Press, 1971); A.D. Couper, *The Geography of Sea Transport* (London: Hutchinson, 1972), p. 121.

278. Ibid.

279. Legault, "Licence to Pollute?" p. 218.

280. N.J. Healy, "The CMI and IMCO Draft Conventions on Civil Liability for Oil Pollution," *Journal of Maritime Law and Commerce* 1 (1969):93.

281. Ibid.

282. Ibid.

283. See IMCO Doc. LEG/WG(2), (1969), pp. 1-2.

284. J.C. Sweeney, "Oil Pollution on the Oceans," *Fordham Law Review* 37 (1968):115, 206.

285. Ibid.

286. Ibid., pp. 206-207.

287. Lilar and van den Bosch, *Comité Maritime International,* p. 114.

288. Ibid., pp. 46-50.

289. Gosovic, *UNCTAD,* p. 150.

290. Lilar and van den Bosch, *Comité Maritime International,* p. 48.

291. Ibid., p. 50.

292. Ibid.

293. At that time the CMI had fewer than thirty states as members.

294. Lilar and van den Bosch, *Comité Maritime International,* pp. 50-52.

295. Ibid., pp. 52-56.

296. Ibid., p. 52.

297. Ibid., pp. 56-74.

298. Ibid., p. 64 ("He who benefits shares in the burden").

299. Ibid., pp. 74-76.

300. Ibid., p. 76.

301. Ibid., pp. 82-84.

302. Ibid., pp. 76-82.

# 7

# New Challenges for Marine Transport

*If all states asserted and were protected in extravagant, disproportionate, exclusive claims, there would be little, if any, net total of inclusive use for common enjoyment.*

—Myres S. McDougal (*Yale Law Journal* 67, 1958)

*. . . neither a single State nor a single ideal, whether in the religious field or one of political belief, can spread its canopy throughout the world. The possible instrumentalities for world peace symbolized by the concept of Cakravartin, or Pax Romana or that of World Christendom or Dar-ul-Harb or even Napoleon or Hitler have been discarded one by one in the course of human history proving beyond doubt that path to progress lies in the direction of rule by and through international organizations.*

—Nagendra Singh (*Achievements of UNCTAD I and UNCTAD II in the Field of Shipping and Invisibles*, 1969)

## Introduction: Shipping and the Lessons of History

In our introduction we began with the Third United Nations Conference on the Law of the Sea (UNCLOS III) and the "decade of the ocean." In this concluding chapter, we will have to close the circle. In other words, not only will this chapter serve to chronicle rapidly the final decades of our examination, but it will also attempt to provide some answers to the lessons of history by summarizing and, perhaps, even looking ahead.

At the outset we must state our usual caveat that an in-depth analysis cannot be attempted. UNCLOS III is probably one of the most well-chronicled, analyzed, and criticized conferences in history; we could not, and certainly should not, add much further general comment here.[1] What we will attempt, instead, is a look at marine transport during this final period against the background of UNCLOS III—an infinitely easier task—as well as against the background of further developments of some of the organizations already examined.

In addition, of course, the environmental concern of the international community during this period would have a certain effect on world shipping and will thus require a rapid glance. Finally, as we look ahead, we will have

307

to gather the insights gained in this lengthy examination and see what the future holds for this most ancient of all industries in an ever more complex and complicated, as well as unequally divided, world. As we begin this final chapter, there is no doubt in our mind that marine transport is probably facing its greatest challenge ever from a variety of directions. The question we will attempt to answer is whether the industry's great living history has prepared it for this challenge well enough so that it can survive in an era of competing ocean uses among which it will no longer be the principal user or perhaps even a *primus inter pares*.

## The Beginnings of New Ocean Interests

Generally, the commencement of UNCLOS III is considered to be Ambassador Pardo of Malta's brilliant initiative in the United Nations General Assembly in 1967.[2] Without detracting in the slightest from Pardo's idealistic intervention, such an assessment can be described as rather simplistic. There is no doubt that the failures of UNCLOS I and II, and the unfinished business remaining, virtually dictated a new round of international debates within a comparatively short time.[3] Furthermore, the rapid increase in the world's nation-states, brought about by the continuous emergence of newly independent nations,[4] ensured a new conference on the law of the sea at an early date. Of course, the increasing dependence of much of the world on fisheries resources, in addition to the already perceptible world shortage of resources such as oil, gas, and minerals, provided a new approach to oceanic interests. We say "new" because it seems clear that UNCLOS I and II were not really "functionally" resource oriented, whereas during much of the latter part of the 1960s such concerns were being increasingly projected.[5]

Interestingly enough, this perception can best be traced to nongovernmental sources in the years immediately preceding the Pardo proposals. The idea of exploitation of the deep seabed beyond national jurisdiction was probably first put forward in public in Washington in 1965, at a meeting of the Committee on Natural Resources Conservation and Development.[6] In its report, the committee, in referring to the ambiguity relating to the outer limit of the continental shelf created by UNCLOS I, advocated the creation of a special U.N. agency to deal with marine resources, particularly mineral resources.[7] In retrospect, this appears to be a milestone in the modern law of the sea and, without question, the beginning of the end for marine transport's role as the leading use of the sea.

In addition, fishing, the other ancient sea use, was also assuming a newer and ever more central role as the world's swelling population depended more on the living resources of the sea for its protein needs.[8] Henceforth, man's main interest in the ocean would be in terms of the living and nonliving resource wealth available. Navigation was effectively sidelined to a secondary position. It is, of course, questionable whether the world's shipping industry, now completely isolated from other marine-policy questions, was even aware of the important changes that were taking place and would eventually affect it so profoundly. The signposts of the new resource emphasis were being placed with ever greater frequency.

In 1965, the Law of the Sea Institute (LSI) was established in the United States at the University of Rhode Island, under the direction of one of the world's foremost marine geographers assisted by an executive board of marine experts in law, science, politics, and economics.[9] The LSI eventually became one of the leading nongovernmental forums in which "new" oceanic ideas were tried out, and the proceedings of its annual meetings would become required reading for anyone interested in the new oceanic debate.[10] The first LSI meeting discussed the control of international-seabed resources, and the clash that took place between what have been termed the "idealistic" and the "realistic" approaches makes remarkable retrospective reading some fourteen years later as we still struggle with similar principles.[11] Further studies by a variety of organizations, such as the Commission to Study the Organization of Peace; the American Bar Association's National Institute of Marine Resources; the Deep-Sea Mining Committee of the International Law Association; and the World Peace Through Law Center, all pointed to the new "resource orientation" toward the oceans.[12] The trouble was that even the drafters of the 1958 Continental Shelf Convention had not foreseen what was in fact foreseeable. It was felt that the question of exploitation of the deep seabed would not be of importance.[13] The convention, therefore, does not specifically mention the freedom to exploit. Instead, a vague catch-all phrase was inserted in the High Seas Convention:

These freedoms and others which are recognized as the general principles of international law shall be exercised by all states with reasonable regard to the interests of other states and their exercise of the freedom of the seas.[14]

Without a doubt, this was Congress of Vienna language in the jet age. If the High Seas Convention was of little help, the definition applicable to deep-sea exploitation had to be found in the Continental Shelf Convention:

. . . the term 'continental shelf' is used as referring (a) to the seabed and subsoil of the submarine areas adjacent to the coast but outside the area of the territorial sea, to a depth of 200 metres or, beyond that limit, to where the depth of the superjacent waters admits of the exploitation of the natural resources of the said areas. . . .[15]

This meant that exploitation and exploration of the deep seabed was, like navigation, left to the enforcement and control of the flag state. Furthermore, resource activities would not be subject to any existing treaty law; like navigation, they would be an exercise of freedom of the seas under customary international law.[16] Yet in 1952 Dr. John S. Mero had already pointed to the future importance of the manganese nodule found on the surface of the deep seabed.[17] In 1965 Mero published *Mineral Resources of the Sea*, which not only substantiated much of his earlier work but also pointed to the rapid progress of the deep-seabed research undertaken by several major U.S. mining companies.[18]

The race to the seabed had begun in earnest, and soon politics would creep in—also correctly forecast by the first LSI meeting.[19] Many of the newly independent developing nations quickly saw such a race as a new colonization and feared neoimperialism of the oceans by the developed world. By 1966 U.S. President Johnson attempted to reassure them by rejecting "a new form of colonial competition among the maritime nations," insisting that the seas remain "the legacy of all human beings."[20] Nevertheless, he did not address himself to the issue of exactly how the deep-seabed gains would benefit the international community. The result was, of course, a two-pronged argument over whether deep-seabed resources were "the common heritage of all mankind" or to be grabbed and carved up on a first-come, first-served basis, as was the African continent in the previous century.[21]

This difficult issue was further complicated by the continental-shelf dispute between Denmark, the Federal Republic of Germany, and the Netherlands, which ended up in the International Court of Justice in 1976.[22] The court ruled that Germany, which had not ratified the 1958 Continental Shelf Convention, was not bound by its provisions. This ruling meant, simply, that all countries that had not ratified the convention were not bound by it and thus were not bound by even the vaguest principles of law relating to the deep seabed, unless the high-seas article previously cited could be considered a protector. In other words, the time appeared right for some clearly understood and widely accepted international regime, along the lines of the Outer Space Treaty concluded early in 1967, to be put forward.[23]

*The United Nations and the Seabed: New
Implications for Traditional Ocean Uses*

As a result, Arvid Pardo, Malta's ambassador to the United Nations, rose in that forum's General Assembly in August 1967 to make his historic intervention. He requested the inclusion of an item on the agenda of the Twenty-second Session of the General Assembly entitled:

Declaration and treaty concerning the reservation exclusively for peaceful purposes of the seabed and of the ocean floor underlying the seas beyond the limit of present national jurisdiction, and the use of their resources in the interests of mankind.[24]

By way of explanation, Pardo stressed that in view of the rapid progress in technology there was a general fear that the area beyond the continental shelf would become subject to national appropriation.[25] The result might be the militarization of the accessible ocean floor through fixed military installations, as well as the exploitation of immense resources solely for the national advantage of technologically developed states.

To prevent this, Pardo considered that the time had come to declare the ocean floor to be the "common heritage of mankind" and proposed that immediate steps should be taken to draft a treaty embodying five basic principles: (1) that the seabed and ocean floor beyond the limits of national jurisdiction are not subject to national appropriation; (2) that the exploration of the area shall be undertaken in a manner consistent with the principles and purposes of the United Nations Charter; (3) that the use of the area and its economic exploitation shall be undertaken with the aim of safeguarding the interests of mankind, and the benefits shall be used primarily to promote the development of poor countries; (4) that the area will be reserved exclusively for peaceful purposes; and (5) that an international agency be created to assume jurisdiction over the area and ensure that exploration and exploitation activities conform with the provision of the treaty.

Despite the fact that the Maltese initiative was not the first effort in the United Nations to discuss the subject,[26] it was the one with the most far-reaching results. The timing had been perfect. The deep seabed was being discussed simultaneously in a variety of international, national, public, private, governmental, and nongovernmental forums. The era of the deep seabed, which still continues today, had begun. Of course, for quite some time, the debates centered on the resoures of the deep seabed alone. The rest of the law of the sea, despite its unsatisfactory post-UNCLOS I and II status, was not open for further debate—at least not just then.

Accordingly, a number of important "ifs" can be added here. If the major maritime states had been just a little more forthcoming and a little less intransigent, particularly on the territorial-sea issue, the Geneva conventions would have been more acceptable. If the International Law Commission had been a little more realistic in its legal assessments, a more equitable draft might have forestalled future difficulties. If the major shipping states had not seen any change in the law of the sea as an attack on sacrosanct, inviolate principles of international law, agreement might have been reached—if not in 1958, then perhaps in 1960.

In other words, agreement at UNCLOS I and II would probably have resulted in the seabed issue being isolated from most other law-of-the-sea discussions, which might have eased the difficulties of the following decade. However, it did not turn out that way; and the unrealistically hard negotiating position of the major maritime states at UNCLOS I and II (and, to a great extent, in other forums such as IMCO and UNCTAD) on shipping matters would eventually haunt them years later on quite different law-of-the-sea issues. Once an inequity has been established, those who defend even a tiny part of it are tainted with all of it. The conservative defense of the status quo, perhaps for economically defensible reasons but without a full view of the policy implications, would henceforth be viewed in moral terms. The Group of 77, in particular, having only numbers of states as its weapon, would attempt to impose an "oceanic code of conduct" in almost every aspect of ocean affairs within the decade.[27]

It is submitted that these underlying policy implications were never considered by the major maritime states and that, even if they were, they were not understood. Once again, for ocean shipping, now completely separated from public law and policy related to ocean affairs, the isolation was complete and would be felt only much later. The whole seabed debate, although originally, and for some years, seen by many only as a legal question, was a political problem from the beginning. This was certainly known to Pardo, his disciples, and his opponents. However, the North-South encounter was then only in its infancy; and UNCTAD II, as we have seen, was to provide the answers to the questions posed at UNCTAD I. Certainly, in the developed world the belief that things economic, legal, and political could be placed in neat, watertight compartments, to be debated and negotiated separately and at different levels, persisted.

In retrospect it is clear that this was a "fool's paradise," out of touch with the realities of the latter part of the twentieth century. Yet the "Congress of Vienna" syndrome continued while the ranks of newly emergent independent, developing states swelled.[28] It was hardly an auspicious climate within which to discuss the "common heritage of mankind," let alone equitable principles related to the law of the sea.

However, the wheels of the United Nations, once started, cannot be stopped; they grind on slowly and surely. With remarkable speed, the U.N. General Assembly had, in the latter part of 1967, enthusiastically accepted Pardo's proposal and had ordered the

> . . . examination of the question of the reservation exclusively for peaceful purposes of the seabed and the ocean floor and the subsoil thereof, underlying the high seas beyond the limits of national jurisdiction and the use of their resources in the interests of mankind.[29]

This work was to be undertaken by the U.N.'s First Committee. A short while later, after some procedural discussions, a twenty-seven-member working group was set up to study the matter.[30] This, in turn, resulted in the establishment of a thirty-five-state ad hoc Seabed Committee by early December 1967. Finally, on December 18, 1967, the U.N. General Assembly, in a unanimous resolution, incorporated the instructions to the First Committee, as just cited, and formalized the establishment of an ad hoc Seabed Committee, which was to study the peaceful uses of the seabed and the ocean floor beyond the limits of national jurisdiction.[31]

## The U.N. Seabed Committee: Preparation for
## A New Law of the Sea

The U.N. Seabed Committee commenced work in 1968, meeting three times during that year and subsequently reporting its progress to the Twenty-third U.N. General Assembly.[32] In 1969 it met four times and in 1970 twice.[33] However, by that time the committee's studies of the long-term expanded program for oceanic exploration; of the ways and means of promoting the exploration, exploitation, and use of the resources of the international seabed area; and of the problems of the international machinery were in serious difficulties. The main problem was, of course, that the jurisdictional question, left undecided by UNCLOS I and II, made it simply impossible even to define the deep-seabed area beyond national jurisdiction when that very jurisdictional limit was without agreement.

In the broader context, however, the Seabed Committee had realized that there were three main problems preventing it from dealing with the deep seabed in isolation. First, there was the realization that the political and economic realities of the late 1960s had allied themselves with modern scientific and technological advances, thus establishing the need for progressive, as well as functional, development of the law of the sea. Second, the fact that many of the newer U.N. members had taken no part in the Geneva conferences of 1958 and 1960, made these states quite determined to participate fully in *all* decisions relating to the law of the sea. Finally, there was the perfectly valid consideration of studying the problem of ocean space as a whole—that the sea needed to be treated conceptually as part of the total marine environment. This latter consideration brought humankind almost back to its early beginnings, and an elaboration of it would have quickly shown how the ocean uses had become disparate and separated. However, as we shall see, this view was considered to be least valid and received little elaboration apart from isolated diplomatic rhetoric.

When the Seabed Committee reported its difficulties to the Twenty-fifth U.N. General Assembly, the resulting action of that body was a foregone conclusion. The United Nations is a servant of its world membership, the majority of which wanted a complete reexamination of the whole law of the sea.[34] Accordingly, by adopting four historic resolutions, the assembly first laid down a very broad declaration of principles relating to the seabed, which considerably broadened previously accepted limits of discussion;[35] second, requested the Secretary-General of the United Nations to examine the economic implications of seabed mineral production;[36] third, requested the Secretary-General to make an up-to-date study of the question of free access to the sea by, and special problems of, landlocked countries;[37] and finally, expanded the membership of the Seabed Committee to eighty-six states and convened the Third United Nations Conference on the Law of the Sea.[38] In the latter resolution the General Assembly stated quite clearly that a new law-of-the-sea conference, to be convened in 1973, should deal with the very wide spectrum of marine issues:

> . . . the establishment of an equitable international regime—including an international machinery—for the area and the resources of the seabed and the ocean floor and the subsoil thereof beyond the limits of national jurisdiction, a precise definition of the area, and a broad range of related issues including those concerning the regime of the high seas, the continental shelf, the territorial sea (including the question of its breadth and the question of international straits) and contiguous zones, fishing and conservation of living resources of the high seas (including the question of the preferential rights of coastal states), the preservation of the marine environment (including inter alia, the prevention of pollution), and scientific research.[39]

With this formidable, perhaps impossible, agenda, the politicization of the law of the sea appeared to have reached a new level. This greatly simplifies our examination of the international law and policy of marine transport, however, since UNCLOS III would henceforth be only of *political* importance to shipping. Conversely, and more accurately, shipping was of little concern to UNCLOS III, as can be seen clearly from the resolution and as was confirmed later by the actual conference agenda.[40] Only pollution prevention and the law-and-order high-seas rules for ships, which we already have suggested were out of place in this type of treaty, would actually affect shipping.

At first glance, it might even be considered beneficial that marine transport would not figure prominently on the agenda of this difficult conference. Could it not get on with its ocean business in the splendid isolation created by its own history? After all, of what concern were the riches of the deep seabed, the breadth of the territorial sea, the width of the continental shelf, the boundaries of an archipelago, the access problems of a coastless state to the everyday operation of the international shipping industry? Or had that industry by now become the victim of its own history, to be left almost completely without a voice at a conference that, for the first time ever, was dedicated to *every* other important aspect of ocean use? It would seem, almost by implication, that any interest not represented before such a forum would lose something. Given the fact that marine transport had been typecast as intransigent at other forums, its virtual absence at UNCLOS III helped neither its image nor, as will be seen, its future.

Thus the newly enlarged U.N. Seabed Committee commenced its work in 1971, holding two sessions that year, two in 1972, and two in 1973.[41] The committee had, in the interim, virtually become a preparatory committee for UNCLOS III as well as an excellent political organ. This was very different from the preparatory work for UNCLOS I carried out in an atmosphere of scholarly deliberation and academic polemics by the International Law Commission. The Seabed Committee established three working groups: Subcommittee I to deal with all issues relating to the seabed (that is, to continue the work of the original ad hoc Seabed Committee); Subcommittee II to deal with general questions related to law of the sea; and Subcommittee III to deal specifically with problems related to the marine environment as well as marine-scientific research.[42]

The work achieved by the Seabed Committee, which after 1970 was a full preparatory committee for UNCLOS III, has so far received undeservedly less recognition than it deserves.[43] Its achievement was considerable, particularly if viewed against the background of the international situation of the late 1960s and early 1970s. The Seabed Committee somehow had to reconcile the opposing views of the developing world with those of the developed states. The former soon saw the law of the sea as another important link in the confining chain that had to be broken in order to achieve a new international economic order.[44] The latter, as usual, declined to be involved in what they considered an emotional and often subjective debate, regardless of its merits. Furthermore, they simply did not favor the convening of an all-embracing law-of-the-sea conference, nor did they want a strong authority to manage the international seabed.[45] The maritime powers, particularly the United States, the USSR, and the European Economic Community (EEC) states felt that the new moves toward a 200-mile exclusive economic zone (EEZ) as well as a powerful international seabed authority, which could also control marine pollution and scientific research, would endanger the freedom-of-the-seas concept, which they had to protect.[46] These basic difficulties faced the Seabed Committee, which had to resort to a whole new system of compromise diplomacy. Congress of Vienna-style diplomacy could not operate within a politically motivated eighty-six-member body that was, nevertheless, expected to deal with many highly technical questions.[47] However, the work of the committee is too well chronicled to need elaboration here.

The basic difficulty, as old as the law of the sea itself, of where to draw the line of a coastal state's jurisdiction, was almost magically resolved by an African initiative that called for a 12-mile territorial sea and a 200-mile EEZ within which the coastal state would have rights and privileges for functional purposes, which were, however, less than those of the 200-mile territorial sea advanced by some of the Latin American states in 1958 and 1960.[48] Although at first rejected or treated cautiously by most of the developed states, the EEZ idea soon became a rallying point of agreement.[49] On the other hand, it can also be said that for the developed states the 200-mile EEZ was easier to live with than a strong international seabed regime.

After some study, it was discovered that most of the great powers would gain handsomely through the new extension.[50] Landlocked, shelflocked, straitlocked, and other "geographically disadvantaged" states would gain little.[51] The United States, for example, having two long coastlines, as well as the Hawaiian, Micronesian, and Alaskan archipelago, would acquire more offshore resources than any other state.[52] Henceforth the envisaged EEZ would encompass about one-third of total ocean space.[53]

Somehow Pardo's "common heritage of mankind" had gotten off the rails in the Seabed Committee.[54] It is difficult to pinpoint when or why this happened, but the common-heritage principle appeared to be a victim of the growing politicization of the states. When UNCLOS III actually began in late 1973, having finally found a home for its first substantive meeting, the EEZ principle was well on the way to general acceptance and the "common heritage" was suffering in the compromise debate on the deep seabed.[55]

### The Third United Nations Conference on the Law of the Sea

UNCLOS III was faced with a staggering agenda of almost 130 items, many of which could have formed the subject matter of a separate conference.[56] No in-depth examination of marine transport, shipping, or navigation was included. The conference began in late 1973 with a short procedural session, which elected the conference's officers along the lines of political and geographical distribution.[57] At the same time, a "gentlemen's agreement" was concluded to resort to voting only when no other decision-making procedure was left.[58] It was realized that in order to reach agreement for a world ocean treaty, the lowest common denominator of compromise had to be reached by negotiation. The fact that the major powers would in effect have veto power was thus recognized.

The first substantive session of the conference took place in Caracas, Venezuela during a twelve-week period in 1974.[59] The Caracas session allowed national positions by states, which had not been Seabed Committee members, to be brought forward together with the opening statements of national positions on a variety of issues. The conference continued to work in the three groupings established by the Seabed Committee: First Committee—seabed; Second Committee—general aspects of the law of the sea;

Third Committee—marine environment, marine scientific research, and a new agenda item relating to the transfer of marine technology. There appeared a subtle narrowing of differences at the end of the Caracas session. This was reflected in a set of documents that summarized the "main trends" of the negotiations in the three committees.

The third session of UNCLOS III took place in Geneva for eight weeks in 1975.[60] By this time negotiations had begun in earnest. This was reflected in the first comprehensive informal treaty draft issued at the end of this session.[61] The fourth session, in New York in 1976, further refined the Geneva text as set out in a "Revised Single Negotiating Text."[62] Again in New York, the fifth and sixth sessions in 1977 further narrowed differences into an "Informal Composite Negotiating Text" (ICNT), which was slowly beginning to resemble one of the most comprehensive international treaties ever undertaken.[63] The seventh session, which was split between Geneva and New York in 1978, resulted in further consolidation and compromise on the more than 300 articles in the ICNT. The eighth session, in 1979 in Geneva, resulted in a completely revised ICNT being issued.[64] This text underwent further refinement during subsequent sessions in 1979 and 1980 which not only produced a revised text but, most significantly, a draft convention.[65]

Obviously, this rapid chronicling of events does little justice to this tremendous undertaking and provides little more than a calendar schedule. The attempt in the latter part of the twentieth century, by more than 150 states, to draw up a new code for the oceans was bound to be fraught with complexity, difficulty, and frequent deadlock. The work of the conference, in session, between sessions, and in its preparatory stage in the Seabed Committee, has taken well over a decade so far. Its many uninformed critics point to this so-called lack of progress, to the time spent in endless negotiation, to the absence of concrete results, and to the great expense, particularly for some of the smaller countries of the Third World. They tend to forget that law reform in the late twentieth century will take longer than ever before. There are simply more actors in the play. It should be kept in mind that the ILC, with much narrower terms of reference and with relatively little politicization, took close to fifteen years to prepare for UNCLOS I!

In any case, the draft convention is indeed a compromise document, and there is agreement on over 90 percent of its articles. That is certainly an achievement. Even if the conference should fail completely, there is much to be salvaged; new customary international law of the sea has been created throughout this period.

Of course, serious disagreement still exists in several key areas. The ideological North-South encounter relating to the riches of the seabed has not yet been resolved; the actual status of the EEZ has not been decided to the satisfaction of the major maritime states; some questions relating to passage through straits require solutions to satisfy the superpowers; the difficult issue of marine-scientific research remains unresolved; the rights of landlocked states in the EEZ will require better definition; the rights relating to the continental margin—beyond 200 miles—are so far undefined. These and several other issues will require further work in 1981, and perhaps even beyond. However, the point was probably reached in 1980 where further negotiation appeared basically impossible and political decisions were urgently required. The willingness of states to make political concessions will, therefore, decide the final outcome of UNCLOS III.

Considering the history of the international law and policy of marine transport chronicled in this book, it would have been surprising if UNCLOS III had concerned itself in some detail with shipping. In almost abstract terms, the conference discussed questions related directly to ships' use of ocean space, such as transit and passage rights, as well as the controls coastal states may exert over shipping in order to preserve the marine environment. "Abstract" appears to be the most suitable term, because it seems at times that these discussions envisaged ships passing from point A to point B for the sake of making the trip rather than in the pursuit of the economic activities that are the very basis of their existence.

Certainly, the question of commercial viability, which is marine transport's very foundation, has rarely been raised, or raised only as a somewhat emotional defense of the maritime states' status quo. In reality, the private-law aspects of marine transport were now quite far removed from international consideration and were debated instead in forums such as IMCO and UNCTAD and, to some extent, at the nongovernmental CMI level. As we have said, the UNCLOS III beginnings brought about by Arvid Pardo's brilliant, if ideologically unrealistic, initiative were at first strictly related to the seabed. However, the whole public law of the sea was soon reopened for discussion when the Seabed Committee found itself unable to confine itself to its international terms of reference in view of the "unfinished business" of UNCLOS I and II. Nevertheless, marine transport, the most traditional use of the ocean, was noticeably absent from the agenda of a world conference that set out to recodify *all* aspects of the law of the sea and that would soon become a global law-of-the-sea reform movement, with all the commensurate difficulties faced by any law reform.[66]

## Law-of-the-Sea Reform and Marine Transport

Shipping—or at least questions relating to the navigational use of the ocean—featured in only three main agenda items at UNCLOS III. First, the Second Committee debated questions relating to the traditionally difficult issue of marginal-seas jurisdiction. Nevertheless, a relatively satisfactory regime relating to transit rights and innocent passage of ships in spatial zones under the control, or quasi-control, of coastal and island states was slowly worked out.[67] Unfortunately, even this debate took the form of defending and attacking the principle of the so-called freedom of the seas—by then so redundant. Yet the maritime states would paint coastal-state expansionism in the most sinister colors of "anti-Grotian" sentiment and intention. On the other side, many coastal states, particularly of the "territorialist" group, would rattle the brittle skeleton of "creeping jurisdiction" in their cupboards.

In reality, though, the "freedom of navigation" was hardly at issue. The history of the law of the sea and its interpretation has taught us that "free transit," "the right of free transit," and "free passage" are all expressions used interchangeably to delineate basic rights under the principle of free navigation on the seas.[68] Little if any attempt has been made to assert that such a right is not part of the principle of freedom of the seas as first enunciated by Hugo Grotius. Free transit for international merchant shipping should, and could, simply have been viewed as quite separate from the spatial concern of territorial-sea jurisdiction. Then the functional character of such a navigational right would remain secure regardless of any new widths of territorial seas or exclusive economic zones.

Lamentably, this ocean-use functionality was hardly ever considered at UNCLOS III. In any case, there is also little if any evidence that even the most extreme of the territorialist-expansionist states wished to interfere with shipping or the free transit thereof. The right of transit appears to be well established in international law and seems in little danger of being altered in principle from the rule enunciated by Grotius as: "land, rivers and any part of the sea that has become subject to ownership of a people ought to be open to those who, for legitimate reasons, have need to cross over them."[69]

The second area relating to marine transport on the UNCLOS III agenda was a variety of articles relating to rules governing vessels on the high seas.[70] With the exception of some modernization, there appear to be few substantive changes from the 1958 High Seas Convention. Despite the fact that the futility of attempting to establish a genuine link between flag state and ship has been universally accepted, and that the rather murky reasons behind this so-called theory of international maritime law have, as already pointed out, been conclusively and decisively discredited, the principle remains with us.[71] Along with many of the high-seas articles, it is a strange collection of fairly technical rules of conduct and customary norms of behavior. Their utility within a global ocean treaty is questionable, as they now fit much more within IMCO's sphere of interest.

Finally, in its Third Committee, UNCLOS III concerns itself with ship-generated marine pollution. After much painstaking work, and to the credit of the Third Committee, a consensus appears to be close.[72] However, in the past decade great difficulties had to be overcome. The unequal struggle between coastal and maritime states over the prevention of marine pollution, so familiar to us from our IMCO discussion, had to be repeated endlessly at UNCLOS III. Once again, the battleground would have to be the principle of the freedom of the seas rather than the community interest of reducing marine pollution to its lowest common denominator.[73] Coastal-state antipollution regulation was seen as direct interference with legitimate shipping patterns and the "crazy patchwork quilt" of differing, overlapping, and adjoining national legislation was frequently put forward as an extreme argument by the maritime states at the urging of bodies, such as the International Chamber of Shipping, as well as national shipping bodies.[74]

Such arguments did their own interests, those of the conference, or for that matter those of the various maritime states, little service. Everyone accepted the fact that environmental problems could best be solved by internationally accepted measures, except that the maritime states had shown, at IMCO, as well as at some of the CMI liability meetings, that such measures would be reduced to the lowest common denominator. Coastal states demanded still relatively modest but higher standards. The result of this long and at times unnecessary debate is a less-than-satisfactory consensus reflected in the draft convention. The attempt to build in unnecessary safeguards makes the language tortuous and many measures unenforceable.[75] As a result, it must be hoped that dissatisfied coastal states will implement their own simpler rules for safety's sake.[76] It is unlikely that any attempt will be made to interfere with shipping, except perhaps with shipping that is so substandard in terms of safety that it ought not to be permitted into any state's coastal waters in the first place.

In this area of the new law of the sea there will, therefore, be discernible changes for marine transport. In coastal waters, new regulatory patterns will be established, such as special tanker zones, compulsory traffic-separation systems, mandatory pilotage areas, and offshore safety checks.[77] From the point of view of safety these are probably desirable changes, particularly if they will drive substandard shipping from the ocean trade routes or generally upgrade the present low international standards.

However, as in IMCO's sessions, UNCLOS III in its Third Committee had the full opportunity to lay down in a widely accepted code form entirely new and innovative measures to prevent further deterioration of the marine environment. As a matter of fact, IMCO, because of its structure as already described, needed the higher intergovernmental level of the Law of the Sea Conference to do exactly that. However, once again marine transport had no clear policy, either at the international or at most national levels. Instead of working with the coastal states to produce a package containing a universally acceptable high common denominator of safety standards, the all-too-familiar delaying tactics prevailed. Somehow the industry appeared to have learned little, and least of all in the area of international diplomacy relating to ocean affairs, where the intransigent attitude of one forum can lead to disadvantage in another.

At UNCLOS III there was an opportunity for the industry to recoup some of the severe losses suffered in other forums. There was an opportunity once again to become an important, if not essential, partner in the great ocean business—to lend the experience acquired over several millennia to the new directions that the ocean debate was taking. However, by now it was too late.

We have spoken of the shipping industry, international shipping, and marine transport interchangeably, without defining it or describing this entity any further. That is precisely the problem of the industry at this time. There is no longer a central spokesperson who has all the answers, or is at least attempting to find them. The various national transportation ministries and shipping bodies have some of the answers; the International Chamber of Shipping has others, as does the CMI. However, all are limited by self-interest and by their own terms of reference. Thus, sadly ocean shipping for UNCLOS III would be largely a rhetorical issue, which it faced as disjointedly as ever. However, as we shall now see, there were other pressures that marine transport would also have to face in this most recent period in its long history.

## The Environment: New Challenges for a Fragile System

In our earlier discussion of marine pollution and IMCO's efforts at preventing it, we have already alluded to the quickening interest of the international community in the environmental deterioration of the world. This concern reached its peak in the early 1970s, which was seen by many as the "decade of ecology."[78] In the Western developed world, this took the form of a quickly spreading groundswell of concern, often with grass-roots origins, about the general deterioration of the human environment.[79]

Although "pollution" became the key word in this new consciousness, environment as a whole encompasses a much larger area than is envisaged when speaking of the ecological dangers of pollution. For example, for most of the developing countries poverty, hunger, disease, and urban squalor are real and palpable environmental problems, yet they are not pollution problems in the ecological sense, although they certainly are signs of environmental deterioration. Yet as has already been pointed out:

> Pollution is not a modern phenomenon. It is not peculiar to man and may indeed have preceded him. Pollution by man in the twentieth century is

a reflection of population growth, development of technology and a resulting increase in living standards, and consumption habits associated with economic growth. The most serious effects of these trends include the increasing spread of waste and the destruction of nature. Since pollution can be traced to many causes, some of which are political and highly emotional, its solution will not come easily. Most pollution problems are further complicated by the fact that merely national approaches, though important, are too limited to provide lasting assurance of prevention and control. Most forms of pollution are transnational in scope and must be treated within a modern system of international law suitable to the needs of the interdependent world community in the late twentieth century.[80]

Obviously, the "environmental decade" is too well chronicled to need much elaboration here and is, in any case, an area of complexity and of a magnitude far beyond our present scope.[81] It has, however, had a certain effect on the international law and policy of marine transport during the past decade; and it is worth examining purely in that context.

The chief contributing factor to the overall problem of environmental deterioration has been the dramatic increase in the world's population. From a mid-nineteenth century figure of 1 billion, the population of the world has increased to almost 4 billion with a projection of over 6 billion for the turn of the century.[82] This has resulted directly in a new impact of technology and industry, particularly in the sprawling urban centers of the world. In addition, modern technology has increased the demands of this growing population, mainly in the developed world, for goods, materials, and services. Estimates for North America show that the economy, excluding construction and earth-moving equipment, consumes over 2.5 billion tons of material per year.[83] That is the equivalent of over 10 tons for every man, woman, and child.

Considering the importance of marine transport in the modern industrial society, the environmental link to that industry is obvious. The byproducts of the modern world are untreated or inadequately treated sewage; impure water; inadequate housing; inefficient transportation; insufficient educational, medical, and recreational facilities; and noise and noxious fumes. The social, political, and psychological implications may thus be even more pernicious than the inadequate environment in which a great part of the world's population must live. Certainly during the early part of the environmental debate, the countries of the Third World were far from convinced of the urgency of what they considered basically a Northern problem. To them, "pollution" meant factories, transportation, better living conditions.[84] If more pollution was the result of international development, then they might actually welcome it as the unpleasant but inevitable byproduct of what they desired and needed. More realistically, Third-World states were concerned that the effort of the industrialized world to reduce pollution might, in turn, affect the expansion of raw-material exports from developing countries and thus further slow down their development. Environment and development were not considered to be entirely compatible. As the Secretary-General of the then soon-to-be-created United Nations Environment Program would state:

> ... if environment has acquired ... political potency in the more industrialized countries it is endowed with no such magic in much of the developing world, where it is still viewed by many as a rich man's disease they would be prepared to risk if it is the necessary accompaniment to the economic growth they want and urgently need.[85]

Yet at the same time, from the beginning, pollution was considered a transnational problem and thus a further link in the growing politicization of international intercourse.

### The United Nations and the Environment

By mid-1968, the time for concerted international action at the highest level appeared to be ripe. A Swedish proposal for a United Nations Conference on the Human Environment provided the catalyst for a United Nations response.[86] In December 1968, at a time when the ad hoc U.N. Seabed Committee had been in operation for only a year, the Twenty-third U.N. General Assembly decided to convene in 1972 a conference "to provide the framework for comprehensive considerations ... of the problems of the human environment in order to focus the attention of Governments and public opinion on the importance and urgency of this question."[87] Within a year conference preparations had undergone considerable changes of emphasis, reflecting a greater appreciation that although much remained to be done in promoting environmental concern, particularly in developing countries, the conference should also initiate practical as well as ameliorative steps.[88]

Accordingly, the Twenty-fourth U.N. General Assembly decided that the forthcoming conference, to be held at Stockholm, should "serve as a practical means to encourage, and to provide guidelines for, action by Governments and international organizations designed to protect and improve the human environment, and to remedy and prevent its impairment by means of international cooperation."[89] In addition, a twenty-seven-member preparatory committee for the conference was set up, and a conference secretariat was authorized.[90] By early 1971 the preparatory committee had elaborated the details of the conference program, together with an action plan, which was expected to make recommendations to governments and other appropriate bodies for specific actions as well as institutional arrangements for their implementation.[91]

Considerable further preparatory work took place before the United Nations Conference on the Human Environment finally met for twelve days in June of 1972.[92] Twelve hundred delegates from 113 states thus met to discuss a highly political, as well as emotional, issue, giving the world a foretaste of what was to come at UNCLOS III, which was to convene just over a year later. Although the conference addressed itself to all aspects of environmental deterioration, one of its main agenda items covered marine pollution; and that is where marine transport, as one of the sources of this pollution, became involved.

There was ample evidence that ship-generated marine pollution contributed only about 10-20 percent of all marine pollution.[93] The rest is land generated—the outflow of human existence. But the other 80-90 percent were, of course, much more difficult to cope with internationally in a world of sovereign states, as the conference soon discovered. It decided, therefore, that the United Nations should form an organization to deal with the implementation of what became known as the "Stockholm Recommendations." This resulted in the formation of the United Nations Environment Program (UNEP) with its headquarters in Nairobi, Kenya and in existence since 1973.[94] Like its originator, the Stockholm Conference, UNEP has had difficulties since its inception straddling, as it did, a whole array of U.N. specialized agencies with some environmental responsibilities. In addition, of course, the difficulty of laying down international standards for sovereign states had its built-in political difficulties which were not assisted by the continuing question of Third-World interest, or at least priority, in this whole debate.

In our narrower context, however, Stockholm recognized that marine-pollution control did not fit neatly into the terms of reference of marine law, ocean science, or politics, but was really a part of what has been termed "international environmental policy."[95] In other words, the implementation of preventative measures would have to be the responsibility of an array of international organizations as well as private industry. For example, Stockholm Recommendations 86 to 94 dealt directly with marine pollution. They contained requests to governments to cooperate in various ways not only with each other, but also with international groups and organizations such as the Joint Group of Experts on the Scientific Aspects of Marine Pollution (GESAMP), the Food and Agricultural Organization (FAO), the World Health Organization (WHO), the Intergovernmental Oceanographic Commission (IOC), the International Atomic Energy Agency (IAEA), the World Meteorological Organization (WMO), the Inter-Governmental Maritime Consultative Organization (IMCO), the International Hydrographic Organization (IHO), and the International Council for the Exploration of the Sea (ICES).[96] Particular reference was made also to the need for the fullest cooperation with, and participation in, the scheduled 1973 IMCO Marine Pollution Conference, as well as in UNCLOS III. It was recommended that:

Any mechanism for coordinating and stimulating action of the different U.N. organs in connection with environmental problems includes among its functions overall responsibility for ensuring that needed advice on marine pollution problems should be provided to Governments.[97]

*Marine Pollution: The Special Problem*

Most important, however, were the recommendations that governments accept the Stockholm principles both for UNCLOS III and for the 1973 IMCO Marine Pollution Conference. These principles were based almost completely on those adopted at the second session of the preparatory Intergovernmental Working Group on Marine Pollution, which met at Ottawa in late 1971.[98] At that time a declaration was made stating that every state has a duty to protect and preserve the marine environment and, furthermore, to prevent pollution in protected areas where an internationally shared resource, such as a fishery, is located.[99] It was further agreed that such state should ensure that its national legislation provides adequate sanctions against those who infringe on existing regulations on marine pollution.

At the same time, states were requested to assume joint responsibility for environmental protection of the marine environment beyond national jurisdiction. Coastal states were required to protect not only the marine areas within their territorial seas, but also adjacent marine areas, from damage resulting from activities within their territory, internal waters, and territorial seas.

Of direct relevance to our analysis is the enjoinder to states to ensure that vessels under their registration comply with all internationally agreed-on rules and standards relating to ship design and construction, operating procedures, and other relevant factors.[100] The states would be required to cooperate fully in the development of such rules, standards, and procedures through the appropriate international bodies. For example, in the event of an accident on the high seas, which might be expected to result in major damage from pollution, a coastal state, facing serious and imminent danger to its coastline and coastal interests, is permitted to take appropriate measures that may be necessary to prevent, mitigate, and even eliminate such dangers—but always in accordance with international rules and standards.

In other words, the "rise of the coastal state in the law of the sea," to which we have already referred, was nowhere more prominent than in the area of marine-pollution prevention.[101] Yet coastal-state rights had difficulty in achieving even relatively modest recognition at Stockholm or at the many preparatory sessions. Coastal-state demands were practical, based on experience, and far from radical in context. For example, at the Ottawa meeting already referred to, the host state submitted the following proposals:

1. A state may exercise special authority in the areas of the sea adjacent to its territorial waters where functional controls of a continuing nature are necessary for the effective prevention of pollution which could cause damage or injury to the land or marine environment under its exclusive or sovereign authority.

2. A coastal state may prohibit any vessel which does not comply with internationally agreed rules and standards or, in their absence, with reasonable national rules and standards of the coastal state in question, from entering waters under its environmental protection authority.

3. The basis on which a state should exercise rights or powers, in addition to its sovereign rights or powers, pursuant to its special authority in areas adjacent to its territorial waters, is that such rights or powers should be deemed to be delegated to that state by the world community on behalf of humanity as a whole. The rights and powers exercised must be consistent with the state's primary responsibility for marine environmental protection in the areas concerned: they should be subject to international rules and standards and to review before an appropriate international tribunal.[102]

As may be expected, the usual coastal-versus-maritime-state confrontation was the only result. As we have already suggested, when discussing the post-*Torrey Canyon* period at IMCO, the maritime states somehow saw marine pollution as the greatest danger to the freedom-of-the-seas principle, which they, for reasons by then generally obscure, were determined to protect. Once again, a little forthcoming compromise in the Stockholm or pre-Stockholm period by these states would have prevented many of the difficulties on other issues they were to face in many other forums.

The marine-transport industry was ill prepared for the complex environmental issue. The discussion itself ranged from the emotional rhetoric of some segments of the ecology movement, to the practical, hard-fact evidence of the ocean-science community. The sociological, economic, political, technological, and scientific content required constant research by those who wanted to have some understanding of the issue.

But as we have seen, during the *Torrey Canyon* period the industry decided to resist environmental concern with a hard-line approach that was entirely unsuitable for that type of issue. The shipping industry felt justifiably outraged at being singled out as a perpetrator of what was considered to be only about 10-20 percent of the problem. It felt that it was providing a traditional and valuable service and that it was about as careful as it could be in preventing pollution. It could and should have known that this sort of approach was not suitable in the environmentally conscious early 1970s.[103] Ship-generated marine pollution was much too visible in the era of massive media coverage. Dead seabirds with their crude-oil-slicked feathers were, after all, so much more poignant than the evidence of a thousand city sewers emptying into the Atlantic Ocean. In addition, at regular intervals a spectacular tanker disaster would occur, alerting the world and, of course, the coastal states, to the dangers of catastrophic marine pollution.[104] The evidence of oil from tank-cleaning operations was widely available on every recreational beach in the world.[105]

Still the industry, either directly or through the maritime states it owed allegiance to, resisted efforts to establish stricter standards and shift the burden of liability more equitably. With reference to liability, the marine-insurance industry had, almost from the beginning, a fear of "strict liability" because of its unknown content.[106] This was unusual for one of the shipping industry's most flexible, innovative, and financially responsible partners, which would, within a foreseeably short time, be able to underwrite the huge risks involved in wide-bodied aircraft, liquid-natural-gas carriers, supercontainer ships, and oil-exploration and -production platforms, but which would balk at giving shipowners the full coverage they needed for major marine-pollution incidents.[107]

We are not pointing to any fault or shortcoming on the part of the insurance industry, but rather to the general difficulty the whole shipping industry faced on this issue. There was simply no clear policy, based on thorough research, that would have shown clearly that ship-generated marine-pollution problems could be solved by cooperative efforts between maritime and coastal states and aided by the innovative ability of the shipping industry itself. The absence of both research and policy provided sufficiently vague intangibles to put the underwriters on guard. As a result, the whole problem has been treated with extreme and undeserved caution by the marine-insurance industry ever since.

## The Marine Transport of Pollutants

Mentioning the innovative ability of the shipping industry brings us to another point that has a direct bearing on the pollution issue. In the period under discussion, that is, the late 1960s to the late 1970s, marine transport has been undergoing revolutionary changes that can be equated with the change from sail to steam. We have already spoken about the change to oil from coal as the world's prime energy source. More than half of the oil consumed has to be moved by sea.[108] In 1920 the figure was about 100 million tons; but fifty years later, by 1970, this had risen to 1 billion tons. By 1977, 1.7 billion tons of oil moved in international seaborne trade.[109] Obviously, these considerable increases would be reflected in the rise of the world's tanker tonnage. In the decade 1960-1970, world tanker tonnage increased by 100 percent, whereas, as we have seen, the number of ships increased by only about 12 percent.[110] This was caused predominantly by growth in the capacity of tankers and the great improvement in loading and discharging facilities for oil cargoes. Table 7-1 illustrates the growth of the world tanker

**Table 7-1**
**Growth in the World Tanker Fleet, 1900-1969**

| Year | Number of Ships | Size | Deadweight |
|------|-----------------|------|-----------|
| 1900 | 109 | 2,000 Dwt + | 531,000 |
| 1919 | 467 | 2,000 Dwt + | 3,681,000 |
| 1939 | 1,571 | 2,000 Dwt + | 16,600,000 |
| 1955 | 2,693 | 2,000 Dwt + | 39,015,000 |
| 1961 | 2,671 | 10,000 Dwt + | 60,616,000 |
| 1966 | 2,814 | 10,000 Dwt + | 88,585,000 |
| 1969 | 2,991 | 10,000 Dwt + | 121,016,000 |

Source: Petroleum Information Bureau, 1969. See also A.D. Couper, *The Geography of Sea Transport* (London: Hutchinson, 1972), p. 112.

fleet between 1900 and 1970. Not only was the requirement of tanker tonnage dramatically increased by this new demand for oil and oil products, but a change in oil-refining locations in the postwar period brought about the separation of crude-oil carriers from product carriers and a subsequent increase in the size of the former. The change in refining locations came about for four main reasons:

First, there was a greatly increased demand in the industrial countries for all types of oil, for use in transport, electricity-generating stations, heavy industry, petro-chemicals and for thermal purposes. Second, refining techniques had advanced sufficiently to allow an output of grades of oil more closely related to local market requirements. Third, with technical advance there was no longer an excessive amount of unusable waste to be disposed of from a crude-oil cargo. And fourth, following the nationalization of Anglo-Iranian refineries in Persia during 1951, there was a reinforcement of an already existing trend towards security of assets by building more home-based refineries.[111]

The natural result of these changes was the appreciation in tanker size. In 1951 almost 80 percent of all tankers in the world were less than 17,000 tons. But within five years, by 1956, half of the world's fleet was about this size, with the largest vessels reaching 50,000 tons.[112] However, the closure of the Suez Canal, because of the 1956 Middle East War, removed the major constraint on the construction of large tankers. The first 100,000-ton vessels were ordered that year, and within a decade 150,000-ton vessels were in operation. By 1970 over 130 tankers exceeding 200,000 tons deadweight were in service throughout the world.[113] Within a comparatively short period of time, the simple tank ship would become the "supertanker," then the very large crude carrier (VLCC), and eventually the ultra large crude carrier (ULCC).[114] The economies of scale that make these very large vessels highly economical on the long routes—Persian Gulf to North Europe via the Cape of Good Hope, or Persian Gulf to Japan—boosted the greatest expansion of shipping the world has seen since World War II, which in tonnage alone exceeded anything World War II could produce. Table 7-2 should illustrate this remarkable expansion.

As in previous periods, the promise of high profitability in the shipping industry usually results in heavy investment and new construction in an atmosphere composed of a strange and unique combination of lack of economic foresight, greed, and speed. As always, such a period would be followed by an entirely foreseeable shipping slump caused by overtonnaging.[115] The free-enterprise competitiveness of the industry prevents any concerted international shipping policy from being considered. However, the possibility of a major slump in 1966-1967 was diverted by a new Middle East war, which caused freight rates to rise again sharply to new heights.[116] With feverish activity the world's shipyards began to construct larger tankers even more quickly, and by the early 1970s the first ULCC of over 300,000 tons had been built. Within a few years the 500,000-ton vessel size was reached, and a 1,000,000-ton "megaton" tanker was in the advanced design stage.[117]

The speed of construction together with the rapid increase in size allowed for scant attention of safety research into this phenomenon, which not only was entirely new but had not even had the time required to develop internationally accepted construction standards. These were left almost entirely to the shipyards and classification societies. However, before a new slump could occur, the overtonnaged industry was again saved by a new crisis. This was caused by the restructuring of oil prices by the Oil Producing and Exporting Countries (OPEC), which in late 1973 plunged the world

**Table 7-2**
**The World Tanker Fleet in Relation to the Total World Fleet**

|  | Tankers (Million grt) | Other Vessels (Million grt) | Total World (Million grt) | Tanker Fleet as Percentage of World Fleet |
|---|---|---|---|---|
| 1914 | 1.5 | 42.5 | 43.0 | 3 |
| 1939 | 11.4 | 48.7 | 60.1 | 19 |
| 1950 | 17.1 | 44.6 | 61.7 | 28 |
| 1956 | 28.4 | 57.6 | 86.0 | 33 |
| 1962 | 44.5 | 76.5 | 121.0 | 37 |
| 1966 | 62.0 | 93.6 | 155.6 | 40 |
| 1968 | 71.5 | 108.0 | 179.5 | 40 |
| 1976 | 168.1 | 200.7 | 368.8 | 45 |
| 1977 | 174.1 | 219.6 | 393.7 | 44 |

Source: Report, *Committee of Inquiry into Shipping* ("Rochdale Report") (London: HMSO, 1970), p. 154; and OECD, *Maritime Transport 1977* (Paris: OECD, 1978), p. 135.

into an "oil crisis." A new and feverish demand for tanker tonnage resulted in further construction, as the energy-hungry world sought to stockpile huge oil reserves.

Obviously there would be an end to this activity as the new prices would affect the world and cause one of the most severe economic recessions since the Great Depression. The demand for oil would consequently slacken, and by 1975 the shipping slump had arrived. It was a severe one, reminiscent of the post-World War I and post-World War II period; it resulted in VLCCs and ULCCs lying idle at anchorages ranging from the fjords of Norway to the inlets of Sri Lanka.[118] As in other areas of its existence, marine transport seems to learn little from its own economic history. However, we are still attempting to talk about marine pollution as it affected the international law and policy of marine transport. We simply had to give a brief survey of the world tanker industry to illustrate the inherent pollution danger of that type of vessel. Tankers are, after all, the major cause of ship-generated pollution:

> There are three basic causes of pollution by oil tankers. First, the accidental spillage during cargo working, which is an infrequent occurrence and seldom leads to extensive pollution. Second, the ship may be involved in a collision or become stranded, leading to catastrophic and widespread pollution. With the high concentration of shipping in certain areas these accidents are probable, but the risks can be enormously reduced, if not eliminated, by stringent routeing, efficient personnel on every vessel, and the shore control of dense traffic. The third cause stems from the discharge of oily water from the tanker during tank cleaning operations which take place en route between the discharging ports. This source of pollution can be completely eliminated.[119]

Since the *Torrey Canyon* incident in 1967, there have been enough other "spectacular" incidents to keep the environmentally conscious world aware that there are serious safety questions relating to these vessels. Disasters involving the *Arrow* in 1971,[120] the *Metula* in 1974,[121] the *Argo Merchant* and *Sansinena* in 1977,[122] the *Amoco Cadiz* in 1978,[123] and the *Betelgeuse* in 1979,[124] were all *causes célèbres*, receiving wide publicity in the news media, which, regardless of the actual causes of these accidents, pointed to the inherent pollution danger of a relatively frail vessel carrying a very large cargo of pollutants. The efforts by those concerned about the dangers of what has been termed the "tanker bomb" have been concentrated in four areas—three being preventative and one ameliorative.[125]

The first area includes training and manning standards of those actually operating vessels, the standard of construction of vessels, and the responsibility for both by the flag state. Obviously, the very high degree of human error in ship accidents, which have decreased only marginally despite innovative new technology, has been of great concern, both inside and outside the industry.[126] However, there has been little international cooperation, and that which has occurred has been of the lowest-common-denominator variety. Despite the clearly recognized problem, despite the fact that marine transport is definitely an international enterprise, where one state's operation can cause another state's calamity, ship operation has always been a very private matter of concern only to shipowner and flag state. Internationally agreed-on standards thus have been difficult to achieve.

Of course, many maritime states do take the allocation of their flag to vessels very seriously and do enforce acceptably high standards. Unfortunately, many more do not. For example, training standards for certificated, as well as uncertificated, seamen vary from highly skilled university-level standards to none at all.[127] Yet either extreme is "qualified" to operate the largest vessels in the world. As a general rule, therefore, it can be said that ships in the late twentieth century—often fitted with twenty-first-century technology—are operated by men who are trained to nineteenth-century standards, or at least with that century's mentality.

In this area also, the shipping industry has not been able to establish a clear policy. The aviation analogy must again be made. In that industry training was standardized almost from the beginning, and qualifications of airmen are usually easily transferable from state to state. In general, ICAO has been able to lay down the highest possible denominator of training and has had its rules accepted with little or no argument. In marine transport, on the other hand, the fight for better conditions for seamen, begun by Plimsoll and now in the hands of the ILO, has not yet been concluded. At IMCO, the battle for basic standards of training, certification, and watchkeeping for seafarers is still in an early stage. The conclusion of a recent IMCO convention appears to be a commendable start for a new approach.[128] Obviously, it will take many years before the human element of the operating part of ocean transportation will have reached standards required not only by the new technology they are operating but also by the increasingly complex environment in which they are operating it. In an essentially conservative industry, it will probably take a further half-century to catch up to present-day aviation training standards.

For countries in the Third World with embryonic fleets, of course, the increase in training standards comes at a bad time in their development plans. Having previously usually been the suppliers of unskilled sea personnel to developed maritime states, they now seek to establish their own shipping industry in a very competitive business. With new standards, they will now be required to establish training schools and academies with sophisticated equipment in order to meet new international standards. This will add to their development problems and will cause some of these states to fight the imposition of new standards for simple economic reasons.

IMCO's technical-assistance program could help but is at present woefully underbudgeted and unable to face the demands made on it.[129]

The construction standards of vessels is another factor with a direct bearing on safety at sea. Ship construction seems to have become part of a marketing system like that for automobiles, where marketability and customer appeal take priority. In the very competitive ship-construction business, the shipyards have little choice but to produce vessels that are not only commercially viable but also customized for each particular buyer. Vessels built must also be capable of meeting such international safety standards as are in force and, at the same time, be attractively priced.

This seemingly impossible situation has prevailed in the industry for many years. The supertanker, VLCC, ULCC, LNG carrier, supercontainer vessel, and large oil-exploration and -exploitation rigs were all developed in a remarkably short period of time with a minimum amount of research on overall and specific safety aspects. It would seem that this methodology is, in economic terms, probably the most expensive way to build ships. There has been almost no attempt at standardization of ship models together with an upgrading of overall construction standards. Again, the aviation analogy—there are probably not much more than a dozen different basic large commerical jet-airliner types in operation today. Airlines usually request design modifications to conform to the type of service the aircraft is to provide: passenger, freight, combination, short-, medium-, or long-haul, and so on. However, most of the basic engineering is unchanged; and airframe and power plant, already well tested before marketing, becomes then well tried in service and well known by those who operate them.

Of course, this whole approach was not taken by the aviation industry out of some altruistic sense of efficiency and standardization. It makes sound economic sense in an extremely high-cost industry, which appears not to have suffered from this "lack of individuality." On the other hand, in shipping rugged individualism prevails—today undoubtedly at the cost of safety, efficiency, and actual cost. The almost 400 million grt of shipping, which makes up the present world fleet,[130] is composed almost entirely of individually different vessels, each one "custom designed" according to the owner's particular requirements of service and cost.

The aviation analogy can take us only so far, as marine transport is a very different industry. On the other hand, we would suggest that the industry could probably get along quite easily with two to three dozen different ship types, as long as they were adaptable for simple modification. That would provide a strong additional safety factor on the high seas, as within a comparatively short time the full operational ability of such vessels would be apparent and well known to all.

The possibility of the marine-transport industry taking such an approach is remote, however. Even research into such new directions is probably decades away. The cost and profit orientation of the industry, dictated by the built-in competitiveness of the ocean business, is still too strong. As a result, the shipbuilding industry is forced to comply with the demands of its customers and construct at the lowest common denominator of safety rather than the highest.

The continuing argument about double-bottom construction for tankers is a good example.[131] When IMCO made some suggestions along such lines, the shipbuilders of Japan, which has the largest shipbuilding industry in the world, raised an outcry about cost increases and effectively destroyed the proposals or set them back at least a decade.[132] Thus the basic ship-construction standards, binding both builder and potential owner, remain those set down by the classification societies, which are themselves an integral part of the industry they are supposed to safeguard. Furthermore, it must be remembered that the classification societies compete for business among themselves.[133] Once again, the results may very well be something less than the highest standard of international safety.

The aviation analogy can also be made regarding on-board equipment, particularly electronic devices assisting navigation, traffic control, communication, collision avoidance, automatic control, and so on. In the air, standardization has been considerable, stimulating research into better and safer equipment, which has as a result propelled the aviation-equipment industry to the frontiers of outer space. The users of aircraft are generally anxious to have the latest, safest, and best equipment available, which can often be obtained on a lease system until superseded by newer models. Of course, equipment standards are strictly enforced by the aviation regulatory bodies, which themselves carry out in-depth test research.[134] On the other hand, on the ocean we seem to have advanced relatively little in the past century, and there are as yet few internationally accepted rules requiring vessels to carry even the simplest electronic navigational aids.[135] Of course, many ships do carry a great variety of sophisticated equipment, ranging from the trusty radar set to satellite navigation systems. However, such equipment can be fitted simply at the whim of the shipowner. He is not required to use it and often does not. Decisions to fit equipment are often based on cost rather than efficiency or even necessity. At the same time, the ship-equipment industry is basically uncontrolled and can manufacture whatever it thinks will sell. As a result, there is today a veritable conglomeration of electronic aids, presenting the industry with decisions it is often not capable of making. Standardization appears to be seen as opposed to free-enterprise competitiveness in the industry. Again, it will be up to organizations such as IMCO eventually to create some order in what is essentially chaos.

In the field of ship construction and ship equipment, Third-World states will fare badly in their emerging shipping ambitions. As shipping standards rise, as they undoubtedly will, costs will escalate. Access to ship construction via international financial arrangements and hard loans has never been easy for the poorer countries, and in the future it will be even harder.[136] Such states will have to make a policy choice of whether to go into the shipping business at all, or whether to go into it as cheaply as possible. Naturally, the latter will be the more attractive alternative. The result is that Third-World states will become the operators of vessels discarded by the traditional shipping states because: (1) such ships are no longer economical or (2) such ships can no longer comply with rising international safety standards. This, in turn, will put such Third-World states in a "catch-22" dilemma of pleading with bodies such as IMCO and ILO to relax standards so that they can operate substandard ships manned by substandard crews.

*Flag-State Responsibility for Shipping:*
*Pollution Prevention*

From what we have just said, it would be surprising if there were much to add about the flag state's responsibility for training, manning, constructing, and setting equipment standards for its vessels. There are essentially four groups of states to consider. First, the traditional developed maritime state sees its shipping industry essentially as a free-enterprise competitive business operation like any other major corporation operating in its territory. There is usually as little control as possible, as the shipping-industry lobby, at the government-industry interface, has convinced legislators that control is essentially interference. Legislation is, therefore, usually initiated from the industry rather than from government, and thus cannot be expected to contain measures not approved by the industry. Such states usually present a very conservative attitude at international conferences that attempt to change the status quo. As most of the major maritime states can be included in this group, the lack of change in the areas under discussion is directly attributable to the attitude of these states.

The second group comprises the quickly expanding shipping interests of the states of the Socialist bloc and China. As we know, the essentially planned economies of these countries have resulted in a highly motivated marine policy linked to political, as well as commercial, considerations. Naturally, state control is complete, with the state's shipping enterprises considered a part of the overall planning strategy of the state itself. However, in our area of discussion—ship operation, construction standards, and training—there are only marginal differences from the first group of states. There is no question that their training and manning standards are very high, because seamen (and even fishermen) are operating under paramilitary conditions.[137] Nautical training and education is standardized and efficient, but probably not innovative, as it is based on internationally accepted norms, which as suggested, are very conservative. Construction standards are no better than in the first group because, certainly at this stage, technology in the Socialist countries still lags behind that of the West. As a result, many ships of the Socialist states are still built in Western shipyards.[138] In any case, since much of the Socialist shipping is run for entirely sound commercial—and thus nonsocialist—profits, the built-in competitive requirement would preclude most raising of standards. In these states, therefore, the approach is essentially conservative, albeit under strict government control, which enables the state to speak very directly about *its* main interests at international gatherings. At such meetings, this group's posture is dictated to a great extent by political considerations, although there is good evidence of compliance with international measures and standards once accepted.

The third group of states comprises the so-called flag-of-convenience states, which in 1978 had some 28 percent (112.8 million grt) of the world fleet under their flags.[139] We have already examined the flag-of-convenience phenomenon, and can simply add that it continues to expand at the rate of roughly 1 percent per year. That appears to indicate that these states are offering something the traditional flag states cannot. We know, of course, that they do offer minimum state controls to those who register ships with them. There is now ample evidence that the majority of flag-of-convenience operators have "fled their flag" simply for tax reasons.[140] The fact that there has simply not been the required support of governments in the traditional maritime states for their shipping industries is, of course, a commentary on the industry's loss of status in the general economic policy of many of these states.

However, there are, unfortunately, still a variety of other motivations to flee to a "convenient flag." These reasons relate to the subjects under discussion at present. There is no question that low operation as well as construction and equipment standards of ships are not as rigidly enforced in flag-of-convenience states as in most other states.[141] The motivation for flag-of-convenience states simply is not there. Even the largest of these (in terms of registered tonnage), the Republic of Liberia, which has a fairly vigorous ship-safety program, must at the same time continue to attract vessels to its flag for the basic economic reasons that it provides the flag in the first place.[142] In addition, many owners are fleeing their own flags because of rising labor costs and standards. Flag-of-convenience states have no interest in enforcing trade-union regulations and requirements.

Thus there is a weak link in the international law and policy of marine transport in this area. Until substandard vessels and unskilled seamen can no longer find this loophole, this weakness will persist. One must add, of course, that the plugging of the loophole combined with the tax incentives of the flag of convenience may eventually result in wholesale flight from traditional flags, unless some severe restructuring of marine policy takes place in such states. At the international level, the posture of the flag-of-convenience states has been conservative, following the lines taken by the traditional maritime states.

The final group comprises states in the developing world with emergent fleets. For some years to come this will remain a very small part of the world fleet, but there is a discernible trend particularly in the nonliner services.[143] New developments at UNCTAD, which we will discuss shortly, will undoubtedly strengthen this role further. On the regulatory side, however, there is so far little to report. Naturally, at a time when these states wish to encourage the growth of their shipping industries, they will do so by nurturing and facilitating rather than by regulating. Developing states with a Western orientation or political system thus follow the traditional approach, and those with a socialist orientation follow that pattern.

At the same time, the difficulties of development are superimposed on either approach. We have already referred to the tendency of developing states to become the operators of the world's discarded tonnage. That will undoubtedly result in a pattern, already discernible at IMCO meetings, of Third-World states asking special considerations when new safety measures are discussed. This might range from outright opposition to new innovations, which are considered to be luxuries suitable only for the technologically advanced countries, to the demand for double standards.[144] In practical terms, much of the older fleet acquired by these new states will soon simply be unable to meet increasing international standards. The periodic shipping slumps, which will result in large-scale "dumping" of second-hand and excess tonnage into the market, will continuously exacerbate this problem. Once again, solutions are neither easy nor imminent. One of the basic purposes of this book has been to show that the international marine-transport industry, and the law and policy directing and regulating it, has become flawed by its own history. There is simply not the structure, organization, or cohesion within the industry to direct a concerted approach to dealing with some of these most pressing problems facing it. At the same time, the industry's continued opposition to an external intergovernmental structure that might provide new directions amplifies this whole problem.

*The Law and Policy of Marine-Pollution
Compensation*

Having briefly discussed the three preventative aspects of international ship safety, particularly related to the ship-generated-pollution problem, we are left with the ameliorative approach, which has received perhaps more than its fair share of attention. That comment in itself reflects the compensatory system devised by man, which places more value on compensation than on prevention. As every first-year law student is told in his first tort-law class: "... if you can't restore a subject to its original predamaged condition, the next best thing that man has devised is money to compensate for the loss." That has been the general approach in world shipping and has created, as part of the industry, the marine-insurance business, which has evolved since the dawn of history along with shipping itself. Some of the problems that plague shipping today thus also affect the marine-insurance industry.

Like the insurance business generally, the marine-insurance arm is, quite rightly, a conservative one. As there are few uninsured ships on the sea, owing to the risk exposure for uninsured owners, the marine-insurance industry has become a very powerful body. If a shipowner cannot find insurance for his ship; if the cargo owner cannot have his goods insured; if the carrier cannot find coverage for all the myriad risks he is exposed to, simply because he is in the business he is in, then the operation will not get underway. It is as simple as that. Thus marine insurance could operate as a very powerful regulatory control for safety at sea. The fact that it never has been in that position, and would even denounce such a role strongly, is further confirmation of the overcommercialization of the international law and policy of marine transport.[145] Like its counterparts in other areas of marine transport, marine insurance is essentially a commercial enterprise. The transaction operates between the insured, who wants his "ocean venture" covered as fully, widely, and cheaply as possible, and the insurer, who seeks a premium commensurate with the risk exposure. Although the insurance market is basically competitive, the variance in rates is usually not considerable, particularly in the London market which still controls the major portion of this whole business.[146]

Marine insurance, therefore, basically seeks to keep premium income sufficiently above loss expenditure to allow a healthy commercial profit on the investment exposed. As long as this balance exists, the insurance market asks few further questions and relies on its own commercial experience and intelligence built up over a long period. It does not see itself as having any role in the regulatory process. Controls are left to the classification societies, which operate as a technical arm of marine insurance. If, for example, an owner's record is poor, or his trade risky, the premium rates will be higher. However, he will hardly ever be refused insurance. A "moral code of conduct" relating to safety does not exist. Obviously, this is not the place to discuss whether or not it should exist. The structure in existence today in the marine-insurance business has been dictated by its history, and changes will be difficult. In our opinion, the marine underwriter's role as a reliable and expert part of marine transport has not been utilized sufficiently in the attempt to impose a better regulatory process. The result has been unnecessary confrontation and nowhere more so than in the area of ship-generated pollution and its compensatory aspects.

Until the *Torrey Canyon* incident of 1967, no adequate national or international legal regime for compensating victims of oil-pollution damage existed at all.[147] Since then, however, four major schemes have been established, two by the shipping industry and two by IMCO. Firstly, the Tanker Owners' Voluntary Agreement Concerning Liability for Oil Pollution (TOVALOP), which is an agreement among shipowners under which each owner is obliged to pay compensation for oil-pollution damage, came into operation in 1969.[148] This agreement was followed in 1971 by a Contract Regarding an Interim Supplement to Tanker Liability for Oil Pollution (CRISTAL), which provides additional compensation to be paid by the oil industry after other means have been expended.[149] From IMCO came the 1969 International Convention on Civil Liability for Oil Pollution Damage, also known as the "Civil Liability Convention," which imposes on shipowners the liability to pay compensation for claims arising from oil-pollution incidents.[150] This instrument entered into force only in 1975. It was supplemented by the International Convention on the Establishment of an International Fund for Oil Pollution Damage ("Fund Convention"), which was adopted in 1971 but entered into force only in late 1978.[151] The Fund Convention provides for additional compensation for oil-pollution damage in excess of the amount covered by the 1969 Civil Liability Convention.

Of course, oil pollution has presented the marine-insurance industry with special problems. The industry had to find a balance between commercially viable premiums for insuring against oil-pollution damage, and the unknown factor of possible extent of damage. Quite understandably, insurers do not like unknown quantities in their equations, and their caution with respect to oil-pollution coverage has been somewhat vindicated by several recent catastrophic oil spills.[152]

To balance any possible injustices, the ability of the shipowner (and thus his insurer) to limit liability has been devised. This traditional principle of maritime law, although frequently under attack, only recently emerged unscathed from its most searching examination ever.[153] The principle states that if the shipowner engages in a maritime adventure as a service to all who might benefit from it, then he ought not to be exposed to all the risks such an adventure might entail. This principle comes to us from seventeenth-century Dutch commercial practice and, at that time, undoubtedly had a sound commercial basis. Whether it still does is, however, doubtful.[154] Again, it is not for us to examine this complex maritime-law area here. Suffice it to say that the basic battle relating to oil-pollution-damage compensation, since the problem was first recognized, has been fought in terms of the upper limit of financial risk to which a shipowner (and his insurer) should be exposed if a pollution incident takes place.[155] This has, in the past decade, resulted in simply haggling over what the figure should be, between those most exposed to such risks, particularly states with vulnerable coastlines, and the shipping (marine-insurance) industry.

There is no question that the liability situation has improved because of this debate, as is reflected by the entering into force of the conventions previously referred to.[156] On the other hand, there is also ample evidence that the present upper limits of compensation are probably far from adequate to deal with really major pollution damage, multiple accidents, or incidents in particularly fragile environments.[157] To us, this whole debate appears to have been wasteful, as well as inconclusive. The energy, as well as the costs expended, could have benefited a preventative discussion much more. However, that is where the public-law-and-policy and private-maritime-law schism appears again. Public law and policy related to oil-pollution prevention and the preservation of the human environment generally, which is debated very much at the intergovernmental level, is here in conflict with private maritime law and policy related to commercial expediency and financial compensation. The end product will obviously be conflict.

At the same time, there is ample evidence that the marine-insurance industry is perfectly capable of meeting new challenges and carrying new risks. We have already spoken of examples such as wide-body passenger aircraft, the $1 billion risks covered for some of the new North Sea oil-production platforms, and the nuclear and other major risks covered by the insurance industry today. In these areas, however, the industry was able to muster its full resources and present a viable as well as a constructive private view to emerging public policy and thus to become part of the new policy and law-making process. To us this would also indicate that despite the gulf that separates the public and private areas of maritime law and policy by now, all may not be lost.

## IMCO: The Second Important Decade

We have already described the first decade of IMCO's operation and have referred to some of the important work that organization has undertaken in its second decade. Despite its modest size and very inadequate budget, IMCO came into its own in the 1970s.[158] It lost its reputation as a "shipowners' club," gained quite undeservedly in its early years, and was also regarded with much less suspicion by the major maritime states, which had expended such great efforts to prevent its establishment. It was seen, particularly during this period, that there was a vital need for this type of organization in the shipping field; many wondered how the industry had managed without it before. Nevertheless, IMCO was still fettered by its narrow constitution, which required it to be nothing more than a consultative and advisory body. However, there is much to consult and advise on in an industry of ever-increasing complexity and importance. By 1980 the organization had 116 member states, ranging in size from the Seychelles to China, all with maritime interests.[159] IMCO had assumed the responsibility for some twenty-one international conventions, most of which resulted from preparatory work in conferences convened by the organization. These conventions are a perfect illustration of the central place IMCO now occupies in the international law and policy of marine transport.[160]

1. International Convention for the Safety of Life at Sea, 1960 (SOLAS)
2. International Regulations for Preventing Collisions at Sea, 1960
3. International Convention for the Prevention of Pollution of the Sea by Oil, 1954
4. Convention on Facilitation of International Maritime Traffic, 1965
5. International Convention on Loadlines, 1966
6. International Convention on Tonnage Measurement of Ships, 1969
7. International Convention Relating to Intervention on the High Seas in Cases of Oil Pollution Casualties, 1969
8. International Convention on Civil Liability for Oil Pollution Damage, 1969
9. International Convention Relating to Civil Liability in the Field of Maritime Carriage of Nuclear Material, 1971
10. Special Trade Passenger Ships Agreement, 1971
11. International Convention on the Establishment of an International Fund for compensation for Oil Pollution Damage, 1971
12. International Convention for Safe Containers, 1972
13. International Convention for Prevention of Pollution from Ships, 1973
14. Protocol Relating to the Intervention on the High Seas in Cases of Marine Pollution by Substances other than Oil, 1973
15. International Convention for the Safety of Life at Sea, 1974
16. Athens Convention Relating to the Carriage of Passengers and their Luggage at Sea, 1974
17. Convention on the International Maritime Satellite Organization (INMARSAT), 1976
18. Convention on the Limitation of Liability for Maritime Claims, 1976
19. Torremolinos Convention for the Safety of Fishing Vessels, 1977
20. Convention on the International Regulation of Preventing Collisions at Sea, 1977
21. International Convention on Standards for Training, Certification and Watchkeeping for Seafarers, 1978

To be a little more specific, IMCO concentrates its resources in some fourteen separate areas of importance to the international law and policy of marine transport today:

1. *Bulk cargoes and chemicals*: Continuous research into safety measures necessary for the safe carriage of cargoes such as grain, ores, coal, and concentrates, which are carried in increasingly large bulk quantities, has been one of IMCO's priorities for a long time. In addition, standards for procedures and arrangements for the discharge of noxious liquid substances and guidelines on the reception facilities of such substances are under active consideration. The increasingly complex world problem regarding the dumping of international waste is directly related to IMCO's work on safety requirements for ships engaged in dumping and incineration at sea. Consideration is also given to the updating of bulk-chemical and gas carrier codes.[161]

2. *Carriage of dangerous goods*: IMCO has published the first comprehensive, universally accepted, International Maritime Dangerous Goods Code (IMDGC) which is designed to assist compliance with provisions regarding the carriage of dangerous goods by sea contained in the SOLAS convention. This important publication is frequently updated and has established considerable international uniformity in the identification of characteristics of most of the many dangerous substances carried at sea today.[162]

3. *Facilitation of travel and transport*: The object of the 1965 Convention on Facilitation of International Maritime Traffic, which has been in force since 1967, but has so far only been accepted by some forty-four governments, is to eliminate the chaos that exists owing to the many different governmental formalities in international travel and trade, as well as to simplify documentary requirements connected with the arrival, stay, and departure of ships, persons, and cargo in ports. The convention's aim is to achieve standardization of documents required by national authorities by the establishment of the "IMCO model form" concerning general declarations, cargo declarations, ships' stores declarations, crews' effects declarations, crew lists, and passenger lists. Periodic meetings of contracting parties to the convention seek to update these efforts.[163]

4. *Fire safety of ships*: In addition to the general interest in safety of ships under the SOLAS convention, IMCO has been carrying out special work on fire safety for mobile offshore-drilling units as well as the protection of tanker cargo pumprooms. Fire-safety measures for the newest generation of RoRo ships are also under development.[164]

5. *Life-saving appliances*: In the face of the haphazard development of ships' equipment, to which we have already referred, IMCO is attempting to facilitate a more standardized development of life-saving equipment and appliances in conjunction with the continuous revision of the relevant parts of the SOLAS convention.[165]

6. *Marine pollution*. As has been indicated, this politically volatile marine-policy area has received perhaps the greatest share of attention in the past decade and, undoubtedly, catapulted IMCO into its present-day prominence. A Marine Environmental Protection Committee (MEPC) has been established, and the work of IMCO and of this committee is moving directly toward implementing the various marine-pollution resolutions and conventions that have become the organization's responsibility. Work is being carried out on a comprehensive oil-pollution manual. Sections of the manual dealing with prevention and with measures for dealing with spillages have been published. Other sections on contingency planning, salvage, and legal aspects are in progress. In addition, the provision for adequate reception facilities in ports for waste generated on board ships continues to be studied. The lack of adequate facilities in many parts of the world was, and is, a major contribution to the pollution problem. In 1977, the MEPC developed "procedures for the control of discharge" which were adopted by the tenth IMCO assembly. The procedures outline new methods whereby evidence of violations may be obtained and measures taken by all parties involved, particularly port or flag states. Voluntary in-port inspection schemes are expected to be an additional source of evidence of contravention of pollution-convention requirements. Finally, in early 1978 the International Conference on Tanker Safety and Pollution Prevention, organized by IMCO, adopted a protocol for the 1973 Marine Pollution and the 1974 SOLAS conventions.[166] Agreement was obtained for target dates for the entry into force of these instruments by June 1981 and June 1979, respectively. These new requirements will become an annex to the 1973 Marine Pollution Convention and will affect new and existing tankers of certain tonnages and cover such measures as segregated ballast tanks (SBT), clean ballast tanks (CBT), crude-oil washing (COW), and improved inspection and certification standards.

In this area, therefore, IMCO has become an organization of crucial importance in the international law and policy of marine transport. This progress is hampered in only two areas. First, there is still considerable opposition to IMCO's role in preventative measures, as evidenced by the painfully slow acceptance and ratification of the necessary conventions.[167] Second, as already indicated, the slow codification process of UNCLOS III, which will affect much of what IMCO is attempting to do, has affected the progress also. Undoubtedy the conclusion of UNCLOS III will shift many new responsibilities in the marine and environmental protection area to the organization.

7. *Navigation*: Traditionally, navigation consisted of the means of enabling the vessel to proceed from point A to point B by the most expeditious ocean route. That is probably still the basic principle today. However, superimposed on the basic principle are the complexities of in-

ternational marine transport. The increase of the world's fleet in tonnage, numbers of vessels, types of vessels, and size of individual ships long ago called for regulatory measures similar to those affecting the air. Once again, opposition was strong; and regulation and control is so far embryonic or voluntary. Nevertheless, IMCO is attempting to lay down new ship-routing systems, traffic-separation schemes, deep-water routes, and areas of the seas to be avoided. The 1972 Collision Avoidance Regulations, which for the first time recognized such measures, will undoubtedly aid these efforts.[168]

8. *Procedures for the control of ships*: These are intended to identify possible deficiencies in ships and to ensure that remedial measures are taken. They were controversial, as any attempt to achieve standardization or uniformity will obviously offend the individualism so prevalent in the shipping industry. Nevertheless, such measures are necessary if treaties such as the SOLAS and the Load Line conventions are to be effective.[169]

9. *Radio communications*: The prolific expansion of communication methods throughout the world has not had the benefit to shipping that it might have. Once again the commercial, rather than the safety, appeal was allowed to be the industry's main guideline. Different types of equipment, often with minimal testing, proliferated; and standardization measures were haphazard at best. IMCO has been working in this area in conjunction with the International Telecommunications Union (ITU) and took part in the 1979 ITU World Administrative Radio Conference.[170] IMCO has also collaborated with the International Hydrographic Organization (IHO) on the completion of a plan for a worldwide navigation warning system. In addition, the INMARSAT convention of 1976, although not yet in force, has brought the shipping world, through IMCO, to the future world of satellite communications in navigation. However, real progress in this area is still some years away.[171]

10. *Search and rescue*: Modern marine technology notwithstanding, the oceans continue to present to those who use them a considerable peril. Ship (as well as aircraft) losses and accidents require an efficient search-and-rescue mechanism to be established throughout the world; and, despite some of the political-military implications involved, IMCO has taken up this important humanitarian consideration with vigor. The organization's widely accepted Marine Search and Rescue Manual (IMCOSAR) gives guidance to governments on the establishment, organization, and operation of search-and-rescue services. As a result, in 1979 an international conference on maritime search and rescue was held under IMCO auspices.[172]

11. *Ship design and equipment*: We have already referred to the ad hoc approach and individual whims that pervade this area of international shipping. Reform is only in its very early stages, as there simply has been insufficient thought given by many of the major maritime states to substantial

changes in ship-design and ship-equipment standards. However, IMCO has been able to be more effective in the newer technology and has established a Code of Safety for Dynamically Supported Craft, applicable to air-cushion and hydrofoil vehicles. Work is also carried out to finalize a Code of Safety for Mobile Offshore Drilling Units as well as for better safety-construction measures for offshore supply vessels, other special ships, and nuclear-powered propulsion units.[173]

12. *Subdivision, stability, and load lines*: In this area, IMCO has problems similar to those it faces in the standardization and upgrading of ship design and equipment. Of assistance, if it can be called that, has been the upsurge of major tanker disasters such as those involving the *Sansinena, Argo Merchant, Amoco Cadiz*, and *Betelgeuse* in recent years. This contributed, in the past, to some measure of agreement on recommendations concerning tonnage and tonnage measurement of ballast spaces and segregated-ballast oil tankers, of which there are, to date, far too few. Work is also in progress on subdivision requirements for nuclear vessels and other types of ships.[174]

13. *Technical cooperation*: Technical assistance in the maritime field to developing countries by IMCO is considered to be of considerable importance. As a result, a special division within the organization is charged with implementing a comprehensive technical-assistance program to provide the fullest possible training in areas as diverse as maritime-safety administration; training and legislation; shipbuilding and ship repairs; marine pollution; radio communication; hydrography; navigational aids; and port development. For Third-World states the developmental gap from the major maritime states in this area is as immense as everywhere else; and IMCO's efforts, although highly effective, are minimal at best. There is at present relatively little funding available for large-scale projects, and almost all funding must come out of the already overextended resources controlled by the U.N. Development Program (UNDP). A fairly successful feature of this assistance program has been IMCO's part in establishing national and regional training institutions as well as expert missions and fellowships for students from developing countries.[175] For this purpose the organization has established regional advisors in Africa, Latin America, Asia, and the Pacific Ocean area, who are expected to recognize and pinpoint specific needs in their regions.

Considering that this whole examination of the international law and policy of marine transport is intended to emphasize the special problems Third World states face in this, the oldest use of the oceans, it would have been of some comfort to show at this stage an "equalizing process" in action. Unfortunately, it has been quite clear from the moment we began to speak of the devoloping world, that no such process is taking place in any forum concerned with international shipping. Here at IMCO, as well as at UNCTAD, to which we shall come shortly, such a process is certainly being attempted but has become very much a part of the North-South debate. Once again, the constitutional terms of reference of IMCO are also hampering the making of clear policy at the highest level, which would place a much greater emphasis on the organization's technical-assistance efforts. As marine technology advances quickly and international marine transport becomes more and more complex, at a time when its developmental gap is actually widening, much greater assistance will be needed by an increasing number of states.[176]

14. *Training and certification*: As already indicated, IMCO has finally entered this field, and in 1978 successfully concluded the International Convention on Standards of Training, Certification and Watchkeeping for Seafarers. Preparatory work has been carried out by the organization in close conjunction with the International Labor Organization (ILO). In other words, work in this very crucial field is only in its infancy.[177]

*IMCO's Task in International Maritime Law
and Policy*

Even this very rapid glance at IMCO's present work must indicate the very central place the organization now occupies in international marine transport. Despite the limitation of its constitution, IMCO has truly entered the realm of policy formulation and guidance, as well as law making, in international shipping. Its very schedule of work shows that if IMCO does not do it, nobody else will. Unfortunately, much of the organization's work is still related to the very technical areas in which other international bodies simply are not interested. Thus, at this stage, IMCO has only limited commercial implications and interests. Cooperation between IMCO and the CMI, for example, should by now be much further developed. This is not the fault of IMCO, which long ago recognized the ability of the private body, but is rather caused by the self-limiting structure of the CMI, which has little or no means to work in the public sector.[178] Much of IMCO's success, on the other hand, has been the result of the ability of its secretariat. The very low-key posture adopted by earlier secretaries-general, who came from traditional maritime states and who themselves had a background in the shipping industry in such states, was replaced by the very highly visible and progressive posture of the latest secretary-general, an individual from a developing country who, at the same time, is widely respected in international shipping circles.[179]

IMCO's very important legal division, under the guidance of one of Africa's foremost jurists, has had a particularly difficult role to fulfill. Given that it received its breath of life only in the post-*Torrey Canyon* period, this

division has had the formidable task of seeking a legal denominator that
will make the many IMCO conventions as widely acceptable as possible. On
the other hand, IMCO also faces all the problems that the United Nations
and all of its specialized agencies and related bodies face today. The intense
politicization of a very complex world of sovereign nation states, regional
and political and economic alliances, pervade IMCO's corridors as well as
everywhere else. The result is often decision making based on political ac-
ceptability, geographical prerogative, and administrative expediency, rather
than on the highest common denominator the organization should seek. It
is an unfortunate byproduct of the present world system that will cause increasing difficulties to IMCO and other international organizations in the
years to come.

**UNCTAD and the New International
Economic Order**

We have already referred to the important responsibilities given to
UNCTAD for establishing a more equitable developmental regime
throughout the world. The "one-shot" Geneva conference in 1964 had
become an integral part of the United Nations system; and the conference
reconvened, as already mentioned, at New Delhi in 1968.[180] In the period
under discussion, three further meetings would take place: UNCTAD
III—Santiago, Chile, 1972; UNCTAD IV—Nairobi, Kenya, 1976; and
UNCTAD V—Manila, Philippines, 1979.[181] In addition to the periodic
U.N. special sessions dealing with developmental aspects, regional meetings
of nonaligned nations, and nongovernmental conferences, UNCTAD had
quickly become the main forum of discontent; for here the developmental
gap, which continued to grow, could be demonstrated with hard economic
facts, emotional rhetoric, and much political undertone.

We cannot go into details about UNCTAD and its many important
achievements and occasional failures. It is a story that has only partially
been told—or told only by UNCTAD itself—in its rather businesslike and
laconic communiqués.[182] Nevertheless, there is no doubt that UNCTAD has
become the most important center at which the North-South encounter has
been, is, and will continue to be demonstrated. If solutions are to be found,
it will be at UNCTAD, which will convene at increasingly frequent intervals
as the economic problems of the Third World increase.[183] Unfortunately, as
already noted, developed states have either never quite understood the basic
purpose of UNCTAD—despite the fact that they created it—or have not
given the organization and its possibilities their fullest support.

Of course, UNCTAD has become a very public forum that discusses
essentially technical and commercial private matters relating to every im-
aginable aspect of international trade. Discussions often proceed at dif-

ferent levels—the "public political" for developing countries and the "private commercial" for the industrialized states. It is thus not surprising that rhetoric and polemics, rather than agreement and change, often appear to be the net result of UNCTAD sessions. There seems to be general agreement that a considerable economic gap exists between North and South, but attempts to narrow that gap seem doomed to failure. Obviously, the "New International Economic Order," which had become the slogan of the more radical and more demanding of the Third-World states, required major changes and mass transfer of wealth and resources, but was simplistic in its approach and politically unacceptable to the Western industrialized states.

That was the one extreme. On the other, the South could not accept the developmental promises, ad hoc approaches, and alignment necessities of the developed world, which on the whole had consistently failed to raise even the modest 1 percent of GNP to aid demands.[184] These difficulties were exacerbated by the fact that major international economic realignments and changes had put new pressures on a very outdated economic system during this period. As usual, the repercussions of these changes, such as the 1973-1974 oil crisis, major currency fluctuations and revaluations, and industrial undercapacity would have the worst effect on developing states, which as a consequence would plunge further into insurmountable debt and national poverty. For example, UNCTAD IV at Nairobi discussed a possible agreement for an integrated commodity program, including a common-funding mechanism for the establishment of buffer stocks to stabilize the world prices for nineteen core commodities.[185]

All this, just by way of reintroducing UNCTAD's growing importance in world shipping and to place this importance in its proper perspective. There should be no doubt that for most of the Third World, despite its importance, shipping is just one of many pressing developmental problems. As states fight for their very economic survival, vis-à-vis mounting international indebtedness, shortages of food and other resources, increasing population, and lack of industrial capacities, other problems tend to diminish.

*The UNCTAD Shipping Committee: Spokesman*
*for the Third World*

We have seen that despite the opposition of the developed and major maritime states, UNCTAD's Committee on Shipping had become well established and embarked on a variety of areas of investigation following UNCTAD II. There continued to be conflict between the shipping states and the Group of 77 regarding international shipping legislation. The developing states suggested that in order for a comprehensive approach to shipping to succeed, the legal rules under which it operated needed also to be examined.[186] On the other hand, UNCTAD's "B Group" objected strongly and suggested that existing mechanisms were much more suitable for this legal examination.[187] They referred to the CMI and IMCO as such mechanisms. That appeared to be an almost perverse attempt to obstruct. As we have seen several times already, the CMI was a totally unsuitable body to examine political or even policy questions related to shipping legislation. The CMI was simply a very powerful interest group, quite incapable of making the type of equitable policy decisions UNCTAD needed.

On the other hand, IMCO was in that context not much better. Having consistently refused IMCO the right to be anything but a consultative and advisory technical body, the developed states now expected it to make decisions exactly along lines previously closed to it. However, the developing states refused to accept this solution, saying

> . . . that IMCO deals with purely technical questions of shipping and their legal implications, and that the IMCO Council which runs this organization is not representative, since the majority of its members are elected from countries owning the largest merchant marines.[188]

At that time the B Group states suggested that the newly formed UNCITRAL,[189] with its terms of reference covering international trade law, should take over because UNCTAD's Shipping Committee was not specialized and the UNCTAD secretariat was not competent enough to handle the new tasks.[190] It was, however, quickly shown that UNCITRAL had other priorities, and that the whole examination would be unduly delayed unless UNCTAD took the initiative. As a result, the Group of 77 requested

> . . . that a standing committee on international shipping legislation be formed within UNCTAD for the purpose of reviewing the commercial and economic aspects of shipping in relation to legislation; to indicate what modification and what new legislation might be necessary; and to issue directives for UNCITRAL to follow. If UNCITRAL's work proves unsatisfactory, or if it is not capable of fulfilling the task, the Standing Committee should itself undertake the drafting of legislation. The revised draft of the 77 asked for a working group in lieu of a committee. However, no meeting ground could be established, primarily because of the United Kingdom's inflexibility, and as a result, the resolution asking the Board to establish the working group was voted through at the plenary of the Conference.[191]

In the intervening period before UNCTAD III, the UNCTAD Committee on Shipping worked feverishly to acquire whatever expertise it may have lacked in order to become a tour de force in international shipping. During this period, the maritime states missed another opportunity to become a viable part of another law-reform movement—just as they had missed being part of the major reforms taking place at IMCO and later at UNCLOS III. They continued to be intransigent and protective of their status quo and would soon be faced with reforms that placed them in real difficulties. The pattern was not really very different. Overall ocean policy appeared to be completely missing, and coordination was barely discernible. At IMCO the shipping states would be discussing policy issues in technical terms, at UNCTAD in commercial terms, and at UNCLOS III at the political-diplomatic level. At all three forums the demands put to them were basically the same. Demands were made to reform a basically anachronistic system relating to ocean uses in their totality. Even if this fact were known at the top decision-making level of the government of the developed states, it rarely filtered down to those responsible for the negotiations at the three forums. The division between the public and the private law and policy we have said so much about is here most clearly visible, as it precluded any clear policy being made or even attempted.

We have already spoken about the complete absence of the private aspects of marine transport being represented at UNCLOS III. On the other hand, at UNCTAD the reverse can be seen. That forum's Committee on Shipping painstakingly avoided any involvement in public law and policy questions, despite the fact that the UNCLOS III and IMCO debates had a very direct relationship to overall policies being taken at UNCTAD.[192] For a politically oriented body such as UNCTAD to believe that it could achieve its aims in the area of shipping by working within strictly confined "private legal, economic and commercial bounds" was not only strange, but also naive and unrealistic. Even here, the public-private division appears to be affecting the decision- and policy-making process. Only IMCO seems to have seen some of these changes by attempting close liaison with all maritime-oriented forums even remotely connected with its own aims and objectives.[193]

### UNCTAD's Task in International Maritime Law and Policy

By the time UNCTAD III convened at Santiago de Chile,[194] the organization's Committee on Shipping had achieved very substantial preparatory work in several crucial areas that were discussed in the conference's Fourth Committee. To outline some of this work:

1. *Code of Conduct for the Liner-Conference System*: We have already referred to the liner-conference system, which because of its discriminatory propensities had been under increasing criticism from the users of shipping services ever since its inception.[195] To cite the best definition of the conference system yet written:

A conference is an association of competing liner owners engaged in a particular trade who have agreed to limit the competition existing among
themselves. As a minimum, they will have agreed to charge freight rates or
passenger fares for each class of traffic according to an agreed schedule of
charges and to show no discrimination between shippers. To the agreement
foreswearing all forms of price competition may be, and usually is, added
an agreement to regulate sailings according to a predetermined pattern and
to recognize the berth rights of other members. A further step may be to
add a full pooling agreement under which profits and losses on the trade
covered by the conference are shared between the member lines. When this
stage is reached competition between the conference lines has ceased completely. In addition to these internal arrangements, each conference may
have an agreement with the shippers, that is, with its customers. This is
known as a loyalty contract and is designed to secure the continued custom
of the shipper and to prevent the entry of outside competition. When such
a contract has been completed the conference usually agrees to provide a
regular service, either by each member acting independently or by collective
action. The conference does not agree to, although members usually will,
provide additional sailings when trade is at a peak, while shippers have no
sanctions under the contract against shipowners who fail to provide the
contract sailings.[196]

Developing countries, as we have seen, are not shipping states but depend
on the shipping services provided by the maritime states. As exporting countries, they are often completely dependent on this service and are vulnerable
to the vagaries of the conference system.[197] As a result, over a number of
years, the idea has been developed by Third-World states to create a "Code
of Conduct for the Liner Conference System," which appeared in draft
form at UNCTAD III.[198] At that time there was almost total support for
such a code from the Group of 77, but fairly strong opposition from the B
Group states. Of course, as its very name implied, such a code was an attempt to rectify unacceptable practices in international commerce, in fairly
strong moral terms.

This was a heady mixture for maritime states to contend with. The fact
was that they themselves found many aspects of the conference system want-
ing and wished to put limited controls on it.[199] Yet accepting an international
moral code originating in the Third World, which by implication indicated
wrongdoing, was a different matter. There was considerable debate at
UNCTAD III, but by 1975 a convention had been completed and was opened
for signature.[200]

Many of the difficulties that had bedeviled the convention in its
preparatory, discussion, and postsignature stages once again reflect the
public-private-law division. Given the fact that the conference system is
built on strong economic, commercial principles proved in operation for
over a century, there is also the additional fact that its wider public responsibility appears, at first glance, to have little bearing on those operating

the system. Such operators are governed by private maritime law and commercial policy. But as soon as moral-conduct questions are raised by the users of the system, the whole picture changes. An internationally accepted convention, which looks at shipping as a public service with wide community implications, alters the position of those who operate the system. They are now called on to take a position on something in which they have little interest and which will undoubtedly alter their commercial position. Public-maritime-law and -policy considerations will thus be superimposed on what has previously been privately regulated. Nevertheless, the new convention is an important step forward in the search for greater internationalization of the shipping industry. It may eventually alter the whole structure of world shipping to an extent not entirely foreseen.[201] Of course, the maritime states have so far exercised a "veto" by nonratification.[202] Ratification from twenty-four states with 25 percent of the world tonnage is required before the convention can enter into force. That figure has not been reached, although a new EEC shipping policy may very well boost acceptance in the near future.[203]

2. *Technological development in shipping—international combined transport of goods*: This is the second area proposed for discussion at UNCTAD III by the Organization's Committee on Shipping. It continues to be an important area of debate and negotiation. We have already referred to the remarkable technological progress in world shipping in the last decade and the fact that this progress has direct implications for less-developed states. For example, uncertainties exist regarding the application and the economic effect of modern cargo-handling methods for shipping and ports, and in the land-leg of transport. Developments in container traffic, LNG carriers, and other fields are expected eventually to lead to lower transport costs. However, uncertainties and indecisions on the right policy toward technological progress exist, particularly in Third-World states where, owing to the heavy investment often required, the problems faced are particularly acute. Furthermore, an international convention on combined transport appears to be urgently required by states on both sides of the developmental gap. This work is still in progress at the present time.[204]

3. *Development of ports*: Placed at the beginning and end of the seaborne part of international transportation, ports play a vital role for all countries. Since before 1972, UNCTAD's Shipping Committee has recognized this by noting particularly the paramount importance of port development to the economies of developing countries. Efforts are being made to bring about port improvements that would lead to faster turnaround of ships and lower operating costs in shipping generally. To achieve this, concerted national as well as international action is needed to provide financial and technical assistance to developing countries for port improvement. New port installations and services should then be utilized effectively by ship-

ping companies and should be reflected in lower freight costs. The special needs of landlocked developing countries must also be considered in this context. Here, in a fairly technical area such as port development, the public international law of the sea, with its specific concern for landlocked states and transit and territorial rights, suddenly appears. As we have reiterated time and time again, the users of ocean space—here at the landward reach—are not divisible. However, in this area UNCTAD's work is also continuing in cooperation with major port-development funding from the World Bank and its subsidiaries.[205]

4. *Development of merchant marines*: Naturally, this is the area of most vital interest to the Third World as a whole as it seeks to become more equal to the developed world. We have shown how the North had literally floated to prosperity on a fleet of ships, and that the provider of the sea-transport system soon controlled the seas and with it the commerce that moved on them. In the latter part of the 1970s, this undoubtedly changed, as the commercial infrastructure of shipping assumed an even more important role than shipping itself. Nevertheless, access to shipping for many Third-World coastal states, with considerable maritime tradition as well as need, has been an important part of their developmental program. Naturally, UNCTAD and its Shipping Committee has been deeply involved. At UNCTAD III the Group of 77 first voiced their demands that by the end of the century at least 10 percent of world tonnage should be owned by state members of their group.[206] This was essentially a modest target when compared to the Third-World share in international seaborne trade. In order to reach the target, however, in addition to needed technical and other assistance, commercial credits for purchasing new and second-hand vessels must become more readily available on better terms than ever before. It was also recognized that the inadequacies of shipbuilding and ship-repairing facilities in developing countries hampers the proper development of these new merchant fleets. Since 1972 this debate has continued, although it lessened somewhat owing to the shipping slump period of 1975-1977. The 10-percent target has not yet been reached, and there is doubt that it can be reached by 1985.[207] As we can see from table 7-3, Third-World shipping does not as yet figure prominently on the world shipping ladder. However, the combination of advantages such as labor costs, the "Code of Conduct" convention provisions, quasi-flag-of-convenience registration, and new ports and repair facilities, may alter the scales in future years.

5. *Cooperation in merchant shipping*: This subject, first brought forward at UNCTAD III,[208] was one of considerable imagination and scope but appeared much too late in the history of the international law and policy of marine transport to be very effective. The idea was to examine the fea-

**Table 7-3**
**World Fleet, Mid-1978, Vessels over 100 grt**

| Country | Gross Registered Tonnage (in Millions of Tons) | Remarks |
|---|---|---|
| 1. Liberia | 81.1 | Flag of convenience |
| 2. Japan | 39.1 | Member, UNCTAD B Group |
| 3. Greece | 33.9 | Member, UNCTAD B Group |
| 4. United Kingdom | 30.9 | Member, UNCTAD B Group |
| 5. Norway | 26.1 | Member, UNCTAD B Group |
| 6. USSR | 22.2 | COMECON Socialist Group |
| 7. Panama | 20.7 | Flag of convenience |
| 8. United States | 16.1 | (includes U.S reserve and inland fleet) Member, UNCTAD B Group |
| 9. France | 12.1 | Member, UNCTAD B Group |
| 10. Italy | 11.5 | Member, UNCTAD B Group |
| 11. Federal Republic of Germany | 9.7 | Member, UNCTAD B Group |
| 12. Spain | 8.1 | Member, UNCTAD B Group |
| 13. Singapore | 7.5 | Flag of convenience |
| 14. Sweden | 6.5 | Member, UNCTAD B Group |
| 15. India | 5.8 | Member, Group of 77 |
| 16. Denmark | 5.5 | Member, UNCTAD B Group |
| 17. Netherlands | 5.1 | Member, UNCTAD B Group |
| 18. People's Republic of China | 5.1 | Central-planning Member: Group of 77 |
| 19. Brazil | 3.7 | Member, Group of 77 |
| 20. Poland | 3.5 | COMECON Socialist Group |
| 21. Republic of Korea | 2.9 | Member, Group of 77 |
| 22. Canada | 2.9 | (includes Canadian inland fleet) Member, UNCTAD B Group |
| 23. Cyprus | 2.6 | Flag of convenience |
| 24. Yugoslavia | 2.3 | Nonaligned |
| 25. Finland | 2.3 | Member, UNCTAD B Group |
| Rest of the world | 35.3 | |
| Total | 402.5 | |

Source: OECD, *Maritime Transport 1978* (Paris: OECD, 1979), p. 152.

sibility of drafting a general instrument on maritime transport and development, dealing with international relations in shipping. This appeared to be based on a perceived need to harmonize national shipping policies in order to achieve the common denominator of the international shipping policy of benefit for all states. As could be expected, some of the originating proposals in this area came from countries with centrally planned economies, where governments were already playing a major role in national shipping policy. For most other countries, particularly the major maritime states, it was not as simple as that. The division between public and private maritime law and policy was complete, and the public sector was effectively isolated from private shipping-policy decision making. The idea remained alive in UNCTAD, but it has not been seriously considered since.

6. *Freight rates*: This important subject appeared on UNCTAD III's agenda as a draft resolution,[209] the aim of which was to introduce fairness and to relieve, as far as possible, the economies of developing countries from the massive outflow of foreign exchange to developed countries for the payment of shipping services. This approach was called a search for a "freight-rate charter" to induce shipowners to relinquish anachronistic methods for deciding freight rates, the basis of which was usually known only to themselves.[210] At the base of the whole debate, of course, was the general problem that was faced by all in the shipping industry—the problem of escalating costs and an inflationary economic system. However, what was not understood by the Group of 77 was that their demands could not be met by the major states even if they had wanted to acquiesce. Shipping was still a competitive business, very much in the private domain and thus generally not subject to governmental control or interference. As a business, it was run on a profit-making basis; as costs rose, so would rates, which would simply pass higher costs along to the consumer—the user of the shipping services. The fact that this simple economic equation might have political repercussions on the shipping state in other forums, which should have been part of an overall maritime policy if there had been one, was not a consideration. This is part of the basic problem of international shipping, with which the industry has not yet come to terms. As the constant rise in freight rates changes the trade of many Third-World states, it will remain high on UNCTAD's agenda in a difficult inflationary world. Of course, the new directions in an ever more competitive shipping trade, which pits the traditional shipping states against: (1) continually increasing flag-of-convenience operations; (2) rapidly expanding commercial shipping of the Socialist states; and (3) the modest fleets of some of the Third-World states will contribute to whatever stability the freight market will experience in the years to come.

*The Future of UNCTAD in World Shipping*

Thus UNCTAD has given ample notice to the shipping world that a major U.N. organ dedicated to correct some of the imbalances in the world's economy is truly on the road to making major changes in the international law and policy of marine transport. With a dedicated and able secretariat, which has become a full-fledged division within UNCTAD, the Committee on Shipping is as yet far from its full potential. Its main product so far, the "Code of Conduct" convention, as important an instrument as it is, is only a sign of future directions. UNCTAD IV, which took place in Nairobi in 1976, did not discuss shipping as a separate agenda item. As already indicated, the world's economic crisis led to crucial discussion on the common-fund mechanism, which occupied almost all of the conference's energies. In any case, UNCTAD III's shipping aim was fully occupying its shipping division and would continue to do so for some time to come. UNCTAD V, meeting at Manila in 1979, provided a further world forum at which many of these questions were discussed. The eighth session of UNCTAD's Committee on Shipping has been preparing since 1977, and has adopted resolutions on and a program of work to study:

1. Fleet development
2. Landlocked developing countries
3. Port problems
4. Freight rates and consultation machinery
5. Technical and financial assistance in shipping and ports[211]

Furthermore, decisions of a more far-reaching nature were also taken by two other resolutions:

1. To convene an ad hoc intergovernmental group to review the economic consequences of the existence or lack of a genuine link between vessel and flag of registry.
2. To review institutional arrangements within the United Nations system on transport problems and to review the terms of reference of the Committee on Shipping.[212]

In other words, both the important area of flags of convenience and that of its own effectiveness will come under the scrutiny of the Committee on Shipping in the future. Undoubtedly, controversial and far-reaching decisions are yet to come.

We should also mention in this connection that UNCTAD has actively taken up the crucial area of transfer of technology, which is the only hope for most of the developing world.[213] The transfer of marine technology has also been taken up by UNCLOS III's Third Committee,[214] although almost all the independent work has been done by UNCTAD.[215] The many problems inherent in this subject range from the usual North-South rhetoric to highly legal and technical difficulties concerning international patent and trademark law.[216] The U.N. Conference on Transfer of Technology for Development, which took place in 1979, discussed without success some of the international problems in this area.[217] Much of the *real* future for the Third World will lie in the ability of the developed states to transfer technology—"the gift that lasts."[218]

Finally, although we see UNCTAD and its shipping interests in positive terms as an important influence in the future of the international law and policy of marine transport, we must also sound a word of caution. Probably more than any other U.N. organ, UNCTAD suffers from the political malaise that affects most of the U.N. system. It is, after all, an organ spawned by discontent and inequality and owes its continued existence to the continuing inequity in the human existence. As such, it is a microcosm of the United Nations as a whole, with all the partisan politics, regional alliances, and other international systems thrown together. In order to be geographically representative, it often casts merit aside; in order to be politically acceptable, it may suppress common sense; in order to appear commercially aware, it may leave policy implications to take care of themselves. It is not a perfect body—far from it—but it appears to work, and for the maritime aspirations of the developing world it is all there is.

### The New Direction of Marine Transport

*Marine Transport in the U.N. System*

Almost as an epilogue to the U.N. system and its interests in the international policy of marine law and transport, we should also mention those organizations, in addition to IMCO, ITU, and UNCTAD, which in one way or another have increasing responsibility in the marine transport field:

1. *The International Bank group* [International Bank for Reconstruction and Development (IBRD); International Development Association (IDA); International Finance Corporation (IFC)]: has a massive impact on port development and on feeder transport systems throughout the world. Bank reports for 1977 indicate investments of $156 million in marine projects, the total cost of which are expected to exceed $500 million.[219]

2. *U.N. Development Program (UNDP)*: the main U.N. developmental funding agency, which supports projects affecting the marine sector implemented through FAO, IMCO, UNCTAD, WMO, and so on.[220]

3. *United Nations Educational, Scientific, and Cultural Organization (UNESCO)*: is involved, among other things, in governmental efforts to promote teaching, study, and research into marine matters through its suborgan, the International Oceanographic Commission (IOC), and bodies such as the Scientific Commission on Oceanic Research (SCOR), the International Council of Scientific Unions (ICSU), and the International Council for the Exploration of the Sea (ICES).[221]

4. *World Meteorological Organization (WMO)*: The elements, which remain the seafarer's greatest challenge, are the responsibility of this organization, which maintains weather stations and forecasts and seeks to spread meteorological information as widely and freely as possible.[222]

5. *International Labor Organization (ILO)*: One of the oldest and most influential specialized agencies in the U.N. system, the ILO has taken over Samuel Plimsoll's task of seeking acceptable working conditions and standards of training and manning for seamen. Its Joint Maritime Committee is concerned with every aspect of the welfare of those who go to sea.[223]

6. *World Health Organization (WHO)*: studies the epidemiology and monitors the quality of coastal waters, supports projects of pollution control, and keeps under review questions regarding the health of seafarers.[224]

7. *International Atomic Energy Agency (IAEA)*: works in conjunction with IMCO regarding the transport of radioactive materials as well as the operation of nuclear ships.[225]

## Marine Transport in the Nongovernmental System

Outside the U.N. system there are many regional organizations, such as the Organization for Economic Co-operation and Development (OECD), which also take a major interest in world shipping. In other words, at the public international level marine transport now comes within the terms of reference of a great variety of bodies and organizations in an ever more complex world. As the world's most important means of trade and communication, marine transport deserves no less.

On the nongovernmental and private side, organization of the marine-transport industry has, not surprisingly, been much less pronounced. Despite its name, the International Chamber of Shipping (ICS), formed in 1921 and said to represent over two-thirds of the world's shipping industry, remains far removed from being the overall spokesman of the industry. Be that as it may, the ICS has generally used a "lobby-like" approach rather than the constructive input that should have emanated from the organization.

The very fact that the operation of shipping on a free-enterprise basis is a precondition for ICS membership explains its philosophy and its approach to protection of the status quo approach.[226] The ICS secretariat is traditionally provided by the staff of one of the ICS's largest and more conservative members, the General Council of British Shipping (GCBS), a senior member of which is always designated as ICS secretary-general. This organization appears to have tremendous potential as a viable part of the international law and policy of marine transport. This potential has not been realized and the ICS has, instead, acquired a reputation, at times deserved, of being a rather shrill pressure group with inflexible attitudes, at forums such as IMCO, UNCTAD, and even UNCLOS III. Its very loose organizational structure, lack of proper funding, and differing international components contribute to its difficulties, which with a little imaginative change could easily be removed. The ICS could then become a strong and respected spokesman for the operational side of shipping, which is presently so badly represented.

Other organizations, such as the International Shipping Federation (ISF); the Council of European and Japanese Shipowners (CENSA); the International Chamber of Commerce (ICC); the EEC Shipowners' Association (CAACE); the Hongkong Shipowners' Association (HKSOA); the Baltic and International Maritime Conference (BIMCO); the International Association of Independent Tanker Owners (INTERTANKO); the Oil Companies' International Marine Forum (OCIMF); and many others all represent particular areas of interest (usually self-interest) in a very fragmented field.[227] The International Union of Marine Insurance (IUMI), which ought to have a very strong voice commensurate to its importance to the ocean business, which cannot operate without adequate insurance coverage, has also never been the contributor to the international law and policy of marine transport that it should have been. Its essentially private and at times almost secretive approach is the incorrect one at a time when all aspects of marine transport are under the scrutiny of a highly politicized critical community of nations. Perhaps the difficulties that international shipping will have to face in the coming years will result in better and closer coordination and less fragmentation of interests in this important group of private organizations.

*Marine Transport and the CMI*

We cannot leave our conclusions, however brief, about the "internationalization" of the law and policy of marine transport without returning to the Comité Maritime International (CMI), to which we have referred frequently. In the latest decade, the CMI continued to be one of the most important influences in the private maritime law-making process of the industry, and its search for greater uniformity would at times even bring it close to the sort of public role it ought to have played long ago. In the last decade the CMI met four times.[228]

XXVIIIth    Conference:   New York 1965
           Agenda:     *Torrey Canyon*—marine pollution
                     Combined transport
                     Coordination of the international convention relating to carriage by sea of passengers and their luggage

XXIXth     Conference:   Antwerp 1972
           Agenda:     Revision of the constitution of the CMI
                     Revision of the 1957 international convention relating to the limitation of liability of owners of seagoing vessels

XXXth      Conference:   Hamburg 1974
           Agenda:     Limitation of the liability of owners of seagoing vessels
                     Revision of York/Antwerp rules 1950
                     Revision of the Hague rules
                     Shipbuilding contracts
                     International maritime arbitration

XXIst       Conference:   Rio de Janeiro 1977
           Agenda:     Unification of certain rules concerning civil jurisdiction, transit law, and recognition and enforcement of judgment in matters of collision
                     Draft international convention on offshore mobile craft
                     Rio de Janeiro charter party (laytime) definitions

Thus one can see at a glance that the CMI is continuing the work it began before the turn of the century. Its methodology appears to be much the same as that which has previously resulted in many fairly widely accepted conventions. A deeper examination reveals, however, that the organization has undergone some important changes in the last decade. As can be seen, the 1972 Antwerp conference had as an agenda item the revision of the CMI constitution. This was because the government of Belgium was no longer prepared to convene the Brussels Diplomatic Conferences, which in the past had provided the apex on which CMI's preparatory work would be con-

verted into international convention. Belgium, quite rightly, felt that the
U.N. system was now more appropriate for providing the forum required.
However, the CMI still had an important leading role to play because

> . . . the private interests which are involved in the vicissitudes to which
> practitioners are daily subjected, be they shipowners, carriers, shippers,
> merchants, importers or exporters, brokers, bankers, average adjusters,
> must continue to make themselves heard as they constitute the base and
> web of the decisions which, on the political, economic and social level,
> Governments are called upon to take.

> As it remains true and is still acknowledged that CMI is, by virtue of its
> structure and vocation, the forum *"par excellence"* which allows those
> voices to express themselves in complete liberty, it is important, nay essen-
> tial, that its scope embrace the greatest number of interested parties
> wherever they come from, without any discrimination, and that a fruitful
> coordination be established between its work and the work of the Instances
> who are responsible on a governmental and intergovernmental level.[229]

It would be interesting, but probably difficult, to conjecture what
would have occurred had the CMI adopted this approach long ago instead
of remaining an isolated and rather exclusive self-interest group. Its "new
skin" could then have been grafted on slowly instead of by force of external
circumstances over which the organization had virtually no control. We
have already referred to the viable contribution of the CMI to the IAEA in
completing the International Convention on the Liability of Operators of
Nuclear Ships. That, obviously, appeared to be the route the CMI had to
take. However, important momentum was lost; and a precious decade
would pass before the CMI decided to take its first substantive inward look
in 1972. By that time it was probably a little too late. IMCO and the post-
*Torrey Canyon* pollution debate presented an opportunity in 1968-1969 that
was, however, not fully exploited because of what was essentially bickering
over liability limits. Nevertheless, IMCO, still convinced of the basic importance and ability of CMI, conferred consultative status on the organization
and some cooperative work, such as on the Limitation of Liability Convention, has existed ever since.[230]
    However, the days when the CMI would be able to singlehandedly pro-
duce a draft convention and see it through to its diplomatic acceptance were
over. The CMI would henceforth be just another private international
nongovernmental organization with an interest in shipping. It is not considered to be a body that can equitably represent *all* aspects of world shipping interests. In particular, out of the present CMI membership of a mere
thirty-three states, only six are from the Third World. Out of the six, five
are long-established Latin American states, and the remaining state is
India.[231] There are no African members at all. Yet at the 1972 Antwerp Conference, the CMI unanimously adopted a new structural reform for the
organization, consisting of:

1. The will to serve all private interests, their own personal requirements as well as their relations with the Government of (sic) which they might depend.

2. The desire to cooperate with the Governmental or Intergovernmental Authorities with a view to seeking and finding common objectives in the field of activities touching the maritime province and sectors connected therewith.

3. An appeal and overture to all interested quarters wherever they come from in any shape or form, to enable them to gain access to an international forum where they shall be able to freely express themselves and ventilate any claims.

4. The establishment of a flexible, efficient and diversified organism—the Executive Council—and the appointment of a highly qualified officer with a view to fostering and fructifying the contacts that are indispensible between the public and the private sector, with the object to serve best the entire community of maritime interests.[232]

It should seem to us that these undoubtedly admirable aims are not realistic, given the present composition of the organization itself, its governing body, its limited funding, and the basic conservatism of its national-association membership. In particular, considering the general international climate, the North-South debate, and the general disarray of world shipping, great difficulties will face the CMI in the future. Owing to the death of the last CMI president, who had been associated with the founder of the organization,[233] the equilibrium of the CMI has shifted from its traditional Belgian base to Italy.[234] Whether the new president, an eminent Italian maritime jurist and scholar, can bring his considerable influence to bear to steer CMI into the mainstream of international maritime law and policy in the late twentieth century remains to be seen. To be sure, the expertise as well as the power base is there, but nowhere is the isolation created by the division between public maritime law and policy and its private counterparts more pronounced than in this organization. Changes will require a very radical restructuring, which are not at all feasible within the present CMI operation. On the other hand, if there are no changes—if the CMI does not broaden its membership, extend its spheres of influence, and widen its consultative status with related intergovernmental bodies—it will simply become one of many self-interest-motivated lobbies, scrambling for an ever-decreasing share of the tenuous resource known as ocean use. As we have already said, the magic words "freedom of the seas" no longer exist.

## Conclusions: The International Law and Policy of Marine Transport in a Changing World

This has been a very far-ranging chapter, which has attempted to pull many aspects of this whole examination together in a loose summary. It is meant to be nothing more. Each section of the final chapter could merit its own full examination. We were merely attempting to pinpoint the present state of international law and policy of marine transport in all its complexities, matched only by the state of the world itself. This last chapter could thus be seen as a beginning rather than as an end. We are ending this examination, begun in prehistory when man the sailor first set out in his frail craft. And we see also the end to an era on which we, as well as marine transport and its law and policy makers, must turn our backs. It has served us well. From reed boat to 400 million tons of ships of every variety in the world—from small craft hugging unknown coasts to the present when no part of the ocean is inaccessible to man—the world has floated to prosperity in a fleet of long-forgotten ships sailed by long-forgotten people. The open road between nation-states and continents has been the ocean, which itself has been the inspiration for freedom and enterprise. Like the great highroads of Europe at its height, the ocean roads had their merchants and traders, as well as their brigands and pirates, and, we should not forget, the slavers who carried whole nations in chains to unknown lands. Violence has never been far from the sea; and ambition, greed, and intolerance have caused much blood to be shed, into the waters of every ocean.

The ocean is thus a great neutralizing element, but one that has seen little equality in its uses. Ocean uses and ocean rules evolving from prehistory have always favored the more powerful nations, and the whole international law and policy of marine transport has evolved accordingly.[235] The "freedom of the seas" ostensibly applied to all states equally in the use of man's greatest resource. In reality, as we have seen, it has never been that simple. Yet such slogans have undoubtedly contributed to the great global prosperity that made every part of the world accessible and every resource obtainable. The marine-transport system evolved and prospered, and all of man's considerable ingenuity was brought to bear on its technical, commercial, and legal development until it appeared that nothing could ever change it. However, milestones of history, such as the Congress of Vienna and World Wars I and II, did herald change; and change there was, both perceptible and imperceptible. The small family club of nations would, within a historically short time, become an extensive community of very unequal states. Political and regional alignments of nations would soon be superseded by geographical groups and economic alliances. All this came at a time when the world's population was heading toward the 6-billion mark, and resources of every kind, whether living or nonliving, were becoming scarcer and of increasing strategic value. Human ingenuity had, of course, also produced weapon systems that could destroy the earth; but this had also led humanity to the frontier of outer space. It seemed that such complexities would force people into a more cooperative attitude with one another and that, accordingly, the era of global conferences would arrive.

However, old rivalries and older differences would persist, and inequities and inequalities would remain. We have simply examined one aspect of these. It is a good example.

Marine transport and the international law and policy that govern it have come a long way from their distant and modest beginnings. As an industry, marine transport evolved as a fiercely independent and private enterprise and over the years proved to the public interest, through its achievements, that it could work that way. Its development was thus left to its own devices and its own rule making. On the other hand, "ocean use," as a whole, requires public rules, which therefore evolved outside the primary transportation-use system. As we have seen, two monoliths were thus created, which in the conference halls of the world of the 1960s and 1970s would address each other in a language neither could understand nor comprehend. Thus marine transport and the laws and policies that regulate and govern it have become victims of its history—the history chronicled herein. Culminating in the still-incomplete Third U.N. Law of the Sea Conference—the most ambitious law-reform attempt so far—marine law and policy has reached the end of an era; new directions must now be taken. This is why we have also spoken of this final chapter as a beginning.

It is a beginning for a new era for marine transport as well as for the rules within which it operates. The ocean industry will have to rise to what may be its greatest challenge ever to become a viable part of twenty-first-century commerce and communication. We are certain that it can do so. Its history is its best reference. As was recently pointed out:

> The drama of merchant shipping's transition from a loosely organized, contentious, nationally-oriented family of small and medium size firms to today's highly mechanized systems-conscious international enterprise has unfolded with remarkable vigor and speed. It represents a global revolution in business methodology analagous to the displacement in the 1930's of the independent grocery by national supermarket chains. That such pervasive changes could be accomplished are indicative of the flexibility and adaptability of shipping institutions.[236]

In order to have a viable future, the division between the public and private aspects of the shipping system must become supportive rather than confrontative. Industry must have an understanding of *overall* national and international marine policy with respect to all competing ocean uses. In particular, there will be no stability in the area as long as the interests of developing states are not taken into account in the board rooms of the world's shipowning, underwriting, and major commercial corporations. If the moral challenge is insufficient, then sound business practice requiring such stability should provide additional incentive. Private maritime law can no longer simply service the needs of what is essentially a powerful minority.

It now has a much larger constituency, and failure to take these additional interests into account will make even the best laws unacceptable, and certainly unenforceable.

For example, on the thorny environmental question, the interests of the community as a whole will have to take precedent over business expediency and traditional practice. On the other hand, the public sector—governments and intergovernmental organizations—must take account of the problems that marine transport faces. Without question, no nation today can expect to build up and maintain a fully competitive fleet solely through its own resources.[237] If there are exceptions today, there will be none tomorrow. The industry's most successful operators today are those who have mobilized capital, vessels, manpower, and markets on an international basis, usually under a flag of convenience. Other exceptions, such as the continued buildup of Socialist state-owned fleets, will exacerbate this problem further and might present a separate challenge to the traditional free-flag operation. In the 1980s, the traditional concept of the wholly national merchant fleet may well become a complete anomaly.[238] This will result in a truly complex and international shipping industry, sensitive to political pressures, trade policies, and regulatory practices.

It has been suggested that in the past the industry has enjoyed a certain mystique and that government policies toward it have been colored by a mixture of national pride and nostalgic recollections of the past.[239] The shipping industry of today and tomorrow is moving, and will move further, away from its romantic and historical roots into the world of transnational business operations. This means that marine transport, and the law and policy within which it operates, must be seen as very similar to other international undertakings operating on a transnational scale. Accordingly, national and international policy must not only recognize this essentially transnational character, but must also protect competition and operation on fair and equal terms, respecting the needs and interests of all who operate within its confines. The establishment of such a climate of cooperation will herald for the international shipping industry the beginning of an era to which there may very well be no end.

## Notes

1. See "Bibliography," section A. In particular the periodically updated U.N. bibliographic series illustrate the large amount of material generated by UNCLOS III. See United Nations, *The Sea: A Select Bibliography on the Legal, Political, Economic, and Technological Aspects*, E/F.76.I.6., New York, 1976. On the other hand, a truly comprehensive, multilanguage bibliography with a regular updating service remains to be compiled.

2. Shigeru Oda, *The Law of the Sea in Our Time*, II. *The United Nations Seabed Committee, 1968-1973* (Leiden: Sijthoff, 1977), p. 3ff.

3. Shigeru Oda, *The Law of the Sea in Our Time*, I. *New Developments, 1966-1975* (Leiden: Sijthoff, 1977), ch. 1.

4. By the late 1960s there were some 150 independent sovereign nations in the world—almost 50 percent of this group had become independent since World War II.

5. Michael T. Barrett, "Issues in International Law Created by the Scientific Development of the Ocean Floor," *Southwestern Law Journal* 19 (1965):97; cf. T.A. Garaioca, "The Continental Shelf and the Extension of the Territorial Sea," *Miami Law Quarterly* 10 (1956):490; and Edwin Borchard, "The Resources of the Continental Shelf," *American Journal of International Law* 40 (1946):53.

6. Oda, *Law of the Sea in our Time*, I, p. 4.

7. Ibid.

8. Francis T. Christy, *The Common Wealth in Ocean Fisheries* (Baltimore, Md.: Johns Hopkins University Press, 1965).

9. The LSI remained at the University of Rhode Island until 1977, when it moved to the University of Hawaii at Honolulu.

10. First LSI Conference Proceedings, 1966. *The Law of the Sea: Offshore Boundaries and Zones*, edited by Lewis M. Alexander (Columbus: University of Ohio Press, 1967). Second LSI Conference Proceedings, 1967. *The Law of the Sea: The Future of the Sea's Resources*, edited by Lewis M. Alexander (Kingston: University of Rhode Island, 1967). Third LSI Conference Proceedings, 1968. *The Law of the Sea: International Rules and Organization for the Sea*, edited by Lewis M. Alexander (Kingston: University of Rhode Island, 1968). Fourth LSI Conference Proceedings, 1969. *The Law of the Sea: National Policy Recommendations*, edited by Lewis M. Alexander (Kingston: University of Rhode Island, 1969). Fifth LSI Conference Proceedings, 1970. *The Law of the Sea: The United Nations and Ocean Management*, edited by Lewis M. Alexander (Kingston: University of Rhode Island, 1970). Sixth LSI Conference Proceedings, 1971. *The Law of the Sea: A New Geneva Conference*, edited by Lewis M. Alexander (Kingston: University of Rhode Island, 1971). Seventh LSI Conference Proceedings, 1972. *The Law of the Sea: Needs and Interests of Developing Countries*, edited by Lewis M. Alexander (Kingston: University of Rhode Island, 1972). Eighth LSI Conference Proceedings, 1973. *Law of the Sea: The Emerging Regime of the Oceans*, edited by John K. Gamble, Jr. and Giulio Pontecorvo (Cambridge, Mass.: Ballinger, 1973). Ninth LSI Conference Proceedings, 1975. *Law of the Sea: Caracas and Beyond*, edited by Francis T. Christy et al. (Cambridge, Mass.: Ballinger, 1975). Tenth LSI Conference Proceedings, 1976. *Law of the Sea: Conference Outcomes and Problems of Implemen-*

*tation*, edited by Edward Miles and John K. Gamble, Jr. (Cambridge, Mass.: Ballinger, 1976). Eleventh LSI Conference Proceedings, 1977. *Regionalization of the Law of the Sea*, edited by Douglas M. Johnston (Cambridge, Mass.: Ballinger, 1978). Twelfth LSI Conference Proceedings, 1978. *Law of the Sea: Neglected Issues*, edited by John K. Gamble, Jr. (Honolulu: University of Hawaii, 1979).

11. Alexander, *First LSI Proceedings*, pp. 299-309.

12. Oda, *Law of the Sea in Our Time*, I, pp. 7-12.

13. Edgar Gold, "The Rise of the Coastal State in the Law of the Sea," in *Marine Policy and the Coastal Community*, edited by D.M. Johnston (London: Croom Helm, 1977), p. 21. For an analysis of this problem see E.D. Brown, *The Legal Regime of Hydrospace* (London: Stevens, 1971), ch. 3.

14. High Seas Convention, art. 6.

15. Continental Shelf Convention, art. 1.

16. Brown, *Legal Regime of Hydrospace*, ch. 3.

17. John L. Mero, "Manganese," *North Dakota Engineer* 27 (1952):28.

18. John L. Mero, *The Mineral Resources of the Sea* (Amsterdam: Elsevier, 1965).

19. Alexander, *First LSI Proceedings*, pp. 310-320.

20. "Law for the Sea's Mineral Resources," cited by Louis Henkin, in *Uses of the Seas*, edited by Edmund A. Gullion (Englewood Cliffs, N.J.: Prentice-Hall, 1968), p. 38.

21. See, for example, Gamble and Pontecorvo, *Eighth LSI Proceedings*.

22. *North Sea Continental Shelf Cases*, [1969] I.C.J. Repts. 3.

23. Gyula Gal, *Space Law* (Leiden: Sijthoff, 1969), p. 283.

24. Oda, *Law of the Sea in Our Time*, II, cited p. 3.

25. Ibid., pp. 3-4.

26. Oda, *Law of the Sea in Our Time*, I, p. 3.

27. Already a misnomer at that time, as some 100 states were members of the group.

28. Ibid.

29. U.N. General Assembly Resolution 2340(xxii), December 18, 1967.

30. Oda, *Law of the Sea in Our Time*, II, p. 7.

31. Ibid.

32. Ibid., pp. 11-48.

33. Ibid., pp. 49-152.

34. Ibid., p. 132ff.

35. U.N. General Assembly Resolution 2749(xxv), December 17, 1971.

36. U.N. General Assembly Resolution 2750 A(xxv), December 17, 1971.

37. U.N. General Assembly Resolution 2750 B(xxv), December 17, 1971.

38. U.N. General Assembly Resolution 2750 C(xxv), December 17, 1971.

39. Ibid.

40. U.N. Doc. A/CONF.62/69.

41. United Nations, *Report of the Committee on the Peaceful Uses of the Sea-Bed and the Ocean Floor Beyond the Limits of National Jurisdiction.* General Assembly, 26th and 27th Sessions. Supplements no. 21 (A/8421 and 8721), 1971 and 1972.

42. Oda, *Law of the Sea in Our Time*, II, pp. 153-300.

43. The recently published *The Law of the Sea in Our Time*, II. *The United Nations Seabed Committee, 1968-1973* compiled and collected by Judge Shigeru Oda is a notable exception.

44. See, for example, Michael A. Morris, "The New International Economic Order and the New Law of the Sea," in *The New International Order*, edited by Karl P. Sauvant and Hajo Hasenpflug (Boulder, Colo.: Westview, 1977), pp. 175-189.

45. Ibid.

46. Ibid.

47. Also with scientific questions relating to marine-scientific research.

48. Douglas M. Johnston and Edgar Gold, *The Economic Zone in the Law of the Sea: Survey, Analysis and Appraisal of Current Trends*, LSI Occ. Paper no. 17 (Kingston: University of Rhode Island, 1973), pp. 6-7.

49. Gerard A. Mangone, *Marine Policy for America* (Lexington, Mass.: Lexington Books, D.C. Heath and Company, 1977), p. 206.

50. *Ninth LSI Conference Proceedings*, pp. 136ff.

51. T.M. Franck, M. El Baradei, and G. Aron, "The New Poor: Land-Locked, Shelf-Locked and Other Geographically Disadvantaged States," *New York University Journal of International Law and Policy* 7 (1974):33.

52. John K. Gamble, Jr., *Global Marine Attributes* (Cambridge, Mass.: Ballinger, 1974), p. 191.

53. *Tenth LSI Conference Proceedings*, p. 133ff.

54. A.L. Danzig, "A Funny Thing Happened to the Common Heritage on the Way to the Sea," *San Diego Law Review* 12 (1975):655.

55. Gold, "The Rise of the Coastal State," p. 29.

56. U.N. Doc. A/CONF. 62/69.

57. Edgar Gold, "The Third United Nations Conference on the Law of the Sea: The Caracas Session, 1974," *Maritime Studies and Management* 2 (1974):102, 104.

58. Ibid.

59. Ibid.; John R. Stevenson and Bernard G. Oxman, "The Third United Nations Conference on the Law of the Sea: The 1964 Caracas Session," *American Journal of International Law* 69 (1975):1.

60. Edgar Gold, "The Third United Nations Conference on the Law of the Sea: The Geneva Session, 1975," *Maritime Studies and Management* 3 (1975):117; John R. Stevenson and Bernard G. Oxman, "The Third United Nations Conference on the Law of the Sea: The 1975 Geneva Session," *American Journal of International Law* 69 (1975):763.

61. United Nations, *Third U.N. Conference on the Law of the Sea.* Official Records, vol. 4, 1975, p. 137 (DOC. A/CONF. 62/WP.8).

62. Edgar Gold, "The Third United Nations Conference on the Law of the Sea: The 4th and 5th Sessions, New York 1976," *Maritime Policy and Management* 4 (1977):171.

63. Ibid.; Edgar Gold, "The Third United Nations Conference on the Law of the Sea: The Sixth Session, New York 1977," *Maritime Policy and Management* 5 (1978):63.

64. Informal Composite Negotiating Text/Revision 1. U.N. DOC. A/CONF.62/WP.10/Rev. 1, April 28, 1979.

65. Informal Composite Negotiating Text/Revision 2 U.N. DOC. A/CONF.62/WP.10/Rev. 2, April 11, 1980; and Draft Convention on the Law of the Sea (Informal Text). U.N. DOC. A/CONF.62/WP.10/Rev. 3, August 27, 1980.

66. Edgar Gold, "The 'Freedom' of Ocean Shipping and Commercial Viability," in *Law of the Sea: Neglected Issues*, edited by John K. Gamble. Proceedings, Law of the Sea Institute Twelfth Annual Conference (University of Hawaii, Honolulu, 1979), pp. 248-258.

67. Ibid., p. 255.

68. Ibid.

69. E. Lauterpacht, "Freedom of Transit in International Law," *Grotius Society Transactions* 44 (1958-1959), cited p. 313.

70. Draft Convention on the Law of the Sea (Informal Text), Part VII.

71. Ibid., art. 91. It is of considerable interest to note in this connection that the shipping deliberations of UNCTAD V in Manila, 1979, resulted in several resolutions aimed at reducing the "open-registry" problem. One of these, proposed by the Soviet bloc Group D called for "criteria for a genuine link between vessels and their countries of registry. . . ." See Editorial, "High Stakes in Manila," *Seatrade* 9 (June 1979):3, 4.

72. Draft Convention on the Law of the Sea (Informal Text), Part XII.

73. Gold, "Ocean Shipping and Commercial Viability," p. 256.

74. J. Wardley-Smith, ed. *The Control of Oil Pollution* (London: Graham and Trotman, 1976).

75. Draft Convention on the Law of the Sea (Informal Text), Part XII, Sections 6 and 7.

76. Gold, "Ocean Shipping and Commercial Viability," p. 257.

77. Edgar Gold, "New Directions in International Maritime Law," in *Proceedings of the Nautical Institute Conference on International Shipping* (London: Nautical Institute, 1979).

78. D.M. Johnston, "Marine Pollution Control: Law, Science and Politics," *International Journal* 28 (1972-1973):69.

79. E.D. Brown, "The Conventional Law of the Environment," *Natural Resources Journal* 12 (1973):203.

80. James Barros and Douglas M. Johnston, *The International Law of Pollution* (New York: Free Press, 1974), p. xv.

81. Kenneth A. Hammond, George Macinko, and Wilma B. Fairchild, eds. *Sourcebook on the Environment: A Guide to the Literature* (Chicago: University of Chicago Press, 1978); Margaret Galey, *Marine Environmental Affairs Bibliography*, Special Publication no. 6, Law of the Sea Institute: University of Rhode Island, 1977.

82. J.J. Greene, "Policy on the Environment," *University of Toronto Law Journal* 21 (1971):241, 242.

83. Ibid.

84. See "The Environment," in "Issues before the 26th General Assembly," *International Conciliation* no. 584, September 1971, p. 73.

85. Ibid.

86. Ibid., p. 72.

87. U.N. General Assembly Resolution 2398(xxiii), December 3, 1968.

88. "Issues before the 26th General Assembly," p. 72.

89. U.N. General Assembly Resolution 2581(xxiv), December 18, 1969.

90. Ibid.

91. "Issues before the 26th General Assembly," p. 74.

92. United Nations, *Report of the United Nations Conference on the Human Environment*, Stockholm, 1972. E.73.II.A.14 (1973).

93. Johnston, "Marine Pollution Control," p. 70.

94. Arthur S. Banks, ed. *Political Handbook of the World: 1977* (New York: McGraw-Hill, 1978), p. 543.

95. Johnston, "Marine Pollution Control," p. 89ff.

96. Ibid.

97. *UNEP Report*, p. 48.

98. *Report of the Intergovernmental Working Group on Marine Pollution on its Second Session.* U.N. DOC.A/CONF.48/1WGMP.II/5., p. 7.

99. Johnston, "Marine Pollution Control," p. 90.

100. Ibid.

101. Ibid.

102. *Proceedings, Intergovernmental Working Group on Marine Pollution, Ottawa 1971.* Cited Ibid., p. 91.

103. L.H.J. Legault, "The Freedom of the Seas: A License to Pollute?" *University of Toronto Law Journal* 21 (1971):210.

104. IMCO, "Where the Oil was Spilled: 1962-1978," *IMCO News* 1 (1979):12-13.

105. Usually in the form of coagulated tarry lumps. See ICS/OCIMF, *Clean Seas Guide for Oil Tankers* (London: ICS, 1978).

106. Nicholas J. Healy, "The International Convention on Civil Liability for Oil Pollution," *Journal of Maritime Law and Commerce* 1 (1969-1970):317.

107. Robert A. Shinn, *The International Politics of Marine Pollution Control* (New York: Praeger, 1974).

108. A.D. Couper, *The Geography of Sea Transport* (London: Hutchinson, 1972), p. 110.

109. Ibid.

110. Ibid.

111. Ibid., p. 113.

112. Ibid., p. 114.

113. Ibid., cited p. 115.

114. ULCC is usually a tanker with a deadweight tonnage over 300,000 tons.

115. C. Ernest Fayle, *A Short History of the World's Shipping Industry* (London: Allen and Unwin, 1933), p. 294 et seq.

116. Couper, *Geography of Sea Transport*, p. 117.

117. Plans were scrapped because of the impending shipping slump of the late 1970s.

118. What to do with idle VLCCs and ULCCs was a new problem that had received almost no consideration before the slump.

119. Couper, *Geography of Sea Transport*, p. 121.

120. Report, *Royal Commission: Pollution of Canadian Waters by Oil and Formal Investigation into Grounding of Steam Tanker 'ARROW'* (Ottawa: Information Canada, 1971). See also "Where the Oil was Spilled," *IMCO News* 1 (1979):12-13.

121. "In Chile's Strait of Magellan." *IMCO News* 1 (1979):12-13.

122. "Off Nantucket Shoal on the U.S. East Coast and in San Pedro, California," *IMCO News* 1 (1979):12-13

123. "Off the Northwest Coast of France," *IMCO News* 1 (1979):12-13.

124. "In Bantry Bay, Ireland," *IMCO News* 1 (1979):12-13.

125. Noel Mostert, *Supership*. A recent serious disaster involving a collision between two VLCCs, the *Atlantic Empress* and the *Aegean Captain* in the Caribbean, appears to lend credence to the continuing danger of major oil spills.

126. *IMCO News* 1 (1979):18.

127. As was evident from the deliberation of the recent IMCO Conference on Standards of Training, Certification and Watchkeeping for Seafarers.

128. International Convention on Standards of Training, Certification and Watchkeeping for Seafarers, 1978.

129. IMCO, *IMCO and Its Activities* (London: IMCO, 1978), p. 19.

130. OECD, *Maritime Transport 1977*, p. 135.

131. IMCO, *IMCO and Its Activities*, pp. 14-17.

132. Tanker Construction revisions were put forward as far back as 1968, after the *Torrey Canyon* disaster.

133. R.S. Doganis and B.N. Metaxas, *The Impact of Flags of Convenience* (London: Polytechnic of Central London, 1976), p. 109.

134. Banks, *Political Handbook 1977*, p. 560.

135. For example, the Convention on International Regulations for Preventing Collisions at Sea, 1972, in force since July 15, 1977, does not even make the fitting of radar compulsory on board ships.

136. C.T. Grammenos, *Bank Finance for Ship Purchasing* (Bangor: University of Wales Press, 1979).

137. Usually serving on merchant and fishing vessels in lieu of compulsory military service.

138. Usually in Scandinavian countries.

139. OECD, *Maritime Transport 1978*, p. 152.

140. Donald A. Kerr and Edgar Gold, "Flags of Convenience: The 'Offshore' Registration of Ships," in *New Directions in Maritime Law 1978*, edited by Edgar Gold (Halifax: Dalhousie Univesity, Faculty of Law, 1978), pp. 85-103.

141. Ibid.

142. Ibid.

143. OECD, *Maritime Transport 1977*, pp. 13-14.

144. See Founex Report, *Environment and Development. International Conciliation* no. 586 (1972).

145. The marine-insurance industry, having been a strong member of the CMI, has basically followed that organization's general philosophy.

146. The London market controls between 65 and 75 percent of marine-insurance "invisibles."

147. Edgar Gold, *Oil Pollution: A Survey of Worldwide Legislation* (Arendal: Assuranceforeningen Gard, 1971).

148. Ibid.; see also *IMCO News* 4 (1978):4-5.

149. Ibid.

150. Ibid.

151. Ibid.

152. Present claims, related to the *Amoco Cadiz* disaster, stand at over $1 billion.

153. See Convention on the Limitation of Liability for Maritime Claims, 1976.

154. Ibid.; see also F.J.J. Cadwallader, "The New Convention on Limitation on Liability," in *New Directions in Maritime Law 1978*, edited by Edgar Gold, pp. 5-19.

155. Healy, "International Convention on Civil Liability."

156. *IMCO News* 4 (1978):4-5.

157. Such as oil pollution in "ice-infested" waters.

158. See IMCO, *IMCO and its Activities*.

159. Hong Kong is an associate member.

160. *Lloyd's Nautical Yearbook and Calendar, 1979* (London: Lloyd's, 1979), p. 311.

161. Ibid., p. 313.

162. Ibid.

163. Ibid., pp. 314-315.

164. Ibid., p. 313.

165. Ibid., p. 312.

166. Ibid., pp. 313-314.

167. Robin Churchill, "Why do Marine Pollution Conventions take so long to enter into Force?" *Maritime Policy and Management* 4 (1976):41.

168. *Lloyd's Nautical Year Book*, p. 311.

169. Ibid., p. 312.

170. Ibid.

171. J.D. Parker, "International Radio Communications at Sea: Order or Chaos for the Next 25 Years?" *Proceedings, Nautical Institute Conference on International Shipping* (London: Nautical Institute, 1979).

172. *Lloyd's Nautical Year Book*, p. 312.

173. Ibid., pp. 312-313.

174. Ibid., p. 312.

175. Ibid., p. 315.

176. IMCO, *IMCO and its Activities*, pp. 19-21.

177. *IMCO News* 4 (1978):6-7.

178. We have already referred to the CMI's basic philosophy vis-à-vis "public" matters. In addition, the CMI's modest secretarial infrastructure and budget permits very little public involvement.

179. Mr. C.P. Srivastava, of India.

180. B. Gosovic, *UNCTAD: Conflict and Compromise* (Leiden: Sijthoff, 1972), pp. 80-83.

181. Report and Annexes, *UNCTAD—Third Session, Santiago de Chile*, vol. 1; Report and Annexes, *UNCTAD—Fourth Session, Nairobi*; Editorial, "High Stakes at Manila," *Seatrade* 9 (June 1979):3.

182. Gosovic, *UNCTAD*.

183. See UNCTAD, "Economic Co-operation Among Developing Countries," in *The New International Order*, edited by Sauvant and Hasenpflug, p. 437ff.

184. Ibid.

185. Report, *UNCTAD—Fourth Session, Nairobi*. UNCTAD Doc. TD/217.

186. R.A. Ramsay, "The Organization of Shipping," in *Ocean Yearbook I*, edited by Elisabeth Mann Borgese and Norton Ginsburg (Chicago: University of Chicago Press, 1978), p. 211ff.

187. The developed states of the OECD.

188. Gosovic, *UNCTAD*, pp. 24-28.

189. Ibid.

190. Ibid.

191. Ibid., pp. 248-249.

192. In an interview with the late Dr. W.R. Malinowski, the head of UNCTAD's Shipping Division in 1973, we had this point specifically confirmed.

193. IMCO gives observer status to all marine-oriented organizations and attempts close liaison with the CMI.

194. See Report and Annexes, *UNCTAD—Third Session, Santiago*.

195. S.G. Sturmey, "The Development of the Code of Conduct for Liner Conferences," *Marine Policy* 3 (1979):133.

196. S.G. Sturmey, *British Shipping and World Competition* (London: Athlone Press, 1962), p. 322.

197. Gosovic, *UNCTAD*, pp. 142-143.

198. Convention on a Code of Conduct for Liner Conferences; see *International Legal Materials* 13 (1974):912.

199. Gosovic, *UNCTAD*, p. 143. n. 20.

200. Sturmey, "Development of the Code of Conduct," p. 139.

201. Ibid.

202. OECD, *Maritime Transport 1977*, p. 16.

203. It has recently been announced that the EEC states have indeed acceded to the new convention on May 8, 1979. However, the EEC decision was to ratify a modified version of the code. See Editorial, "High Stakes in Manila," *Seatrade* 9 (June 1979):3.

204. Ramsay, "Organization of Shipping"; see also Report and Annexes, *UNCTAD—Third Session, Santiago*, vol. 1, p. 261ff.

205. Ibid., pp. 262-263.

206. Ibid., pp. 263-267.

207. Although shipping statistics are usually at least 12-18 months behind, there is every indication that the desired figure will not be reached.

208. Report and Annexes, *UNCTAD—Third Session, Santiago*, vol. 1, pp. 266-267.

209. Ibid., pp. 267-269.

210. Gosovic, *UNCTAD*, p. 142.

211. C. French, "Poor Nations may rock the Boat at Manila Conference," *Globe and Mail* (Toronto), March 22, 1979, p. B10.

212. Ibid. Unfortunately, UNCTAD V in this area was inconclusive but laid the groundwork for much further work and debate. See Editorial, "High Stakes in Manila," *Seatrade* 9 (June 1979):3.

213. Edgar Gold, "The International Transfer and Promotion of Technology," in *The International Law and Policy of Human Welfare*, edited by R. St.J. Macdonald, D.M. Johnston, and G.L. Morris (Alphen aan den Rijn: Sijthoff and Noordhoff, 1978), pp. 549-582.

214. Ibid., pp. 562-567.

215. UNCTAD, *Guidelines for the Study of the Transfer of Technology to Developing Countries*. Doc. E.72.II.D.19. (1972).

216. D. Lall, "The Patent Systems and the Transfer of Technology to Less Developed Countries," *Journal of World Trade Law* 10 (1976):1.

217. The Conference met in September 1979 in Vienna, Austria.

218. Gold, "Transfer of Technology," p. 575.

219. Banks, *Political Handbook of the World: 1977*, pp. 558-559.

220. Ibid., p. 542.

221. Ibid., pp. 567-568.

222. Ibid., pp. 571-572.

223. Ibid., pp. 562-564.

224. Ibid., pp. 569-570.

225. Ibid., p. 574.

226. Nagendra Singh and Raoul Colinvaux, *Shipowners*, British Shipping Laws, vol. 13 (London: Stevens, 1967), pp. 145-148.

227. *Lloyd's Nautical Year Book 1979*, pp. 325-333.

228. Albert Lilar and Carlo van den Bosch, *Le Comité Maritime International* (Anvers: CMI, 1972), pp. 115-116; CMI, *Documentation* (Anvers: CMI, 1972-1979).

229. Lilar and van den Bosch, *Le Comité Maritime International*, pp. 98-100.

230. CMI, *Documentation 1972-1979*.

231. Argentina, Brazil, Chile, Colombia, Mexico, Peru, Venezuela. See also CMI, *Yearbook 1978* (Anvers: CMI, 1978).

232. Lilar and van den Bosch, *Comité Maritime International*, pp. 104-105.

233. Albert Lilar of Belgium.

234. Francesco Berlingieri of Italy.

235. Edgar Gold, "The Rise of the Coastal State in the Law of the Sea," in *Marine Policy and the Coastal Community*, edited by D.M. Johnston (London: Croom Helm, 1976), p. 17.

236. S.A. Lawrence, *International Sea Transport: The Years Ahead* (Lexington, Mass.: Lexington Books, D.C. Heath and Co., 1972), p. 253.

237. Ibid.

238. Ibid.

239. Ibid., p. 254.

# Bibliography

This bibliography is not intended to be comprehensive enough to cover adequately *all* the areas studied in this book. It is, however, intended to indicate the sources consulted for research and reference.

For convenience, the bibliography has been divided into thirteen categories. However, each book, document, or article is (with a few exceptions) only included once. It is likely that in many cases sources might easily fit into two or more categories. In such cases inclusion will be in the category in which the source has made its major contribution.

A. Anthologies, bibliographies, yearbooks, encyclopedias
B. General world history: Sources and general works
C. The ocean: Geography, science, and technology
D. Maritime history: General works
E. Maritime history: Law and policy
F. International law and policy: Sources and general works
G. International law and policy of the sea
H. Maritime law and policy
I. Maritime commerce and economics
J. Ocean-resources law and policy
K. Marine-environmental law and policy
L. Intergovernmental and governmental documents
M. United Nations documents

## A. Anthologies, Bibliographies, Yearbooks, Encyclopedias

Banks, Arthur S. *Political Handbook of the World: 1978*. New York: McGraw-Hill, 1978.

"Bibliography of Marine Affairs I and II." *Ocean Management* 2 (1974-1975):147, 267.

Blaustein, A.P., and Beede, B.R. "African Legal Periodicals: A Bibliography." *African Legal Studies* 11 (1974):71.

Delupis, Ingrid. *Bibliography of International Law*. London: Bowker, 1975.

Firth, Frank E., ed. *The Encyclopedia of Marine Resources*. New York: Van Nostrand, 1969.

Galey, Margaret. *Marine Environmental Affairs Bibliography*. Special Publication no. 6. Law of the Sea Institute, University of Rhode Island, 1977.

Gamble, John K., Jr. *Global Marine Attributes*. Cambridge, Mass.: Ballinger, 1974.

Hammond, Kenneth A.; Macinko, George; and Fairchild, Wilma B. *Sourcebook on the Environment: A Guide to the Literature*. Chicago, Ill., University of Chicago Press, 1978.

Hollick, Ann L. *Marine Policy, Law and Economics. Annotated Bibliography*. Kingston, R.I.: Law of the Sea Institute, 1970 (1st supplement, 1971).

Koers, Albert W. *The Debate on the Legal Regime for the Exploration and Exploitation of Ocean Resources: A Bibliography for the First Decade, 1960-1970*. Special Publication no. 1. Law of the Sea Institute, University of Rhode Island, 1970.

Langer, William L., ed. *An Encyclopedia of World History*. 4th ed. Boston: Houghton Mifflin, 1968.

Lay, S.H.; Churchill, Robin; and Nordquist, Myron, eds. *New Directions in the Law of the Sea*. 8 vols. Dobbs Ferry, N.Y.: Oceana, 1973-1979.

*Lloyd's Nautical Yearbook and Calendar*. London, 1979.

Mann Borgese, Elisabeth, and Ginsburg, Norton. *Ocean Yearbook 1*. Chicago: University of Chicago Press, 1978.

Mathias, P., and Pearsall, A.W.H. *Shipping: A Survey of Historical Records*. Newton Abbot: David and Charles, 1971.

*Ocean Affairs Bibliography*. Ocean Series 302. Woodrow Wilson International Center for Scholars, Washington, D.C., 1971.

Oda, Shigeru, ed. *The International Law of the Ocean Development—Basic Documents*. 4 vols. Alphen aan den Rijn: Sijthoff, 1972-1978.

Pfeil, Helena P. von. *Oceans, Coasts and Law: Holdings of Eighteen Libraries with Union List, Plus Selected Additional Books, Papers, Foreign and U.S. Articles Categorized by Topic*. 2 vols. Dobbs Ferry, N.Y.: Oceana, 1976.

Syatauw, J.J.G. *Decisions of The International Court of Justice—A Digest*. Leiden: Sijthoff, 1969.

Szekely, Alberto. *Bibliography on Latin America and the Law of the Sea*. Special Publication no. 5. Law of the Sea Institute, University of Rhode Island, 1976.

"The Law of the Sea: A Selective Bibliography of Articles, Documents and Monographs." *Columbia Journal of Transnational Law* 13 (1974):173.

United Nations. *The Sea: Legal and Political Aspects. A Select Bibliography*. E/F.74.I.9. New York, 1974.

————. *The Sea: A Select Bibliography on the Legal, Political, Economic, and Technological Aspects*. E/F.76.I.6. New York, 1976.

Wigmore, John H. *A Panorama of the World's Legal Systems*, vols. I and II. St. Paul, Minn.: West Publishing Co., 1928.

## B. General World History: Sources and General Works

Bailyn, Bernard, Davis, David B., Donald, David H., Thomas, John L., Wiebe, Robert H., Wood, Gordon S., *The Great Republic. A History of the American People.* Toronto: Little, Brown, 1977.

Bibby, Geoffrey. *Looking for Dilmun.* New York: Knopf, 1969.

Braudel, Fernand. *The Mediterranean.* 2 vols. New York: Harper and Row, 1972-1973.

Craig, Gordon A. *Germany 1866-1945.* New York: Oxford University Press, 1978.

Condliffe, J.B. *The Commerce of Nations.* New York: Norton, 1950.

Davidson, Basil. *Let Freedom Come. Africa in Modern History.* Boston, Mass.: Little, Brown, 1978.

Day, Clive. *A History of Commerce.* 2nd ed. New York: Longman's, Green, 1919.

Galbraith, John Kenneth. *The Age of Uncertainty.* London: André Deutsch, 1977.

Grant, Michael. *History of Rome.* New York: Scribner, 1978.

Hagen, Victor W. von. *The Ancient Sun Kingdoms of the Americas.* New York: World Publishers, 1957.

Herm, Gerhard. *The Phoenicians: The Purple Empire of the Ancient World.* New York: Morrow, 1975.

Horne, Alistair. *A Savage War for Peace: Algeria 1954-1962.* New York: Viking, 1977.

James, R.R. *The British Revolution 1880-1934.* New York: Knopf, 1977.

Jones, Gwyn. *A History of the Vikings.* London: Oxford University Press, 1968.

July, Robert W. *A History of the African People.* 2nd ed. New York: Scribner, 1974.

Landels, J.G. *Engineering in the Ancient World.* Berkeley: University of California Press, 1978.

Lane, Frederic C. *Venice, A Maritime Republic.* Baltimore, Md.: Johns Hopkins University Press, 1973.

Louis, William Roger. *Imperialism at Bay. The United States and the Decolonization of the British Empire, 1941-1945.* New York: Oxford University Press, 1978.

Mansfield, Peter. *The Arab World—A Comprehensive History.* New York: Crowell, 1976.

Merk, Frederick. *History of the Westward Movement.* New York: Knopf, 1978.

Pallottino, Massimo. *The Etruscans.* Edited by D. Ridgway. Bloomington: Indiana University Press, 1975.

Reischauer, Edwin O. *The Japanese*. Cambridge, Mass.: Harvard University Press, 1977.

Sealey, Raphael. *A History of the Greek City States: 700-338 B.C.* Berkeley: University of California Press, 1976.

Seton-Watson, Hugh. *Nations and States*. Boulder, Colo.: Westview, 1977.

Sherwood, Robert E. *Roosevelt and Hopkins: An Intimate History*. New York: Harper Brothers, 1948.

Stern, Fritz. *Gold and Iron: Bismarck, Bleichröder and the Building of the German Empire*. New York: Knopf, 1977.

Thomas, Hugh. *The Spanish Civil War*. Rev. ed. New York: Harper and Row, 1977.

Wolpert, Stanley, *A New History of India*. New York: Oxford University Press, 1977.

## C. The Ocean: Geography, Science, and Technology

Beattie, J.H. "Traffic Routing at Sea, 1857-1977." *Journal of Navigation* 31 (1978):167.

Bello, E. "The Present State of Marine Science and Oceanography in the Less Developed Countries." *International Lawyer* 8 (1974):231.

Brophy, Patrick. *Sailing Ships*. London: Hamlyn, 1974.

Cockcroft, A.N., and Lameijer, J.N. *A Guide to the Collison Avoidance Rules*. 2nd ed. London: Stanford Maritime, 1976.

Cotter, Charles H. *The Atlantic Ocean*. Glasgow: Brown, Son and Ferguson, 1974.

Deacon, G.E.R., gen. ed. *Oceans*. 2nd ed. Toronto: Hamlyn, 1968.

Engel, Leonard. *The Sea*. New York: Time-Life Inc., 1961.

Freuchen, Peter. *Peter Freuchen's Book of the Seven Seas*. London: Jonathan Cape, 1958.

Horsfield, Brenda, and Stone, Peter B. *The Great Ocean Business*. London: Hodder and Stoughton, 1972.

Kay, David. "International Transfer of Marine Technology: The Transfer Process and International Organizations." *Ocean Development and International Law* 2 (1974-1975):351.

King, Cuchlaine A.M. *Introduction to Physical and Biological Oceanography*. London: Edward Arnold, 1975.

La Feber, Walter. *The Panama Canal. The Crisis in Historical Perspective*. New York: Oxford University Press, 1978.

McCulloch, David. *The Path Between the Seas. The Creation of the Panama Canal, 1870-1914*. New York: Simon and Schuster, 1977.

Moorehead, Alan. *Darwin and the Beagle*. New York: Harper and Row, 1964.

Mostert, Noel. *Supership*. London: Macmillan, 1975.

Munro-Smith, R. *Merchant Ship Types*. London: Marine Media Management, 1975.

———. *Ships and Naval Architecture*. London: Institute of Marine Engineers, 1973.

*Oceanology International '78*. Special issue. *Ocean Management* 4 (1978):107.

Page, R.C., and Gardner, A. Ward. *Petroleum Tankship Safety*. London: Maritime Press, 1971.

Parker, John F. *Sails of the Maritimes*. Aylesbury: Hazell, Watson, 1961.

Phillips-Birt, Douglas. *A History of Seamanship*. London: Allan and Unwin, 1971.

*Safety at Sea*. Proceedings of the 2nd West European Conference on Marine Technology, 1977. London: Royal Institute of Naval Architects, 1977.

*Safety in Shipping*. A Seatrade Study. London: Seatrade, 1978.

Schlee, Susan. *The Edge of an Unfamiliar World: A History of Oceanography*. New York: Dutton, 1973.

Smith, Robert W. "An Analysis of the Strategic Attributes of International Straits." *Maritime Studies and Management* 2 (1974):88.

Taylor, L.G. *Seaports: An Introduction to their Place and Purpose*. Glasgow: Brown, Son and Ferguson, 1974.

Villiers, Allan. *Man, Ships and the Sea*. Washington: National Geographic, 1973.

Wooster, Warren S., ed. *Freedom of Oceanic Research*. New York: Crane, Russak, 1973.


## D. Maritime History: General Works

Allen, Oliver E. *The Windjammers*. Alexandria, Va.: Time-Life, 1978.

Bass, George F. *Archeology Beneath the Sea*. New York: Walker and Co., 1975.

———, ed. *A History of Seafaring—Based on Underwater Archeology*. New York: Walker and Co., 1972.

Beaglehole, J.C. *The Life of Captain James Cook*. Stanford, Calif.: Stanford University Press, 1974.

Botting, Douglas. *The Pirates*. Alexandria, Va.: Time-Life, 1978.

Burwash, Dorothy. *English Merchant Shipping: 1460-1560*. Toronto: University of Toronto Press, 1947.

Casson, Lionel. *The Ancient Mariners*. New York: Macmillan, 1959.

———. *Ships and Seamanship in the Ancient World*. Princeton, N.J.: Princeton University Press, 1971.

Cavendish, Marshall. *The History of the Sailing Ship*. New York: Arco Publications, 1975.

Cipolla, Carlo M. *Guns, Sails and Empires*. New York: Pantheon, 1965.

Colby, Charles C. *North Atlantic Arena*. Water Transport in the World Order. Carbondale: Southern Illinois University Press, 1966.

Cornewall-Jones, R.J. *The British Merchant Service*. London: Sampson, Low and Marston, 1898.

Culican, William. *The First Merchant Venturers: The Ancient Levant in History and Commerce*. London: Thames and Hudson, 1966.

Davis, Charles G. *Ships of the Past*. New York: Bonanza Books, 1929.

Davis, Ralph. *The Rise of the English Shipping Industry in the 17th and 18th Centuries*. London: Macmillan, 1962.

Fayle, C. Ernest. *A Short History of the World's Shipping Industry*. London: Allan and Unwin, 1933.

Howarth, David. *Sovereign of the Seas: The Story of Britain and the Sea*. New York: Atheneum, 1974.

_____ . *The Men-of-War*. Alexandria, Va.: Time-Life, 1978.

Hughes, Terry, and Costello, John. *The Battle of the Atlantic*. New York: Dial, 1977.

Humble, Richard. *The Explorers*. Alexandria, Va.: Time-Life, 1978.

LeScal, Yves. *The Great Days of the Cape Horners*. New York: New American Library, 1966.

Lewis, Archibald R. *Naval Power and Trade in the Mediterranean—A.D. 500-1100*. Princeton, N.J.: Princeton University Press, 1951.

Lucie-Smith, Edward. *Outcasts of the Sea—Pirates and Piracy*. New York: Paddington, 1978.

Maddocks, Melvin. *The Great Liners*. Alexandria, Va.: Time-Life, 1978.

Mitchell, Donald W. *A History of Russian and Soviet Seapower*. New York: Macmillan, 1974.

Morison, Samuel E. *Admiral of the Ocean Sea. A Life of Christopher Columbus*. 2 vols. New York: Time, 1962.

_____ . *The European Discovery of America: The Northern Voyages*. New York: Oxford University Press, 1971.

_____ . *The European Discovery of America: The Southern Voyages*. New York: Oxford University Press, 1974.

Pitt, Barrie. *The Battle of the Atlantic*. New York: Time-Life, 1977.

Randier, Jean. *Man and Ships around Cape Horn*. New York: McKay, 1969.

Rao, S.R. "Shipping and the Maritime Trade of the Indus People." *Expedition* 7 (1965):30.

Stevens, W.O., and Westcott, A. *A History of Sea Power*. New York: Doubleday, 1944.

Villiers, Allan. *Captain James Cook*. New York: Scribner, 1967.

Walder, David. *Nelson—A Biography*. New York: Dial, 1978.

Wernick, Robert. *The Vikings*. Alexandria, Va.: Time-Life, 1979.

Whipple, A.B.C. *Fighting Sail*. Alexandria, Va.: Time-Life, 1978.

Williamson, J.A. *The Ocean in English History*. Oxford: Clarendon, 1941.

Wilson, Derek. *The World Encompassed. Francis Drake and his Great Voyage*. New York: Harper and Row, 1977.

### E. Maritime History: Law and Policy

Alexandrowicz, C.H. "Freitas Versus Grotius." *British Year Book of International Law* 35 (1959):162.

Barclay, Thomas. "The Antwerp Congress and the Assimilation of Mercantile Law." *Law Quarterly Review* 2 (1886):66.

Benedict, Robert D. "The Historical Position of the Rhodian Law." *Yale Law Journal* 18 (1909):223.

Bradshaw, Richard E. "The Politics of Soviet Maritime Security: Soviet Legal Doctrine and the Status of Coastal Waters." *Journal of Maritime Law and Commerce* 10 (1979):411.

Brown, Philip Marshall. "Editorial Comment: 'The Law of Territorial Waters'." *American Journal of International Law* 21 (1927):101.

Cohen, Edward E. *Ancient Athenian Maritime Courts*. Princeton, N.J.: Princeton University Press, 1973.

Comment, "Territorial Seas—3000 Year Old Question." *Journal of Air Law and Commerce* 36 (1970):73.

Crecraft, E.W. *Freedom of the Seas*. Freeport, N.Y.: Books for Libraries Press, 1935.

Crichton, G.H. "Grotius on the Freedom of the Seas." *Juridical Review* 53 (1941):226.

DePauw, Frans. *Grotius and the Law of the Sea*. Brussels: Université de Bruxelles, 1965.

Dumbauld, Edward. *The Life and Legal Writings of Hugo Grotius*. Norman: University of Oklahoma Press, 1969.

Franck, Louis. "Collision at Sea in Relation to International Maritime Law." *Law Quarterly Review* 12 (1896):260.

Fulton, Thomas W. *The Sovereignty of the Sea*. London: Blackwood, 1911.

Galibourg, Henri. *L'Unification du droit maritime commercial*. Angers: J. Siraudeau, 1912.

Gormley, W. Paul. "The Development of the Rhodian-Roman Maritime Law to 1681—With Special Emphasis on the Problem of Collision." *Inter-American Law Review* 3 (1961):317.

_____ . "The Development and Subsequent Influence of the Roman Legal Norm of 'Freedom of the Seas'." *University of Detroit Law Journal* 40 (1963):561.

_____ . "The Unilateral Extension of Territorial Waters: The Failure of the United Nations to Protect Freedom of the Seas." *University of Detroit Law Journal* 43 (1966):695.

Hale, Richard W. "Territorial Waters as a Test of Codification." *American Journal of International Law* 24 (1930):65.

Hjertonsson, Karin. *The New Law of the Sea: Influence of the Latin American States on Recent Developments in the Law of the Sea*. Leiden: Sijthoff, 1973.

Ito, Fujio. "The Thought of Hugo Grotius in the *Mare Liberum*." *Japanese Annual of International Law* 18 (1974):1.

Jados, Stanley S. *Consulate of the Sea and Related Documents*. University, Ala.: University of Alabama Press, 1975.

Johnson, D.H.N. "The Geneva Conference on the Law of the Sea." *Year Book of World Affairs* 13 (1959):68.

———. "IMCO: The First Four Years (1959-1962)." *International and Comparative Law Quarterly* 12 (1963):31.

Kent, H.S.K. "The Historical Origins of Three-Mile Limit." *American Journal of International Law* 48 (1954):537.

Krieger, K.-F. "Die Entwicklung des Seerechts im Mittelmeerraum von der Antike bis zum Consulat de Mar." *Jahrbuch für Internationales Recht* 16 (1973):179.

Lapidoth, R. "Freedom of Navigation—Its Legal History and its Normative Basis." *Journal of Maritime Law and Commerce* 6 (1975):259.

Lilar, Albert, and van den Bosch, Carlo. *Le Comité Maritime International: 1897-1972*. Antwerp: CMI, 1973.

Lobingier, C.S. "The Maritime Law of Rome." *Juridical Review* 47 (1935):1.

Mahan, A.T. *The Influence of Sea Power upon History—1660-1783*. 22nd ed. Boston: Little and Brown, 1911.

Marsden, R.G., ed. *Documents Relating to the Law and Custom of the Sea*. Vol. I: *1205-1648*. London: Navy Research Society, 1916.

———, ed. *Documents Relating to the Law and Custom of the Sea*. Vol. II: *1649-1797*. London: Navy Research Society, 1915.

Masterson, William E. "Territorial Waters and International Legislation." *Oregon Law Review* 8 (1929):309.

Miller, Hunter. "The Hague Codification Conference." *American Journal of International Law* 24 (1930):101.

Morris, Michael A. "Brazilian Ocean Policy in a Historical Perspective." *Journal of Maritime Law and Commerce* 10 (1979):349.

Note. "Law of the Sea." *International Conciliation*, no. 520 (November 1958).

O'Connell, D.P. *The Influence of Law on Sea Power*. Manchester: University of Manchester Press, 1975.

Parry, Clive. "The Inter-Governmental Maritime Consultative Organization." *British Year Book of International Law* 25 (1949):437.

Quéguiner, J. "The Mediterranean as a Maritime Trade Route." *Ocean Management* 3 (1978):179.

Reddie, James. *An Historical View of the Law of Maritime Commerce.* Edinburgh: Blackwood, 1841.

————. *Researches, Historical and Critical in Maritime International Law.* 2 vols. Edinburgh: Clark, 1844-1855.

Reeves, Jesse S. "The Codification of the Law of Territorial Waters." *American Journal of International Law* 24 (1930):486.

Reppy, Alison. "The Grotian Doctrine of the Freedom of the Seas Reappraised." *Fordham Law Review* 19 (1950):243.

Sanborn, Frederic R. *Origins of the Early English Maritime and Commercial Law.* New York: Century, 1930.

Scott, Sir Leslie, and Miller, Cyril. "The Unification of Maritime and Commercial Law through the Comité Maritime International." *International Law Quarterly* 1 (1947):482.

Singh, Nagendra. *Achievements of UNCTAD-I (1964) and UNCTAD-II (1968) in the Field of Shipping and Invisibles.* New Delhi: Chand, 1969.

Smith, George P. II. "The Concept of Free Seas: Shaping Modern Maritime Policy within a Vector of Historical Influence." *International Lawyer* 11 (1977):355.

Sørensen, Max. "Law of the Sea." *International Conciliation,* no. 520 (November 1958).

Standard, W.L. "Maritime Conventions and World Peace through Law." *Inter-American Law Review* 1 (1959):387.

Teclaff, L.A. "Shrinking the High Seas by Technical Methods—from the 1930 Conference to the 1958 Conference." *University of Detroit Law Journal* 39 (1962):660.

Trimble, E.G. "Violations of Maritime Law by the Allied Powers during the World War." *American Journal of International Law* 24 (1930):79.

Vallega, A. "International Relations and Maritime Dependence." *Maritime Policy and Management* 4 (1976):107.

Walker, Wyndham L. "Territorial Waters: The Cannon Shot Rule." *British Year Book of International Law* 22 (1945):210.

Watt, Donald C. "First Steps in the Enclosure of the Oceans—The Origins of Truman's Proclamation on the Resources of the Continental Shelf, 28 September, 1945." *Marine Policy* 3 (1979):211.

Wortley, A.A. "Great Britain and the Movement for the Unification of Private Law since 1948." *Tulane Law Review* 32 (1958):541.

## F. International Law and Policy: Sources and General Works

Abi-Saab, G. "The Third World and the Future of the International Legal Order." *Revue Egyptienne de Droit International* 29 (1973):27.

Amuzegar, Jahangir. "The North-South Dialogue: From Conflict to Compromise." *Foreign Affairs* 54 (1976):547.

Bos, Maarten, ed. *The Present State of International Law and other Essays.* Deventer: Kluwer, 1973.

Brierly, J.L. *The Law of Nations.* 6th ed. Edited by Sir Humphrey Waldock. Oxford: Clarendon Press, 1963.

Brownlie, Ian. *Principles of International Law.* 2nd ed. Oxford: Clarendon Press, 1973.

_____ , ed. *Basic Documents in International Law.* 2nd ed. Oxford: Clarendon, 1972.

Castel, J.G. *International Law. Chiefly as interpreted and applied in Canada.* 3rd ed. Toronto: Butterworths, 1976.

de Montbrial, Thierry. "For a New World Economic Order." *Foreign Affairs* 54 (1975):61.

Dopfer, Kurt, ed. *Economics in the Future.* London: Macmillan, 1976.

Falk, Richard A. *The Status of Law in International Society.* Princeton, N.J.: Princeton University Press, 1970.

Falk, Richard A., and Black, Cyril E., eds. *The Future of the International Legal Order.* Vols. I-IV. Princeton, N.J.: Princeton University Press, 1969-1972.

Foighel, Isi. "Aid to Developing Countries—A Legal Analysis." *Nordisk Tidskrift of International Ret*, 40 (1970):87.

Friedmann, Wolfgang. *The Changing Structure of International Law.* London: Stevens, 1964.

_____ . *Law in a Changing Society.* 2nd ed. New York: Columbia University Press, 1972.

Goodrich, L.M.; Hambro, Edvard; and Simons, Patricia. *Charter of the United Nations.* Commentary and Documents. 3rd rev. ed. New York: Columbia University Press, 1969.

Gosovic, Branislaw. *UNCTAD: Conflict and Compromise.* Leiden: Sijthoff, 1972.

Green, L.C. *International Law through the Cases.* 4th ed. Toronto: Carswell, 1978.

Hargrove, John L., ed. *Law, Institutions and the Global Environment.* Dobbs Ferry, N.Y.: Oceana, 1972.

Hawthorne, Edward P., ed. *The Transfer of Technology.* Paris: OECD, 1970.

Hazzard, Shirley. "Where Governments Go to Church." *New Republic*, March 1, 1975, pp. 11-14.

Koul, A.K. *The Legal Framework of UNCTAD in World Trade.* Bombay: Tripathi, 1977.

Lauterpacht, Hersch. *International Law: Collected Papers* 1. *General Works.* Edited by E. Lauterpacht. Cambridge: University Press, 1970.

_____ . *International Law: Collected Papers.* 2. *The Law of Peace,* pt. I. Edited by E. Lauterpacht. Cambridge: University Press, 1975.

_____ . *International Law: Collected Papers.* 3. The Law of Peace, pts. II-VI. Edited by E. Lauterpacht. Cambridge: University Press, 1977.

Macdonald, R. St. J.; Morris, Gerald L.; and Johnston, Douglas M., eds. *Canadian Perspectives on International Law and Organization.* Toronto: University of Toronto Press, 1974.

Macdonald, R. St. J.; Johnston, Douglas M.; and Morris, Gerald L., eds. *The International Law and Policy of Human Welfare.* Alphen aan den Rijn: Sijthoff and Noordhoff, 1978.

Nussbaum, Arthur. *A Concise History of the Law of Nations.* Rev. ed. New York: Macmillan, 1967.

O'Connell, D.P. *International Law.* 2 vols. 2nd ed. London: Stevens, 1970.

Oppenheim, L. *International Law.* I. *Peace.* 8th ed. Edited by H. Lauterpacht. London: Longman, 1952.

_____ . *International Law.* II. *Disputes, War and Neutrality.* 7th ed. Edited by H. Lauterpacht. London: Longman, 1955.

Patel, S.J. "The Technological Dependence of Developing Countries." *UNITAR News* 6 (1974):19.

_____ . "The Technological Dependence of Developing Countries." *Journal of Modern African Studies* 12 (1974):1.

Reddie, James. *Inquiries in International Law.* Edinburgh: Blackwood, 1842.

Report. *Issues before the 26th General Assembly. International Conciliation,* no. 584. 1971.

Röling, B.V.A. "International Law and the Maintenance of Peace." *Netherlands Year Book of International Law* (1973):1.

Ruddy, F.S. "Res Nullius and Occupation in Roman and International Law." *University of Missouri at Kansas City Law Review* 36 (1968):274.

_____ . *International Law in the Enlightenment.* New York: Oceana, 1975.

Sauvant, Karl P., and Hasenpflug, Hajo, eds. *The New International Order: Confrontation or Co-operation between North and South.* Boulder, Colo.: Westview, 1977.

Schwarzenberger, Georg. *A Manual of International Law.* 5th ed. London: Stevens, 1967.

_____ . *International Law and* Order. London: Stevens, 1971.

Sen, Sudhir. *United Nations in Economic Develoment—Need for a New Strategy.* Dobbs Ferry, N.Y.: Oceana, 1969.

Shihata, Ibrahim F.I. "Arab Oil Policies and the New International Economic Order." *Virginia Journal of International Law* 16 (1976):261.

Stone, Julius. *Of Law and Nations: Between Power Politics and Human Hopes.* Buffalo, N.Y.: Hein, 1974.

Tunkin, G.I. *Theory of International Law.* Translated by W.E. Butler. London: George Allan and Unwin, 1974.

Udokang, Okon. *Succession of New States to International Treaties.* Dobbs Ferry, N.Y.: Oceana, 1972.

Uri, Pierre. *Development without Dependence.* New York: Praeger, 1976.

Verwey, Wil D. *Economic Develoment, Peace and International Law.* Assen: Van Gorcum, 1972.

Vreeland, Hamilton. *Hugo Grotius.* New York: Oxford University Press, 1917.

White, Robin C.A. "A New International Economic Order." *International and Comparative Law Quarterly* 24 (1975):542.

## G. International Law and Policy of the Sea

Adie, W.A.C. *Oil, Politics and Seapower. The Indian Ocean Vortex.* New York: Crane Russak, 1975.

Alexander, Lewis M. *The Law of the Sea: Offshore Boundaries and Zones.* Columbus: Ohio State University Press, 1967.

_____ . "Regional Arrangements in the Oceans." *American Journal of International Law* 71 (1977):84.

_____ . *Regional Arrangements in Ocean Affairs.* Kingston: University of Rhode Island, 1977.

_____ , ed. *The Law of the Sea: International Rules and Organization for the Sea.* Proceedings, Law of the Sea Institute 3rd Annual Conference, 1968. Kingston, R.I.: Law of the Sea Institute, 1968.

_____ , ed. *The Law of the Sea: National Policy Recommendations.* Proceedings, Law of the Sea Institute 4th Annual Conference, 1969. Kingston, R.I.: Law of the Sea Institute, 1969.

_____ , ed. *The Law of the Sea: The United Nations and Ocean Management.* Proceedings, Law of the Sea Institute 5th Annual Conference, 1970. Kingston, R.I.: Law of the Sea Institute, 1970.

_____ , ed. *The Law of the Sea: A New Geneva Conference.* Proceedings, Law of the Sea Institute 6th Annual Conference, 1971. Kingston, R.I.: Law of the Sea Institute, 1971.

_____ , ed. *The Law of the Sea: Needs and Interests of Developing Countries.* Proceedings, Law of the Sea Institute 7th Annual Conference, 1972. Kingston, R.I.: Law of the Sea Institute, 1972.

_____ , ed. *Gulf and Caribbean Maritime Problems.* Kingston, R.I.: Law of the Sea Institute, 1973.

Alexander, Lewis M.; Cameron, Francis; and Nixon, Dennis. "The Costs of Failure at the Third Law of the Sea Conference." *Journal of Maritime Law and Commerce* 9 (1977):1.

Alvarado Garaioca, T. "The Continental Shelf and the Extension of the Territorial Sea." *Miami Law Quarterly* 10 (1956):490.

Amerasinghe, C.F. "The Problem of Archipelagoes in the International Law of the Sea." *International and Comparative Law Quarterly* 23 (1974):539.

Anand, R.P. "Freedom of Navigation through Territorial Waters and International Straits." *Indiana Journal of International Law* 14 (1974): 160.

_____ . *Legal Regime of the Sea-Bed and Developing Countries.* Leiden: Sijthoff, 1976.

Arnold, R.P. "The Common Heritage of Mankind as a Legal Concept." *International Lawyer* 9 (1975):153.

Auburn, F.M. "The International Seabed Area." *International and Comparative Law Quarterly* 20 (1971):173.

Bardonnet, Daniel. "La dénonciation par le Gouvernement Sénégalaïs de la Convention sur la Mer Territoriale et la Zone Contigue et de la Convention sur la Pêche et la Conservation des Ressources Biologiques de la Haute Mer." *Annuaire Francais de Droit International* 1 (1972):123.

Bethill, C.D. "Peoples' China and the Law of the Sea." *International Lawyer* 8 (1974):724.

Blecher, M.D. "Equitable Delimitation of the Continental Shelf." *American Journal of International Law* 13 (1979):60.

Boczek, B.A. *Flags of Convenience. An International Legal Study.* Cambridge, Mass.: Harvard University Press, 1962.

Böhme, Eckart, and Kehden, Max I. *From the Law of the Sea towards an Ocean Space Regime.* Frankfurt/Main: Metzner, 1972.

Booth, K. *Navies and Foreign Policy.* London: Croom Helm, 1977.

Bouchez, Leo J. *The Regime of Bays in International Law.* Leiden: Sijthoff, 1964.

_____ . "Some Reflections on the Present and Future Law of the Sea." *The Present State of International Law and Other Essays.* Edited by Maarten Bos. Deventer: Kluwer, 1973.

Bowett, D.W. "The Second United Nations Conference on the Law of the Sea." *International and Comparative Law Quarterly* 9 (1960):415.

Brown, E.D. *The Legal Regime of Hydrospace.* London: Stevens, 1971.

_____ . *Passage through the Territorial Sea. Straits used for International Navigation and Archipelagoes.* London: David Davies Memorial Institute, 1975.

Brown, Seyom, and Fabian, Larry L. "Diplomats at Sea." *Foreign Affairs* 52 (1974):301.

Burke, William T. *Contemporary Law of the Sea: Transportation,*

*Communication and Flight.* Occasional paper no. 28, Law of the Sea Institute, University of Rhode Island, 1975.

Burke, William T.; Legatski, Richard; and Woodhead, William W. *National and International Law Enforcement in the Ocean.* Seattle: University of Washington Press, 1975.

Burns, Thomas S. *The Secret War for the Ocean Depths. Soviet-American Rivalry for the Mastery of the Seas.* New York: Rawson, 1978.

Castañeda, Jorge. "The Concept of Patrimonial Sea in International Law." *Indiana Journal of International Law* 12 (1972):535.

Castines, L. de. "La mer patrimoniale." *Revue Generale de Droit International Public* 79 (1975):447.

Charney, J.I., "The International Regime for the Deep Seabed: Past Conflicts and Proposals for Progress." *Harvard International Law Journal* 17 (1976):1.

Christy, Francis T.; Clingan, Thomas A. Jr.; Gamble, John K. Jr.; Knight, H. Gary; and Miles, Edward. *Law of the Sea: Caracas and Beyond.* Proceedings, Law of the Sea Institute 9th Annual Conference, 1975. Cambridge, Mass.: Ballinger, 1975.

Colombos, C. John. "The Unification of Maritime International Law in Time of Peace." *British Year Book of International Law* 21 (1944):96.
————. *The International Law of the Sea.* 6th rev. ed. London: Longmans, 1967.

Couper, A.D.; Burger, W. Jun.; and Abdelgalil, S. "Shipping Control and the Changing Use of Marine Space." *Maritime Policy and Management* 4 (1977):409.

Dean, Arthur H. "The Geneva Conference on the Law of the Sea: What was Accomplished." *American Journal of International Law* 52 (1958):607.
————. "The Second Geneva Conference on the Law of the Sea: The Fight for Freedom of the Seas." *American Journal of International Law* 54 (1960):751.

Draper, J.A. "The Indonesian Archipelagic State Doctrine and the Law of the Sea: 'Territorial Grab' or Justifiable Necessity?" *International Lawyer* 11(1977):1, 3.

Dupuy, René-Jean. *The Law of the Sea: Current Problems.* Dobbs Ferry, N.Y.: Oceana, 1974.

Finlay, L.W., and McKnight, M.S. "Law of the Sea: Its Impact on the International Energy Crisis." *Law and Policy in International Business* 6 (1974):639.

Franck, T.M.; El Baradei, M.; and Aron, G. "The New Poor: Land-Locked, Shelf-Locked and other Geographically Disadvantaged States." *New York University Journal of International Law and Policy* 7 (1974):33.

Friedmann, Wolfgang. "Selden Redivivus—Towards a Partition of the Sea?" *American Journal of International Law* 65 (1971):757.

————. *The Future of the Oceans.* New York: Braziller, 1971.

Gamble, John King Jr., and Pontecorvo, Giulio. *Law of the Sea: The Emerging Regime of the Oceans.* Proceedings, Law of the Sea Institute, 8th Annual Conference, 1973. Cambridge, Mass.: Ballinger, 1973.

————. *Marine Policy: A Comparative Approach.* Lexington, Mass.: Lexington Books, D.C. Heath and Co., 1977.

————. *Law of the Sea: Neglected Issues.* Proceedings, Law of the Sea Institute 12th Annual Conference, 1978. Honolulu: Law of the Sea Institute, University of Hawaii, 1979.

Garcia Amador, F.V. *Latin America and the Law of the Sea.* Occasional Paper no. 14. Law of the Sea Institute, University of Rhode Island, 1972.

————. "The Latin-American Contribution to the Development of the Law of the Sea." *American Journal of International Law* 68 (1974):33.

Garrett, Michael T. "Issues in International Law created by Scientific Development of the Ocean Floor." *Southwestern Law Journal* 19 (1965):97.

Gitelson, S.A. "UNDP Technical Assistance." *Journal of World Trade Law* 5 (1971):533.

Gold, Edgar. "The Third United Nations Conference on the Law of the Sea: The Caracas Session, 1974." *Maritime Studies and Management* 2 (1974):102.

————. "The Third United Nations Conference on the Law of the Sea: The Geneva Session, 1975." *Maritime Studies and Management* 3 (1975):117.

————. "The Third United Nations Conference on the Law of the Sea: The 4th and 5th Sessions, New York, 1976." *Maritime Policy and Management* 4 (1977):171.

————. "The Third United Nations Conference on the Law of the Sea: The Sixth Session, New York, 1977." *Maritime Policy and Management* 5 (1978):63.

————. "The 'Freedom' of Ocean Shipping and Commercial Viability." In *Law of the Sea: Neglected Issues.* Proceedings, Law of the Sea Institute, 12th Annual Conference, 1978. Edited by John K. Gamble, Jr., p. 248. Honolulu: Law of the Sea Institute, University of Hawaii, 1979.

Gullion, Edmund A., ed. *Uses of the Seas.* Englewood Cliffs, N.J.: Prentice-Hall, 1968.

Gutteridge, J. "Beyond the 3 Mile Limit: Recent Developments affecting the Law of the Sea." *Virginia Journal of International Law* 14 (1973-1974):195.

Hardy, Michael. "Regional Approaches to Law of the Sea Problems: The European Community." *International and Comparative Law Quarterly* 24 (1975):336.

Hargrove, John L. "New Concepts in the Law of the Sea." *Ocean Development and International Law* 1 (1973-1974):5.

Hedberg, H.D. "The National-International Jurisdictional Boundary on the Ocean Floor." *Ocean Management* 1 (1973):83.

Heinzen, Bernard G. "The Three-Mile Limit: Preserving the Freedom of the Seas." *Stanford Law Review* 11 (1959):597.

Hollick, Ann L. "The Origins of 200-Mile Offshore Zones." *American Journal of International Law* 71 (1977):494.

Janis, Mark W. *Sea Power and the Law of the Sea.* Lexington, Mass.: Lexington Books, D.C. Heath and Co., 1976.

Janis, Mark W., and Daniel, Donald C.F. "The U.S.S.R.: Ocean Use and Ocean Law." *Maritime Studies and Management* 2 (1974):71.

Jessup, Philip C. *The Law of Territorial Waters and Maritime Jurisdiction.* New York: Jennings, 1927.

_____ . "The United Nations Conference on the Law of the Sea." *Columbia Law Review* 59 (1959):234.

Johnson, Barbara, and Zacher, Mark W. *Canadian Foreign Policy and the Law of the Sea.* Vancouver: University of British Columbia Press, 1977.

Johnston, D.M. "The Economic Zone in North America: Scenarios and Options." *Ocean Development and International Law Journal* 3 (1975):53.

_____ . "The New Equity in the Law of the Sea." *International Journal* 31 (1975-1976):79.

_____ , ed. *Marine Policy and the Coastal Community: The Impact of the Law of the Sea.* London: Croom Helm, 1976.

_____ , ed. *Regionalization of the Law of the Sea.* Proceedings, Law of the Sea Institute 11th Annual Conference, 1977. Cambridge, Mass.: Ballinger, 1978.

Kassim, A.F. "The Law of the Sea: Conflicting Claims in the Persian Gulf." *Journal of International Law and Economics* 4 (1969-1970):282.

_____ . "The Law of the Sea: Conflicting Claims in the Persian Gulf." *Journal of International Law and Economics* 4 (1975):782.

Kehden, Max I. *Die Inanspruchnahme von Meereszonen und Meeresbodenzonen durch Küstenstaaten.* 2nd ed. Frankfurt/Main. Metzner, 1971.

Kingham, J.D., and McRae, D.M. "Competent International Organizations and the Law of the Sea." *Marine Policy* 3 (1979):106.

Knauss, John A. *Factors influencing a U.S. Position in a Future Law of the Sea Conference.* Occasional paper no. 10. Law of the Sea Institute: University of Rhode Island, 1971.

Knight, H. Gary. *Consequences of Non-Agreement at the Third U.N. Law of the Sea Conference.* ASIL Studies in Transnational Legal Policy no. 11. Washington: ASIL, 1976.

————, ed. *The Law of the Sea: Cases, Documents and Readings.* Washington, D.C.: Nautilus, 1975.

Kolodkin, A.L. "Territorial Waters and International Law." *International Affairs* 8 (Moscow, 1969):78.

Kolodkin, A.L., and Molodcov, S. V. *Seefriedensrecht.* Frankfurt/Main.: Metzner, 1973.

Kronfol, Z.A. "The Exclusive Economic Zone: A Critique of Contemporary Law of the Sea." *Journal of Maritime Law and Commerce* 9 (1978):461.

Krüger-Sprengel, F. *The Role of NATO in the Use of the Sea and the Seabed.* Ocean Series 304. Washington, D.C.: Woodrow Wilson International Conference for Scholars, 1972.

Lapidoth, R. "Freedom of Navigation and the New Law of the Sea." *Israel Law Review* 10 (1975):456.

Larson, David, ed. *Major Issues in the Law of the Sea.* Durham: University of New Hampshire Press, 1976.

*Law of the Sea I—XI.* Special Issues, vols. 6-16. *San Diego Law Review* (1969-1980).

Levy, J.-P. "Ocean Management and a New Law of the Sea." *Ocean Management* 2 (1973):129.

Lindemayer, Bernd. *Schiffsembargo und Handelsembargo.* Baden-Baden: Nomos Verlag, 1975.

Logue, John J., ed. *The Fate of the Oceans.* Villanova, Pa.: Villanova University Press, 1972.

Mangone, Gerald J. *Marine Policy for America: The United States at Sea.* Lexington, Mass.: Lexington Books, D.C. Heath and Co., 1977.

Mann Borgese, Elisabeth, ed. *Pacem in Maribus.* New York: Dodd, Mead, 1972.

McDougal, Myres S. "The Law of the High Seas in Time of Peace." *Denver Journal of International Law and Policy* 3 (1973):45.

McDougal, Myres S., and Burke, William T. "Crisis in the Law of the Sea: Community Perspectives versus National Egoism." *Yale Law Journal* 67 (1958):539.

McDougal, Myres S., and Burke, William T. "The Community Interest in a Narrow Territorial Sea: Inclusive versus Exclusive Competence over the Oceans." *Cornell Law Quarterly* 45 (1960):171.

————. *The Public Order of the Oceans.* New Haven: Yale University Press, 1962.

McDougal, Myres S.; Burke, William T.; and Vlasic, Ivan A. "The Maintenance of Public Order at Sea and the Nationality of Ships." *American Journal of International Law* 54 (1960):25.

Miles, Edward, and Gamble, John King Jr., eds. *Law of the Sea: Conference Outcomes and Problems of Implementation.* Proceedings,

Law of the Sea Institute 10th Annual Conference, 1976. Cambridge,
    Mass.: Ballinger, 1977.
Moore, J.N. "The Law of the Sea: A Choice and a Challenge." *Virginia
    Journal of International Law* 15 (1974-1975):791.
Nelson, L.D.M. "The Patrimonial Sea." *International and Comparative
    Law Quarterly* 22 (1973):668.
Nweihed, Kaldone G. *La Vigencia del Mar.* 2 vols. Caracas: Equinoccio,
    1973-1974.
Nwogugu, E.I. "Problems of Nigerian Offshore Jurisdiction." *Inter-
    national and Comparative Law Quarterly* 22 (1973):349.
Ochan, Ralph. *Marine Policy and Developing Landlocked States: The
    Search for a new Equity in the Law of the Sea.* Unpublished master of
    law thesis, Dalhousie University, 1977.
Oda, Shigeru. *The Law of the Sea in our Time.* I. *New Developments
    1966-1975.* Leiden: Sijthoff, 1977.
Oda, Shigeru, Johnston, Douglas M., Hollick, Ann L., and Holst,
    Johann. *A New Regime for the Oceans.* Triangle Paper no. 9. New
    York: Trilateral Commission, 1975.
Opoku, K. "The Law of the Sea and Developing Countries." *Revue
    de Droit International* 51 (1973):28.
Orrego Vicuña, Francisco, ed. *Politica Oceanica.* Santiago: Editones Uni-
    versitaria, 1977.
Osieke, E. "The Contribution of States from the Third World to the
    Development of the Law of the Continental Shelf and the Concept of
    the Economic Zone." *Indiana Journal of International Law* 15
    (1975):313.
Oudendijk, J.K. *Status and Extent of Adjacent Waters.* Leiden: Sijthoff,
    1970.
Oxman, Bernard H. "The Third United Nations Conference on the Law of
    of the Sea: The 1976 New York Sessions." *American Journal of Inter-
    national Law* 71 (1977):247.
_____ . "The Third United Nations Conference on the Law of the Sea:
    The 1977 New York Session." *American Journal of International Law*
    72 (1978):57.
_____ . "The Third United Nations Conference on the Law of the Sea:
    The Seventh Session (1978)." *American Journal of International Law*
    73 (1979):1.
Padelford, Norman J., ed. *Public Policy for the Seas.* Cambridge,
    Mass.: Massachusetts Institute of Technology Press, 1970.
Papadakis, N. *The International Legal Regime of Artificial Islands.*
    Leiden: Sijthoff, 1977.
Pardo, Arvid. "A Statement on the Future Law of the Sea in Light of Cur-
    rent Trends in Negotiations." *Ocean Development and International
    Law* 1 (1973-1974):315.

Peyroux, E. "Les Etats africains face au questions actuelles de droit de la mer." *Revue Generale de Droit International Public* 78 (1974):623.

Pharand, Donat, "The Law of the Sea: International Straits." *Thesaurus Acroasium* 7 (1977):59.

Plasil-Wenger, Franz. "UNIDO: The United Nations Industrial Development Organization." *Journal of World Trade Law* 5 (1971):188.

Platzöder, Renate, and Vizthum, Wolfgang Graf. *Zur Neuordnung des Meeresvölkerrechts auf der Dritten Seerechtskonferenz der Vereinten Nationen.* Eggenberg: Stiftung Wissenschaft und Politik, 1974.

Ratiner, Leigh. "United States Oceans Policy: An Analysis." *Journal of Maritime Law and Commerce* 2 (1970-1971):225.

Rembe, N.S. "Law of the Sea: Conflicts over Limits of National Jurisdiction." *Eastern Africa Law Review* 7 (1974):65.

————. *"Africa and the International Law of the Sea: A Study of the Contribution of the African States to the Third United Nations Conference on the Law of the Sea."* Alphen aan den Rijn: Sijthoff and Noordhoff, 1980.

Rosenne, S. "The Third U. N. Conference on the Law of the Sea." *Israel Law Review* 11 (1976):1.

Rozakis, C. L. *The Greek-Turkish Dispute over the Aegean Continental Shelf.* Occasional Paper no. 27. Law of the Sea Institute, University of Rhode Island, 1975.

Sebek, Viktor. *The Eastern European States and the Development of the Law of the Sea.* 2 vols. Dobbs Ferry, N.Y.: Oceana, 1977, 1979.

Slouka, Z. J. *International Custom and the Continental Shelf.* The Hague: Nijhoff, 1968.

Smith, H.A. *The Law and Custom of the Sea.* London: Stevens, 1959.

Sohn, L. "A Tribunal for the Seabed or the Oceans." *Zeitschrift für Ausländisches Öffentliches Recht und Völkerrecht* 32 (1972):253.

Stevenson, John R., and Oxman, Bernard H. "The Preparations for the Law of the Sea Conference." *American Journal of International Law* 68 (1974):1.

Stevenson, John R., and Oxman, Bernard H. "The Third United Nations Conference on the Law of the Sea: The 1974 Caracas Session." *American Journal of International Law* 69 (1975):1.

Stevenson, John R., and Oxman, Bernard H. "The Third United Nations Conference on the Law of the Sea: The 1975 Geneva Session." *American Journal of International Law* 69 (1975):763.

Swing, John T. "Who Will Own the Oceans?" *Foreign Affairs* 54 (1976):527.

Szekely, Alberto. *Latin America and the Development of the Law of the Sea.* 2 vols. Dobbs Ferry, N.Y.: Oceana, 1976 and 1978.

"The Exclusive Economic Zone and the Law of the Sea." Special Issue. *Maritime Policy and Management* 4 (1977):313.

Vali, F.A. *Politics of the Indian Ocean Region.* New York: Free Press, 1976.

Vizthum, W.G. "Auf dem Wege zu einem neuen Meeresvölkerrechts." *Jahrbuch für Internationales Recht* 16 (1973):229.

Wenk, Edward. *The Politics of the Ocean.* Seattle: University of Washington Press, 1972.

Zacklin, Ralph, ed. *The Changing Law of the Sea: Western Hemisphere Perspectives.* Leiden: Sijthoff, 1974.

## H. Maritime Law and Policy

Admiralty Law Institute. Tulane University. "Symposium on American Law of Collision." *Tulane Law Review* (1977):759.

_____ . "Symposium on Maritime Law." *Tulane Law Review* 35 (1960):5.

_____ . "A Symposium on the Hull Policy." *Tulane Law Review* 41 (1967):233.

_____ . "A Symposium on the P. and I. Policy." *Tulane Law Review* 43 (1969):457.

_____ . "Symposium on Carriage of Goods by Water." *Tulane Law Review* 45 (1971):697.

_____ . "Symposium on Maritime Liens and Securities: Ship Sales and Finance." *Tulane Law Review* 47 (1973):489.

_____ . "Symposium on Charter Parties." *Tulane Law Review* 49 (1975):743.

_____ . "Symposium on American Law of Collision." *Tulane Law Review* 51 (1977):759.

Bar-Lev, Joshua. "The UNCTAD Code of Practice for the Regulation of Liner Conferences." *Journal of Maritime Law and Commerce* 3 (1971-1972):783.

Baxi, Upendra. "Unification of Private Maritime International Law through Treaties—An Assessment." *Indian Year Book of International Law* (1966-1967):72.

Becker, Gordon L. "A Short Cruise on the Good Ships Tovalop and Cristal." *Journal of Maritime Law and Commerce* 5 (1973-1974): 609.

Behnam, A.Y. "A Study of the Value of National Fleets and Shipping Policies in Developing Countries." Unpublished Master's thesis, University of Wales, 1974.

_____ . "Political Factors and the Evolution of National Fleets in Developing Countries." *Maritime Studies Management* 3 (1976):131.

Berlingieri, Francesco. "International Maritime Arbitration." *Journal of Maritime Law and Commerce* 10 (1979):199.

Braekhus, Sjur, and Rein, Alex. *Handbook of P. and I. Insurance.* Arendal, Norway: Assuranceforeningen Gard, 1972; Supplement, 1975.

Braekhus, Sjur, and Rein, Alex. *P. and I. Insurance for Drilling Vessels.* Arendal, Norway: Assuranceforeningen Gard, 1976.

*Britain and the Sea.* The Collected Papers and Records of the Conference held at the Royal Naval College, Greenwich, 1973.

Butler, William E. *The Soviet Union and the Law of the Sea.* Baltimore, Md.: Johns Hopkins University Press, 1971.

Chorley, Lord, and Giles, O.C. *Shipping Law.* 6th ed. London: Pitman, 1970.

Chrispeels, Erik, and Graham, Thomas. "The Brussels Convention of 1924 (Ocean Bills of Lading)." *Journal of World Trade Law* 7 (1973):680.

Chrzanowski, E. "Current Aspects of International Shipping Policy." *Maritime Policy and Management* 5 (1978):289.

Clingan, Thomas, and Alexander, Lewis M. *Hazards of Maritime Transit.* Cambridge, Mass.: Ballinger, 1973.

Coghlin, T.G. "Protection and Indemnity Insurance: The P. and I. Clubs." *Journal of World Trade Law* 5 (1971):591.

Colinvaux, Raoul. *Carver's Carriage by Sea.* 2 vols. 12th ed. British Shipping Laws, vols. 1 and 2. London: Stevens, 1971.

Comment. "The Difficult Quest for a Uniform Maritime Law: Failure of the Brussels Conventions to achieve International Agreement on Collision Liability, Liens and Mortgages." *Yale Law Journal* 64 (1955):878.

Comment, "PanLibHon Registration of American-owned Merchant Ships: Government Policy and the Problem of the Courts." *Columbia Law Review* 60 (1960):711.

Couper, A.D. "Commentary: Shipping Policies and the EEC." *Maritime Policy and Managment* 4 (1977):129.

Diplock, Lord. "Conventions and Morals—Limitation Clauses in International Conventions." *Journal of Maritime Law and Commerce* 1 (1969-1970):525.

Donaldson, Hon. Sir John; Staughton, C.S., and Wilson, D.J. *The Law of General Average and the York-Antwerp Rules.* 10th ed. British Shipping Laws, vol. 7. London: Stevens, 1975.

Dover, Victor. *A Handbook to Marine Insurance.* 7th ed. Revised by R.H. Brown. London: Witherby, 1970.

Farthing, R.B.C. "UNCTAD Code of Practice for the Regulation of Liner Conferences: Another View." *Journal of Maritime Law and Commerce* 4 (1972-1973):467.

Ghandi, D.S. *Shipowners, Mariners and the New Law of the Sea.* London: Fairplay, 1977.

Gilmore, Grant, and Black, Charles L. Jr. *The Law of Admiralty.* 2nd ed. Mineola, New York: Foundation, 1975.

Gold, Edgar. "Should Canada Ratify or Implement the International Conventions Initiated under the Auspices of the Comité Maritime International?" *Proceedings of the 52nd Conference of the Canadian Bar Association.* Halifax, 1970.

————, ed. *New Directions in Maritime Law 1976.* Halifax, N.S.: Dalhousie University, 1976.

————, ed. *New Directions in Maritime Law 1978.* Halifax, N.S.: Dalhousie University, 1978.

Goldie, L.F.E. "Recognition and Dual Nationality—A Problem of Flags of Convenience." *British Year Book of International Law* 39 (1963):220.

Gorter, Wythze. *United States Merchant Marine Policies: Some International Economic Implications.* Princeton, N.J.: Princeton University Press Essays in International Finance, 1955.

Grime, Robert. *Shipping Law.* London: Sweet and Maxwell, 1978.

Guzhenko, T., and Kwasniewski, K. "Comecon Shipping Policy—A Soviet and a West German Viewpoint." *Marine Policy* 2 (1977):102.

Haji, Iq-bal. "UNCTAD and Shipping." *Journal of World Trade Law* 6 (1972):58.

Healy, Nicholas J., and Sharpe, David J. *Cases and Materials on Admiralty.* St. Paul, Minn.: West Publishing Co., 1974.

Holman, H. *A Handy Book for Shipowners and Masters.* 16th ed. Edited by M.R. Holman. London: Adams, 1964.

Hopkins, F.N. *Business and Law for the Shipmaster.* 3rd ed. Glasgow: Brown, Son and Ferguson, 1974.

International Chamber of Shipping. *Third U.N. Conference on the Law of the Sea—Caracas 1974: The Shipping Issues.* London: I.C.S., 1974.

Jambu-Merlin, Roger. *Les Gens de Mer.* Volume in Series Traité Général de Droit Maritime. Edited by René Rodière. Paris: Dalloz, 1978.

Johnson, D.H.N. "The Nationality of Ships." *Indian Year Book of International Affairs* 8 (1959):3.

Knudsen, O. *The Politics of International Shipping.* Lexington, Mass.: Lexington Books, D.C. Heath and Co., 1978.

Lawrence, S.A. *United States Merchant Shipping Policies and Politics.* Washington: Brookings, 1966.

Lilar, Albert, and van den Bosch, Carlo. "The International Brussels Conventions of May 10, 1952, for the Clarification of Certain Rules relating to Penal and Civil Jurisdiction in Matters of Collision and Arrest of Vessels." *Unification of Law Year Book* (1947-1952):341.

Manca, Plinio. *International Maritime Law.* 3 vols. Antwerp: European Transport Law, 1970-1971.

Mankabady, S. "International and National Organisations concerned with Shipping." *Lloyd's Maritime and Commercial Law Quarterly* 3 (1974):274.

―――――― . *The Hamburg Rules on the Carriage of Goods by Sea.* Boston: Sithoff, 1978.

MccGwire, Michael; Booth, Ken; and McDonnell, John. *Soviet Naval Policy: Objectives and Constraints.* New York: Praeger, 1975.

McConville, J. *The Shipping Industry in the United Kingdom.* Strategic Factors in Industrial Relations Systems Research Series, no. 26. Geneva: International Institute for Labour Studies, 1977.

McGuffie, Kenneth C. *The Law of Collisions at Sea.* 11th ed. British Shipping Laws, Vol. 4. London: Stevens, 1961; Supplement, 1973.

Meijers, H. *The Nationality of Ships.* The Hague: Nijhoff, 1967.

Metaxas, B.N. "Some Thoughts on Flags of Convenience." *Maritime Studies and Management* 1 (1973):162.

OECD, "Study on Flags of Convenience." *Journal of Maritime Law and Commerce* 4 (1972-1973): 231.

Owen, David R. "Origins and Development of Collision Law." *Tulane Law Review* 51 (1977):759.

Padwa, David J. "The Curriculum of IMCO." *International Organization* 14 (1960):524.

Rajwar, L.M.S.; Valente, M.G.; Oyevaar, Jan J.; and Malinowski, W.R. *Shipping and Developing Countries.* International Conciliation no. 582, Carnegie Endowment for International Peace, 1971.

Report. "The UNCTAD Board and Shipping." *Journal of World Trade Law* 5 (1971):714.

Report. "UNCITRAL: Revision of the Hague Rules." *Journal of World Trade Law* 5 (1971):573.

Report. "UNCTAD: Code of Conduct for Liner Conferences." *Journal of World Trade Law* 8 (1974):536.

Ridley, Jasper. *The Law of the Carriage of Goods by Land, Sea and Air.* 4th ed. Edited by Geoffrey Whitehead. London: Shaw and Sons, 1975.

Ripoll, Jose. "UNCTAD and Insurance." *Journal of World Trade Law* 8 (1974):75.

Robinson, G.H. "An Introduction to American Admiralty." *Cornell Law Quarterly* 21 (1935):46.

Rodière, René. *Traité Général de Droit Maritime. Introduction, L'Armement.* Paris: Dalloz, 1976.

Romans, T.J. "The American Merchant Marine—Flags of Convenience and International Law." *Virginia Journal of International Law* 3 (1963):121.

Sassoon, David M. *C.I.F. and F.O.B. Contracts.* 2nd ed. British Shipping Laws, vol. 5. London: Stevens, 1975.

Shah, M.J. "The Implementation of the U.N. Convention on a Code of Conduct for Liner Conferences 1974." *Journal of Maritime Law and Commerce* 9 (1977):79.

Silverstein, Harvey B. "Technological Politics and Maritime Affairs—Comparative Participation in the Intergovernmental Maritime Consultative Organization." *Journal of Maritime Law and Commerce* 7 (1976):367.

_____ . *Superships and Nation States: The Transnational Politics of the Inter-Governmental Maritime Consultative Organization.* Boulder, Colo.: Westview, 1978.

Simmonds, K.R. "The Constitution of the Maritime Safety Committee of IMCO." *International Law Quarterly* 12 (1963):56.

Singh, Nagendra. "The Indian Merchant Shipping Act, 1958, and International Law." *Indian Journal of International Law* 1 (1963):10.

_____ . *Statements by Dr. Nagendra Singh, Representative of India to UNCTAD II in the Fourth Committee on Shipping and Invisibles.* New Delhi: Vigyan Bharan, 1963.

_____ . *International Law Problems of Merchant Shipping.* Leiden: Sijthoff, 1967.

_____ . *The Legal Regime of Merchant Shipping.* Bombay: University of Bombay Press, 1969.

_____ . *Maritime Flag and International Law.* Leiden: Sijthoff, 1978.

Singh, Nagendra, and Colinvaux, Raoul. *Shipowners.* British Shipping Laws, vol. 13. London: Stevens, 1967.

_____ . *International Conventions on Merchant Shipping.* 2nd ed. British Shipping Laws, vol. 8. London, Stevens, 1973.

Stanton, L.F.H. *The Law and Practice of Sea Transport.* Glasgow: Brown, Son and Ferguson, 1964.

Steinicke, Dietrich. *Handelsschiffahrt und Prisenrecht.* Frankfurt/Main: Metzner, 1973.

Sturmey, S.G. *British Shipping and World Competition.* London: Athlone, 1962.

_____ . "National Shipping Policies." *Journal of Industrial Economics* 14 (1965-1966):14.

_____ . "The Development of the Code of Conduct for Liner Conferences." *Marine Policy* 3 (1979):133.

Sundstrom, G.O. Zacharias. *Foreign Ships and Foreign Waters.* Stockholm: Almquist and Wiksell, 1971.

Szasz, Paul C. "The Convention on the Liability of Operators of Nuclear Ships." *Journal of Maritime Law and Commerce* 2 (1970-1971):541.

Tetley, William. *Marine Cargo Claims.* 2nd ed. Toronto: Butterworths, 1978.

Thomas, Michael, and Steel, David. *The Merchant Shipping Acts.* 7th ed. British Shipping Laws, vol. 11. London: Stevens, 1976.

Watts, A.D. "The Protection of Merchant Ships." *British Year Book of International Law* 33 (1957):52.

Wilner, Gabriel. "Survey of the Activities of UNCTAD and UNCITRAL in the Field of International Legislation on Shipping." *Journal of Maritime Law and Commerce* 3 (1971):129.

Wong, J. "Container Transport—Position under the F.C.L. System and Marine Insurance Law." *Malaya Law Review* 17 (1976):270.

Yiannopoulos, A.N. "The Unification of Private Maritime Law by International Conventions." *Law and Contemporary Problems* 30 (1965):370.

Ying, C.A. "The Hague Rules and the Carriage of Goods by Sea Act 1972: A Caveat." *Malaya Law Review* 17 (1976):86.

Zamora, Stephen. "UNCTAD III—The Question of Shipping." *Journal of World Trade Law* 7 (1973):91.

## I. Maritime Commerce and Economics

Alderton, P.M. *Sea Transport—Operation and Economics.* London: Thomas Reed, 1973.

Alexandersson, Gunnar, and Norstrom, Goran. *World Shipping—An Economic Geography of Ports and Seaborne Trade.* Stockholm: Almquist and Wiksell, 1963.

*Arab Shipping 1979.* A Seatrade Guide. Colchester: Seatrade, 1979.

Behnam, A.Y. "Political Factors and the Evolution of National Fleets in Developing Countries." *Maritime Studies Management* (1975):131.

———. "Ocean Freight Rates and the Developing Economy—A Consumer of Shipping Services Policy." Unpublished Ph.D. dissertation, University of Wales, 1976.

———. *Liner Conferences, Developing Countries and Consumer Policy.* Special Meeting of the Club of Rome on the New International Order, *Pacem in Maribus VII.* Algiers, 1976.

Bess, David. *Marine Transportation.* Danville, Ill.: Interstate Printers, 1976.

Branch, Alan E. *The Elements of Shipping.* 4th ed. London: Chapman and Hall, 1977.

Bryan, I.A., and Kolowitz, Y. *Shipping Conferences in Canada.* Ottawa: Consumer and Corporate Affairs Department, 1978.

Cellineri, Louis E. *Seaport Dynamics: A Regional Perspective*. Lexington, Mass.: Lexington Books, D.C. Heath and Co., 1976.

Cohen, D., and Shneerson, D. "The Domestic Resource Costs of Establishing/Expanding a National Fleet." *Maritime Studies and Management* 3 (1976):221.

Couper, A.D. *The Geography of Sea Transport*. London: Hutchinson, 1972.

_____ . "The New Economic Order and African Shipping Policies." *Maritime Policy and Management* 5 (1978):267.

Cufley, C.F.H. *Ocean Freights and Chartering*. London: Crosby Lockwood Staples, 1970.

Deakin, B.M. *Shipping Conferences: A Study of their Origins, Development and Economic Problems*. Cambridge: University Press, 1973.

_____ . "Shipping Conferences: Some Economic Aspects of International Regulation." *Maritime Studies and Management* 2 (1974):5.

Dover, Victor. *A Handbook to Marine Insurance*. 8th ed. Revised by R.H. Brown. London: Witherby, 1975.

*EEC Shipping 1978*. A Seatrade Guide. Colchester: Seatrade, 1978.

Goss, R.O. *Advances in Maritime Economics*. London: Cambridge University Press, 1977.

Grammenos, Costas Th. *Bank Finance for Ship Purchasing*. Bangor: University of Wales Press, 1979.

Hearn, George H. "Cargo Preference and Control." *Journal of Maritime Law and Commerce* 2 (1970-1971):481.

Kendall, Lane C. *The Business of Shipping*. Cambridge, Maryland: Cornell Maritime Press, 1973.

King, Thomas A. "The Value of Shipping to the U.S. Economy." *Maritime Policy and Management* 4 (1977):163.

Lawrence, S.A. *International Sea Transport: The Years Ahead*. Lexington, Mass.: Lexington Books, D.C. Heath and Co., 1972.

"Liner Shipping in the U.S. Trades." Special Issue. *Maritime Policy and Management* 5 (1978):141.

Mance, Sir Osborne. *International Sea Transport*. London: Oxford University Press for Royal Institute of International Affairs, 1945.

Marlow, P.B. "The Indirect Benefits of Shipping in a National Economy." *Maritime Policy and Management* 4 (1978):117.

Marx, Daniel J. *International Shipping Cartels: A Study of Industrial Self-Regulation by Shipping Conferences*. New York: Greenwood, 1953.

McDowell, C.E., and Gibbs, H.M. *Ocean Transportation*. New York: McGraw-Hill, 1954.

Metaxas, B.N. "Notes on the Internationalization Process in the Maritime Sector." *Maritime Policy and Management* 5 (1978):51.

Moreby, David H. *The Human Element in Shipping*. Colchester: Seatrade Publications, 1975.

Naess, Erling D. *The Great PanLibHon Controversy*. The Fight over the Flags of Shipping. Epping, Essex: Gower Press, 1972.

O'Loughlin, Carleen. *The Economics of Sea Transport*. Oxford: Pergamon, 1967.

Pedrick, John L., Jr. "Tankship Design and Regulation and its Economic Effect on Oil Consumers." *Journal of Maritime Law and Commerce* 9 (1978):377.

Pontecorvo, Giulio, and Wilkinson, Maurice. "An Economic Analysis of the International Transfer of Marine Technology." *Ocean Development and International Law* 2 (1974-1975):255.

Rinman, Thorstan, and Linden, Rigmor. *Shipping—How it Works*. Gothenburg: Rinman and Linden A.B., 1978.

Schmeltzer, Edward, and Peavy, Robert A. "Prospects and Problems of the Container Revolution." *Journal of Maritime Law and Commerce* 1 (1969-1970):203.

Sturmey, S.G. *Shipping Economics. Collected Papers*. London: Macmillan, 1975.

Vamberg, R.G. "Nationalism in Shipping." *Maritime Studies and Management* 1 (1974):243.

Van den Burg, G. *Containerization and Other Unit Transport*. London: Hutchinson Benham, 1975.

Wanhill, S.R.C. "Freight Rates, Conferences and Developing Countries." *Maritime Studies and Management* 2 (1975):231.

Williams, D., ed. *The Operational Challenge*. Proceedings of a Conference on Shipping Tomorrow, London, 1977. London: Nautical Institute, 1977.

Wood, J.N. "Shipping and the U.K. Economy." *Maritime Studies and Management* 3 (1975):71.

Woods, James R. *"The Container Revolution." Journal of World Trade Law* 6 (1972):661.

Zimmerman, E.W. *Ocean Shipping*. New York: Prentice-Hall, 1922.

## J. Ocean Resources Law and Policy

Adede, A.O. "Settlement of Disputes arising under the Law of the Sea Convention." *American Journal of International Law* 69 (1975):798.

Alexander, Lewis M. ed. *The Law of the Sea: The Future of the Sea's Resources*. Proceedings—Law of the Sea Institute 2nd Annual Conference, 1967. Kingston, R.I.: Law of the Sea Institute, 1967.

Andrassy, Juraj. *International Law and the Resources of the Sea*. New York: Columbia University Press, 1970.

Boasson, Charles. "Resources of the Sea and International Law." *Israel Law Review* 6 (1971):292.

Borchard, Edwin. "Resources of the Continental Shelf." *American Journal of International Law* 40 (1946):53.

Burke, William T., ed. *Towards a Better Use of the Ocean*. New York: Humanities Press, 1969.

Buzan, Barry. *Seabed Politics*. New York: Praeger, 1976.

Clark, Wilson. *Energy for Survival*. Garden City, N.Y.: Anchor, 1975.

Friedheim, Robert L., and Kahane, Joseph B. "Ocean Science in the United Nations Political Arena." *Journal of Maritime Law and Commerce* 3 (1971-1972):473.

Garcia Amador, F.V. *The Exploitation and Conservation of the Resources of the Sea*. 2nd ed. Leidon: Sijthoff, 1963.

George, G.W.P. *Australia's Offshore Resources: Implications of the 200-Mile Zone*. Canberra: Australia Academy of Science, 1978.

Gold, Edgar. "Law of the Sea and Ocean Resources." *Introduction to Physical and Biological Oceanography*. Edited by C.A.M. King. London: Edward Arnold, 1975.

Johnston, Douglas M. *The International Law of Fisheries*. New Haven, Conn.: Yale University Press, 1965.

Jones, Erin Bain. *Law of the Sea: Oceanic Resources*. Dallas: Southern Methodist University Press, 1972.

Knight, H. Gary. *Managing the Sea's Living Resources*. Legal and Political Aspects of High Seas Fisheries. Lexington, Mass.: Lexington Books, D.C. Heath and Co., 1977.

Koers, Albert W. *International Regulation of Marine Fisheries*. London: Fishing News (Books) Ltd., 1973.

Luard, Evan. *The Control of the Seabed*. London: Heinemann, 1974.

Mann Borgese, Elisabeth. *The Drama of the Oceans*. New York: Abrams, 1975.

Oda, Shigeru. *The Law of the Sea in Our Time*. II. *The United Nations Seabed Committee 1968-1973*. Leiden: Sijthoff, 1977.

Odidi Okidi, C., and Westley, Sydney, eds. *Management of Coastal and Offshore Resources in Eastern Africa*. Occasional paper no. 28. Nairobi, Kenya: Institute for Developmental Studies, University of Nairobi, 1978.

Park, Choon-ho. "The Sino-Japanese-Korean Sea Resources Controversy and the Hypothesis of a 200-Mile Economic Zone." *Harvard International Law Journal* 16 (1975):27.

Riesenfeld, Stefan A. *Protection of Coastal Fisheries under International Law*. Washington, D.C.: Carnegie Endowment, 1942.

Rothschild, Brian J. *World Fisheries Policy. Multidisciplinary Views*. Seattle: University of Washington Press, 1972.

Sampson, Anthony. *The Seven Sisters*. New York: Viking, 1975.
Sohn, L. "Die Ausbeutung des Meeresgrundes Jenseits des Kontinental-schelfs." *Jahrbuch für Internationales Recht* 14 (1969):101.

## K. Marine Environmental Law and Policy

Barros, James, and Johnston, Douglas M. *The International Law of Pollution*. New York: Free Press, 1974.
Bergman, Samuel. "No Fault Liability for Oil Pollution Damage." *Journal of Maritime Law and Commerce* 5 (1973-1974):1.
Boczek, B.A. "International Protection of the Baltic Environment against Pollution." *American Journal of International Law* 72 (1978):782.
Bradley, Paul G. "Marine Oil Spills: A Problem in Environmental Management." *Natural Resources Journal* 14 (1974):337.
Brown, E.D. "The Lessons of the *Torrey Canyon*." *Current Legal Problems* (1968):113-136.
_____. "The Conventional Law of the Environment." *Natural Resources Journal* 12 (1973):203.
Caflisch, L. "International Law and Ocean Pollution: The Present and the Future." *Revue Belge de Droit International* 8 (1972):7.
Churchill, Robin. "Why do Marine Pollution Conventions take so long to enter into Force?" *Maritime Policy and Management* 4 (1976):41.
Cummins, Philip A., Logue, Dennis E., Tollison, Robert D., and Willett, Thomas D. "Oil Tanker Pollution Control: Design Criteria vs. Effective Liability Assessment." *Journal of Maritime Law and Commerce* 7 (1975-1976):169.
D'Amato, Anthony, and Hargrove, John L. *Environment and the Law of the Sea*. A.S.I.L. Studies in Transnational Legal Policy, no. 5. Washington, D.C.: A.S.I.L., 1974.
Danzig, A.L. "Marine Pollution—A Framework for International Control." *Ocean Management* 1 (1973):347.
Dinstein, Yoram. "Oil Pollution by Ships and Freedom of the High Seas." *Journal of Maritime Law and Commerce* 3 (1971-1972):363.
Fitzmaurice, Victor E. "Liability for North Sea Oil Pollution."*Marine Policy* 2 (1978):105.
Fleischer, C.A. "Pollution from Seaborne Sources." Collected Papers, vol. 3. *New Directions in the Law of the Sea*. Edited by Robin Churchill, K.R. Simmonds, and Jane Welsh. Dobbs Ferry, N.Y.: Oceana, 1973.
Founex Report. *Environment and Development*. International Conciliation no. 586. Carnegie Endowment for International Peace, 1972.
Franck, Richard A. *Deepsea Mining and the Environment*. A.S.I.L. Studies in Transnational Legal Policy, no. 10. Washington, D.C.: A.S.I.L., 1976.

Gold, Edgar. "Pollution of the Sea and International Law: A Canadian Perspective." *Journal of Maritime Law and Commerce* 3 (1971-1972): 13.

‗‗‗‗‗ , ed. *Oil Pollution: A Survey of Worldwide Legislation*. Arendal, Norway: Assuranceforeningen Gard, 1971.

Hargrove, John L., ed. *Who Protects the Ocean? Environment and the Law of the Sea*. St. Paul, Minn.: West Publishing Company, 1975.

Healy, Nicholas J. "The C.M.I. and IMCO Draft Conventions on Civil Liability for Oil Pollution." *Journal of Maritime Law and Commerce* 1 (1969-1970):93.

‗‗‗‗‗ . "The International Convention on Civil Liability for Oil Pollution." 1 *Journal of Maritime Law and Commerce*, (1969-70), 317.

Horrocks, J.C.S. "The 1973 Marine Pollution Convention—Problems and Solutions." *Marine Policy* 1 (1977):52.

ICS/OCIMF, *Clean Seas Guide for Oil Tankers*. London: ICS, 1978.

Johnston, D.M. "Marine Pollution Control: Law, Science and Politics." *International Journal* 28 (1972-1973):69.

Legault, L.H.J. "Freedom of the Seas: A Licence to Pollute?" *University of Toronto Law Journal* 21 (1971):211.

Livingston, David. *Marine Pollution Articles in the Law of the Sea Single Informal Negotiating Text*. Occasional Paper no. 31. Law of the Sea Institute, University of Rhode Island, 1976.

Lowe, A.V. "The Enforcement of Marine Pollution Regulations." *San Diego Law Review* 12 (1975):624.

Lowry, P.D. "Maritime Pollution: Canada's Approach." *International Business Lawyer* 4 (1976):365.

Matthews, G. "Pollution of the Oceans: An International Problem?" *Ocean Management* 1 (1973):161.

McDougal, Myres, and Schneider, Jan. "The Protection of the Environment and World Public Order: Some Recent Developments." *Mississippi Law Journal* 45 (1974):1085.

McManus, Robert J., and Schneider, Jan. "Shipwrecks, Pollution and the Law of the Sea." *National Parks and Conservation Management*, June 1977, pp. 10-15.

Mendelsohn, Allan I. "Ocean Pollution and the 1972 United Nations Conference on the Environment." *Journal of Maritime Law and Commerce* 3 (1971-1972):385.

Nanda, Ved P. "The Torrey Canyon Disaster: Some Legal Aspects." *Denver Law Journal* 44 (1967):400.

Neuman, Robert H. "Oil on Troubled Waters: The International Control of Marine Pollution." *Journal of Maritime Law and Commerce* 2 (1970-1971):349.

Nweihed, Kaldone G. *La Contaminacion Marina ante el Derecho Internacional*. Caracas: Edition Presidencia de la Republica, 1978.

Oudet, L. *In the Wake of the* Torrey Canyon. London: Royal Institute of Navigation, 1972.

Petaccio, Victor. "Water Pollution and the Future Law of the Sea." *International and Comparative Law Quarterly* 21 (1972):15.

Petrow, Richard. *The Black Tide*. London: Hodder and Stoughton, 1968.

Price, H. Marcus III. "Making an Analysis of the Torrey Canyon Incident as a Model. *International Lawyer* 8 (1974):219.

Ramcharan, B.G. "The International Law Commission and International Environmental Law." *Ocean Management* 2 (1974-1975):315.

Ritchie-Calder, Lord, ed. *The Pollution of the Mediterranean Sea*. Berne: Herbert Lang, 1972.

Sanger, Clyde. "Environment and Development." *International Journal* 28 (1972-1973):103.

Schachter, Oscar, and Serwer, Daniel. "Marine Pollution Problems and Remedies." *American Journal of International Law* 65 (1971):84.

Schiras, J. "L'Affaire de Torrey Canyon sept ans après: Essai d'une synthèse." *Revue Hellenique de Droit International* 26-27 (1973-1974):254.

Shinn, Robert A. *The International Politics of Marine Pollution Control*. New York: Praeger, 1974.

Sweeney, Joseph C. "Oil Pollution of the Oceans." *Fordham Law Review* 37 (1968-1969):155.

Teclaff, Ludwik A., and Utton, Albert E. *International Environmental Law*. New York: Praeger, 1974.

Waldichuk, M. "International Approach to the Marine Pollution Problem." *Ocean Management* 1 (1973):211.

Wardley-Smith, J., ed. *The Control of Oil Pollution*. London: Graham and Trotman, 1976.

## L. Intergovernmental and Governmental Documents

Comité Maritime International. *International Conventions on Maritime Law*. Anvers: CMI.

_____ . *Documentation*. Anvers: CMI, 1972-1979.

_____ . *Yearbook—Annuaire 1978*. Anvers: CMI, 1978.

Committee of Inquiry into Shipping. Report. Viscount Rochdale, chairman. CMND. 4337. London: HMSO, 1970.

OECD. *Maritime Transport 1976*. Paris: OECD, 1977.

_____ . *Maritime Transport 1977*. Paris: OECD, 1978.

_____ . *Maritime Transport 1978*. Paris: OECD, 1979.

*Protocol of Proceedings of the International Marine Conference, 1889.* 3 vols. Washington, D.C.: U.S. Government Printing Office, 1890.

Report. *Royal Commission: Pollution of Canadian Waters by Oil and*

*Formal Investigation into Grounding of Steam Tanker* Arrow. Ottawa:
Information Canada, 1971.

The League of Arab States. *Regional Maritime Training Institute.*
Alexandria, 1972.

Transport Canada Marine. *A Shipping Policy for Canada.* TP-1676
(1979).

United States Congress, Committee on Foreign Affairs. *The Indian Ocean:
Political and Strategic Future.* Hearings before the Sub-committee on
National Security Policy and Scientific Development, 1971.
Washington, D.C.: U.S. Government Printing Office, 1978.


**M. United Nations Documents**


IMCO. *Annual Reports.* 1969-1976.

_____ . *Assembly Resolutions and other Decisions.* 1959-1972.

_____ . *Basic Documents.* Vol. I (1968); vol. II (1969); vol. III (1972).

_____ . *International Conference on Revision of the International
Regulations for Preventing Collisions at Sea, 1972.* Final Act, etc. London: IMCO, 1974.

_____ . *Report of the Symposium on Prevention of Marine Pollution
from Ships, Acapulco, Mexico, 1976.* London: IMCO, 1976.

_____ . *IMCO and its Activities.* London: IMCO, 1978.

IMCO/UNCTAD. *Technical Assistance in Maritime Transport.* London:
IMCO (n.d.).

UNCITRAL. *International Legislation on Shipping.* U.N. Doc.
A/CN.9/105, March 18, 1975.

UNCTAD. *Review of Maritime Transport.* Annual Edition.

_____ . *Shipping and the World Economy.* 67.II.D.12 (1966).

_____ . *Consultation in Shipping.* 68.II.D.1 (1967).

_____ . *Establishment and Expansion of Merchant Marines in Developing
Countries.* 1968.

_____ . *International Legislation on Shipping.* E.69.II.D.2 (1968).

_____ . *Multinational Shipping Enterprises.* E.72.II.D.17 (1972).

_____ . *Shipping in the Seventies.* E.72.II.D.15 (1972).

_____ . *Proceedings of the United Nations Conference on Trade and
Development—Third Session, Santiago de Chile, 1972.* Vol. I. Reports
and Annexes. 1973.

_____ . *United Nations Conference of Plenipotentiaries on a Code of
Conduct for Liner Conferences.* Report of the Conference on the First
Part of its Session, 1973. U.N. Doc. TD/CODE 7.

_____ . *A Transport Strategy for Land-locked Developing Countries.*
E.74.II.D.5 (1974).

———. *Guidelines for the Study of the Transfer of Technology to Developing Countries.* E.72.II.D.19 (1972).

———. *An International Code of Conduct on Transfer of Technology.* U.N. Doc. TD/B/C.6 AC.1/2/Supp.1, February 4, 1975.

———. *Preparation of a Draft Outline of a Code of Conduct on Transfer of Technology.* U.N. Doc TD/B/C.6/AC.1/2/Supp.1, February 4, 1975.

———. *Trade and Development Issues in the Context of a New International Economic Order.* UNCTAD IV Seminar Proposed Discussion Paper, 1976.

———. *UNCTAD IV. Nairobi—Transfer of Technology.* U.N. Doc. TD/490 (1976).

———. *New Directions in International Trade and Development Policies.* E.76.II.D.1 (1976).

UNITAR. United Nations. *The International Development Strategy.* First Over-all Review and Appraisal of Issues and Policies. E/5268 ST/ECA/177.

———. *International Co-operation for Pollution Control.* UNITAR Research Report no. 9.

———. *U.N. Development Aid—Criteria and Methods of Evaluation.* New York: Arno Press, 1971.

United Nations. *National Legislation and Treaties Relating to the Law of the Sea.* United Nations Legislative Series. 10 vols. 1951-1979.

———. *United Nations Conference on the Law of the Sea. Official Records.* Vols. I-VII. 58.V.4 (1958).

———. *Second United Nations Conference on the Law of the Sea. Official Records.* 2 vols. 62.V.3 (1960).

———. *Report of the Committee on the Peaceful Uses of the Sea-Bed and the Ocean Floor Beyond the Limits of National Jurisdiction.* General Assembly, 26th and 27th Sessions. Supplements no. 21(A/8421 and 8721) (1971 and 1972).

———. *Report of United Nations Conference on the Human Environment, Stockholm, 1972.* E.73.II.A.14 (1972).

———. *Report of the Committee on the Peaceful Uses of the Sea-Bed and the Ocean Floor Beyond the Limits of National Jurisdiction.* Vols. I-VI. General Assembly, 28th Session. Supplement No. 21(A/9021) (1973).

———. *Third United Nations Conference on the Law of the Sea.* Official Records. Vols. I-X. E.75.V., 1974-1979.

———. *Committee on Science and Technology for Development.* Report on the Third Session, 1976. E/5777.E/C.8/48 (1976).

———. *Institution Building for Transport Development in Developing Countries.* E.71.VIII.1 (1971).

# List of Statutes

# List of Cases

# Index

# About the Author

**Edgar Gold** is professor of law in the Faculty of Law and executive director of the Dalhousie Ocean Studies Programme, Dalhousie University. After sixteen years of service in the merchant marine, including several years in command, he obtained the B.A. and law degrees in Canada and the doctorate in international marine law in the United Kingdom. He is a member of the Nova Scotia bar and, in addition to his university duties, has practiced admiralty law for several years. He has carried out research and consulting work in many parts of the world and serves on the governing boards of several international associations involved in the marine field. Professor Gold has participated in the Third U.N. Conference on the Law of the Sea since 1973 and has published widely in most areas of marine affairs. He has a particular interest in the marine law and policy of less-developed countries.